HIST

of the

Lincoln Family

An Account of the

Descendants of Samuel Lincoln
of Hingham Massachusetts

1637-1920

COMPILED BY WALDO LINCOLN A. B.
President of the American Antiquarian Society

WORCESTER MASSACHUSETTS
Commonwealth Press
1923

- Notice -

Unfortunately, the page with illustrations (facing p. 16) is missing from this
edition. We feel that the contents of this book warrant its reissue despite this
inconvenience, and hope you will agree and read it with pleasure.

A Facsimile Reprint
Published 2000 by

HERITAGE BOOKS, INC.
1540E Pointer Ridge Place
Bowie, Maryland 20716
1-800-398-7709
www.heritagebooks.com

ISBN 0-7884-1489-5

A Complete Catalog Listing Hundreds of Titles
On History, Genealogy, and Americana
Available Free Upon Request

adahc a. JOHN, son of Mishal (*Thomas, Mordecai, Mordecai, Samuel*) and Rachel (Thompson) Lincoln of Laurelton, Pa., born Jan. or June 30, 1782, in Berks county, Pa.; died Aug. 19, 1862, at Laurelton, "aged eighty years." He was taken by his parents to Buffalo Valley (then in Northumberland, now in Union county), the year after his birth, and received whatever school education he had at Mifflinburg, in the subscription schools then in vogue. After his marriage he owned and resided on a farm about three miles southeast of Mifflinburg. In 1826 his father-in-law gave him a farm in Hartley township, now owned by John-Lincoln Knight, *adahc abb*, on which he made his home until his death. For nearly a half century he and his wife were members of the Methodist Episcopal Church. The cozy church building with cemetery attached, known as the Lincoln Methodist Episcopal Church or Lincoln Chapel, was named in his honor, being located on land given by him for that purpose. (From memoranda furnished by Richard-VanBuskirk Lincoln, *adahc aa*, to James-Minor Lincoln of Wareham, Mass.; Hist. of Susquehanna and Juniata Valleys, vol. ii, p. 1396.)

He married, June 3, 1819, Hannah, daughter of Richard and Hannah (Kelly) VanBuskirk of Mifflinburg, Pa., born March 20, 1801, at Mifflinburg; died March 20, 1880, near Swengel, Lewis township, Pa., "aged seventy nine years." (Records of James-Minor Lincoln, Wareham, Mass.)

Children, born at Mifflinburg:

adahc aa. RICHARD-VANBUSKIRK, born Dec. 18, 1822.

adahc ab. RACHEL-THOMPSON, born Jan. 13, 1825; died Oct. 17, 1875, near Laurelton, Pa.; married, June 29, 1842, Samuel H. Knight of Hartleton Borough, Union county, Pa. He was a physician.
Children:
    a. HANNAH, born June 14, 1843; died 1860.
    b. JOHN-LINCOLN, born June 7, 1849.

adahc ac. CATHERINE-ELIZABETH, born Oct. 20, 1829; married, June 3, 1846, W. R. Halfpenny of Hartley township, Pa., or perhaps of Lewisburgh, Pa. They lived in Union county, Pa.
Children:
    a. MARY-HANNAH, born Aug. 10, 1847.
    b. JOHN-LINCOLN, born May 7, 1850.
    c. JAMES-MILTON, born June 6, 1853.

adahc b. THOMAS, son of Mishal (*Thomas, Mordecai, Mordecai, Samuel*) and Rachel (Thompson) Lincoln of Mifflinburg,

Pa., born Nov. 1, 1795, at Mifflinburg; died 1852, at Circleville, Pickaway county, Ohio, whither he had removed in 1840. He married but nothing has been learned of his wife. Letters to members of this family have received no attention.

Children:

adahc ba. SOLOMON; married at Circleville, Ohio, Malinda Morris and removed to Mt. Pulaski, Ill., in 1853.
    Children:
        a. JOHN.
        b. RACHEL.
adahc bb. JOHN, married, in 1853, at Circleville, Malinda Morris, a niece of his brother Solomon's wife. He removed to Mt. Pulaski, Ill., and was president of the First National Bank there. He had four children, one of whom, C. W. Lincoln, was cashier of the same bank.
adahc bc. SARAH, married, in 1853, at Circleville, Samuel Morris, brother of her brother Solomon's wife. They removed to Mt. Pulaski, Ill. They had six children: three at Circleville and three at Mt. Pulaski.
adahc bd. ROSE, married Samuel Morris, brother of her brother John's wife. They lived at Circleville, where he was cashier of the Third National Bank.

adahf c. JOHN, son of Joseph (*Thomas, Mordecai, Mordecai, Samuel*) and Elizabeth (Dickinson) Lincoln of Rising Sun, Md., born Apr. 18, 1800, at Radnor, Pa.; died June 25, 1864, at Rising Sun. He learned cabinet-making with Abner Taylor, whom he followed to Maryland and in whose shop, at Rising Sun, he worked for many years. He then purchased from Nathan Haines, two hundred and forty acres of land near Rising Sun and, later, from the same an adjoining tract of the same size, which became the Lincoln homestead. In connection with farming he became a tanner.

He married, May 22, 1823, at Rising Sun, Francina, daughter of Henry and Mary E. (Knight) Reynolds, born Dec. 2, 1804; died Sept. 11, 1861, at Rising Sun. (Oxford, Chester county, Pa., "Press," June 18, 1903; Records of John-Joseph Lincoln, *adahf cea.*)

Children, born at Rising Sun:

adahf ca. MARY-ELIZA, born June 8, 1824; died Aug. 14, 1893, at Rising Sun; married, Dec. 23, 1847, at Rising Sun, Ellis-Pusey, son of John-Wardell and Deborah (Brown) Passmore of Nottingham, Pa., born Aug. 4, 1823, at Nottingham, where he died after 1903. He was a farmer and chrome-miner, and was living in 1903. He was a Friend and held no military or civil office. (Records of Lincoln-Knight Passmore, *adahf cab.*)

Children, born at Rising Sun:

a. JOHN-WARDELL, born Dec. 11, 1848; mar. Alice M. Martindale.
b. LINCOLN-KNIGHT, born Sept. 2, 1850; mar. Ellen F. Faxon.
c. LEROY-CHASE, born Jan. 8, 1854; mar. Rebecca E. Hunt.
d. EMMA-FRANCES, born Nov. 16, 1855; mar. John D. Haines.
e. CHARLES-SUMNER, born July 11, 1858; mar. Susan M. Came.
f. WALTER-CHANNING, born Dec. 1, 1860; mar. Lillian P. Haines.
g. ELLIS-PUSEY, born Feb. 1, 1869; mar. Emily-Pusey Shelmire.

adahf cb. JOSEPH-HENRY, born Feb. 11, 1826.

adahf cc. REBECCA-FRANCES, born Jan. 5, 1828; died March 1, 1909, at Rising Sun; married, Aug. 13, 1846, at Philadelphia, Pa., Joseph-Hutton, son of Edwin and Margaret (Hutton) Haines of Rising Sun, born March 27, 1825, at Rising Sun; died Nov. 2, 1867, at Danville, N. Y. They lived at Rising Sun. He was a miller and farmer.

Children, born at Rising Sun:

a. JOHN-LINCOLN, born Oct. 21, 1847; mar. Nellie Taft.
b. ANNA-FRANCES, born Aug. 26, 1849; mar. Basil-Haines Brown.
c. ELIZABETH-DICKINSON, born Oct. 14, 1851; mar. Charles Brown.
d. MARGARET-HUTTON, born March 11, 1854; living, 1914, unmarried.
e. IDA-ELLA, born Sept. 28, 1857; mar. William Addison.
f. SARAH-STUBBS, born July 30, 1859; mar. William Smith.
g. RACHEL-EMMA, born Dec. 21, 1860; mar. George McKinsey.
h. JOSEPH-HUTTON, born Dec. 27, 1866; living, 1914, unmarried.

adahf cd. ELIZABETH, born Feb. 2, 1830; died Nov. 8, 1893, at Rising Sun; married, Feb. 20, 1859, at Oxford, Pa., Jonathan, son of Isaac and Mira (Haines) Reynolds of Rising Sun, born March 29, 1829, at Rising Sun; died there March 19, 1908. They lived at Rising Sun. He was a farmer. (Records of Isaac-Wayne Reynolds, *adahf cdb.*)

Children, born at Rising Sun:

a. MARY-EMMA, born Oct. 19, 1860; died Apr. 9, 1891, unmarried.
b. ISAAC-WAYNE, born Oct. 26, 1863; mar. Letitia Paxon.

adahf ce. ABEL-THOMAS, born Nov. 27, 1831.

adahf cf. MARGARET-WORTHINGTON, born March 27, 1834; living, 1913, at Rising Sun; married, July 22, 1862, at Philadelphia, Pa., James-Henry, son of Samuel and Elizabeth (Kinsey) Scott of Baltimore, Md., born June 15, 1838, at Baltimore; died Nov. 21, 1869, at Rising Sun. He was a dentist. They lived at Baltimore. (Records of Margaret-Worthington [Lincoln] Scott.)

Children, born at Baltimore:

a. GEORGE-MILTENBERGER, born June 14, 1863; died Oct. 11, 1874.
b. MARGARET-LINCOLN, born 1868; died aged three months.
c. FLORENCE-MAY, born May 1, 1870; died Oct. 5, 1890, unmarried.
d. SARAH-ANNA, born Dec. 1, 1872; mar. (1) Walter-Richard Buffington; (2) Samuel Entrikin.

adahf cg. FRANCINA-KNIGHT, born Jan. 22, 1836; living, 1913, at Oxford, Pa.; married, June 5, 1860, at Philadelphia, Pa., Isaac-Stubbs, son of Jacob-Reynolds and Hannah-Brown (Stubbs) Kirk of Oxford, born Aug. 14, 1834, at East Nottingham, Pa.; died Jan. 6, 1908, at Fremont, Pa. He was educated at the District school; the Pugh Boarding School of East Nottingham; and the Henry Ridgeway Boarding School of Bordentown, N. J. He then bought a property in West Nottingham, where he conducted a general store and a farm. In 1856, a post office being established in the township by the name of Fremont, he was appointed postmaster and held the office for fifty years, until the establishment of rural delivery caused abolishment of minor offices. He was a mineralogist of ability and a collector of Indian relics and of postage stamps, of both of which he had a fine collection. (Records of Mrs. Clara-Lincoln [Kirk] Pugh, *adahf cgb.*)

Children, born at Fremont:

    a. JENNIE-HANNAH, born May 20, 1861; mar. William-Preston King.

    b. CLARA-LINCOLN, born March 2, 1866; mar. Harold-Brown Pugh.

    c. CHARLES-BENTON, born Jan. 11, 1870; mar. Elizabeth Rogers.

    d. PINCKNEY-JACOB, born Feb. 28, 1875; mar. Mary Stubbs.

adahf ch. LYDIA-ELMIRAH, born Aug. 13, 1838; married, Feb. 20, 1859, at Oxford, Pa., Edwin H., son of Haines and Phebe-Dinah (Moore) Reynolds of Rising Sun, born March 4, 1837, at Rising Sun, where they were living in 1914. He is a farmer and plumber. (Records of Miss Margaret Reynolds, *adahf chb;* Smedley Family, p. 48.)

Children, born at Rising Sun:

    a. ELLA-FRANCES, born March 23, 1860; mar. Edwin-Marshall Hunt.

    b. MARGARET, born March 10, 1862; living, 1914, unmarried.

    c. SARAH-ROSENE, born Sept. 7, 1864; mar. Benjamin-Passmore Stubbs.

    d. ELIZABETH, born Jan. 1, 1866; mar. Ulysses-Grant Brown.

    e. GEORGIANA, ⎫ born 1868; both died in infancy.
    f. CORNELIA, ⎭

    g. JANETTE, born Aug. 8, 1872; mar. John-Welch Dix.

adahf ci. CORNELIA, born July 12, 1840; living, 1914, at Pleasant Grove, Pa.; married, Oct. 14, 1885, at New York, N. Y., Joseph-Rich, son of Joseph and Rachel (Cutler) Blackburn of Pleasant Grove, born Feb. 14, 1832, at Pleasant Grove; died there Feb. 4, 1909. They were Friends in belief, "just and upright in all their dealings." They lived at Pleasant Grove. He was a farmer. They had no children. (Records of Mrs. Cornelia Blackburn.)

adahf cj. BENTON, born June 11, 1842; living, 1914, at Fremont, Pa., unmarried.

adahf ck. RACHEL-HOUSEKEEPER, born May 7, 1845; married, June 4, 1868, at Philadelphia, Pa., Charles H, son of John and Mary (Jackson) Platt of Wilmington, Del., born Nov. 10, 1845, at Wilmington. He is a bookkeeper. They were living in 1914, at Helena, Mont. (Records of Mrs. Rachel-Housekeeper [Lincoln] Platt.)

Children, born: *a, b* at Rising Sun, Md.; *c-e* at Avondale, Pa.:

    a. MARY-CORNELIA, born March 9, 1870; living, 1914, unmarried.

    b. FLORENCE-FRANCINA, born Oct. 6, 1872; living, 1914, unmarried.

    c. ELIZABETH-REYBOLD, born Oct. 23, 1878; living, 1914, unmarried.

    d. JOHN-LINCOLN, born June 6, 1881; living 1914, unmarried.

    e. HELEN, born Jan. 28, 1887; living, 1914, unmarried.

adahf cl. WILLIAM-PENN, born Apr. 29, 1850; died May 21, 1850.

adahf d. ABEL-THOMAS, son of Joseph (*Thomas, Mordecai, Mordecai, Samuel*) and Elizabeth (Dickinson) Lincoln of Rising

Sun, Md., born May 12, 1803, at Radnor, Delaware county, Pa.; died May 17, 1869, at Philadelphia, Pa. He was a cabinet-maker and lived at Philadelphia. In later life he became a grocer. In a deed given by Abel and his wife, Sept. 18, 1845, he is described as a "grocer of the Northern Liberties."

He married, March 7, 1826, at Chestnut Level, Pa., Rachel³, daughter of Philip² (*Thomas¹*) and Mary (Hickman) House-keeper of Milltown, Chester county, Pa., born Dec. 16, 1799, at Milltown; died Apr. 20, 1890, at Philadelphia. Her mother Mary⁴ Hickman was daughter of Benjamin³ (*Benjamin², Benjamin¹*) and Lucy (Cheyney) Hickman. She was born Apr. 16, 1776; died Apr. 13, 1845, and married Philip Housekeeper, Jan. 19, 1796. (Records of Henry-Philip Lincoln, *adahf daa.*)

Children, born at Philadelphia:

adahf da. CHARLES-SHIPPEN, born June 30, 1827.
adahf db. JOHN-TAYLOR, born Apr. 6, 1829; died Nov. 8, 1851, unmarried.
adahf dc. HENRY-PHILIP, born Oct. 5, 1831; died Oct. 12, 1854, unmarried.
adahf dd. GEORGE-WASHINGTON, born July 21, 1835; died Jan. 16, 1857, unmarried.
adahf de. WILLIAM-PENN, born Aug. 11, 1839; died July 31, 1848.

adaid a. CALEB, son of James (*Abraham, Mordecai, Mordecai, Samuel*) and Elizabeth (Jones) Lincoln of Carnarvon, Pa., born March 4, 1793, at Carnarvon; died Sept. 12, 1831.

He married, March, 1818, Margaret-Amelia, daughter of Clemson and Margaret-Amelia (Moore) Henderson, born July 4, 1800; died March 11, 1871. She married (2) John Long, by whom she had a son, George. (Genealogy of David Jones, p. 106.)

Children:

adaid aa. ELIZABETH, born March 3, 1820; died Apr. 1, 1875; married, March 11, 1841, Richard Pierce.
  Children:
   a. JOHN, born Dec. 9, 1841; died Dec. 1, 1844.
   b. JAMES-LINCOLN, born Nov. 26, 1845; mar. Ella-Ruth Gaul.
   c. MARGARET-AMELIA, born Aug. 20, 1851; mar. Henry-Kupp Spotts.
adaid ab. SAMUEL, born Aug. 26, 1823.
adaid ac. JOHN, born Apr. 16, 1826; left home and has never been heard from since.

adaid b. JOHN, son of James (*Abraham, Mordecai, Mordecai, Samuel*) and Elizabeth (Jones) Lincoln of Carnarvon, Pa., born

Apr. 5, 1796, at Carnarvon; died July 17, 1867, at Churchtown, Pa. He was a farmer and lived between Churchtown, Lancaster county, and Morgantown, Bucks county, Pa.

He married, Nov. 17, 1814, Hannah[4], daughter of John[3] (*Jonathan[2], David[1]*) and Elizabeth (Graham) Jones of Reading Forge, Pa., born Oct. 16, 1793; died Apr. 2, 1869, at Churchtown. (Genealogy of David Jones, pp. 42-3; 106-7.) The will of John Jones of East Nantmeal, Pa., dated Jan. 11, 1816, names: "daughter Hannah," to whom is left a legacy "during the lifetime of her husband John Lincoln, afterwards to be paid to her or her children." (Chester County Wills and Administrations, Abstracts of, with Hist. Soc'y of Penn.)

Children, born at Churchtown:

adaid ba. JAMES, born Oct. 9, 1818; died in infancy.
adaid bb. GEORGE-JONES, born Oct. 28, 1821.
adaid bc. THAMAZINE, born Oct. 10, 1822; married, Dec. 26, 1841, Samuel-Miles Cresswell.
  Children:
      a. HANNAH-ELIZABETH, born 1842; mar. J. Howard Jacobs.
      b. JAMES-ROSS, born May 31, 1843; died March 29, 1848.
adaid bd. REES-EVANS, born May 30, 1825; died Oct. 8, 1858, unmarried.
adaid be. ELIZABETH, born March 2, 1829; died Nov. 16, 1872, unmarried.

adaid c. SAMUEL, son of James (*Abraham, Mordecai, Mordecai, Samuel*) and Elizabeth (Jones) Lincoln of Carnarvon, Pa., born July 13, 1798, at Carnarvon; died Apr. 28, 1882, at Churchtown, Pa. He lived at Churchtown and was a farmer. He is described as a man of earnest purpose and enterprising energy, filled with a spirit of thrift and industry. He was ever foremost in matters of public zeal and took a keen interest in the progressive spirit of the age, cheerfully accepting the burden of such public trusts as came to him in the performance of which he was zealous and faithful. He was for many years identified with the interests of Carnarvon, of which town he was a prominent citizen and highly esteemed. He lived, after his marriage, on the Jackson homestead, near Joanna Furnace. (Hist. of Lancaster County, Pa., p. 696.)

He married, Dec. 24, 1835, at Lancaster, Pa., Maria, daughter of Thomas and Margaret (Hughes) Jackson of Berks county, Pa., born Dec. 14, 1802, at Robeson township, Pa.; died Aug. 6,

1848, at Morgantown, Pa. (Genealogy of David Jones, pp. 107-8; Records of Elizabeth [Lincoln] Hertzler, *adaid cc.*)

Children, born at Churchtown:

adaid ca. EDWARD, born Sept. 12, 1837; died June 5, 1912, at Churchtown; married, March 3, 1874, at Lancaster, Pa., Sarah-Ann, daughter of John and Hannah (Cox) Tripple of Churchtown, born Feb. 12, 1844, at Churchtown; living, 1914. They lived at Churchtown. He was a farmer. They had no children.

adaid cb. MARGARET, born Jan. 1, 1840; married, June 14, 1860, Abner-Evans, son of Jesse and Margaret (Allen) James of Loag, Pa., born Sept. 8, 1831, at Loag. They are living, 1914, at Elverson, Pa. He is a farmer. Children, born: *a, b* not reported; *c* at Isabella, Pa.:

    a. EDWARD-LINCOLN, born Sept. 7, 1861; died Sept. 14, 1865.
    b. CLARENCE-ALAN, born Aug. 30, 1866; mar. Elizabeth-Jane Millard.
    c. BESSIE-LINCOLN, born Nov. 11, 1875; mar. Isaac-Trego Mc-Farland.   (See Bailey Family, p. 306.)

adaid cc. ELIZABETH, born Sept. 8, 1842; married, Nov. 28, 1872, at Lancaster, Pa., John-Zook, son of John and Martha (Reeser) Hertzler of Churchtown, born Feb. 17, 1843, at Churchtown. They are living at Churchtown. He is, 1914, a miller and justice of the peace. Children, born at Morgantown, Pa.:

    a. ALICE-MAY, born June 19, 1875; mar. George-Henry Muhlenberg.
    b. EDWARD-FENDALL, born Nov. 30, 1880; mar. Anna-Mae Millard.

adaid g. ABRAHAM, son of James (*Abraham, Mordecai, Mordecai, Samuel*) and Elizabeth (Jones) Lincoln of Carnarvon, Pa., born July 12, 1812, at Carnarvon; died Feb. 11, 1900, at Whitehall, near Churchtown, Pa.

He married, Nov. 25, 1838, at Churchtown, Sarah-Anderson[4], daughter of David[3] (*John[2], David[1]*) and Mary D. (McCalmant) Jenkins of Churchtown, born June 23, 1819, at Churchtown; died Feb. 17, 1900, at Churchtown, where they had lived. (Jenkins Family Book, p. 98; Genealogy of David Jones, p. 108.)

Child, born at Churchtown:

adaid ga. ELIZABETH-JONES, born Nov. 10, 1840. She was living, 1904, at Churchtown, unmarried, but is reported to have died before 1913.

adaid h. DAVID-JONES, son of James (*Abraham, Mordecai, Mordecai, Samuel*) and Elizabeth (Jones) Lincoln of Carnarvon, Pa., born Jan. 29, 1816, at Carnarvon; died Apr. 10, 1886, at Birdsboro, Pa.

He married, Apr. 15, 1847, Mary-Ives, daughter of Mark Davis. (Gen. of David Jones, pp. 108-9.)

Children, born at Birdsboro:

adaid ha. CLARA, born Sept. 16, 1848; died Feb. 28, 1912, at Leesport, Pa.; married, Aug. 17, 1873, at Birdsboro, Jeremiah-Starr, son of Benjamin and Elizabeth (Starr) Parvin of Leesport, born Sept. 17, 1841, at Leesport; died there Dec. 26, 1909. They lived at Leesport. He was engaged in the manufacture of leather. (Records of Henry-Philip Lincoln, *adahf daa*, and of Mary-Ives Parvin, *adaid had.*)

Children, born at Leesport:

    a. EDWARD-LINCOLN, born Nov. 29, 1874; mar. Elizabeth-Weida Raser.

    b. ELIZABETH-STARR, born Feb. 2, 1877; mar. Richard-Warren Knight.

    c. GEORGE-BROOKE, born Oct. 23, 1878; mar. Mary Noecker.

    d. MARY-IVES, born Feb. 26, 1883; living, 1913, unmarried.

    e. BENJAMIN, born Aug. 8, 1887; living, 1913, unmarried.

    f. LUCIA, born Oct. 10, 1891; living, 1913, unmarried.

adaid hb. JAMES, born May 1, 1851; died Apr. 16, 1893, unmarried. He was a physician.

adaid hc. WILLIAM-IVES, born Sept. 16, 1852.

adaid hd. GEORGE-JONES, born March 16, 1854; died July 14, 1855.

adaid he. MARY-DAVIES, born Apr. 14, 1856; living, 1913, unmarried at Birdsboro.

adaid hf. ANNE-BOONE, born June 10, 1858; living, 1913, unmarried at Birdsboro.

adaid hg. ELIZABETH, born Dec. 9, 1862; married (1), May 21, 1885, Douglas Smith. She married (2), June 7, 1894, Henry-Knabb Harrison. They were living, 1913, at Birdsboro.

    Child, by first husband:

    a. WILLIAM SMITH, born Oct. 22, 1886; died July 4, 1888.

adaii b. JOHN-DEHAVEN, son of Thomas (*Abraham, Mordecai, Mordecai, Samuel*) and Alice (Dehaven) Lincoln of Exeter, Pa., born Jan. 1, 1815 (Sunday), at Exeter; died June 27, 1895, at Lorane, Exeter township, where he had passed his life. He was a farmer.

He married, Jan. 24, 1837, at Exeter, Sarah, daughter of Henry and Elizabeth (Deeter) Gilbert of Exeter, born Jan. 4, 1811, at Exeter; died Apr. 15, 1895, at Lorane. (Family Bible of Harrison-Gilbert Lincoln, *adaii bc.*)

Children, born at Exeter:

adaii ba. AMELIA, born March 28, 1838; died Dec. 14, 1895, unmarried.

adaii bb. ALFRED-GILBERT, born Apr. 21, 1839.

adaii bc. HARRISON-GILBERT, born July 28, 1840.

adaii bd. ELIZABETH, born Nov. 20, 1841; married, Oct. 6, 1864, at Reading,

Pa., Samuel-Romig, son of Mathias and Rachel (Romig) Hafer of Exeter, born July 8, 1840, at Exeter. They were living in 1913 at Reading. He was book-keeper for Hafer Brothers, produce dealers.

Children, born: *a-d* at Exeter; *e* at Birdsboro, Pa.:

    a. AMMON-LINCOLN, born June 3, 1866; mar. Nellie Lebkicker.

    b. ADELE-LINCOLN, born Nov. 20, 1868; mar. John Siegfried.

    c. SAMUEL-LINCOLN, born Sept. 20, 1870; mar. Ida Endy.

    d. MATHIAS-LINCOLN, born July 20, 1873; mar. Cora Brensinger.

    e. RACHEL-LINCOLN, born Sept. 14, 1876; mar. Harry McKinney.

adaii be. JOHN-GILBERT, born March 7, 1843.

adaii bf. RICHARD-GILBERT, born Dec. 5, 1844.

adaii bg. MARTHA, born Dec. 12, 1846; living, 1913, at Reading, Pa.; married, Dec. 22, 1865, at Reading, David, son of Daniel and Catharine (Heming) Focht of Robeson, Pa., born Oct. 30, 1842, at Robeson; died Nov. 7, 1875, at Birdsboro, Pa. He was at first a butcher, but later kept a candy store. They had no children.

adaii bh. ANN, born Feb. 16, 1849; living, 1913, at Reading with her sister Martha. She married, Nov. 17, 1870, at Reading, John-Frederick, son of Joel and Margaret (Jones) Reifsnyder of Exeter, born Apr. 22, 1849, at Unionville, Pa.; died March 17, 1905, at Reading. He lived at Reading and was a produce dealer. They had one daughter who died in infancy. (Hist. of Berks County, Pa., vol. i, p. 596.)

adaii bi. SARAH, born May 24, 1851; living, 1913, at Reading with her sisters, Martha and Ann. She married, in 1875, at Reading, Lewis P., son of Samuel and Elizabeth (Spayd) Ruth of Bern township, Pa., born June 5, 1852, at Bern; died Nov. 15, 1883, at Reading. He lived at Reading and was a laborer. (Records of Mrs. Sarah [Lincoln] Ruth.)

Children, born at Reading:

    a. ELIZABETH, born March 12, 1876; mar. Frederick Haas.

    b. CLARENCE, born May 12, 1877; married Gertrude Brown.

adaii bj. MARY, born Aug. 24, 1852; living, 1913, at Reading, Pa.; married, Dec. 26, 1872, at Reading, Daniel, son of Daniel and Susan (Eidel) Biehl of St. Lawrence, Pa., born 1849, at Oley, Pa.; died Jan. 28, 1893, at Reading. He lived at Reading and was a policeman.

Children, born at Reading:

    a. HENRY-THOMAS, born Sept. 22, 1873; died Sept. 22, 1874.

    b. SARAH-ESTHER, born Apr. 3, 1876; mar. Harry S. Schuck.

    c. SUSAN-REBECCA, born Oct. 2, 1877; mar. J. Harvey Lengel.

    d. MARTHA-LINCOLN, born Aug. 8, 1879; mar. George T. Brown.

    e. MARY-LINCOLN, born Nov. 15, 1883; mar. William-Joseph Stout.

adaii bk. OSCAR, born Feb. 16, 1855; died Apr. 25, 1857.

adbca a. JOHN, son of Abraham (*Jacob, Abraham, Mordecai, Samuel*) and Elizabeth (Shrum) Lincoln of Kingsessing, Pa., now part of Philadelphia, born Aug. 19, 1790, at Kingsessing; died Dec. 20, 1824, at Philadelphia, intestate, and administration on his estate was granted to his widow, Martha Lincoln, Jan. 8, 1825; sureties Isaac Lincoln and George Gesner, both of Philadel-

phia. His estate was valued at $800. (Philadelphia Adminis-
trations, Book N, p. 25.)

He married Martha-Biddle Fimple, of whom nothing has been
learned. According to the "Ogden Genealogy" they were of
Haverford, Pa. (Records of Mrs. Katharine-Rebecca [Paschall]
Styer, *adbca bbd.*)

Children, born at Kingsessing:

adbca aa. ANN, married a Mr. Dylks.

adbca ab. SARAH-NITZEL, born Sept. 4, 1820; married, Apr. 25, 1842, Anning-
Asbury[5], son of Joseph[4] (*Aaron[3], Stephen[2], David[1]*) and Lucretia (Gorman)
Ogden of Newark, Del., born Apr. 24, 1817, at Newark; died May 4, 1894,
at Paschallville, Pa. He was a builder and, later, a merchant. They
lived at Paschallville. (The Quaker Ogdens, p. 128.)

    Children, born at Paschallville:

      a. JOHN-LINCOLN, born Jan. 29, 1843; mar. Jennie Wright.

      b. GEORGE-LYBRAND, born Nov. 12, 1845; mar. Selina Sharp.

      c. JAMES-ASBURY, born March 7, 1848; mar. Helen-Virginia Nor-
ton.

adbca d. ISAAC, son of Abraham (*Jacob, Abraham, Mordecai,
Samuel*) and Elizabeth (Shrum) Lincoln of Kingsessing, Pa.,
now part of Philadelphia, born May 2, 1797, at Kingsessing;
died July 8, 1867, at Waynesville, Ohio, whither he removed
from Darby, Pa., having first lived for a few years at Cincinnati,
Ohio, where his two daughters were born. He was a farmer. He
removed to Waynesville in 1828, and "did much hard labor in
opening up his farm from the woods." The farm is still, 1914,
in the family, being occupied by his grandson.

He married (1), Sept. 12, 1821, at Philadelphia (Records of
First Reformed Church), Margaret Smith, who was born at
Darby, and died March 24, 1829, at Waynesville.

He married (2), May 27, 1830, at Waynesville, Eliza, daughter
of John Robertson of Ohio, born Sept. 7, 1791, in Stafford county,
Va.; died Aug. 3, 1849, at Waynesville, aged 58 years. Her
father was a Scotchman and was drowned at sea while returning
to his native land for a visit. (Records of Mrs. Katharine-
Rebecca [Paschall] Styer, *adbca bbd;* and Isaac-Wilber Lincoln,
adbca dcc.)

Children, by first wife, born at Cincinnati:

adbca da. ELIZABETH, born Sept. 2, 1822; died June 15, 1889, at New Burlington, Ohio; married, Sept. 8, 1842, at Waynesville (Lebanon, Ohio, Rec-

ords), John, son of Absolom and Ellenor Chenoweth of Waynesville, born Aug. 27, 1815; died Nov. 5, 1865, at Harveysburg, Ohio. He was a farmer. They lived at Waynesville, Corwin and Harveysburg, Ohio. (Family Records.)

Children, born: *a-c* at Waynesville; *d-f* at Harveysburg.

- *a.* ISAAC-LINCOLN, born July 16, 1843; died Jan. 2, 1863.
- *b.* MARGARET-ELLENOR, born Jan. 7, 1845; mar. John-Hisey Gard.
- *c.* ELIZA-JANE, born June 22, 1847; mar. Eli-Smith Carroll.
- *d.* JOHN-WILLIAM-HENRY, born Aug. 24, 1851; died Feb. 4, 1854.
- *e.* MARY-ELIZABETH, born Sept. 6, 1854; mar. Benjamin-Milton Anson.
- *f.* CHARLES-ABSOLOM, born Feb. 11, 1860; mar. Mary-Adeline White.

adbca db. JANE, born March 7, 1826; died Jan. 4, 1888, unmarried.

Child, by second wife, born at Waynesville:

adbca dc. JOHN-ROBERTSON, born June 10, 1831.

adbca f. ABRAHAM, son of Abraham (*Jacob, Abraham, Mordecai, Samuel*) and Elizabeth (Shrum) Lincoln of Kingsessing Pa., now part of Philadelphia, born Sept. 5, 1802, at Kingsessing; died Sept. 19, 1892, at Waynesville, Ohio. When a young man he learned the wagonmaker's trade but he removed, in 1824, to Waynesville, where he became a farmer and lived until his death.

He married, Nov. 15, 1834, at Waynesville (Lebanon, Ohio, Records), Ruth, daughter of Zachariah and Elizabeth (O'Neal) Prater of Waynesville, born Aug. 17, 1816, near Waynesville; died there Apr. 19, 1893. (Records of Mrs. Katharine-Rebecca [Paschall] Styer, *adbca bbd.*)

Children, born at Waynesville:

adbca fa. JOSEPH, born Jan. 17, 1836; died Feb. 20, 1867, at Waynesville, unmarried.

adbca fb. ELIZABETH, born June 17, 1838; died Apr. 2, 1897, at Waynesville; married, May 10, 1853, at Waynesville, Albert-Elliot Warwick of Waynesville, a disreputable character who by cruel and abusive treatment of his wife and children drove his wife into a fit of insanity in which she killed him with an axe. For this crime she was imprisoned in the penitentiary but was finally pardoned.

Children, born at Waynesville:

- *a.* EVELYN-OPHELIA, born March 5, 1854; mar. Cassius-Clay Cleaver.
- *b.* JOSEPH-WILKINS, born Feb. 16, 1856; mar. Ella Turner.
- *c.* CLAYTON-RAYMOND, born Jan. 9, 1858; mar. Kate Bloom.
- *d.* CARRIE-EMMA, born June 3, 1860; mar. Albert-Samuel Taylor.

    e. Lizzie-Ada, born Jan. 5, 1862; mar. George-William Goodle.
    f. Ruth-Anna, born July 4, 1865; mar. George-Martin Daugherty.
adbca fc. Benjamin, born March 8, 1844.

adbcf a. Jacob, son of Moses (*Jacob, Abraham, Mordecai, Samuel*) and Barbara (Kinch) Lincoln of Darby, Pa., born 1795, at Darby; died Nov. 18, 1848, at Darby. He lived at Darby and was a stone-mason as shown by a deed, dated March 25, 1840, by which Jacob Lincoln of Darby, stone-mason, and Eliza his wife conveyed to Thomas A. Potts of Kingsessing for $1200 land in Paschallville, formerly belonging to Dr. Henry Paschall and which he conveyed to said Jacob, March 22, 1826. (Philadelphia Deeds, Bk. G. S. 16, p. 46.) He is buried in the Old Swedes Cemetery at Kingsessing, now part of Philadelphia, Pa. His gravestone is inscribed as follows:

"Sacred ‡ to the memory of ‡ Jacob Lincoln ‡ who departed this life ‡ November 18th 1848 ‡ in the 53rd year of his age ‡ Rest in Peace."

His will, dated Feb. 21, 1848, proved Dec. 5, 1848, leaves: "To wife Eliza and son William all money in hand or due me at my death. To son William the plantation in Upper Darby on which he resides containing 21 acres, and my lot in Darby, bought of David Lewis, containing 18 acres. To wife the plantation we live on in Darby containing 24 acres during her life and afterwards to son William. Remainder to William. Executors: wife Eliza and son William." (The Ancestry of Abraham Lincoln, p. 170.)

From the foregoing it is learned that his wife's name was Eliza and that she survived him. It is also evident that if they had other children, none but William was living in 1848. Mrs. Lincoln married (2), before Sept. 24, 1856, Anthony J. Jordan, as appears by the petition for administration on the estate of her son William.

Child, born at Darby:

adbcf aa. William; died before Sept. 24, 1856, intestate. Administration on the estate of William Lincoln was granted to Elizabeth P. Lincoln, Oct. 23, 1856. Her petition in Orphans' Court, dated Sept. 24, 1856, calls her widow and administratrix of William Lincoln and sets forth: "that said William Lincoln died intestate, leaving no issue and as next of kin his mother Eliza Lincoln, now wife of Anthony J. Jordan; George Lincoln, an uncle; and the children of Michael Lincoln, a deceased uncle

viz.; Isaac and Jacob Lincoln, Anna-Eliza wife of Daniel Trites, Rebecca
wife of James Hutchinson, and Elizabeth Lincoln a minor under 21."
(The Ancestry of Abraham Lincoln, p. 179.)

He married, Dec. 16, 1845, at Doe Run, Pa., Elizabeth, daughter of
Joseph and Mary-Ann (Hope) Phipps of Lancaster county, Pa., born
1824, in Lancaster county. She married (2) Atwood Powell. (Bailey
Family, p. 363.) They had no children.

adbcf b. GEORGE, son of Moses (*Jacob, Abraham, Mordecai,
Samuel*) and Barbara (Kinch) Lincoln of Darby, Pa., born Sept.
21, 1798, at Darby; died Aug. 20, 1877, at Darby "in his 80th
year." His gravestone says he was born in 1793, but this must
be an error of the stone-cutter. He was a farmer and lived at
Darby where he was supervisor of roads during nearly all of his
active adult life.

He married, Nov. 9, 1820, at Upper Darby, Phoebe-Speekman, daughter of Henry and Margaret Hoofstitler of Upper
Darby, born Aug. 20, 1800, at Upper Darby; died May 30, 1888,
at Darby. They are both buried in the old Darby cemetery
called "Mt. Zion," their gravestones being inscribed as follows:

"My Husband ‡ George Lincoln ‡ born Sep. 21st 1793 ‡ died
Aug. 20th 1878."

"In Memory of ‡ Phebe S. Lincoln ‡ died May 31, 1888 ‡
aged 88 years."

(Records of Clara-Virginia [Gilbert] Taylor, *adbcf bia;* George-
Lincoln Gilbert, *adbcf bid;* The Quaker Ogdens, p. 126, which
erroneously calls Mrs. Lincoln, Phebe-Shillingford. The gravestone inscriptions do not agree with the family Bible record.)

Children, born at Darby:

adbcf ba. JOHN, born Sept. 9, 1821.
adbcf bb. HENRY, born Dec. 7, 1822; died Oct. 7, 1825.
adbcf bc. JAMES, born Nov. 26, 1824; died Nov. 13, 1826.
adbcf bd. ELIZA, born Nov. 6, 1826; died June 22, 1899, at Kanopolis, Kan.;
married, Jan. 8, 1845, at Darby, Joseph, son of Henry and Catherine
(Lincoln) Paschall, formerly of Concord, Delaware county, Pa., *adbca ba,*
born March 23, 1823, at Darby; died July 8, 1894, at Kanopolis, whither
they removed in 1876.
Children, born: *a-c* at Paschallville; *d-h* at Concordville, Pa.:
a. GEORGE-HENRY, born Sept. 26, 1845; mar. Mary N. Lane.
b. JOSEPH, born Feb. 16, 1848; died young.
c. BEULAH-WORTH, born Sept. 9, 1849; mar. Erskine Becker.
d. CATHARINE-LINCOLN, born May 24, 1852; mar. George W.
Gilkinson.

      e.   JOSEPH-ALBIN, born Dec. 31, 1854; mar. (1) Nellie Sherman; (2) Ellen Weise.

      f.   MOSES-LINCOLN, born Dec. 15, 1857; mar. Jane M. Lane.

      g.   ANNA-FRANCES, born Sept. 19, 1860; mar. Abraham Wise.

      h.   ELIZA-IRENE, born March 10, 1865; died 1872.

adbcf be.   MOSES, born Oct. 24, 1828.

adbcf bf.   JACOB, born Dec. 13, 1830; died Oct. 26, 1832.

adbcf bg.   GEORGE, born May 31, 1834; died Apr. 3, 1835.

adbcf bh.   WILLIAM, born May 28, 1836; died Feb. 20, 1838.

adbcf bi.   PHOEBE, born July 16, 1838; married, May 25, 1859, at Darby, George-Frederick, son of George and Hetty (Chambers) Gilbert of Philadelphia, Pa., born July 18, 1833. They are living, 1915, as they have always, in the Borough of Yeadon, Pa., Lansdowne P. O. He was a farmer but is now retired. (Records of Mrs. Clara-Virginia [Gilbert] Taylor.)

    Children, born at Lansdowne:

      a.   CLARA-VIRGINIA, born Feb. 12, 1860; mar. Edward-Thompson Taylor.

      b.   PHOEBE-ELLA, born June 24, 1861; died March 24, 1863.

      c.   ESTELLE, born Apr. 14, 1864; mar. Horace-Armand Dunk.

      d.   GEORGE-LINCOLN, born June 25, 1866; mar. Gertrude Vandergrift.

adbcf c.   MICHAEL, son of Moses (*Jacob, Abraham, Mordecai, Samuel*) and Barbara (Kinch) Lincoln of Darby, Pa., born May 22, 1801, at Darby; died Oct. 16, 1844, at Darby. He was a farmer and lived at Darby. He died intestate and administration on his estate was granted to his brother Jacob, Jan. 6, 1846.

His wife's name was Rebecca but nothing has been learned of her save what is on her gravestone. She was born in 1801, and died June 14, 1865, at Darby in her 64th year. Mr. Lincoln is buried in the Old Swedes cemetery at Kingsessing, now part of Philadelphia, but his wife is buried in the old burying ground at Darby. Their gravestones bear the following inscriptions:

"Sacred ‡ to the Memory of ‡ Michael Lincoln ‡ who departed this life ‡ October 16th 1844 ‡ aged 43 years 4 months ‡ and 24 days ‡ Rest in peace."

"Our Mother ‡ In Memory of ‡ Rebecca R ‡ Relict of the late ‡ Michael Lincoln ‡ who departed this life ‡ June the 14th 1865 ‡ in the 64th year of her age ‡ Tho' lost to sight to memory dear ‡ Remain in peace."

Children, born at Darby:

adbcf ca.   ISAAC R.

adbcf cb.   JACOB. He is said to have married and to have had a daughter Laura, who became a nurse and was living, 1915, at Logan, Pa., unmarried.

adbcf cc. ANN-ELIZA, married, before 1851, Daniel Trites, but nothing has been learned of them.
    Children:
        a. JACOB-LINCOLN, born Aug. 14, 1851; died Apr. 28, 1858.*
        b. A DAUGHTER, mar. Isaac Custer and was living, 1915, at Colwin, Pa.
adbcf cd. REBECCA, died Feb. 21, 1879, at Philadelphia; married James Hutchinson. Administration on the estate of Rebecca Hutchinson, who died Feb. 21, 1879, was granted March 4, 1879, to Mary-Ann Hutchinson, 1632 Walnut St. Bond $2000. Sureties: Sarah Harkness and Margaret Hutchinson, all of Philadelphia. (Philadelphia Administrations, Bk. W, p. 111.)
adbcf ce. ELIZABETH, under age in 1856.

adbfa b. DANIEL-SAVAGE, son of William (*Mordecai, Abraham, Mordecai, Samuel*) and Lois (Pardee) Lincoln of Middletown Upper Houses, now Cromwell, Conn., born June 21, 1802, at Middletown Upper Houses; died Feb. 6, 1871, at Cromwell, where he had passed his life. He was a farmer and wheelwright and is said to have been a fine workman at his trade.

He married, Nov. 28, 1822, at Middletown, Conn., Florilla[3], daughter of Samuel[2] (*Samuel[1]*) and Ruth (Goodrich) Buck of Chatham and Portland, Conn., born July 31, 1803; died Oct. 31, 1884, at Berlin, Conn., but was buried at Cromwell in the new cemetery by the side of her husband and two of their children. Their gravestones are thus marked:

"Daniel S. Lincoln ‡ died ‡ Feb. 6, 1871 ‡ aged 69 ‡ Florilla B. his wife ‡ died Oct. 31, 1884 ‡ aged 82."

"Children of ‡ Daniel S & ‡ Florilla Lincoln ‡ Eliza M. ‡ died Nov. 9, 1859 ‡ aged 32 ‡ Sherman ‡ died Jan. 10, 1871 ‡ aged 39."

Isaac B. Lincoln was appointed, Feb. 28, 1871, administrator on the estate of Daniel S. Lincoln, his father, the widow declining. The estate was appraised at $3080.50. (Records of Congregational Church, Middletown Upper Houses; Gen. of Samuel Buck Families of Portland, Conn., p. 23; Middletown Probate Records.)

Children, born at Cromwell:

adbfa ba. SHERMAN, born Nov. 16, 1823; died Oct. 20, 1830, at Cromwell and is buried in the old cemetery. His gravestone is inscribed as

*His gravestone at Darby reads thus: "Erected ‡ to the memory of ‡ Jacob L. son ‡ of Daniel & Anna-Eliza Trites ‡ who died April 28th A. D. 1858 ‡ aged 6 years 8 months & 14 days."

25

follows: "Sherman ‡ son of ‡ Daniel S. & ‡ Florilla Lincoln ‡ died Oct.
21, 1830 ‡ ae 7 yrs."

adbfa bb. HANNAH M., born July 19, 1825; died March 3, 1887; married,
Oct. 12, 1846, at Middletown, Hiram Morgan of Berlin, Conn. He was a
blacksmith.

Children:
    a. CLARENCE-AUGUSTUS, died aged 11 months.
    b. EDGAR, living, 1916, at Berlin.

adbfa bc. ELIZA M., born Sept. 15, 1827; died Nov. 9, 1859, at Cromwell,
unmarried.

adbfa bd. ISAAC-BUCK, born Dec. 26, 1829.

adbfa be. SHERMAN, born 1832; died Jan. 10, 1871, at Cromwell. He enlisted
Apr. 19, 1861, in the 1st regiment Connecticut Volunteer Infantry for
three months, and was mustered out July 31, 1861. He re-enlisted as corporal, Aug. 19, 1861, in Company B, 7th Connecticut Volunteer Infantry,
was reduced to the ranks Sept. 1, 1863, re-enlisted as veteran Dec. 22,
1863, was captured at Hatcher's Run, Va., June 17, 1864, paroled March
4, 1865, and was honorably discharged July 20, 1865. He is said to have
been married in Portland, Conn., but nothing definite has been learned of
his wife.

adbfa bf. A CHILD, died May 24, 1834, in infancy.

adbfa bg. DANIEL-SAVAGE, born January, 1843.

adbfa bh. EDWARD-BUCK, born May 26, 1847; died Aug. 16, 1847, aet. 3
mos. Cromwell records say he was born in 1848.

adbfa e. WILLIAM M., son of William (*Mordecai, Abraham,
Mordecai, Samuel*) and Lois (Pardee) Lincoln of Middletown
Upper Houses, now Cromwell, Conn., born 1810, at Middletown;
died previous to 1880, at Cromwell, but there is no record of his
death. He was a farmer, lived at Cromwell and was of rather
dissipated habits.

He married before 1840, probably at Portland, Conn., Julia-
Ann Caldwell of Portland, born 1812. She is said to have died
after 1880, a widow. At the time of the birth of their daughter,
Mary-Jane-Savage, she was aged 35, and Mr. Lincoln was aged
37. (Middletown and Cromwell Records; Cromwell Church
Records.)

Children, born at Cromwell:

adbfa ea. JOSEPH, born 1840. He enlisted Sept. 5, 1862, in Company F,
24th Connecticut Volunteer Infantry, and served until Sept. 30, 1863.
He is called a "sailor" in his marriage record. He married, July 4, 1866,
at Middletown, at the age of 26, Mrs. Mary E. Northorp, who was then
24 years old. No further record has been found of them.

adbfa eb. WILLIAM H., died February, 1843.

adbfa ec. MARY-JANE-SAVAGE, born Nov. 27, 1847; died Dec. 7, 1852.

adbfa ed. ELLA, born March 15, 1850.

adbfa ee. WILLIAM, born June, 1852; died Dec. 6, 1852, aet. 6 months.
adbfa ef. A CHILD, born July 24, 1853; probably died young.
adbfa eg. JOHN, born Oct. 3, 1855; died Oct. 30, 1855.

adbfa f. ASA S., son of William (*Mordecai, Abraham, Mordecai, Samuel*) and Lois (Pardee) Lincoln of Middletown Upper Houses, now Cromwell, Conn., born 1814, at Middletown; died Feb. 13, 1869, at Cromwell, "aged 55 years." He was a farmer and lived at Cromwell.

He married about 1840, probably at Westbrook, Conn., Lucy Post of Westbrook, born 1820, at Westbrook; died May 17, 1894, at Cromwell, "aged 74 years." (Cromwell Records.) Mr. Lincoln's will, dated Dec. 17, 1867, probated March 25, 1869, names only his wife Lucy P. His estate was inventoried at $6032.25. (Middletown Probate Records, vol. xxiv, p. 259.)

Children, born at Cromwell:

adbfa fa. A CHILD, died Nov. 1, 1841, in infancy.
adbfa fb. ANNIE-SARAH, born Sept. 14, 1843; married, Dec. 27, 1859, at Cromwell (Cromwell Church Records say 1858), John-Demming, son of Ellelar and Aurelia Botelle of Cromwell, born Oct. 6, 1837, at Cromwell. His father was a native of France. After their marriage they lived at Cromwell until after 1886. They then removed to Waterbury, Conn., but are now, 1916, living at Oakville, Conn. Mr. Botelle was in earlier life a travelling salesman but, later, became an auctioneer. (Family Records.)
Children, born at Cromwell:
   a. LINCOLN-BELA, born Nov. 22, 1861; died 1871.
   b. ALBERT H., born Dec. 12, 1863; mar. Edith Marendaz.
   c. FANNY, born Jan. 13, 1866; mar. Michael Gleason.
   d. EDWARD M., born Oct. 2, 1867; mar. Mabel Adams.
   e. LUCY, born July 1, 1869; died Apr. 24, 1881.
   f. GRACE, born Oct. 31, 1872; mar. George Boden.
   g. HERBERT-JOHN, born Oct. 28, 1874; mar. Bertha Stoddard.
   h. BELA-LINCOLN, born Oct. 15, 1876; living, 1916, unmarried.
   i. IDA-WILCOX, born Oct. 4, 1878; living, 1916, unmarried.
   j. GERTRUDE-MAY, born Apr. 22, 1880; died Aug. 3, 1900, unmarried.
   k. SARAH S., born Apr. 10, 1883; died Oct. 22, 1884.
   l. PEARL-AMELIA, born Apr. 11, 1886; mar. Charles-Christopher Schreier.
adbfa fc. MARY L., born 1846; died at Deep River, Conn.; married, May 7, 1865, at Cromwell, Edward C., son of Jairus and Eunice (Southworth) Moore, born 1838, at Deep River; died at Deep River, where they had lived. They had no children. She was 19 and he was 27 years old when married.
adbfa fd. LUCY A., born 1849; married, Nov. 27, 1873, at Cromwell, Charles H. Jones, a native of New Brunswick, born 1849 and described as a

laborer in the marriage record. They were both twenty-four years old
when married. They had no children.

adbfa fe.   Asa S., born 1852; died Oct. 20, 1867, "aged fifteen years."

adbfa ff.   John-Egbert, born Aug. 17, 1855; died Feb. 26, 1857.

adbfa fg.   Belle E., born May 10, 1858; died at Deep River, Conn.; married,
June 22, 1876, at Cromwell, W. Arthur, son of John Lane of Deep River,
born 1850, at Winthrop, Conn.; living, 1915, at Middletown. He was a
merchant, twenty-six years old when married.

    Children:

        a. Anna-May, born 1878; died unmarried.

        b. Herbert, died unmarried.

adbfa fh.   Charles-Russell, born Oct. 30, 1862.

adcac b.   Francis, son of Uriah (*Isaac, Isaac, Mordecai,
Samuel*) and Mary (Lincoln) Lincoln of Cohasset, Mass., born
Sept. 13, 1775, at Cohasset; died May 29, 1850, at Cohasset.
He was a farmer and tanner and lived in Cohasset on South Main
street, in a house which he built in 1806, just north of one built
by Mordecai Lincoln, *ad*, for his son Isaac. He carried on his
father's tannery business until the loss of an eye, in 1816, compelled him to abandon the works. He was a member of the
school committee in 1807, 1818 and 1826.

He married, Nov. 29, 1804, at Cohasset, Peggy[6], daughter of
Peter[5] (*Daniel[4], Nathaniel[3], Israel[2], Thomas[1]*) and Molly (Tower)
Nichols of Cohasset, born Apr. 19, 1778, at Cohasset; died Oct.
22, 1858, at Cohasset. (Family Bible with Francis Lincoln,
adcac bab; Cohasset Genealogies, pp. 242, 303; Cohasset Records,
which differ sometimes from the Family Bible.)

Child, born at Cohasset:

adcac ba.   Isaac, born Nov. 12, 1805.

adcac d.   Isaac, son of Uriah (*Isaac, Isaac, Mordecai, Samuel*)
and Mary (Lincoln) Lincoln of Cohasset, Mass., born Jan. 26,
1780, at Cohasset; died March 6, 1868, at Brunswick, Me. He
graduated at Harvard College in the class of 1800, and was its
last surviving member. He studied medicine and began practice
in 1804 at Topsham, Me., but soon removed to Brunswick where
he was in successful practice for more than fifty years, though
he retired from active business some time before his death. He
received an honorary degree of M.D. from Bowdoin College in
1831; was a member of the medical faculty of the Maine Medical

School from 1820 to 1867, and in 1865 was chosen an overseer of Bowdoin College. He was a prominent citizen of the town and a leader of the Congregational Church. He was elected to the Governor's Council but declined to serve. "A man of high character and of sterling integrity, but remarkably firm and decided in his opinions—genial always and cheerful to the last days of his life."

He married, Aug. 24, 1820, at Brunswick, Marcia-Scott, daughter of John and Mary (Tapham) Dunlap of Brunswick, born July 12, 1799, at Brunswick (Cohasset Genealogies and Brunswick records say July 22); died Feb. 2, 1833, at Brunswick. (New Eng. Hist. & Gen. Register, vols. xxiii, p. 201; xxiii, p. 86; Hist. of Brunswick, pp. 760-1; Bangor Hist. Recorder, vol. vi, p. 41; Cohasset Genealogies, p. 242; Brunswick Records.)

Children, born at Brunswick:

adcac da. JOHN-DUNLAP, born June 1, 1821.

adcac db. MARY-ELIZABETH, born May 13, 1823; died March 8, 1908, at Bath, Me.; married, May 24, 1848, at Brunswick, John-Green, son of William and Harriet (Leland) Richardson of Bath, born Dec. 16, 1823, at Bath; died Aug. 29, 1894, at Bath. He is erroneously called John J. in the record of his marriage at Brunswick. He lived in Bath and was in business there until 1857 when he went to Liverpool, England, where he remained until 1874 when he returned to Bath. He was mayor of Bath 1878-9 and presidential elector in 1883. "Richardson Memorial" is in error in saying that he was postmaster of Bath in 1873, as he never held that office in any place. He was a great-nephew of Governor King, Maine's first governor. (Richardson Memorial, p. 627; Bath Records; Records of Miss Marcia Richardson, *adcac dba*.)

   Child, born at Bath:

   a. MARCIA-DUNLAP, born May 3, 1849; living, 1910, at Bath, unmarried.

adcai b. JOHN, son of Lazarus (*Isaac, Isaac, Mordecai, Samuel*) and Fanny (Kilby) Lincoln of Cohasset, Mass., born Jan. 15, 1784, at Cohasset; died Dec. 31, 1832, at Wilmington, N. C., and is buried in Central burying ground, Cohasset. "Cohasset Genealogies" says he died at sea; but this probably means on one of his voyages, as the Cohasset records clearly state that he died at Wilmington and, moreover, his body was brought to Cohasset for burial. He was a master-mariner or sea captain. He lived at Cohasset, in the Cushing Kilby house on South Main street. "Cohasset Genealogies," p. 548, says: "The name of

John Lincoln is given as captain of the following vessels in the registers of the Boston Custom House, but as the name continues on the records after the death of the Cohasset John Lincoln, we cannot be sure that these vessels were actually commanded by him: Schooner Eliza, May, 1819; schooner Mary Ann, 1822; brig Boston, 1823; brig Billow, 1824; brig Chilo, 1828; brig Wave, 1831."

He married (1), Aug. 2, 1807, at Scituate, Mass., Deborah-Otis[4], daughter of Snell[3] (*Issachar[2], Joseph[1]*) and Charlotte (Otis) Wade of Scituate, born May 25, 1786, at Scituate; died Apr. 11, 1818, at Cohasset.

He married (2), Feb. 7, 1819, at Cohasset, Elizabeth[7], daughter of James[6] (*James[5], Jeremiah[4], Jeremiah[3], Samuel[2], John[1]*) and Susanna (Lincoln) Stoddard of Cohasset, *aaffb b*, born, Dec. 13, 1784, at Cohasset; died Jan. 9, 1848, at Cohasset. Both wives are buried in Central burying ground. (Cohasset Genealogies, p. 242; Cohasset Records; Scituate Records; Gravestones.)

Children, by first wife, born at Cohasset:

adcai ba. DEBORAH, born June 2, 1808; died May 8, 1897, at Cohasset; married, Dec. 2, 1829, at Cohasset, John[6], son of Gershom[5] (*Aaron[4], Aaron[3], Aaron[2], Phineas[1]*) and Ruth (Lothrop) Pratt of Cohasset, born July, 1801, at Cohasset; died Jan. 1, 1865, at Cohasset, "aged sixty-three years, six months." He was a mariner but his death was due to a railroad accident. (Cohasset Genealogies, p. 350.)
>   Children, born at Cohasset:
>   *a.* OTIS-LINCOLN, born Aug. 26, 1830; mar. Naomi-Downs Pettis.
>   *b.* JOHN L., born May 11, 1833; mar. Paulina-Snow Joy.

adcai bb. CHARLOTTE-OTIS, born Nov. 5, 1811; died June 6, 1813, but the church records say June 5.

adcai bc. OTIS-WADE, born Oct. 31, 1817; died Feb. 25, 1818. He is erroneously called Otis-Ward in his birth record.

Children, by second wife, born at Cohasset:

adcai bd. JAMES-CARTER, born Nov. 23, 1819; died Oct. 30, 1822. His gravestone in Central burying ground says "aged 5 years."

adcai be. SUSANNAH-STODDARD, born Aug. 21, 1822; died Sept. 13, 1880, at Cohasset; married, Dec. 13, 1840, at Cohasset, Henry[7], son of Henry[6] (*David[5], Anthony[4], John[3], John[2], Nicholas[1]*) and Deliverance (Dyer) Snow of Cohasset, born Sept. 18, 1810, at Cohasset; died Apr. 25, 1904, at Cohasset. His birth is erroneously given as 1814 in Cohasset records. He was a master-mariner and lived at Cohasset on South Main street, in a house which he built south of his father's. (Cohasset Genealogies, p. 391.)
>   Children, born at Cohasset:
>   *a.* A SON, born Apr. 17, 1841; died May 6, 1841.
>   *b.* JAMES H., born June 28, 1842.

    c. ANN-FRANCES, born Aug. 24, 1844; died July 5, 1869, unmarried.
    d. SUSAN-ELIZABETH, born Oct. 20, 1846; mar. Leonard A. Giles.
    e. RUTH-NICHOLS, born June 29, 1848; mar. James-Hall Nichols.
    f. CHARLOTTE-OTIS, born Nov. 8, 1850; mar. George W. Mealy.
    g. BENJAMIN-LINCOLN, born Aug. 2, 1853; died Jan. 24, 1859.
adcai bf. BETSEY-WADE, born Dec. 16, 1824; died March 22, 1828. Her
gravestone says "died March 22, 1826 aged 3 years."
adcai bg. JOHN-JAMES, born Aug. 5, 1827.

adcai f. ANSLEM, son of Lazarus (*Isaac, Isaac, Mordecai, Samuel*) and Fanny (Kilby) Lincoln of Cohasset, Mass., born Jan. 19, 1794, at Cohasset; died Oct. 19, 1888, at Malone, N. Y. He is called "Anselm" in Cohasset Genealogies and Cohasset Records, but he called himself Anslem and named his son the same. He removed to Malone and was a tanner and shoemaker.

He married, Jan. 28, 1829, at Colchester, Vt., Hannah, daughter of Paul and Sabrina (Spencer) Clapp of Colchester, born Nov. 19, 1811, at Colchester; died Sept. 21, 1861, at Malone. (Cohasset Genealogies, p. 238; Winslow Family, vol. ii, p. 594; Records of George-Morton Lincoln, *adcai fba.*)

Children, born at Malone:

adcai fa. EMILY-BEAN, born July 3, 1831; died Oct. 14, 1865, unmarried.
adcai fb. JOHN, born July 26, 1833.
adcai fc. ALFRED, born July 10, 1836; died Apr. 11, 1869, at Malone, unmarried.
adcai fd. MARY-ANNA, born Dec. 31, 1839; died Nov. 29, 1842.
adcai fe. FANNY-KILBY, born July 20, 1843; living, 1912, unmarried.
adcai ff. ANSLEM, born Oct. 26, 1845.
adcai fg. WARREN, born February, 1848; died Dec. 24, 1851.
adcai fh. ELLEN-MARIA, born June 23, 1853; living, 1912, unmarried.

adcak b. WARREN, son of James (*Isaac, Isaac, Mordecai, Samuel*) and Abigail (Mitchell) Lincoln of Cohasset, Mass., born Nov. 2, 1792, at Cohasset; died Nov. 12, 1823, at Cohasset. He lived at Cohasset in a house built by his father and now owned by his grandson, Thomas Doyle, on South Main street.

He married, about 1818, Hannah Hobbs, who was born in March, 1800, and died Jan. 30, 1867, at Cohasset, "aged sixty six years, ten months." She married (2), Nov. 3, 1837, at Arlington, Mass., Daniel Faloon who died of an accident Jan. 21, 1854, at Arlington, though Boston records say he died there and was buried in South Ground. He is described in the record

of his death as "a laborer from Ireland, aged forty years."
There is no record of his having any children. (Cohasset Gen-
ealogies, p. 242; Cohasset Records; Arlington Records; Mass.
Vital Records.)

Children, born at Cohasset:

adcak ba. MARY-ANN, born March 23, 1819; died Apr. 15, 1900, at Cohasset;
married (1), July 18, 1852, at Cohasset, Thomas, son of Daniel Doyle of
Ireland, born 1817, in Ireland; died Aug. 13, 1857, at Cohasset. He was a
master-mariner and lived at Cohasset on South Main street, in the house
which belonged to his wife's father. Captain Doyle was commander of
the schooners Antelope and Abigail, the brigs Eliza Burgess and Almatia,
and the bark Maryland. Cohasset records say he was thirty-five years
old when married. Mrs. Doyle married (2), Aug. 2, 1862, at Cohasset,
Captain Alden Simmons of Duxbury, a widower with one son. He died
in 1880, having had no child by Mary-Ann. (Cohasset Genealogies,
pp. 139, 561.)
  Children, by first husband, born at Cohasset:
    a. WARREN-LINCOLN DOYLE, born Jan. 1, 1855; died June 8, 1856.
    b. THOMAS-WARREN DOYLE, born May 23, 1857; living, 1909, at
      Cohasset.
adcak bb. JAMES-WARREN, born Aug. 25 or 26, 1820; died May 6, 1901, at
Boston, Mass.; married Rebecca, daughter of Joseph and Zerviah (Sweet-
land) Sherburn of Industry, Me., born July 12, 1809, at Industry; died
May 1, 1901, at Boston. They are both buried at South Gardiner, Me.
He was a mason by trade. He moved to Boston when about seventeen
years old and lived there until his death. They had no children. (Mass.
Vital Records.)

adfad b. MARTIN, son of Jacob (*Obadiah, Jacob, Mordecai,
Samuel*) and Chloe (Lincoln) Lincoln of Cohasset and Lancaster,
Mass., born Jan. 23, 1795, at Cohasset; died Dec. 9, 1878, at
Westfield, Mass. He went to New York State in 1816, but
returned to Lancaster, where his parents had settled soon after
his birth, in 1826, and became principal of the Academy. In
1836 he removed to Boston to teach in a private school on
Shawmut avenue. He remained there until 1849, when he
removed to Champion, N. Y., where he engaged in farming.
He returned again to Massachusetts in 1875, living at Westfield
until his death. He was engaged in the War of 1812, but did
not see active service. He was sometimes called "captain."
He is said to have had the physical features of President Lincoln.

He married, Nov. 1, 1818, at Watertown, N. Y., Susan-White,
daughter of Adam and Margaret (White) Freeman, born May 2,
1799, near Utica, N. Y.; died May 7, 1893, at Newton, Mass.,

"aged ninety four years, five days." (Records of Miss Mary-Alice Walton, *adfad bce;* Mass. Vital Records.)

Children, born: *a, b* at Alexandria; *c* at Watertown, N. Y.:

adfad ba. MARTIN-VOLNEY, born Dec. 22, 1819.

adfad bb. MARY-MARIA, born March 19, 1821; living, 1912, at Black River, N. Y.; married, July 22, 1891, at Newton, Mass., Lewis-Harris, son of Horace and Phila (Harris) Loomis of Champion, N. Y., born 1823, at Champion; died June, 1901, at Lyndonville, N. Y. Since his death she has lived at Black River. He was a farmer. He married (1), Apr. 20, 1852, Eliza P. Sheldon, who died March 2, 1890. They had no children but adopted as a daughter, Etta Townsend, who was born March 17, 1857; married a Mr. Brown and is now, 1912, a widow.

adfad bc. ELECTA-NOBLES, born May 12, 1824; died March 15, 1908, at West Newton, Mass.; married, Aug. 27, 1850, at Watertown, N. Y., George-Augustus, son of James and Elizabeth (Bryant) Walton of Wakefield, Mass., born Feb. 20, 1822, at Wakefield; died Nov. 7, 1908, at West Newton. He was educated in Lexington Academy, Reading Academy and Bridgewater Normal School where he graduated in 1844. He received the degree of A.M. at Williams College in 1869. He was a teacher in various towns in Massachusetts and, from 1871 to 1896, was agent of the State Board of Education. He was a member of the American Institute of Instruction from 1846, and has been its treasurer and president. Was alderman of the City of Lawrence. He was the author of numerous books on Arithmetic and of various educational papers and reports. His wife was also a teacher until her marriage. She was a graduate of Lexington, Mass., Normal School. They lived at Lawrence, Westfield and West Newton. (Records of Miss Mary-Alice Walton, *adfad bce;* Who's Who in America, 1908-9.)

Children, born at Lawrence:

a. HARRIET-PIERCE, born Sept. 2, 1852; mar. James-Robert Dunbar.

b. GEORGE-LINCOLN, born March 15, 1854; living, 1912, unmarried.

c. EDGAR-BRYANT, born Oct. 8, 1856; died Sept. 8, 1858.

d. FREDERICK, born Feb. 14, 1859; died May 5, 1860.

e. MARY-ALICE, born Jan. 13, 1865; living, 1912, unmarried.

adfae a. WILLIAM, son of Amos (*Obadiah, Jacob, Mordecai, Samuel*) and Huldah (Kilby) Lincoln of Cohasset, Mass., born Oct. 24, 1785, at Cohasset; died Sept. 20, 1869, at Cohasset. He was a farmer and lived at Cohasset on South Main street, in a house previously occupied by his father and built by his uncle Jacob.

He married, Jan. 2, 1814, at Scituate,* Becky, daughter of Haywood and Judith (Bailey) Pierce of Scituate, born Apr. 3, 1785, at Scituate; died Apr. 15, 1867, at Cohasset. (Cohasset

*Pierce Genealogy says they were married Sept. 25, 1813, but this is probably the date of the intentions.

Genealogies, p. 243; Cohasset Records; Scituate Records; Pierce Genealogy, 1889, p. 63; Mass. Vital Records.)

Children, born at Cohasset:

adfae aa. WILLIAM, born Nov. 2, 1814; died Jan. 11, 1817, and is buried in Central burying ground, where his gravestone says he died June 11, 1817, "aged 2 yrs. 2 ms. 9 ds."

adfae ab. HULDAH, born July 3, 1817; died Aug. 13, 1833.

adfae ac. BETSEY-PIERCE, born Dec. 28, 1819; died Nov. 1, 1872, at Cohasset; married, Oct. 10, 1859, at Cohasset, William, son of Edward and Catherine Donnelly of York, Pa., born December, 1818 or 1819; died 1880, in Colorado. He was aged forty when married. He was a printer in York or Newcastle, Pa., but removed to Cohasset, where he lived in the Obadiah Lincoln house on South Main street, occupied in 1912 by Mrs. Esther-Eliza Lincoln, *adfae ad.*

Children, born at Cohasset:

    a. WILLIAM-LINCOLN, born Jan. 8, 1861; living, 1885, in Idaho unmarried.

    b. EDWARD-PIERCE, born Nov. 13, 1862; living, 1911, at Iditarod, Alaska, unmarried. A Roosevelt rough rider.

    c. GEORGE-GRANVILLE, born Jan. 29, 1864; living, 1911, at Seattle, Wash., unmarried. Cohasset records say born Jan. 20.

adfae ad. WILLIAM, born Dec. 22, 1821.

adfae ae. REBECKAH, born June 25, 1824; died Jan. 29, 1843, at Cohasset, unmarried. "Cohasset Genealogies" says died Jan. 22.

adfae af. HANNAH-JANE, born July 14, 1826; died Dec. 8, 1872, at Hematite, Mo.; married, Aug. 14, 1855, at Cohasset (Family Bible; Cohasset Records say Aug. 13), Alexander-Watson, son of Robert Smith of Scotland, born 1816 or 1817, at Eglan, Scotland. No record of his death has been found but he was drafted into the army and was missing after the battle of Hatch's Run, Va. He was a farmer from Thomasville, Ontario. They lived there for three months after their marriage and then removed to Canastota, N. Y., and thence to Norton, Mich. Mr. Smith is said to have been thirty-eight years old when married. They had no children. (Records of Mrs. William Lincoln, *adfae ad.*)

adfah a. WILLIAM-VINAL, son of Obadiah (*Obadiah, Jacob, Mordecai, Samuel*) and Marcy (Vinal) Lincoln of Scituate, Mass., born Oct. 21, 1796, at Cohasset, Mass.; died March 8, 1865, at Quincy, Mass. He was put under guardianship of his uncle, William Vinal of Scituate, Oct. 4, 1802. He lived at Quincy after his marriage and is called "trader" in the Massachusetts Vital Records.

He married, Nov. 26, 1838, at Quincy, Mrs. Mary (Sampson) Packard, daughter of Joshua and Lucy (Holbrook) Sampson of Braintree, Mass., and widow of Samuel Packard who died Apr. 18, 1837, at Quincy, and by whom she had two children. She

was born Sept. 9, 1810, at Braintree, but the date of her death
has not been learned. (Mass. Vital Records; Quincy Records;
Sampson Family, p. 71; Giles Memorial, p. 466; Winslow Family,
vol. i, p. 178; Vinton Memorial, p. 186; Plymouth County
Probate Records, vol. xxxii, p. 192.)

Children, born at Quincy:

adfah aa. MARY-VINAL, born Dec. 24, 1839; married, Aug. 25, 1867, at
Quincy, Horace W., son of Joshua and Adaline Phelps of Braintree,
born 1840, at Braintree. He was living at Weymouth, Mass., when
married and was a "bootmaker."

adfah ab. LUCY-FRANCES, born Oct. 16, 1841; married, Feb. 5, 1874, at
Quincy, John-Thomas, son of Lewis and Polly (Hathaway) McLauthlin
of Duxbury, Mass., born March 12, 1838, at Duxbury. He was a "ship-
joiner" and in 1876 was living at East Boston. Later he is called "carpenter" and his name appears in the Boston directories until 1904,
after which date it disappears.

adfah ac. MERCY-MARIA, born July 1, 1843; died July 12, 1865, at Quincy,
unmarried.

adffe c. THOMAS, son of Caleb (*Abraham, Jacob, Mordecai,
Samuel*) and Nancy (Bicknell) Lincoln of Cohasset, Mass., born
Nov. 7, 1809, at Dorchester, Mass.; died March 17, 1891, at
Providence, R. I. Dorchester records, as published by the
Boston Record Commissioners, give his birth as Sept. 2, 1810,
which may have been the date of his baptism. "Cohasset
Genealogies" also gives incorrect dates of birth for all the
children of Caleb and Nancy (Bicknell) Lincoln. As given here
they are from the family Bible. Mr. Lincoln lived at the time
of his marriage at East Cambridge, Mass., but soon removed to
Providence, where he passed the remainder of his life. He
engaged in the manufacture of soap, at first with S. R. Jackson
under the firm name of S. R. Jackson & Co., and later with his
brother Samuel, when the firm name became T. & S. Lincoln.

He married, Dec. 3, 1835, at Watertown, Mass., Lucy-Cool-
idge[7], daughter of Asa[6] (*John[5], John[4], Ebenezer[3], Simon[2], Simon[1]*)
and Mary (Coolidge) Stone of Newton, Mass., born July 8, 1815,
at Watertown; died Dec. 12, 1909, at Providence, "in the full
possession of all her faculties, although in her ninety fifth year."
(Providence Records; Newton Records; Watertown Records;
Gen.'s and Hist. of Watertown, pp. 586-7, 951; Boston Evening
Transcript, Dec. 13, 1909; Records of George-Henry Lincoln,
adffe cb.)

Children, born: *a* at Cambridge, Mass.; *b-g* at Providence:

adffe ca. FRANCIS-STONE, born Sept. 11, 1836.
adffe cb. GEORGE-HENRY, born Nov. 18, 1838.
adffe cc. EMMA-BICKNELL, born Sept. 19, 1841; living, 1911, at Providence, unmarried.
adffe cd. THOMAS-MANSON, born Dec. 29, 1843.
adffe ce. LYDIA-MARIA, born Sept. 19, 1846; married, Apr. 28, 1869, at Providence, Herbert-Mortimer, son of Jefferson-Liberty and Mary-Amanda (Gardner) Kimball of Providence, born Sept. 10, 1845, at Coventry, R. I. "Kimball Family" says he was born Sept. 5, and gives March 19, 1870, as the date of his son's birth. He and his wife were both living, 1911, at Providence. He was in the life insurance business. (Providence Records; Kimball Family, p. 805.)
    Child, born at Providence:
      a. HERBERT-FRANCIS, born Feb. 18, 1870; died Nov. 19, 1871.
adffe cf. RICHMOND-JACKSON, born Jan. 3, 1849; died Nov. 23, 1900, at Cranston, R. I., unmarried.
adffe cg. CHARLES-EDWARD, born March 10, 1853.

adffe d. SAMUEL, son of Caleb (*Abraham, Jacob, Mordecai, Samuel*) and Nancy (Bicknell) Lincoln of Cohasset, Mass., born Dec. 7, 1811, bapt. March 20, 1814, at Dorchester, Mass., died Dec. 21, 1859, at Providence, R. I. He lived at Providence where he was at first in the grocery business, but, being unsuccessful in that, he was taken into partnership by his brother Thomas in the soap business, the firm name being T. & S. Lincoln.

He married (1), Apr. 16, 1835, Hannah-Prentiss, daughter of William Perry of Brookline or Brighton, Mass., born March 13, 1811; died July 31, 1837, at Providence. Providence records call her "aged 24 years."

He married (2), Nov. 1, 1838, at Cumberland, R. I., Olive, daughter of Amos and Olive (Darling) Cook of Cumberland, born Jan. 4, 1815, at Cumberland; died May 3, 1862, at Providence, "aged forty-seven years, two months, twenty-nine days." (Dorchester Records; Providence Records; Records of George-Henry Lincoln, *adffe cb;* Family Bible of Clarence-Henry Lincoln, *adffe df.*)

Children, by first wife, born at Providence:

adffe da. SARAH-ELIZABETH, born Jan. 29, 1837; died Sept. 17, 1838, at Providence. She is said to have been buried at Brighton, Mass., with her mother, but their deaths are recorded in Westminster Congregational Church, Providence.

Children, by second wife, born at Providence:

adffe db. WILLIAM-PERRY, born Sept. 17, 1839; died Sept. 27, 1861, unmarried.

adffe dc. CHARLES-EDMUND, born Sept. 3, 1844; died July 23, 1845.

adffe dd. SAMUEL-DARLING, born Sept. 19, 1846; died Feb. 17, 1865, while a private in the 10th regiment, Rhode Island infantry, on duty in the Civil war. He married, Feb. 12, 1865, at Woonsocket, R. I., Laura-Ashbury, daughter of Hanson and Eliza-Ann (Marsh) Arnold of Woonsocket, where she was born. She married (2) a Mr. Sage, a well-known trunk dealer in Boston, and was living, 1912, at Sharon, Mass. Mr. and Mrs. Lincoln had no child.

adffe de. LOVELL-BICKNELL, born March 16, 1850; died July 9, 1867.

adffe df. CLARENCE-HENRY, born Dec. 2, 1853.

adffe dg. LEVI-COOK, born Apr. 15, 1858.

adffe 1.   ABRAHAM, son of Caleb (*Abraham, Jacob, Mordecai, Samuel*) and Elizabeth (Robbins) Lincoln of Cohasset, Mass., born Feb. 3, 1830, at Cohasset; died Oct. 20, 1912, at Cohasset. He was a mason by trade and for twenty-one years was in the employ of William C. Poland of Boston. He lived first at Roxbury, Mass., where he was resident in 1852 and 1853. He afterwards lived at Cambridgeport for a while, but, in 1856, was living in Boston and, in 1867, he returned to Cohasset where he passed the remainder of his life. At Cohasset he lived on Beechwood street, in a house built by his father. "Cohasset Genealogies" says that he was a soldier in the Civil war, but his daughter says this is an error.

He married (1), Apr. 1, 1852, at Boston, Sarah-Janette, daughter of Earl P. and Juline (Everett) White of Norton, Mass., born March 10, 1824, at Norton; died Oct. 23, 1853, at Cohasset. She is called "of Boston" when married.

He married (2), Nov. 17, 1853, at Boston, Mary-Jane, daughter of Robert and Eliza (Campbell) Galbraith of St. John, New Brunswick, born Aug. 11, 1831, at St. John; died Apr. 15, 1901, at Cohasset. She is also called "of Boston" when married. (Cohasset Genealogies, p. 243; Mass. Vital Records; Norton Records; Records of Abraham Lincoln and of his daughter, Mrs. Olive-Augusta [Lincoln] Richards.)

Child, by first wife, born at Cohasset:

adffe la. CHARLES-WHITE, born May 19, 1853; died Dec. 25, 1860.

Children, by second wife, born: *b* at Cohasset; *c* at Boston:

adffe lb.   LIZZIE-ROBBINS, born July 31, 1854, according to Family records, but "Cohasset Genealogies" and Cohasset records both say June 12. She was living, 1911, at Cohasset. She married, Dec. 11, 1873, at Cohasset, Horace-Kingman, son of Shadrach-Sever and Mary-Jane (Kingman) Marden of Weymouth, Mass., born Oct. 2, 1851, at Weymouth; died Feb. 23, 1897, at East Weymouth. They lived at Cohasset on Beechwood street, but the marriage proved unhappy and they separated. He was an organ builder.

    Child, born at Cohasset:

      a.   HARRY-NIXON, born Nov. 29, 1878; living, 1911, unmarried.

adffe lc.   OLIVE-AUGUSTA, born May 2, 1856; married, Nov. 28, 1877, at Cohasset, Frank-Winslow, son of Ebenezer-William and Clarissa-Emeline (Richards) Richards of Weymouth, Mass., born Feb. 17, 1854, at Weymouth. They were living, 1911, at Weymouth. He was a carpenter.

    Child, born at Cohasset:

      a.   FRED-LINCOLN, born Aug. 1, 1878; mar. Florence-Eveline Sulis.

SEVENTH GENERATION

aabcd bc. Nichols, son of Nichols (*Jonathan, Jonathan, Samuel, Samuel, Samuel*) and Deborah (Souther) Lincoln of Hingham, Mass., born Oct. 4, 1816, at Hingham; died May 31, 1885, at Danvers, Mass. He was a shoemaker and lived at Danvers, having removed thither before his marriage.

He married, June 5, 1849, at South Scituate (now Norwell), Mass., Lucy-Ann, daughter of Charles and Rhoda (Reed) Briggs of Scituate, born Aug. 7, 1827, at South Scituate; died Nov. 17, 1878, at Danvers. She was insane at the time of her death.

Mr. and Mrs. Lincoln and two of their children are buried in the cemetery at Danvers Center. Their gravestones bear the following inscriptions:

"Nichols Lincoln ‡ died May 31, 1885 ‡ aet 68 yrs 7 mos ‡ 23 dys."

"Lucy A. Wife of ‡ Nichols Lincoln ‡ died Nov. 17, 1878 ‡ aet 51 yrs 8 mos ‡ 10 dys."

"Lucy Ann ‡ Dau of Nichols & ‡ Lucy Ann Lincoln ‡ died Sept. 13, 1853 ‡ aet 1 yr 11 mos."

"Alvah Lincoln ‡ died Dec 10 1881 ‡ Aet 27 yrs 4 mos." (Danvers Records; Scituate Records; Mass. Vital Records; Gravestones at Danvers.)

Children, born at Danvers:

aabcd bca. Lucy-Ann, born Oct. 14, 1851; died Sept. 13, 1853.

aabcd bcb. Alvah-Thaxter, born Aug. 4, 1854; died Dec. 10, 1881, at Danvers; married, May 28, 1876, at Boxford, Mass., Anna R., daughter of Tobias-Davis and Mary-Ann (Townsend) Reed of Topsfield, Mass., born Sept. 4, 1856, at Topsfield; died Jan. 18, 1878, at Danvers. He was a cordwainer. They lived at Danvers and had no children. Massachusetts Vital Records have an erroneous record of their marriage; they also say that Mr. Lincoln died in 1880, and that his sister, Emma-Souther, was born in 1856.

aabcd bcc. Emma-Souther, born Aug. 31, 1857; married, Dec. 2, 1877, at Danvers, Jerome-Porter, son of Joel F. and Eliza (Thompson) Phelps of Danvers, born Aug. 7, 1853, at Danvers. His father was a shoemaker born at Northfield, N. H.; his mother was a native of Salem, Mass. He is described as a "shoecutter" at the time of his marriage. They were living, 1911, at Rochester, N. H. (Mass. Vital Records; George-Henry Lincoln, *aabcd bcd*.)

Children:
    a. ARTHUR-CHESTER.
    b. ANNIE-MAY, living, 1911, unmarried.
aabcd bcd. GEORGE-HENRY, born June 14, 1869.

aabce ab. JAIRUS-BEALS, son of Peter (*Frederick, Jonathan, Samuel, Samuel, Samuel*) and Anna (Bates) Lincoln of Weymouth, Mass., born March 23, 1815, at Weymouth; died May 1, 1879, at Weymouth. He is described as "bootmaker" in 1844, but in the record of his death he is called "farmer." He lived at Weymouth.

He married, Apr.* 17, 1842, at Weymouth, Priscilla-Shaw[3], daughter of David[2] (*Samuel[1]*) and Polly (Shaw) Pratt of Weymouth, born Jan. 22, 1822, at Weymouth, baptized there Apr. 6, 1828; died Nov. 26, 1898, at Weymouth, "aged seventy six years, ten months, four days." (Weymouth Records; Mass. Vital Records.)

Children, born at Weymouth:

aabce aba. CHARLES-JAIRUS, born Apr. 1, 1844.
aabce abb. HARRIET-PRISCILLA, born June 29, 1846; living, 1912, at Weymouth, unmarried.
aabce abc. DAVID-PRATT, born Oct. 19, 1855.

aabce ad. PETER-WHITMARSH, son of Peter (*Frederick, Jonathan, Samuel, Samuel, Samuel*) and Anna (Bates) Lincoln of Weymouth, Mass., born Aug. 2, 1820, at Weymouth according to Weymouth records; died July 12, 1902, at Boston, Mass., "aged eighty-one years, eleven months, six days," say Massachusetts Vital Records, which would make him born on Aug. 6, 1820. He was a "cordwainer" or shoemaker and later was in the boot and shoe business at Boston. He is buried at North Weymouth.

He married, Nov. 23, 1842, at Weymouth, Nancy-Jane, daughter of Thomas and Nancy (Spence) Porter of Boston, born September, 1819, at Boston; died May 26, 1895, at Boston. (Weymouth Records; Mass. Vital Records, which say they were married Dec. 1, 1842.)

Children, born: *a-d* at Weymouth; *e-i* at Boston.

aabce ada. CHARLES-AUGUSTUS, born Aug. 30, 1843; died Sept. 12, 1843.

*So say Weymouth records, but Massachusetts Vital Records say June.

aabce adb. GEORGE-EDWARD, born Oct. 12, 1844; died Oct. 14, 1848.

aabce adc. SARAH-JANE, born Nov. 3, 1845; died Jan. 1, 1899, at Weymouth, unmarried.

aabce add. JOHN T. (or F.), born Nov. 13, 1847; died Aug. 15, 1848.

aabce ade. ELLA A., born Aug. 5, 1849; died Oct. 6, 1849. Her birth record gives her no middle initial; State records call her "a son."

aabce adf. NANCY-JANE, born Oct. 16, 1850; died Oct. 23, 1851.

aabce adg. GEORGE-PETER, born Nov. 24, 1854; died Oct. 13, 1855, at Boston, "aged ten months, nineteen days." He is called George W. in State records.

aabce adh. WARREN T., born March 11, 1857; died Aug. 8, 1857.

aabce adi. ABRAHAM, born Nov. 7, 1860; died Sept. 2, 1889, at Pembroke, Mass., having taken poison by mistake. He was a "shipper" and unmarried.

aabce ae. OLIVER, son of Peter (*Frederick, Jonathan, Samuel, Samuel, Samuel*) and Anna (Bates) Lincoln of Weymouth, Mass., born March 20, 1824, at Weymouth; died Apr. 7, 1893, at Weymouth, "aged sixty-nine years, seventeen days." He is called "shoemaker" in the Massachusetts Vital Records, except in the record of his death when he is said to be "retired." He lived at Weymouth.

He married (1), Dec. 4, 1848, at Weymouth, Jane-Thaxter, daughter of John and Mary-Ann Burrell of Charlestown, Mass., or Weymouth, born June, 1824; died Aug. 27, 1849, at Weymouth. She is erroneously called daughter of John and Mary-Ann Randall in the record of her death in Massachusetts Vital Records.

He married (2), July 24, 1851, at Weymouth, Hannah-Pratt, daughter of Ebed and Sophia (Nash) Dunbar of Weymouth, born Feb. 19, 1829, at Weymouth; died Sept. 11, 1902, at Weymouth. (Weymouth Records; Mass. Vital Records; Records of Mrs. Edith-Lillian [Lincoln] Case, *aabce aebb.*)

Children, born at Weymouth:

aabce aea. ABIGAIL-FRANCES, born Feb. 26, 1852; died Aug. 11, 1902, at Weymouth, unmarried.

aabce aeb. FREDERIC, born May 16, 1854.

aabce aec. LAFORREST, born July 21, 1857.

aabce bg. GEORGE-FREDERICK-HANDEL, son of Frederick (*Frederick, Jonathan, Samuel, Samuel, Samuel*) and Hepzibah (Bouvé) Lincoln of Boston, Mass., born Jan. 8, 1816, at Boston; died at Albany, N. Y., before the Civil war. He lived at Boston

26

until about 1849, when he removed to Albany and was employed
in the post-office there. In 1840-1 he was engaged in the grocery
and provision business in Boston.

He married, Nov. 28, 1839, at Boston, by Rev. Paul Dean,
Margaret L., daughter of Morton and Elizabeth Beal of Boston,
born June, 1818, at Boston; died Dec. 28, 1869, at Boston, having
returned to Boston after her husband's death with her daughter.
Her father was born at Hingham, Mass.; her mother at Waltham,
Mass. She is called "aged fifty one years, seven months" in the
record of her death. (Boston Records; Mass. Vital Records;
Records of Mrs. Bernard-Whitman Lawrence, *aabce bhb*.)

Children, born at Boston:

aabce bga. FRANCIS-HENRY, born July, 1841; died Aug. 28, 1849, at Boston.
aabce bgb. ELIZABETH-BEAL, born 1844; died Oct. 22, 1911, at Boston,
    unmarried.

aabce cb. WILLIAM, son of Ezekiel (*Frederick, Jonathan,
Samuel, Samuel, Samuel*) and Elizabeth (Fillebrown) Lincoln
of Boston, Mass., born 1812, at Boston; died March 23, 1866, at
Boston, "aged fifty-four years." He lived at Boston and was a
"calker" and "graver."

He married, Nov. 11, 1834, at Boston, by Rev. Sebastian
Streeter, Nancy Barber, who was born in 1815; died Apr. 25,
1842, at Boston and was buried at Weymouth. (Boston Records.)

Children, born at Boston:

aabce cba. WILLIAM. He died after 1905. It is thought that he was married
    but nothing definite has been learned of him.
aabce cbb. ADRIANNA, born 1838; died March 17, 1880, at Hingham, Mass.;
    married, Nov. 16, 1858, at Hingham, Josiah[7], son of Daniel[6] (*Josiah[5],
    Daniel[4], Josiah[3], Anthony[2], William[1]*) and Tamar (Stoddard) Sprague of
    Hingham, born May 21, 1834, at Hingham; living, 1912, at Hingham
    Center. He was a "painter" when married. He married (2), June 7,
    1883, at Hingham, Sarah, daughter of Joshua and Almira (Humphrey)
    Leavitt of Hingham, born in 1846, by whom he had a daughter, Myra-
    Ellen, born July 27, 1887. (Hist. of Hingham, vols. ii, p. 437; iii, p. 177;
    Mass. Vital Records.)
        Child, born at Hingham:
        a. FRED-LINCOLN, mar. Annie W. Vinal.
aabce cbc. MARY.*

    *A Mary, daughter of William Lincoln, was born at Boston Jan. 16, 1849; and died there
June 7, 1849; but unless he had a second wife she could not have been daughter of this William.

aabce cd. JOHN-FILLEBROWN, son of Ezekiel (*Frederick, Jonathan, Samuel, Samuel, Samuel*) and Elizabeth (Fillebrown) Lincoln of Boston, Mass., born March 9, 1817, at Boston; died May 7, 1857, at Quincy, Mass. His gravestone at Mount Auburn says he was born March 8. He was a merchant tailor, doing business in Boston but living at Harrison Square, Dorchester, Mass., from 1846 to 1851, and perhaps longer, but eventually removing to Quincy, where he was living in 1856, when his daughter Hattie was born, though she was born at Charlestown, Mass. He was first lieutenant in the Boston Light Infantry, and prominent in the militia.

He married, Sept. 14, 1840, though Boston records say 1841, at Boston, Ellen-Deane, daughter of John and Mary (Deane) Simonds of Boston, born Nov. 10, 1822, at Boston; died May 22, 1908, at Dorchester, Mass. She married (2), Nov. 7, 1867, at Reading, Mass., Robert B., son of Frederick W. and Harriet H. Moores of Hudson, N. Y., born June 18, 1824, at New York, N. Y.; died by drowning in Neponset river March 28, 1874, "aged fifty years, nine months, ten days." He was a lieutenant in the United States navy, but is called "upholsterer" in the record of his death. (Boston Records; Mass. Vital Records; Records of Edward-Turner Lincoln, *aabce cdb*, who has the family Bible.)

Children, born: *a* at Boston; *b-d* at Dorchester; *e* at Charlestown:

aabce cda. GEORGE-EDMANDS, born Oct. 27, 1841.
aabce cdb. EDWARD-TURNER, born May 19, 1846.
aabce cdc. MARY-EDMANDS, born Oct. 23, 1847; died July 19, 1849.
aabce cdd. MARY-EMMA, born July 13, 1851; married, Aug. 22, 1871, at Quincy, Mass., William-Penn, son of Henry and Elizabeth (Smith) Barker of Quincy, born June 3, 1843, at Quincy; died Jan. 1, 1910, at Quincy. He was a granite worker. She is living, 1912, at Dedham, Mass., with her daughter Lillian.
Children, born at Quincy:
    a. LILLIAN-LINCOLN, born Jan. 25, 1873; mar. Arthur-Peter Benson.
    b. HERBERT-WILLIAM, born May 1, 1877; mar. Anne Roberts.
    c. STELLA, born July 26, 1888; living, 1912, at Quincy, unmarried.
aabce cde. HATTIE-LOUISE, born Feb. 10, 1855; married, Sept. 15, 1879; at Quincy, Mass., Andrew-Wayland, son of Andrew and Caroline (Gower) Hayes of Lebanon, Me., born Aug. 9, 1856, at Sanford, Me.; died Feb. 13, 1894, at Brighton, Mass. He was a lawyer. They lived at Quincy, Revere and Brighton. She is living, 1912, at Dorchester.

Children, born: *a* at Quincy; *b* at Revere; *c* at Brighton:
  a. GERTRUDE-LINCOLN, born Oct. 22, 1881; died October, 1885.
  b. HELENA-VESTA, born July 10, 1885; living, 1912, unmarried.
  c. LINCOLN, born Apr. 21, 1894.

aabcf ac. ROYAL-WATERMAN, son of Royal (*Royal, Jonathan, Samuel, Samuel, Samuel*) and Harriet (McLellan) Lincoln of Portland, Me., born Aug. 25, 1809, at Portland; died Nov. 18, 1891, at Brunswick, Me. He lived at Portland. He was a journalist and became city editor of the "Portland Press." For a number of years he was employed in the Portland post-office.

He married, June 21, 1856, at Portland, Hannah-Mehitabel, daughter of Thomas and Julia (Vose) Brewer of Robbinston, Me., born Nov. 19, 1831, at Robbinston. She was living, 1911, at South Framingham, Mass. (Portland Records; Brunswick Records; Family Bible.)

Children, born: *a-f* at Portland; *g* at Rockland, Me.:

aabcf aca. HENRIETTA-BREWER, born Nov. 11, 1857, according to the family Bible, but Portland records say Aug. 17, 1858. She was living, 1911, at South Framingham, with her mother, unmarried.

aabcf acb. CARRIE-DOWNS, born Oct. 19, 1859; married, Jan. 26, 1886, at Brunswick, Me., John-Henry, son of Henry-Merritt and Lucy (Curtis) Dunning of Brunswick, who died, July 16, 1905, at Brunswick. He was engaged in newspaper work at Brunswick and Bath, Me. His widow was living, 1911, at South Framingham.

  Child, born at Brunswick:
    a. FRANCES-LINCOLN, born Jan. 28, 1895.

aabcf acc. MARY-BALKON, born March 2, 1862; died Aug. 8, 1863.

aabcf acd. HENRY-BREWER, born March 18, 1864; died March 19, 1864.

aabcf ace. MARY-ELIZABETH, born Feb. 11, 1866, according to the family Bible, but Portland records say June 16, 1865. She married, Sept. 21, 1899, at South Framingham, Mass., Howard-George, son of George-Aholiab and Laura-Whitehouse (Decker) Sawyer of Norridgewock, Me., born Oct. 19, 1866, at Norridgewock. They are living, 1911, at Medford, Mass. He is employed as supervisor in the out-patient department of the Boston city hospital. They have no children.

aabcf acf. GEORGE-GIFFORD, born Jan. 1, 1872; living, 1911, unmarried at South Framingham, Mass. He is employed by the Dennison Manufacturing Company.

aabcf acg. FRED-ROYAL, born Dec. 13, 1878; married, June 1, 1910, at South Framingham, Mass., Elsie-Minnie, daughter of Mervin-Emory and Minnie-Elizabeth (Eames) French of South Framingham, born May 23, 1888, at South Framingham, where they were living in 1911.

aabcf ae. WILLIAM-WATERMAN, son of Royal (*Royal, Jonathan, Samuel, Samuel, Samuel*) and Harriet (McLellan) Lincoln of Portland, Me., born Apr. 16, 1814, at Portland; died March 3, 1901, at Newark, N. J. He removed to Savannah, Ga., before his marriage and was in the wholesale and retail drug business there.

He married, Sept. 6, 1852, at Portland, by Rev. James Pratt, Mary-Waite, daughter of George and Mary (Thorla) Lewis of Portland, born Dec. 21, or 31, 1817, at Portland; died Jan. 10, 1910. (Portland Records; Records of George-William Lincoln, *aabcf aea*.)

Children, born at Savannah:

aabcf aea. George-William, born Oct. 4, 1854.
aabcf aeb. Frank-Thorla, born July 5, 1856; died June 27, 1900, at Savannah, where he had lived. He was a physician and was never married.

aabcf da. Thompson, son of Cotton (*Royal, Jonathan, Samuel, Samuel, Samuel*) and Betsey (Thompson) Lincoln of Cornish, Me., born Apr. 30, 1819, at Cornish; died Oct. 4, 1881, at Cornish. He was originally named Joshua-Thompson, but not liking the name "Joshua" he dropped it. He fitted for college at the Parsonfield Academy of Limerick, Me., and the Bridgeton, Me., Academy. He entered Norwich University in 1837, and graduated with the degree of A.B. in 1839. He then read law in the office of C. R. Ayer of Cornish and was admitted to the bar at Alfred, Me., in the spring of 1844, but his health failing he never practised that profession. Later he studied medicine and was the inventor of numerous remedies and specifics. He lived at Cornish and is buried there.

He married, March 2, 1841, at Cornish, Hannah-Farrar-Jewett, daughter of Ira and Lydia (Jewett) Clark of Cornish, born July 8, 1819, at Cornish; died there June 28, 1909. (Hist. of Norwich Univ., p. 218; Records of Miss Fanny-Clark Lincoln, *aabcf dab*.)

Children, born at Cornish:

aabcf daa. Laura-Flint, born March 18, 1845; living, 1913, at Everett, Mass.; married, May 28, 1873, at Portsmouth, N. H., John-Frank, son of George-Frank and Mary-Frances (Moulton) Rand of Cornish, born Apr. 8, 1849, at Parsonfield, Me.; died March 27, 1905, at Cornish, where he had lived. He was a carriage painter. He enlisted in 1864 in Company F, 32nd Maine infantry, and was in eleven big battles.
Child, born at Cornish:

    a. ALICE-LINCOLN, born March 21, 1874; mar. George-Edward Hutchins.

aabcf dab. FANNY-CLARK, born March 18, 1849; living, 1910, at Cornish, unmarried. She is a dress-maker.

aabcf dac. MARTHA, born Oct. 1, 1851; died Aug. 31, 1852.

aabcf dad. BENJAMIN-CLARK, born Sept. 30, 1860. He married, July 15, 1890, at Boston, Mass., Olive-Irvette, daughter of Henry-Bennett and Amanda (Stone) Pike of Cornish, born Feb. 14, 1861, at Cornish. They were living 1910, at Boston. He was employed in the office of Boston Music Hall. They have no children.

aabcg db. BEZA-HOLBROOK, son of Rufus-Warren (*Beza, Jonathan, Samuel, Samuel, Samuel*) and Damietta-Dennison (Clapp) Lincoln of Hingham, Mass., born March 13, 1823, at Hingham; died July 10, 1878, at Concord, N. H. He was a coach-trimmer and lived at Concord. He enlisted Aug. 26, 1864, for one year as private in Company E, 1st heavy New Hampshire artillery; was promoted to be quartermaster sergeant and was honorably discharged May 30, 1865, by General Orders, No. 53.

He married, Dec. 25, 1844, at Boston, Mass., Martha-Josephine, daughter of Levi and Mary-Ann (Nash) Forester of Boston, born Oct. 3, 1824, at Boston; died Sept. 27, 1897, at Providence, R. I. (Boston Records; Hist. of Hingham, vol. ii, p. 473; Records of Miss Fanny-Forester Lincoln, *aabcg dbb.*)

Children, born: *a* at Boston; *b-f* at Concord:

aabcg dba. EDWIN-SAVILLE, born July 11, 1847.

aabcg dbb. FANNY-FORESTER, born July 12, 1851; living, 1911, at Malden, Mass., unmarried. She was then employed by the Malden and Melrose Gas Company.

aabcg dbc. HARRY-WARD, born Feb. 27, 1854.

aabcg dbd. ⎰ GEORGE-LYMAN, born Jan. 13, 1857.

aabcg dbe. ⎱ ETTA-LYMAN, born Jan. 13, 1857; married, June 7, 1883, at Malden, Mass., Everett, son of George Stevens of Steuben, Me., born Nov. 3, 1847, at Steuben; died Sept. 24, 1906, at Malden. His mother was a Miss Allen. He was a brick-mason and lived at Malden, where his widow was living in 1911. He enlisted in 1863 as private in Company K, 2nd regiment, Maine volunteer cavalry.

    Child, born at Malden:

        a. GEORGE-EVERETT, born June 10, 1889; mar. Agnes-Lillian Watson.

aabcg dbf. ANNIE-LEAVER, born Feb. 27, 1864; living, 1911, at Malden, Mass., unmarried.

aabcg dc. RUFUS-WARREN, son of Rufus-Warren (*Beza, Jonathan, Samuel, Samuel, Samuel*) and Damietta-Dennison

(Clapp) Lincoln of Hingham, Mass., born June 8, 1825, at Hingham; died Sept. 6, 1874, at Boston, Mass. He lived at Boston and in the record of his marriage, in 1850, he is called a "furniture dealer," but in 1857, and in the record of his second marriage and of his death, he is called "coachman."

He married (1), according to Massachusetts Vital Records, Apr. 13, 1850, at Charlestown, Mass., Mary, daughter of Patrick and Rosanna McKenly of Charlestown. She is called twenty years old, which would make her born in 1830. But the State vital records have also the following record which conflicts with this, viz.: "Rufus W., son of Rufus W. Lincoln, a coachman of Boston aged 31 years, born at Hingham, and Mary, daughter of Patrick McKenly of Boston, aged 29 years born at Boston, were married Jan. 31, 1857, at Boston; it being his first, her second marriage." This entry has two possible explanations, neither of which, however, may be true; first: that the name "Mary" is an error in one case or the other and that Mr. Lincoln married two sisters, in which case there is another error in calling the second marriage his first; second: that Mary had been secretly married, previous to 1850, and was committing bigamy in her first marriage to Mr. Lincoln and, her first husband dying, she was legally married to Mr. Lincoln in 1857. No record has been found of her death, nor of the birth of any child.

He married (2), July 23, 1867, at Boston, Eugenia L., daughter of Isaiah and Lucretia Barbour of Camden, Me., born 1842, at Camden, being called twenty-five years old at the time of her marriage. No record of her death has been found. (Mass. Vital Records.)

Child, by second wife, born at Boston:

aabcg dca. ADDIE-KIMBALL, born Sept. 26, 1869. Nothing has been learned of her.

aabcg de. GEORGE-BRONSON, son of Rufus-Warren (*Beza, Jonathan, Samuel, Samuel, Samuel*) and Damietta-Dennison (Clapp) Lincoln of Hingham, Mass., born Nov. 10, 1829, at Hingham; died July 25, 1914, at Boston. He lived at Boston and was a varnish-maker, but had retired from business before his death.

He married, Jan. 15, 1874, at Weymouth, Mass., Emma-Hamlin, daughter of Leavitt and Mary L. (Pratt) Torrey of Weymouth, born March 18, 1849, at Weymouth; died Jan. 26, 1916, at Boston and was buried at Hingham. They were married by Rev. W. P. Tilden of Boston. At the time of her marriage she was living at Abington, Mass. (Mass. Vital Records; Records of Mrs. Mary-Warren [Lincoln] Fish, *aabcg deb.*)

Children, born at Boston:

aabcg dea. CHARLES-ELIOT, born Apr. 5, 1880. He graduated at Dwight school, Boston; since then has always been engaged in clerical office work. For the ten years previous to 1912, he was with the United Shoe Machinery Company. He married, Feb. 22, 1903, at Boston, Bertha D, daughter of William-Harrison and Caroline-Matilda (Newton) Eaton of Worcester, Mass., born June 11, 1857, at Worcester. They were living, 1912, at Dorchester, Mass. They have no children. (Records of Charles-Eliot Lincoln.)

aabcg deb. MARY-WARREN, born Jan. 29, 1883; married, Oct. 29, 1904, at Cambridge, Mass., Ozro-Meacham, son of Carlton-Rittenhouse and Ida (Meacham) Fish of Cambridge, born Sept. 21, 1881, at Brandon, Vt. From 1904 to 1906, they lived at Cincinnati, Ohio, but since then they have lived at Somerville, Mass., where they are now, 1911, residing. He is a travelling salesman for the firm of Wells, Richardson & Co., of Burlington, Vt. (Records of Mrs. Ozro-Meacham Fish.)
     Child, born at Somerville:
       a. OZRO-MEACHAM, born June 10, 1909.

aabcg dec. GEORGE-BRONSON, born March 23, 1885; died July 22, 1893.

aabcg ded. WARD-CLAPP, born July 19, 1893; living, 1912, unmarried.

aabcg dg. AMASA-LYMAN, son of Rufus-Warren (*Beza, Jonathan, Samuel, Samuel, Samuel*) and Damietta-Dennison (Clapp) Lincoln of Hingham, Mass., born Sept. 22, 1833, at Hingham; died Feb. 9, 1897, at Santa Barbara, Calif. At the age of eighteen he entered the employ of the Hingham Bank and, afterwards, that of the Shawmut Bank, Boston. About 1857 he went to the Massachusetts Bank, Boston, with which he remained until 1869, when he removed to Santa Barbara. After one year on a ranch he started the First National Bank of Santa Barbara, becoming its cashier, in which position he remained until his death. He was county treasurer for eight years and city treasurer for about fifteen years.

He married, June 12, 1862, at Boston, Abbie-Smith, daughter of Johnson and Mary (Foster) Patrick of Kalamazoo, Mich., born Apr. 4, 1841, at Kalamazoo; died March 26, 1902, at Santa

Barbara. (Mass. Vital Records; Records of Henry-Patrick Lincoln, *aabcg dgb*.)

Children, born: *a, b* at Boston; *c* at Santa Barbara:

aabcg dga. LYMAN-PUTNAM, born July 6, 1863.
aabcg dgb. HENRY-PATRICK, born Sept. 18, 1865.
aabcg dgc. JOHN-SPENCER, born Aug. 11, 1874.

aabcj hb. JOHN-ROBIE, son of Levi-Thaxter (*John, Jonathan, Samuel, Samuel, Samuel*) and Mary-Ann (Brown) Lincoln of Portland, Me., born Jan. 19, 1857, at Yarmouth, Me. He was, in 1910, a hack-driver in the employ of Fernald & Sawyer of Portland.

He married, Nov. 2, 1880, at Portland, Julia-Hall, daughter of Nelson-Collingwood and Grace (Hamlin) Robbins of Portland, born Jan. 18, 1858, at Falmouth, Me. They were living, 1910, at Portland. (Portland Records; Records of John-Robie Lincoln.)

Child, born at Portland:

aabcj hba. ROBIE-THAXTER, born March 18, 1883.

aabck ba. CHARLES-NATHANIEL-MINOT, son of Charles (*Charles, Jonathan, Samuel, Samuel, Samuel*) and Martha-Blake (Minot) Lincoln of Charlestown, Mass., born Aug. 28, 1822, at Boston, Mass.; died Nov. 9, 1889, at Jamaica Plain, Mass. He was educated in the Charlestown public schools, after which he was first engaged in the foreign money department of the Suffolk Bank of Boston. In 1847 he entered the employment of the Merchants Bank of Boston, where he remained until July, 1884, serving for five years of this period as note teller and five years as receiving teller. He then served for a few months as cashier of the Hingham National Bank. He was for many years a deacon of the Central Congregational Church of Jamaica Plain. "He was a modest, generous, faithful man, conscientious and just in all his dealings."

He married (1), Apr. 8, 1847, at Charlestown, Mary-Ann, daughter of Henry and Olive-Pratt (Turner) Shattuck of Deerfield and Amherst, Mass., born Apr. 30, 1820, at Amherst; died Apr. 8, 1860, at West Roxbury, Mass.

He married (2), Oct. 29, 1863, at Amherst, Marcia-Maria,

daughter of Isaac-Howard and Lydia (Turner) Bangs of Amherst, born Feb. 5, 1829, at Leverett, Mass.; died July 20, 1906,
at Boston. (Mass. Vital Records; Shattuck Memorials, p. 241;
Records of Rev. Charles-Lincoln Morgan, *aabck aa.*)

Children, by first wife, born at Jamaica Plain:

aabck baa.   CHARLES-BEZA, born Dec. 29, 1864; died Oct. 12, 1865.
aabck bab.   ELBRIDGE-BANGS, born Aug. 18, 1866.

Child, by second wife, born at Jamaica Plain:

aabck bac.   MARY-SHATTUCK, born Dec. 6, 1869; died June 29 or 30, 1875.

aabck bd. WILLIAM-OLIVER, son of Charles (*Charles, Jonathan, Samuel, Samuel, Samuel*) and Martha-Blake (Minot)
Lincoln of Charlestown, Mass., born June 5, 1827, at Boston;
living, 1911, at Allston, Mass. He attended the public schools
until the age of fifteen when he was apprenticed to Otis Tufts,
a builder of steam engines and printing presses. At the age of
nineteen he removed to East Boston, the shops being removed
thither, and at the age of twenty-three he was made foreman of
the works. He remained with the Tufts until 1850 when the
business was closed, and he then accepted the superintendency
of the manufactory of William Carleton, with whom he remained for twenty-two years, living at Jamaica Plain, Mass.
After Mr. Carleton's death in 1874 he accepted the position of
general superintendent of the Bridgeport Brass Company's
works and resided at Bridgeport, Conn., for five years. Owing
to changes in the company he then removed to Fairhaven, Mass.,
assuming charge of the Fairhaven Iron Works. In 1886 he was
made treasurer of the American Tool and Machine Company of
Boston and removed to Allston, where he was living in 1911.
He was a member of the Massachusetts Charitable Mechanics
Association and served on the board of judges of awards for steam
machinery. At Jamaica Plain he was a member of the Mather
Congregational Church and was a member of its standing committee. He was afterwards connected with the South Congregational Church of Bridgeport and of the Allston Congregational
Church.

He married, Nov. 10 or 27, 1850, at Chicopee, Mass., Sarah-
Jane, daughter of James and Elizabeth Luey of Cornish, N. H.,

born June 1, 1830, at Cornish; died Aug. 12, 1909, at Allston. In the State records of the births of her children she is said to have been born at Dorchester, Mass. (Records of William-Oliver Lincoln.)

Children, born: *a, b* at East Boston; *c, d* at Jamaica Plain:

aabck bda. ELLEN-AUGUSTA, born Sept. 30, 1851; living, 1911, with her father, unmarried.

aabck bdb. EDWARD-LOUIS, born March 28, 1853. He was educated in the public schools, graduating from the High school at the age of sixteen. He then served for two years as clerk in the office of the Philadelphia Steamship Company, and in 1871 became an assistant in the National Bank of Commerce of Boston. In 1878 he was appointed receiving teller and in 1883 assistant cashier, which position he held until 1896. He removed to New York City before 1902 and was living there in 1911, called "manager."

He married, Sept. 19, 1881, at Boston, Anna, daughter of Edward and Anna (Doyle) Wyman of Boston, born Feb. 4, 1862, at Boston. They were living, 1911, at New York, N. Y. They have no children.

aabck bdc. CHARLES-MINOT, born Sept. 15, 1859; died Dec. 13, 1901, at Atlanta, Ga., unmarried.

aabck bdd. KATHARINE-MARIE, born Nov. 25, 1864; living, 1911, with her father, unmarried.

aabck bf. HENRY-BARRY, son of Charles (*Charles, Jonathan, Samuel, Samuel, Samuel*) and Martha-Blake (Minot) Lincoln of Charlestown, Mass., born Jan. 13, 1830, at Charlestown; living, 1911, at Jamaica Plain, Mass. He was educated in the public schools of Charlestown and Dorchester, Mass., and at an early age entered the employ of the Suffolk Bank of Boston, where he remained for one year in the foreign money department. He then entered the employ of Messrs. James W. Page & Company, selling agents for several cotton manufacturing companies of New England, and has since remained in that business, but in 1863 was connected with the treasurer's instead of the selling department. He removed from Charlestown to Jamaica Plain in 1858, and has resided there since then.

He married, May 11, 1852 (Mass. Vital Records say May 4), at Charlestown, Helen-Maria, daughter of Zachariah and Mary (Foster) Shedd of Charlestown, born June 19, 1832, at Charlestown; died Nov. 29, 1885, at Jamaica Plain. (Records of Rev. Charles-Lincoln Morgan, *aabck aa.*)

Children, born: *a, b* at Charlestown; *c, d* at Jamaica Plain:

aabck bfa. HENRY-MOORHEAD, born Apr. 17, 1855; died Oct. 7, 1855.

aabck bfb. HELEN-MARIA, born Apr. 17, 1856; living, 1911, with her father, unmarried. Massachusetts Vital Records say she was born Sept. 17, 1856.

aabck bfc. LAWRENCE-LITCHFIELD, born Sept. 18, 1858.

aabck bfd. FRED E, born Feb. 16, 1866; living, 1911, with his father, unmarried.

aabck bh. JAMES-FRANCIS, son of Charles (*Charles, Jonathan, Samuel, Samuel, Samuel*) and Martha-Blake (Minot) Lincoln of Charlestown, Mass., born Apr. 13, 1836, at Charlestown; died March 11, 1899, at Neponset, Mass. He was educated in the Charlestown and Dorchester public schools and began business life in February, 1859, and continued in various lines until his death. He lived at Neponset, a village in Dorchester.

He married, Oct. 28, 1858, at Neponset, Josephine, daughter of George and Betsy (Adams) Clapp of Quincy, Mass., born Dec. 8, 1835, at Quincy; died Oct. 26, 1907, at Boston, where she was then living and aged, say the Massachusetts Vital Records, "seventy-two years, ten months, and eighteen days," which would make her born Dec. 8, 1834.

Children, born at Dorchester:

aabck bha. WALTER F., born Dec. 14, 1860; died March 10, 1889.

aabck bhb. WILLIAM-HENRY, born Jan. 14, 1865; living, 1911, at Neponset. He is married.

aabck bhc. MARTHA-BLAKE-MINOT, born Jan. 24, 1871; died July 29, 1871.

aabhe ab. HERMAN-CUSHING, son of Jotham (*Cushing, John, Samuel, Samuel, Samuel*) and Adeline F. (Bancroft) Lincoln of Warwick, Mass., born Aug. 2, 1863, at Warwick. At the age of six years he removed with his parents to Orange, Mass., where he attended school until the age of fifteen, after which, for four years, he was employed on various farms in the vicinity. Since then he has been employed on the Boston and Maine railroad, being, in 1912, a freight conductor between East Deerfield, Mass., and Rotterdam Junction, N. Y. He was living in 1912 at Zoar, Mass., but had previously lived at North-field, Fitchburg and North Adams, Mass.

He married, Dec. 21, 1887, at Erving, Mass., Lula-DeEtta, daughter of Ezekiel-Woods and Mary-Adeline (Sibley) Jaynes of Rowe, Mass., born Dec. 17, 1867, at Rowe. (Records of Herman-Cushing Lincoln.)

Children, born: *a* at North Adams; *b* at Charlemont, Mass.:

aabhe aba. HAZEL-ADELINE, born Dec. 23, 1888; living, 1912, unmarried.
aabhe abb. ROY-BANCROFT, born June 15, 1897.

aabhg aa. JOHN, son of John (*John-Barker, John, Samuel, Samuel, Samuel*) and Rachel-Burr (Sprague) Lincoln of Hingham, Mass., born Oct. 24, 1837, at Hingham; living, 1911, at Northbridge, Mass., whither he removed in 1869. He has always been a farmer. He was overseer of the poor at Northbridge for several years, and has been highway surveyor. He was sergeant in Company G, 13th regiment, Connecticut volunteer infantry, in the Civil war.

He married, Nov. 21, 1866, at Hingham, Hannah-Maria[7], daughter of Orin[6] (*Reuben[5], Willard[4], John[3], Paul[2], Richard[1]*) and Hannah-Mayo (Hopkins) Sears of Hingham, born March 29, 1836, at Brewster, Mass.; died July 9, 1888, at Northbridge. (Hist. of Hingham, vol. i, part i, p. 363; vol. ii, p. 474; Mass. Vital Records; Records of John Lincoln.)

Children, born: *a* at Hingham; *b* at Northbridge:

aabhg aaa. WINTHROP, born June 29, 1868.
aabhg aab. LOUISA, born Nov. 10, 1872; living, 1911, unmarried.

aabhg db. HENRY, son of Albert (*John-Barker, John, Samuel, Samuel, Samuel*) and Frances-Gordon (Currier) Lincoln of Hingham, Mass., born March 5, 1852, at Boston; died Jan. 5, 1890, at Hingham. He lived at Hingham and was a book-keeper.

He married, Nov. 6, 1879, at Boston, Mass., Mary-Shepard, daughter of William-Frederick and Caroline (Fernald) Blanchard of Chelsea, Mass., born Sept. 9, 1854, at Chelsea; living, 1911, at Hingham Center, on Leavitt street. Her father was a native of Searsport, Me., her mother of Winterport, Me. (Records of Mrs. Henry Lincoln.)

Children, born at Hingham:

aabhg dba. FREDERICK-EDWIN, born Nov. 3, 1880.
aabhg dbb. FRANCES, born June 20, 1883; married, Dec. 16, 1908, at Hingham, Gurdon-Tucker, son of Josiah-Benjamin and Carrie-Dexter (Colburn) Newell of Newton, Mass., born Feb. 23, 1883, at Newton Upper

Falls, Mass. They were living, 1911, at Hingham Center. He was a bank clerk. No children.

aacbc ac. WILLIAM-SEVER, son of Levi (*Levi, Enoch, Jedediah, Samuel, Samuel*) and Penelope-Winslow (Sever) Lincoln of Worcester, Mass., born Nov. 22, 1811, at Worcester; died Nov. 8, 1889, at .Worcester. He graduated at Bowdoin college in 1830; studied law at Worcester with Newton & Lincoln, both of the partners being his uncles. He was admitted to the bar in September, 1833, and settled as a lawyer in Millbury, Mass., and afterwards at Alton, Ill., where he was city attorney. He returned to Worcester before 1847, and became a farmer at Quinsigamond village, owning the farm formerly belonging to his uncle John-Waldo Lincoln, and afterwards known as the "Ballard farm." After a few years he sold the farm, gave up farming and went into the city to live, but a few years later he bought another farm in the vicinity of Tatnuck village and there resided until his death. In 1858 he was "city marshall" of Worcester, as the chief of police was then called. In 1859 he was elected president of the Worcester County Agricultural Society, which office he held for many years. He was particularly interested in raising pure-blooded Jersey cattle and eventually had a fine herd.

He was commissioned, June 3, 1862, lieutenant colonel of the 34th regiment, Massachusetts volunteer militia, then recruiting for the war, was promoted colonel, Oct. 14, 1864, and for meritorious services in the Shenandoah valley was confirmed brigadier general June 23, 1865. He was wounded in the right shoulder at the battle of Newmarket, May, 1864, and was taken prisoner. While on his way to Andersonville he made his escape, and in his "History of the Thirty-Fourth Regiment" he tells the story of his thrilling adventures while on his way to the Union lines. His right arm was permanently disabled, and he never entirely recovered from the effects of the wound and exposure.

He married, Oct. 22, 1835, at Worcester, Elizabeth[7], daughter of George-Augustus[6] (*Joseph[5], Joseph[4], John[3], Joseph[2], John[1]*) and Louisa (Clap) Trumbull of Worcester, born Aug. 31, 1816, at Worcester; died Feb. 15, 1900, at Worcester. (Family Records; Worcester Records; Trumbull Genealogy, pp. 29-31.)

Children, born: *a*, *b*, at Alton; *c*, *d* at Worcester:

aacbc aca. WILLIAM, born Sept. 25, 1839; died Aug. 13, 1869, at Worcester, unmarried. He served as private in the Worcester Light Infantry, sixth Massachusetts regiment, which responded to the call for three-months volunteers in April, 1861; but as he did not leave Worcester with the company, but with the third battalion of rifles which left some days later, it is uncertain if he joined the regiment in time to accompany it on its historical march through Baltimore on Apr. 19. He was promoted to be sergeant. He returned home much broken in health, and his death was eventually due to hardships endured in this service.

aacbc acb. LEVI, born Apr. 27, 1844.

aacbc acc. GEORGE-TRUMBULL, born Feb. 5, 1847; died Feb. 7, 1869, at Worcester, unmarried.

aacbc acd. WINSLOW-SEVER, born Oct. 31, 1848.

aacbc ad. DANIEL-WALDO, son of Levi (*Levi, Enoch, Jedediah, Samuel, Samuel*) and Penelope-Winslow (Sever) Lincoln of Worcester, Mass., born Jan. 16, 1813, at Worcester; died July 1, 1880, at New London, Conn., being killed by being thrown accidentally from the observation train at the Harvard-Yale boat race, and run over by the cars. He received his education at Leicester academy and Harvard college where he received the degree of A.B. in 1831. After graduation he studied law and was admitted to the bar of Worcester county in 1834. For a short time thereafter he was associated with his uncle, William Lincoln, *aacbc j*, on the staff of the "Worcester Aegis," and then purchased a small farm of about twenty acres on the west side of Worcester, and there devoted himself for nearly thirty years to fruit and flower culture. His farm, though a barren piece of land when he purchased it, became under his exquisite taste a beautiful estate. It comprised the land now bounded by Pleasant, Piedmont, Austin and Bellevue streets and has long been entirely built over. Mr. Lincoln was especially interested in the culture of the pear, and at one of the annual exhibitions of the Worcester Horticultural Society he exhibited one hundred and sixty named varieties of that fruit.

In politics he was, during his early years, a Whig but on the breaking up of that party he became a Democrat and so remained during the remainder of his life, though in his latter years he was inactive in political affairs. He was a member of the State legislature in 1846 as representative; alderman of the city of Worcester in 1858 and 1859; and mayor in 1863 and 1864, being defeated for a third term by a narrow margin, owing to the bitterness engendered against all Democrats, no matter how patriotic, by the events of the Civil war. In 1865 he was chosen trustee of the Worcester Public Library, and at the time of his death was chairman of the sinking fund commissioners of Worcester. He was a director of the Citizens, later Citizens National, Bank from 1855 to 1872, and of the Worcester National Bank from 1879 until his death; a trustee of the Worcester County Institution for Savings, and for much of the time a member of the board of investment; a trustee of Rural Cemetery; director of the Worcester Gas Light Company; trustee of Memorial Hospital; and for several years trustee of the Worcester Polytechnic Institute and its first secretary. He had been president of the Worcester County Agricultural Society and of the Worcester County Horticultural Society. He took an active interest in the local militia and for years was an active member of the Worcester Light Infantry, of which company he was elected ensign, March 15, 1837; lieutenant, July 4, 1837; and captain, Apr. 28, 1838, serving with great credit and honor until his resignation Feb. 11, 1841.

He became a director of the Boston and Worcester Railroad Company in 1858, and was its vice-president, and practically its president in 1867-8, when Hon. Ginery Twichell the president was in Congress. On its consolidation with the Western Railroad Company as the Boston and Albany Railroad Company, he was elected vice-president and in 1878, on the retirement of Chester Chapin, was placed in the position of president, holding that office until his death, and showing in it the great executive ability which has been a marked characteristic of the family.

He resided on his farm on Pleasant street until 1867, when he removed to Ashland street, to the house built by his wife's father, on the estate afterwards of the late J. Edwin Smith, where he lived until 1873, when he removed to his late father's mansion on Elm street, now, 1922, owned by his son, the compiler of this genealogy.

He married, Nov. 30, 1841, at Worcester, Frances-Fiske[6], daughter of Francis-Taliaferro[5] (*Pliny*[4], *Noah*[3], *James*[2], *Thomas*[1]) and Mary-Buckminster (Fiske) Merrick of Worcester, born

DEATH OF CAPTAIN GEORGE LINCOLN (1816-1847) AT THE BATTLE OF BUENA VISTA
February 23, 1847
From a contemporary print

Oct. 5, 1819, at Worcester; died Apr. 8, 1873, at Boston, Mass., where the family had been passing the winter, as had been their custom for several years. Mrs. Lincoln was a very lovely woman, of slight, frail figure. Her portrait by George Fuller is, though somewhat idealized, an excellent likeness of her. There are several portraits of Mr. Lincoln, none of which are entirely satisfactory. (Family Records.)

Children, born at Worcester:

aacbc ada. Frances-Merrick, born July 1, 1843; living, 1922, at Worcester, unmarried. She has been much interested in charities and was a trustee of the Worcester Lunatic Hospital for many years. She is now a trustee of the Worcester Art Museum.

aacbc adb. Mary-Waldo, born Sept. 15, 1845; married Oct. 18, 1870, at Worcester, Joseph-Estabrook⁸, son of Isaac⁷ (*Phineas⁶, Isaac⁵, Simon⁴, Simon³, Samuel², Dolor¹*) and Mary-Holbrook (Estabrook) Davis of Worcester, born Sept. 27, 1838, at Worcester; died Oct. 27, 1907, at Boston, Mass. He was as a young man employed as a clerk in Boston and then went to Buenos Ayres, where he was in business for several years, returning to Worcester about 1864. He then associated himself in business with the Washburn Iron Company of Worcester, which was engaged in the re-rolling of railroad iron and the manufacture of car wheels, and remained with them until 1882. About 1890 he removed with his family to Boston and resided there until his death. His widow is now, 1922, living there.

Children, born at Worcester:

    a. Lincoln, born March 31, 1872; mar. Catharine-Bradlee Crowninshield.

    b. Mabel, born March 25, 1875; mar. John-Reed Post.

aacbc adc. Anne-Warren, born Feb. 6, 1848; died July 21, 1849.

aacbc add. Waldo, born Dec. 31, 1849.

aacbc af. George, son of Levi (*Levi, Enoch, Jedediah, Samuel, Samuel*) and Penelope-Winslow (Sever) Lincoln of Worcester, Mass., born Oct. 19, 1816, at Worcester; died Feb. 23, 1847, at the battle of Buena Vista, Mexico. He was educated at Leicester academy, but got into some boyish scrape there and was sent to sea with Captain James-Warren Sever, his mother's cousin. He sailed to China and returned under the mate, having a very hard time. He made a second voyage and had a similar experience. He returned with the vessel to Holland, where he left it, made his way to Paris and thence returned home. He had had enough of the sea and was appointed by President Jackson, through his father's influence, to a lieutenancy in the United States army, and was immediately

27

sent to Florida, where he arrived a few days after the Fort
Dade massacre. In the Mexican war he distinguished himself
at the battle of Resaca de la Palma, by rescuing Lieutenant
Jordan from a number of Mexicans, killing two of the enemy
unaided, and three others with the assistance of his sergeant.
For this gallantry he was promoted, June 18, 1846, to be assistant
adjutant general, with the brevet rank of captain. His friends
in Worcester presented him with a very handsome dress sword,
as a testimonial of their admiration of his bravery, which sword
he never received, being killed before it reached him. It is
now owned by his nephew, Waldo Lincoln, as is also the dress
sword which he used in service. At the battle of Buena Vista,
Captain Lincoln, who was a member of the 3rd U. S. infantry,
was attached to the staff of General Wool. During the action
he was mounted on a magnificent white horse, and by his distinguished appearance drew more than his share of the enemy's
fire, being mistaken, it is thought, for General Taylor, and, while
leading a charge, was shot through the heart. His remains
were taken to Worcester, being escorted thither by a detachment of Kentucky volunteers, with whose officers he had been
on intimate terms, and were honored by a military funeral
which was long remembered by the inhabitants of Worcester.
Political feeling ran very high in Worcester during the Mexican
war and it is said that, during Captain Lincoln's funeral, a
Mr. Leander Eaton, who kept a store on Main street through
which the procession passed, hung out a sign reading, "No
homage to murderers." There is no portrait of Captain Lincoln in existence, but his brother, Edward-Winslow, described
him to the writer as being six feet two inches tall, with very
large blue eyes and very handsome. A colored print of the
scene of his death was published and is here reproduced.

He married, May 24, 1839, at Ogdensburg, N. Y., Nancy,
daughter of Silvius and Nancy-Mary (Devillers) Hoard of
Ogdensburg, born Oct. 26, 1820, at Antwerp, N. Y.; died Sept.
4, 1852, at Worcester. She married (2), June 25, 1850, at
Worcester, Hon. Stephen Salisbury of Worcester as his second
wife. She had no children by him. Her grandfather was Louis
de Villers, a native of France, who came out in Rochambeau's
expedition to aid this country in the war of the Revolution.

(Family Records; see "Worcester Aegis," March 3, 1847, for poems relating to Capt. Lincoln; *ibid.*, March 10, 1847, and "Worcester Spy" of same date for correspondence about the sword; "Aegis," Apr. 7, 14, May 12, July 14 and 21, for description of the battle of Buena Vista and the funeral.)

Child, born at Worcester:

aacbc afa. GEORGIANNA-DEVILLERS, born May 10, 1840; died Dec. 28, 1861, at Worcester, She was first named "Anne-Devillers" and her name was changed Apr. 26, 1847, by the legislature. She was a very tall and strikingly beautiful woman. She married, Jan. 8, 1861, at Worcester, Francis-Blake[3], son of George-Tilly[7] (*Thomas*[6], *Tilly*[5], *Obadiah*[4], *Jacob*[3], *Edward*[2], *Edmund*[1]) and Elizabeth-Chandler (Blake) Rice of Worcester, born Apr. 12, 1835, at Worcester; died May 25, 1913, at Boston, Mass., where he had been living for a number of years. They had no children. He married (2), June 20, 1869, at Boston, Sally-Blake, daughter of Romeo and Sarah-Chandler (Blake) Austin of Boston, born Jan. 28, 1841, at Boston; living, 1922, at Boston; by whom he had four children: Francis-Blake, Gertrude-Austin, George-Tilly, and Arthur.

aacbc ah. JOHN-WALDO, son of Levi (*Levi, Enoch, Jedediah, Samuel, Samuel*) and Penelope-Winslow (Sever) Lincoln of Worcester, Mass., had his name changed, Apr. 16, 1846, by the Massachusetts legislature to EDWARD-WINSLOW. He was born Dec. 2, 1820, at Worcester and died Dec. 15, 1896, at Worcester. He graduated at Harvard college in 1839, and then went to Alton, Ill., where he studied law with his brother, William-Sever; was admitted to the bar and, for a time, acted as prosecuting attorney for the city. In 1845 he returned to Worcester, gave up the practice of law and purchased an interest in the "Aegis" newspaper and became its editor. In 1849 he was appointed postmaster by President Taylor and held that office for four years. He then spent some time in Illinois and, returning to Worcester, became editor of the "Bay State," a short-lived publication. He devoted the remainder of his life to horticulture, being from 1860 until his death secretary of the Worcester County Horticultural Society. In 1870 he was made chairman of the commissioners of shade trees and public grounds, and, later, of its successor, the Parks Commission. To his wise foresight and personal supervision, Worcester is indebted for many of its beautiful parks. Mr. Lincoln was a forcible and ready writer, witty, keen and scholarly, and his annual reports were always read with interest and pleasure. He became in later life extremely deaf, an affliction which befell many of the family.

He married (1), March 29, 1848, at Philadelphia, Pa., Sarah-Rhodes, daughter of George-Rhodes and Elizabeth (Paddleford) Arnold of Providence, R. I., born March 29, 1827, at Providence; died July 1, 1856, at Worcester.

He married (2), August 4, 1858, at Bristol, R. I., Kate-Von-Weber, daughter of Ward and Mary (Von Weber) Marston, born July 1, 1833, at Charlestown, Mass.; died Dec. 19, 1903, at Worcester. Her father, Ward Marston, was lieutenant colonel of the United States marines. (Family Records.)

Children, by first wife, born: *a* at Worcester; *b-d* in Illinois:

aacbc aha.   ELIZA-PADDLEFORD, born Aug. 31, 1850; died May 7, 1851.
aacbc ahb.   JOHN-WALDO, born Oct. 30, 1852. He was educated in the Worcester public schools and the Worcester Polytechnic Institute, class of 1871, as a civil engineer. On leaving school he became a rodman on the Atchison, Topeka & Santa Fé railroad under Mr. Frank Firth. In 1875 he went to San Francisco, Calif., where he engaged in the commission business and was a member of the Produce Exchange. From 1877 to 1881, he was paymaster and cashier of the Northern Pacific railroad, stationed at Ainsworth and Spokane, Wash. Later he followed his profession of civil engineer on the Croton aqueduct, New York, and in Florida and Oregon. Exposure due to a severe experience in an Oregon survey necessitated his retirement. Since 1887 he has led the quiet life of an orchardist, and in 1901 he retired to Ocean Park, Calif., where he has since resided. He was a director, since organization in 1905, of the First National Bank of Ocean Park and president of the Santa Monica Bay hospital.
    He married, Oct. 31, 1876, at San Francisco, Sarah-Rosetta, daughter of John-Michael and Sarah-Rosetta (Noah) Eberline of Roseburg, Ore., born July 27, 1852, at Des Moines, Iowa. Mr. Eberline, whose father was a general in the Bavarian army, bore the same name as his father and was educated in the Bavarian military school. He came to America in 1838 at the age of nineteen, lived at various places, North and South, finally dying, July 9, 1881, at Roseburg. His wife died at Des Moines, Aug. 9, 1852, and Mr. Eberline then emigrated to Oregon. Mr. and Mrs. Lincoln are living at Ocean Park. They have no children.
aacbc ahc.   ARNOLD, born Oct. 27, 1853; died July 27, 1854.
aacbc ahd.   CHARLES-FREDERIC, born June 16, 1856; died June 17, 1856.

Children, by second wife, born at Worcester:

aacbc ahe.   ANNIE-MARSTON, born Oct. 15, 1859; living, 1921, at Worcester, unmarried.
aacbc ahf.   MARIAN-VINAL, born May 17, 1862; married (1), Sept. 18, 1884, at Worcester, Edward-Langdon, son of Theodore-Peacock and Eliza-Turner (Howe) Bogert of New York, N. Y., born Aug. 18, 1852. The marriage

proved an unhappy one and they were divorced Feb. 24, 1896, at New
York. He died in 1910. She married (2), Dec. 19, 1901, at Worcester,
Marsden-Jasael, son of Horatio-Nelson and Malvina (Wilson) Perry of
Rehoboth, Mass., born Nov. 2, 1850, at Rehoboth. By his first wife,
Jessie McGregor, from whom he was divorced, he had no children. Mr. and
Mrs. Perry are living, 1921, at Providence and Newport, R. I. He is a
successful and wealthy financier, much interested in Colonial furniture
and silver. He was formerly especially interested in Shakesperiana, of
which he succeeded in collecting one of the finest collections in the world,
and at that time the largest in the United States.

Children, by first husband, born at Providence:

    a. EDWARD-LANGDON BOGERT, born Aug. 28, 1885; living, 1921,
unmarried.

    b. PELHAM-WINSLOW BOGERT, born July 19, 1895; living, 1921,
unmarried.

Child, by second husband, born at Providence:

    c. MARSDEN-JASAEL PERRY, born Sept. 5, 1902.

aacbc ahg. MARSTON, born June 23, 1864.

aacbc. ahh. ADALINE-SEVER, born June 17, 1867; married, Dec. 12, 1907, at
New York, N. Y., Henry-Joseph, son of Henry-Joseph and Mary (Hamill)
Graham of Belfast, Ireland, born Feb. 13, 1867, at Belfast. He lived in
England until emigrating to this country about thirty years ago. Mr.
and Mrs. Graham have been engaged in stock-raising since their mar-
riage, raising several fine cows and horses every year for exhibition and
sale. They are living, 1922, at Scarsdale, N. Y. Mr. Graham is of
Scotch descent. They have no children.

aacbc ahi. HELEN, born Apr. 8, 1870; living, 1922, unmarried.

aacbc ahj. PELHAM-WINSLOW, born Dec. 13, 1873. He graduated at Worcester Polytechnic Institute in 1892, and was for some time thereafter
employed by the J. Russel Marble Co. of Worcester, a paint and chemical house. He then became connected with Norcross Brothers, builders
and contractors, with whom he remained for some years, first at Brownville, Me., then at Manchester, Vt., and finally at Cleveland, Ohio.
He is now, 1922, with the Salduro Potash Co. at Salduro, Utah. He married (1), Aug. 5, 1900, at Boston, Mass., while living at Brownville, Mary
E., daughter of Timothy and Ellen (McCarthy) Coffey of Boston, who
was born in 1873 at Boston. They were divorced in 1912, and in 1913 he
married a second wife, named Elizabeth. He has had no children.

aacbc ahk. KATHARINE-VON WEBER, born Apr. 15, 1876; died Oct. 11, 1895,
at Worcester, unmarried.

aacbe da. FREDERIC-WALKER, son of Louis (*Amos, Enoch,
Jedediah, Samuel, Samuel*) and Mary Hathorne (Knight) Lincoln
of Boston, Mass., born Feb. 17, 1817, at Boston (his monument
at Mt. Auburn says Feb. 27); died Sept. 13, 1898, at Boston.
He was educated in Boston public schools and, after the death
of his parents, in a private school at Canton, Mass. He was
then apprenticed to Mr. Gedney King, maker of nautical instruments on State street, Boston. He continued with him and

his successor, Charles-Gedney King, until 1839 when he began business on his own account on Commercial street. He continued for forty-three years, as maker of nautical and surveying instruments and dealer in seamen's charts and equipments, until 1882, when he accepted the position of manager of the Boston Storage Company, which position he held until his death. He was president of the Massachusetts Charitable Mechanics Association from 1854 to 1856, and its treasurer for a term beginning in 1880, and in connection therewith was president of the Revere House Corporation. He was a member of the State legislature in 1837 and 1838, and again in 1872 and 1874. He was appointed on the board of harbor commissioners in 1868 and was chairman of the board for several years. He was chairman of the board of overseers of the poor, and in 1878 its treasurer also. In December, 1857, he was elected mayor of Boston to serve the following year and was again elected in 1858, 1859 and 1862 and each year thereafter until 1865, thus serving for seven years, a longer term than that of any other incumbent of the office. He was energetic and prompt in suppressing the draft riots during the Civil war, his services being recognized by his election to membership in the military order of the loyal legion. He was a director of the Continental National Bank; trustee of the Massachusetts Institute of Technology and of the Museum of Fine Arts; president of the Franklin Savings Bank; president of the Massachusetts Charitable Fire Society, and member of other institutions; treasurer of the Young Men's Benevolent Society; member of the Boston Light Infantry; a founder of the Commercial Club in 1869 and its first president. In 1854 he became a director of the Bunker Hill Monument Association and, for several years, was its president. For more than thirty-five years he was treasurer of the Second Unitarian Church, at whose services he was always a punctual attendant. He received an honorary degree of master of arts from Harvard and Dartmouth universities. He was a member of the New England Historic Genealogical Society from 1847 until his death, though never active in its proceedings. He was of good height, compactly built and of muscular firmness and vigor. "To good judgment, punctuality, firmness and unquestioned integrity, he added a courteous and genial manner that disarmed opposi-

FREDERIC WALKER LINCOLN
1817-1898
From a steel engraving

tion and greatly promoted success in upholding the interests he represented. He was a model citizen and a consistent Christian gentleman." For a complete biography of his life see "In Memoriam, Frederic Walker Lincoln," Boston, 1899. He was buried at Mount Auburn.

He married (1), May 18, 1848, at Boston, according to Boston records,* Emeline[6], daughter of Jacob[5] (*Jacob[4], Stephen[3], Stephen[2], John[1]*) and Mary-Ann (Hall) Hall of Boston, born Nov. 9, 1827, at Boston; died July 21, 1849, at Boston.

He married (2), June 20, 1854, at Boston, Emily-Caroline[7], daughter of Noah[6] (*David[5], David[4], David[3], Stephen[2], Stephen[1]*) and Sally (Howe) Lincoln of Boston, born Feb. 7, 1827, at Boston; died March 26, 1901, at Brookline, Mass. During her residence in Boston she was a constant attendant upon the Second Church in Copley square, and was closely in touch with all the charitable work of the society. (Boston Records; Mass. Vital Records; N. E. Hist. & Gen. Register, vol. liv, pp. xcv-xcvii, 229; Tribute to Noah Lincoln; Halls of New England, p. 345; Records of Frederic-Walker Lincoln, *aacbe dab.*)

Child, by first wife, born at Boston:

aacbe daa. HARRIET-ABBOT, born Feb. 10, 1849; died May 17, 1902, at Baltimore, Md.; married, Nov. 18, 1872, at Boston, George-Austin, son of George and Hepsy-Ann (Seaver) Coolidge of Boston, born Apr. 12, 1845, at Dedham, Mass.; died July 4, 1911, at Belmar, N. J. He was at one time a publisher but had had no occupation for many years. They lived at Boston, Washington, D. C., and Englewood, N. J.
Children:
    a. EMELYN-LINCOLN, born Aug. 9, 1873; living, 1911, unmarried.
    b. FREDERIC-AUSTIN, born Aug. 26, 1877; living, 1911, unmarried.
    c. ERNEST-HALL, born May 4, 1881; mar. Jean-Mellen Thurston.
    d. GEORGE-PERCIVAL, born Oct. 25, 1884; mar. Mabel-Moore Duhring.

Children, by second wife, born at Boston:

aacbe dab. FREDERIC-WALKER, born Aug. 29, 1855.
aacbe dac. MARY-KNIGHT, born March 12, 1858; died March 8, 1901, at Brookline, unmarried.
aacbe dad. LOUIS-REVERE, born June 29, 1862.

aacbe ha. AMOS, son of Amos (*Amos, Enoch, Jedediah, Samuel, Samuel*) and Rebecca-Trevett (Bartol) Lincoln of

---

*N. E. Hist. & Gen. Register, vol. ii, p. 325, says May 29; "Halls of New England" says May 19; a family record says May 20.

Boston, Mass., born September, 1818, at Boston; died July 17, 1870, at Boston in the lunatic hospital. He lived at Boston, his name first appearing in the Boston directories in 1849, when he is described as "ostler"; from 1852 to 1859 he is called "laborer"; and from 1860 to his death he was janitor of the Franklin school, living on Newlands street.

He married, Apr. 2, 1849, at Boston, by Rev. Otis A. Skinner, Mary-Ann Call, born August, 1812, at York, Me., though her marriage record says she was born at Wiscasset, Me.; died July 9, 1896, at Boston, in the Old Ladies Home. She was aged eighty-three years, eleven months when she died, and Mr. Lincoln's age at death is given as fifty-one years, ten months. (Boston Records; Mass. Vital Records.)

Children, born *a, c* at Boston; *b* at Quincy, Mass.:

aacbe haa. AMOS A., born Jan. 14, 1851.

aacbe hab. ADA-TYLER, born Jan. 18, 1853; died Feb. 12, 1855, at Boston.

aacbe hac. LOUIS-RUSSELL, born March 30, 1856; died Oct. 17, 1883, at Boston. He succeeded his father as janitor of the Franklin school. He lived at Boston and is called Louis T. in the Boston directories and also in the Quincy, Mass., records, so perhaps he changed his name to Louis-Trevett.

He married, June 8, 1882, at Quincy, Nancy-Elizabeth, daughter of James and Margaret D. (Taylor) Burke of Quincy, born Apr. 12, 1861, at Quincy; died Oct. 23, 1885, at Quincy, aged twenty-four years, six months, eleven days. Her father, James Burke, who was half brother to Mary-Ann Call, the mother of Louis-Russell Lincoln, was born at York, Me.; her mother was born at Boston. Mr. and Mrs. Lincoln had no children. (Mass. Vital Records; Quincy Records.)

aacbe hb. SAMUEL-RUSSELL-TREVETT, son of Amos (*Amos, Enoch, Jedediah, Samuel, Samuel*) and Rebecca-Trevett (Bartol) Lincoln of Boston, Mass., born in 1820, at Boston; died Dec. 7, 1873, at Boston, aged fifty-two years. He died in the poor-house at Rainsford island. In 1854 he is described as "baker, living at Boston." His daughter thinks that he had other children by his second wife, and that he perhaps married a third wife; but she knows little of him after his separation from her mother.

He married (1), Nov. 7, 1842, at Boston, Mary-Ann, daughter of Baslee and Emma (Jennison) Bennett of Boston, born Apr. 15, 1822, at Boston; died Sept. 6, 1865, at Dedham, Mass., aged

forty-three years, four months, twenty-one days. They separated and were, apparently, divorced.

He married (2), May 3, 1854, at Boston, Susan, daughter of
Henry and Susan (Pickett) Lewis of Lynn, Mass., and widow of
Isaac Mansfield of Lynn, whom she married June 9, 1839, at
Lynn and who died Apr. 7, 1849, at Lynn of dislocation of the
vertebrae. He was son of John 3d and Lydia-Husey (Breed)
Mansfield of Lynn, where he was born N,ov. 29, 1821. Susan
Lewis was born Oct. 18, 1821, at Lynn. No record of Mrs. Susan
Lincoln's death has been found. (Boston Records; Mass. Vital
Records; Lynn Records; Records of Mrs. Lucy-Emma [Lincoln]
McClennan, *aacbe hbb.*)

Children, by first wife, born: *a* unknown; *b* at Charlestown,
Mass.:

aacbe hba. MARY-ELIZABETH, born Jan. 3, 1842; died Oct. 1, 1868, at Cambridge, Mass.; married, Jan. 25, 1863, at Dedham, Mass., Albert-Loammi,
son of Loammi-Walker and Laurana (Pincin) Phipps of Dedham, born
1840, at South Dedham. He was a blacksmith and removed to Cambridge
before September, 1868. (Mass. Vital Records.)
    Children, born: *a* at Dedham; *b* at Cambridge:
    a. CHARLES-WALKER, born Jan. 13, 1865; died Apr. 9, 1869.
    b. GEORGE-ALBERT, born September, 1868; killed July 24, 1885, at
          Jamaica Plain, Mass., on Boston & Providence railroad.
aacbe hbb. LUCY-EMMA, born Nov. 29, 1844; married, June 23, 1868, at
Charlestown, Albert, son of Robert and Mary-Ann (Pigeon) McClennen
of Charlestown, born Dec. 13, 1837, at Boston, Mass.; died Jan. 30,
1906, at Boston. He lived at Boston and was by trade a machinist. He
served for three years during the Civil war as able seaman on board the
flagship "Minnesota." His widow was living, 1911, at Boston.
    Children, born at Boston:
    a. EMMA-GERTRUDE, born June 9, 1869; died Apr. 17, 1870.
    b. ARTHUR-RAYMOND, born March 23, 1871; living, 1911, un-
          married.

aacbe 1d. LEVI-LOUIS, son of Abraham-Orne (*Amos, Enoch,
Jedediah, Samuel, Samuel*) and Hannah-Sprague (Wales) Lincoln
of Bath, Me., born Dec. 4, 1827, at Bath; died May 29, 1903,
at Portland, Me. He lived first at Bath, but removed to Skowhegan, Me., about 1865 and bought a house there of Abner and
Philander Coburn. At that time he was conductor on a train
on the Portland and Kennebec railroad which necessitated his
passing the night at Skowhegan. In 1868 he was transferred to
another train and removed to Portland, selling his house in

Skowhegan. He later became superintendent of the Portland and Kennebec railroad, and on its consolidation with the Maine Central railroad, was made assistant superintendent of that road, and removed to Augusta, Me. He next became superintendent of the Bangor and Bucksport railroad, and, later, of the Rumford Falls railroad, and in 1896 was living at Rumford Falls. He finally gave up active business, bought a place in Portland near the Westbrook line, and passed the rest of his life there.

He married (1), Aug. 22, 1853, at Brunswick, Me., Rachel-Ann, daughter of John and Mary (French) Noble of Brunswick, born Feb. 10, 1831, at Brunswick; died Dec. 21, 1861, at Bath.

He married (2), June 14, 1864, at Boston, Mass., Lydia-Nichols, daughter of Nathaniel-Nichols and Susan (Lincoln) Bates of Boston, born March 19, 1835, at Boston; died Feb. 27, 1896, at Rumford Falls. She was descended through her mother from Stephen Lincoln of Hingham. (Portland Records; Brunswick Records; Bath Cemetery Records; Cohasset Genealogies, p. 28; Hist. of Hingham, vol. ii, p. 479; Records of Rev. Howard-Abbot Lincoln, *aacbe ldd;* Gravestones in Maplegrove Cemetery, Bath.)

Children, by first wife, born at Brunswick:

aacbe lda. FRANK-LOUIS, born July 27, 1855; died Feb. 23, 1899, at Portland, unmarried. He was a travelling agent for a railroad. He is buried at Bath, Me.

aacbe ldb. MARY-AMELIA, born Feb. 25, 1860; died Dec. 14, 1903, at Portland, unmarried.

Children, by second wife, born: *c, d* at Skowhegan; *e, f* at Augusta:

aacbe ldc. A SON, born Apr. 20, 1865; died Apr. 23, 1865.

aacbe ldd. HOWARD-ABBOT, born July 22, 1867. He graduated at Amherst college in 1892 and studied for the ministry at Andover Theological Seminary where he received the degree of B.D. in 1904. In 1911 he was minister of the Congregational church at Wiscasset, Me. He married, July 19, 1910, at Newtonville, Mass., Blanche-Winifred, daughter of Royal-Hopkins and Elizabeth (Carlisle) Wadleigh of Newton, Mass., born May 17, 1871, at Newton. (Records of Rev. Howard-Abbot Lincoln.) No children.

aacbe lde. WALTER-BOWDLEAR, born July 30, 1872; died Sept. 12, 1872, at Augusta, but is buried at Bath.

aacbe ldf. LEVI-BATES, born Feb. 5, 1875.

aacbe 1f. AUGUSTUS-CLARK, son of Abraham-Orne (*Amos, Enoch, Jedediah, Samuel, Samuel*) and Hannah-Sprague (Wales) Lincoln of Bath, Me., born March 12, 1831, at Bath; died May 23, 1902, at Benton Station, Me. He is buried at Bath. He was a railroad conductor on the Portland and Kennebec railroad, living at Bath and, for a short time, at Skowhegan, Me. He afterwards removed to Portland, Me., and on being made station agent at Benton removed thither, and lived there until his death. In his later years he was a signal tender.

He married (1), March 29, 1853, at Bath, Emma-Jane Williams, an English woman who came to America with an aunt. Her father never came to this country and his name is not known to the family, nor is there any record of her birth. Her mother afterwards came to the United States and died here. Mr. and Mrs. Lincoln were divorced about 1856 and she married (2) Thomas Joy, and was thought to have died at Charlestown, Mass., about 1870, but the following record from Massachusetts Vital Records probably refers to her: "Emma Joy, widow, aged forty-five years, six months, born in England and daughter of Edward and Mary A. (surname unknown), living at 46 Walker street, Boston, died Nov. 13, 1880, at Boston."

He married (2), Oct. 5, 1857, at Bath, Mrs. Harriet-Maria (White) Bean, daughter of William-Henry and Susan-Maria (Thornton) White of Bath, and divorced wife of I. X. Bean of Portland by whom she had a son, Edward. She was born Jan. 4, 1838, at Portland and was living, 1911, at Benton Station. (Bath Cemetery and Town Records; Records of Mrs. Anna-Amelia [Lincoln] Hall, *aacbe lfe*, and Mrs. Augusta-Clark [Lincoln] Woodward, *aacbe lfa*.)

Child, by first wife, born at Bath:

aacbe lfa. AUGUSTA-CLARK, born Jan. 8, 1854; married, Dec. 29, 1876, at Brunswick, Me., William-Given, son of Horace and Mary-Elizabeth (Thomas) Woodward of Brunswick, born Nov. 1, 1848, at Brunswick; died Jan. 9, 1901, at Brunswick, where he had always lived. He was a carpenter and farmer. She was living, 1911, at Brunswick.
  Child, born at Brunswick:
    a. HARRY-LINCOLN, born Nov. 23, 1875; mar. Priscilla Talbot.

Children, by second wife, born: *b–e* at Bath; *f, g* at Portland:

aacbe lfb. FREDERIC-REVERE, born Nov. 6, 1858.
aacbe lfc. HARRIET-MARIA, born Apr. 21, 1860; died March 4, 1905, at Ben-

ton, Me.; married, March 1, 1884, at Benton, Ozro, son of Joseph and Almedia (Gerald) Brown of Benton, born March 20, 1854, at Benton; living there in 1911. He is a farmer.

Child, born at Boston:

    a.   EARL-LINCOLN, born Nov. 28, 1885; mar. Ruby-Grace Whitman.

aacbe lfd.   GEORGE-AUGUSTUS, born July 16, 1862; his whereabouts unknown to the family in 1911. In 1898 he was a steam and gas fitter and was living at East Kingston, N. H. He married, June 16, 1898, at Exeter, N. H., Jennie M. Crockett, a divorced woman, living at the time of her marriage at East Kingston. She was born at Malone, N. Y., and as she is called aged 41 when married she was born in 1857. (New Hampshire Vital Records.)

aacbe lfe.   ANNA-AMELIA, born July 21, 1865; married (1), Nov. 24, 1885, at Skowhegan, Me., Herbert, son of Emerson Kilgore of Skowhegan. He was living, 1911, at Skowhegan and was foreman of the lasting department of a shoe shop. They were divorced and she married (2), Nov. 24, 1898, at Bath, Arthur-White, son of Oliver-Gray and Frances (White) Hall of Augusta, Me., born Aug. 12, 1866, at Rockland, Me. He is a printer, living, 1911, at Rockland. They were divorced in 1902. She is living, 1911, at Rockland and is forewoman of a shop.

Child, by first husband, born at Benton, Me.:

    a.   IDA-LINCOLN KILGORE, born July 4, 1887; mar. Verne Battese.

Child, by second husband, born at Rockland:

    b.   ARTHUR-FRANCIS HALL, born July 12, 1900.

aacbe lff.   CARRIE-ABBOT, born Sept. 15, 1867, though Portland records say 1869; died Nov. 2, 1894, at Dexter, Me.; married, Oct. 14, 1890, at Fairfield, Me., Ernest-Eugene, son of Joseph H. and Betsey-Roxanna (Larrabee) Warren of Dexter, born Dec. 19, ——— at Parkman, Me. He was in 1911 a printer, living at Holyoke, Mass. He lived for a year and a half after leaving home at Waterville, Me., and then moved to Dexter and was one of the proprietors of the "Dexter Gazette." For the ten years previous to 1911 he was in the printing business at Holyoke as treasurer and manager of the Anker Printing Company. Mrs. Warren is buried at Bath. He married (2) Miss Julia-Louisa Judd, who died before 1911, without children.

Child, born at Dexter:

    a.   CARL-REED, born Oct. 9, 1894; died Dec. 18, 1895.

aacbe lfg.   HARRY-IRVEN, born January, 1871; died Apr. 25, 1876, at Portland, but is buried at Bath.

aacbg cc.   EZRA, son of Ezra (*Ezra, Enoch, Jedediah, Samuel, Samuel*) and Chastine (Hartwell) Lincoln of Boston, Mass., born March 12, 1819, at Boston; died June 15, 1863, at Belmont, Mass. He was educated in the Boston public schools and in 1835 won a Franklin medal at the English high school. He became by profession a civil engineer and for some time was a commissioner of patents. He filled several offices of honor and trust; representative in the General Court 1850, 1851 and 1852;

member of the common council from ward 10, in 1847, 1851 and 1852; aide to Governors Briggs and Clifford; one of the commissioners on Boston harbor; and State engineer on the Rhode Island boundary and the Hoosac tunnel. On the incoming of a Republican administration in 1861, he was appointed assistant treasurer of the United States in Boston, and held that office when he died. He was an active and earnest politician but extended his urbanity to opponents as well as friends. His moral character was unblemished and he left no personal enemies. (Boston Daily Advertiser, June 16, 1863.)

He married (1), Jan. 4, 1844, at Boston, Helen-Elizabeth, daughter of Charles and Elizabeth (Rand?) Sprague of Boston, born 1819, at Boston; died March 30, 1851, at Boston, "aged thirty two years." (Sprague Family in America, p. 227.)

He married (2), Dec. 2, 1856, at West Roxbury, Mass., Phebe-Maria, daughter of William and Margaret-Elizabeth (Kupfer) Blake of Jamaica Plain, Mass., born May 2, 1835, at Boston; died Jan. 21, 1892, at New York, N. Y. (Mass. Vital Records.)

Children, by second wife, born: *a* at West Roxbury; *b* at Boston:

aacbg cca. CHARLES-SPRAGUE, born Aug. 23, 1857. He removed to New York city in 1878 and remained there until 1888, when he removed to Superior, Wis., where he lived for twelve years. In 1900 he went to St. Paul, Minn., and has lived there since. He is, 1911, an editor in the employment of the West Publishing Company. He married, Dec. 14, 1892, at Stillwater, Minn., Mary-Sophronia, daughter of John-Johnson and Pernicia-Ann (Ranno) Robertson of Stillwater, born Oct. 12, 1868, at Stillwater. They have no children. (Records of Charles-Sprague Lincoln.)

aacbg ccb. HELEN-MARIA, born Oct. 3, 1859; living, 1910, at New York, N. Y., unmarried. She is an invalid.

aacbg ch. JEROM, son of Ezra (*Ezra, Enoch, Jedediah, Samuel, Samuel*) and Chastine (Hartwell) Lincoln of Boston, Mass., born July 16, 1829, at Boston; died Feb. 23, 1896, at San Francisco, Calif., whither he removed soon after his marriage and where he passed the rest of his life. He was a merchant.

He married, Sept. 14, 1854, at Brookline, Mass., Philinda-Gates, daughter of Daniel and Philinda-Gates (Prouty) Bates of Boston, born March 9, 1837, at Boston; living, 1910, at San Francisco. (Mass. Vital Records; Family Records of Miss

Chastine-Lincoln Cushing, *aacbg caa;* and of Mrs. Philinda-Gates Lincoln.)

Children, born at San Francisco:

aacbg cha. JEROME-BATES, born July 29, 1863; died July 4, 1899, unmarried.
aacbg chb. ETHEL, born June 1, 1873; married Nov. 17, 1909, at San Francisco, John-Ralston, son of Alexander and Clara (Smith) Hamilton of Canada, born Oct. 21, 1870, at San Francisco. He is an architect. They were living in 1910 at San Francisco.

aacbg ck. LOWELL, son of Ezra (*Ezra, Enoch, Jedediah, Samuel, Samuel*) and Chastine (Hartwell) Lincoln of Boston, Mass., born June 28, 1836, at Boston. He was educated in the Boston public schools and entered the employ of Lawrence, Stone & Company, manufacturers' agents in Boston, in 1852, with whom he remained four years. In 1856 he went with James M. Beebe of Boston; in 1859 he was admitted as partner in the firm of E. R. Mudge & Company of Boston and, in 1868, was put in charge of their New York branch and removed to New York. In 1880 he was a partner in the house of Joy, Lincoln & Motley with whom he remained until 1885, when he joined the firm of Catlin & Company with whom he still remains. He is, 1910, a director in the German-American Insurance Company and of the Mechanics National Bank of New York, and trustee of the Greenwich Savings Bank.

He married, Dec. 22, 1863, at Boston, Clara-Amanda, daughter of Loring and Amanda-Sophia (Forbes) Lothrop of Boston, born Nov. 18, 1842, at East Cambridge, Mass. They were living, 1910, at New York, N. Y. (Nat'l Cyclopedia of Am. Biography, vol. x, p. 85; Forbes-Forbush Genealogy, p. 75; Mass. Vital Records; Records of Lowell Lincoln.)

Children, born: *a-c* at Boston; *d-f* at New York:

aacbg cka. LOWELL, born Oct. 1, 1864; died Oct. 3, 1864.
aacbg ckb. LOWELL, born Dec. 15, 1865.
aacbg ckc. ARTHUR-HUNTINGTON, born June 27, 1867; died Sept. 28, 1884.
aacbg ckd. A CHILD, unnamed, born and died Apr. 21, 1869.
aacbg cke. EZRA, born Jan. 11, 1871; died Aug. 16, 1907, at Locust, N. J., unmarried.
aacbg ckf. CLARA-LOTHROP, born Feb. 6, 1874; married, Sept. 22, 1896, at New York, James-Parrish, son of Dr. Charles-Carroll and Helen (Parrish) Lee of Maryland and New York city, born June 6, 1870, at New York. He graduated at Harvard college in 1891; studied law and in 1910 was practising that profession in New York, where they were residing.

Children, born at New York:
    a. CLARA-LOTHROP, born March 22, 1898.
    b. HELEN, born Apr. 11, 1900.
    c. CHARLES-CARROLL, born Nov. 27, 1902.
    d. MILDRED, born Oct. 28, 1909.

aacdb bd. SOLOMON-HENRY, son of Solomon (*Otis, William, Jedediah, Samuel, Samuel*) and Eleanor M. (Gove) Lincoln of Perry, Me., born Sept. 3, 1826, at Perry; living, 1910, at Perry with his third wife. He is a farmer.

He married (1), Feb. 20, 1855, at Perry, Anna M. White, adopted daughter of Thomas and Lydia Lowell. She was born May 20, 1835, at Perry; and died there May 21, 1868.

He married (2), March 25, 1869, at Perry, Helen-Martha, daughter of Joel and Hannah (Guptil) Knowlton of Charlotte, Me., born Feb. 27, 1840, at Cherryfield, Me.; died Oct. 10, 1871, at Perry.

He married (3), July 10, 1873, at Perry, Mary-Jane, daughter of John and Harriet (Wilt) Campbell of Bass River, New Brunswick, born Dec. 10, 1838, at Bass River; living, 1910. She was called of Perry in 1873, when she was married. (Perry Records; Records of William-Henry Lincoln, *aacdb gf.*)

Children, by first wife, born at Perry:

aacdb bda. ELLEN-MARIA, born June 9, 1856; died Oct. 1, 1859.
aacdb bdb. GEORGE-LOWELL, born May 9, 1858; died Nov. 22, 1859.
aacdb bdc. ALICE, born Feb. 18, 1860. She was really an adopted child, the daughter of Lydia Hall. She married (1) John O'Brien; (2) Milton Briery; (3) Don Matthews.
aacdb bdd. ADELBERT, born Sept. 1, 1862; living, 1910, with his father, unmarried.
aacdb bde. HENRY, born May 12, 1865; died July 5, 1881.

Children, by second wife, born at Perry:

aacdb bdf. BERTHA-ADELAIDE, born June 10, 1870; married, Feb. 26, 1894, at Perry (also given as Feb. 17), John-Augustine, son of Thomas and Mary (Kirk) Mitchell of St. John, New Brunswick, born Nov. 2, 1871, at St. John. They were living, 1910, at Perry.
    Children, born at Perry:
        a. WALTER-AUGUSTINE, born Dec. 25, 1894.
        b. HARRY-ALLEN, born March 21, 1896.
        c. NELLIE-MAY, born Apr. 3, 1897.
        d. JOHN-LESTER, born July 7, 1900; died Sept. 9, 1907.
        e. DORIS-BLANCHE, born March 30, 1904.
        f. ALICE-JOSEPHINE, born June 29, 1906.
        g. WILLIAM, born March 31, 1910.

aacdb bdg.   WALTER,   } born Oct. 8, 1871; { living, 1910, at home, unmarried.
aacdb bdh.   NELLIE,   }   { married, Dec. 2, 1908, at Blacks
    Harbor, New Brunswick, Robert, son of William and Elinor (Foley)
    Thompson of Queenstown, Ireland, born Sept. 2, 1849, at Blacks Harbor.
    He is a carpenter. They were living, 1910, at Penfield, New Brunswick.
    Child, born at Blacks Harbor:
      a.   CHALLONER-GUILFORD, born Oct. 2, 1909.

Children, by third wife, born at Perry:

aacdb bdi.   MARY-ALMA, born Aug. 23, 1873; living, 1910, at home, unmarried.
aacdb bdj.   HARRIET-AMELIA, born June 12, 1875; married, Dec. 7, 1897, at
    Perry, Arthur-Eugene, son of William and Viola (Johnson) Gilson of
    Perry, born March 24, 1875, at Perry. They are living, 1910, at Boston,
    Mass.
    Children, born: *a, e* at Eastport, Me.; *b-d* at Perry; *f* at Taunton, Mass.:
      a.   TERESA-LENORE, born March 18, 1899.
      b.   LEWIS-DONOVAN, born Jan. 19, 1901.
      c.   ALDA-MAY, born June 12, 1903.
      d.   ANNIE-BERNADETTE, born Aug. 13, 1905 (Aug. 11 in Perry
        records).
      e.   BROOKS-LINCOLN, born July 19, 1907.
      f.   ELTON-LEROY, born Apr. 7, 1909.

aacdb eb.   GEORGE-OTIS, son of Otis (*Otis, William, Jedediah,
Samuel, Samuel*) and Mary-Richards (Jones) Lincoln of Perry,
Me., born May 5, 1830, at Perry; died Apr. 11, 1899, at Milton,
Mass., where he had lived. The record of his death in Massa-
chusetts Vital Records makes the singular error of calling his
mother Ruth Stevens, and giving his father's birthplace as
Liverpool, Nova Scotia. He was a farmer. During the Civil
war he was a private in Company E, 31st Maine infantry.

He married, May 13, 1855, at Eastport, Me., Paulina, daughter
of Jacob and Caroline (Pierce) Stannels of Eastport, born
March 2, 1830, at Eastport; died Jan. 20, 1898, at Eastport.
(Eastport Records; Perry Records; Records of Edmund-Sabine
Lincoln, *aacbd ebg.*)

Children, born: *a, b* at Eastport; *c* at Aroostook; *d* at Patten;
e-g at Dennysville, Me.:

aacdb eba.   JACOB-STANNELS, born March 31, 1856.
aacdb ebb.   GEORGE-HERBERT, born May 15, 1858; is dead. He was married
    and his widow was living in 1912 at Chicago, Ill.
aacdb ebc.   CHARLES, born June 3, 1860; died Jan. 27, 1861, at Aroostook.
aacdb ebd.   CHARLES-OTIS, born June 23, 1862 (he himself says June 25).
    He was living in 1913 at Eureka, Calif., a merchant in books and station-
    ery. He married in 1882 at Eastport, Fannie, daughter of Charles and

Elizabeth (Boynton) Bell of Eastport, born Nov. 16, 1863, at Eastport; living, 1913. They have no children.

aacdb ebe. LEWIS-JONES, born July 1, 1865; died Aug. 17, 1867, at Dennys-**ville.**

aacdb ebf. FREDERICK, born Jan. 27, 1868; died Apr. 26, 1876, at Eastport.

aacdb ebg. EDMUND-SABINE, born Jan. 20, 1869.

aacdb ee. HERBERT-RICHMOND, son of Otis (*Otis, William, Jedediah, Samuel, Samuel*) and Mary-Richards (Jones) Lincoln of Perry, Me., born Sept. 3, 1836, at Perry. He lived until about 1890 at Perry on the old Otis Lincoln farm; then removed to Eastport, Me., and was living there in 1911. He has always been a farmer. He served for nine months during the Civil war as private in Company D, 43d Massachusetts infantry, being enrolled Aug. 25, 1862, and discharged July 30, 1863.

He married (1), Nov. 1, 1863, at Dedham, Mass., Caroline-Matilda, daughter of Belcher-Sylvester and Hannah (Whiting) Wood of Dedham, born Sept. 18, 1839, at Dedham; died Oct. 25, 1876, at Perry.

He married (2), Dec. 19, 1878, at Eastport, Mrs. Lizzie-Smith (Hibbert) Norton, daughter of John and Eliza (Smith) Hibbert of Perry, and widow of Seth B. Norton of Pembroke, Me. She was born Aug. 24, 1843, at Perry and died there July 3, 1890.

He married (3), Apr. 30, 1892, at Lubec, Me., Mrs. Mary-Knight (Hanscom) Hoyte of Machias, Me., daughter of Peter and Lydia (Huntly) Hanscom of East Machias and widow of Otis Hoyte of Machias. She was born Jan. 28, 1851, at East Machias and was living, 1911. (Perry Records; Dedham Records; Records of Herbert-Richmond Lincoln.)

Children, by first wife, born: *a* at Perry; *b* at Dedham:

aacdb eea. GEORGE-ALBERT, born Oct. 21, 1864.

aacdb eeb. WARREN-SILVESTER, born Feb. 12, 1867; living, 1911, at Cambridgeport, Mass., where he was a watchman in one of the factories. He removed from Eastport to Tewksbury, Mass., and lived there until the death of his wife. In Tewksbury he was a farmer. He married, Sept. 30, 1896, at Tewskbury, Emilia-Carlson, daughter of Martin and Maria (Carlson) Ahlberg of Lowell, Mass. They are so named in the record of her death, but in her marriage record they are called John and Harriet. She was born Jan. 21, 1868, in Sweden, and died Sept. 14, 1899, at Lowell "aged thirty-one years, seven months, twenty-four days." They had no children. (Mass. Vital Records.)

28

Children, by second wife, born at Perry:

aacdb eec. RALPH-HERBERT, born Sept. 13, 1880. He is an optical die maker, living, 1911, at Geneva, N. Y. He married, Sept. 7, 1910, at Pigeon Cove, Rockport, Mass., Helen-Hale, daughter of Herbert-Austin and Martha-Amelia (Hale) Story of Pigeon Cove, born Aug. 3, 1884, at Pigeon Cove. No children. (Records of Ralph-Herbert Lincoln.)

aacdb eed. ARTHUR-FREDERICK, born Apr. 4, 1882; living, 1911, at New York, N. Y., unmarried. He is engaged in the fruit business.

aacdb eee. BENJAMIN-JONES, born June 22, 1885; living, 1911, at New York, N. Y., unmarried. He is in business with his brother Arthur.

aacdb ef. OTIS, son of Otis (*Otis, William, Jedediah, Samuel, Samuel*) and Mary-Richards (Jones) Lincoln of Perry, Me., born March 20, 1842, at Perry; died May 15, 1907, at Milton, Mass. He was a farmer at Perry but removed to Milton about 1890 and engaged in farming there. He enlisted in 1861 as private in Company F, 6th Maine infantry, and served for three years, then re-enlisted and served until the end of the war. He was promoted to be corporal.

He married, March 8, 1864, at Edmunds, Me., Julia-Sophia, daughter of Henry and Hannah (Runnels) Jones of Edmunds, born June 18, 1844, at Edmunds; living, 1911, at Lowell, Mass. (Perry Records; Records of Mrs. Otis Lincoln.)

Children, born *a* at Charlotte, Me.; *b, c* at Perry:

aacdb efa. GRACE-CAROLINE, born March 30, 1866; living, 1911, at Lowell, unmarried.

aacdb efb. FRANKLIN-PHILBROOK, born Nov. 4, 1867.

aacdb efc. OTIS, born May 24, 1875; living, 1911, at Boston, Mass. He is a photographer and lived first at Lowell, Mass., but removed about 1895 to Boston and in 1911 was employed in Purdy's studio. He married, Sept. 8, 1898, at Boston, Gertrude-Abby, daughter of Joseph-Louis and Emma-Louise (Carver) Berry of Livermore Falls, Me., born Nov. 15, 1877, at Livermore Falls. They have no children. (Mass. Vital Records.)

aacdb fc. ALBERT-ROBINSON, son of William (*Otis, William, Jedediah, Samuel, Samuel*) and Maria L. (Copp) Lincoln of Dennysville, Me., born Oct. 3, 1831, at Perry, Me.; died Oct. 18, 1899, at Dennysville. He was a graduate of Sackville academy and New York Medical college; lived at Dennysville and practised his profession there. He was assistant surgeon of Company K, 1st Maine heavy artillery, in the Civil war; commissioned Dec. 15, 1862, and mustered out Sept. 11, 1865. The following account of his life has been furnished by his daughter, Mrs. Elkins:

"He received his early education in the public schools at Eastport, Me., and at Sackville, N. B., Seminary, with one year at Yale. He graduated from the University Medical School of New York (now Columbia University) in 1854, and for one year practised medicine in Minneapolis, Minn. Shortly after the death of his first wife he went back to Dennysville, where he spent the remainder of his life, with the exception of two years in California, in 1859-60. On Dec. 15, 1862, he was commissioned assistant surgeon of the First Maine Heavy Artillery (Dr. Jerome-Bonaparte Elkins being the surgeon), and was stationed at Maryland Heights until May, 1864, when he joined the Army of the Potomac. In October, 1864, Dr. Lincoln was made surgeon in charge of hospitals and, for a short time, was surgeon-in-chief of artillery. After the close of the war he returned to Dennysville and resumed the practice of medicine, in which he continued actively engaged until September, 1896. He was a Republican, voting for Abraham Lincoln under rebel fire at Fort Sedgwick. For twenty years he was a member of the school committee of his native town, was president of the Washington County Agricultural Society for three years, and served four years as a member of the State Board of Agriculture. He served one term as representative to the State legislature. He was a master mason, commander of Theodore Lincoln Post, G. A. R., for eight years, and a member of the Loyal Legion. In September, 1896, while attending the national encampment of the G. A. R. at Minneapolis, he became critically ill of a lingering disease which continued till his death. As the 'Old Doctor,' a title given him more from respect and love than for age, he was known over a large territory. No call for aid was ever refused by him. No night was too dark, no storm too severe, no snow drifts too deep for him to start out at the call for help. His cheerful face brought hope and courage to the sufferer on the sick bed and to the watcher beside it. He was a faithful friend to the old soldiers, having an affection for them which was ardently returned. As Ian McLaren says in his story of the 'Country Doctor': 'Death was, after all, the victor for the man who had saved others, but would not save himself'; and he was laid to rest beneath the folds of the flag he loved so well."

He married (1), Sept. 14, 1854, at Eastport, Me., Elizabeth-Jacobs, daughter of Samuel J. Clarke of Eastport, perhaps also of New Haven, Conn. She died Dec. 3, 1855, at Dennysville and is buried at Eastport. She had no children.

He married (2), Feb. 19, 1857, at Dennysville, Deborah-Reynolds, daughter of Solomon and Eliza (Wilder) Foster of Dennysville, born Feb. 27, 1832, at Dennysville; died there March 3, 1901, "aged sixty-nine years, four days." (Perry Records; Dennysville Records; Records of Albert-Edward Lincoln, *aacdb fcb*.)

Children, by second wife, born at Dennysville:

aacdb fca. ELIZABETH-MARIA, born Nov. 11, 1857; married, Jan. 15, 1884, at Dennysville, Augustus-Jerome, son of Jerome-Bonaparte and Olive-Esther (Blanchard) Elkins of Oldtown, Me., born Nov. 1, 1856, at Lincoln, Me. He graduated at the University of Maine in 1877, taking the degree of Bachelor of Mechanical Engineering. They lived at Fergus Falls, Minn., from 1884 to 1892, and since then have lived at Minneapolis, Minn. He is a book-keeper. (Records of Mrs. Elizabeth-Maria Elkins.)

Child, born at St. Paul, Minn.:

a. PHYLLIS-MAXWELL, born Jan. 1, 1890; unmarried, 1911.

aacdb fcb. ALBERT-EDWARD, born Oct. 15, 1859.

aacdb fcc. MARY-GILLIGAN, born Sept. 18, 1866; died same day.

aacdb fcd. HARRY-FOSTER, born Aug. 31, 1867.

aacdb fce. OLIVE-ELKINS, born Oct. 3, 1875; married, Oct. 6, 1909, at Minneapolis, Minn., Edgar-Arnold, son of James-Roscoe and Ellen-Elizabeth (Arnold) Swain of Minneapolis, born May 17, 1868, at Saratoga, Minn. They lived first at Minneapolis where he was a tailor, but in 1913 they were living at Twodot, Mont., where he was a Congregational minister and missionary. (Records of Mrs. Olive-Elkins [Lincoln] Swain.)

Child, born at Minneapolis:

a. EDGAR-ARNOLD, born Feb. 23, 1911; died March 7, 1911.

aacdb gc. JOHN-MELVIN, son of Thompson (*Otis, William, Jedediah, Samuel, Samuel*) and Sarah-Leighton (Jones) Lincoln of Perry, Me., born Aug. 25, 1833; died Jan. 8, 1866, being lost at sea on the coast of Florida with his whole family, while on his way to Florida where he had intended to settle. He lived at Pembroke, Me., and like all his brothers was a sailor. He served in the Civil war and was first lieutenant in Company F, 6th Maine infantry, and captain in the 2nd Maine cavalry.

After the war, deciding to emigrate to Florida, he took passage in the brig "Neva" of East Machias, Me., which sailed from New York for Jacksonville and, arriving off St. John's bar and having taken aboard her pilot, was unable to cross the bar in a terrible gale from the northeast and was lost with all on board.

He married, June 1, 1855, at Pembroke, Mehitable-Ellen, daughter of Bela and Mercy (Hersey) Wilder of Pembroke, born Apr. 11, 1837, at Pembroke; died Jan. 8, 1866, at sea. (Perry Records; Boston and Maine newspapers for January, 1866; Records of William-Henry Lincoln, *aacdb gf.*)

Children, born at Pembroke:

aacdb gca. JOHN-THOMPSON, born 1859; died Jan. 8, 1866.
aacdb gcb. LEWIS-WADSWORTH, born 1861; died Jan. 8, 1866.
aacdb gcc. WILLIAM-HENRY, born 1863; died Jan. 8, 1866.

aacdb gf. WILLIAM-HENRY, son of Thompson (*Otis, William, Jedediah, Samuel, Samuel*) and Sarah-Leighton (Jones) Lincoln of Perry, Me., born Nov. 2, 1839, at Perry; living, 1911, at Perry but in poor health. He was in early life a sailor but, later, became a farmer. He was orderly sergeant in Company F, 6th Maine infantry, from 1861 to 1864, and was wounded in the battle of St. Mary's Heights, Va. He is a much respected citizen of Perry and, though a great sufferer from cancer of the throat, always cheerful. He has taken a great interest in this compilation and has furnished considerable information about the Perry branch of the family.

He married, June 20, 1865, at Dennysville, Me., Sarah-Maria, daughter of John and Sarah-Leighton (Hersey) Campbell of Pembroke, Me., born March 9, 1846, at Pembroke; died Apr. 4, 1911, at Perry. (Perry Records; Records of William-Henry Lincoln.)

Children, born at Perry:

aacdb gfa. IDA-ELLA, born Apr. 28, 1866; living, 1910, at Perry; married, July 5, 1888, at Perry, Herbert-Stanley, son of Stanley and Harriet (Stoddard) Frost of Perry, born Dec. 6, 1867, at Perry; died Jan. 4, 1904, at Perry, where he had always lived. He was a farmer.
    Children, born at Perry:
      a. AUSTIN-LEROY, born June 12, 1889; unmarried, 1910.
      b. WILLIAM-STANLEY, born Apr. 7, 1891.
      c. ETHEL-MAY, born Aug. 24, 1894.
      d. LINCOLN-STODDARD, born Oct. 7, 1903.

aacdb gfb. NELLIE-MAY, born Aug. 8, 1868; married, June 27, 1894, at Perry, Frank-Herbert, son of Joseph and Ann-Maria (Wedgewood) Woodbury of Litchfield, Me., born June 10, 1869, at Litchfield. He is a jeweler. They were living, 1911, at Gardiner, Me. They have no children.

aacdb gfc. SARAH-CAMPBELL, born July 29, 1872; married, June 24, 1896, at Perry, Stephen-Emerson, son of James and Mary (Vose) Cox of Robbinston, Me., born Feb. 28, 1866, at Robbinston, where they were living in 1911. He is a merchant and in 1911 was town clerk and postmaster.
   Children, born at Robbinston:
   a. GERTRUDE-LINCOLN, born Sept. 30, 1903.
   b. HELEN-GENEVA, born Apr. 10, 1907.

aacdb gfd. JOHN-THOMPSON, born Apr. 3, 1879; died Aug. 28, 1899, from drowning in the river at Perry.

aacdb gfe. ANNIE-MAY, born March 23, 1887; married, Oct. 29, 1908, at Perry, Oscar-Elmer, son of Robert and Laura (Leach) Newcomb of Perry, born Aug. 4, 1880, at Perry. They are living, 1911, at Perry. He is a farmer.
   Child, born at Perry:
   a. LAURA-ANNIE, born Oct. 11, 1909.

aacdb ic. NATHAN-PATTANGALL, son of Ezekiel (*Otis, William, Jedediah, Samuel, Samuel*) and Sophia (Gibbs) Lincoln of Perry, Me., born Sept. 26, 1840, at Perry. He enlisted Sept. 6, 1861, at Readville, Mass., in the 1st Massachusetts cavalry, Company G, and was honorably discharged in Boston, May 16, 1865. His regiment was a part of the Army of the Potomac. In June, 1864, he was captured in a cavalry raid near Orange Court House, Va., and was imprisoned at Andersonville until March 25, 1865, when all the prisoners were released. In 1866 he was a farmer living at West Roxbury, Mass., but, later, he removed to Bridgewater, Mass., and was living there in 1913.

He married, March 28, 1866, at West Roxbury, Serena-Morgan, daughter of Andrew and Nancy-Ann (Gove) Brown of Newburyport, Mass., born May 3, 1839, at Pittston, Me., though her marriage record says she was born at Newburyport; living, 1913. (Perry Records; Mass. Vital Records; Records of Nathan-Pattangall Lincoln.)

Children, born: *a* at Newburyport; *b* at Vineland, N. J.; *c* at Cambridge, Mass.:

aacdb ica. WINTHROP-CLINTON, born July 22, 1867. (Mass. Vital Records say July 22, 1866, at Boston.)

aacdb icb. LILLIAN-GERTRUDE, born July 13, 1869; married, Apr. 4, 1900, at East Douglas, Mass., Walter-Edgar, son of Edmund and Barbara (Aldrich) Carpenter of East Douglas, born Oct. 20, 1856, at East Douglas.

They were living, 1914, at East Douglas. He is a farmer. (Records of
Mrs. Lillian-Gertrude Carpenter.)

Children, born at East Douglas:

    a. WALTER-LINCOLN, born Jan. 22, 1901.
    b. BARBARA-SERENE, born Sept. 26, 1902.
    c. EDGAR-NATHAN, born Aug. 24, 1904; died Aug. 31, 1904.
    d. ROSWELL-DONALD, born Feb. 17, 1907.
    e. MARGARA-LORRAINE, born Apr. 24, 1908.
    f. EDGAR-ALDRICH, born Feb. 28, 1914.

aacdb icc. CLARA-EUDORA, born Feb. 11, 1877; living, 1914, at Bridgewater,
Mass., unmarried. She is a teacher and has taught in Texas, Georgia,
Illinois, Rhode Island and Massachusetts.

aacdb ig. JOHN-HOWARD, son of Ezekiel (*Otis, William,
Jedediah, Samuel, Samuel*) and Susan (Haymon) Lincoln of
Perry, Me., born Apr. 10, 1852, at Calais, Me.; died Feb. 10,
1905, at St. Stephens, New Brunswick, being attacked with
heart disease on the train, while returning from work on which
he had been engaged in New Brunswick. He was a farmer and,
later, a granite worker. He lived at Robbinston, Me., and, after
July, 1888, in the village of Red Beach.

He married (1), Nov. 8, 1873, at Perry, Mary-Eliza, daughter
of John and Nancy (Carlow) Trumbull of Robbinston, born
July 14, 1846, at Robbinston; died there Jan. 28, 1876.

He married (2), March 9, 1878, at Perry, Martha, daughter
of Robert and Martha-Ann (Smith) Golding of Perry, born Aug.
22, 1855, at Perry; living, 1911, at Red Beach, Robbinston.
(Perry Records; Records of Mrs. Martha [Golding] Lincoln.)

Child, by first wife, born at Robbinston:

aacdb iga. BERTHA, born Jan. 13, 1875; married, May 18, 1901, at Red
Beach, William, son of Clowds and Agnes (Kennedy) Warnick of Red
Beach, born Oct. 19, 1872, at Red Beach. He is, 1911, captain of a
sloop. His father, Clowds Warnick, was a native of St. John, N. B.
Mr. and Mrs. Lincoln were living, 1911, at Red Beach.

    Child, born at Red Beach:

      a. ERNEST-HOWARD, born March 3, 1903.

Children, by second wife, born: *b-f* at Robbinston; *g* at Red
Beach:

aacdb igb. GORHAM-EDGAR, born Apr. 2, 1879.
aacdb igc. ROBERT-GOLDING, born Jan. 14, 1881.
aacdb igd. LOUIS-DEWOLF, born Dec. 22, 1882.
aacdb ige. ANDREW, born Dec. 13, 1884; died Sept. 13, 1888.
aacdb igf. CHARLES-WILLIS, born June 5, 1888.
aacdb igg. WILLIAM-CURTIS, born Jan. 2, 1893.

aacdb ih. GEORGE-POTTLE, son of Ezekiel (*Otis, William, Jedediah, Samuel, Samuel*) and Maria (Watson) Lincoln of Perry, Me., born Oct. 6, 1856, at Perry; living, 1911, at Perry. He is a farmer.

He married, Jan. 6, 1878, at Perry, Clementina, daughter of William and Lidia (Hurd) Hibbard of Perry, born May 14, 1846, at Perry; living, 1911. The Perry records are much confused as to this marriage and the date may be Dec. 6, 1877. Their intentions were published Nov. 26, and certificate was given Dec. 1, 1877.

Child, born at Perry:

aacdb iha. CHARLES, born Dec. 28, 1878; living, 1911, at Portland, Me., where he was in the employ of the Eastern Steamship Company. He is married but no particulars have been obtained. He calls himself "Charles W."

aacdc ea. WILLIAM-HENRY, son of Henry (*Henry, William, Jedediah, Samuel, Samuel*) and Charlotte-Ann-Lewis (French) Lincoln of Boston, Mass., born June 13, 1835, at Boston; living, 1911, at Brookline, Mass. He was then a shipping merchant and steamship agent in Boston. In 1861 he joined in partnership with Frank N. Thayer under the firm name of Thayer & Lincoln as ship-chandlers and ship-owners. Between 1866 and 1882 the firm built or purchased forty ships. In 1870 they established a line of fortnightly sailing ships between Boston and Liverpool, England. In 1872 they established a steamship line to Liverpool and, in 1876, became interested in the Leyland line of steamships of which Mr. Lincoln became the Boston agent and, later, a director. In 1879 he established the Allan line to Glasgow. He was one of the best-known men in the trans-Atlantic trade in Boston; every movement for the commercial improvement of the city has had his endorsement, and he was highly esteemed by the business men of Boston. He has held many offices of trust and honor. From 1857 to 1861 he was secretary of the Young Men's Christian Association and in 1860 its vice-president. He was for many years a director in the National City Bank. In 1873 he was first elected a member of the Brookline school board in which he remained for twenty-two years, being for sixteen years its chairman. From 1890 to 1899 he was a member of the board of park commissioners of Brookline, finally declining a re-election. He was president of the Brookline Savings Bank from 1877 to 1904, when he resigned the office; a member of the State nautical commission from 1892 to 1896, and its chairman for two years; president of the Boston Commercial Club, 1883 to 1886; president of Boston Chamber of Commerce, 1900 to 1904; director of the Boston Insurance Company from 1881; and a member of the corporation of the Massachusetts Institute of Technology from 1895. He was a trustee of Wellesley College; trustee and president of the Episcopal Theological School at Cambridge; and president of the Economic Club of Boston from its formation in 1901. When a young man he joined the Independent Corps of Cadets and in May, 1862, was sworn into the service of the United States and went to Fort Warren on garrison duty. In July of the same year he was mustered out of service, with the company.

He married, Apr. 21, 1863, at New York, N. Y., Celia-Frances, daughter of James-Wiggin and Eliza-Folsom (Robinson) Smith of New York, born July 1, 1838, at New York; living, 1911. (Records of William-Henry Lincoln.)

Children, born at Brookline:

aacdc eaa. HENRY, born Feb. 25, 1864; living, 1911, at Palestine, Tex. He engaged in hotel business, first at Los Angeles, Calif., and later at San Francisco, Calif., in which business he was very successful. He left that business to go into mining in Nevada and, later, into farming in Texas, in which latter occupation he says that he and his friends were ruined by George-Graham Rice, "now on trial in New York as one of the swindlers of the Scheftel outfit." He is at present, 1911, manager of the "Highland Farms" at Palestine, but says that he intends to return, early in 1912, to the hotel business, "for which nature has adapted him." He married, May 7, 1910, at Houston, Tex., Anna-Mae, daughter of Jacob and Adaline (Buchanan) Billette of Newport, Ky., born Feb. 16, 1885, at Newport. (Records of Henry Lincoln.)

aacdc eab. HELEN-FRANCES, born Apr. 8, 1866; married, Jan. 6, 1904,* at Brookline, Burdette-Loomis, son of Henry-Martyn and Sarah-Jane (Closson) Arms of Springfield, Vt., born Sept. 27, 1869, at Springfield. He is a graduate of the University of Vermont. He is a physician, a specialist in bacteria. The marriage was unhappy and they are separated. No children. (Hist. of Springfield, Vt., pp. 293-4.)

aacdc eac. ALEXANDER, born Oct. 31, 1873.

aacdc ead. ELSIE, born July 18, 1875; married, Apr. 18, 1899, at Brookline, Samuel-Cushing, son of Gilbert-Russell and Althea (Train) Payson of Watertown, Mass., born Apr. 20, 1875, at Belmont, Mass. They are

*Massachusetts Vital Records say 1905 and that Mr. Arms was then aged 34.

living, 1911, at Brookline. He is treasurer of the American Finishing and Machine Company.

Children, born at Brookline:

    a. WILLIAM-LINCOLN, born June 3, 1901.

    b. EDITH-CUSHING, born March 31, 1904.

aacdc ec. RICHARD-MITCHELL, son of Henry (*Henry, William, Jedediah, Samuel, Samuel*) and Charlotte-Ann-Lewis (French) Lincoln of Boston, Mass., born Dec. 26, 1838, at Boston. He was engaged in mercantile business in Boston until 1865 when he removed to the West and engaged in stock ranching in Texas and Colorado until 1894, when he returned to Massachusetts and settled in Southborough.

He married, March 9, 1876, at Rosita, Colo., Virginia-Mabel, daughter of William-Lewis and Mary-Elizabeth (Lacey) Murray of Sweetwater, Tenn., born July 19, 1859, at Springfield, Mo. They are living, 1911, at Southborough. (Records of Richard-Mitchell Lincoln.)

Children, born at Gardner, Colo.:

aacdc eca. HENRY-RICHARDSON, born Nov. 30, 1876.

aacdc ecb. CHARLOTTE, born March 4, 1878; married, Nov. 5, 1901, at Southborough, Mass., Harry-Austin, son of Henry-Austin and Mary-Celia (Rhymes) McMaster of Southborough, born March 13, 1876, at Sharon, Mass. They are living, 1912, at Southborough. He is a merchant.

    Children, born at Southborough:

        a. EDITH, born Dec. 21, 1908.

        b. CHARLOTTE, born Sept. 4, 1910.

        c. VIRGINIA, born Apr. 24, 1912.

aacdc ecc. MARY-ELIZABETH, born Apr. 26, 1880; married, June 10, 1908, at Southborough, Mass., Walter-Ellis, son of Charles-Augustus and Laura-Josephine (Ellis) Fiske of Marlborough, Mass., born Feb. 16, 1880, at Chelsea, Mass. They were living, 1912, at Southborough. He was then in the shoe manufacturing business.

    Child, born at Southborough:

        a. WALTER-ELLIS, born June 8, 1910.

aacdc ecd. MABEL, born March 1, 1883; died Apr. 7, 1883.

aacdc ece. RICHARD, born Sept. 9, 1884; living, 1912, unmarried.

aacdc gb. WILLIAM-EDWARDS, son of William (*Henry, William, Jedediah, Samuel, Samuel*) and Mary-Moore (Francis) Lincoln of Brookline, Mass., born July 17, 1842, at Boston, Mass. He has always been engaged in real estate and insurance business, and in 1911 was treasurer of the Brookline Savings Bank.

He married, Oct. 20, 1880, at Brookline, Caroline-Alma, daughter of Zenas-Franklin and Julia-Frances (Tilden) Brett of Brookline, born Oct. 4, 1850, at Wareham, Mass. They are living, 1911, at Brookline. (Mass. Vital Records; Records of William-Edwards Lincoln.)

Children, born at Brookline:

aacdc gba. WILLIAM-OTIS, born Aug. 29, 1881; died May 31, 1899.
aacdc gbb. HELEN-ALMA, born March 11, 1883; married, Dec. 18, 1915, at Brookline, Augustus, son of Augustus W. and Martha (Perkins) Locke, born Aug. 22, 1883. He graduated at Harvard college in 1904 with the degree of A.B., and in 1913 received the degree of B.S. as mining geologist. They were living, 1915, in Montana. (Hist. & Genealogy of Capt. John Locke, p. 481.)

aacdc ge. JAMES-OTIS, son of William (*Henry, William, Jedediah, Samuel, Samuel*) and Mary-Moore (Francis) Lincoln of Brookline, Mass., born Feb. 1, 1851, at Boston. He was educated in the Brookline public schools and at Harvard college where he received the degree of A.B. in 1873, and A.M. in 1881. He then studied in the Berkeley Divinity school where he graduated in 1884. He taught for one year at De Veaux college, Suspension Bridge, N. Y., and then for six years at St. Mark's school, Southborough, Mass. He was made deacon, 1884; priest, 1885, and served at Williamstown, Mass., Troy and Whitehall, N. Y., and at Topeka, Kan. Since 1893 he has been resident professor at the Church Divinity school of the Pacific coast at San Mateo and San Francisco, Calif. He and Mrs. Lincoln founded St. Dorothy's Rest for Convalescents, in 1901, at Camp Meeker, Calif., in memory of their daughter Dorothy. This charity, which is especially for children, is held by the Protestant Episcopal bishop of California as corporation sole, and is managed by five managers. Mr. Lincoln is the treasurer.

He married, Oct. 6, 1885, at Middle Haddam, Conn., Nellie-Olmsted, daughter of Robert and Sarah (Knox) Pitkin of New Orleans, La., born Nov. 8, 1860, at New Orleans. They were living, 1911, at San Francisco. (Mass. Vital Records; Records of Rev. James-Otis Lincoln; Pitkin Genealogy, p. 70, which says Mrs. Lincoln was born Nov. 8, 1861.)

Children, born: *a* at Troy, N. Y.; *b* at Kansas City, Mo.:

aacdc gea. KATHARINE, born Sept. 22, 1886; died Sept. 29, 1886.
aacdc geb. DOROTHY-PITKIN, born Dec. 10, 1891; died Feb. 19, 1900, at San
    Francisco.

aacdc gf. WALTER-MOORE, son of William (*Henry, William,
Jedediah, Samuel, Samuel*) and Mary-Moore (Francis) Lincoln
of Brookline, Mass., born Nov. 10, 1852, at Boston, Mass.

He married (1), Nov. 27, 1883, at Cambridge, Mass., Susan-
Congdon, daughter of Avery-Tucker and Lydia-Atearn (Morton) Allen of Nantucket, Mass., born Sept. 2, 1847, at Nantucket;
died June 2, 1902, at Brookline.

He married (2), Sept. 21, 1903, at Medford, Mass., Elisabeth-
Lincoln[8], daughter of Job[7] (*Job[6], Job[5], Samuel[4], Matthew[3],
Daniel[2], Matthew[1]*) and Salome (Abbott) Cushing of Medford,
born Sept. 13, 1865, at Medford. See *abbea je.* They were
living, 1911, at Brookline. (Records verified by Walter-Moore
Lincoln.)

Children, by first wife, born: *a* at Medford; *b* at Auburndale,
Mass.:

aacdc gfa. MORTON-FRANCIS, born Apr. 11, 1888; died Aug. 3, 1888.
aacdc gfb. MARY, born March 14, 1890; died Jan. 5, 1891, at Auburndale.

Child, by second wife, born at Brookline:

aacdc gfc. WILLIAM, born Dec. 27, 1906.

aacdd da. WILLIAM-OTIS, son of William-Otis (*Solomon,
William, Jedediah, Samuel, Samuel*) and Adeline (Lincoln)
Lincoln of Hingham, Mass., born Apr. 20, 1838, at Hingham;
died Apr. 14, 1907, at Hingham. His early life was spent in
Hingham and he always lived there even while in business in
Boston, his home being on South street, near Thaxter's bridge.
In the Civil war he was commissary sergeant of Company A,
1st Massachusetts cavalry. After the war he became connected
with Wadsworth & Howland in Boston, dealers in paints and
varnishes, and retired from active business about fifteen years
before his death. For several years he was town auditor. He
was a devoted layman of the Episcopal church, his activities
not being confined to St. John's parish, Hingham, which he
was largely instrumental in founding about 1882, and to which
he gave unselfish and faithful service as vestryman and treasurer

until his death. He was interested in the churches in the diocese, was annually elected a delegate to the diocesan convention, and had been appointed to important committees. He was a member of Edwin Humphrey Post, G. A. R., and of Old Colony Lodge, F. and A. M.

He married, Aug. 17, 1870, at Albany, N. Y., Mary-Rogers, daughter of John-Rogers and Sarah-Royce (Haskell) Hoar of Pawtucket, R. I., born June 11, 1841, at Warren, R. I.; living, 1911, at Hingham. (Hist. of Hingham, vol. i, pt. i, p. 349; vol. ii, p. 475; Newspaper Notice, April, 1907; Records of Selwyn-Randall Lincoln, *adcdd dae*.)

Children, born: *a–d* at Boston; *e* at Hingham:

aacdd daa.	FLORA-PAGE, born Feb. 19, 1873; died July 31, 1873.		
aacdd dab.	HELEN-REVERE, born Aug. 17, 1875; died May 9, 1876.		
aacdd dac.	LILLIAN-HASKELL,	⎫	both graduated, Wellesley College, 1899;
aacdd dad.	BLANCHE-ADELINE,	⎬ born July 9, 1877;	both living, 1911, unmarried.
aacdd dae.	SELWYN-RANDALL, born Dec. 3, 1879.		

aacdd dd. REVERE, son of William-Otis (*Solomon, William, Jedediah, Samuel, Samuel*) and Adeline (Lincoln) Lincoln of Hingham, Mass., born Dec. 2, 1846, at Hingham; died Oct. 9, 1910, at Oak Park, Ill., where he had been a resident for twenty-two years and was much respected. He enlisted at Readville, Mass., July, 12, 1864, in Company F, 5th Massachusetts infantry, for one hundred days' service and was mustered in July 28, 1864. He served with his regiment at Fort McHenry, Baltimore, Md., on garrison duty and in guarding prisoners, and new recruits who were being sent to their regiments, and was mustered out Nov. 16, 1864, at Readville, by reason of expiration of service. He then became a clerk in a mercantile house in Boston, but removed to Chicago, Ill., in 1884, and became a buyer in the linen department of Schlesinger & Mayer's store, a position he held for eight years, when he undertook a similar position with Marshall Field & Company, with whom he remained until his death. In his business relations he was known as a man loyal to duty and to his associates. He was a member of the G. A. R., the Columbian Knights, and General Grant council Royal Arcanum. He had held all the offices in the lodge and was selected several times as delegate to the grand council. He belonged to no church.

He married, Aug. 5, 1868, at Woonsocket, R. I., Amanda-Melvina, daughter of Horace-Martin and Anna-Helen (Maxey) Pierce of Woonsocket, born Apr. 16, 1847, at Woonsocket; living, 1910, at Oak Park. Mr. and Mrs. Lincoln had no children, but a young woman, named Isabel R., lived with them and was generally regarded as their daughter. (Records of Mrs. Revere Lincoln.)

aacdd ea. SOLOMON, son of Solomon (*Solomon, William, Jedediah, Samuel, Samuel*) and Mehitable (Lincoln) Lincoln of Hingham, Mass., born Aug. 14, 1838, at Hingham; died Oct. 15, 1907, at Boston, Mass. He graduated at Harvard college in 1857, and was the valedictorian of his class. He was tutor at Harvard in Greek, Latin and mathematics from 1858 to 1863, at the same time studying in the Law school, receiving the degree of A.M. in 1860 and of LL.B. in 1864. He was immediately admitted to the bar and for the next eighteen years he practised law in partnership with Stephen-Bradshaw Ives, Jr., at Salem, Mass., and Boston, but after 1882 was alone. He served as aide on Governor Talbot's staff 1874-9, and in the last year was commissioner to the meeting of governors of the original thirteen states. He was president of the trustees of the Boston public library from 1899 to his death, having been vice-president for the two previous years. In 1882 he was elected an overseer of Harvard college, and for several years was president of the board. He had been president of the Boston bar association and was a prominent member of the American bar association. He was a member of the Massachusetts Historical Society and of the American Antiquarian Society; director of the Boston Athenæum; president of the Unitarian club; and president of the Bunker Hill Monument Association. As a lawyer his practice was large and lucrative but always scrupulously honorable. "Personally he combined a fine dignity with many genial qualities. His presence was notable and the outer man was an index of the character of which it was the temple." (Boston Evening Transcript, Oct. 16, 1907; N. E. Hist. & Gen. Register, vol. lxii, p. lxxvi.) He was buried at Haydenville, Mass., but a cenotaph was erected to him at Hingham.

He married, Feb. 15, 1865, at Williamsburg, Mass., Ellen B., daughter of Joel and Isabella-Weir (Smith) Hayden of Hayden-ville, Mass., born 1838 at Haydenville, died March 18, 1897, at Boston. Her father was lieutenant-governor of the State in 1863-6. (Mass. Vital Records.)

Child, born at Salem, Mass.:

aacdd eaa. BESSIE, born June 28, 1868; married, Apr. 17, 1900, at Boston, Mass., Murray-Anthony, son of Edward-Edmund and Susan (Anthony) Potter of Clifton Springs, Ill., born March 15, 1871, at Clifton Springs; died May 17, 1915, at Lancaster, Mass., his summer home, his winter home being in Boston. He graduated at Harvard college in the class of 1895, and was a graduate student from 1896 to 1899, receiving the degree of A.M. in 1897, and Ph.D. in 1899. At the time of his marriage he was teaching at Dartmouth college, but returned to the Harvard faculty after one year and became a member of its teaching staff as assistant professor of Spanish and French. He published two or three Spanish text books for use in his classes. Mrs. Potter is, 1922, living in Boston. They had no children.

aacdd eb. ARTHUR, son of Solomon (*Solomon, William, Jedediah, Samuel, Samuel*) and Mehitable (Lincoln) Lincoln of Hingham, Mass., born Feb. 16, 1842, at Hingham; died Dec. 11, 1902, at Boston, Mass. He graduated at Harvard college in 1863, and then entered the law school, receiving the degree of A.M. in 1866, and of LL.B. in 1865. He practised his profession in Boston, first entering the office of Lothrop & Bishop Jan. 1, 1866, but in the following January opening an office alone. In November, 1867, he became a partner with Lothrop and Bishop, the firm name being Lothrop, Bishop & Lincoln, and continued a member of this firm until its dissolution in 1879, after which he was in practice by himself. In 1876 he delivered the Memorial Day address at Hingham. In 1879 and 1880 he was representa-tive to the General Court from the first Plymouth district. On July 30, 1877, he was commissioned judge advocate, with the rank of captain, on the staff of Brigadier General Eben Sutton, and on March 3, 1882, he resigned and was discharged. He was manager, secretary and treasurer of the Boston dispensary; treasurer of the industrial School for Girls at Dorchester, Mass.; clerk and treasurer of the Proprietors of the Social Law Library in Boston; trustee of the Derby academy, Hingham; trustee and president of the Hingham public library; trustee of the Massachusetts State library; director of the Hingham Mutual Fire Insurance Company; and director and secretary of the Alumni Association of Harvard college. He is buried at Hingham.

He married, Dec. 17, 1863, at Boston, Serafina[8], daughter of Joseph-George[7] (George[6], Joseph[5], Benjamin[4], Thomas[3], John[2], Thomas[1]) and Serafina (Martinez) Loring of Malaga, Spain, born Aug. 27, 1849, at Malaga; living, 1914, at Boston. Her grandfather, Mr. George Loring, who was a native of Hingham, settled in business at Malaga, lived a long life there and left a large family of children, of whom Joseph-George, who was born in 1818, was the only one to come to this country, which he did in 1856 and settled in Boston. (Hist. of Hingham, vol. i, pt. i, p. 374; pt. ii, p. 332; vol. ii, p. 475; vol. iii, p. 35; Boston Evening Transcript, Dec. 12, 1902; Records of Mrs. Arthur Lincoln.)

Child, born at Boston:

aacdd eba.   SERAFINA, born Sept. 2, 1884. She has always been called "Serita," the Spanish diminutive of Serafina. She married, Oct. 4, 1911, at Boston, Matthew, son of Nelson-Slater and Isabel-Hazard (Bullock) Bartlett of Boston, born Apr. 2, 1879, at Boston. He graduated at Harvard college in 1901. They live at Beverly Farms, Mass.

Child, born at Brookline, Mass.:
   a.   SERITA, born Dec. 9, 1912.

aacdd ec.   FRANCIS-HENRY, son of Solomon (Solomon, William, Jedediah, Samuel, Samuel) and Mehitable (Lincoln) Lincoln of Hingham, Mass., born Apr. 14, 1846, at Hingham; died July 7, 1911, at Boston, Mass. He was educated at Derby academy, Hingham, and at Harvard college, receiving the degree of A.B. in 1867, and A.M. in 1871. In 1873 he was elected secretary of his class, retaining the office until his death. After graduation he was associated with the dry-goods firm of A. Hamilton & Company of Boston until they were burned out in the great fire of 1872. He then went into the real estate business with Alexander S. Porter and in June, 1873, opened an office for himself to conduct general real estate and insurance business. In this he continued during his life, but he had many outside interests. He was president and director of the Hingham Mutual Fire

Insurance Company; president of the Massachusetts Mutual Fire Insurance Union; president and trustee of the Hingham Institution for Savings; director of the Hingham Cemetery; and trustee of Loring Hall in Hingham and of the Hingham public library. He served for many years on the school committee of Hingham. He belonged to the Society of Colonial Wars; the Massachusetts Society of the Sons of the American Revolution, of which he was long State historian; the Bunker Hill Monument Association, which he had served as treasurer; the Colonial Society; the New England Historic-Genealogical Society; and the Society for the Propagation of the Gospel among the Indians and Others of North America. He was also treasurer of the American Unitarian Association. He contributed nine chapters to the History of Hingham, being the greater portion of part two of volume one and all of great historical value. He was much interested in the family genealogy and was expected to be of great assistance in the compilation of this volume. He lived all his life in Hingham.

He married, June 1, 1875, at Hingham, Anna-Francis[8], daughter of Abner-Loring[7] (*John*[6], *John*[5], *James*[4], *John*[3], *John*[2], *Richard*[1]) and Lydia-Jacobs (Ripley) Baker of Hingham, born March 22, 1845, at Hingham; living, 1913, at Hingham. (Boston Evening Transcript, July 7, 1911; Hist. of Hingham, vol. ii, pp. 19, 475.)

Child, born at Hingham:

aacdd eca. FRANCIS-HENRY, born Dec. 2, 1876.

aafff gh. FREDERICK-LEWIS, son of Lewis (*Elisha, Ezekiel, Elisha, Samuel, Samuel*) and Mary-Avery (Souther) Lincoln of Cohasset, Mass., born Feb. 8, 1856, at Cohasset. He is a carpenter, living, 1909, at Cohasset on Sohier street.

He married, July 1, 1886, at Cohasset, Mary-Adella, daughter of James-Edward and Catherine-Amelia (Walker) Ward of North Alton, Nova Scotia, born Oct. 6, 1869, at North Alton; living, 1909. (Cohasset Genealogies, p. 246; Records of Sarah-Lewis Lincoln, *aafff gha.*)

Child, born at Cohasset:

aafff gha. SARAH-LEWIS, born March 2, 1887; living, 1909, at Cohasset, unmarried.

29

abbea ca. FRANCIS-MAYHEW, son of Jerome (*Jerome, Francis, Hezekiah, Daniel, Samuel*) and Nancy (Pratt) Lincoln of Cohasset, Mass., born Dec. 20, 1804, at Cohasset, though "Cohasset Genealogies" says Jan. 7, 1805, probably the date of baptism. He died June 29, 1862, at Cohasset. He was a farmer and lived at Cohasset on Beechwood street, corner of Doane street, but in the record of his death he is called "carpenter." "Cohasset Genealogies" is in error in stating that he was wrecked on the fishing schooner "Maine" in 1846 in Massachusetts Bay, when his son Ezekiel was lost, having confused him with his son, Francis-Mayhew, Jr.

He married, June 7, 1824, at Scituate, Mass., Sarah[6], daughter of Samuel[5] (*William[4], John[3], Thomas[2], Thomas[1]*) and Hannah (Studley) Hyland of Scituate, born March 23, 1797, at Scituate; died May 13, 1863, at Cohasset. Both Mr. and Mrs. Lincoln are buried in Beechwood cemetery and their gravestones are thus inscribed:

"Francis M. Lincoln ‡ died June 29, 1862 ‡ aged 57 years. ‡ Ezekiel his son lost at sea ‡ Aug. 16, 1846 ‡ aged 11 yrs."

"Sarah ‡ wife of ‡ Francis M. Lincoln ‡ died May 13, 1863 ‡ aged 66 yrs."

(Cohasset Records; Cohasset Genealogies, p. 244; Scituate Records; Hist. of Cohasset, pp. 428-431.)

Children, born at Cohasset:

abbea caa. ALMIRA, born July 24, 1824; died Apr. 5, 1903, at Cohasset; married, Feb. 18, 1844, at Cohasset, Thomas Williams who was born April, 1818, in England and died Sept. 28, 1890, at Cohasset. His parents died in his childhood and he came to America alone. He was a mariner living, at the time of his marriage, at Boston, but he removed immediately to Cohasset and became a fisherman and farmer. (Cohasset Genealogies, p. 482.)

Children, born at Cohasset:
- a. GEORGE, born May 7, 1845; died Dec. 4, 1899, at Tewksbury, Mass.
- b. LOUISA-JANE, born Aug. 10, 1847; mar. William Litchfield.
- c. JAMES-FRANKLIN, born Sept. 8, 1849; mar. Mary-Elizabeth Rich.
- d. SAMUEL-LINCOLN, born Sept. 10, 1851; mar. Augusta Burbank.
- e. SARAH-FRANCIS, born July 27, 1854; mar. Robert-Lorenzo Curtis.
- f. NANCY-CAROLINE, born Oct. 28, 1856; died Nov. 4, 1873, unmarried.
- g. EZEKIEL-THOMAS, born Sept. 1, 1859; mar. Caroline-Adelaide Manuel.
- h. IDA-MAY, born Jan. 6, 1862; mar. Howard-Ellms Litchfield.

  i. CHARLES-HERBERT, born Sept. 13, 1866; mar. Jennie Walker.
  j. WALLACE-CLARENCE, born Dec. 4, 1870; mar. Addie Leonard.
abbea cab. ISAIAH, born Jan. 31, 1826.
abbea cac. FRANCIS-MAYHEW, born Apr. 29, 1827.
abbea cad. SAMUEL, born Jan. 1, 1828.
abbea cae. HANNAH, born Dec. 7, 1830; living, 1911, at Cohasset; married, Nov. 24, 1853, at Hingham, Mass. (according to Massachusetts Vital Records but the intentions were published at Cohasset Nov. 26), Franklin-Jacobs[3], son of Isaac-Newton[2] (*Stephen*[1]) and Judith-Litchfield (Damon) Damon of Scituate, Mass., born Apr. 10, 1826, at Scituate; died May 29, 1882, at Cohasset. He was a blacksmith and lived at Cohasset on Pleasant street. (Cohasset Genealogies, p. 127; Scituate Records.)
  Children, born at Cohasset:
   a. IDA-MAY-CUSHING, born May 1, 1854; died Jan. 12, 1861.
   b. FRANKLIN-WALLACE, born Dec. 23, 1855; died Sept. 6, 1861.
   c. MARIETTA-LINCOLN, born Apr. 24, 1858; died Sept. 7, 1862.
   d. NEWCOMB-LINCOLN, born Oct. 31, 1860; mar. Amelia-Ripley Snow.
   e. EDWARD-JACOB, born Aug. 2, 1869; died June 29, 1876.
abbea caf. ELIZA-JAMES, born Nov. 16 or 18, 1832; died Jan. 11, 1894, at Norwell, Mass.; married, Dec. 26, 1851, at Cohasset, George-Edward, son of William-Garrett and Margaret (Powers) Ainslie of Halifax, Nova Scotia, born Jan. 20, 1831, at Halifax; died Feb. 6, 1905, at Norwell. They are buried in Beechwood cemetery, Cohasset. He was first a mariner but, later, a shoemaker. They lived at first at Cohasset but removed to Norwell after the birth of their children. (Cohasset Genealogies, p. 2; Mass. Vital Records.)
  Children, born at Cohasset:
   a. SUSAN-ELLEN, born Oct. 12, 1852; mar. Wilbur-Francis Gardner.
   b. HENRIETTA-MARIA, born March 22, 1855; mar. William-Wallace Apts.
   c. GEORGE-WILLIAM, born July 30, 1857; mar. Belinda Arnold.
   d. ATWOOD-INGALLS, born March 23, 1860; mar. Sarah Haskell.
   e. A SON, born Sept. 30, 1862; died soon.
   f. MARY-EVA, born July 16, 1868; mar. Benjamin-Sewell Litchfield.
   g. HENRY-WILBUR, born Dec. 31, 1870; died same day.
   h. A CHILD, born March 15, 1873; died March 16, 1873.
   i. ALBERT-WALLACE, born June 10, 1875; mar. Mary-Jane Emerson.
abbea cag. MARY, born Feb. 2, 1835; living, 1911, at Beechwoods, Cohasset; married, Nov. 27, 1853, at Cohasset, William-Osborn[3], son of Osborn[2] (*Ziba*[1]) and Silence-Tower (Lincoln) Wood of Cohasset, born Oct. 11, 1827, at Cohasset; died there Feb. 21, 1904. His mother was descended from Daniel Lincoln, the sergeant. He was a shoemaker. They lived at Cohasset on King street. (Cohasset Genealogies, p. 488.)
  Children, born at Cohasset:
   a. MARY-SNOW, born Sept. 11, 1854; died Sept. 19, 1858.
   b. EMMA-MELVILLE, born June 1, 1856; died Sept. 9, 1858.
   c. CYRUS-WILLIAM, born Nov. 6, 1859; mar. Martha-Franklin Curtis.
   d. MARTHA-COTTLE, born March 9, 1867; mar. Henry-Herbert Gardner.*

---

*Cohasset Genealogies gives them Emma E., but this is said to be an error.

abbea cah.   EZEKIEL, born Aug. 30, 1837; drowned in the wreck of the "Maine," Aug. 16, 1846.

abbea cai.   ELLEN-MARIA, born June 20, 1839; living, 1911, at Beechwoods, Cohasset; married (1), published Dec. 6, 1856, at Cohasset, Silas-Damon[8], son of Freeman[7] (*Silas[6], Daniel[5], Josiah[4], Nicholas[3], Josiah[2], Lawrence[1]*) and Lucy (Damon) Litchfield of Scituate, Mass., born Oct. 29, 1830, at Scituate; died Aug. 25, 1910, at Scituate. He was a shoemaker. They lived at Beechwoods, but the marriage proved unhappy and they were divorced in 1869.

She married (2), May 20, 1871, at Cohasset, Warren[4], son of Silas[3] (*Silas[2], Silas[1]*) and Ruth (Cook) Newcomb of Hingham, Mass., born March 16, 1832, at Hingham; died Feb. 17, 1904, at Cohasset. She was his second wife, he having married (1), Nov. 30, 1854, Ann-Maria Arnold, who died July 21, 1867, and by whom he had two children. He served in the Civil war in Company D, Massachusetts heavy artillery. He was a shoemaker and lived at Cohasset. (Cohasset Genealogies, pp. 258, 296; Scituate Records; Mass. Vital Records; Hist. of Hingham, vol. iii, p. 81.)

Children, by first husband, born at Scituate:

    a.   LIZZIE-MARIA LITCHFIELD, born Oct. 24, 1857; died June 27, 1860.

    b.   MARY-ELIZABETH LITCHFIELD, born Aug. 12, 1862 (or Oct 29); mar. William-Webster Bates.

    c.   SILAS-DAMON LITCHFIELD, born Apr. 19, 1864; mar. Lily W. (Petersen) Eldred.

Children, by second husband, born at Cohasset:

    d.   ELLEN-FRANCES NEWCOMB, born July 26, 1869; mar. Joseph Ruso.

    e.   HATTIE-COLBERTH NEWCOMB, born Oct. 20, 1872; living, 1911, unmarried.*

abbea mb.   MARTIN-JEROME, son of Martin (*Jerome, Francis, Hezekiah, Daniel, Samuel*) and Nancy (Jenkins) Lincoln of Cohasset, Mass., born Apr. 17, 1836, at Cohasset; living, 1911, at Taunton, Mass., whither he had removed from Cohasset about 1864. He is a machinist.

He married, Jan. 30, 1862, at Cohasset, Ann-Jane[5], daughter of George[4] (*James[3], James[2], Richard[1]*) and Cynthia (Collier) Hall of Cohasset, born Jan. 31, 1839, at Cohasset; living, 1911. (Cohasset Genealogies, pp. 175, 244; Cohasset Records; Halls of New England, p. 650, which says Ann-Jane was born Jan. 30, 1839.)

Children, born: *a* at Cohasset; *b-e* at Taunton:

abbea mba.   EDWARD-HALL, born May 24, 1863.

abbea mbb.   WINSLOW-HALL, born March 17, 1865; died Sept. 6, 1865.

abbea mbc.   WILLIAM-ELLIS, born June 27, 1868; died Nov. 10, 1868.

*A family record says she was born 1873 and that Silas-Damon Litchfield was born in 1866.

abbea mbd. GEORGE-MARTIN, born March 28, 1873.

abbea mbe. CHARLES-JAMES, born July 8, 1878; living, 1911, unmarried.

abbea mh. CHARLES-CUSHING, son of Martin (*Jerome, Francis, Hezekiah, Daniel, Samuel*) and Nancy (Jenkins) Lincoln of Cohasset, Mass., born Jan. 8, 1847,* at Cohasset; died May 16, 1913, at New York. He was a merchant and lived at Brooklyn, N. Y.

He married, Jan. 8, 1874, at Dover, N. H., Flora-Estella, daughter of Ivory and Olive (Plummer) Hayes of Brooklyn, born June 3, 1854; died Sept. 9, 1907, at Westport, Conn. (Records of Miss Annie-Elizabeth Lincoln, *abbea mi.*)

Children, born at Brooklyn:

abbea mha. EDITH-ESTELLE, born Oct. 21, 1874; died Feb. 2, 1875.

abbea mhb. FLORENCE-HAYES, born March 7, 1876; died Nov. 15, 1889, at Springfield, Mass.

abbea mhc. FRED-JEROME, born March 6, 1881.

abbea mhd. HARRY-FRANCIS, born Oct. 14, 1882.

abbec bb. HENRY, son of Joseph (*Zenas, Francis, Hezekiah, Daniel, Samuel*) and Mary-Humphrey (Nichols) Lincoln of Cohasset, Mass., born Oct. 1, 1812, at Cohasset; died Nov. 9, 1842, at Boston, Mass., and was buried at Cohasset. He was, according to his son Richard, a carpenter and builder and lived at Boston, but "Cohasset Genealogies" says that he lived on Elm street, Cohasset, and that his children were born there.

He married, Nov. 24, 1839, at Boston, by Rev. Edwin Burnham, Ophelia, daughter of William and Hepzibah (Lincoln) Whittington of Cohasset, *aaffi j*, born Feb. 21, 1813, at Cohasset; died Oct. 17, 1898, at Dedham, Mass. She married (2), Jan. 18, 1852, at Cohasset, James, son of Thomas and Susannah (Stoddard) Willcutt of Cohasset, born Sept. 27, 1801, at Cohasset; died there Dec. 8, 1864. He was a cooper and lived on Elm street, Cohasset. His first wife, Priscilla-Nichols Lothrop, by whom he had five children, died Aug. 3, 1845, at Cohasset. (Cohasset Records; Cohasset Genealogies, pp. 245, 479-80; Boston Records.)

---

*The Cohasset records call the child of his parents born on this date Andrew-Jackson, but this is an error of the records according to all the members of the family, who agree that Martin had no child of that name.

Children, born at Cohasset:

abbec bba. RICHARD-HENRY, born Oct. 12, 1840.

abbec bbb. ALFRED-WHITTINGTON, born March 25, 1843, but "Cohasset Genealogies" says March 2. He died Jan. 24, 1875, at Cohasset, unmarried. He was a salesman. He served in the Civil war in the U. S. navy as a landsman on the S. S. "Montgomery."

abbec be. JOSEPH, son of Joseph (*Zenas, Francis, Hezekiah, Daniel, Samuel*) and Mary-Humphrey (Nichols) Lincoln of Cohasset, Mass., born Dec. 15, 1819, at Cohasset; died Jan. 28, 1880, at Boston, Mass. He lived at Boston and was a carpenter.

He married, July 6, 1840, at Boston, by Rev. Robert Turnbull, Elizabeth, daughter of William-Henry and Elizabeth (Northey) Neville of Boston, born March 10, 1822, at Boston; living, 1911, at Roxbury, Mass., with her son Winthrop, and remarkably well preserved at the advanced age of ninety years. Her father was an Englishman by birth and a skilled wood-carver. (Cohasset Genealogies, p. 241; Boston Records; Mass. Vital Records; Records of Mrs. Elizabeth [Neville] Lincoln.)

Children, born at Boston:

abbec bea. GUY-ALVIN-THEODORE, born Oct. 27, 1850; died July 29, 1895, at Boston, unmarried. He was a homœopathic physician.

abbec beb. LUCY-JOSEPHINE-ELIZABETH, ⎫ born Sept. 5,* 1857; ⎧ died Dec. 13, 1857.
abbec bec. WINTHROP-DALLAS, ⎭ ⎩ he is living, 1911, at Roxbury, Mass., with his mother, unmarried. He is employed by Doud, Blake and Company, wholesale druggists, in Boston.

abbec bg. ZENAS-DALLAS, son of Joseph (*Zenas, Francis, Hezekiah, Daniel, Samuel*) and Mary-Humphrey (Nichols) Lincoln of Cohasset, Mass., born Sept. 23, 1823, at Cohasset; died March 22, 1902, at Cohasset. He was in 1861 engaged in the clothing business in Boston, Mass., and lived there, but he returned to Cohasset and was engaged in the coal business.

He married (1), Apr. 17, 1850, at Cohasset, Frances-Ellen, daughter of Charles and Ann Coney of Portland, Me., born March 15, 1830, at Portland; died Jan. 9, 1871, at Cohasset. Her father was a native of Roxbury, Mass.; her mother was born at Haverhill, Mass.

He married (2), Nov. 27, 1890, at Cohasset, Nina-Elizabeth,

*Massachusetts Vital Records say Sept. 21.

daughter of Joseph-Henry and Alice-Susan (Crawford) Higgins of Charlestown, Mass., born June 28, 1868, at Charlestown; living, 1911, at Cohasset. She has had no children. Mr. Lincoln and his first wife are buried in Central burying ground, Cohasset. (Cohasset Genealogies, p. 245; Mass. Vital Records.)

Child, by first wife, born at Boston:

abbec bga. FANNY-ELLEN, born May 4, 1861; died Nov. 19, 1871, at Cohasset.

abbec bi. LOUIS-NICHOLS, son of Joseph (*Zenas, Francis, Hezekiah, Daniel, Samuel*) and Mary-Humphrey (Nichols) Lincoln of Cohasset, Mass., born Jan. 27, 1827, at Cohasset; died Aug. 10, 1899, at Cohasset. He lived at Cohasset on Elm street, in the house of his father and of his grandfather Nichols. He was engaged in coal business with his brother, Zenas-Dallas. He was selectman, 1870-1877; assessor for the same period and an overseer of the poor, 1871-1877.

He married, Nov. 15, 1850, at Cohasset, Eliza-Ann, daughter of John and Abigail Livingston of Boston, Mass., born 1827 at Boston; died Dec. 28, 1903, at Cohasset "aged seventy-five years." (Cohasset Genealogies, pp. 245, 509; Mass. Vital Records.)

Child, born at Cohasset:

abbec bia. EFFIE-FLORENCE, born Sept. 25, 1852; died Oct. 21, 1872, at Cohasset, unmarried.

abbec bl. EZEKIEL-WALLIS, son of Joseph (*Zenas, Francis, Hezekiah, Daniel, Samuel*) and Mary-Humphrey (Nichols) Lincoln of Cohasset, Mass., born Nov. 26, 1832, at Cohasset; died July 14, 1871, at Boston, Mass. He was a "salesman" and lived at Boston.

He married, Oct. 12, 1854, at Boston, Nancy-Franklin, daughter of Thomas-Webb and Sarah-Duxbury (Wyatt) Brown of Boston, born May 30, 1835, at Boston; living, 1911. (Cohasset Genealogies, p. 241; Mass. Vital Records; Records of Leon-Girard Lincoln, *abbec bla.*)

Child, born at Boston:

abbec bla. LEON-GIRARD, born June 27, 1856; living, 1911, at Boston, an assistant wharfinger at 50 Central wharf. He married, Aug. 17, 1907, at Boston, Frances-Louisa, daughter of Charles-Harris and Louisa-Frances

(Adams) Smith of Boston, born Sept. 25, 1862, at Boston. Her father was born at Foxborough, Mass., her mother at Medford, Mass. They have no children.

abbec fb. ALLEN, son of Thomas (*Zenas, Francis, Hezekiah, Daniel, Samuel*) and Nancy (Norcross) Lincoln of Cohasset, Mass., born Nov. 24, 1814, at Cohasset; died July 5, 1889, at Woburn, Mass. He was a graduate of Dartmouth college in the class of 1839, and was an intimate friend of Edward Webster, son of Daniel Webster. In his college days he published a "Student Account Book," showing in those days a bent of mind of which he availed himself in his business life. He entered the ministry and became pastor of the Congregational church at Gray, Me., where he remained for fourteen years until 1859 or 1860, when he accepted the pastorate of a mission church in Lynn, Mass., which he held for about four years. His voice failing he retired from the ministry and entered business life as book-keeper for a roofing company, which position he held until about a year before his death, living at Woburn.

He married (1), May 20, 1840, at Manchester, N. H., Lucy, daughter of Stephen and Almira (Kendall) Richardson of Woburn, born Jan. 11, 1820, at Woburn; died July 25, 1846, at Gray. "Vinton Memorial" and "Richardson Memorial" give May 21 as the date of marriage. In their intentions, published at Cambridge, Mass., Apr. 11, she is called of Goffstown, N. H.

He married (2), Aug. 17, 1847, at Auburn, Me., Julia-Ann, daughter of Asa and Mary (Beals) Holmes of Auburn, born May 5, 1821, at Minot, Me.; died Oct. 10, 1855, at Gray. The Portland, Me., Commissioners' records give Aug. 7 as the date of the marriage, but this was probably the date of publishing the intentions.

He married (3), Apr. 16, 1856, at Woburn, Martha, daughter of Joseph and Patty (Pierce) Gardner of Woburn, born July 2, 1816, at Woburn; died Dec. 28, 1891, at Woburn. (Mass. Vital Records; New Hampshire Records; County Commissioners' Records at Portland, Me.; Woburn Records; Medway Records; Vinton Memorial, p. 233; Richardson Memorial, p. 444; Pierce Genealogy, 1882, p. 107; Records of Miss Julia-Holmes Lincoln, *abbec fbc.*)

Children, by first wife, born at Gray:

abbec fba. Lucy-Allen, born Aug. 7, 1842; died Apr. 21, 1883, at Woburn;
married, Nov. 1, 1865, at Woburn, Cyrus-Bowen, son of Cyrus and Ellen
Richardson of Cambridge, Mass., born, 1842, at Cambridgeport. He was
an engineer, living, 1865, at Woburn and then aged twenty-three years.
Children:
    a. Charles-Marshall.
    b. Frank-Lincoln, born Aug. 21, 1878.
    c. Lucy-Allen, born Jan. 6, 1883; died Aug. 19, 1883.
abbec fbb. A son, born and died June 7, 1846.

Children, by second wife, born at Gray:

abbec fbc. Julia-Holmes, born Apr. 2, 1850; living, 1911, unmarried.
abbec fbd. Charles-Hobart, born Oct. 6, 1855.

Child, by third wife, born at Gray:

abbec fbe. Joseph-Gardner, born Dec. 4, 1858; died Jan. 22, 1877, at Amherst, Mass., where he was attending college.

abbec fd. Thomas, son of Thomas (*Zenas, Francis, Hezekiah,
Daniel, Samuel*) and Nancy (Norcross) Lincoln of Cohasset,
Mass., born Dec. 9, 1817, at Cohasset; died May 22, 1882, at
Somerville, Mass. He lived at first at Saugus, Mass., and at the
time of his marriage is described as an "expressman." He
afterwards removed to Somerville and was engaged in the fur-
niture and upholstery business with A. H. Allen in Dock square,
Boston.

He married, June 14, 1840, at Medford, Mass., Harriet,
daughter of John and Abigail Tufts of Somerville, born Sept.
19, 1819, at Somerville; died June 24, 1883, at Taunton, Mass.,
in the Insane Hospital, having become insane after her husband's
death. (Cohasset Genealogies, p. 242; Saugus Records; Medford
Records; Goldthwaite Genealogy, pp. 258, 315; Records of Mrs.
Edward-Maynard Lincoln, *abbec fdc.*)

Children, born at Saugus:

abbec fda. Mary P., born 1841; died Apr. 19, 1891, tat Boston; married, Apr.
8, 1862, at Lynn, Mass., Nathan-Albert, son of Elbridge (or Eldridge)
and Eliot Merriam of Billerica, Mass., born 1840, at Boxford, Mass.
They lived at Somerville and at Charlestown, Mass. He was a farmer.
(Mass. Vital Records.)
    Child, born at Lynn:
      a. Harriet E., born March 26, 1868; died March 16, 1875, at
Boston, "aged 7 years, 11 months, 18 days."
abbec fdb. Madeline, born May 4, 1848 (Mass. Vital Records say 1849;
family records say 1847); died June 28, 1910, at Dorchester, Mass.;

married, Nov. 24, 1875, at Charlestown, Mass., Simon, son of Jacob
and Mary-Ann ([McCloud] Burns) Goldthwaite of Bangor, Me., born
Apr. 22, 1851, at Bangor. He is, 1911, in the furniture and upholstery
business in Roxbury district, Boston, living at Dorchester. He married
(1) Annie B., daughter of George B. and Mary Robertson, who died Feb.
15, 1873, at Somerville.
Children, born at Somerville:
   a.   ALICE-LINCOLN, born Aug. 25, 1876; mar. Sewell-Albert Carroll.
   b.   BERENICE-FRANCES, born Apr. 20, 1881; living, 1911, unmarried.
   c.   RALPH-PERCIVAL, born Oct. 14, 1882; mar. Lillian Heyward.
abbec fdc.   EDWARD-MAYNARD, born Sept. 25, 1858.

abbhc db.   ROBERT-BEALS, son of Robert-Beals (*Obadiah,
Hezekiah, Hezekiah, Daniel, Samuel*) and Susan (Knott) Lincoln
of Boston, Mass., born Nov. 3, 1844, at Boston; died June 9,
1909, at Waltham, Mass. He was a machinist in early life but
became a manufacturer of machinery and was president of the
Waters Governor Company. He lived at Boston.

He married, Oct. 8, 1866, at Boston, Helen-Francenia, daugh-
ter of Ira-Rowell and Louisa (Daniels) Philbrick of Boston, born
Jan. 9, 1845, at Nashua, N. H.; living, 1912, at Boston. (Mass.
Vital Records; Records of Mrs. Helen-Francenia Lincoln.)

Children, born: *a, e-g* at Boston; *b-d* at Kittery, Me.:

abbhc dba.   FREDERICK-HERBERT, born May 28, 1867; died July 11, 1910, at
Philadelphia, Pa. He was an electrical engineer and lived at Philadelphia.
He married, Apr. 16, 1890, at Richmond, Ind., Addie, daughter of
Josiah-Campbell and Rebecca (Young) Long of Richmond, born Apr.
19, 1865, at Richmond; living, 1912. They had no children.
abbhc dbb.   EDITH-HATTIE, born Jan. 25, 1870; living, 1912, unmarried.
abbhc dbc.   SUSAN-RUSSELL, born March 22, 1872; married, Jan. 31, 1898,
at Waltham, Mass., Nathan-Ellsworth, son of Nathan and Susan-Hardy
(Chadbourne) Smith of Waltham, born Jan. 31, 1866, at Lexington,
Mass. They are living, 1912, at Waltham. He is a farmer.
Children, born at Waltham:
   a.   MABEL-EDITH, born Aug. 3, 1898.
   b.   NATHAN, born Nov. 11, 1900.
abbhc dbd.   FANNIE-BIDDLE, born Aug. 25, 1874; married, July 31, 1907,
at Worcester, Mass., Harry-Austin, son of Taylor-Fillmore and Maria-
Jane (Hall) Smith of Wakefield, Mass., born Apr. 11, 1877, at Melrose,
Mass. They are living, 1912, at Waverly, Mass. He is a book-keeper.
Child, born at Roxbury, Mass.:
   a.   FLORENCE-JEANNETTE, born Feb. 24, 1908.
abbhc dbe.   EDWARD-REYNOLD, born July 4, 1878; married, Sept. 14, 1905,
at Waltham, Mass., Ethel-Agnes, daughter of Clarence-Llewellyn and
Edith (Ashley) Wentworth of Waltham, born Feb. 22, 1883, at Waltham.
They are living, 1912, at Waltham. He is a book-keeper. They have
no children.

abbhc dbf. ALICE-LOUISE, born May 30, 1882; living, 1912, unmarried.
abbhc dbg. ROBERT-BEALS, born May 11, 1885; died May 3, 1892, at Boston.

abbhc dc. GEORGE-HENRY, son of Robert-Beals (*Obadiah, Hezekiah, Hezekiah, Daniel, Samuel*) and Susan (Knott) Lincoln of Boston, Mass., born July 3, 1846, at Boston. He is, 1911, an iron-founder, living at Boston.

He married, Oct. 29, 1871, at Boston, Adeline-Louise, daughter of Charles-Andrew and Adeline (Tall) Bodge, of Boston, born June, 1851, at Boston; living, 1911. Massachusetts Vital records call her aged twenty-five years when married. (Mass. Vital Records; Boston Records; Records of George-Henry Lincoln.)

Child, born at Boston:

abbhc dca. GEORGE-LUTHER, born Oct. 8, 1874. He graduated at Harvard college in 1896, taking the degree of A.B., and in 1897 he received the degree of A.M. In 1899 and 1900 he was instructor in French at Leland Stanford University, and in the latter year was appointed assistant professor of French at Kansas University, which position he resigned in 1905, returning to Cambridge where he pursued a graduate course at Harvard until 1909, when he was appointed instructor in Romance languages. He is living, 1911, with his father in Boston. He married, July 27, 1910, at Madrid, Spain, Elizabeth-Marian, daughter of William-Hooker and Alice (Gordon) Gulick of Madrid, born Aug. 5, 1879, at Santander, Spain. Mr. Gulick is an American by birth. (Records of George-Luther Lincoln.)

adaaa aa. ABRAHAM, son of Mordecai (*Abraham, John, Mordecai, Mordecai, Samuel*) and Mary (Mudd) Lincoln of Washington county, Ky., born probably in Washington county; died March, 1852, at Fountain Green, Hancock county, Ill., whither he is said to have removed before 1830. His name first appears in the Hancock county records March 15, 1836, when he and his wife Elizabeth sold for $100 the north west ¼ of the south west ¼ of section 25 township 6, containing forty acres. He was then called of Hancock county and the deed was witnessed by Benjamin Mudd, who was probably his wife's brother. (Hancock County Deeds, Book B, p. 221.) Mr. Lincoln was a farmer and held the office of justice of the peace, which shows that he was a man of standing in the community.

His will dated Oct. 14, 1851, filed for probate March 25, 1852, calls him of Fountain Green and names: daughters Mary-Jane

Lincoln, Parmelia Lincoln and Ellen Lincoln, to whom is left "the farm upon which I now reside so long as they remain unmarried"; sons Hezekiah Lincoln and Nicholas Lincoln, to whom is left "one horse saddle and bridle worth $75. and to each one yoke of oxen"; and son Robert Lincoln to whom is left "such sums of money as I may have given him."

Mr. Lincoln married Elizabeth Mudd, of whom nothing has been learned. She was probably a cousin and evidently died before him as she is not named in his will. Four of their children are buried at La Harpe, Ill., their gravestones being inscribed as follows:

"Nicholas ‡ Lincoln ‡ 3rd Son & 6th child ‡ of ‡ Abraham ‡ Lincoln ‡ of Fountain Green ‡ Township ‡ Died ‡ Mar. 7, 1888 ‡ aged ‡ 53 y's, 9 Ms. ‡ & 11 Ds. ‡ Eternal Rest grant to him O Lord ‡ And let perpetual light shine on him."

"Mary J ‡ Lincoln ‡ 2nd Dau. & 3rd Child ‡ of ‡ Abraham ‡ Lincoln ‡ Died ‡ Aug. 29, 1888 ‡ Call not back the dear departed ‡ Anchored safe where storms are o'er. ‡ On the border land we left them ‡ Soon to meet and part no more."

"Hezekiah Lincoln ‡ Died ‡ Sept. 25, 1888 ‡ Aged ‡ 59 Yrs. 1 Mo. 16 Ds."

"Permelia A. ‡ Lincoln ‡ Died ‡ Dec. 12, 1895."

Children, born: *a-e* in Kentucky; *f-g* in Illinois:

adaaa aaa. PRISCILLA, married John Smith and removed to Kentucky, where her only daughter was born whose children were living in 1895 at Springfield, Ky. Mrs. Hezekiah Lincoln says that she never removed to Illinois, with her parents, but remained in Kentucky and was married there.

Child, born in Kentucky:
   a. PRISCILLA-FLORIDA, married (1) John Anderson; (2) Charles C. McGill.

adaaa aab. PARMELIA, died Dec. 12, 1895, at La Harpe, Ill., unmarried. The petition of Charles C. McGill of Springfield, Ky., represents that Permelia Lincoln, late of Hancock county, Ill., died at La Harpe Dec. 12, 1895, intestate, leaving real and personal estate . . . and no husband nor brothers and sisters; that her sole and only heirs, so far as known, are John O. L. Anderson, Clement C. McGill, Mary E. McGill and Robert J. McGill, all of whom are minor children of Priscilla-Florida, who was a daughter of Priscilla Smith, who was a sister of Permelia Lincoln, deceased, all of which children now live in Springfield, Ky., and are under age. Your petitioner, the father of the three last and step father of the first . . . etc. (Probate Records of Hancock County, Ill.)

adaaa aac. MARY-JANE, died Aug. 29, 1888, at La Harpe, Ill., where she is buried.

adaaa aad. ROBERT, died Sept. 5, 1868, in Hancock county, Ill., unmarried and intestate, and George W. Bachelder was appointed his administrator. In the settlement of his estate the following are named as his only heirs at law: "Mary Jane Lincoln of whom said administrator is conservator, Hezekiah Lincoln, Nicholas Lincoln, Priscilla Smith, Pamelia Lincoln, and Ellen Sullivan, being his brothers and sisters."

adaaa aae. HEZEKIAH, born Aug. 9, 1829; died Sept. 25, 1888, at La Harpe, Ill. He was a farmer, lawyer and merchant, living first at Fountain Green, on the old homestead, and, later, at La Harpe. His will, dated Sept. 23, probated Oct. 23, 1888, names wife Phoebe A. Lincoln and leaves to her "my undivided one half interest in the home farm at Fountain Green, known as the 'Abraham Lincoln Farm.' "

He married, Jan. 14, 1869, at Peoria, Ill., Phoebe-Ann, daughter of Peter and Ann (Hyers) Brewer, born Nov. 26, 1833, at Williamson, N. Y.; living, 1916, at La Harpe. They had no children. (Information of Mrs. Hezekiah Lincoln; Hancock County Records.)

adaaa aaf. NICHOLAS, born May 24, 1834; died March 7, 1888, unmarried, at La Harpe, Ill., where he is buried.

adaaa aag. ELLEN, died before Dec. 12, 1895, at Fort Worth, Tex., married, Nov. 28, 1861, in Hancock county, Ill., John Sullivan. They removed to Texas and lived at Dallas and Forth Worth. (Hancock County Records.) They had no children.

adaaa ab. JAMES-BRADFORD, son of Mordecai (*Abraham, John, Mordecai, Mordecai, Samuel*) and Mary (Mudd) Lincoln of Washington county, Ky., and Hancock county, Ill., born in Washington or Grayson county, Ky.; died November, 1837, at Fountain Green, Ill. He received no school education but, nevertheless, is said to have been better educated in the common branches of learning than most men of his time with whom he was associated. He was a carpenter by trade and lived in Grayson county, Ky., until October, 1829, when he removed to Sangamon county, Ill., and thence in 1831 to Fountain Green, Hancock county, Ill., where he passed the few remaining years of his life. He held the office of U. S. Land Commissioner; was county commissioner of Hancock county, and was the first justice of the peace of that county.

From the records of Hancock county we learn that on Dec. 28, 1835, he purchased of John Williams for $50 the southeast ¼ of the southeast ¼ of section 35, township 36 north, containing 40 acres, and in the same month he sold, with his wife Frances, for $100 to Jonathan Prior, 80 acres in township 6. (Hancock County Deeds, Book B, pp. 111, 117.) He died intestate and on Nov. 13, 1837, Daniel Prentiss gave bonds as administrator on the estate of James B. Lincoln. (County Clerk's Records.)

He married in 1821 in Grayson county, Ky., Frances, daughter of William and Frances (Childers) Day of Grayson county, born Jan. 1, 1799, in Mercer county, Ky.; died Nov. 1, 1884, at Fountain Green. This family are all Roman Catholics, having inherited that religion from James-Bradford's mother, Mary (Mudd) Lincoln, who was a devout member of that church. (Records of Mrs. Mary-Rowena [Lincoln] Bowman, *adaaa abc.*)

Children, born: *a-c* at Leitchfield, Ky.; *d* in Sangamon county, Ill., *e, f* at Fountain Green:

adaaa aba. THOMAS-JEFFERSON, born Apr. 20, 1822; died Apr. 26, 1914, at Fountain Green. He lived on the home farm at Fountain Green. He married (license given Jan. 1, 1855), Martha-Jane Bures.

adaaa abb. ELIZABETH, born 1825; died in Allen county, Kan.; married William Dickerson.

adaaa abc. MARY-ROWENA, born Oct. 22, 1827; died January, 1918, at Tennessee, Ill.; married (1), Jan. 16, 1848, according to the county records but Mrs. Bowman says Jan. 21, 1847, at Fountain Green, William, son of John and Mary (French) Lovely of Colchester, Ill., born at Maysville, Ky.; died June, 1853, at Fountain Green. He was a farmer. She was brought by her parents from Kentucky to Illinois when she was three years old and lived until her second marriage at Fountain Green.

She married (2), Apr. 18, 1861, at Macomb, Ill., Charles-Newton, son of John and Catherine (Zwingler) Bowman of Madison county, Tenn., born July 14, 1818, at Jackson, Tenn.; died Sept. 6, 1904, at Tennessee, Ill., where he had lived. He was a farmer. This family are all Roman Catholics.

Child, by first husband, born at Fountain Green:
    a. WILLIAM LOVELY, born Sept. 24, 1853; mar. Amanda Burrow.

Children, by second husband, born at Tennessee, Ill.:
    b. ELIZA BOWMAN, born Apr. 23, 1862; mar. George Scheifly.
    c. ROBERT-LEE BOWMAN, born May 7, 1864; died September, 1882.
    d. ROSA-MAY BOWMAN, born Oct. 13, 1866; died Sept. 17, 1867.
    e. EMILY-NORA BOWMAN, born July 17, 1868; died Dec. 20, 1870.
    f. CHARLES-NEWTON BOWMAN, born Nov. 1, 1870; died Nov. 24, 1870.
    g. THOMAS-EDWARD BOWMAN, born Sept. 24, 1871; mar. Evaline Hardy.

adaaa abd. EMILY-SUSAN, born April, 1830; died May 20, 1892, at Fountain Green, unmarried.

adaaa abe. JAMES-RILEY, born 1832; died Nov. 12, 1906, at Carthage, Ill. He married Margaret Tibbons (or Gibbons).

adaaa abf. CHARLES-PRENTISS, born 1837; died Apr. 4, 1858, at Fountain Green, unmarried.

adaaa bb. Thomas, son of Josiah (*Abraham, John, Mordecai, Mordecai, Samuel*) and Catherine (Barlow) Lincoln of Harrison county, Ind., born 1806, in Washington county, Ky.; died Jan. 26, 1849, in Harrison county, Ind. He was a farmer and lived most of his life in Harrison county. On Oct. 21, 1840, he purchased of his brother and sisters, "all their right, title and claim, as the heirs of Josiah Lincon deceased, in the northwest quarter section, N° 12, of Township N° 2, South of range N° 2 East, in Harrison Co. Ind." being the home farm, the consideration being three hundred dollars. (Harrison County Land Records, Bk. N, p. 219.)

He married about 1825 at Leavenworth, Crawford county, Ind., Sarah, daughter of Benjamin and Mary (Bullington) Weathers of Crawford county, born about 1810 in Crawford county; died Feb. 18, 1892, in Harrison county. (Records of Joseph-David Lincoln, *adaaa bbcg.*)

Children, born at Milltown, Ind.:

adaaa bba. Rachel, born Apr. 8, 1827 (one record says July 12, 1829); died July 10, 1908, at Handcock Chapel, Ind. She was married Aug. 26, 1847, by Samuel M. Ott, J. P. in Harrison county, to Joseph-Davis Ott of Handcock Chapel, where he was born Aug. 12, 1826, and died Sept. 20, 1908, having passed his whole life there. He was a farmer. (Records of Henry-Thomas Ott, *adaaa bbac.*)
Children, born at Handcock Chapel:
- *a.* Amanda-Marthaette, born Sept. 13, 1848; mar. John-Robert Totton.
- *b.* Sarah-Elizabeth, born Jan. 4, 1850; died Oct. 21, 1850.
- *c.* Henry-Thomas, born Aug. 8, 1852; mar. Harriet-Anna Seacat.
- *d.* John-Patterson, born July 7, 1854.
- *e.* Mary-Abigail, born May 27, 1856; mar. Edward Routh.
- *f.* Joseph-Marion, born June 20, 1858.
- *g.* Harriet-Anne, born Feb. 10, 1860; living, 1916, unmarried.
- *h.* Hester-Rosanna, born Oct. 3, 1863.
- *i.* George-McLean, born Dec. 1, 1866; mar. Dora Campbell.
- *j.* Florence-May, born May 3, 1869; died May 6, 1869.

adaaa bbb. Benjamin, born Jan. 3, 1830.

adaaa bbc. Mordecai, born March 2, 1832.

adaaa bbd. Jacob, born about 1834.

adaaa bbe. Washington, born Oct. 25, 1835.

adaaa bbf. Warden, born March 4, 1841.

adaaa bbg. Joseph, born Dec. 30, 1842.

adaaa bbh. William, died long ago. Was married and had a son but nothing is known of him.

adaaa bbi. James, born Jan. 29, 1848.

adaaa be. JACOB, son of Josiah (*Abraham, John, Mordecai, Mordecai, Samuel*) and Catherine (Barlow) Lincoln of Harrison county, Ind., born July 16, 1815, at Blue River, Ind.; died Aug. 10, 1889, in Wayne county, Mo. He removed from Indiana to Missouri and was a farmer.

He married, Nov. 20, 1839, in Harrison county, Ind., Martha Gibbs of Crawford county, Ind., born Jan. 9, 1820, in Crawford county; died in Harrison county after 1865. (Information of Joseph Lincoln, *adaaa beg*, and Jonathan-Jones Lincoln, *adaaa bef.*)

Children, born in Harrison county:

adaaa bea. MARY, born Aug. 15, 1840; died March 18, 1885, in Wayne county, Mo. She married and had six children, but nothing further is known of her.

adaaa beb. THOMAS, born March 13, 1842.

adaaa bec. WILLIAM, born Sept. 25, 1844.

adaaa bed. JAMES-WASHINGTON, born Feb. 6, 1846; died Oct. 6, 1896, in Wayne county, Mo. He married, Oct. 10, 1872, in Harrison county, Ind., Martha J. Kennedy.

adaaa bee. ELIZABETH, born Apr. 6, 1848.

adaaa bef. JONATHAN-JONES, born Sept. 26, 1850.

adaaa beg. JOSEPH, born Nov. 6, 1852.

adaaa beh. MATILDA, born Sept. 20, 1857; died July 6, 1884, in Harrison county, unmarried.

adaaa bei. KATHARINE, born Jan. 10, 1860; married, Feb. 16, 1882, in Harrison county, Isaac-Wilford, son of John-Jacob and Julian-Ann (Soner) Walk of Harrison county, born Sept. 5, 1854, in Harrison county; died Jan. 21, 1911, at Arab, Mo. He was a farmer. She is living, 1916, at Arab. (Records of Mrs. Katharine [Lincoln] Walk.)

Children, born: *a, b* in Harrison county; *c-h* at Arab:

    a. CHARLES-EDDY, born Apr. 26, 1883; mar. Ettie McDonald.

    b. ANDY-GROVER, born Oct. 21, 1884; died Sept. 9, 1891.

    c. IVY-MAY, born Apr. 12, 1887; died Jan. 9, 1888.

    d. CLAUDE-ELMER, born May 29, 1889; died Oct. 26, 1897.

    e. LOLA-FLORENCE, born Sept. 16, 1893; died Feb. 11, 1912, unmarried.

    f. DESSY-MAY, born Feb. 29, 1896; mar. Edgar-Lee Sweet.

    g. CHLOE-MARIE, born Nov. 27, 1898.

    h. OSCAR-ALONZO, born Nov. 28, 1901.

adaaa bej. CHARLES, born March 6, 1862.

adaaa bek. ROSANNA, born Jan. 12, 1865; died Apr. 16, 1886, in Harrison county, unmarried.

adaaa db. ABRAHAM, son of Thomas (*Abraham, John, Mordecai, Mordecai, Samuel*) and Nancy (Hanks) Lincoln of Kentucky, Indiana and Illinois, born Feb. 12, 1809, near Hodgenville,

Ky.; died Apr. 15, 1865, at Washington, D. C., while President of the United States, the victim of an assassin's bullet. Little has been learned of his early life and education. His first teacher is said to have been Zachariah Riney, whose school he attended for two or three months at the age of seven, and his second was Caleb Hazel, with whom he studied for about three months. If it is true that "the boy actually learned to write an intelligent letter at this time," as claimed by his biographers, he must have been very precocious. After the removal of the family to Indiana he went to school successively to Hazel Dorsey, Andrew Crawford and a Mr. Swazey, the last named keeping a school about 1826, four and a half miles from Lincoln's home. After this Lincoln was entirely self taught. In 1816 his father removed with all his family to Indiana and settled in Spencer county, near Gentryville, and in 1825 Abraham was employed by James Taylor for nine months, at six dollars per month, his principal employment being the management of a ferry boat across the Ohio at Anderson's creek. The next year he was employed by Mr. Gentry at Gentryville, and was sent by him to New Orleans in charge of a flat-boat laden with produce. For this service he received eight dollars per month. In 1830 the family removed to Macon county, Ill., and settled on the Sangamon river, about ten miles from Decatur, where they arrived on March 1. Here he first assisted his father to build a cabin and then, being twenty-one years of age, went to work on his own account, acquiring at this time the title of "rail-splitter" by which he was familiarly called in his political campaigns. His father removed in the spring of 1831 to Coles county, Ill., and Abraham never returned to live under the paternal roof.

In 1831 he made a second flat-boat trip to New Orleans, with his cousin John Hanks and his step-brother John Johnson, with a cargo of hogs. They were employed by Denton Offutt of New Salem, Ill. They built the boat on Spring creek and rafted it to the Sangamon and thence to the Mississippi. On neither of these flat-boat trips is there any evidence of an adventure in behalf of kidnapped negroes, such as has recently been depicted in moving pictures. On returning from this trip Lincoln became a clerk in Mr. Offutt's store at New Salem and first acquired the sobriquet "Honest Abe," by his scrupulously fair treatment

30

of all customers. That fall he served as clerk of elections, his first public office.

In April, 1832, he enlisted in a militia company from Sangamon, Ill., for the Black Hawk war, and was chosen its captain on April 21, but the volunteers proved unsatisfactory and were mustered out on May 27. Lincoln immediately re-enlisted as a private in Capt. Elijah Iles's Company of independent rangers for twenty days, the mustering officer being Major Robert Anderson who, thirty years later, defended and surrendered Fort Sumter. On the expiration of this service Lincoln was again mustered in, on June 20, as a member of an independent company under Capt. Jacob M. Early which was disbanded on July 10, three weeks before the massacre of Bad Axe ended the war. During his whole service Lincoln saw no actual fighting.

In the fall of this year he ran for the legislature on the Whig ticket but was defeated. He then went into partnership with William F. Berry in keeping a general store. Berry turned out to be a worthless drunkard, and, as Lincoln had little business capacity, the enterprise failed within a year, and it was not until 1849 that he discharged all the resulting obligations. On May 7, 1833, he was appointed postmaster of New Salem by President Jackson and held that office until 1836, when it was abolished. He is said to have kept the office in his hat, the revenue not being sufficient to pay for larger quarters. After his failure in business he became deputy land surveyor to John Calhoun, who was the official surveyor of Sangamon county, which position he retained until his removal to Springfield, Ill., at the same time he commenced the reading of law, having been during all his life a constant student and voracious reader of all the books and newspapers he could lay his hands on.

In 1834 he was elected to the legislature and was re-elected in 1836, 1838 and 1840, after which he declined to be again a candidate, though he was again elected in 1854 but resigned before taking his seat. In the campaign of 1836 he established his reputation as a public speaker and at the following session he first met Stephen A. Douglas in debate. It was at this session he subscribed a protest against pro-slavery resolution and commenced his anti-slavery record.

He was admitted to the bar in the autumn of 1836 and removed to Springfield the following spring, where, on Apr. 27, 1837, he became the law partner of Major John T. Stuart. This partnership continued until Apr. 14, 1841, Stuart having been elected to Congress, and Mr. Lincoln formed a business association with Judge Stephen T. Logan of Springfield which was dissolved Sept. 20, 1843; and on the same day he became senior partner in a new firm with William H. Herndon, which was never formally dissolved except by Mr. Lincoln's death.

In 1840 Mr. Lincoln became involved in a quarrel with James Shields, who held Lincoln responsible for certain articles which had appeared in the Sangamon "Journal," which offended Mr. Shields. The writer of the articles was really a young woman, a friend of Lincoln's and by many thought to have been Miss Mary Todd, to whom Lincoln was then, or soon after, affianced and who afterwards became his wife. Mr. Shields challenged him to fight a duel and Lincoln selected broadswords as the weapons, and took preparatory instruction in that arm. The duel was prevented by the action of mutual friends, at the scene of the proposed fight on Bloody island.

In 1844 he was a candidate for presidential elector for Henry Clay. In 1846 he was elected representative to Congress by a majority of 1511, the only Whig member from Illinois. In 1848 he was a member of the national Whig convention. In this year, after the adjournment of Congress on Aug. 14, he went to New England and made various campaign speeches. In the course of this journey he stopped at Worcester, Mass., and was entertained at dinner by ex-Governor Levi Lincoln, *aacbc a*, a distant cousin, though the family connection was unknown to them both. In 1852 he was again on the Whig electoral ticket, this time for General Scott, and was defeated for the third time.

In October, 1854, he made a powerful speech against Mr. Douglas at Springfield on the Kansas-Nebraska bill, and did this again at Peoria. This was instrumental in bringing about the election of a Whig legislature; and Lincoln and Lyman Trumbull were candidates for the nomination to the United States senate, but Lincoln withdrew and Trumbull was chosen. On May 29, 1856, he assisted in organizing the Republican party of Illinois, and his name was presented to the national Republican convention for vice-president, but he was defeated by Mr. Dayton.

In 1858 he had his remarkable contest with Mr. Douglas for the senatorship, in which at first they attended each other's meetings in order to reply later, and finally met each other in seven joint meetings at Ottawa, Freeport, Jonesboro, Charleston, Galesburg, Quincy and Alton. The result was a Democratic legislature and the election of Douglas, though Lincoln's popular vote was four thousand over Douglas's.

Late in 1859 and early in 1860 he made several journeys through various portions of the country on lecturing tours, visiting Ohio, Kansas, New York and New England. Meanwhile his name became prominently mentioned for the presidential nomination, his principal competitor being William H. Seward. The Republican convention met at Chicago, June 16, 1860, in an immense building called the "Wigwam." Lincoln's name was placed in nomination by the Illinois delegation, and on the first ballot he received 102 votes to 173½ for Seward, the remaining votes being divided among several other candidates. On the third ballot Lincoln was triumphantly nominated, and in the ensuing election he received 180 votes in the electoral college to 123 for his three opponents, the Democratic votes being divided between Douglas and Breckenridge, the Whig candidate, John Bell, receiving 39. Lincoln's popular vote, however, was far from being a majority of the whole vote cast, his three opponents receiving nine hundred and thirty thousand votes more than he, and the joint vote of the two Democrats exceeding Lincoln's by nearly three hundred thousand. At his re-election in 1864, however, the seceding states of course not voting, he received a popular majority of over four hundred thousand.

It is unnecessary here to relate any of the incidents of his official life as President, or the circumstances of his tragic assassination at the hands of John-Wilkes Booth, which filled the whole nation with mourning. These have been told and retold in his many biographies to which the reader is here referred, none of which, however, are to be entirely relied upon for the incidents of his early life, or for the details of his parentage and ancestry.

Shortly after his nomination to the presidency Mr. Lincoln furnished to Mr. J. W. Fell a brief account of his life. The manuscript of this has been preserved. It bears no date. On March 20, 1872, it was certified to by David Davis, Lyman Trumbull and Charles Sumner as being in the handwriting of Abraham Lincoln and is undoubtedly authentic. It has been published in facsimile several times and is here given in full:

"I was born Feb. 12, 1809, in Hardin County, Kentucky. My parents were both born in Virginia, of undistinguished families, second families perhaps I should say—My mother, who died in my tenth year, was of a family of the name of Hanks, some of whom now reside in Adams, and others in Macon counties, Illinois. My paternal grandfather, Abraham Lincoln, emigrated from Rockingham County, Virginia, to Kentucky, about 1781 or 2, where, a year or two later he was killed by indians, not in battle, but by stealth, when he was laboring to open a farm in the forest—His ancestors, who were quakers, went to Virginia from Berks County, Pennsylvania—An effort to identify them with the New England family of the same name, ended in nothing more definite, than a similarity of Christian names in both families, such as Enoch, Levi, Mordecai, Solomon, Abraham and the like.

"My father, at the death of his father, was about six years of age; and he grew up, literally without education—He removed from Kentucky to what is now Spencer County, Indiana, in my eighth year—We reached our new home about the time the State came into the Union—It was a wild region, with many bears and other wild animals still in the woods.—There I grew up—There were some schools, so called; but no qualification was ever required of a teacher, beyond 'readin, writin', and cipherin' to the Rule of Three—If a straggler, supposed to understand latin, happened to sojourn in the neighborhood, he was looked upon as a wizzard—There was absolutely nothing to excite ambition for education. Of course when I came of age I did not know much—Still somehow, I could read, write and cipher to the Rule of Three, but that was all—I have not been to school since—The little advance I now have upon this store of education, I have picked up from time to time under the pressure of necessity—

"I was raised to farm work, which I continued till I was twenty two—At twenty one I came to Illinois, and passed the first year in Illinois, Macon County—Then I got to New Salem at that time in Sangamon, now in Menard County, where I remained a year as a sort of Clerk in a store—Then came the Black Hawk war; and I was elected a Captain of Volunteers— a success which gave me more pleasure than any I have had since—I went the campaign, was elated [elected?], ran for the Legislature the same year (1832) and was beaten—the only time I ever have been beaten by the people—The next and three succeeding biennial elections, I was elected to the Legislature— I was not a candidate afterwards. During this Legislative period I had studied law, and removed to Springfield to practice it— In 1846 I was once elected to the lower House of Congress—Was not a candidate for re-election—From 1849 to 1854, both inclusive, practiced law more assiduously than ever before— Always a whig in politics, and generally on the Whig electoral ticket, making active canvasses—I was losing interest in politics, when the repeal of the Missouri Compromise aroused me again—What I have done since then is pretty well known—

"If any personal description is thought desirable, it may be said, I am, in height, six feet, four inches, nearly; lean in flesh, weighing, on an average, one hundred and eighty pounds; dark complexion, with coarse black hair, and grey eyes,—no other marks or brands recollected—

"Yours very truly
"Hon. J. W. Fell   A. Lincoln"

He married, Nov. 4, 1842,* at Springfield at the residence of Ninian W. Edwards, brother-in-law of the bride, Mary[3], daughter of Robert-Smith[2] (*Levi*[1]) and Ann-Eliza (Parker) Todd of Lexington, Ky., born Dec. 13, 1818, at Lexington; died July 16, 1882, at Springfield of paralysis. "She was of the average height, rather compactly built, had a well rounded face, rich dark brown hair, and bluish-grey eyes. In her bearing she was proud, but handsome and vivacious. Her education had been in no wise defective; she was a good conversationalist, using with equal fluency the French and English languages. When she used a pen, its point was sure to be sharp, and she wrote with wit and ability. She not only had a quick intellect but an intuitive judgment of men and their motives. Ordinarily she was affable and even charming in her manners; but when offended or

---

*This date is from Lincoln's family Bible and is accepted by most authorities, but "Bard Family," pp. 446-7, says the marriage occurred March 4, 1842, and gives the birth of Mary Todd as Dec. 12, 1818.

ABRAHAM LINCOLN
1809-1865
From a photograph taken February 9, 1864

antagonized, her agreeable qualities instantly disappeared beneath a wave of stinging satire or sarcastic bitterness, and her entire better nature was submerged. In her figure and physical proportions, in education, bearing, temperament, history—in everything she was the exact reverse of Lincoln." (Herndon's "Abraham Lincoln," vol. i, p. 194.)

Children, born at Springfield:

adaaa dba. ROBERT-TODD, born Aug. 1, 1843.
adaaa dbb. EDWARD-BAKER, born March 10, 1846; died in infancy.
adaaa dbc. WILLIAM-WALLACE, born Dec. 21, 1850; died Feb. 20, 1862, at Washington, D. C., in the White House.
adaaa dbd. THOMAS, born Apr. 4, 1853; died July 15, 1871, at Chicago, Ill.

adaae ab. PRESTON, son of David (*Jacob, John, Mordecai, Mordecai, Samuel*) and Catherine (Bright) Lincoln of Lacey Spring, Va., born Dec. 11, 1811, at Dayton, Va.; died Apr. 17 (or May 15), 1848, at Dayton. He is buried at New Erection, Va. He was a farmer and lived at Dayton and at Mt. Crawford, Va.

He married at Mt. Crawford, Elizabeth, daughter of Christian and Catharine (Lincoln) Coffman of Dayton, born Feb. 10, 1814, at Dayton; died Apr. 9, 1856, at Dayton. She married (2) a Mr. Morris, by whom she had one son, Walter, who died at White Sulphur Springs, Va. Mrs. Catharine (Lincoln) Coffman was daughter of Thomas (*John, Mordecai, Mordecai, Samuel*) and Elizabeth (Casner) Lincoln of Lexington, Ky., *adaah c.* (Records of Mrs. Virginia-Catherine [Lincoln] Taylor, *adaaf aga*, and of Mrs. Luther E. Chapman, *adaae abbc.*)

Children, born at Mt. Crawford:

adaae aba. ALBERT-CURTIS, born Apr. 25, 1840 (or 1839).
adaae abb. JOSEPHINE-ELIZABETH, born Jan. 9, 1842;* died May 1, 1908, at Lacey Spring, Va.; married, June 30, 1859, at Washington, D. C., John-William, son of John-William and Susan (Miller) Stearn of Lacey Spring, born Aug. 3, 1836, at Mill Creek, Va.; living, 1915, at Lacey Spring. He is a cordwainer and harness-maker. (Records of John-William Stearn.)

Children, born at Lacey Spring:
    a. SUSAN-PANSY, born Apr. 1, 1860; died Dec. 19, 1861.
    b. CHARLES-ALBERT, born Jan. 10, 1862; mar. Betty Fridley.
    c. VIRGINIA-DAVIS, born Apr. 2, 1866; mar. Luther E. Chapman.

*Mr. Stearn says that Josephine-Elizabeth and her twin sister Mary-Catherine were born in 1841, but this is hardly likely if their brother Albert was born in 1840.

    d. BISHOP-WEAVER, born Feb. 12, 1872; mar. Lucy Doval.
    e. STUART-SAMUEL, born Aug. 7, 1878; mar. Maud Vanpelt.
adaae abc. MARY-CATHERINE, twin of the foregoing, born Jan. 9, 1842;
    died aged about eight years.
adaae abd. FANNY-ELIZABETH, born Aug. 11, 1844; died Nov. 18, 1909,
    at Lima, Ohio; married at Lacey Spring, John-Dickerson, son of Gabriel
    and Delilah (Cole) Wood of Lacey Spring, born Dec. 3, 1837, at Lacey
    Spring; died Apr. 5, 1914, at Harrisonburg, Va. He was a farmer. They
    lived at Lacey Spring. (Records of Fred-Edward Wood, *adaae abda.*)
    Child, born at Lacey Spring:
        a. FRED-EDWARD, born March 24, 1872; living, 1914, at Lima,
        Ohio.
adaae abe. ISABEL. She died at Crawfordsville, Ind. She is said to have
    married John Ruebush and to have had a son, Frank, who served one
    or two terms in the regular army, and whose last known address was
    Crawfordsville.
adaae abf. DAVID-FRANKLIN. He is said to have died, unmarried, at Kansas
    City, Mo.

    adaae ag. JACOB-NICHOLAS, son of David (*Jacob, John, Mordecai, Mordecai, Samuel*) and Catherine (Bright) Lincoln of Lacey Spring, Va., born Apr. 3, 1821, at Dayton, Va.; died Feb. 21, 1880, at Lacey Spring. He was found unconscious at his mill door by his brother Abraham, suffering from a wound on the head, and died without recovering consciousness. It is supposed he had been left for dead by his assailants. Two men were tried for the crime and were found guilty and sent to the penitentiary. Mr. Lincoln was a farmer and miller and lived at Lacey Spring.

    He married, Oct. 16, 1849, at Broadway, Va., Caroline-Thomas, daughter of Michael and Leannah (Thomas) Homan of Broadway, born July 19, 1828, at Broadway; living, 1914, at Lacey Spring in excellent health and in full possession of her faculties. (Records of Mrs. Virginia-Catherine [Lincoln] Taylor, *adaaf aga.*)

    Children, born at Lacey Spring:

adaae aga. VIRGINIA-CATHERINE, born Aug. 2, 1850; married, May 21,
    1868, at Lacey Spring, John-Wesley, son of Zachary and Nancy (Eppard)
    Taylor of Stonewall, Va., born Oct. 28, 1835, at Stonewall. He received
    the degree of A.M. at Randolph-Macon college in 1860; served as private
    in Company I, 2nd Virginia infantry, in 1862 for about a year, and then
    became a farmer and surveyor. Since his marriage he has been a teacher
    and principal of the Lacey Spring school. He and his wife are living,
    1914, at Lacey Spring. They have no children.

adaae agb. MARY-LEANNAH, born Oct. 22, 1852; married, May 30, 1872, at Lacey Spring, Jefferson-Jacob, son of Jacob-Bright and Elizabeth (Coiner) Nicholas of Stonewall, Va., born Aug. 13, 1847, at Port Republic, Va. He is a farmer and miller. He served in McNeal's regiment, C.S.A., near the close of the Civil war. He and his wife are living, 1914, at Port Republic.

Children, born at Port Republic:
- *a.* BESSIE-LINCOLN, born Sept. 6, 1873; mar. Stuart M. Yancey.
- *b.* CARRIE-TAYLOR, born Nov. 23, 1875.
- *c.* JACOB-BRIGHT, born Oct. 4, 1879; died Sept. 8, 1894.
- *d.* JOHN-HOMAN, born Feb. 7, 1882; living, 1916, unmarried.
- *e.* GROVER-CLEVELAND, born Oct. 22, 1884; mar. Rosalie Baxter.
- *f.* EDNA-VIRGINIA, born March 6, 1887; died May 8, 1896.

adaae agc. HARVEY-PRESTON, born July 11, 1855.

adaae agd. ELIZABETH-THERESA, born Dec. 18, 1859; married, Nov. 27, 1879, at Lacey Spring, Charles-Henry, son of Jacob-Bright and Elizabeth (Coiner) Nicholas of Port Republic, Va., born Oct. 10, 1853, at Port Republic. They have lived at Lacey Spring but recently removed to Harrisonburg, Va., where they are now, 1914, residing. (Records of Mrs. Elizabeth-Theresa [Lincoln] Nicholas.) He is a farmer and miller.

Children, born at Lacey Spring:
- *a.* WILLIAM-FRANKLIN, born June 10, 1882; mar. Bernice-Luin Moore.
- *b.* ELIZABETH-LINCOLN, born Nov. 12, 1883; living, 1914, unmarried.
- *c.* GEORGIA-WINIFRED, born Feb. 3, 1891; living, 1914, unmarried.

adaae age. HEROD-FRANKLIN, born Nov. 26, 1861; died Jan. 29, 1863.

adaae agf. EFFIE-AMELIA-FLORENCE, born May 23, 1864; married, Oct. 15, 1885, at Lacey Spring, Philip-Miller, son of Simon and Margaret (Miller) Coiner of Waynesboro, Va., born July 15, 1853, at Waynesboro. He is a farmer. They are living, 1914, at Waynesboro.

Children, born at Waynesboro:
- *a.* CASPER-CECIL, born Oct. 8, 1886; living, 1914, unmarried.
- *b.* HORTIE-MARGARET, born Sept. 30, 1889, living, 1914, unmarried.

adaae agg. CAROLINE-HOMAN, born Oct. 23, 1866; married, Dec. 7, 1886, at Lacey Spring, John-William, son of John and Sally (Bowers) Weaver of Lima, Ohio, born March 22, 1864, at Lima. He is a mechanic and is employed in the railroad shops at Lima, where they are now, 1914, living.

Children, born at Lima:
- *a.* RHEA-LOVETTA, born Nov. 18, 1887; living, 1914, unmarried.
- *b.* ROBERT-LINCOLN, born Sept. 24, 1894; living, 1914, unmarried.

adaae agh. NORA-ABIGAIL, born Oct. 2, 1869; living, 1914, unmarried.

adaae agi. JACOB-THOMAS, born Apr. 3, 1872.

adaae ah. ABRAHAM, son of David (*Jacob, John, Mordecai, Mordecai, Samuel*) and Catherine (Bright) Lincoln of Lacey Spring, Va., born Dec. 19, 1822, at Dayton, Va.; died May 5, 1905, at Harrisonburg, Va. He was a farmer and lived at Lacey Spring until his wife's death. He was captain of a company of

Virginia militia in the Civil war, serving at Winchester, and was a heavy sufferer by the destruction done in the Valley during the war. After the war he became the first postmaster of Lacey Spring. As an instance of his unassuming modesty it is related that when the government decided to establish a post office at what is now Lacey Spring, Mr. Lincoln was asked by the department to suggest a name and, at the desire of his friends he wrote suggesting Lincoln Spring, from the spring so called, which gushed from the ground in great volume immediately below his house. His writing not being very good the officials misread the name and without further inquiry named the spring Lacey instead of Lincoln, and Mr. Lincoln, though urged to have the error corrected, refused to do so on the ground that, as he said, one name was as good as the other. Though having no middle name he always signed his name "A. B. Lincoln."

He married, July 10, 1855, at Bristol, Tenn., Mary-Elizabeth, daughter of Edward and Mary (Henton) Hughes of Bristol, born June 26, 1836; died Dec. 25, 1902, at Lacey Spring. (Records of Jetson-Jackson Lincoln, *adaae ahc;* Family Bible with Mrs. Lucy-Knox [Lincoln] Bradford, *adaae ahe.*)

Children, born at Lacey Spring:

adaae aha. JOHN-EDWARD, born July 22, 1856.

adaae ahb. DIANA-MCKELVA, born Oct. 26, 1858; died May 3, 1862.

adaae ahc. JETSON-JACKSON, born Apr. 27, 1863.

adaae ahd. SAMUEL-WALDEN, born Oct. 30, 1864; is a farmer living, 1914, at Broadway, Va., near Lacey Spring. He married, at Lacey Spring, Ella-Lee Long of Melrose, Linville township, Va. They have four children.

adaae ahe. LUCY-KNOX, born Apr. 30, 1869; married, Dec. 27, 1892, at Lacey Spring, Robert-Winfield, son of James-Mortman and Elizabeth (Miller) Bradford of Orkney Springs, Va., born Aug. 17, 1857, at Orkney Springs. He is a machinist. They are living, 1914, at Harrisonburg, Va., which has always been their home except in 1912-13 when they lived at McGaheysville, Rock county, Va. (Records of Mrs. Lucy-Knox [Lincoln] Bradford.)

Children, born: *a, c-f* at Lacey Spring; *b* at Harrisonburg:

    a. NORRIS-LINCOLN, born July 24, 1895.

    b. EDITH-LUCILE, born Feb. 29, 1898; died Oct. 25, 1905.

    c. CLAUDE-WINFIELD, born Aug. 5, 1900.

    d. MILLER-HUGHES, born Oct. 18, 1903.

    e. MARY-ELIZABETH, born Feb. 12, 1905.

    f. CATHERINE-KNOX, born June 2, 1906.

adaae ahf.   KATIE-BRIGHT, born Nov. 15, 1875; married S. S. Gordon, of whom nothing is known. She was thought to be living, 1914, either at New Orleans, La., or at Denver, Colo. They have had no children.

adaae hf. JACOB-BROADDUS, son of Jacob (*Jacob, John, Mordecai, Mordecai, Samuel*) and Nancy ([Lionberger] Rhodes) Lincoln of Linville, Va., born Sept. 8, 1830, at Linville Creek; died Feb. 17, 1898, at Tye River, Nelson county, Va. He was a farmer and lived in Rockbridge county, Va., near Lexington.

He married (1), Nov. 22, 1853, at Fairfield, Va., Mary-Isabella, daughter of William-Woodson and Eliza (Holtzman) Jasper of Rockingham county, Va., and later of Huntington, W. Va., born in Rockingham county; died Aug. 24, 1879, at Lexington. Mrs. Jasper's father, James Holtzman, and his wife Barbara came from Germany.

He married (2), Oct. 18, 1880, at Tye River, Mrs. Sarah (Jones) Shipman, daughter of George and Sarah (Pendleton) Jones of Tye River, and widow of John Shipman of Newmarket, Va., who died Jan. 28, 1858, at Newmarket in the twenty-eighth year of his age. She was born Apr. 22, 1836, at Tye River, and died there Oct. 18, 1890.

He married (3), Dec. 14, 1892, at Linville Creek, Dorcas-Sarah-Emeline, daughter of Richard-Snow and Mary-Elizabeth (Lincoln) Maupin, *adaae iac*, of Linville Creek, born Sept. 2, 1851, at Linville Creek; living, 1915, at New York City, but with a summer home at Tye River. Mr. Lincoln had no children by his second and third wives. (Records of Mrs. Jacob-Broadus Lincoln.)

Children, by first wife, born: *a* at Raphine, Va.; *b–i* at Lexington:

adaae hfa. WILLIAM-EFFIAH, born Apr. 27, 1855.
adaae hfb. JOHN-DAVID, born Nov. 24, 1856.
adaae hfc.   GEORGE-THOMAS, born Feb. 1, 1859; died in infancy.
adaae hfd.   IDA-ELIZA, born May 20, 1861; married, 1879, at Harpers Ferry, Va., Erasmus, son of David and Susan (Miller) Pultz of Lexington, born Sept. 5, 1856, at Lexington. He is a farmer. They are living, 1915, at Lexington.

Children, born at Lexington:
    a. ASHBY-LINCOLN, born March 23, 1881.
    b. GRAHAM-MOORE, born July 21, 1883.
    c. MAMIE-BELL, born Oct. 17, 1885.
    d. JACOB-DEWITT, born Apr. 12, 1887.

adaae hfe. SALLIE-JOSEPHINE, born Aug. 25, 1863; died in infancy.

adaae hff. MATTIE-BELLE, born Nov. 30, 1865; married, March 4, 1884,
    at Lexington, Charles-Preston, son of Greenberry and Mary-Hans-
    barger (Anderson) Rodes of Afton, Va., born Sept. 10, 1856, at Afton.
    They lived for ten years after marriage at Terre Haute, Ind., and then
    returned to Lexington, where they are now, 1915, living. He is a farmer.
        Children, born: *a-c* at Terre Haute; *d* at Lexington:
        a. MARY-ANNA, born Nov. 24, 1885.
        b. CHARLES-LINCOLN, born Jan. 29, 1889; mar. Mamie-Rhodes
            Printz.
        c. HELEN-MARGARET, born Jan. 19, 1895; died Aug. 7, 1895.
        d. ROBERT-PRESTON, born Dec. 4, 1904.

adaae hfg. "BABY," died in infancy.

adaae hfh. ASHBY-ABRAHAM, born Dec. 23, 1871.

adaae hfi. CHARLES-BROADDUS, born Apr. 4, 1873.

adaae hi. ABRAHAM-RANDOLPH, son of Jacob (*Jacob, John,
Mordecai, Mordecai, Samuel*) and Nancy ([Lionberger] Rhodes)
Lincoln of Linville, Va., born June 14, 1835, at Linville Creek;
died Oct. 20, 1875, at Denver, Colo., where he had lived. He
was for a time county treasurer, but retired before his death.

He married at Independence, Mo., Celia-Helen, daughter of
Dr. Joshua and Lucretia-Lurena (Drake) Hobbs. She was born
at New Franklin, Mo.; and died June 24, 1910, at Boonville,
Mo., where she had been living with her daughter. The family
records having been destroyed by fire, other dates are not ob-
tainable. (Records of Mrs. Nancy [Lincoln] Wallace.)

Child:

adaae hia. NANCY; married Arthur-Andrew Wallace. They are living,
    1914; at Boonville, Mo., and have no children.

adaaf ab. JOHN-MORDECAI, son of Jesse (*John, John, Mordecai, Mordecai, Samuel*) and Nancy (Brown) Lincoln of Eagle
Furnace, Tenn.; born Sept. 18, 1837, at Eagle Furnace; died
Aug. 25, 1914, at Nashville, Tenn. He was educated in the
Marysville, Tenn., preparatory school and the University of
Tennessee. He entered the Confederate army at the age of
nineteen, at first in the infantry, later in the cavalry. He served
through the entire war and was in prison at Camp Douglas for
two years. He was made deaf by the hardships he endured in
the war. He had no settled home, nor had he any definite occupation. He taught school some and farmed a little, but did
neither very long. In 1883 he was living at Chattanooga, Tenn.

He married, probably in Washington county, Tenn., Mrs. Sarah (Guinn) Wright, daughter of Thomas Guinn of Washington county. Her first husband's Christian name has not been learned, nor the dates of her birth and death. Her mother, Mrs. Thomas Guinn, was a daughter of Sydney Hale of Washington county, who is said to have belonged to the Massachusetts Hales. (Records of Miss Nannette-Brown Lincoln, *adaaf abd.*)

Children, born in Greene county, Tenn.:

adaaf aba. FELIX-ZOLLICOFFER, born Aug. 22, 1868; married, Sept. 10, 1886, at Gainesville, Ga., Barrington-Symrad, son of William-Monroe and Mary-Earle (Hackett) Sharp of Ringgold, Ga., born July 5, 1861, at Atlanta, Ga. They are living, 1917, at Atlanta. He is in the wholesale dry-goods business. They belong to the Presbyterian church.
  Children, born at Atlanta:
    a. ELIZABETH-EMILY, born March 22, 1888.
    b. McALLEN, born Oct. 19, 1891.
    c. HELEN, born July 3, 1896.
    d. ROBERT, born 1899; died aet. 1 year.
    e. BARRINGTON-SYMRAD, born 1901; died aet. 6 months.
adaaf abb. TENNESSEE, born Apr. 22, 1870; living, 1917, at New York, N. Y., unmarried.
adaaf abc. ADA-LEE, born Aug. 25, 1873; married Campbell-Douglas, son of John-Daniel Easterlin of Charleston, S. C., born in 1875 at Charleston. He was educated at Porter Military Academy, Charleston. They were living, 1917, at New York City.
  Children, born at Atlanta, Ga.:
    a. JOHN-DANIEL, born Aug. 29, 1897; mar. Helen Booth.
    b. DOUGLAS-LINCOLN, born Aug. 30, 1899. He was a first class seaman in the U. S. navy in the World war.
adaaf abd. NANNETTE-BROWN, born Sept. 8, 1875; living, 1917, in New York City, unmarried. She is a magazine writer.
adaaf abe. HUGH-BROWN, died Aug. 28, 1915, unmarried.

adaaf ac. JAMES-HAMILTON, son of Jesse (*John, John, Mordecai, Mordecai, Samuel*) and Nancy (Brown) Lincoln of Eagle Furnace, Tenn., born May 12, 1848, at Sparta, near Eagle Furnace; died June 8, 1899, at Chattanooga, Tenn. He fell from his office window and fractured his skull. He was a dentist doing business at Chattanooga, but living at Lookout Mountain till a short time before his death. He was educated at the University of Tennessee.

He married (1), Dec. 19, 1872, at Ringgold, Ga., Charity-Emma, daughter of Preston-Jornegan and Mary-Henderson (Peck) Lea of Ringgold, born Jan. 10, 1851, near Knoxville,

Tenn., or according to another authority at Dandridge, Tenn.
She died July 24, 1879, at Lookout Mountain. They lived on
an estate of ten acres "on the slope of Lookout Mountain" and
"on the old military road said to have been made by General
Andrew Jackson about 1812," which estate was conveyed, Apr.
21, 1873, by Robert Cravens to Mrs. C. Emma Lincoln, wife of
J. H. Lincoln. (Hamilton County, Tenn., Deeds, vol. O, Book
B, p. 230.) This estate was sold, May 30, 1912, by Jesse Lincoln and wife Mayme Lincoln, W. P. Lincoln and wife Lula
Goodwin Lincoln, and Hugh B. Lincoln (single) "only surviving
heirs of C. Emma Lincoln (deceased)," and was acknowledged
at Electra, Tex., by Hugh B. Lincoln and by Jesse Lincoln and
his wife Mayme, and at Sour Lake, Tex., by W. P. Lincoln and
wife Lula Goodwin. (*Ibid.*, vol. xi, book O, p. 182.)

He married (2), Sept. 6, 1881, at Ringgold, Ida-Beatrice,
daughter of William-Monroe and Mary-Earle (Hackett) Sharp
of Ringgold, born March 16, 1853, at Roswell, Ga.; living, 1917.
(Records corrected by Mrs. Adelia-Lane [Lincoln] Garretson,
adaaf acd.)

Children, by first wife, born at Lookout Mountain:

adaaf aca. JESSE, born Nov. 19, 1873; living, 1912, at Electra, Tex.; married
at Corsicana, Tex., Mayme Presley.
adaaf acb. WILLIAM-PRESTON, born Jan. 3, 1875; living, 1912, at Electra,
Tex.; married at Corsicana, Tex., Lula Goodwin.
Children:
adaaf acba. ABRAHAM, born May 9, 1901.
adaaf acbb. WILLIE-BEATRICE, born March 16, 1906.
adaaf acc. HUGH-BROWN, born March 5, 1877; living, 1912, at Electra,
Tex., unmarried.

Children, by second wife, born at Lookout Mountain:

adaaf acd. ADELIA-LANE, born Feb. 10, 1883; married, May 9, 1914, at
Houston, Tex., Warren-Harris Garretson. They are living, 1917, at
Beaumont, Tex. He is president of the Chamber of Commerce. She
is the society editor of a Beaumont newspaper. No children.
adaaf ace. ROBERT-ABRAHAM, born May 31, 1885.
adaaf acf. FREDERIC-ALBERT, born Dec. 28, 1887.

adaaf db. JOHN-CRAIGIN, son of Mordecai (*John, John,
Mordecai, Mordecai, Samuel*) and Clara (Paul) Lincoln of
Greeneville, Tenn., born Nov. 7, 1815, in Hardy county, Va.
(now West Virginia); died Dec. 24, 1849, at Memphis, Tenn.

He lived at Greeneville and at Eagle Furnace, Tenn., and at Memphis. He was a merchant. He was brought up by his grandfather Lincoln in Lebanon, Ohio, until he was over fifteen years of age, and then went to his father's in Greeneville.

He married, Dec. 7, 1837, at Sparta, Tenn., Jane, daughter of William and Melinda (Jarvis) Usrey of Sparta, born March 18, 1822, at Sparta; died May 4, 1880, in Smith county, Tenn. She married (2), Sept. 10, 1848, at Sparta, Nicholas Mercer, a physician at Alexandria, Tenn., who died Feb. 19, 1868, at Alexandria, and by whom she had two children, viz.: Flora, born Aug. 23, 1851, and Effie, born March 10, 1854. She married (3), Feb. 15, 1874, at Alexandria, Isaac Jones, a farmer living in Smith county, who died there Jan. 27, 1880. She was his second wife and had no children by him. (Records of Mrs. Josephine [Lincoln] Davis, *adaaf dbb.*)

Children, born *a, b* at Eagle Furnace; *c* at Memphis:

adaaf dba. WILLIAM-HENRY, born Feb. 5, 1840.
adaaf dbb. JOSEPHINE, born Jan. 22, 1843; married, Oct. 18, 1876, in Smith county, Tenn., Robert-Gilbert, son of John and Catherine (Redwine) Davis of Rowan county, N. C., born Oct. 15, 1819, at Rowan county; died Aug. 7, 1901, in Smith county. He was a farmer living in Smith county. After his death his widow lived at Alexandria, Tenn., until 1912 when she removed to Nashville, Tenn., where she now, 1916, resides with her daughter. (Records of Mrs. Josephine [Lincoln] Davis.)
    Children, born in Smith county:
      a. ROBERTA, born July 17, 1877; mar. George-Rowland Boyd.
      b. CHARLES-LINCOLN, born Nov. 27, 1879; mar. Willie-May Oliver.
      c. WILLIAM-GAY, born Oct. 12, 1881; mar. Irene Rutland.
      d. HALE-McCLELLAN, born June 3, 1885; living, 1916, unmarried.
adaaf dbc. LEWIS-CRAIGIN, born May 10, 1845.

adaah eb. JOHN-KARSNER, son of George (*Thomas, John, Mordecai, Mordecai, Samuel*) and Juliann (Gatewood) Lincoln of Liberty, Mo., born Dec. 21, 1821, near Lexington, Ky.; died Apr. 13, 1903, at Plattsburg, Mo. A newspaper obituary says he was born Dec. 29.

He was taken by his parents from Kentucky to Clay county, Mo., at the age of six months and, in 1844, he settled on a farm near Plattsburg in Clinton county where he passed the rest of his life, except for ten years, from 1849 to 1859, which he and his family passed in Kentucky. He built up a splendid farm of about seventeen hundred acres, which was cultivated and improved to a high degree. "He was a good neighbor, generous and charitable, honest and just minded," possessing an outspoken disposition and great public spirit. A strong admirer of Jefferson Davis he was grievously disappointed by the failure of the Southern Confederacy, to which he never became really reconciled. He was a Democrat of the old school and always an earnest supporter of his party's policies and, though seeking no office for himself, was ever an active supporter of his political friends.

He married, Jan. 15, 1845, at Liberty, Mo., Elmira-Taylor, daughter of Cullen and Louisiana (Schrader) Melone of Liberty, born June 11, 1828, at Liberty; died March 1, 1903, at Plattsburg. (Records of Mrs. John-Karsner Lincoln, Jr., *adaah ebd.*)

Children, born: *a, b* at Liberty; *c, d* at Lexington, Ky.:

adaah eba. GEORGIA, born Nov. 25, 1847; married, Dec. 24, 1882, on Excelsior farm, four miles south of Plattsburg, Mo., Benjamin-Owen, son of Benjamin and Juliet (Owen) Weller of Henderson, Ky., born Jan. 9, 1844, at Henderson. They have lived at Dallas, Tex., but are now, 1917, residing at Plattsburg. (Records of Mrs. Georgia [Lincoln] Weller.)
    Children, born at Dallas:
       a. JOHN-THERON, born Apr. 21, 1883; died Dec. 7, 1886.
       b. ELMIRA-JULIET, born Feb. 22, 1889; mar. John-Walker Stark.
adaah ebb. CULLEN-MELONE, born Jan. 5, 1850.
adaah ebc. ELLA B, born Feb. 25, 1852; married, June 5, 1877, on Excelsior farm, near Plattsburg, Mo., Washington Adams. He is a lawyer. They are living, 1917, at Kansas City, Mo.
    Child, born near Plattsburg:
       a. JOHN-WASHINGTON, born Aug. 21, 1882; living, 1917, unmarried.
adaah ebd. JOHN-KARSNER, born Apr. 6, 1854.

adaah ec. ROBERT-TALIAFERRO, son of George (*Thomas, John, Mordecai, Mordecai, Samuel*) and Juliann (Gatewood) Lincoln of Liberty, Mo., born Sept. 29, 1823, at Liberty; died Oct. 22, 1876; married in Clay county, Mo., a Miss Sally Thompson and had six children, perhaps in different order from that here given.

Children:

adaah eca. GEORGE, born June 3, 1852; living, 1916, at Trinidad, Colo. He is married and has two children.
    Children:
       a. BIRDIE V.
       b. WILLIAM-HARRY.
adaah ecb. STEPHEN.

adaah ecc. LUCY.
adaah ecd. EDWARD.
adaah ece. SAMUEL.
adaah ecf. WALTER.

adaah ee. PETER-GATEWOOD, son of George (*Thomas, John, Mordecai, Mordecai, Samuel*) and Juliann (Gatewood) Lincoln of Liberty, Mo., born Feb. 22, 1827, at Liberty. He was remembered in the will of his grandfather, Peter Gatewood of Fayette county, Ky., with a legacy of $2000 "because he has lived with me from infancy to manhood."

He married, July 31, 1849, in Fayette county, Ky., Mary-Ann Nelson, of whom nothing further has been learned except that she was a niece of John-Leland Howard who married Peter's sister, Jane-Cordelia. Their marriage is recorded at Lexington, Ky. They removed to Missouri and both died there before their only child was twelve years old.

Child:

adaah eea. EDWINA, married a Mr. Copeland and died *s. p.*

adaah ei. LEMUEL-SAUNDERS, son of George (*Thomas, John, Mordecai, Mordecai, Samuel*) and Juliann (Gatewood) Lincoln of Liberty, Mo., born Aug. 12, 1833, at Liberty; died March 24, 1907, at Excelsior farm, Plattsburg, Mo.

He married, Dec. 7, 1854, Sarah, daughter of John-Trimble and Julia-Ann Allen of Kentucky, born in 1834; died Oct. 21, 1914, at Fort Smith, Ark. Mr. Lincoln made his home at Excelsior farm, formerly the home of his brother, John-Karsner, now the home of Benjamin-Owen Weller, *adaah eba.* They are said to have had five children but the names of two only have been learned.

Children, born at Liberty:

adaah eia. CAROLINE, born 1856; died Oct. 21, 1914, at Fort Smith, Ark.; married, 1883, at Versailles, Ky., James-Chiles, son of Joseph-Chambers and Mary (Chiles) Irwin of Mt. Sterling, Ky., born, 1842, in Kentucky; living, 1915, at Fort Smith. He has been a lumberman, cattle dealer and ranchman. They lived at Versailles, Ky., Flag Ranch, Comanche county, Kan., and at Fort Smith. (Records of Julia-Lincoln Irwin, *adaah eiaa.*)

   Children, born: *a, c* at Flag Ranch; *b* at Versailles; *d* at Fort Smith:
   a. JULIA-LINCOLN, born Oct. 31, 1884; living, 1915, unmarried.

31

      b. FRANCIS-ALLEN, born Oct. 21, 1886; living, 1915, unmarried.

      c. JOSEPH-CHAMBERS, born Aug. 14, 1888; mar. Ruth-Catheryn MacLeod.

      d. SUSAN, born July 18, 1893; living, 1915, unmarried.

adaah eib. ANNA, married L. L. Timmons and was living, 1915, at Mt. Sterling, Ohio.

adaah ek. GEORGE-THOMAS, son of George (*Thomas, John, Mordecai, Mordecai, Samuel*) and Juliann (Gatewood) Lincoln of Liberty, Mo., born Oct. 9, 1836, near Liberty; living, 1917, two and a half miles from Bentonville, Ark., where he is engaged in fruit growing. He attended William Jewell college at Liberty, but did not graduate and in May, 1861, enlisted in the Confederate army and served through the war. He held the rank of captain and was attached to Colonel Joe Blackburn's regiment at one time, but for how long has not been learned.

He married (1), June 20, 1859, at Liberty, Virginia-Morton, daughter of George-Morton and Elizabeth-Curd (Lewis) Pryor of Clay county, Mo., born July 18, 1839, near Liberty; died, 1861, at Liberty. Her father, George-Morton Pryor, was born Feb. 20, 1804, in Trimble county, Ky.; his wife, Elizabeth-Curd Lewis, was born Aug. 4, 1810, in Jessamine county, Ky.

He married (2), in 1864, Mrs. Mattie (Halsey) Davis, widow of Dr. Green B. Davis of northern Louisiana, and daughter of Abraham A. and Elizabeth (LeFlore) Halsey of Rankin, Miss., and New Orleans, La. She was born about 1837 in Carroll county, Miss., and died at Fort Smith, Ark. (Thomas Halsey and Descendants, p. 339.)

He married (3), near Winona, Miss., Ellen S., daughter of Dr. William J. Sykes of Winona, born 1848, at Winona; died Dec. 13, 1910, at Bentonville.

He married (4), November, 1916, Mrs. Mary Lucas of Mayfield, Ky. Mr. Lincoln had no children by his last three wives. (Records of George-Thomas Lincoln and Mrs. George-Morton Lincoln, *adaah eka.*)

Child, by first wife, born at Liberty:

adaah eka. GEORGE-MORTON, born Feb. 5, 1861.

adaah el. CHARLES-HOWARD, son of George (*Thomas, John, Mordecai, Mordecai, Samuel*) and Juliann (Gatewood) Lincoln of

Liberty, Mo., born Feb. 15, 1839, at Liberty; died Jan. 15, 1915, at Plattsburg, Mo. He served as first lieutenant in the Confederate army under General Sterling Price. He was a farmer but had retired at the time of his death. He lived at Plattsburg.

He married, Aug. 20, 1863, at Liberty, Angie, daughter of George and Julia-Ann Smith of Winchester, Va., where she was born. (Records of Benjamin-Owen Weller, *adaah eba.*)

Children, born at South Plattsburg, Mo.:

adaah ela. FLOYD, born June 24, 1864; died 1882, at Plattsburg.

adaah elb. RUSSELL, born March 30, 1866. Has been married but has separated from his wife.

adaah elc. MARGARET, born July 16, 1869; living, 1920, at Kansas City, Mo. She is said to have married Magnus W. Barber of that place.

adaah eld. CHARLES-HOWARD, born Sept. 15, 1874. He has been twice married.

adaah ele. ANGIE, ⎫
⎪
⎬ born Aug. 27, 1879; ⎧ married a Mr. Williams, but they are separated. She is living, 1920, at Plattsburg. They had one child.
adaah elf. JULIA, ⎪
⎭ ⎨ married Col. Willis Wood, who is dead. She is living, 1920, at Kansas City, Mo.

adaah em. JAMES-EDWIN, son of George (*Thomas, John, Mordecai, Mordecai, Samuel*) and Juliann (Gatewood) Lincoln of Liberty, Mo., born Sept. 27, 1840, near Liberty; died March 18, 1896, at Liberty. He was educated in Clay county, Mo., graduating at William Jewell college in 1860. He then studied law at the Louisville, Ky., law school, where he graduated in 1862. He immediately opened a law office in Liberty but soon after went to Montana, where he engaged in trade until 1864, when he returned to Liberty and resumed the practice of law in partnership with Henry L. Routt, which partnership continued until 1867, when it was dissolved and Mr. Lincoln took as a partner Colonel W. H. Woodson, with whom he continued until 1873, after which he conducted his practice alone.

In 1871, he was elected city attorney of Liberty and, in 1872, prosecuting attorney for Clay county, in which latter office he continued two years, declining a re-election. In 1876, he was chosen representative in the General Assembly and took an active part in all the proceedings, being chairman of the special committee appointed to amend and conform the laws to the new constitution, which had just been adopted. In 1878, he was elected probate judge of Clay county, to which office he was re-elected in 1882, without opposition, but from which he resigned in 1884, and was then appointed by the Governor a curator of the University of Missouri, in which position he served for four years. He then removed to Colorado and established a bank at Buena Vista, the firm name being Lincoln, Hockaday and Co., but his health failing he sold out this business and returned to Liberty and resumed the practice of law, and purchasing the Liberty "Tribune" he edited it from May, 1888, to May, 1890.

In September, 1895, he became editor of the Liberty "Herald" and so continued until his death. He was, until 1894, a member of the Democratic party, but in that year he joined the Populist party. He was from his youth an ardent temperance advocate and never faltered in his allegiance to the men who were fighting the saloons in Clay county. In religious connection he was a member of the Christian church, which he joined while in college. He was a Free Mason, becoming a member of Liberty Lodge in 1862, and, in 1873, became identified with Liberty commandery of Knights Templar.

"Tried by all the tests, Mr. Lincoln was a good man and a good citizen. Faithful in all the relations of life, very kindly in feelings toward his fellow men, a good neighbor and friend, genial and pleasant in intercourse, always courteous, respectful of the opinions of others and firm in his own, of large public spirit, loving his country with a native's largest measure of love, without bitterness towards enemies or harshness towards rivals, never claiming as much as he merited, conceding to others all they could justly claim, he was in manners and spirit a gentleman of whom his kindred and friends may well be proud." (From an obituary notice in the Liberty Herald.)

He married, Dec. 7, 1865, at Liberty, Margaret-Pixley, daughter of Greenup and Catherine (Pixley) Bird of Liberty, born Oct. 2, 1845, at Liberty; living, 1915, at Bowling Green, Mo. (Records of Mrs. James-Edwin Lincoln.)

Children, born at Liberty:

adaah ema. LORA-BIRD, born 1866; died Aug. 29, 1869.
adaah emb. KATHARINE-BIRD, born May 10, 1873; married, June 30, 1900,

at Liberty, Robert-Lee, son of Col. M. E. and Mary-Ellen (Duncan) Motley of Bowling Green, Mo., born December, 1873, at Hartford, Mo. He graduated at William Jewell college in 1892, and at Ann Arbor in 1894. He is a lawyer and has been probate judge of Pike county, Mo., since 1902. They are living, 1915, at Bowling Green. Mrs. Motley is a member of the Daughters of the American Revolution, and is General Federation secretary for Missouri. She is a contributor to "The Missouri Woman."

Children, born at Bowling Green:
> a. DOROTHY-MARGARET, born Oct. 3, 1902.
> b. BLANCHE-DUNCAN, born Dec. 1, 1907.

adaah emc. GATEWOOD-SAUNDERS, born Aug. 5, 1875.

adaah emd. JAMES-EDWIN, born June 1, 1879.

adaah eme. CHARLES-PRINCETON, born March 27, 1885; died September, 1888.

adaah gd. ISAAC-WELLS, son of David (*Thomas, John, Mordecai, Mordecai, Samuel*) and America-Sanders (Gatewood) Lincoln of Clay county, Mo., born Oct. 30, 1829, in Fayette county, Ky., where his parents were temporarily living; died at Saint Joseph, Mo. He went to California in 1849, but remained there about a year and a half only, returning to Clay county where he was a farmer and breeder of fine horses until 1862, when he removed to Saint Joseph where he passed the remainder of his life. He was for a number of years the proprietor of the Pacific House in Saint Joseph, but did not run it himself. He was inventor, patentee and sole proprietor of a combination dough kneader, flour chest and sifter, which went by his name, and he was later engaged in manufacturing, making all kinds of machinery.

He married, Sept. 20, 1860, in Clay county, Marie-Louisa, daughter of Charles and Agnes ([Davenport] Barnett) Gilkey of Lexington, Ky., born Sept. 29, 1841, at Lexington; living, 1920, with her daughter at Independence, Mo. (Records of James-Claiborne Lincoln, *adaah gda;* Hist. of Buchanan County, Mo., p. 870.)

Children, born: *a* at Liberty, Mo.; *b-e* at Saint Joseph:

adaah gda. JAMES-CLAIBORNE, born Apr. 5, 1862.

adaah gdb. WILLIAM-DAVID, born May 3, 1864.

adaah gdc. SALLIE-KNIGHT, born Nov. 16, 1869; living, 1920, at Independence, Mo. She married Fleming Pendleton.

adaah gdd. DONIPHAN-RICE, born Feb. 12, 1874; living, 1920, unmarried.

adaah gde. ISAAC-WELLS, born Aug. 9, 1878; living, 1920, at Chicago, Ill., and is engaged in the lumber business, being president and treasurer

of the Lincoln Lumber Company. He married, Nov. 22, 1918, at South
Bend, Ind., Kathryn-Gould, daughter of Arthur-Henry and Ada-Gertrude (Rice) Wait, born March 30, 1885, at Sturgis, Mich.

adaga aa. JAMES-HANDSHAW, son of Thomas (*Benjamin,
Mordecai, Mordecai, Mordecai, Samuel*) and Mary (Evans)
Lincoln of Carmichaels, Pa., born Sept. 15, 1813, at North
Union, Pa.; died March 6, 1877, at Le Roy, Ill., according to his
nephew, Horace-Greely Lincoln, *adaga agf*, but his granddaugh-
ter, Una-Mae Daugherty, *adaga aaga*, says he was born in
February and that he was aged 62 years, 22 days, when he died.
If she is correct he must have died in March, 1875.

Mr. Lincoln taught school for a Mr. Mason who promised to
give him a classical education, but Mr. Mason's sudden death
prevented this. Several years later Mr. Lincoln became part
owner of a newspaper published at Brownsville, Pa., but becoming tired of this he went as second clerk on the steamboat
"Forsythe" to St. Louis, Mo., in 1837, where he secured employment on the "Globe-Democrat," of which paper he afterwards became, it is claimed, part or complete owner. Meeting
with reverses he removed, between 1840 and 1842, to Le Roy,
where he passed the rest of his life, engaged in the drug business.

He married, Sept. 12, 1841, at Buckels Grove, McLean
county, Ill., Nellie Merrifield, who was born Nov. 5, 1820, in
Green county, Ohio, and died March 21, 1898, at Le Roy.
(Records of Horace-Greely Lincoln, *adaga agf*.)

Children, born *a, c-g* at Le Roy; *b* at Buckels Grove:

adaga aaa. THOMAS-ABRAHAM, born June 21, 1843.

adaga aab. BENJAMIN-FRANKLIN, born March 6, 1845; died in Nebraska.
He was married and had three daughters.

adaga aac. MARY-ELLEN, born Apr. 7, 1847; married Alexander Dixon
and was living, 1919, at Le Roy.
  Child:
    a. A DAUGHTER, married Aldo Smith.

adaga aad. MORDECAI, born Jan. 27, 1849; died Feb. 25, 1896, at Cainesville, Mo., unmarried.

adaga aae. EDGAR C., born Oct. 8, 1852; living, 1918, at Farmer City,
Ill., unmarried.

adaga aaf. JAMES T., born Oct. 8, 1855; died July 22, 1916, at Bloomington,
Ill., unmarried.

adaga aag. EMMA-ELIZA, born June 7, 1862; died Feb. 11, 1907, at Maryville,
Mo.; married, Feb. 21, 1882, at Ridgeway, Mo., George-Byron, son of
George and Mary (Wilson) Daugherty of Callensburg, Pa., born Oct. 17,

1851, at Callensburg; living, 1918. He is with the Business Men's Accident Insurance Co. They lived at Ridgeway, Mine LaMotte and Maryville, Mo. (Records of Miss Una-Mae Daugherty.)
    Child:
        a. UNA-MAE, mar. Porter-Palmer Bowsher, Leon, Va.

adaga ag. THOMAS-BOONE, son of Thomas (*Benjamin, Mordecai, Mordecai, Mordecai, Samuel*) and Mary (Evans) Lincoln of Carmichaels, Pa., born March 16, 1825, at North Union, Pa.; died Feb. 14, 1901, at Carmichaels, Cumberland Township, Pa., whither he removed after his marriage and where he passed the rest of his life. He followed farming for several years and, later, was a large stock dealer.

He married, in Cumberland Township, Mariah-Jackson Hart of Cumberland, born Nov. 11, 1826, at Cumberland; died March 25, 1879, at Carmichaels. (Records of Horace-Greely Lincoln, *adaga agf.*)

Children, born at Carmichaels:

adaga aga. VIRGIL-ASHMEAD, born Nov. 6, 1847; died Sept. 8, 1877, at Carmichaels, unmarried. He was a teacher.

adaga agb. JAMES-SILLIMAN, born June 18, 1850; died March 14, 1903, at Carmichaels, where he had lived. He was a carpenter and cabinet-maker. He married Susan Groomes. They had no children.

adaga agc. THOMAS-LIONEL, born Feb. 17, 1856; died Aug. 24, 1902, at Mountain Lake Park, Md. He was by profession an attorney-at-law, also an author and writer. He married Harriet Flenniken, who died before Apr. 30, 1900, on which date he, then living at Carmichaels, gave a quit-claim deed to lands acquired from the Flennikens, the deed being witnessed by his nephew, Robert-Todd Lincoln, *adaga agda.* (Fayette County Deeds, vol. 194, p. 500.) He had no children.

adaga agd. CHARLES-JENNINGS, born Nov. 5, 1857.

adaga age. LUTHER-AXTELL, born Sept. 15, 1859; living, 1915, unmarried. He is a physician and pharmacist.

adaga agf. HORACE-GREELY, born Oct. 10, 1863.

adaga agg. WILLIAM-GRIM, born May 27, 1865; living, 1915, unmarried. He is a music teacher.

adaga ga. HENRY, son of Mordecai (*Benjamin, Mordecai, Mordecai, Mordecai, Samuel*) and Jane (Gilpin) Lincoln of Dunbar, Pa., born, 1832, at Dunbar; died about 1861 or 62, probably at Dunbar.

He married, Apr. 10, 1856, at Smithfield, Pa., Huldah, daughter of Jesse and Susanna Leech of Smithfield, who was born about 1831, at Smithfield. They lived for a few years at Smithfield but separated about five or six years after marriage, each going to his own family, and Mr. Lincoln died soon after. In March, 1863, Jesse Leech removed to Allen county, Ohio, and Mrs. Lincoln went with him, taking her son Charles. She afterwards married a wealthy physician and was living, 1915, at Los Angeles, Calif., aged eighty-four years. (Information of Mrs. Elizabeth [Lincoln] Haldeman, *adaga ge*, and Mrs. Annie-Elizabeth [Carson] Moore, *adaga abd*.)

A deed dated Jan. 14, ———— and recorded July 13, 1870, says: Henry Lincoln of Fayette county "in consideration of certain debts paid for him by Jane Lincoln (his mother) as also his care and expense accrued in this his present and perhaps his last sickness," quit claims all title to one tenth part of the land on which Mordecai Lincoln (his father) died intestate, to Jane Lincoln. No wife signed this deed. (Fayette County Deeds, Book 22, p. 425.)

Children, born at Smithfield:

adaga gaa. CHARLES-BENTON-FREMONT, died in 1912 or 1913, at Los Angeles, Calif. He remained with his grandfather until maturity, receiving a common school education. He then entered the employ of the Fort Wayne and Chicago Railroad Company, in the ticket office at Lima, Ohio. After a few years he procured a position with the Southern Pacific Railroad Company at Denver, Colo., where he remained for three or four years, when he removed to San Francisco, Calif., serving the same company until 1905, in several positions among which was that of general passenger accountant of the entire system. When the new railroad, commonly known as Senator Clark's road, was built from Salt Lake City to Los Angeles, he left the Southern Pacific and entered the employ of the new road, being in the general offices at Los Angeles, and remained there until his death.

He married at Denver a Miss Kerr. (Information of Snyder Leech, of Smithfield, Pa.)

adaga gab. A DAUGHTER, who died about the same time as her father, aged two years.

adaga gd. MORDECAI, son of Mordecai (*Benjamin, Mordecai, Mordecai, Mordecai, Samuel*) and Jane (Gilpin) Lincoln of Dunbar, Pa., born Sept. 1, 1838, at Dunbar; died Jan. 14, 1912, at Uniontown, Pa. He was for sixteen years a teacher in the district schools; after that a farmer and agent for nursery stock. In 1861, he enlisted in Company C, 85th Pennsylvania infantry, and was discharged in September, 1862, for incapacity, having been wounded in the hand. He was frequently called Mordecai S Lincoln, but apparently had no middle name, and perhaps used the initial "S" to distinguish him from his father.

He married, Apr. 23, 1863, at Uniontown, Mary-Elizabeth, daughter of Edward and Mary (Martin) Rose of North Union, Pa., born Oct. 11, 1848, at North Union; living, 1915, at Uniontown. After their marriage they lived at North Union for twenty-five years, then for twelve years at McLellantown, Pa., until 1900, and after that at Uniontown. (Records of Mrs. Mordecai Lincoln.)

Children, born at North Union:

adaga gda. EDWARD-ROSE, born June 3, 1864.

adaga gdb. CHARLES-HENRY, born June 3, 1867; married, June 26, 1890, Lizzie, daughter of Conrad and Elizabeth (Bowman) Deffenbaugh of Nicholson, Pa. He is an engineer on the Baltimore and Ohio Railroad. They are living, 1915, at Connellsville, Pa. They have no children.

adaga gdc. MARY-JANE, born Oct. 8, 1869; married, Oct. 17, 1890, Isadore-Lincoln, son of David and Mary (Poundstone) Kauffman of Jumonville, Pa., born 186– at Jumonville. They are living, 1915, at Uniontown, Pa. He is a plumber.

    Children:
       a. MABEL-MARIE, born Apr. 2, 1895; unmarried, 1915.
       b. CATHERINE, born Aug. 15, 1897; unmarried, 1915.
       c. KENNETH, born July, 1908.

adaga gdd. SARAH-ANN, born May 16, 1871; living, 1915, unmarried.

adaga gde. CLARA, born July 22, 1877; died Apr. 26, 1878, and is buried in the Lincoln burying ground at North Union.

adaga gdf. BELLE, born July 4, 1879; died Jan. 24, 1880, and is buried in the Lincoln burying ground at North Union.

adaga gdg. LILLIAN-HOGSETT, born June 24, 1881; married, Jan. 30, 1904, at Brownsville, Pa., James-Bailey, son of James and Elizabeth (Moxley) Davis of Tippecanoe, Pa., born July 13, 1880, at Tippecanoe. They are living, 1915, at Uniontown, Pa. He is a clerk in a shoe store.

    Children, born at Uniontown:
       a. CHARLES-LINCOLN, born Dec. 17, 1905.
       b. ROBERT-FRANKLIN, born Dec. 21, 1908.
       c. JAMES-BAILEY, born March 21, 1911.

adaga gdh. HARRY-BENJAMIN, born May 4, 1884; married, Apr. 23, 1905, at Waynesburg, Pa., Mary, daughter of Gordon and Henrietta (Campbell) Howard of Waynesburg. They are living, 1915, at Connellsville, Pa. He is a locomotive engineer on the Baltimore and Ohio Railroad. They have no children.

adaga gf. EDWARD-GILPIN, son of Mordecai (*Benjamin, Mordecai, Mordecai, Mordecai, Samuel*) and Jane (Gilpin) Lincoln of Dunbar, Pa., born Aug. 27, 1844, at Dunbar; died

July 14, 1906, at Dunbar, where he had passed his whole life. He was a stone-mason.

He married about 1867, at Uniontown, Pa., Lucy-Ann, daughter of Zebley and Mary (Sweitser) Moast of Mount Braddock, Pa., born in 1855. They were married before Jan. 6, 1868, on which date Edward G. Lincoln and Lucy his wife of Dunbar conveyed to Joseph T. Shepler of Dunbar one half acre of land and a one story house "now occupied by said Lincoln." (Fayette County Deeds, Book xxxvii, p. 363.)

On Jan. 13, 1908, the homestead in Dunbar was sold and the deed signed by the following: Lucy Lincoln, B. F. Lincoln and Cora Lincoln, Ella Stutler and Hiram Stutler her husband, Matilda Keffer and Albert Keffer her husband, Elias H. Lincoln and Alice Lincoln his wife, Charles Lincoln and Elizabeth Lincoln his wife, M. J. Lincoln and Isabella Lincoln his wife, all of Dunbar Borough, Connellsville and Dunbar township. (*Ibid.*, Book cclxxxii, p. 47.)

Mrs. Lincoln married (2), December, 1914, at Dunbar, John Gengerich of Brownsville, Pa., where they are now, 1915, living. (Information of Mrs. Mary-Elizabeth [Rose] Lincoln, *agada gd.*)

Children, born at Dunbar:

adaga gfa. BENJAMIN-FRANKLIN, born May 28, 1869.

adaga gfb. NELLIE-JANE, born Jan. 22, 1872; married (1), Aug. 27, 1897, at Dunbar, William-Jacob, son of Thomas-Jefferson and Hannah (Davis) Farr, born about 1868; died March 6, 1898, at Dunbar, aged about 30 years. He was a blacksmith and lived at Dunbar. They had no children.

She married (2), Oct. 14, 1902, at Dunbar, Hiram-Lakin, son of William-Winfield and Olive (Pope) Stutler, who was born in Doddridge county, W. Va. They are living, 1915, at Dunbar. He is a car finisher.

Children, by second husband, born: *a, b* at Coalton, W. Va.; *c-e* at Dunbar:

    a.   HAYWARD-LAWRENCE STUTLER, born Apr. 20, 1904.
    b.   WILLIAM-EDWARD STUTLER, born March 6, 1906.
    c.   CECIL-ERNEST STUTLER, born Jan. 2, 1908.
    d.   NELLIE-ESTELLE STUTLER, born Aug. 2, 1910.
    e.   LILLA-PEARL STUTLER, born Jan. 6, 1914; died Apr. 18, 1914.

adaga gfc. MATILDA-CRAIG, born Aug. 3, 1874; married Albert Keffer. He is a carpenter. They live, 1915, at Brownsville, Pa.

adaga gfd. CHARLES-EDWARD, ⎫   ⎧ married Elizabeth Alderson; lives at Dunbar. A stone-cutter.

adaga gfe. ELIAS-HUDSON, ⎬ born June, 1877; ⎨ married Alice Rout; lives at Hampton, Va. A stone-mason.

adaga gff. JAMES-McCAIN, born 1879; married Isabella McCain. They are living, 1915, at Peachem P. O., Dunbar. He is an engineer.

adaga gh. BENJAMIN-FRANKLIN, son of Mordecai (*Benjamin, Mordecai, Mordecai, Mordecai, Samuel*) and Jane (Gilpin) Lincoln of Dunbar, Pa., born June 11, 1847, at Dunbar. At the age of sixteen he commenced to teach school in Fayette county, Pa., at which he continued for three years. He then went for a year to Michigan University at Ann Arbor, and at the age of twenty went to La Salle county, Ill., where he taught school for two years. He then studied law at Ottawa, Ill., and was admitted to the bar in 1872. Since then he has practised his profession. In 1890 he was elected county judge for La Salle county, which office he held for four years. He then formed a partnership with William H. Stead, under the firm name of Lincoln & Stead, which continued until Mr. Stead's election as Attorney General of the State in 1905, since which he has practised alone. For several years he was Mr. Stead's chief assistant and participated in the preparation of several very important cases. He has built up a large and successful law practice and, aside from that, was chiefly instrumental in establishing on a permanent basis Ottawa's most important industrial institution, the Federal Plate Glass factory.

He married (1), Apr. 24, 1873, at Ottawa, Nellie, daughter of Russell-Kendall and Susan (Wakey) Brown of La Salle county, born Nov. 24, 1855, in La Salle county; died Nov. 13, 1885, at Ottawa.

He married (2), Feb. 3, 1887, at Ottawa, Mary-Elizabeth, daughter of William and Mary-Elizabeth (Hise) Osman of Ottawa, born Dec. 24, 1858, at Ottawa. Her parents were natives of Pennsylvania and removed to Illinois about 1840, before their marriage. Mr. Osman was editor for over fifty years of "The Ottawa Free Trader." Mr. and Mrs. Lincoln are living, 1915, at Ottawa. (Records of Benjamin-Franklin Lincoln.)

Children, by first wife, born at Ottawa:

adaga gha. WALTER-KENDALL, born Oct. 11, 1876.

adaga ghb. MAUDE-ANNE, born Nov. 12, 1879. She is unmarried. She spent four years in Vienna and Paris in the study of piano music. She is now, 1915, living at Hollidaysburg, Pa., where she has charge of the department of music in a school in that city.

Child, by second wife, born at Ottawa:

adaga ghc. KATHERINE-MARY, born Feb. 2, 1892; living, 1915, unmarried.

adaga gi. THOMAS-JEFFERSON, son of Mordecai (*Benjamin, Mordecai, Mordecai, Mordecai, Samuel*) and Jane (Gilpin) Lincoln of Dunbar, Pa., born July 7, 1849, at Dunbar; died Jan. 3, 1900, at South Connellsville, Pa. These dates are from the family Bible, except that his birth is given therein as 1847, which is probably an error for 1848 or 1849, the latter perhaps more likely. He was a stone-mason and lived at Dunbar.

He married, June 30, 1870, Margaret-Ellen Yaw, who was born Oct. 31, 1851, and died Jan. 1, 1908, or 1909.

March 11, 1876, Thomas J. Lincoln and Ellen his wife of Connellsville sold land in Dawson, Pa., for $600. In this deed she signs herself Maggie E. Lincoln. On March 23, 1885, and May 24, 1887, Margaret E. Lincoln and Thomas J. Lincoln, her husband, sold land in West Vanderbilt, Pa., purchased in 1883 of Joseph Oglenee and Rebecca his wife of East Liberty, Pa. (Fayette County Deeds, Books 32, p. 94; 65, p. 183; 72, p. 488.)

Children, born at Dunbar:

adaga gia. MARY-ELIZABETH, born Jan. 27, 1871; died in a home for the feeble minded.
adaga gib. JOSEPH H., born Sept. 11, 1872; died Oct. 5, 1872.
adaga gic. JAMES-DERNELL, born March 22, 1875.
adaga gid. WILLIAM-ROGERS, born Oct. 18, 1878.
adaga gie. GEORGE-WASHINGTON, born Apr. 1, 1881. He is a brick-layer by trade and was living until 1916, at Connellsville, Pa., but removed that year to Youngstown, Ohio. He is married and has one child.

adagb de. BENJAMIN-FRANKLIN, son of Jesse (*John, Mordecai, Mordecai, Mordecai, Samuel*) and Hannah (Jones) Lincoln of Uniontown, Pa., born Sept. 17 or 20, 1820, at Uniontown; died Feb. 8, 1868, at Columbus, Ohio. He was married and his wife's name was Martha, but nothing further has been learned of her save that she is said to have married (2) a Mr. Huston. (Genealogy of David Jones, pp. 88-9.)

Children:

adagb dea. BELLE. She died in 1916 or 1917, at St. Petersburg, Fla. She married John Miller.
adagb deb. EDITH, married Willis Pyatt and was living, 1916, at St. Petersburg, Fla.

adafb dh. JOHN-PATTERSON, son of Jesse (*John, Mordecai, Mordecai, Mordecai, Samuel*) and Hannah (Jones) Lincoln of Uniontown, Pa., born Feb. 18, 1828, at Uniontown.

He married (1), in 1852, Amy Trout.

He married (2), Sept. 15, 1882, Ellen Kennedy, by whom he had no children. (Genealogy of David Jones, pp. 89-90.)

Child, by first wife:

adagb dha. HESTER, born Oct. 17, 1853; married, Apr. 16, 1873, John-Henry Collins. They were said to be living, 1915, at Lancaster, Fairfield county, Ohio.
Children:
a. HELEN-REBECCA, born Aug. 2, 1874.
b. ROSALIA-AMY, born Jan. 25, 1875; mar. Albert J. Rundio.

adagb dj. RICHARD-STOKES, son of Jesse (*John, Mordecai, Mordecai, Mordecai, Samuel*) and Hannah (Jones) Lincoln of Uniontown, Pa., born Feb. 18, 1832, at Uniontown; died in 1871, being lost in a severe snowstorm that winter in the mountains of West Virginia. His body was never recovered. He was a tinsmith and lived at Uniontown. He served in the Union army in the Civil war.

He married, Apr. 10, 1857, at Uniontown, Hannah-Ann, daughter of Leroy and Sallie (Sutton) Haymaker of Uniontown, born Oct. 9, 1830, at Uniontown; died Dec. 30, 1909, at Uniontown. (Genealogy of David Jones, p. 90; Records of Leroy-Sherman Lincoln, *adagb dje.*)

Children, born at Uniontown:

adagb dja. MARGARET-JANE, born Sept. 27, 1858; married, July 15, 1874, at New Salem, Pa., Lacy-Evans, son of George and Ruth (Moore) Dearth of New Salem, born Jan. 2, 1856, at New Salem. They are living, 1915, near New Salem. He is a farmer.
Children, born near New Salem:
a. MINNIE-LINCOLN, born Nov. 4, 1875; living, 1915, unmarried.
b. SALLIE-PEARL, born May 26, 1877; living, 1915, unmarried.
c. GEORGE-BAIRD, born June 28, 1883; living, 1915, unmarried.
d. BLANCHE-MOORE, born June 26, 1890; living, 1915, unmarried.
e. MARGUERITE-EVANS, born Apr. 9, 1892; living, 1915, unmarried.
adagb djb. RICHARD-ELLSWORTH, } born May 24, 1861; { died June, 1861.
adagb djc. JESSE-LEROY, } { died June, 1861.
adagb djd. SALLIE-HAYMAKER, born June 24, 1862; living, 1915, at Uniontown, unmarried.
adagb dje. LEROY-SHERMAN, born Aug. 21, 1866.

adagb fb. WILLIAM-HARRISON, son of William (*John, Mordecai, Mordecai, Mordecai, Samuel*) and Diadama (Briggs) Lincoln of Westville Center, N. Y., born Dec. 14, 1837, at Westville Center. He was a farmer, living at West Constable, N. Y., until about 1886, when he removed to Plattsburg where he was living in 1915, and where he was working for the city as foreman.

He married, March 31, 1862, at Bombay, N. Y., Frances-Louisa, daughter of Stephen-Vanranselar and Mary-Araminta (Trumbull) Parr of Bombay, born March 7, 1844, at Bombay; living, 1915. (Records of William-Harrison Lincoln.)

Children, born: *a-d* at West Constable; *e* at Plattsburg:

adagb fba. FRANCES-ELOISE, born March 31, 1863; married, Jan. 24, 1884, at Lyon Mountain, N. Y., George-Henry, son of Joseph-Conrad and Mary (Ayres) Myers of Dannemora, N. Y., born Nov. 19, 1856, at Dannemora. Mary Ayres was descended from Robert Ayres, a sergeant in the Revolution, who was the messenger, according to family tradition, who conveyed to Jane McCrea a message from her lover, Lieut. David Jones, urging her to submit to an Indian escort to convoy her to Burgoyne's army to be married. Mr. and Mrs. Lincoln are living, 1916, at Plattsburg. He is a merchant.

Children, born at Lyon Mountain:
  a. HELEN-MARY, born Sept. 8, 1885.
  b. FLORENCE-EDNA, born Jan. 21, 1887; mar. John H. Brandt.
  c. MARY-FRANCES, born Jan. 30, 1889; died Sept. 15, 1910.
  d. CHARLES-RALPH, born Aug. 3, 1893.

adagb fbb. CHARLES-EGBERT, born Feb. 7, 1865; married, Nov. 18, 1895, at Lee, Mass., Mary, daughter of Langham and Anna (Summerfield) Booth of Albany, N. Y., born Jan. 1, 1870, at Liverpool, England. Her parents came from England with their family in the early seventies. Mr. Lincoln has been connected with the United States Railway mail service for thirty years. He is now, 1916, chief clerk of that service at Albany, where he has lived since Jan. 15, 1912. They have no children.

adagb fbc. EDNA-ALICE, born June 29, 1867; married, Jan. 29, 1903, at Plattsburg, Eugene-Malcome, son of James and Catherine (Wilkins) Bishop of Mayfield, N. Y., born Oct. 9, 1848, at Mayfield. They were living, 1915, at Gloversville, N. Y. He was a glove manufacturer, and died early in April, 1916. They had no children.

adagb fbd. HELEN-MARY, born Jan. 18, 1871; married, Jan. 5, 1909, at Gloversville, N. Y., William-Wilson, son of William-Henry and Margaret-Elizabeth (Betts) Conaughty of Cohoes, N. Y., born Dec. 7, 1859, at Cohoes. They have lived since marriage at Watervliet, N. Y. He is a "railroad man." They have no children.

adagb fbe. DAISY-MAY, } born Feb. 6, 1876; { died June 6, 1877.
adagb fbf. DORA-DELL, }   { died June 15, 1876.
adagb fbg. WILLIAM-ANDREW, born June 14, 1878; died same day.
adagb fbh. WILLIAM-HENRY, born Aug. 20, 1886; died Feb. 21, 1913, unmarried.

adahb bb. GEORGE-VASHTINE, son of William (*Thomas, Thomas, Mordecai, Mordecai, Samuel*) and Lydia (Myers) Lincoln of Atglen, Pa., born Nov. 11, 1811, at Atglen; died Oct. 19, 1888, at Philadelphia, Pa. He was a farmer and passed practically his whole life on a farm about four miles from Atglen, near Parkesburg.

He married, Sept. 4, 1834, at Lancaster, Pa., Mary, daughter of Stacy and Mary (Smith) Morris of New Jersey and Pennsylvania, born Nov. 14, 1810, in Chester county, Pa.; died Apr. 5, 1896, at Philadelphia. Her will dated Aug. 22, 1893, says she was then living in Philadelphia and names her six living children. (Philadelphia Wills, vol. 185, p. 417.) Her grandfather, Edward Smith of Philadelphia, was a sea-captain; her father, Stacy Morris, was born Apr. 7, 1780, and her mother, Mary Smith, was born in May, 1786. (Records of Samuel-Wilson Lincoln, *adahb bbi.*)

Children, born at Atglen:

adahb bba. RUTH-ANN, born June 28, 1835; died May 28, 1902, at Philadelphia; married, Sept. 19, 1872, at Parkesburg, Pa., John, son of James Stewart of county Tyrone, Ireland, born in 1833, in Ireland; died May 17, 1903, at Philadelphia, where he had lived. He was a painter. They had no children.

adahb bbb. NEWTON, born October, 1837; died October, 1837.

adahb bbc. THOMAS-OSBORN, born Nov. 6, 1839; died Apr. 19, 1842.

adahb bbd. LYDIA-PRISCILLA, born Oct. 15, 1841; died March 15, 1863, at Parkesburg, Pa., unmarried.

adahb bbe. SARAH-JANE, born Feb. 22, 1844; living, 1916, at East Downington, Pa.; married, Nov. 25, 1869, at Parkesburg, George-Washington Wagner, born June 29, 1829, at Compassville, Chester county, Pa.; died Jan. 30, 1893, at Philadelphia. They lived first at Parkesburg, where he was a farmer, but removed, later, to Philadelphia.

Child, born at Parkesburg:

    a. GRACE-OLIVIA, born Feb. 3, 1871; mar. William Carey.

adahb bbf. OLIVIA-ELIZABETH, born Sept. 29, 1845; living, 1913, at Atglen; married, Nov. 18, 1869, at Parkesburg, Pa., Andrew-Jackson, son of Charles and Nancy (Kirkpatrick) Irwin of Parkesburg, born March 2, 1837, at Newcastle, Del.; died July 22, 1912, at Atglen. They lived at Atglen and he was by trade a blacksmith. He served in the Civil war, a member of Company L, Pennsylvania volunteer cavalry. He was at one time postmaster of Atglen.

Children, born at Atglen:

    a. RUTH-LILLIAN, born Apr. 26, 1871; mar. John Thompson.

    b. ANNA-ELIZABETH, born Feb. 6, 1873; died Feb. 21, 1873.

    c. MARY-LINCOLN, born Jan. 23, 1876; living, 1913, unmarried.

    d. HELEN-CECILIA, born May 5, 1885; living, 1913, unmarried.

adahb bbg. Mary-Cecilia, born Apr. 6, 1847; died Oct. 23, 1913, at Chicago,
Ill.; married, Apr. 26, 1883, at Parkesburg, Pa., Alfred-Lea, son of Joseph
and Mary-Ann (Caldwell) Carey of Chester county, Pa., born Oct. 1,
1841, in Delaware county, Pa.; died Dec. 23, 1892, at Philadelphia, Pa.
He was a lawyer. They lived at Philadelphia. They had no children.
adahb bbh. George-Eckert, born Sept. 2, 1848; died January, 1918, at
Chicago, Ill. He left his father's farm as a boy and became an apprentice
in the printing establishment of Ashmead and Company, Philadelphia,
the first office in the United States to use a power printing press. On
the completion of his apprenticeship in his twenty-first year, Mr. Lincoln
took a trip to the far West and then travelled back and forth across the
country, working as a printer in many towns and cities. He was at one
time part owner of the "North Missouri Courier" of Hannibal, Mo.,
and, afterwards, publisher of a chain of Colorado mining town newspapers. Tiring of the printing business he joined the "J & J" outfit
as a plainsman and, in this capacity, travelled through the West and
Northwest, particularly in the Black Hills region. In 1880 he went on
the road selling printing material and in 1886 entered the employ of the
Mergenthaler Linotype Company, becoming its Chicago agent in 1902,
which position he held until his death.

He married (1), March 17, 1870, at Hannibal, Mary-Loreno, daughter
of Philip and Barbara (Miller) Heiss of Hannibal, born 1850, at Hannibal;
died in 1908, at St. Louis, Mo. They were divorced in 1875, having had
one child who died an infant in 1871. Philip Heiss was a native of Paris,
France, and emigrated to Hannibal where he died before his daughter's
marriage.

Mr. Lincoln married (2), Feb. 28, 1889, at Philadelphia, Mary, daughter
of Washington and Mary (Vandever) Yates of Philadelphia, born Nov. 9,
1845, at Philadelphia. They had no children.

adahb bbi. Samuel-Wilson, born July 18, 1852.

adahb bc. Thomas, son of William (*Thomas, Thomas, Mordecai, Mordecai, Samuel*) and Lydia (Myers) Lincoln of Atglen,
Pa., born March 7, 1813, at Atglen; died March 4, 1857, at
Gordonville, Pa. He was a cabinet-maker and lived at Leacock
and Gordonville, Lancaster county, Pa.

He married at Reading, Pa., Elizabeth, daughter of John and
Elizabeth (Good) Erb of Strasburg, Pa., born July 16, 1823, at
Strasburg; died Feb. 17, 1910, at Intercourse, Pa. (Records of
Mrs. Margaret-Priscilla [Lincoln] Rutter, *adahb bce.*)

Children, born: *a, d* at Leacock; *b, c* at New Milltown; *e* at
Gordonville:

adahb bca. George-Lewis, born Feb. 16, 1841; died May 1, 1860, unmarried.
adahb bcb. Elizabeth-Ann, born Nov. 9, 1842; married, Dec. 9, 1875, at
Lancaster, Pa., Jonathan-Roland, son of Cyrus and Elizabeth-Anna
(Eaby) Miller of Millcreek, Pa., born Sept. 25, 1841, at Millcreek. He
was in the harness business for twenty-eight years at Intercourse, Pa.,

then a farmer at Spring Garden, Pa. They are living, 1914, at Intercourse.
Children, born at Intercourse:
- a. MARGARET-MAE, born June 22, 1878; mar. Harry-Reaux-Martin Kissenger.
- b. JOSEPH-CLYDE, born Apr. 14, 1883; mar. Elsie-Reidenbach Eberly.

adahb bcc. EMMA-FRANCES, born Dec. 2, 1844; died in the Spring of 1902; married James Scott.
Children:
- a. IRA,
- b. DAISY,
- c. RALPH, } all died before 1914.
- d. HOWARD,
- e. LEWIS,
- f. JAMES, living, 1917, at Lancaster, Pa.
- g. GROVER, living, 1917, at Gordonville, Pa.

adahb bcd. JOHN-ERB, born Aug. 1, 1847.

adahb bce. MARGARET-PRISCILLA, born Sept. 16, 1849; living, 1914, at East Downington, Pa.; married, Dec. 27, 1871, at Compassville, Pa., Jacob R., son of Eli and Elizabeth (Skiles) Rutter of Intercourse, Pa., born Nov. 14, 1842, at Milltown, Pa.; died June 23, 1911, at Intercourse, where they had lived. He was a farmer. He held the office of County Commissioner from 1893 to 1896, and was a bank director.
Children, born at Intercourse:
- a. MINNIE-LYTLE, born Sept. 29, 1872; mar. John-Harry Martin.
- b. ELIZABETH-SKILES, born Aug. 15, 1874; mar. Frederick Leibfreid.
- c. JACOB-BLANCE, born Apr. 9, 1876; died Apr. 11, 1879.
- d. ELI, born Jan. 11, 1878; died Apr. 17, 1879.
- e. WILLIAM-EVANS, born Jan. 24, 1880; mar. Lydia-Magdaline Bair.
- . CARRIE-LINCOLN, born Oct. 22, 1882; mar. Walter-Franklin Mylin.
- g. HARRIET-CLEVELAND, born Nov. 8, 1884; died Dec. 29, 1901.
- h. EFFIE-THORNTON, born Feb. 23, 1889; mar. Park-Leaman Plank.
- i. MAGGIE-CAREY, born Dec. 4, 1890; died Nov. 3, 1891.

adahb bd. GERMAN-DICKENSON, son of William (*Thomas, Thomas, Mordecai, Mordecai, Samuel*) and Elizabeth (Duross) Lincoln of Lancaster county, Pa., born Apr. 9, 1822, in Sadsbury township, Lancaster county; died Dec. 11, 1891, at Wilmington, Del., where he had lived. He was a ship-joiner.

He married (1), Sept. 2, 1846, at Wilmington, Rachel-Potts, daughter of William and Rachel (Dubois) Holston of Naaman's Creek, Newcastle county, Del., born 1824, at Naaman's Creek; died Apr. 15, 1864, at Wilmington.

He married (2), Jan. 18, 1866, at Wilmington, Mary-Rebecca, daughter of Henry-Gregg and Rachel-Logan (Brown) Missimer

32

of Strickersville, Pa., born Feb. 23, 1844, at Strickersville. This family is buried in Brandywine cemetery. (Records of Miss Anna T Lincoln, *adahb bde.*)

Children, by first wife, born at Wilmington:

adahb bda. WILLIAM-TAYLOR, born Aug. 30, 1848; died Apr. 14, 1906, at Wilmington, unmarried.

adahb bdb. MARY-EMMA, born 1851; died Nov. 8, 1860.

adahb bdc. HARRY, born 1857; died July 23, 1859.

adahb bdd. LILLIE-JANE, born June 14, 1860; married, March 29, 1894, at Wilmington, Hubert-Armitage, son of Francis-Asbury and Keziah-Jane (Stewart)* Roop of Wilmington, born June 30, 1846, at Pencador Hundred, Del. They are living, 1919, at Wilmington. He is a job printer.
  Child, born at Wilmington:
    a. ALICE-LINCOLN, born Oct. 20, 1897.

Children, by second wife, born at Wilmington:

adahb bde. ANNA T, born June 13, 1870; living, 1919, at Wilmington, unmarried.

adahb bdf. HARRY-DAVIS, born July 5, 1875; died March 30, 1878.

adahb db. SAMUEL, son of Thomas (*Thomas, Thomas, Mordecai, Mordecai, Samuel*) Lincoln of Montfort, Wis., by his first wife, Miss McNeal. He was born May 7, 1819, in Chester county, Pa.; and died June 10, 1888, at Custer, S. D. He was a farmer and tanner and lived successively in Illinois, at Montfort, Wis., in Iowa, Missouri, and at Custer.

He married, in 1852, at Montfort, Sarah-Jane, daughter of James and Sarah (Pennington) David. Some say the name was Daniel not David. James David or Daniel is said to have been a native of Massachusetts. Sarah-Jane was born July 15, 1834, in Ohio and was living in 1915.

The two oldest children are buried at a place known as the "Old Rock Church," a little country church near Montfort, which was built in 1849. Many Lincolns are said to be buried there. (Records of Miss Mattie Lincoln, *adahg fag.*)

Children, born : *a-g* at Montfort; *h-k* in Iowa:

adahb dba. JOHN, born 1853; died Feb. 11, 1856.

adahb dbb. MARY, born 1855; died Sept. 9, 1859.

adahb dbc. LAVINA, born 1857; died 1871.

adahb dbd. LODENA, born 1859; married a Mr. McFarland of Moorcroft, Wyo.

adahb dbe. OLIVER, } born 1861; { died in 1912(?).

adahb dbf. OLIVE, } { died in infancy.

*Keziah-Jane Stewart was descended from the old Delaware family of Ferris.

adahb dbg. FRANCES, born 1864; married H. Hickman of Moorcroft, Wyo.
adahb dbh. GRANT, born 1866; living, 1920, at LaGrande, Ore. He is married.
adahb dbi. ADDIE, born 1868; died 1868.
adahb dbj. EMMA, born 1871; died 1882.
adahb dbk. CHARLOTTE, born 1874; living, 1920, at Billings, Mont., unmarried.

adahb dc. JOHN, son of Thomas (*Thomas, Thomas, Mordecai, Mordecai, Samuel*) Lincoln of Montfort, Wis., by his first wife, Miss McNeal. He was born in 1821, in Chester county, Pa., and died November, 188–, at Gloucester, N. J. He was a ship-carpenter and lived at Wilmington, Del., until about 1874, when he removed to Gloucester.

He married, March 19, 1857, at New Hope, Pa., Elizabeth Lovett, whose parentage has not been learned. She was born Feb. 15, 1833, and died March 10, 1914, at Gloucester. (Records of Miss Anna T Lincoln, *adahb bde.*)

Children, born: *a-i* at Wilmington; *j* at Gloucester:

adahb dca. SAMUEL-THOMAS, born Dec. 10, 1859; died Nov. 7, 1861.
adahb dcb. GEORGE-WASHINGTON, born May 3, 1860; died July 16, 1860.
adahb dcc. MATILDA-MAY, born June 4, 1861; died Apr. 12, 1919, at Gloucester; married, Jan. 10, 1885, at Gloucester, William, son of Robert and Mary (Thomson) Gardiner, born Feb. 19, 1862, at Glasgow, Scotland. He is an electrician, living, 1920, at Gloucester.
    Children, born at Gloucester:
      a. JOHN-WALLACE, born Aug. 24, 1886; mar. Mrs. Ella (Shallcross) Cline.
      b. ROBERT-LINCOLN, born June 12, 1893; died January, 1894.
adahb dcd. FRANK-ALVIN, born Apr. 10, 1863.
adahb dce. JOHN-WESLEY, born March 10, 1865; married, Jan. 1, 1916, at Gloucester, Mrs. Elizabeth (Agner) Whartenby, daughter of Conrad and Sarah Agner of Philadelphia, Pa., born in 1862, at Philadelphia. They are living, 1920, at Gloucester. He is a pipe-fitter. They have no children.
adahb dcf. WILLIAM-DICKINSON, born Jan. 4, 1867; died May 1, 1889, at Gloucester, unmarried.
adahb dcg. ROBERT-ALLEN, born Oct. 11, 1868.
adahb dch. MARGARET-JANE, born March 31, 1871; married, Jan. 14, 1894, at Leominster, Mass., Frank-Andrew, son of Harvey and Sarah (Palmer) Bradley of Dickinson Center, N. Y., born Sept. 28, 1864, at Dickinson Center. He is a machinist. They were living, 1920, at Fitchburg, Mass.
    Children, born at Fitchburg:
      a. ETHEL-ELIZABETH, born Oct. 28, 1894; mar. (1) Steven Russell; (2) Rexford-LeRoy Myers.
      b. FRANK-LINCOLN, born May 14, 1900.
adahb dci. HOWARD, born Jan. 1, 1874; died Jan. 25, 1914, at Gloucester.

He married Eva Mohring, who is living, 1920, at Gloucester.   They had one child:

    a. ANNA.

adahb dcj.   HARRY-REAVES, born May 3, 1876.

adahb fa.   JAMES-MOORE, son of Samuel (*Thomas, Thomas, Mordecai, Mordecai, Samuel*) and Eliza (Moore) Lincoln of Mount Vernon, Ohio, born May 13, 1832, near Parkesburg, Pa.; died March 4, 1901, at Amity, Mo.   He removed with his parents to Ohio and thence to Wisconsin, Illinois, Iowa and Missouri, finally settling at Amity.   He was a farmer.

He married, Sept. 3, 1857, at Montfort, Wis., Hannah-Elizabeth, daughter of Enoch and Sarah-Ann (Steigers) Johnson, *adahb eb,* born Sept. 23, 1832, in Chester county, Pa.; died Feb. 18, 1915, at Amity.   (Records of Edith-Olivia [Lincoln] Beatty, *adahb fad.*)

Children, born: *a-c* at Montfort, Wis.; *d* at Millersburg, Ill.; *e* in Iowa; *f, g* at Amity:

adahb faa.   SARAH-ELIZABETH, born Feb. 1, 1859; married, Nov. 9, 1882, at Osborn, Mo., James-Christopher, son of Charles-Strawther and Catharine-Ann (Dunn) Whitescarver of Stanberry, Mo., born Feb. 28, 1858, at Hiawatha, Kan.   They are living, 1915, at Olathe, Kan.   He is a teacher.
    Children, born at Stanberry:
        a.   ETTA-ELIZABETH, born Nov. 4, 1884; living, 1915, unmarried.
        b.   CLARA-MAY, born Feb. 3, 1888; living, 1915, unmarried.
adahb fab.   ETTIE-FRANCES, born June 7, 1861; married, Sept. 15, 1881, at Osborne, Mo., Maltimore-Edward, son of Robert-Edward and Anna-Maria (Anderson) Beane of Kilmarnock, Va., born July 18, 1859, at Kilmarnock.   They are living, 1915, at Rock Island, Tex.   He is a farmer. (Records of Mrs. Beane.)
    Children, born: *a* at Maysville; *b* at Barton; *c* at Lamar; *d, e* at Amity, Mo.; *f, g* at Rock Island, Tex.:
        a.   JAMES-ROBERT, born Sept. 25, 1882; mar. Iris Curry.
        b.   ATHA-ELIZABETH, born Nov. 15, 1885.
        c.   RALEIGH-EDWARD, born Oct. 14, 1888.
        d.   CLAUDE-LINCOLN, born May 29, 1890.
        e.   GUY-ARVAL, born Sept. 7, 1895.
        f.   BESSIE-LUE-EMMA, ⎫
        g.   JESSE-LEO,   ⎬ born June 1, 1898.
adahb fac.   EMMA-LOUISA, born Sept. 6, 1862; died March 6, 1891; married, March 12, 1885, at Osborne, Mo., Adam-Henry, son of John and Annie Ferguson of Canada, born near Toronto.   He is a farmer, living, 1915, at Amity, Mo.
    Children, born at Amity:
        a.   JOHN-SAMUEL, born Apr. 12, 1887; mar. Mary-Louisa Matters.
        b.   ARTHUR-HAROLD, born Feb. 3, 1889; living, 1915, unmarried.

adahb fad. EDITH-OLIVIA, born Oct. 9, 1864; married, Sept. 15, 1891, at Amity, Mo., George-Henry, son of John and Caroline (Nixon) Beatty of Fergus, Canada, born Feb. 9, 1865, at Fergus. They are living, 1915, at Monte Vista, Colo., where Mr. Beatty is proprietor of the Hotel Grand, but he is in poor health and his wife runs the business.

Children, born at Monte Vista:
- *a.* OMIE-LINCOLN, born Nov. 29, 1892; died Feb. 18, 1898.
- *b.* OLIN-GEORGE, born May 20, 1894.
- *c.* HANNAH-OLIVIA, born July 12, 1899.
- *d.* JOHN-HENRY, born Aug. 14, 1901.

adahb fae. SAMUEL-ENOCH, born Aug. 6, 1869.

adahb faf. JAMES-WESLEY, born Sept. 23, 1871; living, 1915, at Del Norte, Colo., unmarried.

adahb fag. MARTHA-ELIZABETH, born Nov. 5, 1874; living, 1915, at Amity, unmarried.

adahb gb. THOMAS, son of Azariah (*Thomas, Thomas, Mordecai, Mordecai, Samuel*) and Mary (Miles) Lincoln of Montfort, Wis., born Jan. 7, 1822, at Atglen, Pa.; died June 1, 1890, at Mount Gilead, Ohio. He lived in Grant and Iowa counties, Wis., and at Mount Gilead. He was a farmer and merchant.

He married, Apr. 10, 1844, in Iowa county, Wis., Rachel-Malinda, daughter of William and Sarah (Fought) Kay of Iowa county, born Dec. 4, 1824, in Richland county, Ohio; died Apr. 27, 1896, at Mount Gilead. (Records of Azariah-William Lincoln, *adahb gbc.*)

Children, born: *a-e* in Iowa county; *f* at Montfort; *g* at Mount Gilead:

adahb gba. MARY-ELIZABETH, born Dec. 19, 1845; died Feb. 24, 1900, at Mount Gilead; married, February, 1863, at Boscobel, Wis., Thomas, son of Thomas and Mary (Symmons) Coles of Coburgh, Canada, born Aug. 19, 1840, at Cornwall, England; died Aug. 19, 1890, at Bellefontaine, Ohio. They lived at Boscobel. He was a tinner.

Child, born at Boscobel:
- *a.* RICHARD-ERNEST, born Oct. 3, 1864; mar. Frances-Louise Donaldson.

adahb gbb. SARAH-ADALINE, born Dec. 22, 1847; married, March 29, 1869, at Mount Gilead, Lehigh, son of Ebenezer and Elizabeth (Sheffer) Dakan of Reeder's Mills, Iowa, born March 17, 1840, at Williamsport, Ohio; died Feb. 15, 1909, at Logan, Iowa. He was a farmer. They lived at Mount Gilead and Logan.

Children, born: *a-c* at Mount Gilead: *d* at Logan:
- *a.* WILLIAM-LOCKWOOD, born Apr. 29, 1870; mar. Mary Larson.
- *b.* NELLIE, born Dec. 22, 1871; mar. Clark Cooper.
- *ɔ.* HARRY-LESTER, born July 27, 1874; mar. Mame Stoker.
- *d.* PEARL, born Sept. 27, 1875; mar. Thomas Doyle.

adahb gbc. AZARIAH-WILLIAM, born Sept. 25, 1851.
adahb gbd. JOEL-KAY, born Apr. 22, 1853.
adahb gbe. DAVID-HOLLIS, born Apr. 28, 1855.
adahb gbf. LYDIA-AUGUSTA, born Nov. 5, 1857; died Feb. 25, 1914, at
   Delaware, Ohio; married, Jan. 1, 1885, at Mount Gilead, Ohio, John M.,
   son of Isaac and Mary (Finley) Hull of Morrow county, Ohio, born
   May 15, 1857, in Congress township, Morrow county. They lived at
   Mount Gilead until 1901, when they moved to Mount Vernon and
   thence, in 1909, to Washington Court House and, in 1911, to Delaware.
   He is a dealer in fast horses and follows the circuit races.
      Children, born at Mount Gilead:
         a. THOMAS, born Apr. 22, 1886; mar. Flossie-May Hart.
         b. MARY, born March 2, 1888; living, 1915, unmarried.
adahb gbg. JESSIE-BELLE, born Sept. 20, 1864; died Apr. 13, 1916, in the
   Deaconess Hospital at St. Louis, Mo., and was buried at Mount Gilead.
   She married (1), Feb. 15, 1889, at Mount Gilead, John-Harvey-Carlton,
   son of Amos B. and Laura-Carlton (McFarland) Lerch of Mount Gilead,
   born March 12, 1864, at Ringgold, Pa.; died Aug. 15, 1896, at Mount
   Gilead, where they had lived. She married (2), Sept. 24, 1908, at Logan,
   Iowa, Zachary-Taylor, son of Edwin-Allen and Hannah-Maria (Hosford)
   Bradley of Canton, Ill., born Oct. 31, 1848, at Canton. She was his
   second wife. They lived at Springfield, Mo. He is a jeweler. She had no
   children by either husband.

adahb gc. DICKINSON, son of Azariah (*Thomas, Thomas,
Mordecai, Mordecai, Samuel*) and Mary (Miles) Lincoln of Atglen, Pa., born Oct. 11, 1823, at Atglen; died Nov. 1, 1913, at
Pueblo, Colo. He went with his father from Atglen to Wayne
county, Ohio, in 1833, and thence in 1839 to Lawrence county,
Ill., and in 1843 to Platteville, Wis. After his marriage he
settled in Mifflin, Wis. He was a farmer.

He married, July 3, 1851, at Mifflin, Elizabeth, daughter of
William and Sarah (Fought) Kay of Iowa county, Wis., born
Nov. 11, 1833, in Wayne county, Ohio; living, 1915. (Records
of Abraham-Dickinson Lincoln, *adahb gcd.*)

   Children, born at Mifflin:

adahb gca. EVA-MALISSA, born Apr. 6, 1853; died Jan. 18, 1860.
adahb gcb. WILLIAM, born Aug. 10, 1854; died Sept. 10, 1854.
adahb gcc. MARGARET-ELLEN, born July 16, 1858; died Feb. 3, 1860.
adahb gcd. ABRAHAM-DICKINSON, born July 3, 1861.

adahb ge. JOSEPH-HOLLIS, son of Azariah (*Thomas, Thomas,
Mordecai, Mordecai, Samuel*) and Mary (Miles) Lincoln of Montfort, Wis., born Feb. 10, 1827, at Atglen, Pa.; died July 2, 1906, at
Montfort. He was a wheelwright and blacksmith and always
lived at Montfort.

He married, Dec. 15, 1861, at Montfort, Margaret, daughter of Thomas and Elizabeth (Twining) Laird of Montfort, born Dec. 4, 1841, in Delaware; died May 16, 1871, at Boscobel, Wis., but the "Kirk Family," p. 236, says she died May 19, 1871. (Records of Azariah-Thomas Lincoln, *adahb ged.*)

Children, born at Montfort:

adahb gea. MARY-ELIZABETH, born Oct. 5, 1862; married, at Montfort, Stephen-Harvey Taylor. They are living, 1920, at Lancaster, Wis., and are reported to have had six children.

adahb geb. EVA-ORILLA, born Nov. 13, 1864; living, 1915, at Fredericksburg, Pa.

adahb gec. JOHN-THOMAS, born June 6, 1866; died Dec. 15, 1869.

adahb ged. AZARIAH-THOMAS, born June 20, 1868; living, 1921, at Troy, N. Y. He is a consulting and analytical chemist at the Rensselaer Polytechnic Institute, with which institution he has been connected since 1908, first as assistant professor of chemistry, and since 1912 as professor of physical chemistry. He received the degree of B.S. at the University of Wisconsin in 1894; M.S. in 1898; and Ph.D. in 1899. He was assistant in chemistry at the same university 1896-8, and Fellow in chemistry, 1898-9; research assistant in physical chemistry, Cornell University, 1899-1900; instructor in chemistry, University of Cincinnati, 1900-1; University of Illinois, 1901-2; and assistant professor of chemistry, University of Illinois, 1903-8. He has published many important articles on chemistry.

He married, June 30, 1904, at Mansfield, Ohio, Jennette-Emeline, daughter of William-Barney and Emeline (Grove) Carpenter of Mansfield, born 1868, at Newville, Ohio. They have no children. (Who's Who in America, 1920-1.)

adahc. aa. RICHARD-VANBUSKIRK, son of John (*Mishal, Thomas, Mordecai, Mordecai, Samuel*) and Hannah (VanBuskirk) Lincoln of Laurelton, Pa., born Dec. 18, 1822, in Hartley township, Pa.; died June 18, 1901, at Laurelton. He attended subscription schools and Mifflinburg, Pa., Academy until he was sixteen years old, when he entered the sophomore class at Dickinson college, Carlisle, Pa., where he graduated in 1841, the second in his class of twenty-three members. After graduation he taught school for a number of years until 1845, after which he followed the occupation of farming. He was school director for many terms and a justice of the peace for twenty-five years. He was county commissioner from 1855 to 1860, and filled many county offices. In politics he was, in early life, a Whig, but on the formation of the Republican party he at once became an active member thereof and was, at one time, a candidate for

State senator and, in 1876, a candidate for Congress, but the district being Democratic he failed of election though running several hundred votes ahead of his ticket. He was one of the organizers of the Mifflinburg Bank and continuously one of its directors. He was owner of three fine farms, containing four hundred and eighty acres of land under a high state of cultivation. (Hist. of Susquehanna and Juniata Valleys, vol. ii, p. 1396; Records of John-Wesley Lincoln, *adahc aaa*.)

He married, Aug. 18, 1852, at Mifflinburg, Anna-Maria, daughter of Samuel and Mary (Wolfe) Pellman of Berks county, Pa., born May 29, 1831, near Mifflinburg; died May 4, 1909, at Mifflinburg. Their home was at Laurelton. (Records of James-Minor Lincoln, Wareham, Mass.)

Children, born at Laurelton:

adahc aaa. JOHN-WESLEY, born May 24, 1853.

adahc aab. SAMUEL-PELLMAN, born Oct. 5, 1856; died July 29, 1866.

adahc aac. MARK-HALFPENNY, born Sept. 13, 1860; died Nov. 26, 1898, at Philadelphia, Pa. He was a graduate of the University of Pennsylvania Medical School, became a physician and lived at Natrona, Pa., and at Philadelphia. He married, Apr. 14, 1886, Carrie H., daughter of Cromwell and Sarah H. (Taylor) Pierce of Laurelton, born 1865 in New York State. They had no children.

adahc aad. HANNAH-MARY, born Sept. 7, 1863; died Feb. 10, 1900, at Milton, Pa.; married, Sept. 7, 1887, S. B. Evans. He was a minister of the Methodist-Episcopal church at Lockhaven, Pa. They lived in Hartley township, Union county, Pa.

Children:
- *a.* LUCILE, born June 2, 1889.
- *b.* VINCENT-GOODSELL, born July 11, 1890.
- *c.* GRACE-WINIFRED, born Nov. 18, 1893.
- *d.* MARIAN-GRAY,
- *e.* MIRIAM-GERTRUDE, } born Nov. 6, 1895.

adahc aae. LOUIS-PELLMAN, born Aug. 8, 1866.

adahc aaf. RUFUS-VANBUSKIRK, born Apr. 17, 1871.

adahc aag. ANNA-REBECCA, born Feb. 16, 1873; living, 1913, unmarried.

adahf cb. JOSEPH-HENRY, son of John (*Joseph, Thomas, Mordecai, Mordecai, Samuel*) and Francina (Reynolds) Lincoln of Rising Sun, Md., born Feb. 11, 1826, at Rising Sun; died Feb. 23, 1904, at Rising Sun. He was a farmer and lived at Rising Sun, on "Pigeon Hill."

He married (1), Jan. 4, 1856, at Lancaster, Pa., Sarah-Anna, daughter of John and Annie (Cutler) Stubbs of Peach Bottom,

Pa., born Sept. 18, 1826, at Peach Bottom; died Sept. 30, 1889, at Rising Sun.

He married (2), March 30, 1892, at Richardsmier, Md., Elizabeth, daughter of Stephen and Rebecca (Stubbs) Richards of Richardsmier, born Jan. 7, 1848, at Rising Sun; living, 1913, at Colora, Cecil county, Md. (Records of Annie-Stubbs [Lincoln] Stubbs, *adahf cba;* Smedley Family, p. 528.)

Children, by first wife, born at Rising Sun:

adahf cba. ANNIE-STUBBS, born Nov. 30, 1856; married, May 17, 1881, at Rising Sun, Isaac-Hopper, son of Vincent-Gilpin and Elizabeth (Pierson) Stubbs of Delta, Pa., born Oct. 25, 1855, at Delta. They are living, 1913, at Delta. He is a merchant.

    Children, born at Delta:

        a. HARVIE-LINCOLN, born Apr. 25, 1885; mar. Clarence Galbreath.

        b. RUPERT-ISAAC, born Feb. 24, 1888; mar. Cornelia Winterson.

adahf cbb. HARVIE-GILPIN, born Dec. 18, 1860; died Aug. 24, 1875, at Rising Sun.

adahf ce. ABEL-THOMAS, son of John (*Joseph, Thomas, Mordecai, Mordecai, Samuel*) and Francina (Reynolds) Lincoln of Rising Sun, Cecil county, Md., born Nov. 27, 1831, at Rising Sun; died March 2, 1885, at Sharon Farm, Farmington, Md. He entered Union college, N. Y., in the class of 1857, but left college at the end of his junior year and went to Missouri, where he became a surveyor. He then went to California, where he was a gold miner. He returned East and settled at Oak Hill, Lancaster county, Pa., removing later to Farmington, where he continued to live until his death. He was a farmer, dairyman and miner of chrome. At Oak Hill he was proprietor of the Hub Spoke Works.

He married, Feb. 16, 1864, at Philadelphia, Pa., Elizabeth, daughter of Nathan and Lydia (Pierce) Haines of Oak Hill, born June 10, 1840, at Oak Hill. She married (2), Nov. 9, 1895, at Philadelphia, Henry-Longfellow, son of Joseph and Elizabeth (Hackett) Brinton of Birmingham, Pa., born Aug. 5, 1836, at Birmingham; living, 1913, at Philadelphia in Kirkbrides asylum. His wife is living, 1913, at Oxford, Pa. (Bailey Family, p. 549.)

Child, born at Oak Hill:

adahf cea. JOHN-JOSEPH, born Oct. 11, 1865.

adahf da. CHARLES-SHIPPEN, son of Abel-Thomas (*Joseph,
Thomas, Mordecai, Mordecai, Samuel*) and Rachel (Housekeeper)
Lincoln of Philadelphia, Pa., born June 30, 1827, at Philadelphia;
died Apr. 11, 1901, at Philadelphia. He was educated in the
Philadelphia public schools; studied law with John Cadwallader
and was admitted to the bar. He practised his profession until
1857, when he was appointed assistant coiner of the United
States Mint, which office he held until 1862, when he was appointed deputy clerk of the United States district court, and in 1865
was appointed clerk, which office he held until his death.

He married, May 27, 1857, at Oxford, Pa., Anna[6], daughter of
Jacob[5] (*Jacob[4], Jacob[3], Henry[2], Henry[1]*) and Anna (Moore)
Reynolds of Rising Sun, Md., born July 23, 1835, at Rising Sun;
died Feb. 2, 1908, at Philadelphia. Henry[1] Reynolds emigrated
in 1676 from Chichester, England, to Burlington, N. J. Anna[4]
Moore was daughter of Joseph[3] (*Joseph[2], Andrew[1]*) and Mercy
(Cutler) Moore, born Aug. 31, 1793, in Cecil county, Md.; died
Sept. 19, 1874, at South Vineland, N. J. Her ancestor, Andrew[1]
Moore, emigrated from Ballinacree, Ireland, in 1723. (Records
of Henry-Philip Lincoln, *adahf daa.*)

Children, born at Philadelphia:

adahf daa. HENRY-PHILIP, born March 4, 1858.
adahf dab. WILLIAM-REYNOLDS, born Jan. 28, 1862.
adahf dac. WALTER-RODMAN, born Apr. 9, 1867.
adahf dad. MARY-AGNES, born June 28, 1871; died March 31, 1875.
adahf dae. GEORGE-WASHINGTON, born Feb. 22, 1873.

adaid ab. SAMUEL, son of Caleb (*James, Abraham, Mordecai,
Mordecai, Samuel*) and Margaret-Amelia (Henderson) Lincoln,
born Aug. 26, 1823.

He married, Jan. 13, 1853, Rachel, daughter of Lot and Martha
(Jenkins) Rogers of Churchtown, Pa. Her mother, Martha
Jenkins, was a native of Churchtown and was born there, in
1805. (Genealogy of David Jones, p. 106; Jenkins Family Book,
p. 95; Records of James-Minor Lincoln, Wareham, Mass.)

Children:

adaid aba. MARTHA-ROGERS, born Dec. 4, 1853.
adaid abb. MARGARET-HUDSON, born May 12, 1856; died Dec. 1, 1865.
adaid abc. JAMES-BOONE, born Aug. 16, 1859.
adaid abd. LOT-ROGERS, born Sept. 17, 1861; married, June 1, 1899, Mary-
Ermina Buchanan. "Jenkins Family Book" calls him Linford-Rogers.

adaid bb. GEORGE-JONES, son of John (*James, Abraham, Mordecai, Mordecai, Samuel*) and Hannah (Jones) Lincoln of Churchtown, Pa., born Oct. 28, 1821, at Churchtown; died June 28, 1860.

He married, Jan. 9, 1855, Emily-Virginia Mawson. (Genealogy of David Jones, p. 107.)

Children:

adaid bba. GEORGE-JONES, born Feb. 27, 1857.
adaid bbb. HELEN-CONOLY, born Aug. 19, 1858; married, Sept. 15, 1885, William-Hammersley Gilroy.
    Children:
      a. ROBERT-LINCOLN, born Nov. 11, 1887.
      b. GLADYS-DRAPER, born Oct. 16, 1891.
adaid bbc. ROSALIE-MORGAN, born March 28, 1860; died Nov. 11, 1866.

adaid hc. WILLIAM-IVES, son of David-Jones (*James, Abraham, Mordecai, Mordecai, Samuel*) and Mary-Ives (Davis) Lincoln of Birdsboro, Pa., born Sept. 16, 1852, at Birdsboro. He lives, 1913, at Birdsboro and is cashier of the First National Bank there.

He married, June 12, 1901, at Pottsville, Pa., Emily-Burling, daughter of Louis-Paleskie and Mary (Evans) Garrigues of Pottsville, born Nov. 8, 1872, at Pottsville; living, 1913. (Records of William-Ives Lincoln; Genealogy of David Jones, p. 108.)

Child, born at Birdsboro:

adaid hca. MARY-GARRIGUES, born Jan. 9, 1909.

adaii bb. ALFRED-GILBERT, son of John-Dehaven (*Thomas, Abraham, Mordecai, Mordecai, Samuel*) and Sarah (Gilbert) Lincoln of Exeter, Pa., born Apr. 21, 1839, at Exeter; living, 1913, at Lorane, Exeter township, where he has passed his whole life. He worked for about twenty years on the railroad, but since then has been a farmer. He was road-master of Exeter from 1895 to 1898, and, again, from 1905 to 1913; he served also as school director for Exeter 1895-8, and 1908-11. In 1863, he served for three months as private in Company K, 48th regiment, Pennsylvania infantry.

He married, Aug. 5, 1860, at Reading, Pa., Anna-Louisa, daughter of Samuel-Warren and Mary (Yost) Hemmig of

Spring township, Pa., born Oct. 1, 1841, at Spring; living, 1913.
(Records of Albert-Gilbert Lincoln.)

Children, born at Lorane:

adaii bba.   SARAH-CLARA, born May 19, 1861; living, 1913; married, March 1,
1884, at Reading, Pa., Caleb-Ruth, son of Samuel-Quinter and Elizabeth
(Ruth) Killian of Robeson, Pa., born Nov. 9, 1861, at Robeson; died
July 31, 1912, at Robeson.   They lived at Reading, where he was a
"spannerman'" in a rolling mill.

> Children, born *a-d* at Robeson; *e-h* at Reading:
> *a.*   SAMUEL-LINCOLN, born Aug. 16, 1885; living, 1913, unmarried.
> *b.*   RALPH-LINCOLN, born Sept. 11, 1887; mar. Nora Holl.
> *c.*   OSCAR-LINCOLN, born Feb. 27, 1890; died Apr. 13, 1894.
> *d.*   ALFRED-LINCOLN, born Feb. 24, 1892; died June 16, 1902.
> *e.*   CALEB, born Sept. 24, 1894.
> *f.*   LUKE, born July 25, 1897.
> *g.*   MARK, born Dec. 22, 1899.
> *h.*   HEISTER, born Aug. 5, 1903.

adaii bbb.   OSCAR-HEMMIG, born Apr. 2, 1863.

adaii bbc.   MARY-CATHERINE, born May 27, 1865; married, Nov. 20, 1886,
at Reading, Pa., Charles-Carl, son of Eli and Jane (Parker) Boughter of
Pottstown, Pa., born June 6, 1865, at Reading.   They are living, 1913,
at Reading.   He is employed in an iron mill.

> Child, born at Robeson, Pa.:
> *a.*   CARL, born March 18, 1893; living, 1913, unmarried.

adaii bbd.   ANNA-AMELIA, born Nov. 5, 1867; married, May 26, 1894, at
Reading, Pa., Cyrus, son of Jonathan and Sarah (Huyett) Ruppert of
Exeter, Pa., born Nov. 14, 1865, at Neversink, Exeter township.   They
are living, 1913, at Neversink.   He is a farmer.

> Children, born at Exeter:
> *a.*   ADAM-LINCOLN, born Oct. 20, 1894; died Oct. 25, 1894.
> *b.*   EARL-LINCOLN, born Oct. 2, 1895.
> *c.*   CLARA, born Apr. 25, 1898; died Aug. 17, 1898.
> *d.*   HELEN-LINCOLN, born Aug. 29, 1899.
> *e.*   GEORGE-LINCOLN, born Jan. 9, 1902; died Nov. 27, 1902.
> *f.*   FRANK-LINCOLN, born Feb. 8, 1904.
> *g.*   FLORENCE, born Oct. 21, 1906.

adaii bbe.   MARGARET-PERMILLA, born Dec. 1, 1872; died June 2, 1910, at
Neversink, Exeter township, Pa.; married, June 19, 1892, at Reading,
Henry-Moyer, son of John and Sarah (Moyer) Hafer of Exeter, born Oct.
20, 1870, at Lorane; living, 1913, at Neversink.   He is a carpenter.

> Children, born at Neversink:
> *a.*   SARAH-LINCOLN, born Dec. 25, 1893; living, 1913, unmarried.
> *b.*   LOUISA-LINCOLN, born Jan. 17, 1895; living, 1913, unmarried.
> *c.*   AGNES-LINCOLN, born June 29, 1896; living, 1913, unmarried.
> *d.*   BERTHA-LINCOLN, born July 22, 1897; living, 1913.
> *e.*   CLAYTON-LINCOLN, born Aug. 17, 1898; living, 1913.
> *f.*   JOHN-LINCOLN, born Jan. 12, 1900; died Dec. 25, 1901.
> *g.*   DORA-LINCOLN, born June 12, 1901.
> *h.*   IRMA-LINCOLN, born July 2, 1903; died Apr. 16, 1909.
> *i.*   VICTOR-LINCOLN, born March 20, 1904.

  j. MARTHA-LINCOLN, born Nov. 9, 1905.
  k. ALICE-LINCOLN, born Dec. 19, 1907.
  l. HENRY-LINCOLN, born Apr. 13, 1909.
  m. MARGARET-LINCOLN, born May 16, 1910; died July 23, 1910.
adaii bbf. BERTHA-MAY, born Sept. 2, 1881; married, Apr. 14, 1906, at Reading, Pa., Harry-Llewellyn, son of Harry and Rebecca (Price) Boone of Exeter township, Pa., born March 21, 1879, at Stonersville, Exeter, one half mile north of thebirthplace of Daniel Boone, the Kentucky pioneer. They are living, 1913, at Lorane. He is a stone-mason.
  Children, born: *a, b* at Neversink, Pa.; *c* at Lorane:
  a. GRACE-MINERVA, born Nov. 1, 1906.
  b. ROBERT, born Feb. 27, 1909.
  c. WAYNE, born Aug. 15, 1910; died Aug. 23, 1911.

adaii bc. HARRISON-GILBERT, son of John-Dehaven (*Thomas, Abraham, Mordecai, Mordecai, Samuel*) and Sarah (Gilbert) Lincoln of Exeter, Pa., born July 28, 1840, at Exeter. He was a farmer, living at Exeter until 1885, when he removed to Reading, Pa., where he has since been employed by Huyett Brothers, box-makers, as a teamster. He owns the original notebook of his great-grandfather, Abraham Lincoln, to which reference has been previously made; see *adai.*

He married, Dec. 20, 1870, at Reading, Hannah, daughter of Joseph and Esther (Tobias) Ritter of Exeter, born Aug. 30, 1851, at Reading. They were both living, 1913, at Reading. (Records of Mrs. Harrison-Gilbert Lincoln.)

Children, born at Poplar Neck, Pa.:

adaii bca. SALLY-ANDORA, born June 11, 1871; married (1), Dec. 31, 1890, at Reading, Pa., Edwin-Harrison, son of Fidel and Amelia (Wentzel) Webber of Reading, born Jan. 13, 1869, at Reading; died Oct. 23, 1902, at Reading, where he had always lived. He was a salesman in the hardware business.
  She married (2), May 2, 1912, at Reading, Christin-Christian, son of George and Ellen (Christian) Esterly of Exeter, Pa., born Dec. 15, 1869, at Exeter. They are living, 1913, at Reading. He is a grocer.
  Children, by first husband, born at Reading:
  a. HARRISON-FIDEL WEBBER, born Dec. 17, 1891; mar. Emma Mowry.
  b. ROBERT-EMERY WEBBER, born March 1, 1898.
  c. ESTHER-IRENE WEBBER, born Jan. 9, 1901.
  Child, by second husband, born at Reading:
  d. JOHN-LINCOLN ESTERLY, born Aug. 12, 1913.
adaii bcb. A SON, born July 20, 1872; died July 21, 1872.
adaii bcc. A SON, born May 3, 1873; died same day.
adaii bcd. ESTHER-NORA, born Feb. 5, 1876; living, 1913, unmarried. She is a nurse at Ramapo Sanatorium.

adaii bce. MARTHA, born Jan. 4, 1882; living, 1913, at Reading, unmarried. She is book-keeper of the Pennsylvania Shoe Company.

adaii bcf. A DAUGHTER, born Jan. 12, 1890; died same day.

adaii be. JOHN-GILBERT, son of John-Dehaven (*Thomas, Abraham, Mordecai, Mordecai, Samuel*) and Sarah (Gilbert) Lincoln of Exeter, Pa., born March 7, 1843, at Exeter; died July 19, 1876, at Exeter, where he had passed his life. He was employed on the Philadelphia and Reading Railroad.

He married Catherine, daughter of Daniel and Susan (Eidel) Biehl of St. Lawrence, Pa., born at Mt. Penn., Pa. She married (2) Charles Leimbach and they are living, 1913, at St. Lawrence. (Records of Mrs. Harrison-Gilbert Lincoln, *adaii bc.*)

Children, born at Exeter:

adaii bea. HOWARD. He lives, 1913, at Reading, Pa.
adaii beb. WALTER, living, 1913, at Reading, unmarried.
adaii bec. SUSAN-PERMILLA, is married and lives, 1913, at Philadelphia, Pa.
adaii bed. HARRISON-TILDEN, living, 1913, at Reading.

adaii bf. RICHARD-GILBERT, son of John-Dehaven (*Thomas, Abraham, Mordecai, Mordecai, Samuel*) and Sarah (Gilbert) Lincoln of Exeter, Pa., born Dec. 5, 1844, at Exeter. He was educated in the public schools of Exeter and in the Buttertown school. After a few years of farming he opened the "Red Lion" Hotel at Baumstown, Pa., and remained there thirteen years. He then removed to Birdsboro, Pa., where he was employed in a company store as clerk for three years, and then for a similar length of time with the E. & G. Brooke Iron Company. In 1886 he removed to Reading, Pa., where he has since lived, being first employed as clerk in the freight depot of the Philadelphia and Reading Railroad. Since 1892 he has been in the employ of Reuben Hoffer, in the lumber business. Mr. Lincoln is a Democrat and has served as tax collector of the ninth ward. In religion he is a member of St. Stephen's Reformed Church. He is an Odd Fellow. In 1909 he was owner of the old Lincoln homestead in Exeter. (See page 46.)

He married, May 26, 1866, at Reading, Hannah-Young, daughter of George and Catherine (Young) Stoner of Exeter, born July 26, 1844, at Exeter; living, 1913. (Records of Richard-Gilbert Lincoln; Hist. of Berks County, vol. ii, p. 1147.)

Children, born at Exeter:

adaii bfa. ROSWELL-STONER, born Nov. 24, 1866; living, 1913, at Reading, unmarried.

adaii bfb. VIRGINIA, born July 24, 1868; living, 1913, at Reading, unmarried.

adbca dc. JOHN-ROBERTSON, son of Isaac (*Abraham, Jacob, Abraham, Mordecai, Samuel*) and Eliza (Robertson) Lincoln of Waynesville, Ohio, born June 10, 1831, at Waynesville; died Aug. 1, 1895, at Waynesville. He lived and died on his father's farm, a farmer.

He married, March 24, 1870, at Waynesville, Harriet-Ann, daughter of George and Eunice (Kelley) Zell of Waynesville, born Oct. 30, 1837, at Crosswick, Warren county, Ohio. She is living, 1915, at Waynesville on the old farm with her son. (Records of Mrs. Katharine-Rebecca [Paschall] Styer, *adbca bbd*, corrected by Isaac-Wilber Lincoln, *adbca dcc.*)

Children, born at Waynesville:

adbca dca. EUNICE-ELIZA, born July 22, 1872; married, Sept. 21, 1898, at Waynesville, Frank, son of Christopher and Jane (Decker) Miltenberger of Franklin, Ohio. They are living, 1916, at Lytle, Ohio. He is a farmer. Children:
    a. MILDRED, born Aug. 28, 1902.
    b. MILO, born Jan. 16, 1912.

adbca dcb. GRACE-ANN, born March 10, 1876; married, June 10, 1899, at Waynesville, John-Henry, son of Nathaniel and Susan (Ellis) Smith of New Vienna, Ohio, born Dec. 20, 1869, at New Vienna. They are living, 1916, at Waynesville. He is a barber. She is a milliner. They have no children.

adbca dcc. ISAAC-WILBER, born Oct. 12, 1877. He married, Nov. 3, 1915, at Waynesville, Mrs. Mabel (Anson) Hammer, daughter of Frank Anson of Waynesville and widow of Jesse Hammer of Waynesville. She was born March 17, 1893, near Waynesville. He is a farmer. They are living, 1916, at Waynesville.

adbca fc. BENJAMIN, son of Abraham (*Abraham, Jacob, Abraham, Mordecai, Samuel*) and Ruth (Prater) Lincoln of Waynesville, Ohio, born March 8, 1844, at Waynesville. He is a farmer.

He married, Jan. 8, 1890, at Morrow, Ohio (by Rev. Charles A. Hicky of St. Francis de Sales Church), Frances-Ann, daughter of James and Mary (Purcell) Brown of Oregonia, Ohio, born Dec. 1, 1864, in Warren county, Ohio. They are living, 1915, at Lebanon, Ohio. (Records of Benjamin Lincoln.)

Child, born at Lebanon:

adbca fca.   MARY-RUTH, born Dec. 12, 1893.

adbcf ba.   JOHN, son of George (*Moses, Jacob, Abraham, Mordecai, Samuel*) and Phoebe-Speekman (Hoofstitler) Lincoln of Darby, Pa., born Sept. 9, 1821, at Darby.

He married, Feb. 22, 1849, at Darby, Maria, daughter of George and Sarah Brandt.   Their grandson, Alfred-Wiles Lincoln, thinks that they are buried in the Old Swedes cemetery at Kingsessing, Pa., but no stones mark their graves there. They are said to have had several children, but no trace has been found of any save Alfred.

Children, born at Darby:

adbcf baa.   ALFRED.
and others.

adbcf be.   MOSES, son of George (*Moses, Jacob, Abraham, Mordecai, Samuel*) and Phoebe-Speekman (Hoofstitler) Lincoln of Darby, Pa., born Oct. 24, 1828, at Darby; died July 14, 1879, at Darby.   He was a farmer and lived at Darby.   For many years he was tax collector for the town.

He married, May 6, 1858, Amanda, daughter of Amer and Rebecca (Weed) Ogden of Paschallville, now part of Philadelphia, Pa., born Feb. 27, 1838; died June 10, 1905, at Darby. They are buried in the old burying ground at Darby.   His gravestone bears the following inscription:

"In Memory ‡ of ‡ our father ‡ Moses Lincoln ‡ born Oct. 24, 1828 ‡ died July 14, 1879 ‡ in the 51st year of his age ‡ Whilst in this tomb our father lies ‡ His Spirit rests above; ‡ In realms of bliss it never dies ‡ But knows a Savior's love."

No stone has been erected to Mrs. Lincoln.   (Family Bible with Mrs. Mary-Rebecca [Lincoln] Garrett, *adbcf bea;* The Quaker Ogdens, p. 126; Sharpless Family, p. 854; Gravestone.)

Children, born at Darby:

adbcf bea.   MARY-REBECCA, born Sept. 5, 1859; married, June 16, 1881, at Paschall, Philadelphia, Pa., Jesse-Sharpless, son of Edwin-Thatcher and Alice-Ann (Priest) Garrett of Williston, Pa., born July 27, 1857, in Oregon, while his parents were in the gold regions of that State; died June 19, 1907, at Lansdowne, Pa.   He was in the paper-making business, employed in his father's mill. They lived at Lansdowne, where she is now, 1915, living with all her unmarried children.

Children, born at Lansdowne:

    a. LAURA-ALICE, born Feb. 10, 1883; living, 1915, unmarried.

    b. FRANKLIN-LINCOLN, born June 5, 1885; died May 30, 1892.

    c. FLORENCE-AMANDA, born Apr. 19, 1887; living, 1915, unmarried.

    d. ROBERT-PUSEY, born Nov. 15, 1889; living, 1915, unmarried.

    e. JESSE-SHARPLESS, born May 5, 1892; died May 10, 1892.

    f. GEORGE-SHARPLESS, born Oct. 27, 1893; living, 1915, unmarried.

    g. HENRY-LYNDALL, born Apr. 2, 1896; living, 1915, unmarried.

    h. EDNA-MAY, born Nov. 25, 1898.

adbcf beb. GEORGE-HENRY, born Jan. 23, 1861.

adbcf bec. ANNA-PHOEBE, born Nov. 23, 1862; married, Nov. 23, 1881, at Darby, William, son of John and Mary McConnell of Darby, born Sept. 28, 1854, at Chester, Pa. They are living, 1915, at West Philadelphia. He is a machinist and is employed in Brill's Car Shops. (Records of Mrs. Anna-Phoebe [Lincoln] McConnell.)

Children, born at Darby:

    a. BESSIE-AMANDA, born Dec. 24, 1882; mar. William-Harry King.

    b. HARRY-BONSALL, born Dec. 15, 1884; mar. Lida Leeds.

    c. SUSAN-BAILEY, living, 1915, unmarried.

    d. LOUISA-JONES, born Dec. 29, 1886; mar. George-Conant Kaufmann.

    e. CHARLES-MAXWELL, born Jan. 14, 1888; mar. Rose-Lelia Small.

adbcf bed. AMER-OGDEN, born Dec. 25, 1864.

adbcf bee. JOSEPH-HOWARD, born Nov. 20, 1866.

adbcf bef. SADIE-COUNTAS, born Jan. 10, 1869; married, Aug. 28, 1891, at Camden, N. J., Louis-Daniel, son of John and Eliza (Carver) Blythe of Darby, born July 3, 1871, at Darby. They are living, 1915, at Darby. He is a painter.

Children, born at Darby:

    a. AMANDA-LINCOLN, born July 31, 1893; living, 1915, unmarried.

    b. HORACE-LINCOLN, born July 3, 1896; died Oct. 28, 1907.

    c. ROY-LOUIS, born March 17, 1899.

    d. IDA-MAY, born Oct. 11, 1902.

    e. LIDIE-CARVER, born Sept. 14, 1905.

    f. LOUIS-WILMER, born June 17, 1907.

adbcf beg. WILLIAM-OGDEN, born Oct. 21, 1871.

adbcf beh. PASCHALL-HOOPES, born Dec. 24, 1872; died July 5, 1873.

adbcf bei. CLARA-GILBERT, born Jan. 6, 1874; married (1) Dec. 25, 1891, at Camden, N. J., Charles-Edward Blythe of Darby, born November, 1871 (?), at Darby; died in 1900 at Darby. They lived at Darby. He was a machinist. She married (2), July 3, 1907, at Darby, Charles-Markley, son of Caleb and Sarah (Markley) Staley of Darby, born Oct. 19, 1865, at Darby. They are living, 1915, at Darby. He is in the real estate business. Mr. and Mrs. Staley have no children.

Children, by first husband, born at Darby:

    a. WILLIAM-LINCOLN BLYTHE, born June 25, 1892.

    b. CHARLES-BAIRD BLYTHE, born July 24, 1896; died Jan. 16, 1897.

    c. RALPH-EDWARD BLYTHE, born May 18, 1898.

adbcf bej. HORACE-McKEE, born March 16, 1875; died Aug. 23, 1898, unmarried.

33

adbcf bek. JESSIE-AMANDA, born May 9, 1878; married, March 15, 1899, at
Darby, John, son of Oram and Mary-Jane (McClain) Bleacher of Darby,
born Sept. 14, 1878, at Darby. They are living, 1915, at Darby. He is a
granite-cutter.

Children, born at Darby:
  a. MAZIE-JANE, born Aug. 31, 1900.
  b. LEROY-CLYDE, born July 19, 1903.
  c. ALBERTA-MAY, born Jan. 6, 1906.
  d. OHRAM-ABRAM, born Sept. 14, 1908.

adbcf ca. ISAAC R., son of Michael (*Moses, Jacob, Abraham,
Mordecai, Samuel*) and Rebecca Lincoln of Darby, Pa. He was
living, Sept. 24, 1856, when he is named as an heir of his cousin,
William Lincoln, *adbcf aa.*

He married Elizabeth Noble, who died Oct. 31, 1883, at Darby
and is buried there in the old burying ground, her gravestone
being inscribed as follows: "Mother ‡ Elizabeth Noble ‡ wife of
‡ Isaac R. Lincoln ‡ died Oct. 31, 1883."

Children:

adbcf caa. SUSAN; she was living, 1915, in California, unmarried.
adbcf cab. ANNA, married a Mr. Fields and is said to be living, 1915, at
North Woodbury, N. J.

adbfa bd. ISAAC-BUCK, son of Daniel-Savage (*William,
Mordecai, Abraham, Mordecai, Samuel*) and Florilla (Buck)
Lincoln of Cromwell, Conn., formerly Middletown Upper
Houses, born Dec. 26, 1829 at Cromwell; died Feb. 4, 1911, at
Middletown, Conn. He was a housewright and carpenter and
lived at Cromwell.

He married, Oct. 3, 1860, at Cromwell, Augusta-Caroline,
daughter of Heman L. and Emily (Eno) Nearing of Middletown,
born Dec. 20, 1840, at Middletown; living, 1916, at Waterbury,
Conn.

Mr. Lincoln is buried in the new cemetery at Cromwell with
three of his children, in the same lot as his father and mother.
His monument bears the following inscription: "Isaac B. Lincoln ‡ died ‡ Feb. 4, 1911 ‡ aged 82." (Records of Howard-
Nearing Lincoln, *adbfa bdf.*)

Children, born at Cromwell:

adbfa bda. HERBERT-HENRY, born Nov. 1, 1862.
adbfa bdb. HATTIE A., born Jan. 31, 1866; died June 10, 1866.

adbfa bdc. HATTIE-SIMONS, born Dec. 8, 1867; mar. Nov. 5, 1896, at Middletown, Conn., Norman-Porter, son of Thomas-Knowlton and Almira (Mills) Work of Hartford, Conn., born Feb. 14, 1864, at Hartford. He was, when married, secretary of the Young Men's Christian Association at Hartford. They were living, 1919, at Yonkers, N. Y. He was a teacher.

Children, born *a*, *b* at Hartford; *c*, *d* at Yonkers:

    a. LINCOLN-THOMAS, born Dec. 28, 1898.
    b. HAROLD-KNOWLTON, born May 22, 1901.
    c. RUTH-LINCOLN, born Jan. 11, 1904.
    d. ALICE-MILLS, born Dec. 25, 1911.

adbfa bdd. A SON, born Nov. 6, 1871; died same day.

adbfa bde. REMINGTON-KING, born Aug. 22, 1873; died Apr. 16, 1906, unmarried.

adbfa bdf. HOWARD-NEARING, born May 30, 1880.

adbfa bdg. EDWARD G., born Apr. 9, 1883; died Aug. 5, 1883.

adbfa bg. DANIEL-SAVAGE, son of Daniel-Savage (*William, Mordecai, Abraham, Mordecai, Samuel*) and Florilla (Buck) Lincoln of Cromwell, formerly Middletown Upper Houses, Conn., born January, 1843, at Cromwell; died Nov. 14, 1897, at Zoar, Mass., "aged 54 years, 10 months." He enlisted Sept. 10, 1862, in Company F, 24th regiment, Connecticut volunteer infantry, and served until Sept. 30, 1863. He was a moulder by trade.

He married (1) Katharine Dorflinger of Middletown, Conn., who was born in 1858 at Middletown. He is said to have married (2) Amanda Collins of Collinsville, Conn., from whom he was divorced.

Children, by first wife, born at Cromwell:

adbfa bga. DANIEL-BERTIE, born Feb. 12, 1888; died Sept. 5, 1888.

adbfa bgb. CHARLES-CLEVELAND, born Sept. 4, 1893; living, 1919, at Middletown.

adbfa fh. CHARLES-RUSSELL, son of Asa S. (*William, Mordecai, Abraham, Mordecai, Samuel*) and Lucy (Post) Lincoln of Cromwell, formerly Middletown Upper Houses, Conn., born Oct. 30, 1862, at Cromwell; living, 1916, at Cromwell. He is a farmer but works sometimes at the moulder's trade.

He married, Jan. 12, 1904, at Cromwell, Mrs. Laura-Caroline (Larsen) Anderson, daughter of Rasmus and Mahn (Hansen) Larsen of Denmark and widow of William Anderson of Portland, Conn., who died March 24, 1897, and by whom she had a son

and two daughters. She was born July 13, 1870, at Odeneser
Fyn, Denmark. (Records of Mrs. Charles-Russell Lincoln.)

Children, born at Cromwell:

adbfa fha.   LUCY-ISABELLA, born Jan. 12, 1905; died Jan. 24, 1905.
adbfa fhb.   ASA-CARL, born Sept. 2, 1906.

adcac ba.   ISAAC, son of Francis (*Uriah, Isaac, Isaac, Mordecai, Samuel*) and Peggy (Nichols) Lincoln of Cohasset, Mass.,
born Nov. 12, 1805, at Cohasset; died March 10, 1883, at Cohasset. He was a farmer and lived at Cohasset in a house built
by Mordecai Lincoln about 1717, which he inherited from his
grandfather, Uriah Lincoln.

He married, Nov. 27, 1827, at Cohasset, Sarah[8], daughter of
Daniel[7] (*Zealous[6], Joshua[5], Joshua[4], Joshua[3], Joseph[2], Clement[1]*)
and Sarah (Tower) Bates of Cohasset, born Dec. 18, 1809, at
Cohasset; died there Oct. 13, 1890. (Cohasset Genealogies,
pp. 40, 245; Cohasset Records; Records of Francis Lincoln,
adcac bab.)

Children, born at Cohasset:

adcac baa.   URIAH, born Aug. 25, 1828; died Dec. 20, 1857, unmarried.
adcac bab.   FRANCIS, born Nov. 17, 1830; died Feb. 28, 1916, at Cohasset.
      He was a carpenter but retired before his death. He lived at Boston
      from 1846 to 1887, and was never married.
adcac bac.   DANIEL-WEBSTER, born Apr. 9, 1833.
adcac bad.   SARAH-VINAL, born Apr. 30, 1835; died Dec. 10, 1895, at Chelsea,
      Mass.; married, Feb. 1, 1858, at Cohasset, James-Thomas[7], son of
      Waterman[6] (*Joseph[5], Caleb[4], Joseph[3], Joseph[2], John[1]*) and Rebecca (Gan-
      nett) Bailey of Scituate, Mass., born March 17, 1833, at Scituate (Bailey
      Genealogy, p. 362, says 1823); died June 8, 1910, at Scituate station, but
      was living at the time at Cohasset with Francis Lincoln. He was at first
      a gold-beater but, later, went into the roofing business with his brother-in-
      law, John-Hobart Lincoln. He lived at Chelsea until he retired from
      business. They had no children. (Cohasset Records; Scituate Records.)
adcac bae.   ISAAC-WARREN, born Sept. 3, 1837; died Sept. 18, 1839.
adcac baf.   JOHN-HOBART, born March 15, 1840.
adcac bag.   ISAAC-NEWTON, born Nov. 8, 1842; died Feb. 6, 1872, at Lynn,
      Mass. He was a shoemaker and lived at Lynn.
         He married, Oct. 18, 1866, at Lynn, Lydia-Ellen, daughter of George
      and Harriet (Downing) Breed of Lynn, born Apr. 24, 1845, at Lynn. They
      had no children. She married (2), Apr. 27, 1892, at Lynn, Ira-Newton,
      son of Daniel and Persis (Stevens) Plumer of Goffstown, N. H., born
      Feb. 8, 1857. They are living, 1911, at West Lynn. He was then a
      motorman on the Boston and Northern Electric Railroad. They have no
      children. (Records of Mrs. Ira-Newton Plumer.)

adcac bah. JAMES-DALLAS, born Feb. 4, 1845; died Nov. 11, 1910, at Cohasset in the old Lincoln house, where he had lived. Massachusetts Vital Records erroneously say he was born May 4, 1844. He was never married.

adcac bai. GEORGE-HENRY, born Dec. 16, 1847.

adcac baj. LOVELL-BICKNELL, born Aug. 9, 1850.

adcac da. JOHN-DUNLAP, son of Isaac (*Uriah, Isaac, Isaac, Mordecai, Samuel*) and Marcia-Scott (Dunlap) Lincoln of Brunswick, Me., born June 1, 1821, at Brunswick; died June 3, 1877, at Brunswick, in the old mansion built by his father, in which he had been born and bred and had passed his life. He graduated at Bowdoin college in 1843 and three years later received the degree of M.D. at the Maine Medical School. He at once commenced the practice of his profession, being associated with his father until the latter's death in 1868, and obtained a thorough and comprehensive understanding of his occupation, acquiring a wide reputation as a physician. The following brief abstract is taken from a lengthy obituary notice published in the "Boston Evening Transcript" at the time of his death:

"After success was assured and his professional engagements were all engrossing, he found time to keep even with the age in new discoveries and appliances for the amelioration of human suffering. He was long a member of the school committee of Brunswick, was for many years and at his death a member of the board of overseers of Bowdoin college, served on the faculty of the Maine Medical School and for years was one of the Republican State central committee. He held various town offices, was director of the First National Bank from its organization, and to his efforts is due much of the excellent condition of the roads and public grounds of the town.

"But these functions were his relaxation, his real devotion was to his profession. His daily practice being in a radius of twenty miles, from early morning till night, and not infrequently at night, he was riding from farm to farm, not only giving advice and medicine, but, by his genial presence, mirthful ways and keen sense of humor, cheering the sick room and giving impulse and new inspiration to all the households he visited. He was ever ready with his sage advice in practical matters, and his long intimacy with families made him a frequent peacemaker in social and public quarrels. No man called on him in vain.

No matter how stormy or dark the night, if there was suffering humanity that needed his skill, he proceeded on his errand of mercy without delay. Many and many a time has he driven at the dead of night in such a storm as often comes up on our bleak coast, ten miles to the dreary shore and then been rowed to some lone island, to tend a sick child; and no reward which this world affords can fulfill the prayers of the mother as he wrapped his cloak about him and went out into the darkness, unpaid save in thanks and the satisfaction to his own warm heart."

He married, June 11, 1862, at Portland, Me., Ellen-Elizabeth-Longfellow, daughter of Gen. Samuel and Deborah (Chandler) Fessenden of Portland, born Apr. 21, 1833, at Portland; died Nov. 27, 1890, at Brunswick. (Brunswick Records; Portland Records; Hist. of Brunswick, pp. 760-1; Records of Mrs. Mary-Richardson [Lincoln] Baxter, *adcac dab.*)

Children, born at Brunswick:

adcac daa. ISAAC, born March 29, 1863; living, 1910, at Aberdeen, S. D., where he is in real estate business with A. E. Boyd, under the firm name of Lincoln and Boyd. He married, June 30, 1906, at St. Paul, Minn., Mrs. Margaret (Ringrose) McHugh, who was born Nov. 8, 1863, at Appleton, Wis. No record has been received of her parentage or first husband. They have no children.

adcac dab. MARY-RICHARDSON, born Jan. 24, 1865; married, Sept. 29, 1886, at Brunswick, Hartley-Cone, son of James-Phinney and Sarah-Kimball (Lewis) Baxter of Portland, Me., born July 19, 1857, at Portland. He graduated at Bowdoin college in 1878, and is a member of the Phi Beta Kappa. They are living, 1910, at Brunswick. He is in business as a corn packer.

Children, born at Brunswick:
  a. SARAH-LEWIS, born Feb. 9, 1890.
  b. ELLEN-LINCOLN, born Aug. 22, 1891.
  c. JOHN-LINCOLN, born May 28, 1896.
  d. EMILY-WEST, born May 7, 1898.

adcac dac. CHARLES-STUART-FESSENDEN, born Aug. 13, 1869.

adcai bg. JOHN-JAMES, son of John (*Lazarus, Isaac, Isaac, Mordecai, Samuel*) and Elizabeth (Stoddard) Lincoln of Cohasset, Mass., born Aug. 5, 1827, at Cohasset; died July 10, 1893, at Cohasset. He was a carpenter and ship-joiner. He lived at Cohasset on South Main street.

He married, Dec. 15, 1851, at Cohasset, Ruth-Bates, daughter of John and Hannah (Worrick) Barker of Cohasset, see *aaffh a,* born March 1, 1832, at Cohasset; died Jan. 16, 1911, at Taunton,

Mass. Her father, John Barker, was one of Cohasset's deep-sea captains. He was an Italian and changed his name from Batista to Barker, and was commonly known as Teesta Barker. Mr. and Mrs. Lincoln are buried at Cohasset, their monument being inscribed simply with their names and with the dates of birth and death as here given, except that Mrs. Lincoln's death is given "Jan. 16, 1912." (Cohasset Genealogies, pp. 17, 246; Cohasset Records; Mass. Vital Records.)

Children, born at Cohasset:

adcai bga. WYMAN-RUSSELL, born July 28, 1852.

adcai bgb. CLARA-FRANCES, born May 2, 1854; married, May 3, 1875, at Cohasset, Stillman-Hewens, son of Edward and Hannah (Hewens) Willis of Easton, Mass., born Dec. 14, 1846, at Easton. He was at the time of his marriage a locomotive engineer, living at Boston. They have no children. (Mass. Vital Records.)

adcai bgc. JOHN-ANSELM, born Nov. 23, 1856; married Mrs. Mary (Brightman) Gifford. They live, 1913, at Hyde Park, Mass. They have no children.

adcai bgd. JAMES-CARTER, born March 26, 1862; died Oct. 21, 1862.

adcai bge. FANNY-KILBY, born Dec. 22, 1863; married, March 14, 1883, at Hingham, Mass., William-Elmer, son of George and Caroline-Elizabeth (Groves) Crocker of Provincetown, Mass., born 1860, at Provincetown. In 1883 he was called "yachtsman." They were living, 1913, at Cohasset on South Main street. He is a "utility man." (Mass. Vital Records; Cohasset Genealogies, p. 118.)

Child, born at Cohasset:

a. BESSIE-LINCOLN, born Aug. 18, 1884; mar. Henry-Beals Bates.

adcai bgf. HARRY-WILLARD, born Sept. 30, 1872. He married, Dec. 18, 1900, at Cohasset, Mary-Jane, daughter of Patrick and Ellen (Keefe) Downes of Cohasset, born Feb. 11, 1870, at Cohasset. He is a master-builder. They are living, 1913, at Cohasset on South Main street. They have no children. (Cohasset Genealogies, pp. 139, 246.)

adcai fb. JOHN, son of Anslem (*Lazarus, Isaac, Isaac, Mordecai, Samuel*) and Hannah (Clapp) Lincoln of Malone, N. Y., born July 26, 1833, at Malone; died Jan. 17, 1908, at Malone, where he had passed his life. He was a leather manufacturer and dealer, of the firm of Lincoln and Miller.

He married, Oct. 18, 1870, at Williston, Vt., Mary-Huntington, daughter of Albert-Jonathan and Mary-Anna (Morton) Fuller of Williston, born March 4, 1848, at Williston; living, 1911, at Malone. (Winslow Family, vol. ii, p. 594; Records of Mrs. John Lincoln.)

Children, born at Malone:

adcai fba. GEORGE-MORTON, born July 31, 1872.

adcai fbb. FREDERIC-FULLER, born June 13, 1875. He was educated at Franklin academy, Malone, and at Vermont University, where he graduated in 1897, and immediately took a position on the "New York Sun" as a reporter, continuing in that position two years. For one year he was assistant secretary of the committee for perpetuating the Dewey arch. For six years he was employed on the "Army and Navy Journal" as advertising manager. In December, 1906, he purchased an interest in the "Cement Age," and is president of the company which publishes that magazine and in charge of its business department. He is a member of the Congregational church and in politics an independent Republican. He is, 1912, unmarried and lives in New York City.

adcai fbc. ANNA-MARY, born Apr. 15, 1881; married, Sept. 21, 1908,* at Malone, Orville-William Kellogg, son of Luman-Edwin and Emily-Augusta (Lawrence) Phelps of Fort Jackson, N. Y., born Sept. 29, 1878, at North Lawrence, N. Y. His mother married (2) a Mr. Kellogg and he legally took that name. He is a furniture dealer at Plattsburg, N. Y., where they are living, 1911. She was educated at Franklin academy, Malone, and at the Burnham school, Northampton, Mass. She also took a course and graduated at the Boston School of Gymnastics, after which she taught physical culture for one year in the Young Women's Christian Association at Dayton, Ohio.

    Child, born at Plattsburg:

    a.   MARY-ISABEL, born Dec. 9, 1910.

adcai ff. ANSLEM, son of Anslem (*Lazarus, Isaac, Isaac, Mordecai, Samuel*) and Hannah (Clapp) Lincoln of Malone, N. Y., born Oct. 26, 1845, at Malone; living, 1912, at Malone, where he is employed in the tannery and leather mills.

He married, Apr. 11, 1876, at Malone, Emma-Jane, daughter of Alexander and Adeline-Elizabeth (Hawley) Spicer of Malone, born Nov. 10, 1852, at Malone; living, 1912. (Records of Mrs. John Lincoln, *adcai fb.*)

Children, born *a* at Burke; *b-d, f-h* at Malone; *e* at Nicholville, N. Y.:

adcai ffa. JOHN-ANSLEM, born March 19, 1877; living, 1912, at Bozeman, Mont., unmarried. He is a ranchman.

adcai ffb. JESSIE-MARY, born Dec. 7, 1879; living, 1912, unmarried.

adcai ffc. EDWIN-LITCHFIELD, born Dec. 12, 1881; died Sept. 23, 1884.

adcai ffd. LUCY-AGNES, born July 6, 1884; living, 1912, at Belgrade, Mont., unmarried. She is a teacher.

adcai ffe. CHARLES-SANFORD, born Apr. 7, 1888; living, 1912, unmarried.

adcai fff. WILLARD-MOORE, born March 16, 1893; living, 1912, at Bozeman, Mont., unmarried, with his brother, John-Anslem.

adcai ffg. SARAH-ADELINE, born Feb. 20, 1896; living, 1912, unmarried.

*"Genealogy and Family History of Northern New York" says Sept. 28, 1907.

adfad ba. MARTIN-VOLNEY, son of Martin (*Jacob, Obadiah, Jacob, Mordecai, Samuel*) and Susan-White (Freeman) Lincoln of Lancaster, Mass., born Dec. 22, 1819, at Alexandria, N. Y.; died Oct. 4, 1885, at Boston, Mass. He engaged first in book-binding and, later, became publisher of "The True Flag," a weekly paper issued at Boston, where he lived.

He married (1), Apr. 6, 1843, at Boston, Eliza-Jackson, daughter of Thomas and Susan-Elizabeth (Thayer) Copeland of Savannah, Ga., and Boston, born Oct. 26, 1818, at Savannah; died Feb. 12, 1872, at Boston.

He married (2), Oct. 8, 1872, at Boston, Elizabeth, daughter of Samuel and Elizabeth G. (Joy) Severance of Boston, born Aug. 30, 1835, at Boston; died Sept. 1, 1903, at Montague, Mass., "aged sixty-eight years, two days." She was buried at Boston. Her father was born at Gill, Mass., her mother at Townshend, Vt. She had no children. (Mass. Vital Records.)

Children, by first wife, born at Boston:

adfad baa. SUSAN-ELIZABETH, born March 25, 1847, she says at West Newton, Mass., but her birth is not recorded there. She married, Apr. 30, 1884, at Boston, Eliot-Belknap, son of Edward-Richards and Nancy-Pierce (Reed) Mayo of Boston, born July 3, 1848, at Boston; died June 21, 1896, at Canton, Mass. He was in real estate business and lived at Boston. She is living, 1912, at Jamaica Plain, Mass. (Records of Mrs. Susan-Elizabeth [Lincoln] Mayo.)

Children, born at Boston:
  a. LINCOLN, born Sept. 26, 1885.
  b. AMY-ELIOT, born June 9, 1889.
adfad bab. CHARLES-RAPP, born May 27, 1849.

adfae ad. WILLIAM, son of William (*Amos, Obadiah, Jacob, Mordecai, Samuel*) and Becky (Pierce) Lincoln of Cohasset, Mass., born Dec. 22, 1821, at Cohasset; died Aug. 26, 1864, at Norton, Mich. He was a farmer and lived at Cohasset on South Main street, in the house of his father. In 1864 he went West with his family, intending to live at Norton, but he died soon after his arrival and the family returned to Cohasset.

He married, May 5, 1850, at Cohasset, Esther-Eliza[8], daughter of Francis-Lincoln[7] (*Ambrose[6], Joshua[5], Joshua[4], Joshua[3], Joseph[2], Clement[1]*) and Esther (Johnson) Bates of Cohasset, born March 19, 1828, at Boston, Mass.; living, 1911. (Cohasset Genealogies, p. 246; Cohasset Records; Family Records.)

Children, born at Cohasset:

adfae ada. WALTER-FOSTER, born June 3, 1851.
adfae adb. HENRY-THOMAS, born Nov. 7, 1844; living, 1911, at Cohasset, unmarried, with his mother and sister. He is a mason by trade.
adfae adc. GEORGE-CUMMINGS, born Aug. 22, 1856.
adfae add. PRISCILLA-BATES, born June 16, 1860; living, 1911, unmarried.

adffe ca. FRANCIS-STONE, son of Thomas (*Caleb, Abraham, Jacob, Mordecai, Samuel*) and Lucy-Coolidge (Stone) Lincoln of Providence, R. I., born Sept. 11, 1836, at Cambridge, Mass.; died May 5, 1905, at Providence. He was educated in the public schools of Providence and was in the soap manufacturing business with his father. He lived at Providence.

He married, May 1, 1861, at Newport, R. I., Mary-Elizabeth, daughter of Joseph and Mary-Cathlin (Moore) Cottrell of Newport, born July 28, 1839, at Newport; died Sept. 13, 1877, at Providence. (Records of George-Henry Lincoln, *adffe cb;* Providence Records.)

Children, born at Providence:

adffe caa. ANNIE-COTTRELL, born March 24, 1864; married, June 30, 1897, at Providence, Edwin-Luther, son of Edwin-Luther and Mary (Hillman) Barney of New Bedford, Mass., born Apr. 14, 1870, at New Bedford. They are living, 1911, at New Bedford. He is a lawyer; clerk of the District Court. They have no children.
adffe cab. FRANCIS-HERBERT, born Oct. 11, 1865; died Sept. 12, 1866, at Providence. Providence records say he was born Oct. 13, 1865.
adffe cac. MARY-ELIZABETH, born Dec. 11, 1867; living, 1911, at Providence, unmarried. She is a school teacher.
adffe cad. HELEN-FRANCIS, born Sept. 6, 1869; died Nov. 7, 1870.

adffe cb. GEORGE-HENRY, son of Thomas (*Caleb, Abraham, Jacob, Mordecai, Samuel*) and Lucy-Coolidge (Stone) Lincoln of Providence, R. I., born Nov. 18, 1838, at Providence. He was a soap manufacturer at Providence from 1853 to 1877, then a box manufacturer under the name of Elmwood Paper Box Company until 1908, when he retired. He is living, 1915, at Providence, with his daughter, Mrs. Charles-Weed North.

He married, Nov. 23, 1859, at Providence, Clarissa-Emily, daughter of Thomas and Rosa-Anna (Wright) Greenwood of Attleboro, Mass., born Apr. 15, 1843, at Attleboro; died Apr. 14, 1914, at Providence. Her parents were English, but emigrated to this country soon after their marriage. (Records of George-Henry Lincoln.)

Children, born at Providence:

adffe cba. HENRY-GREENWOOD, born Sept. 14, 1860, but Providence records say May 14. He was living, 1912, unmarried. He is in business with B. B. and R. Knight at Pontiac, R. I.

adffe cbb. LUCY-COOLIDGE, born Nov. 22, 1861; married, Oct. 20, 1886, at Providence, Ashbell-Tingley, son of Beriah and Lucretia (Cole) Wall of Providence, born March 1, 1861, at Providence. He is president of the A. T. Wall Company, manufacturers of jewellers' supplies in Providence. He graduated at Brown university in 1885. They are living, 1912, at Providence.

    Children, born at Providence:
- *a.* HELEN-LINCOLN, born Feb. 28, 1888; mar. Emerus-Donaldson Clapp.
- *b.* CONSTANCE-COLE, born Dec. 28, 1890; living, 1912, unmarried.
- *c.* ASHBELL-TINGLEY, born Feb. 2, 1892; a student, 1911, at Princeton, N. J.

adffe cbc. MINERVA-WRIGHT, born Dec. 29, 1869; married, Oct. 21, 1890, at Providence, Charles-Weed, son of Gideon-Leeds and Sarah-Ann (Weed) North of Rockville, Conn., born Sept. 1, 1865, at Rockville. They are living, 1911, at Providence. He is superintendent of the National Ring Traveller Company. (Genealogy of the Bostwick Family, p. 857.)

    Children, born at Providence:
- *a.* MILDRED-BROWN, born Feb. 16, 1893; unmarried, 1911.
- *b.* HOWARD-LINCOLN, born Feb. 15, 1894; a student, 1911.

adffe cbd. HOWARD-BICKNELL, born Oct. 3, 1871; died March 17, 1873.

adffe cd. THOMAS-MANSON, son of Thomas (*Caleb, Abraham, Jacob, Mordecai, Samuel*) and Lucy-Coolidge (Stone) Lincoln of Providence, R. I., born Dec. 29, 1843, at Providence. He was in the soap manfacturing business with his father and uncle at Providence, and lived at Providence until 1910 when he removed to East Greenwich, R. I., where he and his wife were both living in 1911.

He married, Apr. 5, 1866, at Providence, Augusta-Eugenie, daughter of Daniel-Anthony and Mary-Sampson (Bogman) Prentice of Providence, born July 13, 1846, at Blackstone, Mass. (Providence Records; Records of George-Henry Lincoln, *adffe cb.*)

Child, born at Providence:

adffe cda. LOUIS-MANSON, born May 13, 1870.

adffe cg. CHARLES-EDWARD, son of Thomas (*Caleb, Abraham, Jacob, Mordecai, Samuel*) and Lucy-Coolidge (Stone)

Lincoln of Providence, R. I., born March 10, 1853, at Providence. He ·was for many years a reporter for the "Providence Journal," and a correspondent of the "Boston Herald." He is now, 1911, manager of the Providence board of trade "Journal," living at Providence.

He married (1), May 29, 1875, at Albany, N. Y., Julia-Maria, daughter of Ichabod-Henry and Elsie (Briggs) Ross of Black-stone, Mass., born Apr. 10, 1858, at Blackstone; died July 10, 1885, at Providence. Her mother was a native of Warwick, R. I.

He married (2), July 11, 1886, at Providence, Ada-Maude, daughter of Archibald-Arnold and Harriet (Kirby) McLaughlin of Montreal, P. Q., born June 22, 1861, at Montreal; living, 1911. Her father was from Greenock, Scotland; her mother was a native of Boston, Mass. (Providence Records; Records of George-Henry Lincoln, *adffe cb*.)

Children, by first wife, born at Providence:

adffe cga. WILLIAM-CROWELL, ⎫ born Aug 29, 1876; ⎰ died Jan. 26, 1886.
adffe cgb. FRANK-BOYNTON, ⎭   ⎱ living, 1911, unmar-
ried. In the Spanish war he enlisted at Providence in Battery A and served during the war. He then enlisted as musician and served for three years at Fort Adams, R. I. In 1910 he enlisted as musician in Battery A, National Guard, for three years.

adffe cgc. RALPH-HAMILTON, born Aug. 29, 1881; died Apr. 6, 1886.

Child, by second wife, born at Providence:

adffe cgd. HOPE-KIRBY, born Oct. 17, 1889; living, 1911, unmarried.

adffe df. CLARENCE-HENRY, son of Samuel (*Caleb, Abraham, Jacob, Mordecai, Samuel*) and Olive (Cook) Lincoln of Providence, R. I., born Dec. 2, 1853, at Providence. He lived at Providence until May 14, 1862, when he removed to Cumberland Hill, R. I., where he remained until May 12, 1875. He then removed to East Blackstone, Mass., where he is now, 1911, living. He is a farmer.

He married (1), Dec. 2, 1874, at Woonsocket, R. I., May-Anna-Adelaide, daughter of Christopher and Abigail-Triphena (Hope) Schultz of Boxboro, Mass., born Feb. 14, 1854, at Boxboro; died Aug. 1, 1892, at East Blackstone.

He married (2), Oct. 16, 1895, at Woonsocket, Amy-Gaskill (Daniels) Norwood, daughter of Andrew-Jackson and Amy-

Gaskill (Darling) Daniels of Blackstone, Mass. She was born
Jan. 26, 1862, at Blackstone and married (1) Eugene Martin of
Woonsocket and (2) a Mr. Norwood of Blackstone. She has no
children by Mr. Lincoln. (Records of Clarence-Henry Lincoln.)

Children, by first wife, born at East Blackstone:

adffe dfa. ABBY-HOPE, born March 18, 1879; married, Sept. 27, 1899, at East
Blackstone, Horace-Richmond, son of Francis-Nicholas and Nancy-Arm-
strong (Paine) Thayer of Blackstone, born Sept. 3, 1873, at Blackstone.
He graduated at Massachusetts Institute of Technology in 1898, and at
Lehigh University in 1906. He is, 1911, professor of civil engineering at
Carnegie Technical School, Pittsburgh, Pa., and they are living at Pitts-
burgh. (Records of Mrs. Abby-Hope [Lincoln] Thayer.)
  Children, born: *a, b, d* at Pittsburgh; *c* at South Bethlehem, Pa.:
    a. CLARENCE-RICHMOND, born June 11, 1901.
    b. FRANCIS-LINCOLN, born June 16, 1903; died Nov. 5, 1903.
    c. DONALD-FRANCIS, born Feb. 2, 1905; died May 5, 1905.
    d. RICHARD-NELSON, born June 5, 1907.
adffe dfb. SAMUEL-BICKNELL, born May 14, 1882.
adffe dfc. RALPH-EDWARD, born Oct. 16, 1884.

adffe dg. LEVI-COOK, son of Samuel (*Caleb, Abraham, Jacob,
Mordecai, Samuel*) and Olive (Cook) Lincoln of Providence,
R. I., born Apr. 15, 1858, at Providence. He is living, 1913, at
Providence, where he is State manager of the Manhattan Life
Insurance Company. He previously lived at Woonsocket, R. I.

He married, Apr. 27, 1877, at Woonsocket, Anjanette, daughter of Joseph-Riley and Cornelia (Skinner) Bailey of Woonsocket,
born Dec. 4, 1858, at Higganum, Conn.; died Aug. 1, 1913, at
Providence. (Records of Levi-Cook Lincoln.)

Child, born at Woonsocket:

adffe dga. FLORENCE-CORNELIA, born May 14, 1878; married, Oct. 17, 1900,
at Woonsocket, Eugene-Capron, son of Luther-James and Ellen (Capron)
Hamlett of Woonsocket, born Feb. 3, 1874, at Woonsocket. They were
divorced in 1909. They had no children. She is living, 1911, at Woonsocket.

aabcd bcd. GEORGE-HENRY, son of Nichols (*Nichols, Jonathan, Jonathan, Samuel, Samuel, Samuel*) and Lucy-Ann (Briggs) Lincoln of Danvers, Mass., born June 14, 1869, at Danvers. He removed to East Rochester, N. H., but is living, 1911, at Rochester, N. H. He is a shoe-cutter.

He married, Aug. 29, 1891, at Rochester, Susie-Ella, daughter of Emerson-Greenleaf and Mary-Elizabeth (Emmons) Thompson of Kennebunk Port, Me., where she was born. (Records of George-Henry Lincoln.)

Children, born: *a* at Springvale, Me.; *b-d* at East Rochester:

aabcd bcda. RAYMOND-EMERSON, born March 9, 1894.
aabcd bcdb. HAROLD-GEORGE, born June 23, 1896.
aabcd bcdc. GLADYS-MAIE, born Aug. 5, 1898.
aabcd bcdd. FRED-EUGENE, born Jan. 5, 1900.

aabce aba. CHARLES-JAIRUS, son of Jairus-Beals (*Peter, Frederick, Jonathan, Samuel, Samuel, Samuel*) and Priscilla-Shaw (Pratt) Lincoln of Weymouth, Mass., born Apr. 1, 1844, at Weymouth; died Aug. 26, 1911. He graduated at Harvard college, 1865, and from 1867 to 1869 was engaged in professional study at Columbia college school of mines. He was instructor at the English high school in Boston, Mass., from 1871 to 1885; headmaster of the East Boston high school 1885 to 1889; and of the Dorchester, Mass., high school, 1889 until his death. He was a deacon of Phillips Congregational Church, Boston, 1878 to 1888; and was a member of the Brookline, Mass., school committee from 1887 to 1891. He lived at Brookline from 1885 to 1891, the rest of his mature life at Boston. At the time of his death he was engaged in looking up dates and names for this genealogy, in which he was much interested.

He married, Apr. 5, 1871, at Boston, Lucy-Ellen, daughter of Alvan and Lucy-Whitney (Day) Simonds of Boston, born March 9, 1845, at Boston; living, September, 1911, at Braintree, Mass. (Weymouth Records; Mass. Vital Records; Records of Charles-Jairus Lincoln.)

Children, born at Boston:

aabce abaa. MARION-WHITNEY, born June 9, 1874; graduated at Radcliffe college in the class of 1897; married, Dec. 28, 1898, at Dorchester, Mass., Leslie-Manly, son of Ariel-Manley and Florence-Matilda (Bates) Cain of Dorchester, born Oct. 20, 1872, at Dorchester. He was educated in the Dorchester schools. They are living, 1911, at Brookline, Mass. He is a salesman.

Children, born at Dorchester:
  a. LINCOLN-SIMONDS, born Aug. 21, 1903.
  b. ELIZABETH, born Jan. 19, 1908.

aabce abab. MAUDE-WINTHROP, born Jan. 7, 1876; graduated at Radcliffe college, class of 1898; married, June 22, 1903, at Dorchester, Mass., Arthur-Welles, son of John-William and Mary-Ellen (Wells) Kirkpatrick of Dorchester, born June 24, 1879, at Newburyport, Mass. He was educated in Boston. They are living, 1911, at Braintree, Mass. He is a salesman. His father was a native of Nova Scotia.

Children, born at Braintree:
  a. PRISCILLA, born July 19, 1908.
  b. GORDON-WELLES, born June 21, 1910.

aabce abc. DAVID-PRATT, son of Jairus-Beals (*Peter, Frederick, Jonathan, Samuel, Samuel, Samuel*) and Priscilla-Shaw (Pratt) Lincoln of Weymouth, Mass., born Oct. 19, 1855, at Weymouth. He was at first a mason by trade and lived at Weymouth until a few years ago, when he removed to Maine. He is now, 1912, a farmer living at Atkinson, Me.

He married (1), Nov. 28, 1878, at Weymouth, Cordelia-Etta, daughter of Horace-Mann and Mary-Julia (Parker) Makepeace of Weymouth, born March 18, 1857, at Weymouth; died there May 28, 1897.

He married (2), March 1, 1899, at Weymouth, Clara-Wentworth Makepeace, sister of his first wife, born June 11, 1863, at Weymouth; living, 1912. (Mass. Vital Records; Records of Charles-Jairus Lincoln, *aabce aba.*)

Children, by first wife, born at Weymouth:

aabce abca. JAIRUS-HORACE, born Oct. 9, 1878.
aabce abcb. A SON, born May 24, 1880; died May 25, 1880.
aabce abcc. MILDRED, born March 28, 1884; married, Sept. 21, 1904, at Braintree, Mass., Irving-Weston Morgan, son of Freeman-Weston and Augusta (Norton) Fairbanks, but an adopted son of Michael and Sarah-Jane Morgan. He was born Oct. 23, 1874, at Gorham, Me., and was living at Braintree when married. He is a shoe-cutter. They are living, 1911, at Weymouth.

Children, born: *a* at Braintree; *b* at Weymouth:
  a. HAROLD-FAIRBANKS, born Aug. 26, 1905.
  b. ALICE, born Dec. 28, 1908.

aabce abcd.   ROYAL, born Jan. 25, 1886; died Jan. 25, 1894.
aabce abce.   CHARLES-HAROLD, born Oct. 23, 1892.
aabce abcf.   ESTHER, born Nov. 16, 1895.

Children, by second wife, born at Weymouth:

aabce abcg.   ETTA-HARRIET, born Jan. 7, 1900.
aabce abch.   LESLIE-PARKER, born Jan. 12, 1901.
aabce abci.   DAVID-ROOSEVELT, born Aug. 14, 1902.

aabce aeb. FREDERIC, son of Oliver (*Peter, Frederick, Jonathan, Samuel, Samuel, Samuel*) and Hannah-Pratt (Dunbar) Lincoln of Weymouth, Mass., born May 16, 1854, at Weymouth; died Aug. 9, 1902, at Warren, Mass., where he had lived for the previous twenty-five years, having been employed for twenty-three years at the Knowles Steam Pump Works as a draughtsman. "He was very strict in all his ways, never used liquor or tobacco, and was much beloved by all who knew him."

He married, Dec. 24, 1881, at Springfield, Mass., Alice-Grace, daughter of Francis-Edward and Sarah-Maria (Penhallow) Lewis of Windham, Conn., born May 23, 1861, at Windham. She married (2), Dec. 30, 1903, at Hartford, Conn., Frederick-William Fortune of Springfield, a blacksmith. She is living, 1912, at Springfield. (Records of Mrs. Edith-Lillian [Lincoln] Case, *aabce aebb.*) Her father, Francis-Edward Lewis, died in 1900 at Leonard's Bridge, Conn. "He was a soldier and much of a wanderer, living nowhere very long." His wife died in 1864 at Windham.

Children, born at Warren:

aabce aeba. OLIVER-FRANCIS, born Aug. 28, 1882.
aabce aebb.   EDITH-LILLIAN, born June 27, 1884; married (1), Nov. 18, 1903, at Springfield, Mass., Samuel-Ernest Berrett, son of Charles-Marcus and Ida E. (Soule) Smith of Springfield, born Aug. 25, 1883, at Springfield. His real name was Ernest-Welcome Smith, but he was adopted by his father's sister at the age of seven and his name was changed. The marriage proved unhappy and they were divorced March 16, 1904. She married (2), May 23, 1905, at Enfield, Conn., George-Bacon, son of John-Cahoun and Mary-Bassett (Bacon) Case of Hyannis, Mass., born Sept. 24, 1864, at Centerville, Mass.; died Apr. 20, 1912, at Springfield. He was an expert accountant. They lived at Springfield. Mr. Berrett was a polisher in the Wesson gun shop.

    Child, by first husband, born at Springfield:

       a.   FREDERICK-ERNEST LINCOLN, born Aug. 24, 1904; died Feb. 12, 1905.

Children, by second husband, born at Springfield:
    b.   GLADYS-ZITELLA-ALICE CASE, born Apr. 9, 1907.
    c.   NATHANIEL-BACON CASE, born June 5, 1910; died Jan. 3, 1911.
    d.   A DAUGHTER, stillborn Apr. 21, 1912.

aabce aebc. CLARENCE-FREDERICK, born March 26, 1887.

aabce aebd. VIOLA-ZITELLA, born Dec. 30, 1893; married, July 29, 1911, at Windsor Locks, Conn., Charles-Leighton, son of Charles-Marcus and Emma (Underwood) Dean of Oakland, Calif., born Jan. 6, 1895, at Springfield. He is a book-keeper. They are living, 1912, at Springfield.

aabce aebe. MILTON-WEBBER, born Oct. 24, 1895.

aabce aec. LA FORREST, son of Oliver (*Peter, Frederick, Jonathan, Samuel, Samuel, Samuel*) and Hannah-Pratt (Dunbar) Lincoln of Weymouth, Mass., born July 21, 1857, at Weymouth. He is a shoe-cutter, living, 1912, at East Weymouth.

He married, March 10, 1886, at North Scituate, Mass., Martha-Adelia, daughter of Nathaniel-James and Abigail-Joy (Litchfield) Vinal of North Scituate, born Feb. 2, 1859, at North Scituate; living, 1912. (Records of La Forrest Lincoln.)

Children, born at East Weymouth:

aabce aeca. LA FORREST-WEBSTER, born Sept. 19, 1886; living, 1912, unmarried.
aabce aecb. GLADYS-ADELIA, born Nov. 28, 1889; living, 1912, unmarried.
aabce aecc. FLORENCE-MAY, born July 25, 1893; living, 1912, unmarried.
aabce aecd. HELEN-ABIGAIL, born Oct. 13, 1895; living, 1912, unmarried.

aabce cda. GEORGE-EDMANDS, son of John-Fillebrown (*Ezekiel, Frederick, Jonathan, Samuel, Samuel, Samuel*) and Ellen-Deane (Simonds) Lincoln of Quincy, Mass., born Oct. 27, 1841, at Boston, Mass.; died July 22, 1877, at Somerville, Mass. He was when married a clerk by occupation, but is called "rail-road conductor" in the record of his death. He was a private in Company B, 5th Massachusetts infantry, in the Civil war and his death was due to malarial consumption, contracted while in the army. He lived at Somerville.

He married, Jan. 15, 1868, at Boston, Susan-Louise, daughter of Henry-Parker and Susan (Currier) Edgar of Charlestown, Mass., born Dec. 19, 1842, at Charlestown; living, 1912, at East Somerville. (Mass. Vital Records; Records of Mrs. Susan-Louise Lincoln.)

34

Children, born at Somerville:

aabce cdaa. HENRY, born Dec. 14, 1868; died same day.
aabce cdab. FRANK-ANTONIO, born Aug. 21, 1870; died Feb. 8, 1880.
aabce cdac. JOSEPHINE-RICE, born Sept. 7, 1873; living, 1912, with her mother, unmarried.
aabce cdad. IDA-LOUISE, born July 19, 1875; living, 1912, with her mother, unmarried.

aabce cdb. EDWARD-TURNER, son of John-Fillebrown (*Ezekiel, Frederick, Jonathan, Samuel, Samuel, Samuel*) and Ellen-Deane (Simonds) Lincoln of Quincy, Mass., born May 19, 1846, at Dorchester, Mass. He ran away from home when thirteen years old; went West and became a train-boy on the Illinois Central railroad. He then went to the Plains and became a pony express rider. At the breaking out of the Civil war he enlisted, Apr. 23, 1861, in Company H, 11th Illinois infantry, and was mustered out at Cairo, Ill., in August, 1861. He immediately re-enlisted, Aug. 5, 1861, in Company C, 2nd Illinois light artillery, and served until Aug. 3, 1863. During all this service he was detached from his Company and served as a spy, most of the time being within the Confederate lines. He was finally captured at Waverly, Tenn., tried by court martial and sentenced to be shot the next morning. During that night, however, he succeeded in escaping and made his way into the Union lines, where he reported to General Grant, who refused to let him serve longer as a spy, but had him appointed as master's mate in the navy; and in this capacity he served on the Mississippi river, in the secret service of the United States, until January, 1865, when he resigned. He then entered the secret service in Washington and, in that capacity, arrested Mr. and Mrs. Surratt for complicity in the assassination of President Lincoln. He remained in the service until 1908, when failing health compelled him to resign. After the war he served in Pennsylvania against the notorious whiskey ring and, later, in Kentucky on the same business. In 1893 he was employed at Chicago at the World's Fair. For the last ten years he has been engaged in insurance business in Boston, but during the first six years as a blind to his real occupation.

He married, May 22, 1873, at Louisville, Ky., Mary-Alice, daughter of Thomas-Robinson and Isabel (Vandegraf) Daniell of Louisville, born Aug. 4, 1850, at Louisville. They are living, 1912, at Somerville. (Records of Edward-Turner Lincoln.)

Children, born at Louisville:

aabce cdba. WALTER-DANIELL, born Aug. 7, 1874. He married, Oct. 3, 1901, at Scranton, Pa., Mabel-Harriett, daughter of Wyatt and Celia (St. John) Kelley of Martin, N. H., born 1883, at Lowell, Mass. They are living, 1912, at Roxbury, Mass. He is a photographer. No children. (Mass. Vital Records.)

aabce cdbb. EUNICE-VIOLA, born Jan. 21, 1876; married, June 17, 1902, at Malden, Mass., Edward-Sidney, son of John-Davis and Mary-Annie (Bates) Parker of Salem, Mass., born Dec. 13, 1871, at Salem. He is in the leather business. They were living, 1912, at Everett, Mass., but were about to move to Phillipsburg, Mont. (Records of Mrs. Edward-Sidney Parker.)

Children, born at Everett:
    a. ROBERT-LINCOLN, born Feb. 29, 1904.
    b. JOSEPHINE, born Nov. 12, 1905.
    c. FLORENCE-BATES, } born Nov. 30, 1907.
    d. MARGERY,

aabce cdbc. THOMAS-RANSOM, born Sept. 6, 1877; living, 1912, unmarried. He is a teacher of music.

aabce cdbd. ELMER-ELLSWORTH, born Aug. 6, 1884; living, 1912, unmarried. He is a motorman on an electric railroad.

aabcf aea. GEORGE-WILLIAM, son of William-Waterman (*Royal, Royal, Jonathan, Samuel, Samuel, Samuel*) and Mary-Waite (Lewis) Lincoln of Savannah, Ga., born Oct. 4, 1854, at Savannah. He graduated at Trinity college in 1875, and at Berkeley divinity school in 1878. He is a priest of the Episcopal church and is living, 1911, at Germantown, Pa.

He married (1), Nov. 29, 1883, at Columbus, Ohio, Jennie-Elizabeth, daughter of James and Martha (Hall) Kershaw of Columbus, born Apr. 12, 1859, at Columbus; died November, 1889, at Columbus.

He married (2), Jan. 7, 1892, at Philadelphia, Pa., Julia-Jenks, daughter of Charles and Margaret (Jenks) Handy of Philadelphia. (Records of Rev. George-William Lincoln.)

Children, by first wife, born at Columbus:

aabcf aeaa. THORLA, born Feb. 10, 1885; living, 1911, unmarried.
aabcf aeab. ELIZABETH, born March 10, 1887; living, 1911, unmarried.

aabcg dba. EDWIN-SAVILLE, son of Beza-Holbrook (*Rufus-Warren, Beza, Jonathan, Samuel, Samuel, Samuel*) and Martha-

Josephine (Forester) Lincoln of Concord, N. H., born July 11, 1847, at Boston, Mass. He is living, 1912, at Nashua, N. H., and calls himself a "laborer." He enlisted Aug. 24, 1864, in Company E, 1st New Hampshire heavy artillery, and was honorably discharged, June 15, 1865, at Washington, D. C.

He married, Dec. 29, 1868, at Andover, Me., Jennie-May, daughter of David and Sarah-Shaw (Morton) Morse of Andover, born Sept. 3, 1847, at Andover; living, 1912. (Records of Edwin-Saville Lincoln.)

Children, born: *a* at Concord; *b-d* at Nashua:

aabcg dbaa. LILLIAN-JOSEPHINE, born March 16, 1871; married, Nov. 29, 1890, at Nashua, Leon-Oliver, son of Loren S. and Harriet (Bray) Dow of Essex, Vt., born May 23, 1872, at Essex Junction, Vt. He is a mechanic. They are living, 1912, at Malden, Mass. They have no children.

aabcg dbab. HARRY-GREALY, ⎱ born Aug. 15, 1873; ⎰ living, 1912, unmarried. A painter.

aabcg dbac. HATTIE-GREEN, ⎰ died November, 1885.

aabcg dbad. ETHEL-FORESTER, born Dec. 16, 1885; married, Dec. 16, 1907, at Nashua, Herman, son of Henry and Ellen (Turner) Cherry of Leytonstone, England, born Oct. 1, 1883, at Leytonstone. He is a stationary engineer. They are living, 1912, at Nashua. They have no children .

aabcg dbc. HARRY-WARD, son of Beza-Holbrook (*Rufus-Warren, Beza, Jonathan, Samuel, Samuel, Samuel*) and Martha-Josephine (Forester) Lincoln of Concord, N. H., born Feb. 27, 1854, at Concord. He is a last-maker.

He married, May 15, 1879, at Natick, Mass., Ella-Frances, daughter of Henry and Hannah (Haywood) Ramsdell of Amherst, Mass., born Sept. 14, 1856, at Malden, Mass. They are living, 1911, at Providence, R. I. (Records of Harry-Ward Lincoln.)

Children, born at Malden:

aabcg dbca. CLARENCE-ARTHUR, born Jan. 3, 1881; died March 3, 1881.

aabcg dbcb. HARRY-FRANCIS, born Oct. 19, 1884. He married, Apr. 14, 1910, at Providence, R. I., Ellen-Theresa, daughter of John-Joseph and Mary-Elizabeth (Mullen) McKenna of Warwick, R. I., born July 14, 1883, at Warwick.

aabcg dbd. GEORGE-LYMAN, son of Beza-Holbrook (*Rufus-Warren, Beza, Jonathan, Samuel, Samuel, Samuel*) and Martha-Josephine (Forester) Lincoln of Concord, N. H., born Jan. 13,

1857, at Concord; living, 1911, at Concord, engaged in furniture business.

He married, July 20, 1881, at Concord, Clara-Louise, daughter of Daniel and Ann-Rebecca (Webster) Wyman of Hillsboro, N. H., born Feb. 18, 1856, at Hillsboro; living, 1911. (New Hampshire Records; Records of George-Lyman Lincoln.)

Children, born at Concord:

aabcg dbda. WYMAN-FORESTER, born Dec. 20, 1882; living, 1911, unmarried.
aabcg dbdb. ROBERT-WEBSTER, born Jan. 4, 1892; died Nov. 11, 1901.
aabcg dbdc. ELEANOR-LOUISE, born March 14, 1894; died Dec. 18, 1894.

aabcg dga. LYMAN-PUTNAM, son of Amasa-Lyman (*Rufus-Warren, Beza, Jonathan, Samuel, Samuel, Samuel*) and Abigail-Smith (Patrick) Lincoln of Santa Barbara, Calif., born July 6, 1863, at Boston, Mass. He was by trade a machinist. He lived at one time at Philadelphia, Pa., but is at present, 1911, living, and has been for some years, in the Hawaiian islands. He is postmaster and tax collector at Hookena, and is also a dealer in coffee.

He married, May 12, 1897, at Kailua, Kona, Hawaii, Henrietta Kepilino, who was born Dec. 13, 1878, at Honakua, South Kona, Hawaii. Mr. Lincoln gives the name of his wife's father as Kala-Kepilino Holua and of her mother as Haalou-Kaleikoa Kamakai. (Records of Henry-Patrick Lincoln, *aabcg dgb.*)

Children, born at Hookena, Kona, Hawaii:

aabcg dgaa. HOWARD-AMASA, born Feb. 11, 1898.
aabcg dgab. ABBIE-LUCY, born Aug. 22, 1899.
aabcg dgac. ARTHUR-LYMAN, born July 8, 1901.
aabcg dgad. HARRY-GORDON, born Sept. 15, 1903.

aabcg dgb. HENRY-PATRICK, son of Amasa-Lyman (*Rufus-Warren, Beza, Jonathan, Samuel, Samuel, Samuel*) and Abigail-Smith (Patrick) Lincoln of Santa Barbara, Calif., born Sept. 18, 1865, at Boston, Mass. He entered the service of the First National Bank of Santa Barbara in January, 1884, as messenger, and was promoted from one position to another until after the death of his father in 1897 he was elected cashier, which position he still holds, 1911.

He married, Dec. 3, 1899, at Santa Barbara, Annie-Merton, daughter of William-Henry and Jamesena (Jameson) Stanwood of Santa Barbara, born Oct. 31, 1867, at Brunswick, Me. They are living, 1911, at Santa Barbara. (Records of Henry-Patrick Lincoln.)

Children, born at Santa Barbara:

aabcg dgba.   WARREN-STANWOOD, born Aug. 27, 1897.
aabcg dgbb.   MARGARET-JAMESON, born Sept. 7, 1899.
aabcg dgbc.   ANNA-BLAKE, born Aug. 30, 1904.

aabcg dgc. JOHN-SPENCER, son of Amasa-Lyman (*Rufus-Warren, Beza, Jonathan, Samuel, Samuel, Samuel*) and Abigail-Smith (Patrick) Lincoln of Santa Barbara, Calif., born Aug. 11, 1874, at Santa Barbara. He attended Leland Stanford university but left before graduation to go into business. He has been with Nathan Bentz, Japanese art goods importer, all his business life.

He married, Apr. 18, 1903, at Santa Barbara, Louise, daughter of William-Henry and Jamesena (Jameson) Stanwood of Santa Barbara, born Nov. 4, 1876. They are living, 1911, at Santa Barbara. (Records of Henry-Patrick Lincoln, *aabcg dgb.*)

Children, born at Santa Barbara:

aabcg dgca.   FRANCES, born Feb. 29, 1904.
aabcg dgcb.   MARIAN, born Sept. 1, 1905.

aabcj hba. ROBIE-THAXTER, son of John-Robie (*Levi-Thaxter, John, Jonathan, Samuel, Samuel, Samuel*) and Julia-Hall (Robbins) Lincoln of Portland, Me., born March 18, 1883, at Portland. He is, 1910, a motorman on the railroad between Melrose and Boston, Mass.

He married, Dec. 25, 1903, at Portland, Sarah-Legrow, daughter of Frederic and Jennie (Legrow) Pollock of Deering, Me., born May 10, 1884, at Woodford, Me. They are living, 1910, at Melrose, Mass. Her father, Frederic Pollock, is a native of Nova Scotia. (Records of John-Robie Lincoln, *aabcj hb.*)

Children, born at Portland:

aabcj hbaa.   DONALD-JASON, born March 7, 1905.
aabcj hbab.   WILLIAM-ROBIE, born Dec. 4, 1906.

aabck bab. ELBRIDGE-BANGS, son of Charles-Nathaniel-Minot (*Charles, Charles, Jonathan, Samuel, Samuel, Samuel*) and Mary-Ann (Shattuck) Lincoln of Jamaica Plain, Mass., born

Aug. 18, 1866, at Jamaica Plain. He was educated in the public schools, but from 1886 to 1888 was engaged in the grocery business. He then entered Berkeley school to fit for college, and entered the college of liberal arts, Boston university, from which he graduated in 1893. During the following year he was principal of the high school at Antrim, N. H. He returned to Boston and entered into insurance business. He was living, 1911, at Hyde Park, Mass., but removed in 1913 to Pacific Beach, Calif.

He married, Oct. 20, 1898, at Boston, Mrs. Margaret-Elizabeth (Greene) Merrill, daughter of Julius A. and Abigail-Antoinette (Burridge) Greene of Templeton, Mass., born Nov. 29, 1870, at Templeton. Her first husband, whom she married July 20, 1891, at South Framingham, Mass., was Frank-Allen, son of John-Foster and Frances M. (Allen) Merrill of Athol, Mass., where he was born Apr. 21, 1872. Her father was a native of Farmington, Me.; her mother was born at Templeton. Mr. and Mrs. Lincoln are reported to have had two children. (Mass. Vital Records; Records of Rev. Charles-Lincoln Morgan, *aabck aa.*)

aabck bfc. LAWRENCE-LITCHFIELD, son of Henry-Barry (*Charles, Charles, Jonathan, Samuel, Samuel, Samuel*) and Helen-Maria (Shedd) Lincoln of Jamaica Plain, Mass., born Sept. 18, 1858, at Jamaica Plain.

He married, July 12, 1883, at Jamaica Plain, Lillian-Cora, daughter of John-Jackson and Lydia (Eldredge) Shaw of Jamaica Plain, born Feb. 27, 1864, at West Roxbury, Mass. Her father was a native of York, Me., her mother of Clinton, Me. Mr. and Mrs. Lincoln are living, 1911, at North Cambridge, Mass. He is a clerk. (Mass. Vital Records; Records of Rev. Charles-Lincoln Morgan, *aabck aa.*)

Child, born at Boston, Mass.:

aabck bfca. LILLIAN-SHAW, born Sept. 26, 1884; married, May 1, 1908, at Boston, William-Partelow, son of James-Clegg and Mary-Burns (Partelow) Ingham of Wakefield, Mass., born Nov. 12, 1879, at Wakefield. They are living, 1913, at North Cambridge. He is a buyer. They have no children.

aabhg aaa. WINTHROP, son of John (*John, John-Barker, John, Samuel, Samuel, Samuel*) and Hannah-Maria (Sears)

Lincoln of Hingham, Mass., born June 29, 1868, at Hingham. He removed to Northbridge, Mass., with his parents and became a carpenter. After his marriage he returned to Hingham and is now, 1911, living at Hingham Center, on Hobart street.

He married, Apr. 22, 1893, at Braintree, Mass., Lucy-Jane[8], daughter of Samuel-Cushing[7] (*Daniel[6], Daniel[5], Joseph[4], Joseph[3], Joseph[2], Nathaniel[1]*) and Sarah-Jane (Tower) Souther of Hingham, born May 9, 1873, at Hingham; living, 1911. (Hist. of Hingham, vol. iii, p. 159; Cohasset Genealogies, p. 447; Records of Winthrop Lincoln.)

Children, born at Hingham:

aabhg aaaa.   JOHN-WINTHROP, born Apr. 2, 1894.
aabhg aaab.   GRACE-ISABEL, born Jan. 11, 1896.
aabhg aaac.   ARTHUR-EARLE, born Apr. 29, 1898.
aabhg aaad.   HAROLD-WILBUR, born Nov. 6, 1903.
aabhg aaae.   RALPH-FREEMAN, born Nov. 16, 1906.
aabhg aaaf.   LUCY-ELLEN, born May 13, 1908.
aabhg aaag.   ROY-LESTER, born June 1, 1910.

aabhg dba.   FREDERICK-EDWIN, son of Henry (*Albert, John-Barker, John, Samuel, Samuel, Samuel*) and Mary-Shepard (Blanchard) Lincoln of Hingham, Mass., born Nov. 3, 1880, at Hingham. He is a bookkeeper.

He married, June 11, 1907, at Randolph, Mass., Mary-Florence, daughter of Franklin-Willard and Ida-Adelia (McCarty) Hayden of Randolph, born Nov. 23, 1879, at South Braintree, Mass. They are living, 1911, at Hingham. (Records of Mrs. Henry Lincoln, *aabhg db.*)

Child, born at Randolph:

aabhg dbaa.   EDNA-PHYLLIS, born June 21, 1908.

aacbc acb.   LEVI, son of William-Sever (*Levi, Levi, Enoch, Jedediah, Samuel, Samuel*) and Elizabeth (Trumbull) Lincoln of Worcester, Mass., born Apr. 27, 1844, at Alton, Ill.; died Jan. 17, 1902, at Boston, Mass., after a brief illness, being attacked with pneumonia while on a business trip. He was commissioned July 18, 1862, second lieutenant in Company E, 34th Massachusetts infantry, of which his father was, first, lieutenant colonel and, afterwards, colonel. He was raised to first lieutenant Nov. 9, 1862, and was discharged for disability Aug. 3, 1864, after brave and distinguished service for two years. In 1875 he was made captain of the Worcester Light Infantry and, two years later, retired from the volunteer service. He was at one time president of the regimental association, and commander of the Union Veteran Camp, and was a member of the Loyal Legion. After the war he held a position in the Boston custom house and was afterwards engaged in business in Boston and Worcester. The greater part of his life was passed in Worcester.

He married, Oct. 21, 1867, at Holden, Mass., Mary-Susan³, daughter of Lyman-Allen² (Asa¹) and Susan-Hyde (Walker) Maynard of Brookfield, Mass., born Dec. 26, 1844, at North Brookfield, Mass.; died Nov. 21, 1903, at Worcester. (Family Records; Mass. Vital Records.)

Children, born: *a* at Boston; *b* at Worcester:

aacbc acba. WILLIAM-SEVER, born Apr. 11, 1870.

aacbc acbb. CHARLES-LEVI, born Oct. 16, 1871; died Aug. 19, 1872, at Center Harbor, N. H.

aacbc acd. WINSLOW-SEVER, son of William-Sever (*Levi, Levi, Enoch, Jedediah, Samuel, Samuel*) and Elizabeth (Trumbull) Lincoln of Worcester, Mass., born Oct. 31, 1848, at Worcester; died May 25, 1902, at Worcester. He was educated in Worcester public schools and then associated himself with his father in running the home farm, which he inherited on his parents' death. He was a skilful farmer and, like his father, was much interested in pure-blooded cattle and had a fine herd of Jerseys in which he took great pride. He was always partial to the militia and for a number of years was captain of the Worcester Light Infantry, which his great-uncle, his uncle and his brother had also at one time commanded.

He married, Jan. 1, 1881, at Worcester, Helen-Blake, daughter of Edwin-Augustus and Lydia-McLellan (Blake) Webber of Chicago, Ill., born Nov. 28, 1858, at Chicago; living, 1921, at Worcester. Previous to her marriage she was a school teacher, and she has always been interested in educational affairs, serving for several years on the school committee of Worcester. (Family Records.)

Children, born at Worcester:

aacbc acda. MARGARET-WINSLOW, born July 17, 1882; married, Aug. 20, 1913, at Worcester, William, son of Henry-Sullivan and Emeline-Josephine (Perham) Marcy of Belmont, Mass., born Feb. 15, 1872, at Troy, N. Y. He graduated at the Troy Polytechnic Institute in 1893 and passed the next four years in California as agent of the Nickel Plate Railroad line. Returning to the East he engaged in coal business in company with Thomas-Edward Sterne, under the firm name of The Scranton Coal Company, with office and yards in Worcester, and he has lived in Worcester ever since, with the exception of a few years in New York City. Retiring from the coal business he was for a few years in the employ of the Reed-Prentice Company, manufacturers of machine tools, but since 1919 has been with the Crompton and Knowles Loom Works. They are living, 1921, in Worcester.

Children, born at Worcester:

    a.   HELEN, born June 7, 1914.

    b.   LINCOLN, born Feb. 29, 1916.

aacbc acdb.   ELIZABETH-TRUMBULL, born Nov. 28, 1883; married, Oct. 8, 1906, at Worcester, George-Sumner, son of Charles-Sumner and Eliza-beth-Spring (Holbrook) Barton of Worcester, born Nov. 4, 1881, at Worcester. He graduated at Harvard college in 1903 and immediately after associated himself with the Rice, Barton and Fales Machine and Iron Company of Worcester, makers of paper-making machinery, of which company he has been president and treasurer since the death of his father. They are living, 1921, at Worcester, with a summer residence at Boylston, Mass.

Children, born at Worcester:

    a.   JANET, born July 27, 1907.

    b.   GEORGE-SUMNER, born March 31, 1910.

    c.   CHARLES-SUMNER, born Oct. 9, 1912.

    d.   TRUMBULL, born Aug. 8, 1917.

    e.   PETER, born Nov. 20, 1921.

aacbc acdc.   PENELOPE-WINSLOW, born June 20, 1888; married, July 19, 1917, at Worcester, Richard-Saltonstall, son of William-Greenleaf-Apple-ton and Laura (Saltonstall) Pattee of Quincy, Mass., born Aug. 4, 1889, at Quincy. He graduated at Harvard college in the class of 1911, then entered the Harvard law school, where he received the degree of LL.B. in 1915, and began the practice of law in Boston.

He entered the service of the United States as infantry private Sept. 5, 1917, and was assigned to Company M, 302nd infantry regiment, 76th Division, at Camp Devens, Mass. He was promoted sergeant Sept. 21, and detached to Officers' Training School at Camp Devens, May 15, 1918; was transferred to Officers' Training School at Camp Lee, Va., Aug. 26, and assigned to 154th Depot Brigade at Camp Meade, Md., Sept. 5. He was honorably discharged Jan. 10, 1919. He returned to his profession and is now, 1922, with Ropes, Gray, Boyden and Perkins of Boston. They live at Cohasset, Mass.

Child, born at Worcester:

    a.   PENELOPE-PELHAM, born June 24, 1918.

aacbc acdd.   WINSLOW-SEVER, born Apr. 30, 1893.

aacbc acde.   EDWARD-BLAKE, born May 4, 1898; died Nov. 29, 1908.

aacbc add.   WALDO, son of Daniel-Waldo (*Levi, Levi, Enoch, Jedediah, Samuel, Samuel*) and Frances-Fiske (Merrick) Lincoln

WALDO LINCOLN
From a photograph

of Worcester, Mass., born Dec. 31, 1849, at Worcester. He was educated in the private and public schools of Worcester and at Harvard college, where he graduated in the class of 1870. After graduation he studied chemistry for one year in Lawrence scientific school at Cambridge. In January, 1872, he entered into partnership with his cousin, Joseph-Parker Mason of Worcester, see *aacbc cc*, under the firm name of Mason and Lincoln, for the sale of iron, steel and heavy hardware. This business proving uncongenial to Mr. Lincoln he sold his interest, two years later, to his partner and, with William-Everett Cutter, Harvard 1869, engaged in the manufacture of copperas and Venetian red from the waste sulphuric acid of the Washburn and Moen Manufacturing Company of Worcester, manufacturers of wire. This partnership continued, under the name of W. E. Cutter and Company, until 1889 when it was dissolved, Mr. Cutter retiring on account of impaired health, and Mr. Lincoln continued the business alone, under the name of The Ferric Chemical and Color Company, until 1893 when he sold the business to the Washburn and Moen Manufacturing Company. Since then he has passed his time in historical and genealogical studies and in travel. In May, 1894, he sailed for Europe with his whole family, excepting his eldest son, then a student at Harvard college, and did not return until June, 1896, the time being divided between England, France, Germany and Italy, with excursions to Switzerland, Sweden and Denmark. In 1903 he again visited Europe with his wife and daughters, travelling in Italy, Algeria and Spain. In 1908, with his wife and younger daughter he started for a trip around the world, but after visiting Egypt, India, Ceylon and Burmah, his daughter, Dorothy, was attacked with typhoid fever and died at Singapore on the first of April, 1909, and the bereaved parents hurried home. Since then he and his wife have made several trips to the West Indies, passing two winters there and one in California. In 1902 he published the "Genealogy of the Waldo Family" in two volumes, a work on which he had been engaged for several years and in the compilation of which he travelled extensively through New Hampshire, Vermont, Connecticut and New York. He has given much time during the last twenty years to the preparation of the present volume.

He is a member of the American Antiquarian Society, the Massachusetts Historical Society, the Colonial Society of Massachusetts, the New England Historic Genealogical Society, the American Historical Association, the Prince Society, the Club of Odd Volumes and of several historical societies of minor importance. In 1906 he was elected second vice-president of the American Antiquarian Society and in October, 1907, its president, to the duties of which office he has since devoted much of his time and attention. Passing the winter of 1912-3 in the British West Indies, he was able to secure for the Society's library a large and valuable collection of West Indian newspapers, covering the period from 1790 to 1880, a collection impossible to duplicate.

He was for several years a director of the Merchants and Farmers Mutual Fire Insurance Company of Worcester, of the Worcester Gas Light Company, the Central National Bank of Worcester, and of the Providence and Worcester Railroad Company and, for ten years, trustee and treasurer of the Worcester Polytechnic Institute. He is at present, 1921, a member of the board of investment of the Worcester County Institution for Savings, a trustee of the Memorial Hospital, the Home for Aged Men and the Rural Cemetery, and chairman of the trustees of trust funds of the City of Worcester. From 1910 to 1913 he was chairman of the Massachusetts State Art Commission, to which position he was appointed by Governor Draper in 1910. From 1889 to 1895 he was director of the Worcester Public Library. In politics he was a Democrat until the breaking up of that party over the silver question, since which time he has had no strong party affiliations, though he was in full sympathy with the policies of President Wilson. In 1892 he was on the Democratic electoral ticket, which in Massachusetts was defeated, though successful in the nation at large. In 1896 he was a delegate to the Gold Democratic convention at Indianapolis, and was a candidate for secretary of state of Massachusetts on the Gold Democratic ticket of that year and received a highly complimentary vote. In religion he is a Unitarian, and since his marriage has been a member and active supporter of the First Unitarian Church of Worcester.

He has been a member, and was for two years president, c

HOUSE OF LEVI LINCOLN, JUNIOR (1782-1868), AT WORCESTER, MASS.
Erected in 1836
From a photograph taken about 1865

the Quinsigamond Boat Club of Worcester, and member of the New York Democratic Club and the New York Reform Club of New York City, the Algonquin Club and the Union Club of Boston, and the Colonial Club of Cambridge, Mass. He is at present, 1922, a member of the Worcester Club, the Tavern Club of Boston, and the Tatnuck Country Club of Worcester of which he was a founder and, for seven of the first nine years of its existence, president. He was for several years a member of the Oquossuc Angling Association of Rangeley, Me. During the great war the Worcester Club was particularly active in patriotic service and Mr. Lincoln, whose three sons were in the army, was its president.

He married, June 24, 1873, at Worcester, Fanny[7], daughter of George[6] (*John-Wilkes*[5], *Peter*[4], *Joseph*[3], *John*[2], *William*[1]) and Josephine (Rose) Chandler of Worcester, born Jan. 5, 1852, at Worcester. She was educated in private schools in Worcester; Geneva, Switzerland; and New York City. She is an accomplished French scholar and an exceedingly good judge of paintings and other works of art. She retains to the present day much of the beauty for which she was noted in youth and middle age. She has borne for many years the trying affliction of extreme deafness with extraordinary amiability. Her portrait and that of Mr. Lincoln, both by the late Frederic P. Vinton of Boston, are in the possession of members of the family.

After the death of his father Mr. Lincoln occupied the old family mansion on Elm street, which was built by his grandfather in 1836 and, though somewhat altered and enlarged, is still, through its classical lines, its commanding situation and beautiful surroundings, one of the most striking and imposing residences in central Massachusetts.

Children, born at Worcester:

aacbc adda. MERRICK, born May 25, 1875. He was educated in public and private schools in Worcester and at Harvard university, where he received the degree of A.B. *cum laude* in 1896 and of M.D. *cum laude* in 1900. After graduation at the Medical school he passed eighteen months as house officer of the Massachusetts General Hospital in Boston and then studied for a year in Germany and Vienna. He then began the general practice of medicine in Worcester, in which he still continues, specializing to a large extent in the diseases of children. From 1909 to 1912 he was city physician and he has been since 1911 on the visiting medical staff of Memorial hospital, having been previously on its dispensary staff, and for some years on the visiting staff of the city hospital. He has contributed articles to medical journals and in 1916 published a pocket treatise on the feeding of infants.

On May 19, 1917, he was commissioned first lieutenant in the Medical Reserve Corps of the United States army, and was commissioned captain in the Medical Corps Apr. 24, 1918, and major July 5, 1919. He entered active service July 13, 1917, and was engaged until August in examining candidates for the second reserve officers' training camps. He then passed three weeks at the training camp for medical officers at Fort Benjamin Harrison and on Aug. 27 was sent to Camp Custer, Michigan, as member of infantry regimental detachment 37 of the 85th Division. From Sept. 6, 1917, to Feb. 19, 1918, he served in the detached medical department of the 340th infantry, and for the next month was connected with the 339th Ambulance Corps and the Quartermaster Corps at Camp Custer. On March 15, he was ordered to General Hospital 13 at Dansville, N. Y., where he remained until Apr. 19, when he was ordered to St. Mary's hospital, Hoboken, N. J., on temporary duty. On May 4, he was ordered to the Base Hospital, Camp Mills, Mineola, N. Y., where he remained until Sept. 16, 1919, when he was honorably discharged at Port of Embarkation, Hoboken. While at this hospital he was at first ward surgeon, then assigned to the supervision of the new hospital buildings as administrator and in charge of medical patients; from Dec. 20, 1918, to Jan. 10, 1919, he was acting chief of medical service; from Jan. 11 to June 19, assistant chief of medical service; and from June 20 to his discharge, chief of medical service.

He married, Apr. 29, 1908, at Worcester, Mary, daughter of Charles-Henry and Mary (Grant) Bowker of Worcester, born March 23, 1884, at Worcester. When her husband was ordered to the Base Hospital at Mineola she accompanied him thither, and was actively engaged as secretary in the Y. M. C. A. hut stationed at the Base Hospital, which hut was turned into a ward for pneumonia patients during the epidemic of influenza. She continued in this service until May, 1919. They have no children.

Dr. Lincoln and his brothers are of the fifth consecutive generation in the Lincoln family to graduate at Harvard college, a record which is equalled by few other families and surpassed by but two.

aacbc addb. JOSEPHINE-ROSE, born Feb. 28, 1878; married, Aug. 10, 1904, at Worcester, Frank-Farnum, son of George-Kelley and Maria-Louisa (Farnum) Dresser of Southbridge, Mass., born Oct. 10, 1872, at Southbridge. He graduated at Harvard college in the class of 1894, and received the degree of A.M. in 1897. He studied at the Harvard law school, 1895-7; was admitted to the bar in Worcester and at once began practice there. He is a member of the firm of Smith, Gage and Dresser and recognized as a leader of the Worcester bar. He is an authority on the law of employers' liability and has published a book on that subject. He is living, 1922, in the old Lincoln mansion on Elm street.

Children, born at Worcester:
- a. LOUISA, born Oct. 25, 1907.
- b. ROSE-LINCOLN, born Oct. 9, 1909.
- c. WALDO-LINCOLN, born March 28, 1916.
- d. FRANCES-MERRICK, born Dec. 1, 1918.

aacbc addc. MARY, born and died Dec. 27, 1878.

aacbc addd. DANIEL-WALDO, born Sept. 2, 1882. He graduated at Harvard college in 1904, and received the degree of LL.B. at the Harvard law school in 1907. He was admitted to the bar and at once began practice at Worcester, first in the office of Choate, Hall and Stewart and, later, in partnership with Charles H. Derby under the firm name of Derby and Lincoln. This partnership was dissolved in 1916 and since then Mr. Lincoln has been alone. He was a member of the Worcester Common Council 1913-4, alderman 1915, and representative in the General Court 1916-7.

He attended the officers' training camp at Plattsburg, N. Y., from May 11, 1917, to Aug. 15, 1917, when he received a commission as first lieutenant in the infantry reserve corps and was assigned immediately to the 76th Division, and on Sept. 29 was attached to Company B, 301st regiment of infantry. The division was at Camp Devens, Mass., until July 4, 1918, when it was sent to France and was then broken up, being used as a replacement division. Lieutenant Lincoln was stationed in the classification camp at St. Amand Mond Rond, department of the Cher, and was the executive officer. Early in November the division was ordered to the front, but before it started the armistice was declared and on Nov. 12 Lieutenant Lincoln was transferred to the 163rd infantry, 41st or "Sunset" Division, which was stationed at St. Georges, department of Loire et Cher, and was in command of Company I. On Jan. 25, he left for home via Brest, and sailed, Feb. 5, on the cruiser "Huntington," arriving at Hoboken on Feb. 16, and was honorably discharged on the twenty-first at Camp Dix. He returned to Worcester and resumed the practice of his profession.

He married, Dec. 29, 1917, at Worcester, Harriet-Brayton, daughter of Dr. Charles-Lemuel and Mary-Janette (Brayton) Nichols of Worcester, born Sept. 8, 1891, at Worcester. They have no children.

aacbc adde. GEORGE-CHANDLER, born Aug. 6, 1884. He graduated at Harvard college with the degree of A.B. in 1905, and for the ensuing two years was engaged in telephone business at Kansas City, Mo. He then entered the Harvard medical school, receiving the degree of M.D. in 1911, and for eighteen months thereafter served as house officer in the Worcester City Hospital, following this with a similar service in the Boston Dispensary. He then commenced general practice in Worcester, but in 1916, deciding to specialize in obstetrics, he took a nine months' course in the Boston Lying-In Hospital and returned to Worcester in the winter of 1917. In the following April he enlisted in the Medical Reserve Corps of the United States army, and was commissioned first lieutenant on May 19. He sailed for France on July 28, and was attached to Base Hospital 101 at St. Nazaire, where he remained until Feb. 28, 1919, when he was ordered to the University of Toulouse for a course of instruction. He was commissioned captain Sept. 2, 1918, and major May 2, 1919. Soon after this he was ordered home and arrived at Boston June 9, and was honorably discharged at Camp Dix on June 13. He is now, 1922, practising his profession at Worcester, making a speciality of obstetrics, and is a staff officer of Memorial Hospital.

He married, June 8, 1921, at Woodstock, Conn., Dorothy-Hardy, daughter of Rufus-Byam and Alice-Lyndon (Bowen) Richardson of Woodstock, born Feb. 7, 1887, at Hanover, N. H. She went to France

in February, 1918, as assistant to Miss Winifred Holt in her work among
blinded French soldiers, and was stationed in Paris and Vichy. In
October, 1918, she was put in charge of the re-education of the blinded
soldiers of the American Expeditionary Forces at Base Hospital 8 at
Savenay, and remained there for five months, until March, 1919, when
she returned to America and went to Baltimore as Red Cross worker
at Evergreen, Red Cross Institute for the Blind, where she remained
for one year.

aacbc addf. DOROTHY, born March 4, 1890; died Apr. 1, 1909, at Singapore,
Straits Settlements, while on her way round the world with her parents.
Her body was brought to America and is buried in Rural cemetery,
Worcester. Beautiful in body and more lovely in character, her death
brought desolation to her parents and great grief to a large circle of
relatives and friends. The play room for the children at Memorial
Hospital, Worcester, is dedicated to her memory.

aacbc ahg. MARSTON, son of Edward-Winslow (*Levi, Levi,
Enoch, Jedediah, Samuel, Samuel*) and Kate-Von Weber (Marston) Lincoln of Worcester, Mass., born June 23, 1864, at Worcester. He was educated in the Worcester public schools as
far as the third year in the High School and then took a year's
business course in the Franklin Institute at Philadelphia, Pa.
He then studied law for two years at Providence, R. I., after
which he was for nearly ten years in a real estate office in New
York City. He then returned to Providence, where he was
employed by the Narragansett Electric Light Company and
was, later, treasurer of the Providence, Fall River and Newport
Steamboat Company. His health failing, he went to Denver,
Colo., where he was assistant purchasing agent of the Denver
Tramway company. He finally returned to Providence and is
now, 1922, note teller with the Union Trust Company.

He married, Dec. 8, 1898, at Fall River, Mass., Clara-Ida,
daughter of William-Henry and Mary-Maria (Phelps) Parker of
Fall River, born June 30, 1874, at Pittsfield, Mass. They are
living, 1922, at Providence.

Child, born at Edgewood, R. I.:

aacbc ahga. EDWARD-WINSLOW, born Oct. 30, 1900. Now, 1922, a senior
in Brown University.

aacbe dab. FREDERIC-WALKER, son of Frederic-Walker (*Louis,
Amos, Enoch, Jedediah, Samuel, Samuel*) and Emily-Caroline
(Lincoln) Lincoln of Boston, Mass., born Aug. 29, 1855, at Bos-

ton. He entered into business in connection with the firm of Henry W. Peabody and Company, in Boston, in 1883, and remained in their Boston house until 1891, when he was transferred to their New York house, with which he was still connected in 1913.

He married, Feb. 21, 1895, at New York City, Philena, daughter of William-Packer and Florence (Kelly) Prentice of New York, born June 28, 1868, at New York. Her father was a native of Albany, N. Y.; her mother was born at Naples, Italy. Mr. and Mrs. Lincoln are living, 1913, at New York. (Records of Frederic-Walker Lincoln.)

Children, born at New York:

aacbe daba. FLORENCE, born Jan. 17, 1897.
aacbe dabb. FREDERIC-WALKER, ⎫
aacbe dabc. MARY-KNIGHT, ⎬ born Oct. 15, 1898.
aacbe dabd. PHILENA-HOPE, born June 29, 1901.
aacbe dabe. EMILY-CAROLINE, born March 31, 1906.

aacbe dad. LOUIS-REVERE, son of Frederic-Walker (*Louis, Amos, Enoch, Jedediah, Samuel, Samuel*) and Emily-Caroline (Lincoln) Lincoln of Boston, Mass., born June 29, 1862, at Boston. He was treasurer of the Lux Engraving Company of Boston, living at Brookline, Mass., but in 1896 he formed a partnership with Fred H. Perry under the name of Lincoln and Perry and engaged in printing business. In 1902 the firm was dissolved and he continued in business alone, under the name of the Shawmut Company, but in 1904 this business was merged with that of the Shawmut Paper Manufacturing Company, and he removed to Walpole, N. H., to take charge of the business there, and was living there in 1911.

He married, Oct. 5, 1892, at Boston, Edith-Buckingham, daughter of John-Crafts and Johanna-Paige (Emmons) Morse of Boston, born Apr. 7, 1864, at Boston; living, 1911. (Mass. Vital Records; Crafts Family, pp. 360, 777.)

Children, born at Brookline:

aacbe dada. EVERT-WENDELL, born Dec. 21, 1898; died Dec. 23, 1898.
aacbe dadb. PAUL-REVERE, born May 8, 1901.

aacbe haa. AMOS A., son of Amos (*Amos, Amos, Enoch, Jedediah, Samuel, Samuel*) and Mary-Ann (Call) Lincoln of

35

Boston, Mass., born Jan. 14, 1851, at Boston. He was a "teamster" and lived at Boston until 1889, his name appearing in the
Boston directories until that date, except from 1878 to 1887,
when he was probably living elsewhere. He is said to have removed to New York City, and after having been divorced from
his first wife to have married again, but nothing definite has
been learned of him after 1889. The records of his son's death
and of his daughter's marriage say they were both born in Boston,
but their births are not recorded there nor in Massachusetts
Vital Records, and it is possible they were not born in the
State.

He married, Apr. 1, 1877, at Boston, Mary-Abbie, daughter of
Coleman and Mary A. Hemingway of Grafton, Me., born, 1853,
at Grafton, though in the record of her son's death she is said
to have been born at Portland, Me. She is said to have been
divorced from Mr. Lincoln, but whether before or after his
removal to New York is not known. No record has been found
of her death. (Mass. Vital Records; Boston Directories.)

Children, born at Boston (?):

aacbe haaa. ADDIE L., born 1878; married, Oct. 1, 1898, at the age of 20,
at Orange, Mass., Albert-Luther, son of Otis-Ebenezer and Olive-Richardson (Cole) Covell of Colebrook, N. H., born Aug. 20, 1880, at Colebrook.
At the time of their marriage he was a "teamster" living at Orange;
she was a "housemaid," also living there. They are separated. They
had no children.

aacbe haab. GEORGE W., born February, 1881; died Nov. 15, 1881, at Boston,
aged nine months.

aacbe 1df. LEVI-BATES, son of Levi-Louis (*Abraham-Orne,
Amos, Enoch, Jedediah, Samuel, Samuel*) and Lydia-Nichols
(Bates) Lincoln of Portland, Me., born Feb. 5, 1875, at Augusta,
Me. He is a civil engineer.

He married, June 18, 1902, at Portland, Sarah-Alice, daughter
of Charles and Sarah-Ann (Young) Jackson of Portland, born
Feb. 23, 1877, at Deering, Me. They lived at Portland until
1910, and then removed to Rumford Falls, Me., where they now,
1913, reside. She is described as "sempstress" when married.
(Portland Records.)

Children, born: *a* at Portland; *b* at Rumford Falls; *c* at
Houlton, Me.:

aacbe ldfa. FRANK-LOUIS, born Sept. 22, 1903.
aacbe ldfb. ALICE-REVERE, born Dec. 17, 1906.
aacbe ldfc. ROGER-BATES, born Aug. 12, 1911.

aacbe lfb. FREDERIC-REVERE, son of Augustus-Clark (*Abraham-Orne, Amos, Enoch, Jedediah, Samuel, Samuel*) and Harriet-Maria ([White] Bean) Lincoln of Benton, Me., born Nov. 6, 1858, at Bath, Me. He is a railroad signal tender living, 1911, at Benton Station, Me.

He married, June 11, 1890, at Waterville, Me., Martha-Ann, daughter of Daniel and Louisa (Hall) Hunt of Troy, Me., born Jan. 31, 1856, at Troy, living, 1911. (Records of Mrs. Anna-Amelia [Lincoln] Hall, *aacbe lfe.*)

Child, born at Benton Station:

aacbe lfba. AUGUSTUS-CLARK, born March 15, 1891. He married Eliza Murry of Fairfield, Me., and was living, 1911, at Fairfield.

aacbg ckb. LOWELL, son of Lowell (*Ezra, Ezra, Enoch, Jedediah, Samuel, Samuel*) and Clara-Amanda (Lothrop) Lincoln of New York, N. Y., born December 15, 1865, at Boston, Mass.; died Sept. 19, 1906, at New York. He graduated at Harvard college in the class of 1886. He was, when he died, a member of the firm of Charles Hathaway and Company, bankers, in New York City.

He married, Nov. 24, 1896, at New York, Anna-Jackson, daughter of Dr. Jackson and Mary-Anna (Bogert) Steward of New York, born Aug. 16, 1869, at New York; living 1911. (Records of Lowell Lincoln, Sr.)

Children, born: *a, c* at New York; *b* at Locust, N. J.:

aacbg ckba. MARY-ANNA-LUDLOW, born Aug. 18, 1897.
aacbg ckbb. LOWELL-LOTHROP, born July 4, 1899.
aacbg ckbc. JACKSON-STEWARD, born Feb. 28, 1902.

aacdb eba. JACOB-STANNELS, son of George-Otis (*Otis, Otis, William, Jedediah, Samuel, Samuel*) and Paulina (Stannels) Lincoln of Eastport, Me., born March 31, 1856, at Eastport. He is in the milk business, living, 1912, at Milton, Mass., on Highland street.

He married, Apr. 28, 1886, at Rockland, formerly East Abington, Mass., Emily-Rolfe, daughter of Turner-Reed and Lydia-

Jane (Lindsey) Holbrook of East Abington, born March 25, 1855, at East Abington. (Records of Mrs. Jacob-Stannels Lincoln.)

Children, born at Milton:

aacdb ebaa.   PAULINE, born May 18, 1887; living, 1912, unmarried.
aacdb ebab.   HOLBROOK, born Jan. 8, 1889; living, 1912, unmarried.
aacdb ebac.   JACOB-ARTHUR, born May 2, 1891; died Sept. 25, 1891.
aacdb ebad.   EDITH-MAY, born May 8, 1894; unmarried, 1912.
aacdb ebae.   RUTH-STANNELS, born July 25, 1897; unmarried, 1912.

aacdb ebg. EDMUND-SABINE, son of George-Otis (*Otis, Otis, William, Jedediah, Samuel, Samuel*) and Paulina (Stannels) Lincoln of Eastport, Me., born Jan. 20, 1869, at Dennysville, Me. He removed to Milton, Mass., and is employed, 1911, as shipper in the chocolate factory of Walter Baker and Company.

He married, June 8, 1898, at Charlestown, Mass., Frances-Maud, daughter of John-Wilson and Margaret-Rosetta (Rudolf) Monroe of Dorchester, Mass., born Aug. 8, 1873, at Bridgewater, Nova Scotia. She was a milliner at the time of her marriage. They are living, 1911, at Mattapan, Mass. (Mass. Vital Records; Records of Edmund-Sabine Lincoln.)

Children, born at Dorchester:

aacdb ebga.   ROBERT-EDMAND, born May 17, 1899.
aacdb ebgb.   DOROTHY-MAIE, born Feb. 18, 1903.
aacdb ebgc.   CHARLES-ERNEST, born March 24, 1912.

aacdb eea. GEORGE-ALBERT, son of Herbert-Richmond (*Otis, Otis, William, Jedediah, Samuel, Samuel*) and Caroline-Matilda (Wood) Lincoln of Eastport, Me., born Oct. 21, 1864, at Perry, Me. He was educated at Boynton high school, Eastport, from which he graduated in 1885; at Phillips Exeter academy, where he graduated in 1888; and at Sioux City, Iowa, law school, where he graduated in 1893. He has been a lawyer and travelling salesman. He has lived successively at Sioux City; Wayne, Nebr.; Mitchell, S. D.; and is now, 1912, living at Worthington, Minn.

He married, June 14, 1892, at Minneapolis, Minn., Stella-May, daughter of Josiah-Nelson and Angelina (Darling) Cheney of Garden City, Minn., born Feb. 25, 1863, at Garden City; living, 1912. Her father was a native of Londonderry, Vt.;

her mother was born at Lucerne, N. Y. (Records of George-Albert Lincoln.)

Child, born at Wayne:

aacdb eeaa. GLADYS-VICTORIA, born Oct. 23, 1894; unmarried, 1912.

aacdb efb. FRANKLIN-PHILBROOK, son of Otis (*Otis, Otis, William, Jedediah, Samuel, Samuel*) and Julia-Sophia (Jones) Lincoln of Perry, Me., born Nov. 14, 1867, at Perry, but Perry records say Nov. 4. He was in 1897 a railroad fireman but is now, 1911, janitor of the Milton, Mass., high school.

He married, Nov. 3, 1897, at Woods Hole, Mass., Eliza-Swift, daughter of Joseph-William and Hannah-Boyden (Swift) Gardner of Falmouth, Mass., born Jan. 25, 1877, at Woods Hole. They are living, 1911, at Milton. (Mass. Vital Records; Records of Franklin-Philbrook Lincoln.)

Child, born at Milton:

aacdb efba. DOROTHY-FRANCES, born Sept. 17, 1903.

aacdb fcb. ALBERT-EDWARD, son of Albert-Robinson (*William, Otis, William, Jedediah, Samuel, Samuel*) and Deborah-Reynolds (Foster) Lincoln of Dennysville, Me., born Oct. 15, 1859, at Dennysville. He is a farmer, living, 1911, at Dennysville.

He married, Nov. 1, 1881, at Dennysville, Ellen-Mehitable, daughter of Benjamin-Reynolds and Adaline (Eastman) Jones of Dennysville, born Jan. 26, 1864, at Dennysville; living, 1911. (Dennysville Records; Records of Albert-Edward Lincoln.)

Children, born at Dennysville:

aacdb fcba. PHILIP-JONES, born Sept. 26, 1882; died Jan. 23, 1910, at Dennysville, unmarried.

aacdb fcbb. ALICE-FOSTER, born Oct. 6, 1885; died May 16, 1906, at Dennysville; married, March 11, 1905, at Dennysville, Earl-Rollins, son of John-Ralph and Olive (Barnard) Higgins of Machias, Me., born Jan. 9, 1882, at Calais, Me. He is living, 1911, at Dennysville and is engaged in the lumbering business. He married (2), May 9, 1908, Ethel Johnson. Mrs. Alice-Foster Higgins had no child save one stillborn in May, 1906.

aacdb fcbc. MARY-OTIS, born March 11, 1890; unmarried, 1911.

aacdb fcbd. DONALD-MORTON, born Jan. 22, 1894.

aacdb fcbe. PRISCILLA-EASTMAN, born Nov. 17, 1895.

aacdb fcbf. A DAUGHTER, born and died Aug. 1, 1898.

aacdb fcbg. ALBERT-ROBINSON, born Nov. 13, 1900.

aacdb fcbh. NELLIE-KILBY, born Aug. 23, 1905.

aacdb fcd. HARRY-FOSTER, son of Albert-Robinson (*William, Otis, William, Jedediah, Samuel, Samuel*) and Deborah-Reynolds (Foster) Lincoln of Dennysville, Me., born Aug. 31, 1867, at Dennysville, according to Dennysville records, but he himself says Aug. 30. He graduated with the degree of B.S. at the University of Maine in 1888, and in 1889 received the degree of Mechanical Engineer in electricity. He started in his profession with the Thompson-Houston Company and in 1889 built the first complete electric light and power plant in Cuba, at the city of Cardenas. He has superintended the construction of several electric railroads, but his largest and most important work, previous to 1911, was the construction of a paper-mill plant at Grand Falls, Newfoundland, in 1907. He is living, 1911, at Boston, Mass., but has a summer home at Dennysville.

He married, Oct. 6, 1892, at Millbury, Mass., Florence-Eva, daughter of Rufus-Revilo and Josephine-Augusta (Sutton) Crane of Millbury, born Apr. 14, 1868, at Millbury; living, 1911. (Records of Henry-Foster Lincoln.)

Children, born: *a* at Leicester, Mass.; *b* at St. Albans, Vt.:

aacdb fcda. DOROTHY, born July 19, 1895.
aacdb fcdb. HELEN, born March 28, 1902.

aacdb ica. WINTHROP-CLINTON, son of Nathan-Pattangall (*Ezekiel, Otis, William, Jedediah, Samuel, Samuel*) and Serena-Morgan (Brown) Lincoln of Bridgewater, Mass., born July 22, 1867, at Newburyport, Mass. He was engaged in the drug business from 1887 to 1905, and then entered the college of medicine of Boston University, where he received the degree of M.D. in 1909, and has since then been practising medicine at Providence, R. I. He has lived also at Vineland, N. J., and at East Cambridge, Mass.

He married, Jan. 21, 1894, at Providence, Marie-Rosina, daughter of John and Ella (Blackman) Seissler of Providence, born Oct. 8, 1874, at Sharon, Mass. (Records of Winthrop-Clinton Lincoln.)

Children, born at Providence:

aacdb icaa. WINTHROP-SEISSLER, born Oct. 10, 1894.
aacdb icab. JOHN-NATHAN, born Aug. 5, 1897.
aacdb icac. STEPHEN-MASON, born Aug. 8, 1905.

aacdb igb. GORHAM-EDGAR, son of John-Howard (*Ezekiel, Otis, William, Jedediah, Samuel, Samuel*) and Martha (Golding) Lincoln of Red Beach, Me., born Apr. 2, 1879, at Robbinston, Me. He is an engineer and machinist, living, 1911, at Red Beach.

He married, Oct. 7, 1904, at Calais, Me., Mabel, daughter of John and Alice (Crowley) Sawyer of Jonesport, Me., born Aug. 21, 1883, at Jonesport; living, 1911. (Records of Mrs. Martha [Golding] Lincoln, *aacdb if.*)

Children, born at Red Beach:

aacdb igba. ETHEL, born Aug. 30, 1905.
aacdb igbb. HOWARD-ANDREW, born Jan. 14, 1907.
aacdb igbc. KENNETH, born Aug. 30, 1908.

aacdb igc. ROBERT-GOLDING, son of John-Howard (*Ezekiel, Otis, William, Jedediah, Samuel, Samuel*) and Martha (Golding) Lincoln of Red Beach, Me., born Jan. 14, 1881, at Robbinston, Me. He is a stone-cutter living, 1911, at Red Beach.

He married, Aug. 8, 1904, at St. Andrews, New Brunswick, Bessie Fisher of Robbinston, born May 25, 1889, at Eastport, Me.; living, 1911. (Records of Mrs. Martha [Golding] Lincoln, *aacdb if.*)

Children, born at Red Beach:

aacdb igca. FRANCINA, born Oct. 30, 1905.
aacdb igcb. MARGARET, born Aug. 31, 1908.
aacdb igcc. ROBERT, born March 3, 1911.

aacdc eac. ALEXANDER, son of William-Henry (*Henry, Henry, William, Jedediah, Samuel, Samuel*) and Celia-Frances (Smith) Lincoln of Brookline, Mass., born Oct. 31, 1873, at Brookline. He graduated at Harvard college in the class of 1895, and received the degree of A.M. in 1896, and of LL.B. in 1902. He is, 1911, a member of the law firm of Whipple, Sears and Ogden of Boston and lives at Boston.

He married, June 22, 1909, at North Easton, Mass., Eleanor, daughter of Oliver and Emma (Benson) Ames of St. Paul, Minn., born Feb. 8, 1880, at St. Paul; living, 1911. (Records of William-Henry Lincoln, *aacdc ea.*)

Child, born at Boston:

aacdc eaca. ALEXANDER, born May 25, 1910.

aacdc eca. HENRY-RICHARDSON, son of Richard-Mitchell (*Henry, Henry, William, Jedediah, Samuel, Samuel*) and Virginia-Mabel (Murray) Lincoln of Southborough, Mass., born Nov. 30, 1876, at Gardner, Colo. He continued to live in Huerfano county, Colo., until 1893, when he removed to Southborough and became a farmer and was living there in 1912.

He married, Aug. 29, 1900, at Southborough, Grace-May, daughter of Charles-Leonard and Emma-Baker (Davison) Hawkins of Southborough, born Jan. 21, 1878, at Putnam, Conn. (Records of Richard-Mitchell Lincoln, *aacdc ec.*)

Children, born at Southborough:

aacdc ecaa.   RAYMOND-HENRY, born July 3, 1902.
aacdc ecab.   ETHEL-MAY, born March 28, 1904.
aacdc ecac.   RICHARD-HAWKINS, born Apr. 21, 1906.
aacdc ecad.   RUTH-PEARL, born Oct. 14, 1910; died July 16, 1911.
aacdc ecae.   CHARLES-WILLIAM, born May 14, 1912.

aacdd dae. SELWYN-RANDALL, son of William-Otis (*William-Otis, Solomon, William, Jedediah, Samuel, Samuel*) and Mary-Rogers (Hoar) Lincoln of Boston and Hingham, Mass., born Dec. 3, 1879, at Hingham. He is, 1911, engaged in insurance business at Boston, but lives at Hingham and is town auditor, having succeeded his father in that office. He is battalion sergeant major in fifth regiment, Massachusetts infantry.

He married, June 11, 1902, at Hingham, Adelaide-Gertrude, daughter of John-Thomas and Eunice (Henley) Copithorn of Cambridge, Mass., born Apr. 8, 1879, at Cambridge; living, 1911. (Records of Selwyn-Randall Lincoln.)

Children, born at Hingham:

aacdd daea.   CATHLEEN, born Nov. 12, 1903.
aacdd daeb.   WILLIAM-OTIS, born June 19, 1905.
aacdd daec.   PAULINE-REVERE, born Apr. 19, 1909.

abbea cab. ISAIAH, son of Francis-Mayhew (*Jerome, Jerome, Francis, Hezekiah, Daniel, Samuel*) and Sarah (Hyland) Lincoln of Cohasset, Mass., born Jan. 31, 1826, at Cohasset; died Nov. 25, 1910, at Cohasset. He lived at Cohasset on Doane street, corner of Beechwood. In early life he was a mariner and was wrecked in the schooner "Maine" in 1846 with his brothers, Ezekiel and Francis-Mayhew, when that vessel was run into

by the Cunard steamship "Hibernia," at the entrance to Massachusetts bay, and his brother Ezekiel was lost. Isaiah afterwards became a farmer, giving up seafaring life, and in some
records he is called "shoemaker."

He married, Nov. 22, 1849, at Scituate, Mass., Martha-
Stockbridge, daughter of Meshech and Temperance (Stoddard)
Litchfield of Scituate, born July 26, 1831, at Scituate; died
Feb. 9, 1895, at Cohasset. (Cohasset Records; Cohasset Gene-
alogies, p. 247; Hist. of Cohasset, pp. 428-431; Scituate Records.)

Children, born at Cohasset:

abbea caba. MARY-ELMINA, born Jan. 31, 1850; married, Nov. 26, 1871, at
Cohasset, James-Edward[6], son of James[5] (*James[4], Isaac[3], Isaac[2], George[1]*)
and Susan (Parsons) Dennison of Boston, Mass., born Jan. 21, 1845,
at Boston. They are living, 1911, at Medford, Mass. (Descendants
of George Dennison, p. 349; Cohasset Genealogies, p. 133.)
Children, born: *a-c* at Cambridge, Mass.; *d* at Cohasset:
  a. EDWARD-BERNARD, born Feb. 28, 1872.
  b. FLORENCE-LINCOLN, born Feb. 2, 1876.
  c. IRENE-LOUISE, born Dec. 15, 1878; mar. Arthur-Cameron
    Green.
  d. MARTHA-ALMIRA, born July 13, 1883.
abbea cabb. ORIANNA-AUGUSTA, born May 26, 1853; married, Dec. 18, 1873,
at Cohasset, William-Otis[9], son of John[8] (*Nathan[7], Joseph[6], Joseph[5],
Joseph[4], Joseph[3], Joseph[2], Nathaniel[1]*) and Abigail-Kent (Tower) Souther
of Cohasset, born July 4, 1851, at Cohasset. He is an ice-dealer living,
1911, at Cohasset on King street. (Cohasset Genealogies, p. 396.)
Children, born at Cohasset:
  a. JOHN-ALBERT-LINCOLN, born July 28, 1874; died July 5, 1875.
  b. ORIANNA-AUGUSTA, born Aug. 5, 1876; mar. Arthur-Lincoln
    Marshall.
  c. WILLIAM-OTIS, born Feb. 8, 1879; mar. Louise Stoddard.
  d. DAVID, born June 1, 1881; mar. Mabel-Louisa McKenzie.
  e. BERTHA-ORILLA, born Oct. 18, 1883; living, 1911, unmarried.
abbea cabc. BERTHA-LOUISE, born May 21, 1858; died June 18, 1906, at
Cohasset; married, May 1, 1879, at Cohasset, Edwin-Gleason[3], son of
William-Temple-Stanley[2] (*William[1]*) and Elizabeth-Calief (Damon)
Stewart of Cohasset, born July 9, 1852, at Cohasset. He was living,
1911, at Cohasset on Beechwood street, and died in 1916. He was a
butcher. (Cohasset Genealogies, pp. 405-6.)
Children, born at Cohasset:
  a. ELLA-LOUISE, born May 4, 1880; mar. Frank-Loverell Hunting.
  b. GEORGIANNA-ALMENA, born Sept. 30, 1882; unmarried, 1911.
  c. A DAUGHTER, born and died Feb. 16, 1894.
abbea cabd. ISAIAH-AUSTIN, born May 16, 1864.
abbea cabe. CHESTER-FRANKLIN, born July 9, 1867; died Oct. 12, 1867.
He is called "Charles F." in the State record of his death.
abbea cabf. ALMA G, sometimes called "Alma-Goddess," born Nov. 8,
1868; married, Sept. 5, 1890, at Brookville, Mass., Herbert-Warren, son

of Warren and Josephine (Tilden) Tirrell of Weymouth, Mass., born
May 14, 1866, at Weymouth. He is a graduate of the Massachusetts
Institute of Technology, and in 1911 was in the employ of the Regal
Shoe Company. They were then living at East Weymouth, Mass.

Children, born at Brockton, Mass.:

    a. JENNIE-BAKER, born Feb. 24, 1891.

    b. MARTHA-JOSEPHINE, born June 18, 1895.

abbea cabg. WILLIAM-IRVING, born Oct. 5, 1871.

abbea cabh. MARTHA-MARIA, born March 23, 1875; died Apr. 18, 1916,
at North Scituate, Mass.; married, Dec. 2, 1903, at Cohasset, Wilbur-
Austin, son of William-Davis and Sarah-Frances (Hobson) Carter of
Scituate, born Nov. 23, 1879, at Scituate. He was in 1911 in the employ
of Stone and Webster, Boston, Mass., and lived at North Scituate.

Children, born at North Scituate:

    a. MARTHA-WHITNEY, born May 30, 1914; died June 6, 1914.

    b. WILBUR-AUSTIN, born Apr. 5, 1916.

abbea cabi. ELIJAH-FRANKLIN, born Dec. 14, 1879.

---

abbea cac. FRANCIS-MAYHEW, son of Francis-Mayhew (*Jerome, Jerome, Francis, Hezekiah, Daniel, Samuel*) and Sarah
(Hyland) Lincoln of Cohasset, Mass., born Apr. 29, 1827, at
Cohasset; died March 7, 1905, at Hingham, Mass. He was a
shoemaker, sometimes called a "mechanic." He lived at Hingham on Beal street. He is buried in Fort Hill cemetery. It was
he and not his father who was wrecked on the fishing schooner
"Maine" in 1846, with his brothers Isaiah and Ezekiel, when he
and Isaiah were saved and Ezekiel was lost. "Cohasset Genealogies," p. 244, says it was his father. (Hist. of Cohasset, pp.
428-431.)

He married (1), Jan. 14, 1847, at Cohasset, Caroline-Franklin[8],
daughter of Lewis[7] (*Jessaniah[6], Nathaniel[5], Joshua[4], Joshua[3],
Joseph[2], Clement[1]*) and Deborah (Litchfield) Bates of Cohasset,
born Jan. 22, 1832, at Cohasset; died there Sept. 10, 1848, and
is buried in Beechwood cemetery. She had no children.

He married (2), Apr. 24, 1850, at Cohasset (Mass. Vital Records say at Hingham), Mary-Ann, daughter of Lewis and Almira-
Olive (Dunham) Anderson of Boston, Mass., born July 6, 1832,
at South Boston; died Oct. 30, 1908, at Hingham, aged seventy-
six years, three months, twenty-four days. The record of the
birth of her son, Lewis-Francis, says she was born in Scituate,
Mass. (Cohasset Records; Mass. Vital Records; Cohasset
Genealogies, pp. 43, 244; Hist. of Hingham, vol. ii, p. 475.)

Children, born at Scituate:

abbea caca. CAROLINE-FRANCES, born July 9, 1854; married (1), Nov. 4, 1874, at Quincy, Mass., Robert S., son of Horatio G. and Keziah (Haskins) Cameron of Plymouth, Mass., born Oct. 9, 1853, at Plymouth, The marriage proved unhappy and they were divorced and she resumed her maiden name. Mr. Cameron was a "nailer."

She married (2), Jan. 1, 1877, at Braintree, Mass., Charles-Herbert, son of Pelham W. and Harriet (Swift) Maxim of Fall River, Mass., born in 1854 at Fall River. He also was a nailer and lived at Weymouth, Mass. Mrs. Maxim, who again resumed her maiden name, was living, 1912, with her daughter, at Dorchester, Mass. She is a nurse.

Child by first husband, born at Hingham:

   a. EDITH-VIOLA CAMERON, born 1875; mar. Oliver-Stodder Hayward.

Child, by second husband, born at Hingham:

   b. DWIGHT-THORNTON MAXIM, born March 13, 1877; died Apr. 15, 1903, unmarried.

abbea cacb. LEWIS-FRANCIS, born Sept. 25, 1856; died, 1909, at Hingham. He married (1), Nov. 20, 1876, at Cohasset, Mary-E.-Celia, daughter of William M. and Mary-Elizabeth (Bonney) Crowell of Hingham, born, 1858, at Hingham. They were divorced, and the "History of Hingham" says that she married (2) James Nash and (3) Francis Copeland; but no record of these marriages has been found.

Mr. Lincoln married (2), Aug. 7, 1886, at Hingham, Mary-Lyon, daughter of Enos D. and Mary-Jane (Pratt) Raymond of Weymouth, Mass., born Sept. 16, 1863, at Weymouth. He was a shoemaker and lived at Hingham. He had no children by either wife.

abbea cacc. ALFRED-STONE, born July 16, 1859.

abbea cad. SAMUEL, son of Francis-Mayhew (*Jerome, Jerome, Francis, Hezekiah, Daniel, Samuel*) and Sarah (Hyland) Lincoln of Cohasset, Mass., born Jan. 1, 1828, at Cohasset; died Feb. 15, 1906, at Hampton, Va., in the Soldiers' Home and was buried with military honors. He served for three months during the Civil war in Company A, 42nd regiment, M. V. M. He was a shoemaker before his marriage and lived at South Weymouth, Mass.

He married, Apr. 29, 1857, at South Weymouth, Mary-Ann, daughter of Elisha and Sylvia (Gurney) Sampson of Turner, Me., born Apr. 4, 1829, at Turner; died Jan. 1, 1908, at Whitman, Mass. (Mass. Vital Records; Records of Mrs. Martha-Maria [Lincoln] Carter, *abbea cabh.*)

Child, born at South Weymouth:

abbea cada. AUGUSTA-MARIA, born Nov. 3, 1858; married, June 16, 1879, at Whitman, Mass., James-Andrew, son of John Kennedy of Weymouth, born June 29, 1852, at Cornwallis, Nova Scotia; died Nov. 16, 1891, at Whitman. He was a farmer. They lived at Whitman and had no children. Mrs. Kennedy was living at Whitman in 1911, and was then agent of the Animal Rescue League, and secretary for Whitman of the Massachusetts Audubon Society.

abbea mba. EDWARD-HALL, son of Martin-Jerome (*Martin, Jerome, Francis, Hezekiah, Daniel, Samuel*) and Ann-Jane (Hall) Lincoln of Taunton, Mass., born May 24, 1863, at Cohasset. He is living, 1912, at Snohomish, Wash., having lived previously at Port Blakeley and Winslow in the same State. He is a wagon-maker and dealer in blacksmiths' and wagon-makers' supplies.

He married, May 23, 1896, at Port Blakeley, Jennie-Catherine, daughter of Elof and Ane (Jensen) Elofson of Port Blakeley, born Nov. 10, 1878, at Veile, Denmark. (Records of Edward-Hall Lincoln.)

Children, born at Seattle, Wash.:

abbea mbaa. CHARLES-HENRY, born March 31, 1897.
abbea mbab. GEORGE-WINSLOW, born May 1, 1899.
abbea mbac. ANNIE-ELEONORA, born Jan. 21, 1901.

abbea mbd. GEORGE-MARTIN, son of Martin-Jerome (*Martin, Jerome, Francis, Hezekiah, Daniel, Samuel*) and Ann-Jane (Hall) Lincoln of Taunton, Mass., born March 28, 1873, at Taunton; died Sept. 21, 1910, at Taunton. He was a book-keeper and lived at Taunton.

He married, Feb. 22, 1899, at Taunton, Mabel-Louise, daughter of George-Francis and Elizabeth-Jane (Wilmarth) Champney of Taunton, born Apr. 25, 1871, at Taunton; living, 1911, at Taunton. (Mass. Vital Records; Records of Martin-Jerome Lincoln, *abbea mb*.)

Child, born at Taunton:

abbea mbda. EDWARD-LELAND, born July 12, 1899.

abbea mhc. FRED-JEROME, son of Charles-Cushing (*Martin, Jerome, Francis, Hezekiah, Daniel, Samuel*) and Flora-Estella (Hayes) Lincoln of Brooklyn, N. Y., born March 6, 1881, at Brooklyn. He is living, 1911, at Cohasset.

He married, Oct. 20, 1906, Jennie-Louise, daughter of Gustave and Hilma-Justine (Johnson) Lawson of New York, N. Y., born

Aug. 16, 1885, at Brooklyn; living, 1911. (Cohasset Genealogies, p. 245; Records of Miss Annie-Elizabeth Lincoln, *abbea mi.*)

Children, born at Cohasset:

abbea mhca. DOROTHY-DAVIS, born Aug. 30, 1908.
abbea mhcb. JAMES-MARTIN, born Sept. 22, 1909.

abbea mhd. HARRY-FRANCIS, son of Charles-Cushing (*Martin, Jerome, Francis, Hezekiah, Daniel, Samuel*) and Flora-Estella (Hayes) Lincoln of Brooklyn, N. Y., born Oct. 14, 1882, at Brooklyn. He is a clerk, 1911.

He married, Oct. 20, 1909, at Cohasset, Mass., Marietta-Foster, daughter of Charles-Frederick and Clarinda-Rebecca (Foster) Bennett of Ottawa, Ill., born Nov. 21, 1884, at Ottawa. (Records of Miss Annie-Elizabeth Lincoln, *abbea mi.*)

Child:

abbea mhda. CHARLES-FRANCIS, born March 14, 1911.

abbec bba. RICHARD-HENRY, son of Henry (*Joseph, Zenas, Francis, Hezekiah, Daniel, Samuel*) and Ophelia (Whittington) Lincoln of Cohasset, Mass., born Oct. 12, 1840, at Boston, Mass. He was a private in Company A, 45th regiment, Massachusetts volunteer infantry, in the Civil war. He has been a piano-maker but is now, 1911, retired.

He married, Jan. 7, 1867, at Cohasset, Mary-Elizabeth[8], daughter of Elias[7] (*Thomas[6], Thomas[5], Thomas[4], Thomas[3], John[2], Thomas[1]*) and Mary-Cecilia-Turner (Townsend) Bourne of Cohasset, born May 15, 1843, at Boston. They are living, 1911, at East Dedham, Mass. (Cohasset Genealogies, pp. 82, 245; Records of Richard-Henry Lincoln.)

Child, born at Boston:

abbec bbaa. HENRY-WADSWORTH, born Jan. 1, 1871; died Aug. 15, 1885, at Boston.

abbec fbd. CHARLES-HOBART, son of Allen (*Thomas, Zenas, Francis, Hezekiah, Daniel, Samuel*) and Julia-Ann (Holmes) Lincoln of Woburn, Mass., born Oct. 6, 1855, at Gray, Me.; died Sept. 20, 1904, at East Bridgewater, Mass. He was superintendent of a roofing company and lived at Woburn.

He married, Jan. 7, 1890, at Newton, N. H., Ida-Berenice, daughter of Jotham-Merett and Mary-Jane (Snow) Tabbut of Newton, born Dec. 9, 1866, at Centerville, Me.; died May 14, 1897, at Melrose, Mass. (New Hampshire State Records; Woburn Records; Mass. Vital Records say married Jan. 9.)

Child, born at Woburn:

abbec fbda. ALPHA-BERENICE, born Oct. 11, 1891.

abbec fdc. EDWARD-MAYNARD, son of Thomas (*Thomas, Zenas, Francis, Hezekiah, Daniel, Samuel*) and Harriet (Tufts) Lincoln of Somerville, Mass., born Sept. 25, 1858, at Saugus, Mass. He is living, 1911, at Everett, Mass. For the previous fourteen years he was night watchman for the National Biscuit Company and lived at Somerville and Cambridge, Mass.

He married, Sept. 25, 1880, at Charlestown, Mass., Annie-Emily, daughter of Thomas and Harriet (Hardy) Lindsey of Glasgow, Scotland, born May 6, 1861, at Glasgow; living, 1911. She came to this country in 1871 without her parents to live with an aunt. (Records of Edward-Maynard Lincoln.)

Children, born: *a-c* at Somerville; *d* at Cambridge:

abbec fdca. THOMAS-FRANKLIN, born May 20, 1881. He is an artist, living, 1913, at Boston, Mass. He married, Nov. 1, 1905, at Lexington, Mass., Harriet-Holbrook, daughter of Alvans-Thomas (or Alvano-Thomas) and Laurietta Nickerson of Lexington, born Sept. 1, 1881, at Campobello, Mass.; living, 1913. They have no children. (Mass. Vital Records.)
abbec fdcb. SIDNEY-LINDSEY, born Jan. 3, 1884; living, 1911, at Everett, Mass., unmarried. He is a baggage master on the Boston and Maine railroad at Boston.
abbec fdcc. HARRIET-PRISCILLA, born Jan. 13, 1886; living, 1911, unmarried.
abbec fdcd. ERNEST-FRANCIS, born Dec. 31, 1896.

adaaa bbb. BENJAMIN, son of Thomas (*Josiah, Abraham, John, Mordecai, Mordecai, Samuel*) and Sarah (Weathers) Lincoln of Milltown, Ind., born Jan. 3, 1830, at Milltown; living, 1916, at Oakland City, Ind., where he was a farmer. He remembered nothing of his grandfather. He died in 1920.

He married, July 20, 1854, in Harrison county, Ind., Angeline, daughter of Shird Burton of Harrison county, born October, 1837, in Harrison county; died there Sept. 2, 1879. (Information of Benjamin Lincoln.)

Children, born in Harrison county:

adaaa bbba. SARAH, born Sept. 2, 1855; died July 9, 1886, at Oakland City, unmarried.

adaaa bbbb. RACHEL, born March 23, 1858; died Oct. 14, 1885.

adaaa bbbc. THOMAS, born July 23, 1860; died June 20, 1900, at Oakland City.

adaaa bbbd. MARY, born Oct. 16, 1862; died Dec. 10, 1899, in Knox county, Ind.

adaaa bbbe. GEORGE-WASHINGTON, born Jan. 2, 1865.

adaaa bbbf. HESTER, born Oct. 20, 1869; married a Mr. Dill. They were living in 1916 at Oakland City.

adaaa bbbg. MARGARET, born March 23, 1873; at Depauw, Ind.; married, Jan. 7, 1891, at Oakland City, Ind., William-Jesse, son of A. G. and Mary E. Rutledge of Wheeler, Okla., born Oct. 23, 1871, at Fort Branch, Ind. He is an electrician. They have lived at Oakland City and Petersburg, Ind., but are now, 1916, living at Loogootee, Ind.

Children, born: *a, b, d* at Oakland City; *c, e,* at Petersburg:
- *a.* NELLIE, born May 4, 1891; mar. W. M. Haskins.
- *b.* RALPH-LINCOLN, born Sept. 1, 1894; mar. Marie Hornbrook.
- *c.* RUTH-HESTER, born Nov. 2, 1897; died Aug. 28, 1901.
- *d.* RAY-JESSE, born June 16, 1900.
- *e.* MARY-ISABEL, born Sept. 16, 1909.

adaaa bbbh. EVA, born July 28, 1875; married E. J. Catterill. They were living, 1916, at Oakland City.

adaaa bbc. MORDECAI, son of Thomas (*Josiah, Abraham, John, Mordecai, Mordecai, Samuel*) and Sarah (Weathers) Lincoln of Milltown, Harrison county, Ind., born March 2, 1832, at Milltown; died there March 9, 1911. He was a farmer and passed his whole life in Harrison county.

He married (1), Oct. 13, 1853, at Milltown, Mary-Elizabeth, daughter of James Spencer of Milltown, born Feb. 13, 1836, at Milltown; died there June 27, 1877.

He married (2), Jan. 22, 1878, at Milltown, Mary Schoonover. (Records of Joseph-David Lincoln, *adaaa bbcg.*)

Children, by first wife, born: *a* at Hancock, Ind.; *b-j* at Milltown:

adaaa bbca. JAMES-THOMAS, born Sept. 22, 1855.

adaaa bbcb. MAJOR-WETHERFORD, born Dec. 13, 1858.

adaaa bbcc. RACHEL-ELIZABETH, born June 27, 1860; died Feb. 8, 1902, at St. Louis, Mo.; married, Sept. 5, 1878, at Milltown, James-Monroe, son of Louis and Mary-Elizabeth (Summers) Gott of Mt. Carmel, Ill., born Sept. 18, 1857, at Milltown. He is, 1917, an engine despatcher on the Chicago and Northwestern Railroad, living at Chicago, Ill. They lived at Mt. Carmel; De Soto, Mo.; and St. Louis.

Children, born: *a, b* at Mt. Carmel; *c* at De Soto:
  a. ROSE-ADA, born July 10, 1880; mar. George-Lytton Sexton.
  b. SHELBY-LEE, born July 1, 1883; mar. Lenora Coghlin.
  c. MABEL-MONROE, born Dec. 25, 1893; mar. Elmer Erickson.

adaaa bbcd. SARAH-JANE, born March 15, 1862; died Jan. 8, 1863.

adaaa bbce. MARTHA-ANN, born Nov. 21, 1863; married at Mt. Carmel, Ill., Theodore-Harley, son of Worster P. and Elizabeth-Ann (Reed) Kingsbury, born at Mt. Carmel. They are living, 1916, at Mt. Carmel. He is in the real estate business.
  Children, born at Mt. Carmel:
  a. EVERETT-EARL, born Jan. 11, 1886; mar. Ethel Glick.
  b. GRACE-MAY, born Feb. 29, 1888; mar. Anthony Kuehn.
  c. ELSIE-CORDELIA, born Oct. 27, 1889; mar. Charles Gardner.
  d. VERN-ELDON, born Apr. 4, 1896; living, 1916, unmarried.

adaaa bbcf. WILLIAM-SHERMAN, born Oct. 22, 1865.

adaaa bbcg. JOSEPH-DAVID, born July 31, 1867.

adaaa bbch. MELISSA-ETTA, born Oct. 15, 1870; married, Apr. 17, 1888, at Mt. Carmel, Ill., Socrates-Kelley, son of Charles H. and Aspasia-Ann Christian, born Dec. 5, 1859, in Illinois. They are living, 1916, at Little Rock, Ark. He is a machinist.
  Children, born: *a, b* at De Soto, Mo.; *c, d* at Poplar Bluff, Mo.:
  a. MAGGIE-FERN, born June 24, 1889; mar. Edward-Leslie Salyears.
  b. MAUD-IRENE, born May 7, 1891; died Dec. 15, 1894.
  c. RUTH-MARIE, born Sept. 11, 1895; mar. Guy-Edward Turpin.
  d. CORINNE-KELLEY, born June 22, 1898.

adaaa bbci. MARY-ELLEN, born Nov. 13, 1872; married, Apr. 20, 1892, at Poplar Bluff, Mo., Marion-Ellsworth, son of Thomas-Jefferson and Malinda (Smith) Sanders of Kentucky, born Feb. 28, 1861, in Saline county, Mo. They are living, 1917, at Poplar Bluff. He is a mechanic. (Records of Mrs. Mary-Ellen Sanders.)
  Children, born at Poplar Bluff:
  a. LINCOLN-ELLSWORTH, born Apr. 26, 1894.
  b. ALVIN-VERNETTE, born Jan. 26, 1896.

adaaa bbcj. HARRIET-EVELINE, born Sept. 27, 1874; married, June 25, 1910, at Roscoe, Tex., Edward-Allen, son of Edward-Allen and Kate (Stewart) Warren of Camden, Ark., born July 9, 1869, at Camden. They are living, 1917, at Snyder, Tex. He is a job printer. They have no children. (Records of Mrs. Harriet-Eveline Warren.)

Children, by second wife, born at Milltown:

adaaa bbck. AMANDA-EMELINE, born Nov. 26, 1878; married Norman Bush. They were living, 1916, at Louisville, Ky. He was a clerk in a department store.

adaaa bbcl. ALTHA-MAY, born Jan. 30, 1880; married, Dec. 5, 1901, at Cory-·don, Ind., William-Simon, son of Fred and Lutetia (Byrum) Bergman of Marengo, Ind., born July 11, 1872, at English, Ind. They are living, 1916, at Depauw, Ind. He is a plasterer.
  Children, born: *a-e* at Milltown, Ind.; *f* at Depauw:
  a. ANNA-KATHLEEN, born Sept. 9, 1902.
  b. ERNEST-KNOEFEL, born Dec. 25, 1903.
  c. HARRY-WAYNE, born Aug. 18, 1907.

> *d.* Viola-Fern, born March 17, 1909.
> *e.* Norman-Joseph, born March 6, 1911.
> . William-Lee, born Jan. 26, 1916.

adaaa bbd. Jacob, son of Thomas (*Josiah, Abraham, John, Mordecai, Mordecai, Samuel*) and Sarah (Weathers) Lincoln of Milltown, Harrison county, Ind., born about 1834, at or near Milltown; died at Ottawa, Kan., whither he had removed. He was a farmer.

He married, Oct. 11, 1855, in Harrison county (County Records), Elizabeth Hupp. They were married by Daniel Fowle, minister of the Gospel.

Children. The name of but one has been reported. There are others.

adaaa bbda. George-Thomas. He was living, 1916, at Richland, Kan., and a son-in-law, Henry Hedrick, was living at Quenemo, Kan.

adaaa bbe. Washington, son of Thomas (*Josiah, Abraham, John, Mordecai, Mordecai, Samuel*) and Sarah (Weathers) Lincoln of Milltown, Harrison county, Ind., born Oct. 25, 1835, at Milltown; died Sept. 27 or 29, 1915, at Milltown. He was a farmer and lived at Milltown and Depauw, Ind.

He married (1), February, 1862, in Washington county, Ind., Deborah, daughter of William and Matilda (Jones) Denton of Harrison county, born Feb. 12, 1845, in Harrison county; died March 10, 1873, at Milltown.

He married (2), July, 1884, at Milltown, Deborah-Ann, daughter of Allen and Clara (Foster) Denton of Harrison county, born Aug. 28, 1853, in Harrison county; living, 1916, at Depauw. She was own cousin of his first wife, their fathers being brothers and also brothers of Isom Denton who married Washington Lincoln's aunt, Elizabeth Lincoln, *adaaa bc.* (Records furnished by various members of the family, but with varying dates.)

Children, by first wife, born: *a* at Depauw; *b-f* at Milltown:

adaaa bbea. William-Thomas, born Jan. 16, 1863.
adaaa bbeb. Mary-Ann, born June 23, 1864; died Jan. 19, 1905, at Milltown; married, May 11, 1884, at Milltown, Charles-Mitchell, son of Thomas and Mary-Ann (Rankin) Byrley of Corydon, Ind., born at Corydon or Bradford, Ind.; living, 1916, at Milltown. He is a farmer. (Records of Charles-Edward Byrley, *adaaa bbebb.*)

36

Children, born at Milltown:

    a. Eva-Florence, born Jan. 31, 1885; mar. William-Warner Byrley.

    b. Charles-Edward, born March 11, 1887; mar. Dora-Emma Jenkins.

    c. William-Chester, born July 28, 1889; died May 9, 1890.

    d. Cora-Alice, born July 28, 1891; unmarried, 1916.

adaaa bbec. Joseph, born Dec. 22, 1865; died October, 1866.

adaaa bbed. Margaret, born Sept. 11, 1867; living, 1916, at English, Ind.; married (1), Nov. 25, 1886, at Milltown, William Way of Milltown, who died Dec. 20, 1894, at English.

She married (2), July 21, 1895, at Marengo, Ind., Henry Leach.

She married (3), a Mr. Landers, or Landrill, who was living, 1916, at Saltillo, Ind., by whom she had no children.

Children, by first husband, born at English:

    a. Alva-Washington Way, born Aug. 20, 1887; died 1906.

    b. William-Ilva Way, born Oct. 24, 1889; died August, 1890.

    c. Irva-Franklin Way, born May, 1891.

    d. Pearl-Lucinda Way, born June 4, 1893; mar. a Mr. Doyle.

Child, by second husband, born at Milltown:

    e. Fay Leach, born Apr. 7, 1896.

adaaa bbee. Zeroda, born June 17, 1869; died May 10, 1896; married, March 4, 1891, at Fredericksburg, Ind., Louis Simpson. They lived at Palmyra, Ind., and had three children all of whom died before 1916. He married a second wife who also died before 1916, when he was still living at Palmyra.

adaaa bbef. Alice, born March 2, 1871; married, Feb. 7, 1892, at Marengo, Ind., Willford, son of Jerry and Leah (Hobson) Allen of Paoli, Ind., born Jan. 23, 1867, at Paoli. He is a farmer. They were living, 1916, at Woodrow, Ark.

Children, born: *a-c* at Marengo; *d* at Bradford, Ind.; *e* at Dalton City, Ill.; *f, g* at Bethany, Ill.:

    a. A son, born Dec. 20, 1892; died same day.

    b. Elsie-Irene, born March 24, 1894; mar. Isaac-Thomas Lemarr.

    c. Herschel-Edward, born Nov. 15, 1896; died July 11, 1898.

    d. A son, born Jan. 1, 1901; died same day.

    e. Cecil-Leland, born Jan. 14, 1907.

    f. Frona-Mabel, } born May 29, 1909; { living, 1916.
    g. A son,   }   { died same day.

Children, by second wife, born at Depauw:

adaaa bbeg. Ethel, born Sept. 27, 1885; died Feb. 4, 1912, at Depauw, Ind.; married, Oct. 5, 1907, at Corydon, Ind., James-Roscoe, son of William and Hester (Hughes) Conrad of Depauw, born in Harrison county, Ind.; living, 1916, at Depauw. He is a farmer.

Child, born at Depauw:

    a. William-Washington, born Dec. 18, 1909.

adaaa bbeh. John-Clarence, born Aug. 20, 1890; living, 1916, at Milltown, unmarried.

adaaa bbei. Charlotte-Mabel, born Feb. 8, 1892; living, 1916, unmarried.

adaaa bbf. WARDEN, son of Thomas (*Josiah, Abraham, John, Mordecai, Mordecai, Samuel*) and Sarah (Weathers) Lincoln of Milltown, Harrison county, Ind., born March 4, 1841, at Fredericksburg, Ind. He enlisted in the 17th regiment, Indiana volunteer infantry, in 1861 and was honorably discharged in 1862. He was taken prisoner in one of the battles in Tennessee, he doesn't remember which, and was confined for six months in Libby prison. He is a farmer, living, 1916, at Depauw, Ind.

He married, Apr. 20, 1865, according to the county records though his son says Apr. 11, 1864, at Fairdale (now Ramsey), Ind., Rachel-Ann, daughter of John and Catherine Hurbaugh of Fairdale, born Nov. 2, 1846, at Fairdale; living, 1916. (Records of Warden Lincoln and his son Frank-Abraham.)

Children, born at Leavenworth, Ind.:

adaaa bbfa. CATHARINE, born Dec. 9, 1867; died March 17, 1887, unmarried.
adaaa bbfb. HENRY-PHILIP, born Oct. 11, 1869, also given as Nov. 11.
adaaa bbfc. CHARLES, born Sept. 11, 1871; living, 1916, at Milltown, Ind.
adaaa bbfd. WILLIAM, born Apr. 1, 1876.
adaaa bbfe. WILLARD-EMMANUEL, born Jan. 6, 1879.
adaaa bbff. LELIA, born May 4, 1883; married Apr. 1, 1900, at Depauw, Ind., John-Roscoe, son of Charles C. and Nancy C. (Spencer) Canoles of Milltown, born Dec. 18, 1881, near Milltown. They are living, 1916, at Milltown. He is a farmer.
  Children, born near Milltown:
    a. MARY-ETTA, born March 2, 1901.
    b. BELLA-FLORENCE, born Apr. 8, 1903.
    c. STELLA-RACHEL, born Aug. 9, 1904.
    d. HERMAN-GILBERT, born Nov. 15, 1907.
    e. BLANCHE-ROSELINE, born Sept. 28, 1913.
adaaa bbfg. FRANK-ABRAHAM, born Aug. 16, 1886; living, 1916, at Depauw, Ind., unmarried.
adaaa bbfh. FLORENCE-MARY, born Sept. 1, 1889; married, Oct. 18, 1911, at Corydon, Ind., William-Harvey, son of Samuel and Sarah (Denbo) Austin of Pilot Knob, Ind., born Jan. 22, 1883, at Pilot Knob. (Harrison County Records, which say she was born in 1888.) They are living, 1916, at Milltown, Ind. He is a farmer.
  Child, born at Pilot Knob:
    a. MABEL-IRENE, born Aug. 16, 1912.
adaaa bbfi. EDWARD, born May 20, 1891.

adaaa bbg. JOSEPH, son of Thomas (*Josiah, Abraham, John, Mordecai, Mordecai, Samuel*) and Sarah (Weathers) Lincoln of Milltown, Harrison county, Ind., born Dec. 30, 1842, at Milltown; living, 1916, at Milltown and calls himself a "laborer."

He married, Sept. 5, 1872, at Corydon, Ind., Melissa, daughter of James and Mary-Flora (Ott) Daugherty of Harrison county, born May 16, 1844, in Harrison county; living, 1916. (Records of Joseph Lincoln.)

Children, born in Harrison county:

adaaa bbga.   CARRIE, born July 7, 1873; married (1), March 18, 1894, at Milltown, Ind., Edward-Francis, son of John-William and Sarah (Lang) Lonigan of Milltown, born Apr. 21, 1869, in Harrison county; died Apr. 14, 1902, at Milltown. He was foreman in a saw mill. They lived at Milltown. She married (2), Sept. 23, 1903, at Milltown, George-Andrew Tower, who was born in 1856. They are living, 1916, at Milltown.

     Children, by first husband, born: *a, c* at Milltown; *b* at Marengo, Ind.:
       a.   GUY-LINCOLN LONIGAN, born Aug. 2, 1895.
       b.   ANNA-MABEL LONIGAN, born Apr. 10, 1898.
       c.   JESSIE-MAUD LONIGAN, born Sept. 5, 1901.
     Children, by second husband, born: *d, j* at Milltown; *e-g* at Temple, Ind.; *h* at Freewater, Ore.; *i* at Maunie, Ill.:
       d.   CHARLES-NOEL TOWER, born Dec. 8, 1904.
       e.   JOHN-FRANKLIN TOWER, born Sept. 5, 1906.
       f.   MILDRED-ARLENE TOWER, born March 17, 1908.
       g.   PAUL-HENRY TOWER, born June 7, 1909.
       h.   HARRIET-HOPE TOWER, born March 30, 1911.
       i.   GEORGE-ANDREW TOWER, born Feb. 22, 1913; died Aug. 5, 1913.
       j.   LLOYD-MERLIN TOWER, born Feb. 7, 1916.
adaaa bbgb.   JAMES F, born Oct. 4, 1878.

adaaa bbi.   JAMES, son of Thomas (*Josiah, Abraham, John, Mordecai, Mordecai, Samuel*) and Sarah (Weathers) Lincoln of Milltown, Harrison county, Ind., born Jan. 29, 1848, at Milltown. He has lived during most of his adult life in Knox county, Ind. For five years he was foreman in a handle factory, then for a number of years he was a farmer, and since 1906 he has been in the grocery business at Vincennes, Ind., where he is now, 1922, living. He says of this branch of the family: "The truth about the Lincoln family of this part of the country is, there are none wealthy, nor college graduates, but they are noted for their honesty."

He married, March 12, 1871, at Fredericksburg, Washington county, Ind., Harriet-Ann, daughter of William-Linley and Sarah-Lovisa (Graves) Elliott of Fredericksburg, born March 25, 1854, in Washington county. (Records of James Lincoln.)

Children, born: *a* in Harrison county; *b-d* in Martin county; *e-g* in Dubois county; *h, i* in Knox county, Ind.:

adaaa bbia. MINERVA, born Dec. 14, 1872; married, Aug. 20, 1891, James-Robert, son of Ephraim and Lovina (Johnson) Gilmore of Knox county, Ind., born Jan. 11, 1868, in Knox county. He is a farmer. They are living, 1922, at Vincennes.

Children, born at Vincennes:
  a. EDITH-FLORENCE, born Aug. 20, 1892.
  b. EDNA-PAULINE, born Apr. 27, 1894.
  c. DENNY-OLIVER, born Oct. 16, 1898.
  d. MARY-ANNALEE, born July 13, 1900.
  e. MILDRED-ETHELYN, born Oct. 29, 1902.
  f. JAMES-ELLIOTT, born June 27, 1904.
  g. FRANCIS-LAVERE, born June 13, 1906.
  h. HAROLD-MAURICE, born Jan. 26, 1909.
  i. JOHN-WILLIAM, born Apr. 5, 1912.

adaaa bbib. MAHULDA, born Oct. 4, 1874; married, May 25, 1902, at Vincennes, Howard-William, son of Jeremiah and Elizabeth (Wheeler) Humphreys of Gibson county, Ind., born May 25, 1883, at Hazleton, Ind. He is a farmer. They are living, 1922, at Hazleton, Ind.

Children, born at Hazleton:
  a. HOLLIS-MORDECAI, born July 5, 1905.
  b. RALPH-FRANKLIN, born Dec. 31, 1908.
  c. HARRIETT-ELIZABETH, born Oct. 6, 1912.
  d. SOPHIA-LUCILLE, born Feb. 20, 1914.

adaaa bbic. LAWRENCE, born Dec. 23, 1876.

adaaa bbid. RALPH-PROSSER, born May 3, 1880.

adaaa bbie. SOPHIA-OPAL, born Apr. 30, 1883; married, July 24, 1902, at Vincennes, Elmer-Burton, son of Decker and Sarah (Reel) Cantwell of Vincennes, born March 5, 1882, in Knox county. He is a farmer and dairyman. They are living, 1922, at Vincennes.

Children, born at Vincennes:
  a. DONALD-LINCOLN, born Feb. 5, 1903.
  b. LEGIA-NAOMI, born Oct. 5, 1904.
  c. MARY-ANNALEE, born June 1, 1906.
  d. CHARLES-FREDERICK, born March 11, 1908.
  · e. EDGAR-CLIFFORD, born Aug. 3, 1910.
  f. CATHRYN-MAUDE, born Sept. 2, 1914.
  g. SYLVIA-RUTH-ANN, born Oct. 5, 1916.

adaaa bbif. NATHAN-HARRISON, born Apr. 4, 1885.

adaaa bbig. AMANDA-STELLA, born Feb. 11, 1887; married, July 23, 1906, at Vincennes, Clarence, son of Reuben and Margaret (Flock) Townsley of Vincennes, born July 30, 1882, in Knox county. He is an iron-moulder. They are living, 1922, at Vincennes.

Children, born at Vincennes:
  a. ELMER-ROLAND, born Dec. 6, 1907.
  b. ORVAL-CLARENCE, born June 17, 1909.
  c. CHARLES-BERNARD, born Nov. 13, 1914.
  d. MARGARET-LILLIAN, born June 29, 1921.

adaaa bbih. DAISY-MAUDE, born Aug. 4, 1889; married, Apr. 11, 1909, at Vincennes, Fred-Allen, son of Shadrach and Julia-Ann (Eskew) Parker of Patoka, Gibson county, Ind., born March 18, 1882, in Gibson county. He is a barber. They are living, 1922, at Vincennes. They have no children.

adaaa bbii. EDGAR-THOMAS, born Oct. 18, 1891. He is a barber, living, 1922, at Vincennes. He married, June 25, 1913, at Vincennes, Minnie-Sadie, daughter of Jasper and Mary (Lindsey) Catlett of Vincennes, born Oct. 20, 1893, at Flat Rock, Ill.; died Feb. 22, 1920, at Vincennes. They had no children.

adaaa bef. JONATHAN-JONES, son of Jacob (*Josiah, Abraham, John, Mordecai, Mordecai, Samuel*) and Martha (Gibbs) Lincoln of Harrison county, Ind., and Wayne county, Mo., born Sept. 26, 1850, in Harrison county. He removed to Missouri about 1880 and is now, 1916, living at Arab, Wayne county, Mo. He is a farmer.

He married, in Wayne county, Annie, daughter of Darius Cato of Wayne county, born June 9, 1864, in Wayne county; died June 18, 1897, at Arab. (Records of Jonathan-Jones Lincoln.)

Children, born: *a* in Knox county, Ind.; *b-j* at Arab:

adaaa befa. ETTIE-FRANCES, born Apr. 15, 1877; married a Mr. Sturgeon. They were living, 1916, at Oran, Scott county, Mo.

adaaa befb. ADA-MAY, born Feb. 14, 1881; died Aug. 15, 1882.

adaaa befc. EFFIE-PEARL, born Nov. 9, 1882; died Aug. 15, 1883.

adaaa befd. OLBERSON, born July 8, 1884; living, 1916, unmarried.

adaaa befe. GROVER-JAMES, born July 25, 1886; died March 30, 1906.

adaaa beff. KATHARINE-MAY, born June 19, 1887; died Jan. 19, 1911, unmarried.

adaaa befg. ALBERT-SIDNEY, born March 2, 1889. He was married Nov. 11, 1909, but no particulars have been obtained.

adaaa befh. MAUDE-BELL, born Nov. 17, 1895; married, May 10, 1912, at Arab, Charles Caines or Carnes.

adaaa befi. CHARLES, born June 8, 1897; died June 25, 1897.

adaaa befj. MARY-LOUISE, born June 16, 1900.

adaaa beg. JOSEPH, son of Jacob (*Josiah, Abraham, John, Mordecai, Mordecai, Samuel*) and Martha (Gibbs) Lincoln of Harrison county, Ind., and Wayne county, Mo., born Nov. 6, 1852, in Harrison county. He is a farmer, living, 1916, at Depauw, Ind. According to the records of Harrison county he was twice married, first on Apr. 18, 1875, by Archibald Boslin, J. P., to Martha I. Cook, and second, on Sept. 24, 1879, by E. P. Stevens, M. G., to Rebecca Jones. He himself does not mention his first marriage and calls his wife Rebecca Edmonson of Harrison county, giving no date.

Children, by second wife, born in Harrison county:

adaaa bega. MARINDA-ELLEN, born June 29, 1880; unmarried, 1916.
adaaa begb. CHARLES-WESLEY, born Apr. 8, 1884; died Nov. 1, 1888.

adaaa dba. ROBERT-TODD, son of Abraham (*Thomas, Abraham, John, Mordecai, Mordecai, Samuel*) and Mary (Todd) Lincoln of Springfield, Ill., born Aug. 1, 1843, at Springfield. He was educated at Illinois State university, 1853-9; at Phillips Exeter academy; and at Harvard college, where he was graduated in 1864. He entered the Harvard law school but left it to enter the army, serving until the end of the war as captain on General Grant's staff. He then resumed the study of law and was admitted to the Illinois bar in 1867 and practised at Chicago. He was a delegate to the Republican State convention in 1880, presidential elector the same year, secretary of war 1881-5, and United States minister to Great Britain, 1889-93. After the death of George M. Pullman in 1897 he became president of the Pullman Company, which position he held until 1911 when he resigned and became chairman of the board of directors. He is now, 1919, a director also of the Commonwealth Edison Company, the Continental and Commercial National Bank of Chicago, the Pullman Trust and Savings Bank, and of the John Crerer Library. He resided at Chicago until 1913 and has since lived at Washington, D. C., with a summer residence at Manchester, Vt.

He married, Sept. 24, 1868, at Washington, Mary, daughter of James and Ann-Eliza (Peck) Harlan of Mt. Pleasant, Iowa, born Sept. 25, 1846, at Iowa City, Iowa. Her father, who was born Aug. 26, 1820, in Clark county, Ill., died Oct. 5, 1899, at Mt. Pleasant. He was by profession a lawyer and was one of the prominent founders of the Republican party. He was United States senator from Iowa, 1856-65; secretary of the interior, 1865-7; and again senator, 1867-73. His last official duty was rendered as chief-justice of the second court of Alabama claims. (Records of Robert-Todd Lincoln.)

Children, born at Chicago:

adaaa dbaa. MARY, born Oct. 15, 1869; married, Sept. 2, 1891, at London, England, Charles, son of William-Bradley and Julia (Burhans) Isham of New York, N. Y., born July 20, 1853, at New York. He is a lawyer. They are living, 1919, at New York.

Child, born at New York:

     a. LINCOLN, born June 8, 1892.

adaaa dbab. ABRAHAM, born Aug. 14, 1873; died March 5, 1890, at London, Eng.

adaaa dbac. JESSIE, born Nov. 6, 1875; married (1), Nov. 10, 1897, at Milwaukee, Wis., Warren, son of Warren and Luzina (Porter) Beckwith of Mt. Pleasant, Iowa, born Aug. 8. 1873, at Mt. Pleasant. They were divorced in 1907. She married (2), June 22, 1915, at Manchester, Vt., Frank-Edward, son of Edward-Whiting and Alice (Thomas) Johnson of Norwich, Conn., born July 5, 1873, at Norwich. He is a well-known geographer, connected at one time with the National Geographic Society of Washington, but now, 1919, in the diplomatic service.

     Children, by first husband, born: *a* at Mt. Pleasant; *b* at Riverside, Ill.:

     a. MARY-LINCOLN BECKWITH, born Aug. 22, 1898.

     b. ROBERT-LINCOLN BECKWITH, born July 19, 1904.

adaae aba. ALBERT-CURTIS, son of Preston (*David, Jacob, John, Mordecai, Mordecai, Samuel*) and Elizabeth (Coffman) Lincoln of Mount Crawford, Va., born Apr. 25, 1839, or 1840, at Mount Crawford; died Aug. 26, 1878, at Leadville, Colo. He was a merchant at Lacey Spring, Va., but on his removal to Colorado he became a miner. He was captain in the 17th Virginia cavalry, Company I, from the outbreak of the Civil war until its close and was a near friend of Fitzhugh Lee. So say the family records, but the "History of Rockingham County" says he was a member of Company G, 10th Virginia cavalry, known as the "Valley Guards." After his marriage he was sheriff of Rockingham county for several terms.

     He married, in 1867, at Clifton Hall, near Athlone, Va., Mary-Elizabeth, daughter of Peter-Perry and Betsey-Ann (Lincoln) Koontz of Clifton Hall, *adaae aee,* born Nov. 25, 1845, at Clifton Hall; died Nov. 10, 1914, at Lacey Spring. "Mrs. Lincoln was a member of the Methodist church, having been connected with that denomination since her childhood. The last seven or eight years of her life she resided with her son at Cape Girardeau, Mo., but returned to Lacey Spring shortly before her death to visit her daughter, Mrs. Strickler, at whose house she died after a brief illness. She was well and favorably known to a large circle of acquaintances at Lacey Spring." (From a newspaper obituary; Family records of Mrs. Albertie-Mae [Lincoln] Strickler, *adaae abad.*)

     Children, born: *a-c* at Lacey Spring; *d* at Clifton Hall:

adaae abaa. ANNA-BELLE, born Nov. 8, 1867; married, March 6, 1898, at Carterville, Mo., Albert-Leonard, son of John-Tabro and Annie A. (Haney) Bayless of Springfield, Mo., born Nov. 9, 1872, at Springfield. Mr. Bayless is a machinist. They are living, 1915, at Joplin, Mo. (Records of Mrs. Anna-Belle [Lincoln] Bayless.)

    Children, born at Joplin:

        a. CORA-BELLE, born Apr. 20, 1900; died Nov. 10, 1900.

        b. ALVA-LINCOLN, born Dec. 2, 1901.

        c. FRANK-LEONARD, born Jan. 2, 1904.

        d. ELIZABETH-GRETCHEN, born Dec. 15, 1905.

        e. OPEL-IVEY, born Apr. 8, 1908.

adaae abab. FRANK-FITZHUGH, born March 9, 1869. He says 1868, but this must be an error. He has lived at St. Francis, Ark.; Cape Girardeau, Mo.; Pleasanton, Tex.; and in various other places in these three States, but is now, 1915, living at Stephens, Ark. He has been a railroad station agent and telegrapher for twenty-two years but intends soon to take up farming. He married, May 10, 1905, at Foster, Mo., Maude-Minnie, daughter of William-Wakefield and Andromicha-Wright (Cummins) Russell of Rockville, Ind., born Feb. 25, 1866, at Rockville. They have no children. (Records of Frank-Fitzhugh Lincoln.)

adaae abac. ELIZABETH-GERTRUDE, born May 17, 1872; died July 24, 1914, at Lacey Spring, unmarried.

adaae abad. ALBERTIE-MAE, born Oct. 16, 1874; married, July 27, 1899, at Lacey Spring, Luther-John, son of Benjamin-Franklin and Melvina (Stephens) Strickler of Lacey Spring, born Aug. 15, 1873, at Lacey Spring. They are living, 1915, at Lacey Spring. He is a farmer. (Records of Mrs. Strickler.)

    Children, born: *a* at St. Francis, Ark.; *b-d* at Lacey Spring:

        a. RAYMOND-RUSH, born Dec. 31, 1901.

        b. MARY-GERTRUDE, born Oct. 14, 1904.

        c. EULA-LUCILE, born Feb. 22, 1910.

        d. ETHEL-IRENE, born May 28, 1912.

adaae agc. HARVEY-PRESTON, son of Jacob-Nicholas (*David, Jacob, John, Mordecai, Mordecai, Samuel*) and Caroline-Thomas (Homan) Lincoln of Lacey Spring, Va., born July 11, 1855, at Lacey Spring. He is a farmer and carpenter, living, 1914, at Lacey Spring.

He married, Feb. 27, 1877, at Lacey Spring, Henrietta-Frances, daughter of William C. and Adeline-Margaret (Cave) Grandle of Lacey Spring, born Apr. 27, 1857, at Mauzy, Va.; living, 1914. (Records of Harvey-Preston Lincoln.)

Children, born at Lacey Spring:

adaae agca. ERNEST-ERDINE, born Oct. 2, 1877. He is a wholesale and retail dealer in butter and eggs at Philadelphia, Pa., where he and his wife are now, 1914, living. He was for a while at Pittsburgh, Pa.

He married, Oct. 18, 1911, at New Market Va., Kathleen-Malinda, daughter of Edgar-Leigh and Ellen (Larrick) Zirkle of New Market, born Dec. 4, 1889, at New Market. They have no children.

adaae agcb. ODESSA-OLEON, born Aug. 6, 1879; married, Aug. 14, 1907, at Washington, D. C., Harry R., son of Perry-Samuel and Arbelia (Sibert) Coffelt of Edinburg, Va., born Jan. 3, 1882, near Edinburg. He is a painter and decorator. They are living, 1914, at Dayton, Va. Child, born at Crafton, Pa.:

    a. HARRY-LINCOLN, born June 1, 1912.

adaae agcc. NINI-SIBYL, born Feb. 23, 1883; living, 1914, unmarried.

adaae agcd. WILLIAM-WESLEY, born Oct. 18, 1884. He married, July 20, 1908, at Pittsburgh, Pa., Edna-Earle, daughter of Albert-Sample and Susan-Thompson (Foster) Moreland of Pittsburgh, born July 6, 1883, at Pittsburgh. They are living, 1914, at Washington, D. C. He is a salesman. They have no children.

adaae agce. EDWARD-RETURN, born Sept. 17, 1891. He married, Jan. 1, 1914, at Harrisonburg, Va., Mary-Cornelia, daughter of Frank-Ward and Stella (Sponsellor) Switzer of Marshall, Mo., born Nov. 8, 1890, at Slater, Mo. They are living, 1914, at Harrisonburg. He is a hardware merchant.

adaae agcf. EUNICE-ADALINE, born Sept. 29, 1895; living, 1914, unmarried.

adaae agi. JACOB-THOMAS, son of Jacob-Nicholas (*David, Jacob, John, Mordecai, Mordecai, Samuel*) and Caroline-Thomas (Homan) Lincoln of Lacey Spring, Va., born Apr. 3, 1872, at Lacey Spring. He removed to Lima, Ohio, in 1891, and since 1896 has been a contractor, builder and general superintendent of constructing buildings.

He married, Oct. 26, 1898, at New Market, Va., Emma-Catherine, daughter of Samuel D. and Hetty (Rimer) Hupp of Forestville, Va., born May 22, 1876, at Forestville. They are living, 1914, at Lima. (Records of Jacob-Thomas Lincoln.)

Children, born at Lima:

adaae agia. RALPH-AUGUSTUS, born Aug. 11, 1899.
adaae agib. OPAL-MARIE, born Dec. 20, 1902.

adaae aha. JOHN-EDWARD, son of Abraham (*David, Jacob, John, Mordecai, Mordecai, Samuel*) and Mary-Elizabeth (Hughes) Lincoln of Lacey Spring, Va., born July 22, 1856, at Lacey Spring. He studied medicine at Bellevue Hospital medical college, New York City, where he received the degree of M.D. in 1876. For two years he lived at Cacapon Springs, Hampshire, W. Va., but returned to Lacey Spring after his marriage, and has lived there since, practising his profession. He is a member of the County

Board of Health and of the Shenandoah Valley Medical Society, of which he was president in 1912.

He married, Oct. 22, 1878, at Yellow Spring, W. Va., Amanda-Alice, daughter of Asa and Rebecca (McKeever) Kline of Yellow Spring, where she was born June 9, 1859. (Records of John-Edward Lincoln.)

Children, born at Lacey Spring:

adaae ahaa. ASA-LIGGETT, born May 10, 1891. He received the degree of A.B. at Elon college in 1910 and of A.M. in 1911. He is now, 1914, studying medicine at Johns Hopkins University, Baltimore, Md. He is not married.

adaae ahab. ROBERT-EDSON, born Oct. 3, 1894. In 1914 he was engaged in automobile business at Harrisonburg, Va., unmarried.

adaae ahc. JETSON-JACKSON, son of Abraham (*David, Jacob, John, Mordecai, Mordecai, Samuel*) and Mary-Elizabeth (Hughes) Lincoln of Lacey Spring, Va., born Apr. 27, 1863, at Lacey Spring. He was educated at Elon college, North Carolina, where he received the degrees of M.A. and Ph.B. He is now, 1914, principal of Wakefield, Va., High School.

He married, Dec. 29, 1886, at Linville, Va., Sallie-Stuart, daughter of Emanuel and Penelope-Catharine (Jennings) Sipe of Sparta, Va., born May 25, 1869, at Sparta. Her father was in command of the 12th Virginia cavalry under General Jeb Stuart in the Civil war. (Records of Jetson-Jackson Lincoln.)

Children, born at Port Republic, Va.:

adaae ahca. ABRAHAM-LUCIUS, born Sept. 16, 1887. He is, 1914, State inspector of schools in the department of public instruction, Richmond, Va. He has the degree of A.B. from Elon college.

adaae ahcb. JENNINGS-SIPE, born June 22, 1892. He received the degree of A.B. from Elon college, and, in 1914, was a student at Johns Hopkins University, Baltimore, Md.

adaae hfa. WILLIAM-EFFIAH, son of Jacob-Broaddus (*Jacob, Jacob, John, Mordecai, Mordecai, Samuel*) and Mary-Isabella (Jasper) Lincoln of Lexington, Va., born Apr. 27, 1855, at Raphine, Va.; is living, 1915, at Staunton, Va. He is a farmer. He lived at Lexington, Va., until after the birth of his children.

He married, May 29, 1877, at Rockbridge Baths, Va., Sallie-Ann, daughter of John L. and Hannah-Martha (McGuffin)

Shewey of Nashville, Kan., born Apr. 21, 1858, at Fairfield, Va.; living, 1915. (Records of William-Effiah Lincoln.)

Children, born at Lexington:

adaae hfaa.   ROSA-JOHRTON, born June 19, 1878; living, 1915, unmarried.
adaae hfab.   MARY-ISABEL, born May 7, 1881; married, Oct. 28, 1905, at Washington, D. C., John-DeRosset, son of James-Osborne and Anna (McCullough) Moore of New Hanover county, N. C., born Aug. 27, 1878, in Gaston county, N. C. They are living, 1917, at Glen Allen, Va.
    Children, born: *a* at Staunton; *b, c* at Richmond, Va.:
      a.   JOHN-LINCOLN, born Nov. 8, 1906.
      b.   JAMES-OSBORNE, born Dec. 28, 1908.
      c.   MAURICE-McCULLOUGH, born July 24, 1912.
adaae hfac.   PERCY-WOODSON, born July 25, 1884.
adaae hfad.   NANNIE-MARGARET, born Dec. 13, 1886; married, Jan. 30, 1907, at Staunton, Va., James-Wesley, son of Elisha-Hobson and Mary-Elizabeth (Mullins) Merricks of Charleston, W. Va., born Apr. 18, 1882, at Griffithsville, W. Va. They are living, 1917, at Charleston. He was educated at Dunsmore business college, Staunton, and has been employed by the Standard Oil Company since May 18, 1904.
    Children, born at Charleston:
      a.   JAMES-WESLEY, born Apr. 27, 1908.
      b.   ROBERT-LINCOLN, born March 31, 1913.
adaae hfae.   FLORENCE-LILLIAN, born March 27, 1889; died June 21, 1889.
adaae hfaf.   JANETTE-ANN, born May 3, 1896; married, Feb. 16, 1916, at Staunton, Va., John-Preston, son of Edward-Sylvester and Josephine (Cook) Wickline of Fairfax, Va., born Oct. 26, 1893, at Clifton Forge, Va. He graduated at Dunsmore business college, Staunton, and is a book-keeper and farmer. They are living, 1917, at Fairfax.

adaae hfb.   JOHN-DAVID, son of Jacob-Broaddus (*Jacob, Jacob, John, Mordecai, Mordecai, Samuel*) and Mary-Isabella (Jasper) Lincoln of Lexington, Va., born Nov. 24, 1856, at Lexington. He is a farmer, living, 1917, at Buena Vista, Va.

He married (1) Willie, daughter of William Hill. Her mother's maiden name was Brant.

He married (2) Mrs. Lula (Adams) Brown. (Information of Mrs. Jacob-Broaddus Lincoln, *adaae hf.*)

Child, by first wife:

adaae hfba.   WILLIAM-BRANT, born about 1882.

Child, by second wife:

adaae hfbb.   JOHN-HENRY. He is living, 1917, at Buena Vista.

adaae hfh.   ASHBY-ABRAHAM, son of Jacob-Broaddus (*Jacob, Jacob, John, Mordecai, Mordecai, Samuel*) and Mary Isabella

(Jasper) Lincoln of Lexington, Va., born Dec. 23, 1871, at Lexington. He has lived at Tye River, Va., since he was twelve years old. He is a farmer.

He married, June 1, 1910, at Lowesville, Va., Julia-O'Neal, daughter of Cubus and Rebecca-Rodes (Waddill) Whitehead of Lowesville, where she was born May 3, 1884; living, 1917. (Records of Abraham-Ashby Lincoln.)

Children, born at Tye River:

adaae hfha. JACOB-BROADDUS, born May 9, 1911.
adaae hfhb. SALLIE-REBECCA, born Aug. 11, 1913.

adaae hfi. CHARLES-BROADDUS, son of Jacob-Broaddus (*Jacob, Jacob, John, Mordecai, Mordecai, Samuel*) and Mary-Isabella (Jasper) Lincoln of Lexington, Va., born Apr. 4, 1873, at Lexington. He has passed most of his life at Tye River, Va., but he and his wife are now, 1915, living near Scottsville, Albemarle county, Va. He is a farmer.

He married, Sept. 14, 1890, at Washington, D. C., Kate-May, daughter of William-Andrew and Elizabeth (Mays) Bowles of New Glasgow, Va., born Oct. 29, 1873, at New Glasgow. (Records of Charles-Broaddus Lincoln.)

Children, born at New Glasgow:

adaae hfia. ISABEL, born Sept. 14, 1891; married, Dec. 18, 1907, at Arrington, Va., George W. Moses.
adaae hfib. MAMIE-ELIZABETH, born Feb. 4, 1896; married, Dec. 1, 1913, at Alta Vista, Va., A. Waverly Wingfield.

adaaf ace. ROBERT-ABRAHAM, son of James-Hamilton (*Jesse, John, John, Mordecai, Mordecai, Samuel*) and Ida-Beatrice (Sharp) Lincoln of Chattanooga, Tenn., born May 31, 1885, at Lookout Mountain, Tenn. He lived until 1902 at Chattanooga, where he was employed in the trunk-making business. He then removed to Texas and is a contractor for drilling oil wells.

He married, Aug. 17, 1916, at Austin, Tex., Eugenia-Bryant, daughter of ———— and Eugenia D. (Whitfield) Outlaw of Lilac, Tex., born June 26, 1896, at Lilac. Her father, whose name for some reason has not been given, was a native of North Carolina. Her mother was a Kentuckian. Mr. and Mrs. Lincoln are living,

1917, at Burkburnett, Tex. (Information of Mrs. Robert-Abraham Lincoln.)

Child, born at Burkburnett:

adaaf acea. ROBERTA-BEATRICE, born Sept. 11, 1917.

adaaf acf. FREDERICK-ALBERT, son of James-Hamilton (*Jesse, John, John, Mordecai, Mordecai, Samuel*) and Ida-Beatrice (Sharp) Lincoln of Chattanooga, Tenn., born Dec. 28, 1887, at Lookout Mountain, Tenn. He lived until 1902 at Chattanooga and then removed to Texas. He is a machinist.

He married, March 31, 1915, at Beaumont, Tex., Leona-Adria, daughter of Percy-Elwyn and Nellie (Norman) Parminter, born July 8, 1895, at Everett, Wash. Her father is deceased; her mother resides, 1917, at Fort Morgan, Colo. Mr. and Mrs. Lincoln are living, 1917, at Electra, Tex. (Records of Mrs. Frederick-Albert Lincoln.)

Children, born: *a* at Beaumont; *b* at Electra, Tex.:

adaaf acfa. MARGUERITE-BEATRICE, born Nov. 17, 1915.
adaaf acfb. MILLICENT-ROMA, born Oct. 24, 1917.

adaaf dba. WILLIAM-HENRY, son of John-Craigin (*Mordecai, John, John, Mordecai, Mordecai, Samuel*) and Jane (Usrey) Lincoln of Memphis, Tenn., born Feb. 5, 1840, at Eagle Furnace, Tenn.; died June 10, 1910, in Smith county, Tenn. He was a merchant and lived at Alexandria, Tenn., and in Smith county.

He married (1), Nov. 21, 1867, in Rutherford county, Tenn., Lee, daughter of George and Emma (Pirtle) Moore.

He married (2) Mrs. Alameda (Dougherty) Kennedy of Cannon county, Tenn. She died June 19, 1910, in Smith county. (Records of Mrs. Josephine [Lincoln] Davis, *adaaf dbb.*)

Children, by first wife, born at Alexandria:

adaaf dbaa. MATTIE-JOE, born July 25, 1868; died Aug. 10, 1898, at Gordonsville, Smith county, Tenn.; married, Jan. 5, 1888, in Smith county, Campbell, son of Luther and Betty (Crutchfield) Oliver of Smith county. He is a farmer, living, 1916, at Gordonsville.
    Children, born in Smith county:
      a. WILLIE-LEE, born Nov. 22, 1889; mar. Frank Roy.
      b. ARNETT-STANTON, born Aug. 27, 1894; mar. Mai Morgan.
adaaf dbab. WILLIAM, born Jan. 6, 1873; died June 29, 1873.

Children, by second wife:

adaaf dbac. GUSSIE-LOU, born May 10, 1889; married, Sept. 22, 1911, at Murfreesboro, Tenn., William, son of Charles and Lena (Young) Murphy. He is a farmer. They are living, 1916, in Lebanon, Wilson county, Tenn. They have no children.

adaaf dbad. ABRAHAM, born 1892; died 1904.

adaaf dbc. LEWIS-CRAIGIN, son of John-Craigin (*Mordecai, John, John, Mordecai, Mordecai, Samuel*) and Jane (Usrey) Lincoln of Memphis, Tenn., born May 10, 1845, at Memphis; died Feb. 5, 1893, at Conway, Ark. He was a lawyer, living, first, at Alexandria, Tenn., but removed to Conway before his marriage.

He married, Jan. 13, 1881, at Conway, Effie, daughter of J. E. and Esther (Kerr) Martin of Conway, born Nov. 24, 1863, in Faulkner county, Ark.; living, 1916, at Conway. (Records of Mrs. Effie [Martin] Lincoln.)

Children, born at Conway:

adaaf dbca. JESSE-HAMPTON, born Aug. 16, 1886; living, 1916, unmarried.

adaaf dbcb. ROBERTA-ALICE, born May 7, 1889; died May 11, 1890.

adaah ebb. CULLEN-MELONE, son of John-Karsner (*George, Thomas, John, Mordecai, Mordecai, Samuel*) and Elmira-Taylor (Melone) Lincoln of Liberty, Mo., born Jan. 5, 1850, at Liberty. He graduated from the law department of Kentucky University in 1869, and has practised his profession at St. Joseph, Mo., and at Tucson, Ariz., at which latter place he is now, 1915, living.

He married (1), May 24, 1870, at St. Joseph, Willie-Jane, daughter of William T. and Jane G. (Hayden) Harris of St. Joseph, born 1850, at St. Joseph, and is living there now, 1917. They separated many years ago and were divorced.

He married (2) Mrs. Julia (Brown) Colston, by whom he has no children. (Records of Cullen-Melone Lincoln.)

Children, by first wife, born at St. Joseph:

adaah ebba. DRURY-HARRIS, born Apr. 9, 1873. He was educated at the St. Joseph High School and is now, 1917, a real estate dealer at St. Louis, Mo. He married, Apr. 6, 1910, at St. Louis, Ruth-Eugenia, daughter of Tilley-Alexander and Fannie (Thrash) Martin of St. Louis, born May 18, 1874, at Dalton, Mo. They live at St. Louis and have no children.

adaah ebbb. BOATNER-CHAPMAN, born May 11, 1875; living, 1917, at Los Angeles, Calif., unmarried.

adaah ebd. JOHN-KARSNER, son of John-Karsner (*George, Thomas, John, Mordecai, Mordecai, Samuel*) and Elmira-Taylor (Melone) Lincoln of Liberty and Plattsburg, Mo., born Apr. 6, 1854, at Lexington, Ky. He is a farmer, living, 1915, near Plattsburg.

He married, Oct. 26, 1886, at McFall, Mo., Bash, daughter of John-McClure and Margaret-Elizabeth (Perry) Graham of Albany, Mo., born Aug. 11, 1860, at Trenton, Mo.; living, 1915. (Records of Mrs. John-Karsner Lincoln.)

Child, born at Plattsburg:

adaah ebda. GRAHAM-CULLEN, born Dec. 2, 1890; unmarried, 1915.

adaah eka. GEORGE-MORTON, son of George-Thomas (*George, Thomas, John, Mordecai, Mordecai, Samuel*) and Virginia-Morton (Pryor) Lincoln of Bentonville, Ark., born Feb. 5, 1861, at Liberty, Mo. He passed his youth in Missouri; his early manhood in New Mexico, Arizona and Alaska, where he was a mining prospector; and since 1907 has lived at Bentonville, where he has been engaged in fruit growing with his father.

He married, March 31, 1908, at Bentonville, Emma-Gerard, daughter of John-Newton and Margaret-Trimble (Hays) Lyle of Bentonville, born Jan. 6, 1874, at Fulton, Mo.; living, 1916. (Records of Mrs. George-Morton Lincoln.)

Children, born at Bentonville:

adaah ekaa. NELLIE-PRYOR, born March 16, 1909; died May 25, 1913.
adaah ekab. GEORGE-LYLE, born Nov. 6, 1910.
adaah ekac. JOHN-MORTON, born Aug. 28, 1912.
adaah ekad. CHARLES-GATEWOOD, born Feb. 23, 1914.
adaah ekae. THOMAS-PRYOR, born Aug. 9, 1915.

adaah emc. GATEWOOD-SAUNDERS, son of James-Edwin (*George, Thomas, John, Mordecai, Mordecai, Samuel*) and Margaret-Pixley (Bird) Lincoln of Liberty, Mo., born Aug. 5, 1875, at Liberty. He entered William Jewell college, but receiving an appointment to the United States Naval Academy he entered that institution, where he graduated with honor in 1898, receiving the rank of ensign. On the breaking out of the Spanish war he was promoted as lieutenant on board the

U. S. S. "New Orleans" and was with Admiral Sampson at the taking of Fort Moro. He was promoted lieutenant commander, 1908; commander, 1914; and captain, 1918. In 1915 he was in command of the "Dolphin"; from 1915 to 1917 he was at the head of the department of electrical engineering and physics in the United States Naval Academy. From August, 1917, to August, 1918, he was in command of the "Powhatan," transporting troops to France; and from September, 1918, to October, 1919, he commanded the U. S. S. "St. Louis," for the first two months escorting troop convoys to the English coast.

He married, June 20, 1900, at Liberty, Enfield, daughter of Robert-Miller and Enfield (Peters) Stogdale of Liberty, born Sept. 12, 1881, at Liberty. Her father was a native of Virginia. (Records of Gatewood-Saunders Lincoln; Who's Who in America, vol. xi, p. 1725.)

Child:

adaah emca. CHRISTINE-LEE, born June 22, 1902.

adaah emd. JAMES-EDWIN, son of James-Edwin (George, Thomas, John, Mordecai, Mordecai, Samuel) and Margaret-Pixley (Bird) Lincoln of Liberty, Mo., born June 1, 1879, at Liberty. He has been engaged in railroad service since twenty years of age and is now, 1915, agent of the Kansas City and St. Joseph Electric Railway.

He married, Sept. 1, 1909, at Liberty, Martha-Roy, daughter of Richard-Lee and Martha-Roy (Wilson) Raymond of Liberty, born Dec. 26, 1881, at Liberty. She is a graduate of Liberty Ladies College and is secretary of General Doniphan chapter of the daughters of the American Revolution. They are living, 1915, at Liberty. They have no children.

adaah gda. JAMES-CLAIBORNE, son of Isaac-Wells (David, Thomas, John, Mordecai, Mordecai, Samuel) and Marie-Louisa (Gilkey) Lincoln of Saint Joseph, Mo., born Apr. 5, 1862, near Liberty, Mo. From 1888 until 1906 he was engaged in railroad business, living until 1889 at Atchison, Kan.; from 1889 to 1905 at Saint Louis, Mo.; and from 1905 to 1906 at Kansas

37

City, Mo. From 1906 to 1912 he was traffic manager of the Saint Louis Merchants Exchange and then removed to New York City, where he became traffic manager of the New York Merchants Association, which office he still holds. He is living, 1920, at Wykagyl Park, New Rochelle, N. Y.

He married (1), May 29, 1884, at Saint Joseph, Annie-Shannon, daughter of Moses E. Lard of Lexington, Ky., born Apr. 4, 1863, at Saint Joseph; died Sept. 12, 1899, at Saint Joseph.

He married (2), May 27, 1911, at Saint Louis, Mrs. Helen (Benedict) Burnett, daughter of Emory-Jay and Amelia-Margaret (Scott) Benedict of Memphis, Tenn., and widow of James P. Burnett. She was born June 26, 1876, near Lancaster, Wis., and died Jan. 3, 1917, at New Rochelle. (Records of James-Claiborne Lincoln; Who's Who in America, vol. xi, p. 1725.)

Children, by first wife, born: *a, b* at Saint Joseph; *c* at Saint Louis:

adaah gdaa. JAMES-CLAIBORNE, born Aug. 17, 1889; married, May 28, 1913, at Saint Louis, Margaret Frazer. They are living, 1920, at New York, N. Y., and have two daughters.

adaah gdab. SILAS-WOODSON, born June 22, 1891; died July 2, 1911, at Saint Louis.

adaah gdac. MARY-LOUISE, born Sept. 24, 1894; living, 1920, unmarried.

adaah gdb. WILLIAM-DAVID, son of Isaac-Wells (*David, Thomas, John, Mordecai, Mordecai, Samuel*) and Marie-Louisa (Gilkey) Lincoln of Saint Joseph, Mo., born May 3, 1864, at Smithville, Clay county, Mo. He lived at Saint Joseph until 1889 when he removed to Omaha, Nebr., where he has resided ever since. He is, 1920, car service agent of the Union Pacific Railroad.

He married, May 21, 1885, at Lexington, Ky., Ella-Lightburn, daughter of Alexander-Tennett and Virginia (Oots) Parker of Lexington, born Feb. 11, 1865, at Lexington. (Records of William-David Lincoln.)

Children, born: *a, b* at Saint Joseph; *c* at Omaha:

adaah gdba. WILLIAM-DAVID, born July 18, 1886; died Dec. 31, 1892.

adaah gdbb. LOUISE, born Sept. 2, 1887; died Dec. 26, 1892.

adaah gdbc. FRANK-BUCKINGHAM, born March 11, 1904.

adaga aaa. THOMAS-ABRAHAM, son of James-Handshaw (*Thomas, Benjamin, Mordecai, Mordecai, Mordecai, Samuel*) and Nellie (Merrifield) Lincoln of Leroy, Ill., born June 2 or 21, 1843, at Leroy; died Sept. 21, 1899, at Cainesville, Mo. He was a druggist and lived at Cainesville.

He married, Jan. 2, 1882, at Albany, Mo., Margaret-Alice, daughter of Steven-Decatur and Manda (Moore) Rardin of Ridgeway, Mo., born Nov. 12, 1858, near Cainesville, where she is now, 1919, living. (Records of James-Stephen Lincoln, *adaga aaaa*, and of Una-Mae Daugherty, *adaga aaga*, who gives June 21 as the date of his birth.)

Child, born at Ridgeway:

adaga aaaa. JAMES-STEPHEN, born Oct. 1, 1886. He married, Nov. 3, 1906, at Cainesville, Mo., Nora-Arbel Cain. They are living, 1919, at Portland, Ore., and have no children.

adaga agd. CHARLES-JENNINGS, son of Thomas-Boone (*Thomas, Benjamin, Mordecai, Mordecai, Mordecai, Samuel*) and Mariah-Jackson (Hart) Lincoln of Carmichaels, Pa., born Nov. 5, 1857, at Carmichaels, where he is living, 1915. He is an accountant.

He married Elizabeth Doty. (Information of Horace-Greely Lincoln, *adaga agf.*)

Children, born at Carmichaels:

adaga agda. ROBERT-TODD. He is married and living, 1915, at Santa Cruz, Calif.
adaga agdb. CLIFFORD. He is living, 1915, at Carmichaels, unmarried.

adaga agf. HORACE-GREELY, son of Thomas-Boone (*Thomas, Benjamin, Mordecai, Mordecai, Mordecai, Samuel*) and Mariah-Jackson (Hart) Lincoln of Carmichaels, Pa., born Oct. 10, 1863, at Carmichaels. He is living, 1915, at Washington, Pa., and calls himself a "manager."

He married Frances Nickerson. (Information of Horace-Greely Lincoln.)

Children:

adaga agfa. RALPH-NICKERSON. Living, 1915, unmarried.
adaga agfb. MARIE. Living, 1915, unmarried.
adaga agfc. THOMAS. Living, 1915, unmarried.
adaga agfd. KATHRYN. Living, 1915, unmarried.

adaga gaa. CHARLES-BENTON-FREMONT, son of Henry (*Mordecai, Benjamin, Mordecai, Mordecai, Mordecai, Samuel*) and Huldah (Leech) Lincoln of Smithfield, Pa., born at Smithfield; died 1912 or 1913, at Los Angeles, Calif. He remained with his grandfather Lincoln until maturity, receiving a common school education. He then entered the employ of the Fort Wayne and Chicago Railroad Company, in the ticket office at Lima, Ohio. After a few years he procured a position with the Southern Pacific Railroad Company at Denver, Colo., where he remained for three or four years. He then removed to San Francisco, Calif., serving the same company until 1905 in several positions, among them general passenger accountant of the entire system. When the new railroad, commonly known as Senator Clarke's road, was built from Salt Lake City to Los Angeles he left the Southern Pacific and entered the employ of the new road, being in the general offices at Los Angeles, and remained there until his death.

He married at Denver a Miss Kerr, but nothing has been learned of her or of any children. (Information of Mr. Snyder Leech, Smithfield.)

adaga gda. EDWARD-ROSE, son of Mordecai (*Mordecai, Benjamin, Mordecai, Mordecai, Mordecai, Samuel*) and Mary-Elizabeth (Rose) Lincoln of North Union, Pa., born June 3, 1864, at North Union. He is a farmer, living, 1915, at New Salem, near Brownsville, Pa.

He married, Dec. 22, 1887, at Masontown, Pa., Etta-Belle daughter of William and Caroline (Leclare) Franks of Masontown, born May 22, 1869, at McClellandtown, Pa. (Family Records of Edward-Rose Lincoln.)

Children, born: *a, b* at McClellandtown; *c-e* at Mt. Braddock; *f, g* at Nicholson; *h, i* at Franklin, Pa.:

adaga gdaa. MARY-ELIZABETH, born Feb. 2, 1889; married, June 22, 1914, Lyman B. Jackson. They are living, 1915, at Martinsburg, Pa.

adaga gdab. ELMER-RAY, born June 25, 1890.

adaga gdac. WILLIAM-EDWARD, born June 15, 1892; died Aug. 25, 1903.

adaga gdad. OLIVE-MAY, born Feb. 1, 1896.

adaga gdae. CARL-CLIFFORD, born March 21, 1899.

adaga gdaf. ETTA-BEARL, born Nov. 16, 1901.

adaga gdag. DELLA-FRANCES, born Nov. 4, 1905.

adaga gdah. RUSSELL, born July 3, 1907.
adaga gdai. HAZEL-IRENE, born Sept. 16, 1909.

adaga gfa. BENJAMIN-FRANKLIN, son of Edward-Gilpin (*Mordecai, Benjamin, Mordecai, Mordecai, Mordecai, Samuel*) and Lucy-Ann (Moast) Lincoln of Dunbar, Pa., born May 28, 1869, at Dunbar. From 1900 to 1907 he owned a farm at Summerfield, Pa., on which he lived. He then removed to Pittsburgh, where he remained for two years, and since then he has lived at Collinsville, Pa. He is, 1915, a worker in concrete, employed on one of the railroads.

He married, May 28, 1891, at Cumberland, Md., Cora-Alice, daughter of James-Madison and Sarah-Jane (Lancaster) Tissue of Summerfield, Pa., born Jan. 12, 1870, at Summerfield. (Records of Mrs. Cora-Alice Lincoln.)

Children, born *a* at Dunbar; *b, c* at Collinsville; *d, e* at Summerfield:

adaga gfaa. LUCY-MAY, born Apr. 4, 1892; married, May 2, 1910, at Fairchance, Pa., Elmer-George, son of William and Josephine (Linfield) Wild of Martinsburg, W. Va., born Sept. 15, 1885, at Martinsburg. They live, 1915, at Hanlin Station, Pa. He is a farmer.
Children, born at Collinsville, Pa.:
    a. IDA-MAY, born Feb. 3, 1912.
    b. BENJAMIN-ELMER, born March 12, 1915.
adaga gfab. BENJAMIN-FRANKLIN, born Oct. 19, 1894; unmarried 1915.
adaga gfac. EDWARD-MADISON, born Sept. 8, 1897.
adaga gfad. WINFIELD-SCOTT, born Oct. 23, 1900.
adaga gfae. THOMAS J, born Apr. 13, 1903.

adaga gha. WALTER-KENDALL, son of Benjamin-Franklin (*Mordecai, Benjamin, Mordecai, Mordecai, Mordecai, Samuel*) and Nellie (Brown) Lincoln of Ottawa, Ill., born Oct. 11, 1876, at Ottawa. He was educated in the Ottawa public schools and after graduating from the high school studied law for three years in the office of Lincoln and Stead at Ottawa. He is now, 1915, a member of the prominent law firm of Stead, Lincoln and Fitch of Chicago, Ill., but since 1912 he has lived at Lagrange, Ill.

He married, July 29, 1909, at Chicago, Ruby-Hunt, daughter of Ward-Hunt and Lillie-Loretta (DePue) Dean of Washington, D. C., born Apr. 1, 1882, at Washington. (Records of Walter-Kendall Lincoln.)

Children, born: *a, b* at Chicago; *c* at Lagrange:

adaga ghaa. JANE, born July 15, 1910.
adaga ghab. ANNE-ELIZABETH, born Dec. 1, 1911.
adaga ghac. BARBARA, born Oct. 21, 1913.

adaga gic. JAMES-DERNELL, son of Thomas-Jefferson (*Mordecai, Benjamin, Mordecai, Mordecai, Mordecai, Samuel*) and Margaret-Ellen (Yaw) Lincoln of Dunbar, Pa., born March 22, 1875, at Dunbar. He lived after his marriage until 1907 at Connellsville, Pa., but is now, 1915, living at Hopwood, Pa. He is foreman in the car shops of the West Pennsylvania Railway.

He married, Dec. 24, 1896, at Hopwood, South Union, Pa., Betsey-Viola, daughter of William and Elizabeth (Fell) Kissinger of Brownfield, Pa., born Aug. 28, 1878, at Brownfield. (Records of Mrs. Betsey-Viola Lincoln.)

Children, born at Connellsville:

adaga gica. EDITH-MYRTLE, born Jan. 2, 1898.
adaga gicb. JAMES-PRESTON, born Jan. 4, 1900.
adaga gicc. HELEN-PAULINE, born Jan. 27, 1903.

adaga gid. WILLIAM-ROGERS, son of Thomas-Jefferson (*Mordecai, Benjamin, Mordecai, Mordecai, Mordecai, Samuel*) and Margaret-Ellen (Yaw) Lincoln of Connellsville, Pa., born Oct. 18, 1878, at Dunbar, Pa., has passed most of his life at Connellsville, where he is now, 1915, living, but has lived also at Pittsburgh, Pa., and at Philadelphia. He has been a brick contractor but is now a mason.

He married, July 4, 1903, at Connellsville, Tillie-May, daughter of William and Lurisia (Reece) Zimmerman of Connellsville, born Oct. 18, 1883, at Moyer, Pa.; died May 13, 1914, at Connellsville. (Records of William-Rogers Lincoln.)

Children, born: *a, c* at Connellsville; *b* at Pittsburgh:

adaga gida. MARGARET, born Sept. 17, 1904.
adaga gidb. WILLIAM-ZIMMERMAN, born Feb. 25, 1908.
adaga gidc. ROBERT M, born Feb. 24, 1912.

adagb dje. LEROY-SHERMAN, son of Richard-Stokes (*Jesse, John, Mordecai, Mordecai, Mordecai, Samuel*) and Hannah-Ann (Haymaker) Lincoln of Uniontown, Pa., born Aug. 21, 1866, at Uniontown. He has lived at Uniontown, Connellsville and

Confluence, Pa., and for two years lived at Harrison, Mich. He is now, 1914, manager of the Lincoln Lumber Company of Uniontown.

He married, Nov. 7, 1889, at Wilkinsburg, Pa., Ella, daughter of William-Leroy and Louisa-Ann (Snyder) McClernan of Monongalia county, W. Va., born March 21, 1867, in Monongalia county; died May 7, 1908, at Confluence. (Records of Leroy-Sherman Lincoln; Genealogy of David Jones, p. 90.)

Children, born: *a, b* at Wilkinsburg; *c, d* at Connellsville; *e, f* at Confluence:

adagb djea. LOUISA-ELIZABETH, born Aug. 28, 1891.
adagb djeb. LEROY-SHERMAN, born June 9, 1893.
adagb djec. HENRY-HUSTON, born Feb. 10, 1896.
adagb djed. ELLEN-CLARK, born Sept. 30, 1899.
adagb djee. HANNAH-MARGARET, born March 3, 1902.
adagb djef. VIRGINIA-THORN, born March 20, 1908.

adahb bbi. SAMUEL-WILSON, son of George-Vashtine (*William, Thomas, Thomas, Mordecai, Mordecai, Samuel*) and Mary (Morris) Lincoln of Parkesburg, Pa., born July 18, 1852, at Atglen, Pa.; living, 1913, at Philadelphia, Pa. He was a locomotive engineer on the Pennsylvania Railroad from 1876 to 1880; then for seven or eight years he turned his attention to farming. He afterwards went to New York City for a short time, but returned to Philadelphia and has worked since then in the passenger department of the Pennsylvania Railroad. For twenty years he was ticket inspector and is now, 1913, attendant in the library of the trainsmen's building.

He married (1), March 18, 1880, at Parkesburg, Hannah-Elvina, daughter of Henry and Mary-Dehaven (Squib) Kendig of Sadsburyville, Pa., born Sept. 9, 1856, at Sadsburyville; died Sept. 2, 1881, at Parkesburg. She had no child.

He married (2), March 19, 1891, at Philadelphia, Margaret-Jane, daughter of John and Eliza (Keys) Patrick of Philadelphia, born Apr. 29, 1860, at Philadelphia; died March 17, 1892, at Philadelphia. Her father was a native of Ireland. (Records of Samuel-Wilson Lincoln.)

Child, by second wife, born at Philadelphia:

adahb bbia. RUTH-ELIZABETH, born Jan. 24, 1892; living, 1913, at Philadelphia, unmarried.

adahb bcd. JOHN-ERB, son of Thomas (*William, Thomas, Thomas, Mordecai, Mordecai, Samuel*) and Elizabeth (Erb) Lincoln of Gordonville, Pa., born Aug. 1, 1847, at Leacock, Pa.; died Aug. 15, 1908, by suicide while suffering from mental aberration, at Saint Louis, Mo., where he had been living for some years. He is called "foreman" in the Saint Louis record of his death. His home is given as 4960 Washington boulevard, and in 1909 his widow was living at the same place; but her name does not appear in later directories of Saint Louis.

He was twice married. His first wife's name was Dolly Epstein; and his second wife, who was his widow, is called in the Saint Louis directories "Ada B." Mr. George-Eckert Lincoln, *adahb bbh*, says that John-Erb's second wife was a widow with children when he married her and was a parson's daughter, but he does not remember her name. It is uncertain which wife was the mother of his children.

Children, probably by first wife:

adahb bcda. PAULINE. She is said to have married John Moone of Saint Louis.
adahb bcdb. BEATRICE. She was living, 1909, unmarried.

Child, probably by second wife:

adahb bcdc. ROBERT, died young.

adahb dcd. FRANK-ALVIN, son of John (*Thomas, Thomas, Thomas, Mordecai, Mordecai, Samuel*) and Elizabeth (Lovett) Lincoln of Gloucester, N. J., born Apr. 10, 186– at Wilmington, Del. He is a machinist, living, 1920, at Gloucester.

He married, Nov. 27, 1892, at Chester, Pa., Ellen, daughter of Thomas and Ellen (Meahan) Spencer, born Oct. 31, 1861, at Philadelphia, Pa. (Records of Miss Anna T Lincoln, *adahb bde*.)

Children, born: *a* at Chester; *b* at Gloucester:

adahb dcda. ELLEN-ELIZABETH, born Sept. 28, 1893; married Frank M. Kittenger.
    Children:
      a. FRANK-LINCOLN, born Aug. 4, 1915.
      b. JOHN-ALVIN, born June 3, 1919.
adahb dcdb. MARGARET-MAY, born March 23, 1897; unmarried 1920.

adahb dcg. ROBERT-ALLEN, son of John (*Thomas, Thomas, Thomas, Mordecai, Mordecai, Samuel*) and Elizabeth (Lovett)

Lincoln of Gloucester, N. J., born Oct. 11, 1868, at Wilmington, Del. He is a general contractor, living, 1920, at Gloucester.

He married, Sept. 17, 1905, at Trenton, N. J., Mary-Elizabeth, daughter of Clement-Whitall and Mary-Rebecca (Stetser) Wallace of Red Bank, N. J., born May 4, 1882, at Red Bank. (Records of Miss Anna T Lincoln, *adahb bde*.)

Children, born at Gloucester:

adahb dcga. CLEMENT-ROBERT, born Oct. 22, 1906.
adahb dcgb. JOHN, born March 26, 1910.
adahb dcgc. MARY-ELIZABETH, born Sept. 18, 1914.

adahb fae. SAMUEL-ENOCH, son of James-Moore (*Samuel, Thomas, Thomas, Mordecai, Mordecai, Samuel*) and Hannah-Elizabeth (Johnson) Lincoln of Amity, Mo., born Aug. 6, 1869, in Iowa. He is a farmer, living, 1920, at Osborn, Mo.

He married, Dec. 12, 1894, at Osborn, Della-May, daughter of Daniel and Adeline Coil, born Apr. 11, 1875. (Records of Miss Martha-Elizabeth Lincoln, *adahb fag*.)

Children, born at Osborn:

adahb faea. DANIEL-LEWIS, born Jan. 20, 1896; died Oct. 20, 1918, in France, from wounds received in the Argonne forest. He enlisted May 29, 1917, at Kansas City, Mo., in the 1st Missouri Ambulance Company, 110th sanitary train, 35th division. He was in training at Fort Riley and Fort Sill for nearly a year and left the United States about May 17, 1918. He was wounded Sept. 30 while in action in the Argonne, by a piece of shell which struck him in the breast and penetrated his lung; and he died Oct. 20 at the Base Hospital. His body was brought home and is buried in the cemetery at Osborn.
adahb faeb. JAMES-HUBERT, born Feb. 10, 1898.
adahb faec. MAUDE-OLIVIA, born Sept. 16, 1901.

adahb gbc. AZARIAH-WILLIAM, son of Thomas (*Azariah, Thomas, Thomas, Mordecai, Mordecai, Samuel*) and Rachel-Malinda (Kay) Lincoln of Mount Gilead, Ohio, born Sept. 25, 1851, in Iowa county, Wis. He was graduated from the Ohio Wesleyan university, Delaware, Ohio, in June, 1875; and was superintendent of the public schools at Chesterville, Ohio, from 1876 to 1878, and of the Mount Gilead public schools in 1882 and 1883. In 1884 he removed to Springfield, Mo., and has there practised the profession of law ever since. He was judge of probate for Greene county, Mo., from 1886 to 1894, and judge of the circuit court (criminal division) of that county from 1902 to 1907. He is now, 1915, in partnership with his son Harold-Thomas Lincoln.

He married, Apr. 21, 1885, at Mount Gilead, Jennie-Margaret, daughter of Henry-Hamilton and Isabel-Ugenia (Swaner) Adams of Springfield, born Sept. 13, 1863, at Mount Gilead; living, 1915. (Records of Azariah-William Lincoln.)

Children, born at Springfield:

adahb gbca. WILLIAM-ADAMS, born Jan. 31, 1886.
adahb gbcb. HAROLD-THOMAS, born Nov. 11, 1888.
adahb gbcc. ELWYN-RUSSELL, born Oct. 26, 1896; died Oct. 27, 1913.

adahb gbd. JOEL-KAY, son of Thomas (*Azariah, Thomas, Thomas, Mordecai, Mordecai, Samuel*) and Rachel-Malinda (Kay) Lincoln of Mount Gilead, Ohio, born Apr. 22, 1853, in Iowa county, Wis.; living, 1916, at Mount Gilead.

He married, Aug. 14, 1878, at Mount Gilead, Alta, daughter of James and Rebecca-Jane (Stevens) Schanck of Franklin township, Morrow county, Ohio, born June 6, 1858, at Franklin. (Records of Azariah-William Lincoln, *adahb gbc.*)

Child, born in Congress township, Ohio:

adahb gbda. MARY-BLANCHE, born Dec. 8, 1880.

adahb gbe. DAVID-HOLLIS, son of Thomas (*Azariah, Thomas, Thomas, Mordecai, Mordecai, Samuel*) and Rachel-Malinda (Kay) Lincoln of Mount Gilead, Ohio, born Apr. 28, 1855, in Iowa county, Wis. He is living, 1916, at Marion, Ohio, where he is cashier of the City National Bank.

He married, March 25, 1878, at Williamsport, Ohio, Sylvia-Delphine, daughter of James and Lydia (Hull) Vanatta of Williamsport, born Aug. 22, 1856, at Williamsport; died Sept. 24, 1908, at Marion. (Records of David-Hollis Lincoln.)

Children, born at Williamsport:

adahb gbea. BERYL, born Dec. 27, 1878; married, Aug. 27, 1903, at Marion, Ohio, Harry-Christopher Scherff.
adahb gbeb. ANNIE, born Sept. 28, 1880; married, Sept. 27, 1904, at Marion, Ohio, James-William Knapp.

adahb gcd. ABRAHAM-DICKINSON, son of Dickinson (*Azariah, Thomas, Thomas, Mordecai, Mordecai, Samuel*) and Elizabeth (Kay) Lincoln of Mifflin, Wis., born July 3, 1861, at Mifflin. He was educated in the public schools of Mount Gilead, Ohio, and of Montfort and Boscobel, Wis. In the winters of 1882 and 1883, he taught a country school two miles from Castle Rock, Wis., known as Oak Ridge District. In the spring of 1883 he secured employment in ice and spring water business at Denver, Colo., where he remained until December, when he removed to Grand Island, Nebr., securing employment with a furniture and undertaking establishment with which he remained until the following spring, when he engaged in a confectionery and ice-cream business with his father, who had removed to Grand Island. This business they sold in 1885 and removed to Minneapolis, Kan., where they engaged in a bakery and confectionery business which they carried on until 1890, when, with his father and William Hemenway, his father-in-law, he removed to Cottage Grove, Ore., at that time a small village, and entered into partnership with Mr. Hemenway, under the firm name of Lincoln and Company, to carry on a grocery business. In 1894 he served as first chief of the fire department; and in 1895 he was elected city clerk, which office he held for one year. In 1901, his wife having died and he being afflicted with rheumatism, for which he was advised to seek a dry climate, he sold his business in Cottage Grove and removed to Pueblo, Colo., where he has since resided, being employed at present, 1915, as a locomotive painter by the Denver and Rio Grande railroad company.

He married (1), Sept. 16, 1888, at Minneapolis, Kan., Rose-Jane, daughter of William and Kathareen (McCarger) Hemenway of Cottage Grove, Ore., born Jan. 7, 1870, at Minneapolis; died March 9, 1900, at Cottage Grove.

He married (2), Aug. 18, 1910, at Pueblo, Mary-Etta, daughter of John-Alexander and Martha (Purdy) Kenton of Kansas City, Kan., born Apr. 8, 1871, at Kansas City. Her parents were natives of Kentucky. (Records of Abraham-Dickinson Lincoln.)

Children, by first wife, born at Minneapolis, Kan.:

adahb gcda. GRACE-MAY, born Sept. 6, 1889; married, July 31, 1907, at Cottage Grove, Ore., Harry-Ashley, son of John-Richard and Elinor (McAllister) Matteson of Morris, Ill., born July 20, 1882, at Morris. They are living, 1915, at Seattle, Wash. He is a civil engineer.
  Child, born at Seattle:
    a. JOHN-LINCOLN, born May 4, 1909.

adahb gcdb. ERNEST-WILLIAM, born July 22, 1891; living, 1915, at Seattle, unmarried.

adahc aaa. JOHN-WESLEY, son of Richard-VanBuskirk (*John, Mishal, Thomas, Mordecai, Mordecai, Samuel*) and Anna-Maria (Pellman) Lincoln of Laurelton, Pa., born May 24, 1853, at Laurelton. He was educated in the public schools of Laurelton, the Mifflinburg academy and the Bloomsburg State normal school. After leaving the normal school he worked on his father's farm during the summer and taught school in the winter, until the fall of 1875, when he entered the employ of the Mifflinburg Bank, of which in 1877 he was elected cashier, which office he still held in 1913. He lives at Mifflinburg.

He married, Oct. 7, 1880, Gertrude, daughter of Robert and Caroline (Bergstrasser) Reed of Union county, Pa., and Tiffin, Ohio, born Sept. 19, 1856, near Laurelton. (Records of John-Wesley Lincoln.)

Child, born at Mifflinburg:

adahc aaaa. MARIE-REED, born July 9, 1886; married, Sept. 24, 1913, at Mifflinburg, E. Irland Lawshe. They are living, 1913, at Altoona, Pa.

adahc aae. LOUIS-PELLMAN, son of Richard-VanBuskirk (*John, Mishal, Thomas, Mordecai, Mordecai, Samuel*) and Anna-Maria (Pellman) Lincoln of Laurelton, Pa., born Aug. 8, 1866, near Laurelton. He attended Dickinson college, Carlisle, Pa., from 1883 to 1886, and then, for four years, was a country school teacher. From 1890 to 1892, he was engaged in business as a salesman and, since 1892, he has been in the employ of the Carnegie Steel Company, in various capacities at the Homestead Steel Works. He is now, 1913, superintendent of the structural steel department at Munhall, Pa., where he lives.

He married, Dec. 24, 1896, at Mifflinburg, Pa., Celeste-Jane, daughter of James-Henry and Anna (Trump) Albright of Laurelton, born Nov. 30, 1869, at Laurelton. (Records of Louis-Pellman Lincoln.)

Children:

adahc aaea. RICHARD-VANBUSKIRK, born Dec. 2, 1900.
adahc aaeb. ANNA-ALBRIGHT, born July 18, 1903.
adahc aaec. LOUIS-PELLMAN, born Aug. 10, 1906.

adahc aaf. RUFUS-VANBUSKIRK, son of Richard-VanBuskirk (*John, Mishal, Thomas, Mordecai, Mordecai, Samuel*) and Anna-Maria (Pellman) Lincoln of Laurelton, Pa., born Apr. 17, 1871, at Laurelton. He graduated at Dickinson college, Carlisle, Pa., in 1895, and at the law college in 1896, and was admitted to the bar in 1897. He lived at Iron Mountain, Wyo., from 1898 to 1900; at Denver, Colo., from 1900 to 1911; and since then has lived at Escondido, Calif., where he now, 1914, resides. He is in real estate business.

He married, Jan. 14, 1911, at Denver, Nora-Bell, daughter of Charles-Edmund and Nora-Bell (Berry) Taylor of Denver, born March 12, 1876, at Jersey City, N. J. (Records of Rufus-VanBuskirk Lincoln.)

Child, born at Escondido:

adahc aafa. NORA-ANNE, born Dec. 17, 1912.

adahf cea. JOHN-JOSEPH, son of Abel-Thomas (*John, Joseph, Thomas, Mordecai, Mordecai, Samuel*) and Elizabeth (Haines) Lincoln of Oak Hill, Pa., born Oct. 11, 1865, at Oak Hill. He graduated at Lehigh university in 1889 with the degree of C.E., and became a civil engineer. After graduation he was, for three years, on the United States Geological Survey and for one year a member of the firm of Harris and Lincoln, mining and civil engineers at Elkhorn, W. Va. In 1895 he was appointed chief engineer and superintendent of the Crozer Land Association of Elkhorn, which position he still, 1913, holds. He is also general manager of the Crozer Coal and Coke Company and of the Upland Coal and Coke Company, both of Elkhorn.

He married, Oct. 11, 1899, at Mayberry, W. Va., Rachel-Lloyd, daughter of Edward-Stanley and Clayanna (Lloyd) Hutchinson of Newton, Pa., born May 21, 1873, at Altoona, Pa. (Records of John-Joseph Lincoln; Bailey Family, p. 549; Kirk Family, p. 444.)

Children, born at Elkhorn:

adahf ceaa. LLOYD-STANLEY, born July 20, 1900; died Feb. 21, 1911, at Bluefields hospital, Va., and is buried at Newtown, Pa.
adahf ceab. JOHN-JOSEPH, born Dec. 30, 1901.
adahf ceac. ELIZABETH-HUTCHINSON, born Dec. 26, 1905.
adahf cead. PEMBERTON-HUTCHINSON, born Oct. 15, 1912.

adahf daa. HENRY-PHILIP, son of Charles-Shippen (*Abel-Thomas, Joseph, Thomas, Mordecai, Mordecai, Samuel*) and Anna (Reynolds) Lincoln of Philadelphia, Pa., born March 4, 1858, at Philadelphia. He graduated at university of Pennsylvania in 1880, with the degree of B.S., and is by profession a civil engineer. He has, since graduation, been in the employ of the Pennsylvania Railroad Company and is now, 1913, a division superintendent with headquarters at Williamsport, Pa., where he lives.

He married, March 10, 1885, at Rahway, N. J., Sarah, daughter of Robert-Coddington and Elizabeth (Perrin) Brewster of Rahway, where she was born, March 7, 1864. (Records of Henry-Philip Lincoln.)

Children:

adahf daaa. ROBERT-BREWSTER, born Apr. 16, 1888; died Sept. 1, 1888.
adahf daab. MARION, an adopted daughter, born June 1, 1905.

adahf dab. WILLIAM-REYNOLDS, son of Charles-Shippen (*Abel-Thomas, Joseph, Thomas, Mordecai, Mordecai, Samuel*) and Anna (Reynolds) Lincoln of Philadelphia, Pa., born Jan. 28, 1862, at Philadelphia. He studied medicine at the university of Pennsylvania, receiving the degree of M.D. in 1888. After graduation he studied at Vienna, Austria, and at Boston, Mass., and then practised his profession at Philadelphia until 1895; when he removed to Cleveland, Ohio, where he now, 1913, resides. He is a specialist in the diseases of the ear, nose and throat.

He married, Aug. 20, 1890, at Philadelphia, Virginia-May, daughter of Alexander Gibb of Philadelphia, born May 15, 1868, at Philadelphia; living, 1913. (Records of Henry-Philip Lincoln, *adahf daa.*)

Children, born: *a* at Philadelphia; *b-e* at Cleveland:

adahf daba. DONALD, born Feb. 3, 1894.
adahf dabb. ANNA-REYNOLDS, born Oct. 15, 1896.
adahf dabc. MARY, born Sept. 25, 1898.
adahf dabd. CHARLES-SHIPPEN, born Feb. 22, 1903; died July 29, 1904.
adahf dabe. VIRGINIA, born June 21, 1905.

adahf dac. WALTER-RODMAN, son of Charles-Shippen (*Abel-Thomas, Joseph, Thomas, Mordecai, Mordecai, Samuel*) and

Anna (Reynolds) Lincoln of Philadelphia, Pa., born Apr. 9, 1867, at Philadelphia. He graduated at university of Pennsylvania with the degree of A.B. in 1887, and in 1890 received the degree of M.D. He continued his study of medicine at Vienna, Austria, and at Boston, Mass., and became a gynecologist. He lived for some years at Cocoa, Fla., but after his marriage retired from his profession and removed to Point Pleasant, W. Va., where he was living in 1913.

He married, June 3, 1909, at Point Pleasant, Alice-Ella⁴, daughter of James³ (*James²*, *Philip¹*) and Ella-Catherine (McCullough) Capeheart of Point Pleasant, where she was born, Nov. 5, 1882. (Records of Henry-Philip Lincoln, *adhaf daa.*)

Child, born at Point Pleasant:

adahf daca. JAMES-CAPEHEART, born Sept. 13, 1912.

adahf dae. GEORGE-WASHINGTON, son of Charles-Shippen (*Abel-Thomas, Joseph, Thomas, Mordecai, Mordecai, Samuel*) and Anna (Reynolds) Lincoln of Philadelphia, Pa., born Feb. 22, 1873, at Philadelphia. He became, first, a pharmacist but studied medicine at Jefferson Medical College of the university of Pennsylvania, and received the degree of M.D. in 1902. He had previously received the degree of Ph.G. in 1897 from the Philadelphia college of pharmacy. He practised at first at Philadelphia but, later, removed to Cynwyd, Montgomery county, Pa., where he is now, 1913, living.

He married, June 24, 1908, at Medford, N. J., Effie-Julia, daughter of Israel-Wilkins and Lillie-Willits (Jones) Garwood of Medford, born Feb. 23, 1886, at Medford; living 1913. (Records of Henry-Philip Lincoln, *adhaf daa.*)

Child, born at Cynwyd:

adahf daea. GEORGE-REYNOLDS, born Jan. 29, 1911.

adaid abc. JAMES-BOONE, son of Samuel (*Caleb, James, Abraham, Mordecai, Mordecai, Samuel*) and Rachel (Rogers) Lincoln, born Aug. 16, 1859. He is a physician, living, 1913, at Lancaster, Pa.

He married, Oct. 5, 1898, Alice-Zook Evans. (Genealogy of David Jones, p. 106.)

Child:

adaid abca. MARGARET-EVANS, born June 21, 1899.

adaid bba. GEORGE-JONES, son of George-Jones (*John, James, Abraham, Mordecai, Mordecai, Samuel*) and Emily-Virginia (Mawson) Lincoln, born Feb. 27, 1857. He was for a number of years agent of the Chicago, Milwaukee and Saint Paul Railroad at Philadelphia, Pa., but in 1919 was living at Seattle, Wash.

He married, Sept. 22, 1885, Adelaide-Cook Franklin. (Genealogy of David Jones, pp. 42, 197.)

Children, born at Philadelphia:

adaid bbaa. CLIFFORD-FRANKLIN, born Dec. 9, 1886.
adaid bbab. ALLAN-MAWSON, born June 18, 1888.
adaid bbac. GEORGE-JONES, born Apr. 16, 1890.
adaid bbad. EDITH-MARIAN, born Nov. 22, 1895.
adaid bbae. MARGARET-HOXSON, born Aug. 19, 1897.

adaii bbb. OSCAR-HEMMIG, son of Alfred-Gilbert (*John-Dehaven, Thomas, Abraham, Mordecai, Mordecai, Samuel*) and Anna-Louisa (Hemmig) Lincoln of Lorane, Exeter township, Pa., born Apr. 2, 1863, at Lorane. He is living, 1913, at Potts-town Landing, Pa., where he keeps a store and coal yard.

He married, July 26, 1886, at Reading, Pa., Elizabeth, daughter of John and Mary-Seifert (Wicklein) Ruth of Robeson, Pa., born July 29, 1860, at Robeson; living, 1913. (Records of Alfred-Gilbert Lincoln, *adaii bb.*)

Children, born: *a* at Robeson; *b, c* at Coalsville; *d* at Reading; *e* at West Reading; *f* at Potoxon, Pa.:

adaii bbba. ROBERT-RUTH, born Oct. 21, 1887.
adaii bbbb. LOUISA-GRACE, born Aug. 22, 1889; living, 1913, unmarried.
adaii bbbc. JOHN-RUTH, born May 29, 1892; living, 1913, unmarried.
adaii bbbd. HARVEY-RUTH, born July 22, 1894.
adaii bbbe. GEORGE-RUTH, born Aug. 15, 1898.
adaii bbbf. ELIZABETH, born Apr. 19, 1902.

adbcf baa. ALFRED, son of John (*George, Moses, Jacob, Abraham, Mordecai, Samuel*) and Maria (Brandt) Lincoln of Darby, Pa. He married Ida, daughter of George and Mary Young of Darby. When their youngest son was about eight years old Mr. Lincoln disappeared and was never heard from afterwards. After several years Mrs. Lincoln married again and died Apr. 7, 1907, at Paschallville, Pa.

Children, born at Darby:

adbcf baaa. JOHN, born about 1875. He is married and has two daughters. He was living, 1919, at Astoria, Long Island City, N. Y.

adbcf baab. ALFRED-WILES, born Nov. 12, 1880.

adbcf beb. GEORGE-HENRY, son of Moses (*George, Moses, Jacob, Abraham, Mordecai, Samuel*) and Amanda (Ogden) Lincoln of Darby, Pa., born Jan. 23, 1861, at Darby; died July 4, 1911, at Darby. He was a motorman and lived at Darby.

He married (1), at Darby, Fanny Young of Darby, who died March 8, 1898, at West Philadelphia, Pa.

He married (2), June 26, 1904, at Darby, Hannah-Jane, daughter of Washington and Margaret (Dawson) Taylor of Oxford, Chester county, Pa., and widow of George-Hammond Wiser of Darby. She is living, 1915, at Darby. She had no children by Mr. Lincoln. (Records of Mrs. George-Henry Lincoln.)

Children, by first wife, born at Darby:

adbcf beba. MARY-ELLEN, born Nov. 16, 1891; married, June 26, 1910, at Darby, Alexander, son of David and Martha Founds of Darby. They are living, 1915, at Darby. He works in a chemical laboratory.
　　Child, born at Darby:
　　　a. DAVID, born Oct. 19, 1913.
adbcf bebb. GEORGE-HENRY, born Nov. 10, 1893; living, 1915, at Darby, unmarried.
adbcf bebc. IDA, died in infancy.
adbcf bebd. WILLIAM-WEAVER, born March 8, 1898.

adbcf bed. AMER-OGDEN, son of Moses (*George, Moses, Jacob, Abraham, Mordecai, Samuel*) and Amanda (Ogden) Lincoln of Darby, Pa., born Dec. 25, 1864, at Darby. He is living, 1915, at Darby and is employed in the paper mill at Lansdowne, Pa.

He married, Dec. 24, 1887, at Chester, Pa., Martha-Emma, daughter of George and Margaret Covington of Chester county, Pa., born Oct. 7, 1865, in Chester county. (Records of Amer-Ogden Lincoln.)

Children, born at Darby:

adbcf beda. CLARENCE-AMER, born Nov. 25, 1888; living, 1915, at Darby unmarried. He is a carpenter.

38

adbcf bedb. Horace-William, born May 23, 1890.
adbcf bedc. Raymond-Taylor, born Feb. 14, 1894; unmarried 1915.
adbcf bedd. Herbert-Randolph, born Apr. 4, 1897.
adbcf bede. Norman-Covington, born Jan. 17, 1899.

adbcf bee. Joseph-Howard, son of Moses (*George, Moses, Jacob, Abraham, Mordecai, Samuel*) and Amanda (Ogden) Lincoln of Darby, Pa., born Nov. 20, 1866, at Darby. He is living, 1915, at Darby. He is a teamster.

He married, May 22, 1892, at Darby, Harriet-Cook, daughter of Ephraim and Harriet (Cook) Fithian of Camden, N. J., born Feb. 14, 1873, at Camden. (Records of Mrs. Joseph-Howard Lincoln.)

Children, born at Darby:

adbcf beea. Mary-Amanda, born Oct. 10, 1893; married, Dec. 23, 1909, at Camden, N. J., John, son of Patrick and Margaret Dougherty of Darby, born 1886, at Darby. They are living, 1915, at Darby. He works in a coal yard.
Children, born at Darby:
    a. John, born Aug. 12, 1910.
    b. Mary-Edna, born Sept. 2, 1912.
    c. Harriet-Elizabeth, born Apr. 11, 1915.
adbcf beeb. Joseph-Howard, born Sept. 9, 1895; unmarried, 1915.
adbcf beec. Oscar-Moses, born Aug. 18, 1897.
adbcf beed. Charles-Herman, born Oct. 31, 1903.
aabcf beee. Jessie-Florence, born Aug. 21, 1907.
adbcf beef. George-Washington-Henry, born July 16, 1912.

adbcf beg. William-Ogden, son of Moses (*George, Moses, Jacob, Abraham, Mordecai, Samuel*) and Amanda (Ogden) Lincoln of Darby, Pa., born Oct. 21, 1871, at Darby; died Oct. 13, 1901, at Darby. He was by trade a mason and lived at Darby.

He married, Sept. 4, 1892, at Darby, Lillian, daughter of Edmond H. and Elizabeth (Stewart) Taylor of Darby, where she was born March 21, 1874, and where she died May 29, 1905. (Records of Mr. Edmund H. Taylor, Darby.)

Children, born at Darby:

adbcf bega. William-Edmond, born Aug. 16, 1893; unmarried, 1915.
adbcf begb. Robert-Herman, born Feb. 10, 1895; unmarried, 1915.
adbcf begc. Russell-Phipps, born June 29, 1898.
adbcf begd. Harry-Lewis, born Dec. 18, 1899.

adbfa bdf. HOWARD-NEARING, son of Isaac-Buck (*Daniel-Savage, William, Mordecai, Abraham, Mordecai, Samuel*) and Augusta-Caroline (Nearing) Lincoln of Cromwell, Conn., born May 30, 1880, at Cromwell. He graduated at the New York college of pharmacy in 1900 and is now, 1919, a druggist, living at Middletown, Conn.

He married, July 24, 1907, at New York, N. Y., Ina-Belle, daughter of Frederick-Nelson and Katherine (Lawrence) Porter of Danbury, Conn., born Apr. 24, 1887, at Danbury; living, 1919. (Records of Howard-Nearing Lincoln.)

Child, born at Middletown:

adbfa bdfa. ELIZABETH-ESTHER, born July 23, 1908.

adcac bac. DANIEL-WEBSTER, son of Isaac (*Francis, Uriah, Isaac, Isaac, Mordecai, Samuel*) and Sarah (Bates) Lincoln of Cohasset, Mass., born Apr. 9, 1833, at Cohasset; died Jan. 14, 1900, at Weymouth, Mass. He was a shoemaker and lived during most of his adult life at Weymouth, but for a few years at Stoneham, Mass. He retired from business before his death. He was a private in the Lincoln Light Infantry of Hingham, Mass., which went to the seat of war for three months, Apr. 17, 1861. He afterwards enlisted in the 32nd regiment, Massachusetts volunteer infantry, for three years and served until sometime in 1863, when he was discharged for disability.

He married, Aug. 16, 1863, at Weymouth, Mary-Ann[8], daughter of Nahum[7] (*Sylvanus[6], Daniel[5], Daniel[4], Samuel[3], James[2], James[1]*) and Meribah (Orcutt) Whiton of Weymouth, born March 29, 1845, at Weymouth; died there July 12, 1905. (Mass. Vital Records; Weymouth Records; Cohasset Genealogies, p. 245; Hist. of Hingham, vol. iii, p. 301; Records of Francis Lincoln, *adcac bab.*)

Children, born at Weymouth:

adcac baca. HENRIETTA-WALLIS, born Aug. 29, 1864; married, Dec. 29, 1883, at East Weymouth, Edwin-Ellsworth, son of Elisha and Sarah (Mead) Bass of Rockland, Mass., born Apr. 15, 1861, at Rockland; died Nov. 29, 1890, at East Weymouth. He was a travelling salesman and lived at Stoneham and at Lynn, Mass. She is living, 1911, at Lynn, and is employed in one of the shoe shops.

Child, born at Stoneham:

    a. WALLACE-LINCOLN, born Nov. 27, 1886; died July 27, 1887, at Marlborough, Mass.

adcac bacb. FANNIE-WEBSTER, born Nov. 5, 1866; married, Aug. 17, 1887,
at Lexington, Mass., Henry-Lincoln, son of Edward-Francis and Clara-
Louisa (Cass) Buswell of Stoneham, Mass., born July 27, 1866, at Stoneham. They are living, 1911, at Orient Heights, Mass. He runs a general
store.
  Child, born at Stoneham:
    a. FRANCIS-LINCOLN, born Dec. 24, 1896.

adcac baf. JOHN-HOBART, son of Isaac (*Francis, Uriah,
Isaac, Isaac, Mordecai, Samuel*) and Sarah (Bates) Lincoln of
Cohasset, Mass., born March 15, 1840, at Cohasset; died May
10, 1894, at Chelsea, Mass. He was a gravel-roofer in company
with his brother-in-law, James-Thomas Bailey, *adcac bad*,
having their place of business in Chelsea. He lived at Chelsea.

He married, Nov. 24, 1868, at Chelsea, Margaret-Ellen,
daughter of John-Albert and Eliza-Sparrow (Downing) Thurston
of Lynn, Mass., born Sept. 8, 1845, at Lynn. She married (2),
Sept. 15, 1903, at Lynn, Jesse, son of John-Prout and Almira
(Crosman) Sutherland of Lisbon, Me., born Feb. 13, 1837,
at Freeport, Me. They are living, 1911, at Lynn. (Cohasset
Genealogies, p. 246; Thurston Genealogy, 2nd ed., p. 283;
Mass. Vital Records; Records of Mrs. Ira-Newton Plumer,
adcac bag.)

Child, born at Chelsea:

adcac bafa. HARRIET-MARIA, born Sept. 5, 1870; died March 28, 1901, at
Lynn, unmarried.

adcac bai. GEORGE-HENRY, son of Isaac (*Francis, Uriah,
Isaac, Isaac, Mordecai, Samuel*) and Sarah (Bates) Lincoln of
Cohasset, Mass., born Dec. 16, 1847, at Cohasset. He lived
at Weymouth, Mass., until after his second marriage and was
a shoemaker. He then removed to Scituate, Mass., and was
a painter and carpenter, doing some farming. He is now, 1911,
living at North Scituate.

He married (1), June 16, 1874, at Scituate, Lucy-Ellen,
daughter of John and Lucy-Dunbar (Studley) Marsh of Scituate,
born June 15, 1853, at Scituate; died Feb. 27, 1875, at Weymouth.

He married (2), Jan. 7, 1877, at Scituate, Martha-Jane,
daughter of William-James and Susanna (Cushing) Newcomb

of Scituate, born Oct. 2, 1854, at Scituate; living, 1911. (Cohasset Genealogies, p. 246; Scituate Records; Mass. Vital Records; Records of Francis Lincoln, *adcac bab*, and of Mrs. George-Henry Lincoln.)

Child, by first wife, born at Weymouth:

adcac baia. A DAUGHTER, born Feb. 22, 1875; died Feb. 23, 1875.

Children, by second wife, born at Scituate:

adcac baib. HARRY-NEWTON, born Jan. 20, 1879.
adcac baic. CHARLES-CUSHING, born May 14, 1889; living, 1911, at Boston, unmarried.

adcac baj. LOVELL-BICKNELL, son of Isaac (*Francis, Uriah, Isaac, Isaac, Mordecai, Samuel*) and Sarah (Bates) Lincoln of Cohasset, Mass., born Aug. 9, 1850, at Cohasset. Until 1879 he was a shoemaker and lived at Cohasset. Since his marriage he has lived at North Scituate on what was a part of his father's farm, and since 1880 has been a farmer.

He married, Jan. 1, 1869, at South Scituate, Mass., Mercy-Thomas, daughter of Joseph-Ensign and Hannah (Howard) Merritt of Scituate, born May 14, 1853, at Scituate; living, 1911. (Cohasset Genealogies, p. 246; Mass. Vital Records; Records of Francis Lincoln, *adcac bab*, and of Lovell-Bicknell Lincoln.)

Children, born at Scituate:

adcac baja. NELLIE-THOMAS, born Nov. 23, 1879; married, Nov. 30, 1904, at Scituate, Harry, son of James-Cummings and Henrietta (Bates) Merritt of Scituate, born March 27, 1880, at Scituate. They are living, 1911, at North Scituate. He is a farmer. They have no children.
adcac bajb. FLORENCE-BATES, born June 27, 1884; married, May 3, 1908, at Scituate, Elmer-Stanley, son of Samuel-Lincoln and Augusta (Burbank) Williams of Cohasset, Mass., *abbea caad*, born Apr. 10, 1882, at Cohasset. The marriage proved unhappy and they have separated. She is living, 1911, with her father. They had no children.
adcac bajc. BERTHA-LOVELL, born Jan. 4, 1889; living, 1911, unmarried.

adcac dac. CHARLES-STUART-FESSENDEN, son of John-Dunlap (*Isaac, Uriah, Isaac, Isaac, Mordecai, Samuel*) and Ellen-Elizabeth-Longfellow (Fessenden) Lincoln of Brunswick, Me., born Aug. 13, 1869, at Brunswick. He graduated at Bowdoin college in 1891; received the degree of M.D. at Central university, Kentucky, 1894; was an interne at Salem, Mass., hospital, 1894-5; practised medicine at Louisville, Ky., 1895-9; and since then has been a missionary physician and teacher at St. John's college, Shanghai, China. He was editor of the "China Medical Journal," 1903-7, and was again chosen to that position in 1911, to hold it until 1913. He has been a member of the executive committee of the American Association of China, 1905-6, 1910-1.

He married, Dec. 15, 1903, at Shanghai, Williette-Woodside, daughter of George-Robert and Martha-Josephine (Cowan) Eastham of Harrisonburg, Va., born Dec. 28, 1877, at Harrisonburg. They are living, 1911, at Shanghai. (Records of Charles-Stuart-Fessenden Lincoln.)

Children, born: *a, b* at Shanghai; *c* at Harrisonburg:

adcac daca. MARCIA-DUNLAP, born Dec. 1, 1905.
adcac dacb. JOHN-DUNLAP, born Aug. 25, 1907.
adcac dacc. ELEANOR-FESSENDEN, born Jan. 31, 1911.

adcai bga. WYMAN-RUSSELL, son of John-James (*John, Lazarus, Isaac, Isaac, Mordecai, Samuel*) and Ruth-Bates (Barker) Lincoln of Cohasset, Mass., born July 28, 1852, at Cohasset; died Apr. 20, 1914, at Cohasset. He was a conductor on the New York, New Haven and Hartford Railroad.

He married, July 2, 1878, at Cohasset, Eliza, daughter of Thomas and Jennie (McQueanie) Fraser of West River, Nova Scotia, born 1855 at West River. They lived at Cohasset on Spring street. (Cohasset Genealogies, p. 247; Mass. Vital Records.)

Children, born at Cohasset:

adcai bgaa. JAMES-RUSSELL, born Nov. 25, 1880; died June 11, 1884.
adcai bgab. MARGARET-ELIZA (an adopted daughter), born May 1, 1891.

adcai fba. GEORGE-MORTON, son of John (*Anslem, Lazarus, Isaac, Isaac, Mordecai, Samuel*) and Mary-Huntington (Fuller) Lincoln of Malone, N. Y., born July 31, 1872, at Malone. He graduated from Franklin academy, Malone, in 1890. He was then employed for nine years, 1890-9, in the Farmers National Bank of Malone, and from 1899 to 1903 he was with Farson, Leach and Company, bankers of New York City. He is now,

1911, and has been since February, 1903, treasurer of the F. W. Lawrence Company, wholesale dealers in general merchandise at Malone. He served from Jan. 26, 1892, to Dec. 20, 1897, in the 27th separate company, New York national guard.

He married, June 28, 1906, at Malone, Mabel-Bettina, daughter of Fayette-Washington and Mary (Sargent) Lawrence of Malone, born Feb. 26, 1876, at Bangor, N. Y.; living, 1911. (Records of George-Morton Lincoln.)

Child, born at Malone:

adcai fbaa. GEORGE-MORTON, born Feb. 2, 1910; died Feb. 7, 1910.

adfad bab. CHARLES-RAPP, son of Martin-Volney (*Martin, Jacob, Obadiah, Jacob, Mordecai, Samuel*) and Eliza-Jackson (Copeland) Lincoln of Boston, Mass., born May 27, 1849, at Boston. He removed to New York City in 1873 and remained there until 1893, when he went to Chicago, Ill., but returned to New York in 1897 and again removed to Chicago in 1909 and has been there ever since. He has always been in the sleeping car business, and is now, 1912, assistant to the general superintendent of the Pullman Company.

He married, Nov. 10, 1881, at New York, Charlotte-Wells, daughter of Alfred-Elias and Pauline (Schutt) Brevoort of Fishkill Village, N. Y., born March 29, 1847, at Fishkill Village; living, 1912. (Records of Charles-Rapp Lincoln.)

Child, born at Arlington, N. J.:

adfad baba. HELEN-BREVOORT, born May 9, 1885; married, Jan. 9, 1907, at New York, John-Serpell, son of Frederic and Marion-Orlena Avery of Rochester, N. Y., born Aug. 2, 1876, at Rochester. He received the degree of M.E. at Cornell university in 1899; was general manager of the Rockland Light and Power Company of Nyack, N. Y., until 1912; and is now, 1913, secretary and treasurer of the Bridgeford Machine Tool Works of Rochester. (Records of Mrs. Helen-Brevoort Avery.)
Children, born at New York:
a. JOHN, } born Nov. 2, 1908; { died Nov. 13, 1908.
b. LINCOLN, } { living, 1913.

adfae ada. WALTER-FOSTER, son of William (*William, Amos, Obadiah, Jacob, Mordecai, Samuel*) and Esther-Eliza (Bates) Lincoln of Cohasset, Mass., born June 3, 1851, at Cohasset. He was living, 1911, at Concord, N. H. He has no regular

occupation but "is ready for whatever piece of work comes
first to hand." In other words he is what is called in the country
"a handy man."

He married, Sept. 24, 1884, at Brooklyn, N. Y., Caroline-
Maria, daughter of Edwin-Huntington and Lucy-Jane (Brown)
Barton of Brooklyn, born Aug. 22, 1851, at Brooklyn; living,
1911. (Cohasset Genealogies, p. 246; Records of Walter-
Foster Lincoln.)

Children, born at Hopkinton, N. H.:

adfae adaa. HOWARD-WALTER, born Dec. 14, 1891.
adfae adab. FANNIE-ESTHER, born Feb. 13, 1894.

adfae adc. GEORGE-CUMMINGS, son of William (*William,
Amos, Obadiah, Jacob, Mordecai, Samuel*) and Esther-Eliza
(Bates) Lincoln of Cohasset, Mass., born Aug. 22, 1856, at
Cohasset. After his marriage he lived at Council Grove, Kan.,
for a few years but removed to Portland, Ore., and in 1911
was living at Prosser, Wash., where he had a small ranch.

He married, March 18, 1884, at Council Grove, Arabella-
May, daughter of William and Sylvesta (Whitehead) Whitcomb
of Scituate, Mass., Altoona, Ill., and Council Grove, born May
3, 1865, at Altoona. (Records of Mrs. Esther-Eliza Lincoln,
adfae ad.) Mrs. Lincoln's mother, Sylvesta Whitehead, was
a native of Breogar, England.

Children, born at Council Grove:

adfae adca. IRENE, born Jan. 1, 1885; married, June 30, 1908, at Portland,
Ore., Ralph-Riggs, son of Ezra and Grace (Riggs) Poppleton of Mountain
View, Calif., born June 12, 1881, at Monmouth, Ore. He graduated
at University of Oregon, 1908, and is now, 1911, an electrical engineer
living at Oswego, Ore.
  Child, born at Portland:
    a. GRACE-MAY, born June 6, 1909.
adfae adcb. WARREN, born March 24, 1887; a student, 1911, at State college,
Pullman, Wash.

adffe cda. LOUIS-MANSON, son of Thomas-Manson (*Thomas,
Caleb, Abraham, Jacob, Mordecai, Samuel*) and Augusta-Eugenie (Prentice) Lincoln of Providence, R. I., born May 13,
1870, at Providence. He graduated at Brown university in
1892. He is a dealer in machinery, living, 1912, at Providence.

He married, June 12, 1901, at Providence, Emelyn-Irwin, daughter of Orsemus A. and Caroline-Leland (Irwin) Taft of Providence, born Nov. 4, 1872, at Providence; living, 1912. (Providence Records; Records of George-Henry Lincoln, *adffe cb.*)

Children, born at Providence:

adffe cdaa. HELEN-EUGENIA, born May 31, 1903.
adffe cdab. CAROLINE-TAFT, born March 28, 1911.

adffe dfb. SAMUEL-BICKNELL, son of Clarence-Henry (*Samuel, Caleb, Abraham, Jacob, Mordecai, Samuel*) and May-Anna-Adelaide (Schultz) Lincoln of East Blackstone, Mass., born May 14, 1882, at East Blackstone. He was educated in the public schools of Blackstone and of Woonsocket, R. I., and at the university of Maine, where he graduated as a civil engineer. From 1906 to 1908 he was a member of the firm of Seagrave and Lincoln, engineers, at Woonsocket. Since then he has done general engineering work in Massachusetts, Connecticut and the Southern States. He is living, 1916, at Evanston, Ill.

He married, July 17, 1909, at Moosup, Conn., Carolyn-Louise, daughter of Charles-Henry and Julia M. (Toomey) Whipple of Bellingham, Mass., born Aug. 29, 1882, at Bellingham; living, 1916. (*Ibid.*)

Child:

adffe dfba. ROBERT-BICKNELL, born March 19, 1914.

adffe dfc. RALPH-EDWARD, son of Clarence-Henry (*Samuel, Caleb, Abraham, Jacob, Mordecai, Samuel*) and May-Anna-Adelaide (Schultz) Lincoln of East Blackstone, Mass., born Oct. 16, 1884, at East Blackstone. He is living, 1911, at Whitinsville, Mass., and is a book-keeper.

He married, Sept. 14, 1907, at Brooklyn, N. Y., Leslie-Alberta, daughter of James-Russell and Berta-Evans (Barnes) Bigelow of Los Angeles, Calif., born June 6, 1886, at Blackstone, Mass.; living, 1911. (Records of Ralph-Edward Lincoln.)

Child, born at Whitinsville:

adffe dfca. RICHARD-EDWARD, born Jan. 26, 1910.

aabce abca. JAIRUS-HORACE, son of David-Pratt (*Jairus-Beals, Peter, Frederick, Jonathan, Samuel, Samuel, Samuel*) and Cordelia-Etta (Makepeace) Lincoln of Weymouth, Mass., born Oct. 9, 1878, at Weymouth. He is an express messenger, living, 1911, at Weymouth.

He married, Oct. 28, 1907, at Weymouth, Florence-Alberta, daughter of William-Franklin and Mary-Holmes (McFann) Bartlett of Weymouth, born Dec. 8, 1887, at Weymouth; living, 1911. (Records of Miss Harriet-Priscilla Lincoln, *aabca abb.*)

Child, born at Weymouth:

aabce abcaa. MARGUERITE, born Sept. 8, 1908.

aabce aeba. OLIVER-FRANCIS, son of Frederic (*Oliver, Peter, Frederick, Jonathan, Samuel, Samuel, Samuel*) and Alice-Grace (Lewis) Lincoln of Warren, Mass., born Aug. 28, 1882, at Warren. He was educated at the Warren high school and took a course in electrical science with the Scranton correspondence school. He is an electrician; has lived at Lynn, Mass., and New York City, but is now, 1912, living at Hartford, Conn.

He married, June 21, 1904, at Lynn, Mary-Evangeline, daughter of Carl and Mary (Robishan) Jenson of Halifax, Nova Scotia, born Dec. 4, 1888, at Halifax; living, 1912. (Records of Mrs. Edith-Lillian [Lincoln] Case, *aabce aebb;* Mass. Vital Records say Mary-Evangeline was born at Dartmouth, Nova Scotia.)

Children, born: *a-c* at Springfield, Mass.; *d-e* at Hartford:

aabce aebaa. DOROTHY-EVANGELINE, born Jan. 5, 1905.
aabce aebab. SHIRLEY-ADA, born March 21, 1907; died July 15, 1907.
aabce aebac. A SON, born May 29, 1908; died same day.
aabce aebad. AIDA-GOLDEN, born Nov. 10, 1909.
aabce aebae. CARL-FREDERICK, born Dec. 8, 1911.

aabce aebc. CLARENCE-FREDERICK, son of Frederic (*Oliver, Peter, Frederick, Jonathan, Samuel, Samuel, Samuel*) and Alice-

Grace (Lewis) Lincoln of Warren, Mass., born March 26, 1887, at Warren. He is living, 1912, at New York City. He is a chauffeur and "is a good, honest, temperance man; loved by every one."

He married, Aug. 19, 1908, at Enfield, Conn., Josephine-Amy, daughter of Rufus-Putnam and Josephine (Messier) Wands of Springfield, Mass., born Sept. 24, 1886, at Suffield, Conn.; living, 1912. (Records of Mrs. Edith-Lillian [Lincoln] Case, *aabce aebb.*)

Child, born at Springfield:

aabce aebca. MARION-JOSEPHINE, born Sept. 4, 1909.

aacbc acba. WILLIAM-SEVER, son of Levi (*William-Sever, Levi, Levi, Enoch, Jedediah, Samuel, Samuel*) and Mary-Susan (Maynard) Lincoln of Worcester, Mass., born Apr. 11, 1870, at Boston, Mass. He was for several years landlord of the Paxton Inn at Paxton, Mass., but gave that up in 1910, and purchased a small farm in Boylston, Mass., where he is now, 1922, living, though he was engaged in trucking business at Worcester for a year or two, in company with his son.

He married, March 14, 1894, at Worcester, Villroy-Augusta, daughter of Edward-Payson and Sarah-Jane (Bullock) Goulding of Worcester, born March 5, 1872, at Worcester; living, 1922. (Family Records.)

Child, born at Boston, Mass.:

aacbc acbaa. LEVI, born Aug. 8, 1894.

aacbc acdd. WINSLOW-SEVER, son of Winslow-Sever (*William-Sever, Levi, Levi, Enoch, Jedediah, Samuel, Samuel*) and Helen-Blake (Webber) Lincoln of Worcester, Mass., born Apr. 30, 1893, at Worcester. He enlisted June 26, 1916, in Battery B, First Massachusetts field artillery, as private; was commissioned second lieutenant in the Second Massachusetts field artillery, May 12, 1917; first lieutenant, Sept. 13, 1917; and captain, July 30, 1918. He went to France with the 102nd U. S. field artillery, Sept. 18, 1917, and was stationed at Soissons, Toul and Château-Thierry front, from Feb. 1 to Aug. 12, 1918. He was sent home Sept. 1, 1918, unattached, and ordered to

Camp Kearney with the 42nd field artillery and remained there until discharged Feb. 21, 1919. He returned to Worcester and entered into the employ of the Rice, Barton and Fales Machine and Iron Company, with which company he remained until the summer of 1920, when he removed to Highland, Calif., where he has a small ranch.

He married, Sept. 7, 1919, at Jackson, Ohio, Frances, daughter of John-Ellsworth and Blanche (Armstrong) Jones of Jackson, born Dec. 7, 1893, at Jackson; living, 1922.

Child, born at Worcester:

aacbc acdda. ANN, born Feb. 19, 1920.

abbea cabd. ISAIAH-AUSTIN, son of Isaiah (*Francis-Mayhew, Jerome, Jerome, Francis, Hezekiah, Daniel, Samuel*) and Martha-Stockbridge (Litchfield) Lincoln of Cohasset, Mass., born May 16, 1864, at Cohasset. After his marriage he lived for a while at Somerville, Mass., but is now, 1911, living at Mount Blue, Norwell, Mass. He is a shoe-worker.

He married, Sept. 19, 1894, at Cohasset, Mabel-Gertrude, daughter of James-Henry and Josephine (Palmer) Pinkham of Cohasset, born Sept. 3, 1874, at Somerville; living, 1911. (Records of Isaiah-Austin Lincoln.)

Children, born at Norwell:

abbea cabda. HERBERT-AUSTIN, born Jan. 27, 1898.
abbea cabdb. HELEN-GERTRUDE, born May 8, 1904.
abbea cabdc. BERTHA-LOUISE, born Oct. 27, 1907.

abbea cabg. WILLIAM-IRVING, son of Isaiah (*Francis-Mayhew, Jerome, Jerome, Francis, Hezekiah, Daniel, Samuel*) and Martha-Stockbridge (Litchfield) Lincoln of Cohasset, Mass., born Oct. 5, 1871, at Cohasset. He is in business, 1911, with W. O. Souther, Jr., 6 Province Court, Boston, but lives at North Scituate.

He married, Jan. 16, 1901, at Scituate, Mass., Edwina-Lewis, daughter of Charles and Martha-Jane (Webb) Seaverns of Scituate, born March 12, 1878, at Scituate; living, 1911. (Records of William-Irving Lincoln.)

Children, born at Scituate:

abbea cabga. ALMA-CHIPMAN, born May 24, 1902.
abbea cabgb. MARTHA-KATHLEEN, born Dec. 19, 1905.

abbea cabi. ELIJAH-FRANKLIN, son of Isaiah (*Francis-May-hew, Jerome, Jerome, Francis, Hezekiah, Daniel, Samuel*) and Martha-Stockbridge (Litchfield) Lincoln of Cohasset, Mass., born Dec. 14, 1879, at Cohasset. He is living, 1911, at Cohasset on Beechwood street. He is in the spring-water business.

He married, Aug. 27, 1906, at Cohasset, Ellen-Harriet, daughter of Carl-August and Anna-Maria (Johanson) Johanson of Carls-Krona, Sweden, but by Swedish custom her name was Carlson rather than Johanson. She was born Aug. 22, 1883, at Carls-Krona, and came to America in June, 1900, with a sister. (Records of Elijah-Franklin Lincoln.)

Children, born at Cohasset:

abbea cabia. LAWRENCE-FRANKLIN, born Nov. 27, 1906.
abbea cabib. VIOLA-MARIA, born Feb. 16, 1908.
abbea cabic. JEANNETTE-CARLSON, born Aug. 1, 1909.

abbea cacc. ALFRED-STONE, son of Francis-Mayhew (*Francis-Mayhew, Jerome, Jerome, Francis, Hezekiah, Daniel, Samuel*) and Mary-Ann (Anderson) Lincoln of Hingham, Mass., born July 16, 1859, at Scituate, Mass. In 1893 he was a shoemaker and living at Hingham on Beal street, but nothing has been learned of this family since that date.

He married, July 13, 1879, at Hingham, Mary-Jane[3], daughter of John J.[2] (Henry[1]) and Hannah (Mulligan) Hawke of Hingham, born Dec. 10, 1858, at Boston, Mass. Her father was a native of Ireland. (Hist. of Hingham, vol. ii, pp. 295, 475; Mass. Vital Records.)

Children, born at Hingham:

abbea cacca. ALFRED-HAWKES, born Dec. 5, 1880; died Oct. 13, 1881.
abbea caccb. BERTRAM-FRANCIS, born Apr. 22, 1884.
abbea caccc. A SON, born and died July 10, 1889.

adaaa bbca. JAMES-THOMAS, son of Mordecai (*Thomas, Josiah, Abraham, John, Mordecai, Mordecai, Samuel*) and Mary-Elizabeth (Spencer) Lincoln of Harrison county, Ind., born Sept. 22, 1855, at Hancock, Ind. He lived at Milltown, Ind., until after 1880 and then removed to Overbrook, Kan., and later to Madison, Kan., where he is now, 1916, living. He is a farmer.

He married, Feb. 21, 1878, at Milltown, Annie-Ellen, daughter of Philip-Henry and Rebecca-Green (Bates) Bye of Sharp, Ind., born Jan. 12, 1858, at Sharp; living, 1916. Her father was a private in Company F, 144th regiment, Indiana volunteer infantry, in the Civil war and was discharged July 7, 1865. (Records of James-Thomas Lincoln.)

Children, born: *a, b* at Milltown; *c* at Overbrook:

adaaa bbcaa. MARY-FLORENCE, born Dec. 21, 1878; married, Feb. 21, 1900, at Olpe, Kan., Conrad, son of John-William and Christina (Lautenschlager) Eidman of Emporia, Kan., born Jan. 1, 1875, at Oakville, Ill. He is a farmer. They are living, 1916, at Plymouth, Kan.

Children, born: *a, b* at Olpe; *c, d* at Madison; *e-g* at Plymouth:
   a. ANNA-LEONA, born Dec. 26, 1900; died Nov. 26, 1914.
   b. EDITH-MAY, born May 31, 1903.
   c. ALICE-MAURINE, born Sept. 30, 1906.
   d. FLOYD-THOMAS, born Dec. 26, 1908.
   e. CHESTER-WILLIAM, born June 30, 1911; died Sept. 30, 1912.
   f. NELLIE-FRANCES, born July 9, 1913.
   g. DOROTHY-JOSEPHINE, born Feb. 2, 1916.

adaaa bbcab. HENRY-MORDECAI, born Sept. 20, 1880; living, 1916, unmarried. He is engaged in stock-raising and farming with his brother, in Greenwood county, Kan. He served in Company F, 40th U. S. volunteer infantry, from Sept. 22, 1899, to May 16, 1901, when he was discharged to take a job as horseshoer in the Quartermaster department, where he worked until July 15, 1913.

adaaa bbcac. FREDERIC-ERNEST, born Jan. 31, 1888.

adaaa bbcb. MAJOR-WETHERFORD, son of Mordecai (*Thomas, Josiah, Abraham, John, Mordecai, Mordecai, Samuel*) and Mary-Elizabeth (Spencer) Lincoln of Harrison county, Ind., born Dec. 13, 1858, at Milltown, Ind.; died Jan. 19, 1910, at Chanute, Kan. After his marriage he lived in Colorado, where he was a carpenter contractor.

He married, Feb. 10, 1890, at Colorado Springs, Colo., Mary-Elizabeth, daughter of Daniel and Catherine (Kelly) O'Keefe of White Oak Springs, Wis., where she was born May 3, 1851. She is living, 1917, at Newton, Kan. (Records of Mrs. Mary-Elizabeth [O'Keefe] Lincoln.)

Children, born at La Junta, Colo.:

adaaa bbcba. AGNES-CATHERINE, born Sept. 27, 1891; married, Feb. 21, 1916, at Newton, Kan., William-Harvey, son of William and Mary (Wheatly) Reid of Kansas City, Kan., born Feb. 8, 1890, at Towanda, Kan. He is a clerk. They live, 1917, at Newton.

Child, born at Emporia, Kan.:
   a. WILLIAM-JOSEPH, born Jan. 21, 1917.

adaaa bbcbb. JOHN-MORDECAI, born Dec. 11, 1893; living, 1917, unmarried, at Emporia, Kan. He is a brakeman.

adaaa bbcf. WILLIAM-SHERMAN, son of Mordecai (*Thomas, Josiah, Abraham, John, Mordecai, Mordecai, Samuel*) and Mary-Elizabeth (Spencer) Lincoln of Harrison county, Ind., born Oct. 22, 1865, at Milltown, Ind. He removed to Kansas, living in Osage and Jefferson counties, but is now, 1916, living at Nickerson, Reno county. He is a farmer.

He married, Apr. 6, 1893, at Thompsonville, Kan., Flora-Dell, daughter of Wallace-Ezekiel-Clark and Sarah-Ann (Evans) Mitchell of Ashland, Ohio, born Oct. 25, 1870, at Aleppo, Pa.; living, 1916. (Records of William-Sherman Lincoln.)

Children, born: *a*, *b* at Quenemo; *c*, *d* at Alden, Kan.:

adaaa bbcfa. WILEY-ETHELBERT, born Jan. 29, 1895.
adaaa bbcfb. CLIFFORD-MITCHELL, born Nov. 28, 1896.
adaaa bbcfc. SARAH-MARJORIE, born Nov. 3, 1904.
adaaa bbcfd. EVALYN-MAE, born Nov. 1, 1906; died Oct. 24, 1907.

adaaa bbcg. JOSEPH-DAVID, son of Mordecai (*Thomas, Josiah, Abraham, John, Mordecai, Mordecai, Samuel*) and Mary-Elizabeth (Spencer) Lincoln of Harrison county, Ind., born July 31, 1867, in Harrison county. He lived at Spencer, Harrison county, until about 1906, when he removed to Milltown, Crawford county, Ind., where he is now, 1916, living. He is a farmer.

He married, Oct. 29, 1890, at Whiskeyrun, Ind., Cora, daughter of Abel R. and Sarah-Elizabeth (Craig) Breeden of Milltown, born Apr. 28, 1871, at Scot, Harrison county, Ind. (Records of Joseph-David Lincoln.)

Children, born: *a* at Milltown; *b*, *c* at Spencer:

adaaa bbcga. STELLA, born Feb. 29, 1892; married, Dec. 24, 1912, at Milltown, Joseph M., son of Douglas and Clara E. (Summers) Taylor of Spencer, born Dec. 16, 1889, at Spencer. They are living, 1916, at Spencer. He is a farmer.
  Child, born at Spencer:
    a. DOROTHY E., born Nov. 8, 1915.
adaaa bbcgb. MORDECAI-ABEL, born March 15, 1894.
adaaa bbcgc. THERESA-EVELINE, born July 30, 1900; died Feb. 9, 1901.

adaaa bbea. WILLIAM-THOMAS, son of Washington (*Thomas, Josiah, Abraham, John, Mordecai, Mordecai, Samuel*) and

Deborah (Denton) Lincoln of Depauw, Ind., born Jan. 16, 1863, at Milltown, Ind. He removed to Missouri in 1886 and settled in Bates county, at Adrian, where he is now, 1916, living. He is a farmer.

He married, March 23, 1889, at Fort Scott, Kan., Laura-Elcena, daughter of Preston and Emily-Jane (Evans) Tegarden of Fort Scott, born Aug. 19, 1866, in Orange county, Ind.; living, 1916. (Records of William-Thomas Lincoln.)

Children, born at Adrian:

adaaa bbeaa. ADA-ETHERAGE, born July 23, 1890; married Apr. 23, 1916, at Adrian, Gilbert-Haley Cummings.
adaaa bbeab. EVE-MARIE, born Aug. 19, 1891.
adaaa bbeac. HELEN-GERALDINE, born Sept. 16, 1895.
adaaa bbead. HOWARD-THOMAS, born March 31, 1898.
adaaa bbeae. GLEN-WASHINGTON, born March 5, 1901.
adaaa bbeaf. HARRY-PRESTON, born July 9, 1904.

adaaa bbfb. HENRY-PHILIP, son of Warden (*Thomas, Josiah, Abraham, John, Mordecai, Mordecai, Samuel*) and Rachel-Ann (Hurbaugh) Lincoln of Depauw, Ind., born Oct. 11, 1869, at Leavenworth, Ind. He is a farmer, living, 1916, at Milltown, Ind.

He married, March 26, 1893, at Milltown, Mamie-Maria, daughter of John-Wesley and Caroline (Brawley) Swarens of Milltown, where she was born Oct. 27, 1873. (Records of Henry-Philip Lincoln.)

Child, born at Milltown:

adaaa bbfba. HOMER-FIELDEN, born Feb. 1, 1894; living, 1917, at Lamont, Iowa, unmarried.

adaaa bbfd. WILLIAM, son of Warden (*Thomas, Josiah, Abraham, John, Mordecai, Mordecai, Samuel*) and Rachel-Ann (Hurbaugh) Lincoln of Depauw, Ind., born Apr. 1, 1876, near Leavenworth, Ind. He is a farmer and lived for over thirty years at Milltown, Ind., but is now, 1916, living at Depauw.

He married, in 1894, at Milltown, Alice-Olive, daughter of Thomas and Lucinda (Burgess) Murr of Milltown, born Dec. 11, 1876, at Milltown; living, 1916. (Records of William Lincoln.)

Children, born at Milltown:

adaaa bbfda. GRACE, born Sept. 13, 1894.
adaaa bbfdb. MABEL, born Nov. 30, 1895; married, Aug. 28, 1913, at Corydon, Ind., Shelby E., son of E. J. and Alice (Schoonover) Bye of Milltown, born July 15, 1895, at Milltown. They are living, 1916, at Milltown. He is a farmer. His father was a native of London, England.
adaaa bbfdc. HELEN, born Oct. 21, 1900.
adaaa bbfdd. LILLIAN, born Nov. 14, 1903.
adaaa bbfde. LENA, born Sept. 15, 1908.

adaaa bbfe. WILLARD-EMMANUEL, son of Warden (*Thomas, Josiah, Abraham, John, Mordecai, Mordecai, Samuel*) and Rachel-Ann (Hurbaugh) Lincoln of Depauw, Ind., born Jan. 6, 1879, at Milltown, Ind. He is a farmer, living, 1916, near Milltown.

He married, Dec. 6, 1903, at Milltown, Rosa-Bell, daughter of Louis-Henry and Amelia-Ann (Priest) Mullen of Ireland, Ind., born Nov. 9, 1880, at Ireland; living, 1916.

Child, born near Milltown:

adaaa bbfea. EVA-GWENDOLINE, born Sept. 13, 1910.

adaaa bbfi. EDWARD, son of Warden (*Thomas, Josiah, Abraham, John, Mordecai, Mordecai, Samuel*) and Rachel-Ann (Hurbaugh) Lincoln of Depauw, Ind., born May 20, 1891, at Milltown, Ind. He is a farmer and has always lived near Milltown.

He married, June 11, 1912, at Corydon, Ind., Eva-May, daughter of Louis-Henry and Amelia-Ann (Priest) Mullen of Ireland, Ind., born March 3, 1891 at Ireland; living, 1916. (Records of Edward Lincoln.)

Children, born at Milltown:

adaaa bbfia. JESSE, born March 31, 1913.
adaaa bbfib. BERNICE, born March 11, 1915.

adaaa bbgb. JAMES F, son of Joseph (*Thomas, Josiah, Abraham, John, Mordecai, Mordecai, Samuel*) and Melissa (Daugherty) Lincoln of Milltown, Ind., born Oct. 4, 1878, in Harrison county, Ind. He is a drayman, living, 1916, at Milltown.

He married, Dec. 27, 1903, at Milltown, Lola, daughter of
39

Lewis-Cass and Julia (Priest) Pfeiffer of Crawford county, Ind.,
born Dec. 18, 1884; living 1916. (Records of James F Lincoln.)
Children, born at Milltown:

adaaa bbgba.   GORDON-PFEIFFER, born Dec. 25, 1905.
adaaa bbgbb.   PAULINE, born Dec. 21, 1907.
adaaa bbgbc.   OLIVE, born Apr. 5, 1910.
adaaa bbgbd.   JAMES-MORRIS, born Dec. 7, 1912.

adaaa bbic. LAWRENCE, son of James (*Thomas, Josiah,
Abraham, John, Mordecai, Mordecai, Samuel*) and Harriett-
Ann (Elliott) Lincoln of Vincennes, Ind., born Dec. 23, 1876,
in Martin county, Ind. He is a grocer in company with his
father, living, 1922, at Vincennes.

He married, Oct. 14, 1908, at Vincennes, Jessie, daughter of
John and Lissa (Blister) Schultz of Vincennes, born June 2,
1883, at Vincennes. (Records of James Lincoln, *adaaa bbi.*)
Children, born at Vincennes:

adaaa bbica.   RALPH-ALBERT, born Aug. 14, 1909.
adaaa bbicb.   MARTHA-LOUISE, born March 20, 1912.
adaaa bbicc.   ROBERT-EUGENE, born Oct. 25, 1918.

adaaa bbid. RALPH-PROSSER, son of James (*Thomas, Jo-
siah, Abraham, John, Mordecai, Mordecai, Samuel*) and Harriett-
Ann (Elliott) Lincoln of Vincennes, Ind., born May 3, 1880, in
Martin county, Ind. He is a grocer, living, 1922, at Hazleton, Ind.

He married, March 31, 1901, at Hazleton, Edith, daughter of
Allin W. and Jane (Colman) Anderson of Union, Ind., born
Apr. 17, 1885, at Union; died Dec. 31, 1917, at Hazleton. (Rec-
ords of James Lincoln, *adaaa bbi.*)
Children, born: *a, d-g* at Hazleton; *b, c, h* at Decker, Ind.:

adaaa bbida.   JAMES-ANDERSON, born Feb. 4, 1904.
adaaa bbidb.   CLARENCE-BLANCHARD, born May 20, 1905.
adaaa bbidc.   VIRGIL-EDGAR, born May 5, 1907.
adaaa bbidd.   DIMPLE-MAE, born Apr. 20, 1909.
adaaa bbide.   ROBERT-BURL, } born Dec. 9, 1910; { died 1917.
adaaa bbidf.   ROSCOE-MURL,   died May, 1911.
adaaa bbidg.   HELEN-IRENE, born March 17, 1915.
adaaa bbidh.   BESSIE-MAUDE, born Aug. 25, 1914.

adaaa bbif. NATHAN-HARRISON, son of James (*Thomas,
Josiah, Abraham, John, Mordecai, Mordecai, Samuel*) and

Harriett-Ann (Elliott) Lincoln of Vincennes, Ind., born Apr. 4, 1885, in Dubois county, Ind. He is a machinist, living, 1922, at East Lake, Tenn.

He married, Oct. 23, 1908, Lavina, daughter of Alexander and Lucinda (Robidson) Gibbs of Gibson county, Ind., born June 19, 1885, in Pike county, Ind. (Records of James Lincoln, *adaaa bbi.*)

Children, born: *a, b* at Greencastle, Ind.; *c* at East Lake:

adaaa bbifa. DALLAS-ABRAHAM, born Feb. 25, 1910.
adaaa bbifb. DELORES-ADELINE, born Aug. 20, 1912.
adaaa bbifc. JOHN-RUSSEL, born Jan. 18, 1920.

adaae hfac. PERCY-WOODSON, son of William-Effiah (*Jacob-Broaddus, Jacob, Jacob, John, Mordecai, Mordecai, Samuel*) and Sallie-Ann (Shewey) Lincoln of Staunton, Va., born July 25, 1884, at Lexington, Va. He served for three years, 1904-7, in Troop H, 14th regiment of cavalry, United States army, in the Philippines and California. He is now, 1917, a merchant at San Francisco, Calif.

He married, May 21, 1907, at San Francisco, Lillian, daughter of Edward and Lucia (Ludwig) Steiger of Sonoma, Calif., born July 6, 1884, at Sonoma; living, 1917. (Records of Percy-Woodson Lincoln.)

Children, born at San Francisco:

adaae hfaca. JANET-SALLIE, } born Jan. 27, 1908.
adaae hfacb. RUTH-LILLIAN, }
adaae hfacc. CLAIRE, born July 28, 1909; died Sept. 12, 1910.
adaae hfacd. JOHN-PERCY, born Jan. 25, 1912.
adaae hface. SUSAN-ANNE, born Sept. 15, 1917.

adahb gbca. WILLIAM-ADAMS, son of Azariah-William (*Thomas, Azariah, Thomas, Thomas, Mordecai, Mordecai, Samuel*) and Jennie-Margaret (Adams) Lincoln of Springfield, Mo., born Jan. 31, 1886, at Springfield. He was educated at the Springfield high school and passed two years in Drury college. He is an "abstractor" and is living, 1916, at Kansas City, Mo.

He married, May 6, 1908, at Springfield, Pauline, daughter of Foster-Nathaniel and Mamie-Edith (Fisher) Burns of Tulsa, Okla., born Jan. 19, 1891, at Springfield; living, 1916. (Records of William-Adams Lincoln.)

Child, born at Springfield:

adahb gbcaa. WILLIAM-BURNS, born Jan. 26, 1910.

adahb gbcb. HAROLD-THOMAS, son of Azariah-William (*Thomas, Azariah, Thomas, Thomas, Mordecai, Mordecai, Samuel*) and Jennie-Margaret (Adams) Lincoln of Springfield, Mo., born Nov. 11, 1888, at Springfield. He attended the high school and Drury college at Springfield and in 1906 entered the law department of the university of Missouri, from which he was graduated in 1909 with the degree of LL.B. He passed the State bar examination in January, 1909, and was admitted to practice at that time, but continued in school until graduation the following May. He entered into practice of his profession at Springfield, with his father, and was city tax attorney for two years and served one term as assistant prosecuting attorney. Since then he has been engaged in private practice.

He married, Dec. 6, 1910, at Springfield, Margaret-Louise, daughter of Matthew and Lizzie Sims of Ash Grove, Mo., born March 15, 1890, at Ash Grove. They are living, 1915, at Springfield. (Records of Harold-Thomas Lincoln.)

Child, born at Springfield:

adahb gbcba. MARGARET-LOUISE, born Sept. 28, 1911.

adaii bbba. ROBERT-RUTH, son of Oscar-Hemmig (*Alfred-Gilbert, John-Dehaven, Thomas, Abraham, Mordecai, Mordecai, Samuel*) and Elizabeth (Ruth) Lincoln of Pottstown Landing, Pa., born Oct. 21, 1887, at Robeson, or Gibraltar, Pa.; died July 20, 1912, at Phoenixville, Pa., where he had lived. He graduated from the West Chester high school in 1906; studied electricity with the Scranton correspondence school and became a telegraph operator for the Pennsylvania railroad. He was also a signal repairman.

He married, Oct. 28, 1910, at Lenape, Pa., Hazel-Rees, daughter of Albert-Baldwin and Jennie-Virginia (Green) Huey of Lenape, born June 23, 1890, at Lenape. (Records of Mrs. Robert-Ruth Lincoln.)

Child, born at Phoenixville:

adaii bbbaa. RUTH-JESSIE, born Aug. 12, 1911.

adbcf baab. ALFRED-WILES, son of Alfred (*John, George, Moses, Jacob, Abraham, Mordecai, Samuel*) and Ida (Young) Lincoln of Darby, Pa., born Nov. 12, 1880, at Darby. He has always lived at Darby except for a short time when he lived at Sharon Hill, Pa. His present address, 1919, is Woodbine avenue, Darby. Until August, 1918, he was a florist but since then has been a pipe fitter at the Baldwin Locomotive Works.

He married, Feb. 12, 1902, at Darby, Lillian-May, daughter of Henry and Mary (Schofield) Schuyler of Gloucester, N. J., born Apr. 18, 1884, at Gloucester. (Records of Alfred-Wiles Lincoln.)

Children, born: *a-c, e-i* at Darby; *d* at Sharon Hill:

adbcf baaba. ALFRED-WILES, born Dec. 7, 1902.
adbcf baabb. EDWARD-HENRY, born June 19, 1904; died Oct. 14, 1907.
adbcf baabc. ALEXANDER-SCOTT, born Jan. 5, 1906; died Jan. 24, 1906.
adbcf baabd. EDWARD-HENRY, born Nov. 30, 1908.
adbcf baabe. LILLIAN, born Sept. 28, 1911; died Dec. 5, 1916.
adbcf baabf. MARIETTA, born March 2, 1913.
adbcf baabg. DOROTHY, born May 13, 1916; died Dec. 13, 1917.
adbcf baabh. ELIZABETH, born Aug. 13, 1917; died January, 1918.
adbcf baabi. HENRY, born March 8, 1919.

adbcf bedb. HORACE-WILLIAM, son of Amer-Ogden (*Moses, George, Moses, Jacob, Abraham, Mordecai, Samuel*) and Martha-Emma (Covington) Lincoln of Darby, Pa., born May 23, 1890, at Darby. He is mason by trade and lives at Camden, N. J.

He married Ida P., daughter of Samuel and Clara Jones of Darby.

Child:

adbcf bedba. RUTH.

adcac baib. HARRY-NEWTON, son of George-Henry (*Isaac, Francis, Uriah, Isaac, Isaac, Mordecai, Samuel*) and Martha-Jane (Newcomb) Lincoln of Scituate, Mass., born Jan. 20, 1879, at Scituate. He was living, 1911, at North Scituate, Mass., with his father. He was then employed at Lawley's boat yard at South Boston, Mass.

He married, Feb. 4, 1901, at Gloucester, Mass., Nellie-Josephine, daughter of Perry and Nellie (Tarr) Perkins of Gloucester, born March 8, 1882, at Gloucester. (Records of Mrs. Harry-Newton Lincoln.)

Children, born at Boston, Mass.:

adcac baiba.   DOROTHY-LOUISE, born Nov. 22, 1901.
adcac baibb.   RICHARD-NEWCOMB, born Sept. 22, 1906.

aacbc acbaa. LEVI, son of William-Sever (*Levi, William-Sever, Levi, Levi, Enoch, Jedediah, Samuel, Samuel*) and Villroy-Augusta (Goulding) Lincoln of Boylston, Mass., born Aug. 8, 1894, at Boston, Mass. In 1916 he was a corporal in the Worcester Light Infantry, Company C, 2nd Massachusetts regiment, which Company was mustered into the service of the United States on June 21, 1916. The regiment went to Columbus, N. M., and was under General Pershing's command. Lincoln was promoted to be sergeant July 1, 1916. In the summer of 1917 he attended the Plattsburg school for officers and received his commission as second lieutenant, Aug. 15, 1917. He was attached to the 303rd machine gun battalion and was stationed at Camp Devens, Mass. He was commissioned first lieutenant Dec. 31, 1917, and was sent to Pittsburgh, Pa., as instructor in the University training detachment. He was honorably discharged Dec. 27, 1918. After the war he returned to Worcester and was employed for a time in the shops of S. Porter & Co., last manufacturers. He then engaged in the trucking business with his father, but is now, 1922, in the employ of the Livingston Motor Co. at Worcester.

He married, Dec. 25, 1917, at Ayer, Mass., Josephine-Marion, daughter of Frederick-Brainard and Marion-Inez (Lee) Barnard of Charlestown, Mass., born July 16, 1895, at Brighton, Mass. (Family Records.)

Child, born at Worcester:

aacbc acbaa a.   LEVI, born Aug. 18, 1918.

adaaa bbcac. FREDERIC-ERNEST, son of James-Thomas (*Mordecai, Thomas, Josiah, Abraham, John, Mordecai, Mordecai, Samuel*) and Annie-Ellen (Bye) Lincoln of Madison, Kan., born Jan. 31, 1888, at Overbrook, Kan. He is a farmer, living, 1916, at Madison.

He married, Aug. 24, 1910, at Emporia, Kan., Lizzie, daughter of George W. and Hattie E. (Rosebrooks) Miller of McFall, Mo., born Aug. 19, 1892, at McFall; living, 1916. (Records of Frederic-Ernest Lincoln.)

Child, born at Madison:

adaaa bbcac a.   FERN-BELL, born Feb. 19, 1915.

adaaa bbcgb.   MORDECAI-ABEL, son of Joseph-David (*Mordecai, Thomas, Josiah, Abraham, John, Mordecai, Mordecai, Samuel*) and Cora (Breeden) Lincoln of Milltown, Ind., born March 15, 1894, at Spencer, Ind., where he is now, 1916, living. He is a farmer.

He married, Sept. 15, 1915, at Corydon, Ind., Mary-Gertrude, daughter of George and Adaline (Burgess) Wiseman of Spencer, born Jan. 25, 1898, at Spencer. (Records of Joseph-David Lincoln, *adaaa bbcg.*)

Child, born at Spencer:

adaaa bbcgb a.   GENEVA, born March 9, 1916.

FINIS

INDEX OF PERSONS

Italic letters following a name indicate that the person bearing that name is either a descendant or married a descendant of SAMUEL LINCOLN of Hingham, Mass., the number of letters corresponding to the generation in which the person belongs. Such names may be found under the index letters given and on the page to which the figures following refer. Names not followed by index letters are only mentioned incidentally. For full explanation of the notation employed, see the preface. Names of authorities in the parenthetical notes are not indexed.

ABBOT—Abbott
Agnes-Margaret (Radford) *aacbe lbb* 297
Caroline-Howard (Lincoln) *aacbe lb* 294 297
Elizabeth (Colby) 253
Elizabeth Cushing ([Lincoln] Doane) *aabcd dd* 253-4
Ezra 294 297
Ezra *aacbe lb* 294 297
Ezra-Lincoln *aacbd dba* 294
George 253 294
George *aacbe lbb* 297
Hannah (Poor) 294 297
Harriet-Moody (Lincoln) *aacbe db* 294 297
Jessie-Lincoln (Gunnell) *aacbe lba* 297
John 294
John Colby *aabcd dd* 253
John-Howard *aacbe lba* 297
Joseph 253
Lucy-Amelia *aacbe lbc* 297
Lydia-Almira 253
Lydia-Maria (Breed) 253
Margaret (Armstrong) *aacbe dba* 294
Mary-Ellen (Fuller) 253
Nathan 253
Salome *abbea je* 190 444
Thomas 253
ADAMS
Betsy 412
Ella B. (Lincoln) *adaah ebc* 480
Henry-Hamilton 586
Isabel-Ugenia (Swaner) 586
Jennie-Margaret *adahb gbc* 586
Jerusha 332
John 157 170
John-Quincy 278
John-Washington *adaah ebca* 480
Louisa-Frances 455-6
Lula *adaae hfb* 572
Mabel *adbfa fbd* 387
Mary S. 110 and note
Sarah H *aabcd cj* 141
Washington *adaah ebc* 480
ACKER
Mary-Amelia *adbca ch* 232
ADDISON
Ida-Ella (Haines) *adahf cce* 373
William *adahf cce* 373
AFLICK
Mary *adbcg a* 118
AGNER
Conrad 499
Elizabeth *adahb dce* 499
Sarah (——) 499
AHLBERG
Emilia-Carlson *aacdb eeb* 433
Maria (Carlson) 433
Martin 433

AIKEN
Ann 78 169
James 78
Margaret (Waugh) 78
AINSLIE
Albert-Wallace *abbea cafi* 451
Atwood-Ingalls *abbea cafd* 451
Belinda (Arnold) *abbea cafc* 451
Eliza-James (Lincoln) *abbea caf* 451
George-Edward *abbea caf* 451
George-William *abbea cafc* 451
Henrietta-Maria *abbea cafb* 451
Henry-Wilbur *abbea cafg* 451
Margaret (Powers) 451
Mary-Eva *abbea caff* 451
Mary-Jane (Emerson) *abbea cafi* 451
Sarah (Haskell) *abbea cafd* 451
Susan-Ellen *abbea cafa* 451
William-Garrett 451
ALBRIGHT
Anna (Trump) 588
Celeste-Jane *adahc aae* 588
James-Henry 588
ALCOCK
Elizabeth *akd* 9
ALDEN
Alice-Burrington (Wight) 265
Alice-Wight *aabch dba* 265
Charles-Henry 265
Charles-Henry *aabch db* 265-6
Charles-Henry *aabch dbb* 265
Eliot *aabch dbd* 266
Etta (Estill) *aabch dbd* 266
Katherine-Russell (Lincoln) *aabch db* 265-6
Mary-Lincoln *aabch dbc* 266
ALDERSON
Elizabeth *adaga gfd* 490
ALDRICH
Barbara 438
ALDRIDGE
Matilda *adagb c* 219 220
ALERTON
Mary 114
ALEXANDER
Elizabeth 351
ALLEN—Allyne
miss 406
Aaron H. 457
Alice (Lincoln) *adaaa bbef* 562
Ann (——) 25
Avery-Tucker 444
Cecil-Leland *adaaa bbefe* 562
Ebenezer 86
Edith (Lincoln) *aabhg ee* 278
Elizabeth (Rush) *adbea* 58
Elsie-Irene *adaaa bbefb* 562
Frona-Mabel *adaaa bbeff* 562
Frances M. 535

ALLEN cont'd
Herschel-Edward *adaaa bbefc* 562
James 86
Jerry 562
John-Trimble 481
Joseph 25
Julia-Ann (——) 481
Julius-Bentley 278
Leah (Hobson) 562
Lewis-Eldred *aabhg ee* 278
Lydia-Atearn (Morton) 444
Margaret 377
Mary *agcb* 25
Mary (Lincoln) *agc* 25
Mary-Samantha (Bowen) 278
Rebecca *abae* 86-9
Rebecca (Russel) 86
Samuel 86
Sarah *adaah ei* 481-2
Susan-Congdon *aacdc gf* 444
Susannah (Lewis) 86
Thomas 86
Thomas *agca* 25
Wilford *adaaa bbef* 562
William *agc* 25
William *agcc* 25
William *adbea* 58
ALLMAN—Almond
Josephine ([Lincoln] Stover) *adaee he* 345
Thomas *adaae he* 345
ALLYNE see Allen
ALVEY
John 198 199
AMBROSE
David *adaha de* 224
Sena (Hills) *adaha de* 224
AMES
Eleanor *aacdc eac* 551
Emma (Benson) 551
Oliver 551
ANDERSON
Allin W. 610
Almira-Olive (Dunham) 554
Anna-Maria 500
Edith *adaaa bbid* 610
Jane (Colman) 610
John *adaaa aaaa* 460
John O. L. 460
Laura-Caroline (Larsen) *adbfa fh* 515-6
Lewis 554
Mary-Ann *abbea cac* 554-5
Mary-Hansbarger 476
Priscilla-Florida (Smith) *adaaa aaaa* 460
Robert 466
William *adbfa fh* 515-6
ANDREWS—Andrewes
Abigail *aaib* 12
Anna 172 173
Bertha-Randolph (Hatfield) *aacdb iea* 308
Betsey 263
Catherine-Cushing *aacbh j* 78
Elizabeth 11
Ephraim 10
Fred-Lincoln *aacdb iea* 308
John 308
John-Calvin *aacdb ie* 308
Joseph 34
Ruth 42 121
Sarah (Gibbs) 308
Sophia-Gibbs (Lincoln) *aacdb ie* 307 308
Thomas 10 17 75
William 5
ANSON
Benjamin-Milton *adbca dae* 381
Frank 511
Mabel *adbca dcc* 511
Mary-Elizabeth (Chenoweth) *adbca dae* 381

ANTHONY
Andrew 192
Mary-Birch (Lincoln) *abbhc c* 192
Michael *abbhc c* 192
Susan 447
APPLEBEE—Appleby
Eliza-Ann 180
Elizabeth ([Lincoln] Shackford) *aacdb c* 177 179-80
George *aacdb cc* 180
Gleason 180
Sarah 180
Susan (——) 180
Susan-Maria *aacdb da* 180
Sylvanus *aacdb c* 179-80
Zelinda-Ray *aacdb cb* 180
APPLEBY see Applebee
APPLETON
Catherine-Cushing (Souther) *aabcd ci* 141
William E. *aabcd ci* 141
APTS
Henrietta-Maria (Ainslie) *abbea cafb* 451
William-Wallace *abbea cafb* 451
ARENSBURG
Martha (Barnes) *adaga chd* 360
Theodore *adaga chd* 360
ARMENTROUT
Margaret-Catherine (Lofland) *adaae adb* 343
St. Clair *adaae adb* 343
ARMS
Burdette-Loomis *aacdc eab* 441
Helen-Frances (Lincoln) *aacdc eab* 441
Henry-Martyn 441
Sarah-Jane (Closson) 441
ARMSTRONG
Blanche 604
Margaret *aacbe dba* 294
ARNALL
William 6
ARNOLD
Ann-Maria 452
Belinda *abbea cafc* 451
Eliza-Ann (Marsh) 397
Elizabeth (Paddleford) 420
Ellen-Elizabeth 436
George-Rhodes 420
Hanson 397
Laura-Ashbury *adffe dd* 397
Sarah-Rhodes *aacbc ah* 420
ASHLEY
Dorcas *agje* 27
Edith 458
ASHMEAD
Isaac 496
ATKINSON
George-Henry *adffa k* 133
Nancy (Bates) *adffa k* 133
ATWOOD
Martha 26 note
AUSTIN
Brown *adaaa edb* 204
Florence-Mary (Lincoln) *adaaa bbfh* 563
Lloyd *adaaa eda* 204
Lucretia (Brumfield) *adaaa ed* 204
Mabel-Gertrude (Pinkham) *abbea cabd* 604
Mabel-Irene *adaaa bbfha* 563
Romeo 419
Sally-Blake 419
Samuel 563
Sarah-Chandler (Blake) 419
Sarah (Denbo) 563
William-Harvey *adaaa bbfh* 563
AVERILL
Lydia-Lincoln (Souther) *aabcd cf* 141
Thomas-William *aabcd cf* 141

AVERY
Frederic 599
Helen-Brevoort (Lincoln) *adfad baba* 599
John *adfad babaa* 599
John-Serpell *adfad baba* 599
Lincoln *adfad babab* 599
Marion-Orlena (——) 599
AXTELL
Eliza (McClain) 358
Lillian-May (Gregg) *adaga afd* 359
Luther 358
Luther *adaga af* 358-9
Luther-Melancthon *adaga afd* 359
Mary-Eliza *adaga afc* 358
Sarah (Lincoln) *adaga af* 358-9
Sebastian *adaga afa* 358
Thomas-Lincoln *adaga afb* 358
AYER
C. R. 405
AYRES
Mary 494
Robert 494

BABB
Ann 137
Robert 136 137
BACHE
Richard 266
BACHELDER
George W. 461
BACON
Emeline E. *aafff cb* 315
Joanna E. *aafff cb* 315
Mary Bassett 528
Susanna 16
BAGLEY
Thankful (Burnham) 267
BAILES see Bayless
Jesse-Taylor *adagb di* 365
Martha-Louise (Lincoln) *adagb di* 365
William-Jesse *adagb dia* 365
BAILEY see Bayley
Abner *aafac* 37
Amasa 90
Anjanette *adffe dg* 525
Asa 102 103
Asenath 249
Caleb 516
Cornelia (Skinner) 525
Delila (——) 102
Elizabeth 83
Elizabeth (Nichols) *abcd* 14
Hattie-Eliza *aabcf dbc* 263
Jael (Cushing) 90
James-Thomas *adcac bad* 516 596
John 516
Joseph 516
Joseph-Riley 525
Judith 393
Rebecca 90 91
Rebecca (Gannett) 516
Sarah (Bates) *aafac* 35 37
Sarah-Vinal (Lincoln) *adcac bad* 516
Waterman 516
William *abcd* 14
BAIR
Lydia-Magdalene *adahb bcee* 497
BAIRD
Etta *adaaf dda* 351
James 197
Robert 222
BAKER
Abner-Loring 449
Anna-Frances *aacdd ec* 449
Bethia C. *aacdb da* 180
Deborah 26
Elizabeth 91
Hannah 174

BAKER cont'd
John 26 449
James 449
Lydia-Jacobs (Ripley) 449
Mary-Ann 318
Richard 449
Ruth (Walley) 26
Walter 548
BALCH
Emmeline *adffd b* 133
John 347
BALDWIN
Abigail ([Lincoln] Shaver) *daae af* 344
Christopher-Columbus 290
Henrietta (Lofland) *adaae add* 343
James H. *adaae adc* 343
John *adaae af* 344
Mary-Jane (Lofland) *adaae adc* 343
Mary-Louisa 362
Robert G. *adaae add* 343
Sarah *adfah d* 128
Thomas 297
BALLENTINE
Hannah-Samuels (Lincoln) *adaid e* 230
Jacob-Byler *adaid ea* 230
Thomas-Lincoln *adaid eb* 230
William *adaid e* 230
BANCROFT
Adaline F. *aabhe a* 275-6
Asa 275
Sarah (Clements) 275
BANGS
Edward-Dillingham 170
Isaac-Howard 410
Lydia (Turner) 410
Marcia-Maria *aabck ba* 409-10
BARBER
Christopher 198 199
Dolly *aaflh* 38
Magnus W. *adaah elc* 483
Margaret (Lincoln) *adaah elc* 483
Nancy *aabce cb* 402
BARBOUR
Eugenia L. *aabcg dc* 407
Isaiah 407
Lucretia (——) 407
BARKER
Anne (Roberts) *aabce cddb* 403
Elizabeth (Smith) 403
Francis 34
Hannah (Worrick) *aaffh a* 83 518
Henry 403
Herbert-William *aabce cddb* 403
John *aaffh a* 83 518 519
Joshua 181
Lillian-Lincoln *aabce cdda* 403
Mary-Emma (Lincoln) *aabce cdd* 403
Mary (Jacob) *aac* 32 34
Mary (Lincoln) 34
Robert 34
Ruth-Bates *adcai bg* 518-9
Sarah *aabcf ff* 145
Stella *aabce cddc* 403
Teesta 519
William 126
William-Penn *aabce cdd* 403
BARLOW
Barbara (——) 332
Catharine *adaaa b* 330-3
Christopher 332
Jacob M. 332
BARNARD
Frederick-Brainard 614
Josephine-Marion *aacbc acbaa* 614
Marion-Inez (Lee) 614
Olive 549
Robert 117

BARNES
Abigail 183
Alice-Lou-Myrtle *adaga che* 360
Arthur *adfad ec* 245
Benjamin *adaga chb* 360
Berta-Evans 601
Betsey (Lincoln) *adfad e* 245
Clara-Aspinwall *aacdb eaa* 303
Edward-Lincoln *adfad ea* 245
Edwin *adfad e* 245
Edwin-Cummings *adfad eb* 245
Eliza-Jane *adaga chc* 360
Eliza (Trader) 360
Harriette (Clarke) *adfad eb* 245
J. D. 353
John *adaga ch* 360
John Franklin *adaga cha* 360
Lura A. (Booth) *adfad eb* 245
Lydia-Hersey 261
Margaret (Goff) *adaga chb* 360
Martha *adaga chd* 360
Sophia (Lincoln) *adaga ch* 359 360
Thomas 183 360
BARNETT
Agnes (Davenport) 48
BARNEY
Annie-Cottrell (Lincoln) *adffe caa* 522
Edwin-Luther 522
Edwin-Luther *adffe caa* 522
Mary (Hillman) 522
BARRELL
Lydia 22
BARRETT
Edward *aabcf ahc* 262
Frances-Maria *aabcj ab* 149
Louisa-Harding (Sawyer) *aabcf ahc* 262
Mary 175
BARRY
Charles 152 153
John 152 153
Mary *aabck* 152-4
Mary (Blake) 152
Mary (Vose) 153
Samuel 268
BARTLETT
Daniel 154
Flora-Letitia-Selina *abbhc gb* 193
Florence-Alberta *aabce abca* 602
Isabel-Hazard (Bullock) 448
Mary-Holmes (McFann) 602
Matthew *aacdd eba* 448
Nelson-Slater 448
Serafina (Lincoln) *aacdd eba* 448
Serita *aacdd ebaa* 448
William-Franklin 602
BARTO
Bartholomew *adaic e* 229
Harrison *adaic ea* 229
Isaac *adaic eb* 229
Margaret (Lincoln) *adaic e* 229
Mary *adaic ec* 229
BARTOL
Jonathan-Glover 295
Mary (Chandler) *aabhf a* 70
Rebecca-Trevett *aacbe h* 295
Sally (Trevett) 295
Samuel *aabhf a* 70
BARTON
Caroline-Maria *adfae ada* 600
Charles-Sumner 538
Charles-Sumner *aacbc acdbc* 538
Edwin-Huntington 600
Elizabeth-Spring (Holbrook) 538
Elizabeth-Trumbull (Lincoln) *aacbc acdb* 538
Etta (Baird) *adaaf dda* 351
George-Sumner *aacbc acdb* 538
George-Sumner *aacbc acdbb* 538

BARTON cont'd
Janet *aacbc acdba* 538
Lucy-Jane (Brown) 600
Mordecai-Lincoln *adaaf dda* 349 351
Peter *aacbc acdbe* 538
Sarah-Amelia (Lincoln) *adaaf dd* 351
Sarah (DeBow) *adaaf dda* 351
Trumbull *aacbc acdbd* 538
William *adaaf dd* 348 351
William E. 202 327 341
BASS
Edwin-Ellsworth *adcac baca* 595
Elisha 595
Henrietta-Wallis *adcac baca* 595
Sarah (Mead) 595
Wallace-Lincoln *adcac bacaa* 595
BASSETT
Hannah (Bramhall) 67
Joshua 67
Sarah 67
BATE—Bates
Abigail *aafah* 35 37
Abigail *adffa e* 133
Abigail (Barnes) 183
Abigail (Joy) 36
Abigail (Lincoln) *adffa* 37 62 132-3
Abigail (Nichols) *aafae* 37
Abner 36
Allen *adffa a* 132
Ambrose *aafab* 37 240
Ambrose *aafag* 35 37 90 521
Amos *adcag f* 122
Anna *aabce a* 254
Anna *adffa a* 132
Anna (——) 183
Anna (Bates) *adffa a* 132
Benjamin 60 61
Bessie-Lincoln (Crocker) *adcai bgea* 519
Betty (Beal) *abbad* 41
Caleb 183
Caroline-Franklin *abbea cac* 554
Clement 8 36 90 92 132 183 191 316 516 521 554
Daniel 429 516
David 40
Davis *adffa b* 132
Deborah (Clapp) *afb* 8
Deborah (Litchfield) 554
Edward 254
Ellen *abbed b* 90 125
Enos *aafle* 36 38
Esther *adffa j* 133
Esther-Eliza *adfae ad* 394 521-2
Esther (Hilliard) 8
Esther (Johnson) *abbed g* 90 521
Fanny *abbed d* 90
Florence-Matilda 527
Francis-Lincoln *abbed g* 90 521
Gorham-Parsons *aafff ga* 316-7
Gorham-Parsons *aafff gab* 316
Grace 36
Grace *aafad* 37
Grace (Lincoln) *aafa* 35 36-7 90 132
Gracia *adffa h* 133
Hannah ([Cowing] Pynchon) 36
Hannah (Holbrook) 254
Hannah (Litchfield) *aafaa* 37
Harriet-Melinda *aafff gaa* 316
Harriet-Souther (Lincoln) *aafff ga* 316-7
Hattie-Parsons *aafff gaf* 317
Henrietta 597
Henrietta-Lincoln (Pratt) *adcac of* 239
Henry-Beals *adcai bgea* 519
Hepsibah-Lincoln *abaea ah* 187
Hester *aff* 8 62
Hophney *abbed c* 90
Huldah (Cudworth) 60 61
Isaac *ake* 9

BATE—Bates cont'd
Isabella L. *abbed h* 90
Jacob *akf* 9
James *adcac cf* 239
Jane 320
Jessaniah 554
Jesse 183
Joanna *abaea ae* 187
Job-Tower *aaffi a* 84
John 254
John *abbhe* 92
John *abbec c* 191
Jonathan 191
Jonathan *afc* 8
Joseph 8 36 90 92 132 183 191 316 516 521 554
Joseph *af* 8
Joseph *afb* 8
Joseph *abbah* 41
Joshua 36 90 132 316 516 521 554
Joshua *aafa* 36-7 90 132 316 516
Levi *aafaa* 35 37
Lewis 554
Lewis-Lincoln *aafff gae* 317
Lincoln *abbhe c* 92
Lincoln *adffa d* 132
Lot *aaffj d* 84
Lydia *aacdd* 183-4
Lydia C. *adffa l* 133
Lydia-Nichols *aacbe ld* 426
Margaret (Mackay) *adffa d* 132
Maria *abbed e* 90 125
Martha (Beal) *abbag* 41
Martha (Clark) *ake* 9
Martha (Lincoln) *abbhe* 92
Mary 125
Mary *afa* 8
Mary *aaba* 64-6 78 148
Mary *abbhe b* 92
Mary-Annie 531
Mary (Clark) *akf* 9
Mary-Elizabeth (Litchfield) *abbea caib* 452
Mary (Lincoln) *af* 8
Mercy (Beal) 125
Mercy ([Kent] Stodder) 40
Mordecai *abbad* 41
Nancy *adffa k* 133
Nancy (Sherwin) *adffa g* 133
Nathaniel 554
Nathaniel-Nichols 426
Olive *aaflg* 38
Patience 243
Paul 316
Philinda-Gates *aacbg ch* 429-30
Philinda-Gates (Prouty) 429
Phineas *aafaj* 35 37 132-3
Phineas *adffa g* 133
Polly *abbed i* 90
Priscilla (Lincoln) *abbed* 37 90
Priscilla-Lincoln (James) *aafff eb* 92 185
Priscilla-Stodder *abbed a* 90
Priscilla (Tower) 316
Priscilla-Tower *aafff gac* 316
Rachel *afd* 8
Rachel (Tower) *adffa b* 132
Rebecca-Green 606
Ruth *aacab g* 72
Ruth (Jenkins) *adcag f* 122
Sally *adffa c* 132
Sally (Whitcomb) *aafle* 38
Samuel 8 92 125 191
Samuel *abbag* 41
Samuel *abaea ad* 187
Sarah *aafac* 35 37
Sarah *adcac ba* 516-7
Sarah (Beal) *abbah* 41
Sarah (Collier) *abaea ad* 187

BATE—Bates cont'd
Sarah-Hobart *abbed f* 90
Sarah (Lincoln) *abbec c* 191
Sarah (Lothrop) 92
Sarah (Tower) *aafai* 37 516
Sarah (Whittington) *aaffi a* 84
Silence *aacab g* 72
Susan (Lincoln) 426
Susanna 81
Susanna *afe* 8
Susanna (Beal) *afc* 8
Susanna (Orcutt) 191
Sybil *adffa f* 133
Theophilus *aafai* 35 37
Theophilus *adffa i* 133
Thomas 92
Thomas *abbhe a* 92 185
Urban 254
William-Webster *abbea caib* 452
Winifred (Ellmes) *aafff d* 84
Zealous *aafae* 35 37 316 516
Zealous *aafff gad* 317
Zibiah (Sabiah) *aafaf* 35 37
BATTEESE
Ida-Lincoln (Kilgore) *aacbe lfea* 428
Verne *aacbe lfea* 428
BATTLES
James *adcac ei* 239
Ruth-Nichols (Lothrop) *adcac ei* 239
Susanna 63 note
BAUGH
Henrietta *adaaf aa* 348
BAXTER
Ellen-Lincoln *adcac dabb* 518
Emily-West *adcac dabd* 518
Hartley-Cone *adcac dab* 518
James-Phinney 518
John-Lincoln *adcac dabc* 518
Joseph 81 90
Martha 137
Mary (——) 137
Mary-Richardson (Lincoln) *adcac dab* 518
Rosalie *adaae agbe* 473
Sarah-Kimball (Lewis) 518
Sarah-Lewis *adcac daba* 518
William 137
BAYLESS see Bailes
Albert-Leonard *adaae abaa* 569
Alva-Lincoln *adaae abaab* 569
Anna-Belle (Lincoln) *adaae abaa* 569
Annie A. (Haney) 569
Cora-Belle *adaae abaaa* 569
Elizabeth-Gretchen *adaae abaad* 569
Frank-Leonard *adaae abaac* 569
John-Tabro 569
Opel-Ivey *adaae abaae* 569
BAYLEY see Bailey
Joseph 16
BEAL
Abigail *abca* 14
Abigail (Burr) *abbib* 42
Abigail (James) 260
Abigail ([Marble] Hudson) 71
Andrew 317
Annie L. (Miller) *aafff gbb* 317
Benjamin 317 note
Benjamin *agda* 26
Benjamin *aabca; aabbc* 31 67
Bette 184 187
Betty *abbad* 41
Caleb 67 68 317
Carrie-Jarvis (White) *aafff gbc* 317
Charles *aaffh f* 83
Chloe *abbai* 41 249
Christiana (Simmons) *aabci a* 68
Christopher 317
Clara-Gowing *aafff gbi* 317

BEAL cont'd
Daniel 317
David 260
David *abbib* 42
Ebenezer 72 126
Edith-Angell 317 note
Edith-Loring *aafff gbg* 317 and note
Elijah 67 68
Elizabeth *aaic* 12
Elizabeth *abcf* 14 122
Elizabeth (——) 402
Elizabeth (Burr) *abbia* 42
Emma-Frances (Packard) 317
Ethel M. (Brooks) *aafff gba* 317
Eugene-Willis *aafff gba* 317
Francis-Leander *aafff gbb* 317
George *aaffe e* 82
Hannah 10 65 72
Hannah-Leavitt (Burbank) 317
Harriet-Ripley *aafff gbh* 317
Harry-Winslow *aafff gbd* 317
Henrietta M. (——) 317 note
Henry-Lincoln *aafff gea* 317
Herman-Lincoln *aafff gbc* 317
Hezekiah *abbia* 42
Jacob 260
Jairus 154
Jairus *aabci* 68 142
James 260
Jennie-Warren *aafff geb* 317
Jeremiah 40 42 121 184 317
John 40 42 67 68 121 184 260 317
John *aaij* 12
Jonathan *abba* 40-1
Joshua 67 68 317
Joshua *aabci a* 68
Jotham-Burrell *aafff ge* 316 317
Lazarus 40 42 121 184
Leander *aafff gb* 317
Lorette (Worrick) *aaffh f* 83
Lucy 124
Lucy (Lincoln) *aabca* 66 67
Lydia (Whiton) *aaha* 12
Margaret L. *aabce bg* 402
Martha *abbag* 41
Martha (Hudson) *agda* 25 26
Martha-Lincoln (Burrell) 317
Martha (Thaxter) *aabbc* 31 67
Mary 10 239
Mary *abbae* 41 82
Mary-Elizabeth (Lincoln) *aafff gb* 317
Mary-Gertrude *aafff gbe* 317
Mercy 125
Mercy ([Kent] [Stodder] Bates) 40
Morton 402
Obadiah *abbab* 38 41 71 88 90 132 186 188
Obadiah *abbif* 43
Olive (Lincoln) *aaij* 12
Olive (Pratt) *aaffe e* 82
Percilla *abbaa* 41
Percilla (Lincoln) *abba* 39 40-1
Rachel (Hobart) 68
Rose (Brown) *aafff gea* 317
Ruth 10
Ruth *adca* 121-3 132
Ruth *abbic* 43 88
Ruth (Andrews) 42 121
Samuel 260
Sarah *abbah* 41
Sarah-Ellen *aafff gbf* 317
Sarah-James *aabce h* 260
Sarah (Jones) 67
Sarah-Lewis (Lincoln) *aafff ge* 316 317
Susan *aabci b* 68 142
Susanna *afc* 8
Susanna *abbac* 41 128
Susanna *abbid* 43 184-5

BEAL cont'd
Susanna *aacab a* 72
Susanna (Lewis) 45
Susanna (Lincoln) *abbi* 42-3 88 184
Susanna (Lincoln) *aabci* 66 67-8 142
Tamar *abbaf* 41 191
Thankful *abbig* 43
Thomas *abbi* 42-3 184
Thomas *abbie* 43 88
William M. 317 note
BEALS
Mary 456
BEAN—Beane
Anna-Maria (Anderson) 500
Atha-Elizabeth *adahb fabb* 500
Bessie-Lue-Emma *adahb fabf* 500
Claude-Lincoln *adahb fabd* 500
Edward 427
Ettie-Frances (Lincoln) *adahb fab* 500
Guy-Arval *adahb fabe* 500
Harriet-Maria (White) *aacbe lf* 427-8
I. X. 427
Iris (Curry) *adahb faba* 500
James-Robert *adahb faba* 500
Jesse-Leo *adahb fabg* 500
Maltimore-Edward *adahb fab* 500
Raleigh-Edward *adahb fabc* 500
Robert-Edward 500
BEATTIE—Beatty
Caroline-Cornelia ([Canfield] School-craft) 283
Caroline (Nixon) 501
Edith-Olivia (Lincoln) *adahb fad* 501
George-Henry *adahb fad* 501
Hannah-Olivia *adahb fadc* 501
John 501
John-Henry *adahb fadd* 501
Joseph-Gilmore 283
Olin-George *adahb fadb* 501
Omie-Lincoln *adahb fada* 501
BEAUCHAMP
Ann-Taliaferro (Lincoln) *adaah ea* 354
John A. *adaah ea* 354
John A. *adaah eaa* 354
Robert *adaah eab* 354
BECKER
Beulah-Worth (Paschall) *adbcf bdc* 383
Erskine *adbcf bdc* 383
BECKWITH
Jessie (Lincoln) *adaaa dbdc* 568
Luzina (Porter) 568
Mary-Lincoln *adaaa dbdca* 568
Robert-Lincoln *adaaa dbdcb* 568
Warren 568
Warren *adaaa dbdc* 568
BEEBE
James M. 430
BELCHER
Joseph 70
Lydia-Ann 305
BELL
Charles 432
Elizabeth (Boynton) 433
Fannie *aacdb ebd* 432
Hatevil 303
John 48 468
Lucretia *aacdb ec* 303
Mary 78
Rebecca (Crane) 303
BELLAH
Annie-Du Ross (Evans) *adahb bea* 368
Joseph *adahb bea* 368
BENDALL
Freegrace 4
BENEDICT
Amelia-Margaret (Scott) 578
Emory-Jay 578
Helen *adaah gda* 578

BENNET—Bennett
Baslee 424
Charles-Frederick 557
Clarinda-Rebecca (Foster) 557
Emma (Jennison) 424
Margaret *aacdb b* 77
Marietta-Foster *abbea mhd* 557
Mary 153
Mary-Ann *aacbd e* 77
Mary-Ann *aacbe hb* 424-5
BENSON
Arthur-Peter *aabce cdda* 403
Emma 551
Lillian-Lincoln (Barker) *aabce cdda* 403
BENT
Ann *aabcd ce* 141
BENTZ
Nathan 534
BERGMAN
Altha-May (Lincoln) *adaaa bbcl* 560-1
Anna-Kathleen *adaaa bbcla* 560
Ernest-Knoefel *adaaa bbclb* 560
Fred 560
Harry-Wayne *adaaa bbclc* 560
Lutetia (Byrum) 560
Norman-Joseph *adaaa bbcle* 561
Viola-Fern *adaaa bbcld* 561
William-Lee *adaaa bbclf* 561
William-Simon *adaaa bbcl* 560-1
BERGSTRASSER
Caroline 588
BERLIN
Ann-Maria (Sweetser) 151
BERRETT
Edith-Lillian (Lincoln) *aabce aebb* 528
Samuel-Ernest *aabce aebb* 528
BERRY
Cally (Ewing) 340
Elizabeth 25
Emma-Louise (Carver) 434
Gertrude-Abby *aacdb efc* 434
Jane (——) 25
John 349
Joseph-Louis 434
Lucy (Shipley) 339 340
Nora-Bell 589
Rachel (——) 340
Richard 339 340
William 25
William F. 466
BETTS
Margaret-Elizabeth 494
BICKNELL
John 247
Molly (Pratt) 247
Nancy *adffe* 247-8 395
Zechariah 247
BIEHL
Catherine *adaii be* 510
Daniel 379 510
Daniel *adaii bj* 379
Henry-Thomas *adaii bja* 379
Martha-Lincoln *adaii bjd* 379
Mary (Lincoln) *adaii bj* 379
Mary-Lincoln *adaii bje* 379
Sarah-Esther *adaii bjb* 379
Susan (Eidel) 379 510
Susan-Rebecca *adaii bjc* 379
BIGELOW
Anna (Andrews) 172 173
Berta-Evans (Barnes) 601
Clarissa 173
Clarissa (Bigelow) 173
Daniel 172 173
David 173
Deborah (Heywood) 173
George-Tyler 173
Harriet ([Lincoln] Whitney) *aacbj c* 173

BIGELOW cont'd
James-Russell 601
John 172 173
Joshua 172 173
Leslie-Alberta *adffe dfc* 601
Nancy *aacbj* 172-3
Timothy 172 173
Tyler *aacbj c* 172 173
William-Deford 41
BILLETTE
Adaline (Buchanan) 441
Anna-Mae *aacdc eaa* 441
Jacob 441
BINNEY
Abby *abbea cce* 319
Amos 254
Anna-Bates (Lincoln) *aabce ac* 255
Anna (Lambert) 255
Catherine-Lincoln *aabcd dga* 254
Charles *aabcd dg* 254
Eliza-Ann *aabce acd* 255
Elkanah 255
Fanny-May *aabce acc* 255
John 254 255
John *aabce ac* 255
John-Francis *aabce acb* 255
Judith-Cooper (Russell) 254
Mary 253
Lizzie-Herbert (Ray) *aabce acb* 255
Mary-Ann-Binney (Lincoln) *aabcd dg* 253 254
Omar 254
Sarah *aabce aca* 255
BIRCH
Ann *abbhb d* 92
Eliza *abbhb e* 92
Emily *abbhb g* 92
Ethel *abbhb* 92
Eunice *abbhb f* 92
Eunice *abbhb h* 92
Ithel *abbhb* 92
Loretta *abbhb a* 92
Lucelia *abbhb c* 92
Lucenia *abbhb b* 92
Mary (Lincoln) *abbhb* 92
BIRD
Catherine (Pixley) 484
Greenup 484
Margaret-Pixley *adaah em* 484-5
Mary-Ann *aaffi d* 84
Polly ([Rimel] Swatzel) *adaai c* 102 103
BIRKET see Burkhead
Elizur 203
BISHOP
Catherine (Wilkins) 494
Edna-Alice (Lincoln) *adagb fbc* 494
Eugene-Malcome *adagb fbc* 494
James 494
Robert R. 447
BLACKBURN
Cornelia (Lincoln) *adahf ci* 374
Ellen *adaga cce* 359
Frances (Joab) *adaga cch* 360
George *adaga cch* 360
James *adaga ccb* 359
John *adaga ccg* 360
Joseph 374 482
Joseph-Rich *adahf ci* 374
Kate *adaga ccc* 359
Martha *adaga ccd* 359
Mary-Jane *adaga ccf* 359
Oliver *adaga cc* 359-60
Phoebe *adaga cca* 359
Phoebe (Lincoln) *adaga cc* 359-60
Rachel (Cutler) 374
BLACKMAN
Ella 550

BLACKMER
Washington 245
BLAIR
Rehtse-Louisa (Litchfield) *adcai ei* 241
Robert *adcai ei* 241
BLAISDELL
Mary-Elizabeth *aacdb eac* 303
BLAKE
Edward 153
Elizabeth-Chandler 419
Francis 163
Jonathan 153
Lucy *aabbj* 31
Lydia-McClellan 537
Margaret-Elizabeth (Kupfer) 429
Mary 152 153
Mary (Bennett) 153
Phebe-Maria *aacbg cc* 429
Sarah 193
Sarah-Chandler 419
William 153 429
BLANCHARD
Caroline ((Fernald) 413
Deliverance 300
Mary-Shepard *aabhg db* 413-4
Olive-Esther 436
William-Frederick 413
BLEACHER
Alberta-May *adbcf bekc* 514
Jessie-Amanda (Lincoln) *adbcf bek* 514
John *adbcf bek* 514
Leroy-Clyde *adbcf bekb* 514
Mary-Jane (McClain) 514
Mazie-Jane *adbcf beka* 514
Ohram-Abram *adbcf bekd* 514
Oram 514
BLISS
Adelaide *aacda ha* 175
BLISTER
Lissa 610
BLODGETT
Amos *adffe eb* 248
Anna-Eliza (Champney) *adffe eb* 248
BLOOM
Kate *adbca fbc* 381
BLYTHE
Amanda-Lincoln *adbcf befa* 513
Charles-Baird *adbcf beib* 513
Charles-Edward *adbcf bei* 513
Clara-Gilbert (Lincoln) *adbcf bei* 513
Eliza (Carver) 513
Horace-Lincoln *adbcf befb* 513
Ida-May *adbcf befd* 513
John 513
Lidie-Carver *adbcf befe* 513
Louis-Daniel *adbcf bef* 513
Louis-Wilmer *adbcf beff* 513
Ralph-Edward *adbcf beic* 513
Roy-Louis *adbcf befc* 513
Sadie-Countas (Lincoln) *adbcf bef* 513
William-Lincoln *adbcf beia* 513
BODEN
George *adbfa fbf* 387
Grace (Botelle) *adbfa fbf* 387
BODGE
Adeline-Louise *abbhc dc* 459
Adeline (Tall) 459
Charles-Andrew 459
BODLEY
Sarah-Anne (Shaw) *adagb jd* 219 221
William E. *adagb jd* 221
BODWELL
Bailey 180
BOGARDUS
Amanda *adagb dgi* 365
Annie (Lantz) *adagb dgf* 365
Benjamin-Franklin *adagb dge* 365
Caroline-Winters *adagb dgh* 365

BOGARDUS cont'd
Emily-Elizabeth (Williams) *adagb dgg* 365
Hannah *adagb dgc* 365
Jesse-Lincoln *adagb dgf* 365
Martha-Emily *adagb dgd* 365
Phebe (Lincoln) *adagb dg* 364-5
Philip-Schuyler *adagb dg* 364-5
Philip-Schuyler *adagb dgb* 365
Samuel-Lincoln *adagb dgg* 365
Winfield-Scott *adagb dga* 365
BOGERT
Edward-Langdon *aacbc ahf* 420-1
Edward-Langdon *aacbc ahfa* 421
Eliza-Turner (Howe) 420
Marian-Vinal (Lincoln) *aacbc ahf* 420-1
Mary-Anna 547
Pelham-Winslow *aacbc ahfb* 421
Theodore-Peacock 421
BOGMAN
Mary-Sampson 523
BOHART
Birdie-Pixley *adaah edg* 355
BOND
Amos *adbcg c* 118
Ann-Lincoln (Evans) *adbcg c* 118
Harriet (Loring) 69 note
Lydia *aacba f* 76
Moses 69 note
BONNEY
Mary-Elizabeth 555
BONSTEEL
Maryetta *adcai ef* 241
BOON—Boone
Abigail *adafa* 52 53 and note
Anne *adai* 111-2
Ann (Lea) *adaff* 53
Benjamin 46 52 note
Bertha-May (Lincoln) *adaii bbf* 509
Brigitta (Swanson) 116 note
Catharine 116 and note
Daniel 52 and note 111 194 195 196 222 224
Deborah (Howell) 52 53 note
Dinah *adaeb* 52
Elizabeth *adafh* 53 and note
Elizabeth (Boone) *adafh* 53 and note
Fanny *adaaf dag* 350
George 47 52 53 note 111 229
George *adafe* 53 and note
Grace-Minerva *adaii bbfa* 509
Hannah (Hughes) *adafh* 53 and note
Harry 509
Harry-Llewellyn *adaii bbf* 509
Hezekiah *adafh* 53 and note
James 53 note 111
Jeremiah *adafg* 53 and note
Julian *adaic* 229
Margaret (Mayberry) *adafe* 53 229
Mary 107
Mary *adafd* 52 53
Mary (Foucher) 53 note 111
Mary (Maugridge) 52
Mordecai *adafb* 52 53
Rebecca (——) *adafg* 53
Rebecca (Price) 509
Robert *adaii bbfb* 509
Sarah (Lincoln) *adaf* 52 53 and note
Squire 48
Susanna (——) 52 note
Susanna (Parks) *adafc* 53
Swan 116 note
Thomas *adaff* 53 and note
Wayne *adaii bbfc* 509
William *adaf* 52-3 53 note
William *adafc* 53 and note
BOOTH
Anna (Summerfield) 494

BOOTH cont'd
Elizabeth 91
Helen *adaaf abca* 477
John-Wilkes 468
Langham 494
Lura A. *adfad eb* 245
Mary *adagb fbb* 494
BOSLIN
Archibald 566
BOSWORTH
Beatrice 17
Benjamin 17
Jonathan 8
BOTELLE
Albert H *adbfa fbb* 387
Annie-Sarah (Lincoln) *adbfa fb* 387
Aurelia (——) 387
Bela-Lincoln *adbfa fbh* 387
Bertha (Stoddard) *adbfa fbg* 387
Edith (Marendaz) *adbfa fbb* 387
Edward M. *adbfa fbd* 387
Ellelar 387
Fanny *adbfa fbc* 387
Gertrude-May *adbfa fbj* 387
Grace *adbfa fbf* 387
Herbert-John *adbfa fbg* 387
Ida-Wilcox *adbfa fbi* 387
John-Demming **a**dbfa fb* 387
Lincoln-Bela *adbfa fba* 387
Lucy *adbfa fbe* 387
Mabel (Adams) *adbfa fbd* 387
Pearl-Amelia *adbfa fbl* 387
Sarah S. *adbfa fbk* 387
BOUGHMAN see Bowman
BOUGHTER
Carl *adaii bbca* 508
Charles-Carl *adaii bbc* 508
Eli 508
Jane (Parker) 508
Mary-Catherine (Lincoln) *adaii bbc* 508
BOURNE
Bethia 166
Elias 557
John 557
Mary-Cecilia-Turner (Townsend) 557
Mary-Elizabeth *abbec bba* 557
Relief 318
Thomas 557
BOUVÉ—Bovey
Caroline-Lincoln (Lane) *aabcd acd* 252
Charles-Osborn *aabcd acd* 252
Elizabeth (Scannell) 255
Gibbins 255
Hepzibah *aabce b* 255-6
BOWEN
Mary-Samantha 278
Susan A. (Haskell) *adffd f* 134
BOWERS
Sally 272 473
BOWKER
Charles-Henry 542
Mary *aacbc adda* 542
Mary (Grant) 542
BOWLES
Elizabeth (Mays) 573
Kate-May *adaae hfi* 573
William-Andrew 573
BOWMAN—Boughman
Ann *adbcc b* 117
Anna (Lincoln) *adbcc* 116 117 118
Catherine (Zwingler) 462
Charles-Newton *adaaa abc* 462
Charles-Newton *adaaa abcf* 462
Eliza *adaaa abcb* 462
Elizabeth 489
Emily-Nora *adaaa abce* 462
Evaline (Hardy) *adaaa abcg* 462
Isaac 117

BOWMAN—Boughman cont'd
John 462
Mary-Rowena ([Lincoln] Lovely) *adaaa abc* 462
Peter *adbcc a* 117 118
Robert-Lee *adaaa abcc* 462
Rosa-May *adaaa abcd* 462
Thomas-Edward *adaaa abcg* 462
BOWNE
Hannah 49
John 45 49
Obadiah 45
BOYD
A. E. 518
George-Rowland *adaaf dbba* 479
John-Parker 163
Martha (Swords) *adaga cfc* 360
Roberta (Davis) *adaaf dbba* 479
William *adaga cfc* 360
BOYDEN
Roland-William 538
Safety 53
BOYNTON
Elizabeth 433
BRADFORD
Catherine-Knox *adaae ahef* 474
Claude-Winfield *adaae ahec* 474
Edith-Lucille *adaae aheb* 474
Elizabeth (Miller) 474
James-Mortman 474
Lucy-Knox (Lincoln) *adaae ahe* 474
Mary-Elizabeth *adaae ahee* 474
Miller-Hughes *adaae ahed* 474
Norris-Lincoln *adaae ahea* 474
Robert-Winfield *adaae ahe* 474
BRADLEY
Bedie F. (Catron) *adaah eja* 355
Edwin-Allen 502
Ethel-Elizabeth *adahb dcha* 499
Eugene-Kellar *adaah eja* 355
Fanny *adaah eje* 355
Frank-Andrew *adahb dch* 499
Frank-Lincoln *adahb dchb* 499
George *adaah ejc* 355
Graham-Lincoln *adaah ejb* 355
Guinnie (Uttertrep) *adaah ejb* 355
Hannah-Maria (Hosford) 502
Harvey 499
James 355
Jessie-Belle ([Lincoln] Lerch) *adahb gbg* 502
Julia *adaah ejh* 355
Lucy-Gatewood (Lincoln) *adaah ej* 355
Margaret-Jane (Lincoln) *adahb dch* 499
Marshall *adaah ejf* 355
Nancy (Kellar) 355
Newton *adaah ejd* 355
Robert 355
Sarah (Palmer) 499
Thomas 355
Thomas-Kellar *adaah ej* 355
Zachary-Taylor *adahb gbg* 502
BRAMHALL
Hannah 67
BRANDT
Florence-Edna (Myers) *adagb fbab* 494
George 512
John H. *adagb fbab* 494
Maria *adbcf ba* 512
Sarah (——) 512
BRANSON
William 46
BRANT
miss 572
BRAVARD
Ebenezer *adbce* 117
Rebecca (Lincoln) *adbce* 117-8 232 236

40

BRAWLEY
Caroline 608
BRAY
Harriet 532
Harriet-McLellan (Lewis) *aabcf bb* 144
Jacob *aabcf bb* 144
BRAYTON
Mary-Janette 543
BRAZER
John 283
BREASHA
Eleanor *aacda gd* 175
BRECKENRIDGE
John-Cabell 468
BREED
Aaron 253
George 516
Harriet (Downing) 516
Lydia-Ellen *adcac bag* 516
Lydia-Husey 425
Lydia-Maria 253
Mary (Fillebrown) 253
BREEDEN
Abel R. 607
Cora *adaaa bbcg* 607
Sarah-Elizabeth (Craig) 607
BRENSINGER
Cora *adaii bdd* 379
BRETT
Caroline-Alma *aacdc gb* 443
Julia-Frances (Tilden) 443
Zenas-Franklin 443
BREVOORT
Alfred-Elias 599
Charlotte-Wells *adfad bab* 599
Pauline (Schutt) 599
BREWER
Ann (Hyers) 461
Hannah-Mehitable *aabcf ac* 404
Julia (Vose) 404
Peter 461
Phoebe-Ann *adaaa aae* 461
Thomas 404
BREWSTER
Elizabeth (Perrin) 590
Robert-Coddington 590
Sarah *adahf daa* 590
BRIAN see Bryan
BRIDGE
Thomas 24
BRIDGES
Benjamin 325 326
BRIERY
Alice ([Lincoln] Obrien) *aacdb bdc* 431
Milton *aacdb bdc* 431
BRIGGS
Charles 399
Diadama *adagb f* 365-6
Diadama (———) 365
Elsie 524
George-Nixon 429
Henry-Shaw 360
Ira 365
Joseph 60 61
Judith 84
Lucy-Ann *aabcd bc* 399-400
Mary 60 61
Mary (Garrett) 60-1
Olive 366
Rhoda (Reed) 399
Sarah 63 note
BRIGHT
Catherine *adaae a* 343-4
BRIGHTMAN
Mary *adcai bgc* 519
BRINKMAN
James-George-Waddell *abbea ccg* 319

BRINKMAN cont'd
Mary-Abby-Cushing (Clapp) *abbea ccg* 319
BRINTON
Elizabeth (Hackett) 505
Elizabeth ([Haines] Lincoln) *adahf ce* 505
Henry-Longfellow *adahf ce* 505
Joseph 505
BRISCOE
Anthony-Wayne *adaaa bdc* 333
Francis-Marion *adaaa bde* 333
John *adaaa bd* 330 332 333
Lettie-Ann *adaaa bdb* 333
Margaret-Jane (Soppenfield) *adaaa bdc* 333
Nancy (Lincoln) *adaaa bd* 332 333
Sallie (Totton) *adaaa bde* 333
BRITTEN
James 350
BROCK
Abraham-Edwin *adaae icc* 346
Anna (Windle) *adaae icb* 346
Annie R. (Maynard) *adaae icj* 347
Archibald 346
Arizona-Frances-Virginia-Josephine-Rebecca *adaae icd* 347
Carrie-Lincoln M. *adaae icg* 347
Caroline-Amanda (Lincoln) *adaae ic* 346-7
Charles-Archibald *adaae icb* 346
Edna-Earle *adaae ici* 347
Elizabeth (Hevener) *adaae icb* 346
Elizabeth (Rice) *adaae icc* 346
Hugh-Archibald-Lincoln *adaae icj* 347
John E. *adaae icc* 346
John-Price *adaae ic* 346-7
Mary-Dakota D. *adaae ice* 347
Rebecca-Allemode-LaClyde *adaae ich* 347
Sarah-Aramenta-Nannie *adaae icf* 347
Sarah (Price) 346
BROMLEY
Mary *abbec bae* 321
BRONSDEN
Eliza 166
BROOKS
Eleazer 244
Ethel M. *aafff gba* 317
Louisa 266
Phillips 266
Samuel 266
BROWN—Browne
Almedia (Gerald) 428
Andrew 438
Anna-Frances (Haines) *adahf ccb* 373
Annie-Louise *aacdb hfa* 306
Annie-Robinson (Lincoln) *aacdb hf* 306
Aram 151
Augusta-Lincoln *adaaf dfa* 351
Basil-Haines *adahf ccb* 373
Benjamin 149
Charles *adahf ccc* 373
Deborah 372
Earl-Lincoln *aacbe lfca* 428
Ebenezer 26 note
Elisha *adahf bb* 229
Eliza-Ann (Nutt) 306
Elizabeth (Alexander) 351
Elizabeth-Dickinson (Haines) *adahf ccc* 373
Elizabeth (Reynolds) *adahf chd* 374
Elizabeth (Stephens) *adahf bb* 229
Etta (Townsend) 393
Frances-Ann *adbca fc* 511-2
George T. *adaii bjd* 379
Gertrude *adaii bib* 379
Harriet-Maria (Lincoln) *aacbe lfc* 427-8
Hiram *adahf ba* 229

BROWN—Browne cont'd
James 511
Jethro 306
Jethro *aacdb heb* 306
Joseph 347 348 351 428
Julia *adaah ebb* 575
Levi-Prescott *aacdb he* 306
Lillian-Lillias (Gibson) *aacdb heb* 306
Lorette ([Worrick] Beal) *aaffh f* 83
Lucy-Jane 600
Lula (Adams) *adaae hfb* 572
Lydia 149 274
Marie (Vanier) *aacdb hea* 306
Martha *adfba h* 132
Martha (Biehl) *adaii bjd* 379
Mary-Ann *aabcj h* 267-8
Mary-Gertrude *adaaf dfd* 351
Mary (Harbison) 347 348
Mary ([Johnson] Stover) 351
Mary-Parsons (Lewis) *abaeb a* 87
Mary (Purcell) 511
Mary-Sophia (Lincoln) *adaaf df* 351
Mason-Lincoln *aacdb hea* 306
Miranda (Williams) *adaaf hc* 212
Nancy *adaaf a* 347-8
Nancy-Ann (Gove) 438
Nancy-Franklin *abbec bl* 455-6
Nathaniel 267
Nellie *adaga gh* 491
Ozro *aacbe lfc* 428
Philip *aacbe h* 295
Prudence (——) 149
Rachel-Logan 497
Rebecca 295
Rebecca-Trevett ([Bartol] Lincoln) *aacbe h* 295
Rose *aafff gea* 317
Ruby-Grace (Whitman) *aacbe lfca* 428
Russell-Kendall 491
Ruth-Jane *aabcj i* 151
Ruth (Morse) 151
Samuel *abaeb a* 87
Sarah 306
Sarah-Duxbury (Wyatt) 455
Sarah (Stephens) *adahf ba* 229
Serena-Morgan *aacdb ic* 438-9
Sophie-Bettie *adaaf dfb* 351
Susan-Maria (Lincoln) *aacdb he* 306
Susan (Wakey) 491
Thankful (Burnham) 267
Thomas-Jefferson *aaffh f* 83
Thomas-Webb 455
Ulysses-Grant *adahf chd* 374
William-Heiskell *adaaf dfc* 351
William-Ramsey *adaaf df* 350 351
BROWNFIELD—Brumfield
Elizabeth *adaaa eb* 204
George 337
James 203
Joanna (——) 203
Lucretia *adaaa ed* 204
Nancy (Lincoln) *adaaa e* 203-4
Polly *adaaa ea* 204
Susan *adaaa ec* 204
William *adaaa e* 203-4
BROYLS
Alexander 102
Elisabeth 102
BRUMFIELD see Brownfield
BRYAN—Brian
Cornelius 96
Hannah *adaab a* 95 98
Hannah (Harrison) *adaab af* 101
John 96
Peter 96
William 96
BRYANT
Elizabeth 393

BUCHANAN
Adaline 441
Mary-Ermina *adaid abd* 506
BUCK
Florilla *adbfa b* 385-6
Ruth 59 60 61
Ruth (Goodrich) 385
Samuel 385
BUCKNALL
Benetta *aabcf dca* 263
Benjamin 263
Benjamin-Franklin *aabcf dc* 263
Eliza (Jewett) 263
Frances *aabcf dcb* 263
Martha-Elizabeth (Lincoln) *aabcf dc* 263
BUFFINGTON
Sarah-Anna (Scott) *adahf cfd* 373
Walter-Richard *adahf cfd* 373
BULLINGTON
Mary 463
BULLOCK
Isabel-Hazard 448
Sarah-Jane 603
BURBANK
Augusta *abbea caad* 450 597
Hannah-Leavitt 317
BURES
Martha-Jane *adaaa aba* 462
BURGESS
Adaline 615
Lucinda 608
BURGOYNE
John 190 240 494
BURHANS
Julia 567
BURKE
James 424
Margaret D. (Taylor) 424
Nancy-Elizabeth *aacbe hac* 424
BURKHEAD see Birket
Abraham 203
BURLEIGH
Ann-Augusta *aabcf fe* 145
BURNETT
Helen (Benedict) *adaah gda* 578
James P. 578
BURNHAM
Edwin 453
Mary *aaffi f* 84
Thankful 267
BURNS
Foster-Nathaniel 611
Mamie-Edith (Fisher) 611
Mary-Ann (McCloud) 458
Pauline *adahb gbca* 611-2
BURNWORTH
Eva *adaga gbh* 362
BURPEE
Betsey (Stevenson) *adfag b* 128
John *adfag b* 128
BURR
Abigail *abbib* 42
Elizabeth *abbia* 42
Emma-Frances 277
Eunice 239
Isaac 239
Mary 276
Mary *abea* 15
Mary (Beal) 239
Polly-Stowers *aacbh f* 78
Priscilla *aabce ef* 142
Sarah (Leavitt) *abbda* 42
Thomas 146
Timothy *abbda* 42
BURRELL
Jane-Thaxter *aabce ae* 401
John 401
Martha-Lincoln 317

BURRELL cont'd
Mary-Ann (——) 401
BURRIDGE
Abigail-Antoinette 535
BURROW
Amanda *adaaa abca* 462
BURTNER
Elizabeth *adaae jc* 207
Mary *adaae jc* 207
BURTON
Angeline *adaaa bbb* 558-9
Shird 558
BUSH
Amanda-Emeline (Lincoln) *adaaa bbck* 560
Christopher 341
Norman *adaaa bbck* 560
Sarah *adaaa d* 341
BUSWELL
Clara-Louisa (Cass) 596
Edward-Francis 596
Fannie-Webster (Lincoln) *adcac bacb* 596
Francis-Lincoln *adcac bacba* 596
Henry-Lincoln *adcac bacb* 596
BUTLER
Anna-Maria (Stephenson) *aabcj ec* 150
Benjamin *aabad ga* 139
Cornelia (Little) *aabad ga* 139
Joseph *adage a* 108
Mary (Jones) *adage a* 108
Olive 310
Rebecca-Hill *aacbe d* 293
BUTTERFIELD
John 311
BUTTERS
Edward *abbhc ea* 193
Susanna-Lincoln (Fletcher) *abbhc ea* 193
BYE
Alice (Schoonover) 609
Annie-Ellen *adaaa bbca* 605-6
E. J. 609
Mabel (Lincoln) *adaaa bbfdb* 609
Philip-Henry 606
Rebecca-Green (Bates) 606
Shelby E. *adaaa bbfdb* 609
BYERLY
Peter 330
BYLES
Susanna 144
BYRLEY
Charles-Edward *adaaa bbebb* 562
Charles-Mitchell *adaaa bbeb* 561-2
Cora-Alice *adaaa bbebd* 562
Dora-Emma (Jenkins) *adaaa bbebb* 562
Eva-Florence *adaaa bbeba* 562
Eva-Florence (Byrley) *adaaa bbeba* 562
Mary-Ann (Lincoln) *adaaa bbeb* 561-2
Mary-Ann (Rankin) 561
Thomas 561
William-Chester *adaaa bbebc* 562
William-Warner *adaaa bbeba* 562
BYROM
Phebe *aaffd b* 82
BYRON
Mary *aaffe f* 82
BYRUM
Lutetia 560

CADWALLADER
John 506
CAIN
Ariel-Manley 527
Elizabeth *aabce abaab* 527
Florence-Matilda (Bates) 527
Leslie-Manley *aabce abaa* 527
Lincoln-Simonds *aabce abaaa* 527
Marion-Whitney (Lincoln) *aabce abaa* 527

CAIN cont'd
Nora-Arbel *adaga aaaa* 579
CAINES
Charles *adaaa befh* 566
CALDWELL—Calwell
John 161 197
Julia-Ann *adbfa e* 386-7
Margaret *adcb* 124-6
Mary 124
Mary-Ann 496
Seth 161
CALHOUN
John 466
CALWELL see Caldwell
CALL
Mary-Ann *aacbe ha* 424
CAME
Susan M. *adahf cae* 373
CAMERON
Caroline-Franklin (Lincoln) *abbea caca* 555
Edith-Viola *abbea cacaa* 555
Horatio G. 555
Keziah (Haskins) 555
Robert S. *abbea caca* 555
Virginia-Rolette *adahf ae* 228
CAMPBELL
Dora *adaaa bbai* 463
Eliza 397
Emma *adaae iaa* 346
Harriet (Wilt) 431
Henrietta 489
John 431 437
Mary-Jane *aacdb bd* 431-2
Sarah-Leighton (Hersey) 437
Sarah-Maria *aacdb gf* 437-8
CANBY
Louise R. *adaah edc* 355
CANFIELD
Abraham 283
Augustus 283
Caroline-Cornelia 283
David-Sealy 283
Francis-Allyn 283
Israel 283
Louisa-Cornelia (Seward) 283
Mahlon-Dickerson *aacbc ae* 283
Mary-Seward 283
Penelope-Sever (Lincoln) *aacbc ae* 283
Penelope-Winslow-Sever *aacbc aea* 283
Sarah (Sealy) 283
Thomas 283
CANOLES
Bella-Florence *adaaa baffb* 563
Blanche-Roseline *adaaa bbffe* 563
Charles C. 563
Herman-Gilbert *adaaa bbffd* 563
John-Roscoe *adaaa bbff* 563
Lelia (Lincoln) *adaaa bbff* 563
Mary-Etta *adaaa bbffa* 563
Nancy C. (Spencer) 563
Stella-Rachel *adaaa bbffc* 563
CANON
Daniel *adage d* 109
Elizabeth *adage d* 103 104
John *adage d* 103 104
Nancy (Jones) *adage d* 109
CANTELBURY—Cantlebury
Anna (——) 40
Cornelius 6
Elizabeth 40
Hannah 40
Hester 40
Mary 40
Sarah 40
CANTWELL
Cathryn-Maude *adaaa bbief* 565
Charles-Frederick *adaaa bbied* 565

CANTWELL cont'd
Decker 565
Donald-Lincoln *adaaa bbiea* 565
Edgar-Clifford *adaaa bbiee* 565
Elmer-Burton *adaaa bbie* 565
Legia-Naomi *adaaa bbieb* 565
Mary-Annalee *adaaa bbiec* 565
Sarah (Reel) 565
Sophia-Opal (Lincoln) *adaaa bbie* 565
Sylvia-Ruth-Ann *adaaa bbieg* 565
CAPEHEART
Alice-Ella *adahf dac* 591
Ella-Catherine (McCullough) 591
James 591
Philip 591
CAPRON
Ellen 525
CAREY
capt. 70
Alfred-Lea *adahb bbg* 496
Grace-Olivia (Wagner) *adahb bbea* 495
Joseph 496
Mary-Ann (Caldwell) 496
Mary-Cecilia (Lincoln) *adahb bbg* 496
William *adahb bbea* 495
CARLETON
William 410
CARLISLE
Elizabeth 426
CARLOW
Nancy 439
CARLSON
Ellen-Harriet *abbea cabi* 605
Maria 433
CARMICHAEL
mr. 100 208
CARNES
Ann-Eliza (Gross) *adaaf daj* 351
Charles S. *adaaa befh* 566
Joseph-Malcolm *adaaf daj* 351
Maude-Bell (Lincoln) *adaaa befh* 566
CARPENTER
Ann (——) 233
Barbara (Aldrich) 438
Barbara-Serene *aacdb icbb* 439
Catherine (——) 233
Charles 233
Christiana-Amelia 248
Edgar-Aldrich *aacdb icbf* 439
Edgar-Nathan *aacdb icbc* 439
Edmund 438
Edmund *adbca gc* 233
Emeline (Grove) 503
Frank-Lincoln *adbca ge* 233
Henry 233
Isaac 233
Isaac *adbca g* 233
Jennette-Emeline *adahb ged* 503
John-Lincoln *adbca ga* 233
Joseph *adbca gd* 233
Lillian-Gertrude (Lincoln) *aacdb icb* 438-9
Lincoln 233
Margara-Lorraine *aacdb icbe* 439
Mary (——) 233
Nathan H. 233
Rebecca (Lincoln) *adbca g* 118 233
Roswell-Donald *aacdb icbd* 439
Sarah-Ann *adbca gb* 233
Walter-Edgar *aacdb icb* 438-9
Walter-Lincoln *aacdb icba* 439
William 233
William-Barney 503
CARR
Alonzo-Augustus *aacda ge* 175
Harriet-Maria (Whitney) *aacda ge* 175
Moses 129 130
CARRIER
Hannah (Lincoln) *adaaf b* 210

CARRIER cont'd
Henry *adaaf b* 210
Isaac *adaaf ba* 210
Jesse *adaaf bb* 210
Milton *adaaf bc* 210
Polly *adaaf bd* 210
CARROLL
Alice *adagb dba* 364
Alice-Lincoln (Goldthwaite) *abbec fdaa* 458
Eli-Smith *adbca dac* 381
Eliza-Jane (Chenoweth) *adbca dac* 381
Jacob *adagb db* 364
Lincoln *adagb dbb* 364
Mary-Ann (Lincoln) *adagb db* 364
Sewell-Albert *abbec fdaa* 458
CARSKADON
Charles-Andrew *adaaf ich* 347
Rebecca-Allemode-LaClyde (Brock) *adaae ich* 347
CARSLEY
Abigail-Phinney *aabcf ha* 145
Eliza-Beal (Lincoln) *aabcf h* 145-6
Eliza-Jane *aabcf he* 145
Isaac 145
James-Henry *aabcf hg* 146
James-Mosher *aabcf h* 145-6
Jenny (Mosher) 145
John 145
Mary-Caroline (Greely) *aabcf hf* 146
Royal-Lincoln *aabcf hd* 145
William-Lincoln *aabcf hb* 145
William-Lincoln *aabcf hc* 145
William-Woodbury *aabcf hf* 146
CARSON
Annie-Elizabeth *adaga abd* 358
Elizabeth (Lincoln) *adaga ab* 358
Fannie (Gaddis) *adaga abb* 358
Jennie-Lydia (Crow) *adaga abe* 358
Lucius-Alexandria *adaga abb* 358
Luther-Lincoln *adaga abe* 358
Mary-Bianco *adaga aba* 358
Matilda *adaga abg* 358
Sara-Frances *adaga abc* 358
Smith-Fuller *adaga abf* 358
William 358
William *adaga ab* 358
CARTER
mr. 271
Elizabeth *adbaa b* 114
Hester *adbaa a* 114
James *adbaa* 113 114
Martha-Maria (Lincoln) *abbea cabh* 554
Martha-Whitney *abbea cabha* 554
Rebecca (Lincoln) *adbaa* 113 114
Sarah 114
Sarah-Frances (Hobson) 554
Wilbur-Austin *abbea cabh* 554
Wilbur-Austin *abbea cabhb* 554
William 114
William-Davis 554
CARVER
Emma-Louise 434
Eliza 513
CASE
Edith-Lillian (Lincoln) *aabce aebb* 528-9
George-Bacon *aabce aebb* 528 529
Gladys-Zitella-Alice *aabce aebbb* 529
John-Cahoun 528
Mary-Bassett (Bacon) 528
Nathaniel-Bacon *aabce aebbc* 529
CASELEY
Dorcas (Hamblin) 145
John 145
CASNER
Elizabeth *adaah* 213-5 471
CASS
Clara-Louisa 596

CASS cont'd
Sarah 240
CATLETT
Jasper 566
Mary (Lindsey) 566
Minnie-Sadie *adaaa bbii* 566
CATLIN
Julius 430
CATO
Annie *adaaa bef* 566
Darius 566
CATRON
Bedie F. *adaah eja* 355
CATTERILL
E. J. *adaaa bbbh* 559
Eva (Lincoln) *adaaa bbbh* 559
CAVE
Adeline-Margaret 569
CHADBOURN—Chadbourne
Betsey 262
Mary 25
Susan-Hardy 458
CHAMBERLAIN—Chamberlin
David-Clark *abbhe b* 92
Eleazer D. 273
Job 21
Mary (Bates) *abbhe b* 92
CHAMBERS
Hetty 384
CHAMPNEY
Anna-Eliza *adffe eb* 248
Eliza (Lincoln) *adffe e* 248
Elizabeth-Jane (Wilmarth) 556
Erastus 248
Erastus-Winchester *adffe e* 248
George-Francis 556
Mabel-Louise *abbea mbd* 556
Sarah-Eliza *adffe ea* 248
Sarah L. (Winchester) 248
CHANDLER
Charlotte *aabhf d* 70
Cushing-Lincoln *aabhf g* 70
Edmund 70
Deborah 518
Eliza (Stackpole) 70
Fanny *aacbc add* 541-4
George 541
Jacob *aabhf f* 70
Jane *aabhf e* 70
Joel *aabhf* 70
John 541
John-Wilkes 541
Jonathan 70
Joseph 70 541
Josephine (Rose) 541
Julia-Ann *aabhf h* 70
Mary 282
Mary *aabhf a* 70
Nancy-Deering *aabhf b* 70
Pamela *aabhf c* 70
Pamela (Lincoln) *aabhf* 70
Peter 541
Rachel (Mitchell) 70
William 541
CHAPIN
Mary (Hobart) *ad* 21
Chester 416
Josiah 21
Mary 21 22
Mary (King) 21
Samuel 21
CHAPLIN
Betty 174
CHAPMAN
Carrie D. *adaae idb* 347
Clark-Hiscox *adffe bh* 248
Eliza-Lincoln (Dickinson) *adffe bf* 248
Harriet 268

CHAPMAN cont'd
Josephine-Rebecca (Lincoln) *adaae id* 347
Luther E. *adaae abbc* 471
Mary-Fitch (Dickinson) *adffe bh* 248
Mary-Lincoln *adaae ida* 347
Virginia-Davis (Stearn) *adaae abbc* 471
William *adaae id* 347
William-Hiscox *adffe bf* 248
CHASE
Mary-Maria *abbhc bg* 192
Rufus D. 275
CHECKLEY
Samuel 26
CHELLIS
Reuben 365
CHENEY see Cheyney
Angelina (Durling) 548
Josiah-Nelson 548
Stella-May *aacdb eea* 548-9
CHENOWETH
Absolom 381
Charles-Absolom *adbca daf* 381
Eliza-Jane *adbca dac* 381
Elizabeth (Lincoln) *adbca da* 380-1
Ellenor (——) 381
Isaac-Lincoln *adbca daa* 381
John *adbca da* 381
John-William-Henry *adbca dad* 381
Margaret-Ellenor *adbca dab* 381
Mary-Adeline (White) *adbca daf* 381
Mary-Elizabeth *adbca dae* 381
CHERRY
Ellen (Turner) 532
Ethel-Forester (Lincoln) *aabcg dbad* 532
Henry 532
Herman *aabcg dbad* 532
CHEYNEY see Cheney
Lucy 375
CHICKERING
John W. 267
CHILD—Childs—Chiles
Lydia 188
Mary 481
Phoebe-Gorham 278
CHILDERS
Frances 462
CHIPMAN
Gracia (Bates) *adffa h* 133
John *adffa h* 133
CHOATE
Charles-Francis 543
CHRISMAN
Ann (Harrison) 208
Elizabeth (Lincoln) *adaae k* 206 208
George 201
Jack 208
Jane 208
Jane (Chrisman) 208
John 208
John *adaae ka* 208
Joseph *adaae k* 208
Joseph *adaae ka* 208
Mary *adaae kaa* 208
CHRISTIAN
Aspasia-Ann 560
Charles H. 560
Corinne-Kelley *adaaa bbchd* 560
Ellen 509
Maggie-Fern *adaaa bbcha* 560
Maud-Irene *adaaa bbchb* 560
Melissa-Etta (Lincoln) *adaaa bbch* 560
Ruth-Marie *adaaa bbchc* 560
Socrates-Kelley *adaaa bbch* 560
CHUBBUCK
Alice 31
Mary E. *aabcd cj* 141
Rebecca 9

CHUBBUCK cont'd
Thomas 10
CHURCH
Sarah (Horswell) 15
Thomas 15 33
CLAP—Clapp
Abby (Binney) *abbea cce* 319
Abigail (Monroe) 263
Albert-Otis *abbea cce* 319
Alexander 319
Alexander *abbea cc* 319
Anne-Otis (Lane) *abbea ccb* 319
Bethiah (Litchfield) 319
Betsy (Adams) 412
Charles-Cushing *abbea cca* 319
Damietta-Dennison *aabcg d* 263-4
Deborah *afb* 8
Ebenezer 135
Elizabeth-Ann *abbea ccd* 319
Emeline-Franklyn *abbea ccf* 319
Emerus-Donaldson *adffe cbba* 523
George 412
George-Alexander *abbea ccc* 319
Hannah *adcai f* 391
Helen-Lincoln (Wall) *adffe cbba* 523
Jane 62
Josephine *aabck bh* 412
Louisa 414
Luretta-Cushing (Lincoln) *abbea cc* 319
Mary-Abby-Cushing *abbea ccg* 319
Mary-Jane (Tuttle) *abbea cca* 319
Paul 391
Rachel 241
Sabrina (Spencer) 391
Salma 263
William-Wallace *abbea ccb* 319
CLARE—Clayer—Clayor
John 55
William 54 55
CLARK—Clarke
Abigail *akb* 9
Abigail (Lothrop) 8
Augustus *aabce acd* 255
Eliza-Ann (Binney) *aabce acd* 255
Elizabeth (Alcock) *akd* 9
Elizabeth-Jacobs *aacdb fc* 436
Hannah-Farrar-Jewett *aabcf da* 405-6
Harriette *adfad eh* 245
Ira 405
James 8
James *aka* 9
John *ak* 8
John *akc* 9
Joseph *akd* 9
Lucy 296
Lydia (Jewett) 405
Martha *ake* 9
Mary *akf* 9
Mary (White) 168
Meriba (Tupper) *aka* 9
Rebecca (Hathaway) *akc* 9
Rebecca (Lincoln) *ak* 8 14
Samuel J. 436
Thomas 8 23
Thomas M. 295
William-Andrews 488
William W. 192
CLASE
Humphrey 55
CLAXTON
Augusta (Lincoln) *aabce cc* 258
George *aabce cc* 258
CLAY
Dora (Hockaday) *adaah edb* 354
Henry 467
William-Thomas *adaah edb* 354
CLAYER—Clayor see Clare

CLEAVER
Cassius-Clay *adbca fba* 381
Evelyn-Ophelia (Warwick) *adbca fba* 381
CLEAVES
Benjamin *aabcf be* 144
Jerusha-Lincoln (Lewis) *aabcf be* 144
CLEMENT
miss *adagb gh* 221
Hannah 267
CLEMENTS
Sarah 275
CLIFFORD
John-Henry 429
CLIFT
Joseph 126
CLINE
Ella (Shallcross) *adahb dcca* 499
CLOSSON
Sarah-Jane 441
COAL see Cole
COBURN
Abner 425
Philander 425
COCHRANE—Cochrin
Catharine (Rush) 58
COCKRAN
Jane 301
COE
Cornelia-Woodhull (Little) *aabcf abe* 261
George 261
George-Frederick-Mellen *aabcf ag* 261
Harriet-Lincoln *aabcf aga* 261
John 261
Lydia-Hersey (Barnes) 261
Sargent-Prentiss *aabcf abe* 261
Sophia-Merrill (Lincoln) *aabcf ag* 261
COFFELT
Arbelia (Sibert) 570
Harry-Lincoln *adaae agcba* 570
Harry R. *adaae agcb* 570
Odessa-Oleon (Lincoln) *adaae agcb* 570
Perry-Samuel 570
COFFEY
Ellen (McCarthy) 421
Mary E. *aacbc ahj* 421
Timothy 421
COFFIN
Cornelia-Woodhull ([Little] Coe) *aabcf abe* 261
Francis-Hale *aabcf abh* 261
Jane-Lincoln (Little) *aabcf abh* 261
Joseph-Hale *aabcf abe* 261
Merah 183
COFFMAN
Abigail (Lincoln) *adaae j* 206 207-8
Catharine (Lincoln) *adaah c* 215 471
Christian *adaah c* 215 471
David 207
David *adaae jb* 207
Elizabeth *adaah ca* 215 471-2
Elizabeth (Burtner) *adaae jc* 207
Elizabeth (Strickler) 207
Hannah-Frances *adaae je* 208
Hannah-Frances (Coffman) *adaae je* 207
Hiram *adaae jc* 207
Jacob-Lincoln *adaae ja* 207
Joseph *adaae j* 207-8
Joseph *adaae jd* 207
Joseph-Strickler *adaae je* 208
Josephine-Rebecca-Ann (Evans) *adaae gb* 207
Margaret ([Long] Messick) *adaae jc* 207
Mary (Burtner) *adaae jc* 207
COGHLIN
Lenora *adaaa bbccb* 560
COIL
Adeline (——) 585
Daniel 585

COIL cont'd
  Della-May *adahb fae* 585
COINER
  Casper-Cecil *adaae agfa* 473
  Effie-Amelia-Florence (Lincoln) *adaae agf* 473
  Elizabeth 473
  Hortie-Margaret *adaae agfb* 473
  Margaret (Miller) 473
  Philip-Miller *adaae agf* 473
  Simon 473
COLBURN
  Carrie-Dexter 413
COLBY
  Elizabeth 253
COLE—Coal
  Alice (Stephenson) 124
  Ambrose 22
  Ambrose *ade* 19 22
  Amos 22
  Amos *adeb* 22 23
  Benjamin 22
  Daniel *adaga cca* 359
  Delilah 472
  Elizabeth 360
  Elizabeth 22
  Elizabeth *adea* 23
  Elizabeth (Lincoln) *ade* 18 22
  Enoch 124
  Hannah-Chandler *adcaj g* 123
  Jacob *adaga ccc* 359
  Jonathan *adaaa bdb* 333
  Kate (Blackburn) *adaga ccc* 359
  Lettie-Ann (Briscoe) *adaaa bdb* 333
  Lucretia 523
  Lydia 90
  Martha *adaga c* 359-60
  Mehitable ([Gould] Turner) 22
  Olive-Richardson 546
  Phoebe ([Blackburn] Stewart) *adaga cca* 359
  Polly (James) *adcaj a* 123
  Rachel *adcag d* 122
  Sally 22
  Silence (——) 22
COLEMAN—Colman
  Abigail (——) 124
  Benjamin 174
  Ezekiel *aacda b* 174
  Henry-Wiley 174
  James 124 174
  Jane 610
  Margret 124
  Pamela (Chandler) *aabhf c* 70
  Polly-Otis (Lincoln) *aacda b* 174
  Samuel *aabhf c* 70
  Susanna (Martin) 174
COLES
  Frances-Louise (Donaldson) *adahb gbaa* 501
  Mary-Elizabeth (Lincoln) *adahb gba* 501
  Mary (Symmons) 501
  Richard-Ernest *adahb gbaa* 501
  Solomon 48
  Thomas 501
  Thomas *adahb gba* 501
COLLET
  Tobias 49
COLLIER
  Abigail (Long) 249
  Allyn *abaea af* 187
  Allyn-Lincoln *abaea ab* 187
  Anna (Togue) *abaea ac* 187
  Bridget 82 238
  Christopher *abaea ah* 187
  Cynthia 452
  Elizabeth *abaea ai* 187
  George-Washington *abaea ac* 187

COLLIER cont'd
  Gershom 187 249
  Henry *abaea ag* 187
  Hepsibah-Lincoln (Bates) *abaea ah* 187
  Isaac 187
  James *abaea a* 187
  James *abaea aa* 187
  James *abaea ae* 187
  Joanna (Bates) *abaea ae* 187
  Jonathan 249
  Lucy (Vinal) *adcaj b* 123
  Ruth *adffg* 249
  Sarah *abaea ad* 187
  Sarah (Lincoln) *abaea a* 186-7
  Susan-Caroline (Howe) *abaea af* 187
  Susan-Lothrop (Willcutt) *abaea ag* 187
  Tamsen (Hayden) 187
  Thomas 187 249
  William 187 249
COLLINS
  Amanda 515
  Helen-Rebecca *adagb dhaa* 493
  Hester (Lincoln) *adagb dha* 493
  John-Henry *adagb dha* 493
  Rosalia-Amy *adagb dhab* 493
  Samuel 173
COLMAN see Coleman
COLSTON
  Julia (Brown) *adaah ebb* 575
COMMER
  Lewis-Elmer *adaga gec* 363
  Louisa-Jane (Haldeman) *adaga gec* 363
CONANT
  Charles-Francis *abbhc bd* 192
  Harriet-Lincoln (Shaw) *abbhc bd* 192
CONAUGHTY
  Helen-Mary (Lincoln) *adagb fbd* 494
  Margaret-Elizabeth (Betts) 494
  William-Henry 494
  William-Wilson *adagb fbd* 494
CONEY
  Ann (——) 454
  Charles 454
  Frances-Ellen *abbec bg* 452
  Paulina-Fletcher 303
CONNORS
  Mary-Belle *aabce hab* 260
CONRAD
  Ethel (Lincoln) *adaaa bbeg* 562
  Hester (Hughes) 562
  James-Roscoe *adaaa bbeg* 562
  William 562
  William-Washington *adaaa bbega* 562
COOK—Cooke
  Amos 396
  Charles *adcaj i* 123
  Clarissa (Jenkins) *adcaj i* 123
  Florence-Alphadelle *abbhc gb* 193
  Harriet 594
  Josephine 572
  Martha 301
  Martha I. *adaaa beg* 566
  Mary *aacdb bec* 302
  Olive *adffe d* 396-7
  Olive (Darling) 396
  Ruth 452
  William 222
COOLIDGE
  Emelyn-Lincoln *aacbe daaa* 423
  Ernest-Hall *aacbe daac* 423
  Frederic-Austin *aacbe daab* 423
  George 423
  George-Austin *aacbe daa* 423
  George-Percival *aacbe daad* 423
  Harriet-Abbot (Lincoln) 423
  Hepsey-Ann (Seaver) 423
  Jean-Mellen (Thurston) *aacbe daac* 423
  Louisa (Patterson) 269

COOLIDGE cont'd
Luther 269
Mabel-Moore (Duhring) *aacbe daad* 423
Mary 395
Susan-Patterson *aabck b* 269-71
COOPER
Clark *adahb gbbb* 501
Miriam *adffe jb* 249
Nellie (Dakan) *adahb gbbb* 501
COPELAND
Mr. 481
Edwina (Lincoln) *adaah eea* 481
Eliza-Jackson *adfad ba* 521
Francis 555
Mary E. Celia ([Crowell] [Lincoln] Nash) *abbea cacb* 555
Susan-Elizabeth (Thayer) 521
Thomas 521
COPITHORN
Adelaide-Gertrude *aacdd dae* 552
Eunice (Henley) 552
John-Thomas 552
COPP
mrs. (Peavey) 304
David 304
Maria L. *aacdb f* 304
COTTRELL
Joseph 522
Mary-Cathlin (Moore) 522
Mary-Elizabeth *adffe ca* 522
COULTAS
James 115
COVELL
Addie L. (Lincoln) *aacbe haaa* 546
Albert-Luther *aacbe haaa* 546
Olive-Richardson (Cole) 546
Otis-Ebenezer 546
COVERLY
Edward 273
COVINGTON
George 593
Margaret (——) 593
Martha-Emma *adbcf bed* 593-4
COWAN
Martha-Josephine 598
COWDIN
Elizabeth-Maria *adcai el* 241
COWING
Deborah (Gannett) 36
Hannah 36
Job 36
COX—Coxe
mr. *adaaa cb* 203
Anna-Frances *aacdb jf* 181
E. H. 203 note
Gabriel 197
Gertrude-Lincoln *aacdb gfca* 438
Hannah 377
Helen-Geneva *aacdb gfcb* 438
James 438
Mary (Vose) 438
Nancy 178
Sarah-Campbell (Lincoln) *aacdb gfc* 438
Stephen-Emerson *aacdb gfc* 438
CRAFTS
Thomas 164
CRAIG
Elizabeth (——) 213
Emma *adaah eda* 354
Lewis 213
Matilda-Frances (Lincoln) *adaga gg* 363
Sarah-Elizabeth 607
Stephen *adaga gg* 363
Thomas 363
CRANE
Florence-Eva *aacdb fcd* 550
Josephine-Augusta (Sutton) 550
Lucretia B. 303

CRANE cont'd
Rebecca 303
Rufus-Revilo 550
CRAVERNS
Robert 478
CRAWFORD
Alice-Susan 455
Andrew 465
Charles A. *abbea jf* 190
Mary-Elizabeth (Cushing) *abbea jf* 190
CRESSWELL
Hannah-Elizabeth *adaid bca* 376
James-Ross *adaid bcb* 376
Samuel-Miles *adaid bc* 376
Thamazine (Lincoln) *adaid bc* 376
CRESSY
Daniel 149
Martha-Ellen *aabcj ac* 149
CRILEY
Mary L. *adaga ic* 219
CROADE
Ruth 167
CROCKER
Bessie-Lincoln *adcai bgea* 519
Caroline-Elizabeth (Groves) 519
Charles 136
Fanny-Kilby (Lincoln) *adcai bge* 519
George 519
Job 182
John 182
Josiah 86
Susannah *aacdc* 182-3
Susannah (Robinson) 182
Timothy 182
William 182
William-Elmer *adcai bge* 519
CROCKETT
Jennie M. *aacbe lfd* 428
CROSBY
Dolly 259
Francis-James 152
Frederick 152
Susan (——) 152 153
CROSMAN
Almira 596
CROSS
Eliza (Stevens) 149
William 149
CROUCH
Ann (Birch) *abbhb d* 92
Jacob *abbhb d* 92
CROW
Elizabeth 210
Jennie-Lydia *adaga abe* 358
CROWELL
Mary E. Celia *abbea cacb* 555
Mary-Elizabeth (Bonney) 555
Rebecca *aacdb da* 180
William M. 555
CROWLEY
Alice 551
CROWNINSHIELD
Catherine-Bradlee *aacbc adba* 417
CRUME
Anne (——) 202 203
Daniel 203
Elizabeth 203 and note
James *adaaa caa* 203 note
George L. 203 note
Jesse 203
John 203
Keziah 203
Luella (Jones) *adaaa ca* 203
Mary (——) 203
Mary (Lincoln) *adaaa c* 202-3
Moses 203
Nancy 203
Peggy 203

CRUME cont'd
  Phebe 203
  Philip 202 203
  Ralph *adaaa c* 202-3
  Sally (Popham) *adaaa caa* 203 note
  Sarah 203
  Squire 203
  Susannah 203
  Unice 203
  William 203
  William *adaaa ca* 203
  William-Popham 203 note
CRUTCHFIELD
  Barbara (Lincoln) *adaaa ba* 331 332
  Betty 574
  John *adaaa ba* 330 331 332
  Nora *adaaf dad* 350
CUDWORTH
  Eliza-Lincoln (Pierce) *aabck ab* 154 274
  Huldah 61
  John 60 61
  Mary 91
  Mary (Briggs) 60 61
  Samuel-Curtis *aabck ab* 154 274
CULIN
  Ann (Bowman) *adbcc b* 117 118
CUMMINGS—Cummins
  Abraham 59
  Ada-Etherage (Lincoln) *adaaa bbeaa* 608
  Andromicha-Wright 569
  Gilbert-Haley *adaaa bbeaa* 608
  Isaac 59
  John 59
  Sarah *adc* 59
  Sarah (Wright) 27 59
CUNNINGHAM see Kernoghan
  Anna (Sutton) *adcba e* 125
  Benjamin *adaga ce* 360
  Charles *adcba e* 125
CURRANT
  Frances-Elizabeth *aabce bae* 256
CURRIER
  Benjamin W. 273
  Frances-Gordon *aabhg d* 277
  John-Edward *aabcf abb* 261
  Levi 277
  Martha-Merrill (Little) *aabcf abb* 261
  Moses 277
  Nancy (Gordon) 277
  Susan 529
CURRY
  Iris *adahb faba* 500
CURTIS
  Abigail *adfb* 131
  Abigail (Waters) 131
  Albert-Cushing *aabcd bab* 252
  Ann-Maria (Lincoln) *aabcd ba* 252
  Anna-Maria *aabcd bac* 252
  Clarinda *aabhb b* 69
  Desire (Otis) 252
  Emma (Underwood) *aabcd bae* 252
  Fanny-Leland (Richardson) *aacdc ebd* 309
  Francis J. *aabcd bad* 252
  Frederick *aabcd ba* 252
  Frederick-Nichols *aabcd baa* 252
  Harriet (Kilby) *aaffd g* 82
  Henry W. *aabcd bae* 252
  Isabel (Holly) *aabcd bad* 252
  Jael *adfa* 60 127-8 189 190
  James 252
  John 131
  Joseph 22
  Louis *aacdc ebd* 309
  Lucy 404
  Martha-Franklin *abbea cagc* 451
  Mary-Lee 313
  Mercy-Little (Otis) *adcaj b* 123

CURTIS cont'd
  Miriam 133
  Nehemiah *adcag a* 122
  Persis (Stockbridge) *add* 22
  Polly (Jenkins) *adcag a* 122
  Richard 127
  Robert-Lorenzo *abbea caae* 450
  Ruth (Wade) 60 127
  Sarah 87
  Sarah-Francis (Williams) *abbea caae* 450
  Simeon *aaffd g* 82
  Susan (Ransford) *aabcd baa* 252
  Thomas 60 127
CUSHING
  Abel 31
  Abigail 85
  Abigail-Bailey *abbea jb* 190
  Abigail (Pierce) *abbbd* 189
  Andrew *aacbg ca* 298
  Andrew-Lincoln *aacbg cab* 298
  Anne 270
  Ann-Maria *aabce bab* 256
  Bela *aabce d* 142
  Benjamin 75 167 174 note
  Betsey (Lincoln) *aabce d* 142
  Betsey (Sprague) *aacbf d* 77
  Caroline-Hepzibah *aabce baf* 256
  Catherine *abce* 14 140
  Charles 68
  Charles *abbea ja* 190
  Chastine (Lincoln) *aacbg ca* 298
  Chastine-Lincoln *aacbg caa* 298
  Daniel 1 5 6 30 31 77 142 167 174 189 253 444
  Daniel *aacbf* 77
  Daniel *aacbf a* 77
  David *aabg* 31
  David *aabgb* 31
  Edward *aacbf g* 77
  Edward *aacbf h* 77
  Elijah *aacbf e* 77
  Elijah *aacbf f* 97
  Elisha 142
  Elizabeth *aacbf c* 77
  Elizabeth *aabce baa* 256
  Elizabeth (Lincoln) 77
  Elizabeth (Lincoln) *abbea j* 189-90
  Elizabeth-Lincoln *aacdc gf* 444
  Elizabeth-Scammell (Lincoln) *aabce ba* 256-7
  Elizabeth (Thaxter) 30
  Elizabeth (Thompson) *aabce bag* 257
  Ellen *aabce bad* 256
  Emily M. (——) *abbea jd* 190
  Frances-Elizabeth (Currant) *aabce bae* 256
  Francis *aacbf d* 77
  Frederick-Oliver *aabce bae* 256
  George 298
  Hannah *aabgb* 31
  Hannah (Cushing) *aabgb* 31
  Hezekiah 73
  Isaiah 68 77
  Jael 90
  Jael *aacda* 174-5
  James-Knox-Polk *aabce baj* 257
  Job *abbbd* 36 41 68 77 80 81 83 87 88 124 125 146 188 189 243 444
  Job *abbea j* 189-90 444
  Job *abbea je* 190 444
  John 142 298
  Jonathan *aabgd* 31
  Joseph 91 174 298
  Levi-Lincoln *aacbf i* 77
  Lucy-Woodbury 267
  Lydia *aaha* 12
  Lydia *aabge* 31
  Lydia (——) 91

CUSHING cont'd
Lydia-James *aafff fb* 185
Mabel (Gardner) 31
Marcy 91 246
Martha (Nichols) *abbbd* 41
Martin-Lincoln *abbea jd* 190
Martin-Van-Buren *aabce bag* 256 257
Mary 142
Mary *aabcd d* 253-4
Mary (Binney) 253
Mary-Elizabeth *abbea jf* 190
Mary (Jacob) 31
Matthew 30 31 77 142 167 174 189 253 298 444
Mercy 78 90 91
Molly *aabgc* 31
Nancy 298
Nancy (Cushing) 298
Olive (Lincoln) 142
Otis-Phipps *abbea jg* 190
Patience (Singleton) 256
Perez *aabga* 31
Peter 7 65 77 78 88 90 137 140 190 240 253
Rachel *aacbg* 167 251
Rebecca 250
Ruth *aab* 30
Ruth *aabga* 31
Ruth (Croade) 167
Ruth (Cushing) *aabga* 31
Ruth (Lincoln) *aabg* 29 31
Salome (Abbott) *abbea je* 190 444
Samuel 189 444
Samuel *abbea jc* 190
Samuel-Nichols 256
Samuel-Nichols *aabce ba* 256-7
Sarah 34
Sarah *aacbf b* 77
Sarah *aabce bac* 256
Sarah-Ellen *aabce bai* 257
Sarah (Leavitt) 174
Sarah (Lincoln) *aacbf* 75 77
Sarah (Simmons) *aabgd* 31
Seth 33
Solomon 167 174
Stephen 253
Susan 142
Susan (Staples) *abbea ja* 190
Susanna 596
Susanna (Whiting) 142
Temperance 316
Theophilus 31 73
Thomas-Bouvé *aabce bah* 257
William 160
CUSTER
Isaac 385
Jacob 97
CUTLER
Annie 504
Mercy 506
Rachel 374
CUTTER
William-Everett 539
CUTTING
Lucy *aabab c* 65

DAKAN
Ebenezer 501
Elizabeth (Sheffer) 501
Harry-Lester *adahb gbbc* 501
Lehigh *adahb gbb* 501
Mame (Stoker) *adahb gbbc* 501
Mary (Larson) *adahb gbba* 501
Nellie *adahb gbbb* 501
Pearl *adahb gbbd* 501
Sarah-Adaline (Lincoln) *adahb gbb* 501
William-Lockwood *adahb gbba* 501

DALLOWAY
Jacob *abbhb c* 92
Lucelia (Birch) *abbhb c* 92
DALZELL
William 118
DAMON
Amelia-Ripley (Snow) *abbea caed* 451
Edward-Jacob *abbea caee* 451
Elizabeth-Calief 553
Franklin-Jacobs *abbea cae* 451
Franklin-Wallace *abbea caeb* 451
Hannah (Lincoln) *abbea cae* 189 451
Ida-May-Cushing *abbea caea* 451
Isaac-Newton 451
Judith-Litchfield 451
Judith-Litchfield (Damon) 451
Lucy 452
Lucy (Jenkins) *adcag i* 122
Marietta-Lincoln *abbea caec* 451
Nathaniel *adcag i* 122
Newcomb-Lincoln *abbea caed* 451
Polly *adcbm a* 126
Stephen 451
DANHOWARD
Elizabeth (——) 118
George 118
DANIELL—Daniels
Amey-Gaskill *adffe df* 524-5
Amy-Gaskill (Darling) 524-5
Andrew-Jackson 524-5
Catherine-Turner 318
Isabel (Vandegraf) 530-1
Louisa 458
Mary-Alice *aabce cdb* 530-1
Thomas-Robinson 530-1
DARBY
James *adaga ff* 218
Sarah (Hunt) *adaga ff* 218
DARLING
Amy-Gaskill 524-5
Angelina 548
Olive 396
DARNELL
Elizabeth (Martin) *adaga caf* 359
George *adaga caf* 359
DAUGHERTY see Dougherty
Emma-Eliza (Lincoln) *adaga aag* 486-7
George 486
George *adaga aag* 486-7
George-Martin *adbca fbf* 382
James 564
Mary-Flora (Ott) 564
Mary-(Wilson) 486
Melissa *adaaa bbg* 564
Ruth-Anna (Warwick) *adbca fbf* 382
Una-Mae *adaga aaga* 486 487
DAVENPORT
Agnes 485
DAVID
Elizabeth (Lincoln) *adahb gd* 370
James 370 498
Margaret (Lincoln) *adahb gf* 370
Nancy (McLure) 370
Oliver-Perry *adahb gf* 370
Putnam *adahb gd* 370
Sarah-Jane *adahb db* 498-9
Sarah (Pennington) 498
DAVIS
Catharine Bradlee (Crowninshield) *aacbc adba* 417
Catherine (Redwine) 479
Charles-Lincoln *adaaf dbbb* 479
Charles-Lincoln *adaga gdga* 487
David 468
Dolor 417
Elijah *adahd b* 110
Elizabeth *adah* 109-10
Elizabeth *adahd d* 110

DAVIS cont'd
Elizabeth (Moxley) 489
Green B. *adaah ek* 482
Hale-McClellan *adaaf dbbd* 479
Hannah 490
Hannaniah *adahd c* 110
Irene (Rutland) *adaaf dbbc* 479
Isaac 417
James 489
James *adahd g* 110
James-Bailey *adaga gdg* 489
James-Bailey *adaga gdgc* 489
Jefferson 480
John 57 278 290 479
John *adbch d* 236
Joseph-Estabrook *aacbc adb* 417
Josephine (Lincoln) *adaaf cbb* 479
Joshua *adahd* 110
Lillian-Hogsett (Lincoln) *adaga gdg* 489
Lincoln *adahd h* 110
Lincoln *aacbc adba* 417
Mabel *aacbc adbb* 417
Mark 378
Mary 143
Mary *adahd e* 110
Mary *adbcg f* 118
Mary (———) 109 110
Mary-Holbrook (Estabrook) 417
Mary-Ives *adaid h* 378
Mary (Lincoln) *adbch d* 118 236
Mary-Waldo (Lincoln) *aacbc adb* 417
Mattie (Halsey) *adaah ek* 482
Nancy *adahd a* 110
Phebe *adffd d* 134
Phineas 417
Prudence 144
Robert-Franklin *adaga gdgb* 489
Robert-Gilbert *adaaf dbb* 479
Roberta *adaaf dbba* 479
Samuel 417
Sarah *adahd i* 110
Sarah *aacdc f* 310-11
Sarah (Lincoln) *adahd* 110
Simon 417
Solomon 310
Susan *adahd f* 110
Temperance (Palmer) 310
Thomas 109 216
William-Gay *adaaf dbbc* 479
Willie-May (Oliver) *adaaf dbbb* 479
DAVISON
Emma-Baker 552
DAVY
Edward 333
DAWES
Hattie-Parsons (Bates) *aafff gaf* 317
William *aafff gaf* 317
DAWSON
Margaret 593
DAY
Frances *adaaa ab* 462
Frances (Childers) 462
Lucy-Whitney 526
William 462
DAYTON
William-Lewis 467
DEAN—Deane
Charles-Leighton *aabce aebd* 529
Charles-Marcus 529
Emma (Underwood) 529
Lillie-Loretta (DePue) 581
Mary 403
Paul 166 243 245 259 299 402
Ruby-Hunt *adaga gha* 581-2
Sarah (Lincoln) *adaag* 98 101
Viola-Zitella (Lincoln) *aabce aebd* 529
Ward-Hunt 581

DEARTH
Blanche-Moore *adagb djad* 493
George 493
George-Baird *adagb djac* 493
Lacy-Evans *adagb dja* 493
Margaret-Jane (Lincoln) *adagb dja* 493
Marguerite-Evans *adagb djae* 493
Minnie-Lincoln *adagb djaa* 493
Ruth (Moore) 493
Sallie-Pearl *adagb djab* 493
DEBOW
Sarah *adaaf dda* 351
DECKER
Jane 511
Laura-Whitehouse 404
DECMAN
Catey (Gatewood) 215
DEETER
Elizabeth 378
DEFFENBAUGH
Conrad 489
Elizabeth (Bowman) 489
Lizzie *adaga gdb* 489
DEFOREST
Elizabeth *adffe be* 248
DEHAVEN
Abraham 230
Alice *adaii* 230
DELANO
Ruth *aaffi g* 84
DELAWARE
lord 282
DENBO
Sarah 563
DENNISON
Edward-Bernard *abbea cabaa* 553
Florence-Lincoln *abbea cabab* 553
George 553
Irene-Louise *abbea cabac* 553
Isaac 553
James 553
James-Edward *abbea caba* 553
Martha-Almira *abbea cabad* 553
Mary-Elmina (Lincoln) *abbea caba* 553
Susan (Parsons) 553
DENO
Lucy *adagb fe* 366
DENTON
Allen 561
Clara (Foster) 561
Deborah *adaaa bbe* 561-2
Deborah-Ann *adaaa bbe* 561-2
Elizabeth (Lincoln) *adaaa bc* 332 561
Isom *adaaa bc* 331 332 561
Matilda (Jones) 561
William 561
DePUE
Lillie-Loretta 581
DERBY
Charles-Henry 543
DeROHAN
William 328
DeVILLERS
Louis 418
Nancy-Mary 418
DEWING
Alice *aabck bid* 271
DIBERT
Sarah *adaga ib* 219
DICKERSON
Elizabeth (Lincoln) *adaaa abb* 462
William *adaaa abb* 462
DICKENSON—Dickinson
Azariah 225
Charles 247
Eliza-Lincoln *adffe bf* 248
Elizabeth *adahf* 225 228-9
Elizabeth (DeForest) *adffe be* 248

DICKENSON—Dickinson cont'd
Emeline-Corbett *adffe bd* 248
German 225
Jermyn 225
Joseph 225 228
Lucy-Ashley *adffe bg* 248
Lucy (Pratt) *adffe bb* 247
Margaret 225 370
Margaret (Thomas) 225 228
Mary-Fitch *adffe bh* 248
Nancy-Bicknell *adffe ba* 247
Nancy-Bicknell (Lincoln) *adffe b* 247-8
Priscilla *adahb* 225-6 228
Rufus-Wells *adffe b* 247-8
Rufus-Wells *adffe bb* 247
Sarah 163
Sarah-Adams *adffe bc* 248
Sarah (Wells) 247
William-Greene *adffe be* 248
DILL
Betsy (——) *adcag d* 122
Hester (Lincoln) *adaaa bbbf* 559
DINGES
Amanda (Faucher) *adaaf daa* 350
David-Washington *adaaf dad* 350
Emily-Oneal *adaaf dac* 350
Isaac-Henry *adaaf dab* 350
Nora (Crutchfield) *adaaf dad* 350
Paulina-Emily (Lincoln) *adaaf da* 350-1
William *adaaf da* 350-1
William-Mordecai *adaaf daa* 350
DINSDALE
Alice-Jane *adahb gha* 370
DIX
Janette (Reynolds) *adahf chg* 374
John-Welch *adahf chg* 374
DIXON
Alexander *adaga aac* 486
Elizabeth (Vickery) 79
Mary-Ellen (Lincoln) *adaga aac* 486
DOANE
Elisha 246 253
Elizabeth-Cushing (Lincoln) *aabcd dd* 253-4
Ephraim 253
Frederick 154
Gorham-Lincoln *aabcd ddc* 254
Hezekiah 253
James-Cutler 253
John 253
Mary-Lincoln *aabcd ddb* 254 and note
Susannah-Wendell (Hewes) 253
William-Edward *aabcd dd* 253-4
William-Edward *aabcd dda* 254 and note
DODD
Benjamin 273
George-Lincoln *aabck fea* 273
Horace *aabck fe* 152 273
Maria M. (Faxon) 273
Pauline-Isabelle (Rowe) *aabck fea* 273
Susan-Beals (Lincoln) *aabck fe* 272 273
DODGE
Rebecca 261
DONALDSON
Frances-Louise *adahb gbaa* 501
DONNELLY
Betsey-Pierce (Lincoln) *adfae ac* 394
Catherine (——) 394
Edward 394
Edward-Pierce *adfae acb* 394
George-Granville *adfae acc* 394
William *adfae ac* 394
William-Lincoln *adfae aca* 394
DONELSON see Donaldson
col. 222
DONIPHAN
Margret 354

DORFLINGER
Katharine *adbfa bg* 515
DORING
Elizabeth-Appleby *aacdb beh* 302
Frederic-William *aacdb bec* 302
Ida-May *aacdb bea* 302
Jessie *aacdb beg* 302
John 302
John *aacdb be* 302
John-Henry *aacdb beb* 302
Laura-Matilda *aacdb bef* 302
Lydia-Ellen (Lincoln) *aacdb be* 302
Mary (Cooke) *aacdb bec* 302
Mary-Ellen *aacdb bed* 302
Mary (Molleneaux) 302
Robinson-Lincoln *aacdb bee* 302
Venetia (Glendinning) *aacdb bee* 302
William 302
DORSEY
Hazel 465
DOTY
Elizabeth *adaga agd* 579
DOUGHERTY see Daugherty
Alameda *adaaf dba* 574-5
Harriet-Elizabeth *adbcf beeac* 594
John *adbcf beea* 594
John *adbcf beeaa* 594
Margaret (——) 594
Mary-Amanda (Lincoln) *adbcf beea* 594
Mary-Edna *adbcf beeab* 594
Patrick 594
DOUGLAS
Stephen-Arnold 466 467 468
DOVAL
Lucy *adaae abbd* 472
DOW
Harriet (Bray) 532
Leon-Oliver *aabcg dbaa* 532
Lillian-Josephine (Lincoln) *aabcg dbaa* 532
Loren S. 532
DOWNEY
Jane 221
DOWNES
Ellen (Keefe) 519
Mary-Jane *adcai bgf* 519
Patrick 519
DOWNING
Eliza-Sparrow 596
Harriet 516
DOYLE
Anna 411
Daniel 392
Mary-Ann (Lincoln) *adcak ba* 392
Pearl (Dakan) *adahb gbbd* 501
Pearl-Lucinda (Way) *adaaa bbedd* 562
Thomas *adcak ba* 392
Thomas *adahb gbbd* 501
Thomas-Warren *adcak bab* 242 391 392
Warren-Lincoln *adcak baa* 392
DRAKE
Benjamin-Franklin *adffe gc* 248
Charlotte 211
Elizabeth 211
Elizabeth (Crow) 210
Isaac-Lincoln *adaaf ea* 99 100 210 211 353
Isabel 211
John 211
Joseph 210 211
Lewis 211
Lewis *adaaf e* 210-1 353
Lucretia-Lurena 476
Margaret 211
Mary 211
Mary (Evans) 211
Mary-Leonard (Drown) *adffe gc* 248
Mary (Russell) 211

DRAKE cont'd
Priscilla 211
Rachel (Lincoln) *adaaf e* 99 210-1 353
Samuel 211
Sarah (Evans) *adaaf ea* 211
William-Henry 211
DRAPER
Eben-Sumner 540
DRESSER
Frances-Merrick *aacbc addbd* 542
Frank-Farnum *aacbc addb* 542
George-Kelley 542
Josephine-Rose (Lincoln) *aacbc addb* 542
Louisa *aacbc addba* 542
Maria-Louisa (Farnum) 542
Rose-Lincoln *aacbc addbb* 542
Waldo-Lincoln *aacbc addbc* 542
DRIVER
Nancy *adaae hc* 345
DROWN
Christiana-Amelia (Carpenter) 248
Israel 248
Israel *adffe gb* 248
Leonard *adffe g* 248
Lucy-Lincoln *adffe ga* 248
Mary-Leonard *adffe gc* 248
Mary (Lincoln) *adffe g* 248
DRUMMOND
Charles-Elwell *aabaa dd* 137
David *aabaa d* 135 137
Emma-Ann-Elizabeth *aabaa di* 137
Ezekiel *aabaa dg* 136 137
Frances-Harriet *aabaa dh* 137
Hannah-Jane *aabaa da* 137
James *aabaa df* 134
Jane (Lincoln) *aabaa d* 135 137
Julia-Ann *aabaa de* 137
Mary-Lincoln *aabaa db* 137
Rebecca M. (——) *aabaa df* 137
Susan W. (——) *aabaa dg* 137
William-Butler *aabaa dc* 137
DUANE
Caroline-Elise (Ravenel) *aabch dda* 266
Charles-Willing *aabch dc; aabch dd* 266
Emma-Cushman (Lincoln) *aabch dd* 266
Helen-Frances *aabch ddb* 266
Helen-Frances (Lincoln) *aabch dc* 266
Louisa *aabch ddc* 266
Louisa (Brooks) 266
Mary-Burnside (Morris) *aabch dcb* 266
Russell *aabch dcb* 266
Virginia *aabch dca* 266
William 266
William *aabch dda* 266
William J. 266
DUBOIS
Rachel 497
DUHRING
Mabel-Moore *aacbe daad* 423
DUNBAR
Asa 157
Ebed 401
Hannah-Pratt *aabce ae* 401
Harriet-Pierce (Walton) *adfad bca* 393
James-Robert *adfad bca* 393
Mary 179
Sophia (Nash) 401
DUNCAN
Mary-Ellen 485
DUNHAM
Almira-Olive 554
James P. *aabck bg* 270 274
Harriet-Clementina ([Lincoln] Whittle)
  aabck bg 270 274
DUNK
Estelle (Gilbert) *adbcf bic* 384
Horace-Armand *adbcf bic* 384

DUNKIN
Jenny *adaai f* 103
DUNLAP
John 389
Marcia-Scott *adcac d* 389
Mary (Tapham) 389
DUNN
Catherine-Ann 500
Edmund *adaga if* 219
Rhoda-Louisa (Yeagley) *adaga if* 219
DUNNING
Carrie-Downs (Lincoln) *aabcf acb* 404
Frances-Lincoln *aabcf acba* 404
Henry-Merritt 404
John-Henry *aabcf acb* 404
Lucy (Curtis) 404
DURFEE
Patience 51
DUROSS
Elizabeth *adahb b* 368
DURRETT
R. T. 194 197
DWYER
Fanny O. *abbec bcb* 322
DYE
William 93
DYER
Deliverance 390
Ellen *aabcj cb* 267
James 267
Lucy-Woodbury (Cushing) 267
Matthew *adaae f* 207
Rebecca (Lincoln) *adaae f* 207
Sarah-Ann 346
DYLKS
Ann (Lincoln) *adbca aa* 380

EABY
Elizabeth-Anna 496
EAGLE
Mary-Jane 369
EAMES
Emily *adahf ag* 228
Minnie-Elizabeth 404
EARLE
John 70
EARLY
Jacob M. 466
EASTERLIN
Ada-Lee (Lincoln) *adaaf abc* 477
Campbell-Douglas *adaaf abc* 477
Douglas-Lincoln *adaaf abcb* 477
Helen (Booth) *adaaf abca* 477
John-Daniel 477
John-Daniel *adaaf abca* 477
EASTHAM
George-Robert 598
Martha-Josephine (Cowan) 598
Williette-Woodside *adcac dac* 598
EASTMAN
Adaline 549
Hannah-Baker (Whitcomb) *aacda cg* 175
John B. *aacda cg* 175
EATON
Anna-Maria 322
Anna-Maria (Parker) *aabec bc* 322
Bertha D *aabcg dea* 408
Caroline-Matilda (Newton) 408
Charles-Henry *abbec bcc* 322
David 322
Emily-Catherine (Wood) *abbec bcb* 322
Eva-Moody (Sherriff) *abbec bcc* 322
Fanny O. (Dwyer) *abbec bcb* 322
George-Albert *abbec bcb* 322
Leander 418
Mary-Nichols (Lincoln) *abbec bc* 321-2
Mighell-Smith *abbec bcb* 322
Susannah (Robertson) 322

EATON cont'd
William-David *abbec bc* 321-2
William-Harrison 408
William-Wallis *abbec bca* 322
EBERLINE
John-Michael 420
Sarah-Rosetta *aacbc ahb* 420
Sarah-Rosetta (Noah) 420
EBERLY
Elsie-Reidenbach *adahb bcbb* 497
EDGAR
Henry-Parker 529
Susan (Currier) 529
Susan-Louise *aabce cda* 529-30
EDMONSON
Rebecca *adaaa beg* 566
EDSON
Lydia (Joy) *aaga* 11
Seth *aaga* 11
EDWARDS
Benjamin 168
Betsey *aacbi* 168
Calvin 145
Calvin *aabcf g* 145
Clarissa R. *aabcf gf* 145
Elizabeth M. *aabcf gg* 145
George-Calvin *aabcf gh* 145
Grace 145
Henry-Smith *aabcf gd* 145
Jane G. (Hemenway) *aabcf gd* 145
Louisa F. (Locke) 145
Martha *aabcf ge* 145
Mary (——) 145
Mary H. *aabcf gb* 145
Mary H. (Edwards) *aabcf gb* 145
Mary ([White] Clark) 168
Robert 168
Ninian W. 470
Sophia L. *aabcf ga* 145
Susanna (Lincoln) *aabcf g* 145
Thankful-Lincoln *aabcf gc* 145
William *aabcf gb* 145
EELS
Abiah *adbf* 119-21 237
Abiah (Waterman) 119
Abigail 120
Hannah 120
John 119 120
Joseph 120
Lenthall 120
Lusanna 120
Nathaniel 70 119 120
Samuel 16 119
Sarah 120
Waterman 120
EIDEL
Susan 379 510
EIDMAN
Alice-Maurine *adaaa bbcaa c* 606
Anna-Leona *adaaa bbcaa a* 606
Chester-William *adaaa bbcaa e* 606
Christina (Lautenschlager) 606
Conrad *adaaa bbcaa* 606
Dorothy-Josephine *adaaa bbcaa g* 606
Edith-May *adaaa bbcaa b* 606
Floyd-Thomas *adaaa bbcaa d* 606
John-William 606
Mary-Florence (Lincoln) *adaaa bbcaa* 606
Nellie-Frances *adaaa bbcaa f* 606
ELDRED
Lily W. (Peterson) *abbea caic* 452
ELDREDGE
Lydia 535
ELIOT—Elliot—Elliott
Andrew 88 264
Elizabeth (Langdon) 88
Ephraim 264

ELIOT—Elliot—Elliott cont'd
Harriet-Ann *adaaa bbi* 564-6
Jacob 23
Mary 21 88
Mary (Fleet) 264
Mary-Fleet *aabch d* 264-6
Mary (Pynchem) 88
Sarah-Louisa (Graves) 564
William-Linley 564
ELKINS
Augustus-Jerome *aacdb fca* 436
Elizabeth-Maria (Lincoln) *aacdb fca* 435 436
Jerome-Bonaparte 435 436
Olive-Esther (Blanchard) 436
Phyllis-Maxwell *aacdb fcaa* 436
ELLIOT see Eliot
ELLIS
Abigail (Bates) *adffa e* 133
Eliza W. *aabad ce* 138
Hannah (Whitcomb) *adffd a* 133
Jacob *adffa e* 133
Jeremiah *adffd a* 133
Laura-Josephine 442
Susan 511
ELLMES—Ellms—Ellmms
Ann-Stephen *adffb e* 133
Betsey *aaffj h* 84
Ebenezer-Woodworth 84
Elizabeth (Perry) 84
Elizabeth (Sutton) 62
Elizabeth (Wade) *adfea* 62
Hannah *aaffj c* 84
Hipsabah *aaffj e* 84
John 84
John *aaffj b* 84
Jonathan 62
Joseph 62
Joseph *adfe* 62
Judith (Briggs) 84
Lewis *aaffj f* 84
Lincoln *aaffj a* 84
Lois (Lincoln) *aaffj* 84
Martha *aaffj g* 84
Mary (Lincoln) *adfe* 62
Nathaniel 62
Nathaniel *adfea* 62
Polly *adffj j* 84
Rhodolphus 62
Samuel *aaffj* 84
Sarah *aaffj i* 84
Thomas 62
Winifred *aaffj d* 84
Zoa (Studley) *aaffj f* 84
ELOFSON
Ane (Jensen) 556
Elof 556
Jennie-Catherine *abbea mba* 556
EMERSON
Mary-Jane *abbea cafi* 451
EMMONS
Johanna-Page 545
Mary-Elizabeth 526
ENDY
Ida *adaii bdc* 379
ENO
Emily 514
ENTRIKIN
Samuel *adahf cfd* 373
Sarah-Anna ([Lincoln] Buffington) *adahf cfd* 373
EPPARD
Nancy 472
EPSTEIN
Dolly *adahb bcd* 584
ERB
Elizabeth *adahb bc* 496-7
Elizabeth (Good) 496

ERB cont'd
John 496
ERICKSON
Elmer *adaaa bbccc* 560
Mabel-Monroe (Gott) *adaaa bbccc* 560
ERSKINE
Lucetta 366
ESKEW
Julia-Ann 565
ESTABROOK
Mary-Holbrook 417
ESTERLY
Christin-Christian *adaii bca* 509
Ellen (Christian) 509
George 509
John-Lincoln *adaii bcad* 509
Sally-Andora ([Lincoln] Webber) *adaii bca* 509
ESTILL
Etta *aabch dbd* 266
ESTUS
Frances-Katharine *adaah ge* 357
William *adaah ge* 357
EUSTIS
Anna *aaffe a* 82
William 154 280
EVANS
Alice-Zook *adaid abc* 591-2
Ann-Lincoln *adbcg c* 118
Annie-Du Ross *adahb bea* 368
Benjamin *adbcg* 117 118
Benjamin *adbcg d* 118
Caroline-Elizabeth *adaae ga* 207
Emily-Jane 608
Emily (Worrell) *adbcg e* 118
Grace-Winifred *adahc aadc* 504
Hannah 272
Hannah (Lincoln) *adaae g* 207
Hannah-Lucinda-Dorcas-Cynthia *adaae gc* 207
Hannah-Mary (Lincoln) *adahc aad* 504
Jacob *adbcg g* 118
Joseph *adaae g* 207
Joseph *adbcg a* 118
Josephine-Rebecca-Ann *adaae gb* 207
Lewis *adahb be* 368
Lucile *adahc aada* 504
Margaretta (Lincoln) *adahb be* 368
Marian-Gray *adahc aadd* 504
Mary 507
Mary *adaga a* 358-9
Mary *adbcg b* 118
Mary (Aflick) *adbcg a* 118
Mary (Davis) *adbcg f* 118
Mary (Lincoln) *adbcg* 117 118
Miriam-Gertrude *adahc aade* 504
Nathan *adbcg e* 118
Peter *adbcg f* 118
S. B. *adahc aad* 504
Sarah *adaaf ea* 211
Sarah-Ann 607
Vincent-Goodsell *adahc aadb* 504
EVERETT
Eliza-Jane (Carsley) *aabcf he* 145
George H. *aabcf he* 145
Juline 397
EWELL
Gershom 17
EWIN—Ewing
Cally 340
Henry 96

FAIRBANKS
Augusta (Norton) 527
Freeman-Weston 527
George-Wilder *aacda ce* 175
Sarah-Leavitt (Whitcomb) *aacda ce* 175

FALOON
Daniel *adcak b* 391-2
Hannah ([Hobbs] Lincoln) *adcak b* 391-2
FANNON
Alpha *adaai e* 103
FARNAM—Farnham—Farnum
Charles 26
Daniel 157
David 26
Deborah (Baker) 26
Maria-Louisa 542
Mary *agi* 26 27
FARR
Hannah (Davis) 490
Nellie-Jane (Lincoln) *adaga gfb* 490
Thomas-Jefferson 490
William-Jacob *adaga gfb* 490
FARRAR—Farrow
Elvira *aacda cf* 175
Frances 39
John 39-40
Mary 40
Mary (Hilliard) 39
Percilla *abb* 39-41
FARRELL
Rachel 236, 237
FARRINGTON
Sarah 350
FARROW see Farrar
FARSON
John 598
FAUCHER
Amanda *adaaf daa* 350
FAXON
Ellen F. *adahf cab* 373
Maria M. 273
FEARING
Albert *aacbh j* 78
Alice-Choate (Ingraham) *aabce hac* 260
Aurelia *aacbh e* 78
Aurelia (Fearing) *aacbh e* 78
Benjamin 183
Catherine-Cushing (Andrews) *aacbh j* 78
Chloe (Whiton) *aabad* 138
David *aacbh f* 78
Deborah (Leavitt) *aaeb* 10 11 138
Edwin-Thayer *aabce hac* 260
Elijah 138
Elijah *aada* 10 11 138
Elisha-Pope *aacdc d* 181 183
Hannah (Beal) 10
Harriet A. (Williams) *aacbh g* 78
Hawkes 77 156 260
Hawkes *aacbh* 75 77-8 156 260
Hawkes *aacbh b* 78 260
Helen-Augusta (Miles) *aabce ha* 260
Henry-Lincoln *aabce ha* 67 260
Israel 77 156 260
Jane-Russell (Lincoln) *aabce ha* 260
John 10 73 75 76 77 138 156 260
Leah (Lincoln) *aacbh* 74 75 77-8 156
Lincoln *aacbh g* 78
Lucinda *aacbh d* 78 156
Margaret (Lincoln) 77
Martin *aacbh e* 78
Mary 10
Mary *aabad* 138-9
Mary-Ann (Lincoln) *aacdc d* 182-3
Mary-Belle (Connors) *aabce hab* 260
Mary (Lincoln) *aad* 10
Matilda (Wilder) *aacbh b* 78 260
Morris *aacbh h* 78
Nabby-Fearing (Whiton) *aacbh h* 78
Nathaniel *aad* 10 75 76 138
Olive *aacbh i* 78
Olive *aacbh k* 78
Polly-Stowers (Burr) *aacbh f* 78

FEARING cont'd
Rachel *aacb* 10 75-8
Ruth 10
Sally *aacbh a* 78
Sally *aacbh c* 78
Saloam (Pope) 183
Samuel-James *aabce hab* 260
Sarah 10
Sarah-Jane *aabce haa* 260
Sarah (Johnson) 10 75
FELL
Elizabeth 582
Jesse W. 468 470
FENELLY
Robert 154
FERGUSON
Adam-Henry *adahb fac* 500
Annie (——) 500
Arthur-Harold *adahb facb* 500
Emma-Louisa (Lincoln) *adahb fac* 500
John 500
John-Samuel *adahb faca* 500
Mary-Louisa (Matters) *adahb faea* 500
FERNALD
mr. 409
Caroline 413
FERRILL
Sarah (Carter) 114
FESSENDEN
Deborah (Chandler) 518
Ellen-Elizabeth-Longfellow *adcac da* 518
Samuel 518
FETTERIDGE
Mary 81
FIELD—Fields
Anna (Lincoln) *adbcg cab* 514
Barnum 169 note
Frances-Eliza *aacbi gc* 169
John *aafff gac* 316
Marshall 445
Priscilla-Tower (Bates) *aafff gac* 316
FILLEBROWN
Elizabeth *aabce c* 184 257-8
Elizabeth (Gould) 257
John 257
Mary 253
Thomas 257
FILLERS
Betsy (——) 102
John 102
FIMPLE
Martha-Biddle *adbca a* 380
FINLEY
Mary 502
FIRTH
Frank 420
FISH
Carlton-Rittenhouse 408
Ida (Meacham) 408
Mary-Warren (Lincoln) *aabcg deb* 264 408
Ozro-Meacham *aabcg deb* 264 408
Ozro-Meacham *aabcg deba* 408
FISHER
Bessie *aacdb igc* 551
Caroline-Jones (Lincoln) *aacdb ea* 303
Clara-Aspinwall (Barnes) *aacdb eaa* 303
Daniel-Johnson *aacdb ea* 303
Daniel-Lincoln *aacdb eaa* 303
Ebenezer 303
Edwin *aaffj e* 84
Eliza *adaih c* 112
Fanny A. (Shaw) *aacdb eab* 303
Hipsabah (Ellmes) *aaffj e* 84
Lee-Howard *aacdb eac* 303
Lewis-Beals *aacdb eab* 303
Mamie-Edith 611
Mary *adffd g* 134

41

FISHER cont'd
Mary C. *aacdb ab* 179
Mary-Elizabeth (Blaisdell) *aacdb eac* 303
Mary-Eva *aacdb ead* 303
Nellie B. (Littlefield) *aacdb eae* 303
Rebecca-Morse *aacdb ac* 179
Sally (Johnson) 303
Thomas-Baldwin-Thayer *aacdb eae* 303
FISKE
Charles-Augustus 442
Laura-Josephine (Ellis) 442
Mary-Buckminster 416
Mary-Elizabeth (Lincoln) *aacdc ecc* 442
Walter-Ellis *aacdc ecc* 442
Walter-Ellis *aacdc ecca* 442
FITCH
Joseph E. 581
Murray 173
FITHIAN
Ephraim 594
Harriet (Cook) 594
Harriet-Cook *adbcf bee* 594
FITTS
Emily *aafff cab* 315
FLANIGAN
Jane *adaga ig* 219
FLEET
Mary 264
FLENNIKEN
Harriet *adaga agc* 487
FLETCHER
Betsy 82
Cora-Augusta (Taylor) *abbhc ed* 193
Emma-Frances *abbhc ec* 193
Eunice 151
Harriot (Lincoln) *abbhc e* 192-3
Joel 192
Joel-Parsons *abbhc e* 192-3
Joel-Parsons *abbhc ed* 193
Levi-Lincoln *abbhc eb* 193
Lydia (Hains) 192
Susanna-Lincoln *abbhc ea* 193
FLINT
Jacob 8
Jacob *abaeb d* 87
Susanna ([Lewis] Nickerson) *abaeb d* 87
FLOCK
Margaret 565
FLOWERS
Enoch 99 100
Rebecca *adaa* 99 100
Rebecca (——) 99 100
FOCHT
Catharine (Heming) 379
Daniel 379
David *adaii bg* 379
Martha (Lincoln) *adaii bg* 379
FOGG
Daniel 267
Eliza *aabcj c* 267
Hannah (Clement) 267
FOLEY
Elinor 432
FOLGER
George-Howland *aacdc ab; aacdc af* 182
Mary-Ann (Mitchell) *aacdc af* 182
Susan-Lincoln (Mitchell) *aacdc ab* 182
FORBES
Amanda-Sophia 430
FORESTER
Levi 406
Martha-Josephine *aabcg db* 406
Mary-Ann (Nash) 406
FORTUNE
Alice-Grace ([Lewis] Lincoln) *aabce aeb* 528
Frederick-William *aabce aeb* 528

FOSDICK
Abigail-Reed ([Walker] Lincoln) *aacbe d* 293-4
David 293
James *aacbe d* 293-4
Lincoln 293
Mary-Abby 293
Mary (Frothingham) 293
Sophia (Goodell) 294
FOSS
Anna (Hundevard) 25
Benjamin 25
David-Launtseen 25
Elizabeth ([Berry] Locke) 25
John 24 25
Mary (——) 25
Mary (Chadbourne) 25
Mehitable (Lincoln) *agb* 24 25
Samuel *agb* 24 25
Sarah (Goss) 24 25
Walter 25
FOSTER
Adelaide (Lincoln) *aabhg af* 275 277
Clara 561
Clarinda-Rebecca 557
Daniel 273
Deborah-Reynolds *aacdb fc* 436
Dwight 159
Edith-Lincoln *aabck ffb* 273
Edward 277
Elisha 277
Eliza (Wilder) 436
Evalina-Barry ([Lincoln] Lincoln) *aabck fd* 272 273 274
Frances-Mehitable *aacdb dc* 180
Hatherly 277
John 277
John F. 358
Mary 408 411
Mary-Eliza (Lincoln) *aabck ff* 273
Relief (Sampson) 273
Ruth 138
Seth *aabck ff* 273 274
Seth *aabck ffa* 273
Solomon 436
Susan-Thompson 570
Timothy 277
Walter-Burr *aabhg af* 277
Warren-Lincoln *aabck fda* 273
William 277
FOUGHT
Sarah 501 502
FOULKE
Mary 53 note 111
FOUNDS
Alexander *adbcf beba* 593
David 593
David *adbcf bebaa* 593
Martha (——) 593
Mary-Ellen (Lincoln) *adbcf beba* 593
FOWLE
Daniel 561
FOWLER
Beatrice B. (Gurney) *aabce cea* 258
Edith *aabce ceb* 258
Franklin *aabce cea* 258
James-Lawrence *aabce ce* 258
Louisa-Jane (Lincoln) *aabce ce* 258
FOX
Charles 274
FOXCROFT
Thomas 27
FOY
Ann-Eliza (Taylor) *adagb fa* 366
Lillian 366
FRANCIS
Andrew-Harris *aabck ad* 154
David 12

FRANCIS cont'd
Elizabeth *aafli* 38
Henrietta-Lamson (Pierce) *aabck ad* 154 274
Mary (Moore) 312
Mary-Moore *aacdc g* 312-3
FRANKLIN
Adelaide-Cook *adaid bba* 592
Ann *aaffi c* 84
Benjamin 266
FRANKS
Caroline (Leclare) 580
Etta-Belle *adaga gda* 580-1
William 580
FRASER—Frazer
Eliza *adcai bga* 598
Jennie (McQueanie) 598
Margaret *adaah gdaa* 578
Thomas 598
FREEMAN
Adam 392
Margaret (White) 392
Susan-White *adfad b* 392-3
FRENCH
Charlotte-Ann-Lewis *aacdc e* 309-10
Charlotte (Lewis) 309
Elsie-Minnie *aabcf acg* 404
Leonard 308, 309
Lucy-Lincoln (Litchfield) *adcbm d* 126
Mary 426 462
Mervin-Emory 404
Minnie-Elizabeth (Eames) 404
Moses 147 240
Perez *adcbm d* 126
FRIDLEY—Friedly
Betty *adaae abbb* 471
Peter 103
FROST
Austin-Leroy *aacdb gfaa* 437
Ethel-May *aacdb gfac* 437
Harriet (Stoddard) 437
Herbert-Stanley *aacdb gfa* 437
Ida-Ella (Lincoln) *aacdb gfa* 437
John 24
Lincoln-Stoddard *aacdb gfad* 437
Mary (——) 24
Mehitable *ag* 23-4
Mehitable (——) 24
Stanley 437
William-Stanley *aacdb gfab* 437
FROTHINGHAM
Abigail 170
Ebenezer 292
Eliza-Langdon *aacbe b* 292-3
Ephraim-Langdon 292
Joanna (Langdon) 292
Mary 293
Nathaniel 292
William 292
FULLER
Albert-Jonathan 519
Betsey (Rich) 253
Edward L. *aabcd ddb* 254
George 417
James 253
Mary-Anna (Morton) 519
Mary-Ellen 253
Mary-Huntington *adcai fb* 519-20
Mary-Lincoln (Doane) *aabcd ddb* 254
Mary W. *aabhb a* 69
FURMAN
Abigail-Phinney (Carsley) *aabcf ha* 145
Thomas-Stewart *aabcf ha* 145

GABRIEL
Ann (Jones) *adaig c* 112
Thomas *adaig c* 112
GADDIS
Fannie *adaga abb* 358

GAGE
Thomas-Hovey 542
GALBRAITH—Galbreath
Clarence *adahf cbaa* 505
Eliza (Campbell) 397
Harvie-Lincoln (Stubbs) *adahf cbaa* 505
Mary-Jane *adffe l* 397-8
Robert 397
GALE
Jesse 155
John G. 155
Mary (Smith) *aabhe* 155
GAMBLE
Mary-Jane *adagb jf* 221
GAMMEL
Andrew 178
Robert 178
GANNETT
Deborah 18 36
Elkanah 21 22
Hannah 40
Mary (Chapin) 19 21 22
Matthew 15 16 21 22
Rebecca 516
GARD
John-Hisey *adbca dab* 381
Margaret-Ellenor (Chenoweth) *adbca dab* 381
GARDINER—Gardner
Abel 304
Amos-Allen *aacdb ad* 179
Benjamin A. *aacdb ac* 179
Byron-Leonard *aacdb bed* 302
Charles *adaaa bbcec* 560
Charles-Warren *aacdb ab* 179
Ebenezer 304
Eliza 137
Eliza-Swift *aacdb efb* 549
Eliza-Thompson *aacdb aa* 179
Eliza-Warren *aacdb ai* 179
Ella ([Shallcross] Cline) *adahb dcca* 499
Elsie-Cordelia (Kingsbury) *adaaa bbcec* 560
Francis 31
Frederick-James *aacdb fe* 304
George *aabaa c* 136 137
Hannah-Boyden (Swift) 549
Hannah-Cushing (Wilder) 304
Harriet C. 304
Henry-Herbert *abbea cagd* 451
Hosea 31
John 31
John C. *aacdb ae* 179
John-Wallace *adahb dcca* 499
Joseph 456
Joseph-William 549
Louisa-Maria (Jackman) *aacdb ad* 179
Luke 137
Mabel 31
Maria-Elizabeth (Lincoln) *aacdb fd* 304
Maria L. 304
Mark 137
Martha *abbec fb* 456-7
Martha (Baxter) 137
Martha-Cottle (Wood) *abbea cagd* 451
Mary 137
Mary-Amanda 396
Mary C. (Fisher) *aacdb ab* 179
Mary-Cooper (——) 304
Mary (Dunbar) 179
Mary-Ellen (Doring) *aacdb bed* 302
Mary (Lincoln) *aacdb a* 177 179
Mary-Lincoln *aacdb af* 179
Mary R. (——) *aacdb ae* 179
Mary (Thomson) 499
Mary (Whiting) 31
Matilda-May (Lincoln) *adahb dcc* 499
Patty (Pierce) 450

GARDINER—Gardner cont'd
Rebecca-Morse (Fisher) *aacdb ac* 179
Robert 499
Robert-Lincoln *adahb dccb* 499
Samuel 31 304
Silas-Lincoln *aacdb ah* 179
Susan-Ellen (Ainslie) *abbea cafa* 451
Susan-(Lincoln) *aabaa c* 136 137
Susan-Maria *aacdb ag* 179
Thomas 304
Warren 179
Warren *aacdb a* 179
Wilbur-Francis *abbea cafa* 451
William *adahb dcc* 499
GARFIELD
James-Abram 228 note
GARRARD
James 195
GARRETSON
Adelia-Lane (Lincoln) *adaaf acd* 478
Warren-Harris *adaaf acd* 478
GARRETT
Alice-Ann (Priest) 512
Ann 232
Ann (Knowles) 232
Edna-May *adbcf beah* 513
Edwin-Thatcher 512
Florence-Amanda *adbcf beac* 513
Franklin-Lincoln *adbcf beab* 513
George-Sharpless *adbcf beaf* 513
Henry-Lyndall *adbcf beag* 513
Jael *adc* 59-61
Jesse-Sharpless *adbcf bea* 512-3
Jesse-Sharpless *adbcf beae* 513
Joseph 59 60 61
Laura-Alice *adbcf beaa* 513
Mary 60 61
Mary-Rebecca (Lincoln) *adbcf bea* 512-3
Nathan 232
Richard 59
Robert-Pusey *adbcf bead* 513
Ruth 60 61
Ruth (Buck) 59 60 61
GARRIGUES
Emily-Burling *adaid hc* 507
Louis-Paleskie 507
Mary (Evans) 507
GARWOOD
Effie-Julia *adahf dae* 591
Israel-Wilkins 591
Lillie-Willits (Jones) 591
GARY
Ann *adcai ea* 241
GATES
Elizabeth (Graham) 259
Lucinda *aabce f* 259
Sylvanus 259
GATEWOOD
America-Sanders *adaah g* 356-7
Catey 215
Elizabeth 215
Fanny (Wharton) 354
Hannah (Lincoln) *adaah h* 215
Henry 215
John 215
Juliann *adaah e* 354-6
Larkin 215
Lewis 356
Lucy D. 354 note 355
Nathaniel 215
Peter 215 354 481
Roena 215
Sarah (——) 215
Thomas *adaah h* 215
GAUL
Ella-Ruth *adaid aab* 375
GAY
Ebenezer 157

GAY cont'd
Jotham 68
GAYLORD
Caroline *aaffe f* 82
GAREY—Geary
Alexander *adbcg b* 118
Mary (Evans) *adbcg b* 118
GENGERICH
John *adaga gf* 490
Lucy-Ann ([Moast] Lincoln) *adaga gf* 490
GENTRY
James 465
GEOGHEGAN
Denton 337
GERALD
Almedia 428
GERMAN
Louis 225 228
GESNER
George 379
GIBB—Gibbs
Alexander 590 611
Job 306
Lavina (Robidson) 611
Lucinda (Robidson) 611
Martha *adaaa be* 464
Sarah 308
Sophia *aacdb i* 306-8
Susan (Kingsley) 306
Virginia-May *adahf dab* 590
GIBBONEY
Anna-McKelvin (Lofland) *adaae adg* 343
Cornelia-Smith (Lofland) *adaae adh* 343
J. Haller *adaae adg* 343
Robert *adaae adh* 343
GIBBONS
Margaret *adaaa abe* 462
GIBBS se Gibb
GIBSON
Eunice R. ([Swett] Lincoln) 305-6
Francis J. (——) 306
John 235
John D. 305-6
Lillian-Lillias *aacdb heb* 306
GIFFORD
Mary (Brightman) *adcai bgc* 519
GIGER
Charles *adagc e* 108
Henry *adagc b* 108
Jacob *adagc* 104 108
John *adagc a* 108
Lewis *adagc d* 108
Nancy (Lincoln) *adagc* 104 105 106 108
Polly *adagc g* 108
Sarah *adagc h* 108
Thomas *adagc f* 108
William *adagc c* 108
GILBERT
Clara-Virginia *adbcf bia* 384
Elizabeth (Deeter) 378
Estelle *adbcf bic* 384
George 384
George-Frederick *adbcf bi* 384
George-Lincoln *adbcf bid* 384
Gertrude (Vandergrift) *adbcf bid* 384
Henry 378
Hetty (Chambers) 384
Phoebe-Ella *adbcf bib* 384
Phoebe (Lincoln) *adbcf bi* 384
Sarah *adaii b* 378-9
GILES
Leonard A. *adcai bed* 391
Mary-Jemina (Lincoln) *adagb fc* 366
Susan-Elizabeth (Snow) *adcai bed* 391
GILKEY
Agnes ([Davenport] Barnett) 485
Charles 485

GILKEY cont'd
Marie-Louisa *adaah gd* 485-6
Morgan 198
GILKINSON
Catherine-Lincoln (Paschall) *adbcf bdd* 383
George W. *adbcf bdd* 383
GILL
Benjamin 190 240
Charles *aabab f* 65
Deborah *aabab g* 65 148
Deborah (Lincoln) *aabab* 64 65
Hannah *aabab e* 65 148
Hannah (Beal) 65 72
Jennie-Su'livan (Hockaday) *adaah ede* 355
John *aabab* 65
John *aabab a* 65
John *aabab d* 65
Joshua *aabab c* 65
Lucy (Cutting) *aabab c* 65
Mary *aabab b* 65 147
Mehitable (Lewis) *aabab f* 65
Nathaniel 65 72
Rebecca (Leavitt) *aaea* 11
Samuel *aaea* 11
Susanna 314
Susanna *aba* 13 38-9
Susanna *aahe* 12 72
Susanna (Wilson) 38
Thomas 38 65 72
Thomas-Benton *adaah ede* 355
GILMAN
Sarah 181
GILMORE
Denny-Oliver *adaaa bbiac* 565
Edith-Florence *adaaa bbiaa* 565
Edna-Pauline *adaaa bbiab* 565
Ephraim 565
Francis-Lavere *adaaa bbiag* 565
Harold-Maurice *adaaa bbiah* 565
James-Elliott *adaaa bbiaf* 565
James-Robert *adaaa bbia* 565
John-William *adaaa bbiai* 565
Lovina (Johnson) 565
Mary-Annalee *adaaa bbiad* 565
Mildred-Ethlyn *adaaa bbiae* 565
Minerva (Lincoln) *adaaa bbia* 565
GILPATRICK
James 303
Lucretia B. (Crane) 303
Lydia-Jane *aacdb ec* 303
GILPIN
Elizabeth (Oves) 361
Jane *adaga g* 361-3
Jasper 361
GILROY
Gladys-Draper *adaid bbbb* 507
Helen-Conoly (Lincoln) *adaid bbb* 507
Robert-Lincoln *adaid bbba* 507
William-Hammersley *adaid bbb* 507
GILSON
Alda-May *aacdb bdjc* 432
Annie-Bernadette *aacdb bdjd* 432
Arthur-Eugene *aacdb bdj* 432
Brooks-Lincoln *aacdb bdje* 432
Elton-Leroy *aacdb bdjf* 432
Harriet-Amelia (Lincoln) *aacdb bdj* 432
James 136
Lewis-Donovan *aacdb bdjb* 432
Teresa-Lenore *aacdb bdja* 432
Viola (Johnson) 432
William 432
GIPSON
John 119
GIVIN
Isom 332

GLASGOW
Ann (Lincoln) *adaih* 112
GLEASON
Fanny (Botelle) *adbfa fbc* 387
Michael *adbfa fbc* 387
GLENDINNING
Venetia *aacdb bee* 302
GLICK
Ethel *adaaa bbcea* 560
GLOVER
William 235
GODDARD
Jonathan 38
Susanna ([Gill] Lincoln) 38
GOFF
Margaret *adaga chb* 360
GOLDING—Goulding
Edward-Payson 603
Henry 49
Martha *aacdb ig* 439
Martha-Ann (Smith) 439
Robert 439
Sarah-Jane (Bullock) 603
Villroy-Augusta *aacbc ccba* 603
GOLDSMITH
Hannah 270
GOLDTHWAITE
Alice-Lincoln *abbec fdba* 458
Annie B. (Robertson) *abbec fdb* 458
Berenice-Frances *abbec fdbb* 458
Jacob 458
Lillian (Heyward) *abbec fdbc* 458
Madeline (Lincoln) *abbec fdb* 457-8
Mary-Ann ([McCloud] Burns) 458
Ralph-Percival *abbec fdbc* 458
Simon *abbec fdb* 458
GOOD
Elizabeth 496
Jacob 102
James 112
John 102
GOODELL
Sophia 294
GOODLE
George-William *adbca fbe* 382
Lizzie-Ada (Warwick) *adbca fbe* 382
GOODRICH
Ruth 385
GOODWIN
Arvilla *adaaf fce* 352
Lula *adaaf aca* 478
GOOLD—Gould
Elizabeth 257
Jarvice 3
Mehitable 22
Robert 17
GORDON
Alice 459
Katie-Bright (Lincoln) *adaae ahf* 475
Nancy 277
S. S. *adaae ahf* 475
GORMAN
Lucretia 380
GOSS
James 25
Sarah (——) 24 25
GOTT
James-Monroe *adaaa bbcc* 559-60
Lenora (Coghlin) *adaaa bbccb* 560
Louis 559
Mabel-Monroe *adaaa bbccc* 560
Mary-Elizabeth (Summers) 559
Rachel-Elizabeth (Lincoln) *adaaa bbcc* 559-60
Rose-Ada *adaaa bbcca* 560
Shelby-Lee *adaaa bbccb* 560
GOULD see Goold
GOULDING see Golding

GOVE
Eleanor M. *aacdb b* 301-2
Jacob 301
Martha (Cook) 301
Nancy-Ann 438
GOWAN
Elizabeth *adcah c* 123
GOWER
Caroline 403
GRAHAM
Adaline-Sever (Lincoln) *aacbc ahh* 421
Bash *adaah ebd* 576
Christopher-Columbus 334 342
Elizabeth 259 376
Helen *aabcf abi* 261
Henry-Joseph *aacbc ahh* 421
John-McClure 576
Margaret-Elizabeth (Perry) 576
Mary (Hamill) 421
Sarah *adaig a* 112
GRANDLE
Adeline-Margaret (Cave) 569
Henrietta-Frances *adaae agc* 569-70
William C. 569
GRANT
Mary 542
Ulysses-Simpson 530 567
GRAVES
Sarah-Louisa 564
GRAY—Grey
Nancy *aacab f* 72 note
Rachel *aafhb* 37
Roland 538
GRAYSON
Martha-Hill 345
GREELEY—Greely
Mary-Caroline *aabcf hf* 146
Moses-Reuben *aabck ae* 154 274
Sarah-Robie (Pierce) *aabck ae* 154 274
GREEN—Greene
Abigail-Antoinette (Burredge) 535
Arthur-Cameron *abbea cabac* 553
Benjamin 172
Bethia-Thaxter ([Lincoln] Staples) *aabcj f* 150
Hannah (Kenny) 150
Irene-Louise (Dennison) *abbea cabac* 553
Jennie-Virginia 612
Julius A. 535
Margaret-Elizabeth *abbck bab* 535
Mary (Davis) *adahd e* 110
Samuel 150
Samuel-Denny *aabcj f* 150
GREENWOOD
Clarissa-Emily *adffe cb* 522-3
Rosa-Anna (Wright) 522
Thomas 522
GREGG
Lillian-May *adaga afd* 359
GRENNELL
Hester 163
GREY see Gray
GRIDLEY
Hannah 30
Jeremiah 68
GRIFFIN
Daniel 193
Emma-Adelaide *abbhc gc* 193
Flora-Letitia-Selina (Bartlett) *abbhc gb* 193
Florence-Alphadelle (Cook) *abbhc gb* 193
Harlan-Boyden *abbhc gb* 193
Harlan-Pillsbury *abbhc g* 193
Margaret-Forbes *abbhc ga* 193
Sarah (Blake) 193
Tamar-Nichols (Lincoln) *abbhc g* 193

GRIGSBY
Aaron *adaaa da* 342
Sarah (Lincoln) *adaaa da* 342
GRIM
A. *adaga ae* 358
Matilda ([Lincoln] Watson) *adaga ae* 358
GROCE—Gross
Ann-Eliza *adaaf daj* 351
Fanny ([Boone] Paschall) *adaaf dag* 350
Hugh-Lawrence-White *adaaf dag* 350
Jacob 350
Jesse-Lincoln *adaaf dae* 350
Julia (Seahorn) *adaaf dae* 350
Melvina (Wallace) *adaaf dae* 350
Milton B. *adaaf da* 350-1
Paulina-Emily ([Lincoln] Dinges) *adaaf da* 349 350-1
Sarah (Farrington) 350
Thomas-Montgomery-Brown *adaaf dah* 351
GROOMES
Susan *adaga agb* 487
GROUT
Lewis *adffa l* 133
Lydia C. (Bates) *adffa l* 133
GROVE—Groves
Caroline-Elizabeth 519
Emeline 503
Mary *aacbd a* 77
GUILD
Alice (Dewing) *aabck bid* 271
Almira-Hall *aabck bie* 271
Bertha *aabck bia* 271
Calvin 271
Caroline (Lincoln) *aabck bi* 271
Emmelyn-Ticknor *aabck bic* 271
Israel 271
Jacob 271
Jesse 271
John 271
Mabel-Kellogg *abbck bib* 271
Phineas-Kellogg *aabck bi* 271 274
Phineas-Kellogg *aabck bid* 271
Sally (Kellogg) 271
Samuel 271
Susan-Caroline (Lincoln) *aabck bi* 271 274
GUINN
Sarah *adaaf ab* 477
Thomas 477
GULICK
Alice (Gordon) 459
Elizabeth-Marian *abbhc dca* 459
William-Hooker 459
GUNN
Norton 204
GUNNELL
Jessie-Lincoln *aacbe lba* 297
GUPTIL
Hannah 431
GURNEY
Beatrice B. *aabce cea* 258
John *aaffd f* 82
Sally (Kilby) *aaffd f* 82
Sylvia 555

HAAS
Elizabeth (Ruth) *adaii bia* 379
Frederick *adaii bia* 379
HACKETT
C. H. 317
Elizabeth 505
Mary-Earle 477 478
HAFER
Adele-Lincoln *adaii bdb* 379
Agnes-Lincoln *adaii bbec* 508
Alice-Lincoln *adaii bbek* 509
Ammon-Lincoln *adaii bda* 379

HAFER cont'd
Bertha-Lincoln *adaii bbed* 508
Clayton-Lincoln *adaii bbee* 508
Cora (Brensinger) *adaii bdd* 379
Dora-Lincoln *adaii bbeg* 508
Elizabeth (Lincoln) *adaii bd* 378-9
Henry-Lincoln *adaii bbel* 509
Henry-Moyer *adaii bbe* 508
Ida (Endy) *adaii bdc* 379
Irma-Lincoln *adaii bbeh* 508
John 508
John-Lincoln *adaii bbef* 508
Louisa-Lincoln *adaii bbeb* 508
Margaret-Lincoln *adaii bbem* 509
Margaret-Permilla (Lincoln) *adaii bbe* 508-9
Martha-Lincoln *adaii bbej* 509
Mathias 379
Mathias-Lincoln *adaii bdd* 379
Nellie (Lebkicker) *adaii bda* 379
Rachel-Lincoln *adaii bde* 379
Rachel (Romig) 379
Samuel-Lincoln *adaii bdc* 379
Samuel-Romig *adaii bd* 379
Sarah-Lincoln *adaii bbea* 508
Sarah (Moyer) 508
Victor-Lincoln *adaii bbei* 508
HAGAN
James *adaga e* 217-8
Mary (Lincoln) *adaga e* 217-8
HAINES—Hains
Anna-Frances *adahf ccb* 373
Edwin 373
Elizabeth *adahf cc* 505
Elizabeth-Dickinson *adahf ccc* 373
Emma-Frances (Passmore) *adahf cad* 373
Ida-Ella *adahf cce* 373
John D. *adahf cad* 373
John-Lincoln *adahf cca* 373
Joseph-Hutton *adahf cc* 373
Joseph-Hutton *adahf cch* 373
Lillian P. *adahf caf* 373
Lydia 192
Lydia (Pierce) 505
Margaret (Hutton) 373
Margaret-Hutton *adahf ccd* 373
Mira 373
Nathan 372 505
Nellie (Taft) *adahf cca* 373
Rachel-Emma *adahf ccg* 373
Rebecca-Frances (Lincoln) *adahf cc* 373
Sarah-Stubbs *adahf ccf* 373
HALDEMAN
Bell (Stuterville) *adaga geb* 363
Benjamin-Lincoln *adaga gee* 363
Charles-Baldwin *adaga ged* 363
Cora-Maud (Vittor) *adaga gea* 363
Edward-Allen *adaga ge* 362-3
Elizabeth (Lincoln) *adaga ge* 362-3
Estella (Keyle) *adaga ged* 363
Louisa-Jane *adaga gec* 363
Mary-Louisa (Baldwin) 362
Nellie-May (Harrington) *adaga gee* 363
Peter 362 363
Peter-Shirley 362 363
Stephen-Brown *adaga geb* 363
Thomas-Abraham 362
Thomas-Abraham *adaga gea* 363
HALE
Artemas *aabad d* 138-9
Artemas *aabad dc* 139
Caroline-Augusta *aabad da* 139
Deborah (Lincoln) *aabad d* 138-9
Deborah-Lincoln *aabad db* 139
Eunice (Fletcher) 151
H. W. 151
Harriet (Howard) *aabad dc* 139

HALE cont'd
Harriet (Waite) *aabcj i* 151
Martha-Amelia 434
Mary-Ann (Lincoln) *aabc i* 151 153
Moses 138
Oliver 151
Oliver *aabcj i* 151
Ruth (Foster) 138
Ruth-Jane (Brown) *aabcj i* 151
Sydney 477
HALFPENNY
Catherine-Elizabeth (Lincoln) *adahc ac* 371
James-Milton *adahc acc* 371
John-Lincoln *adahc acb* 371
Mary-Hannah *adahc aca* 371
W. R. *adahc ac* 371
HALL
Abigail *abaec c* 87
Abigail (White) 87
Abraham 186
Abraham-Tower 186
Allyn *abaec b* 87
Ann-Jane *abbea mb* 452-3
Anna-Amelia ([Lincoln] Kilgore) *aacbe lfe* 428
Arthur-Francis *aacbe lfeb* 428
Arthur-White *aacbe lfe* 428
Calvin-Shepard *abbea ccf* 319
Charles 41
Constance 41
Cynthia (Collier) 452
Daniel *abaec* 87
Elizabeth-Lincoln (Lothrop) *adcac er* 239
Emeline *aacbe da* 423
Emeline-Franklyn (Clapp) *abbea ccf* 319
Frances (White) 428
George 40 186 452
George *abaec d* 87
Henry-Knox 186
Isaac 186
Jacob 423
James 186 452
James *abbc* 41-2 186
James *abbca* 42 186
John 41 57 87 423
John-Loomer 543
Louisa 547
Lydia 431
Maria-Jane 458
Martha 531
Mary 186
Mary *abbcd* 42
Mary-Ann 423
Mary-Ann (Hall) 423
Mary (Harrington) *abaec d* 87
Mary (Lincoln) *abbc* 39 41-2 186
Oliver-Gray 428
Persis ([Tower] Lincoln) *abaea* 42 186
Richard 41 186 452
Richard *abbcb* 42
Samuel 186
Sarah *abaec e* 87
Sarah (Lincoln) *abaec* 86 87
Stephen 423
Susanna *abbcc* 42
Thomas *abaec a* 87
William 41
William *adcac ec* 239
HALSEY
Abraham A. 482
Elizabeth (LeFlore) 482
Mattie *adaah ek* 482
HAMBLIN
Dorcas 145
HAMILL
Mary 421

HAMILTON
Alexander 430
Alonzo A. 448
Clara (Smith) 430
Ethel (Lincoln) *aacbg chb* 430
Garvin 208
John-Ralston *aacbg chb* 430
HAMLETT
Ellen (Capron) 525
Eugene-Capron *adffe dga* 525
Florence-Cornelia (Lincoln) *adffe dga* 525
Luther-James 525
HAMLIN
Grace 409
HAMMER
Jesse 511
Mabel (Anson) *adbca dcc* 511
HAMMOND
Caroline-Elizabeth (Evans) *adaae ga* 207
Moses *adaae ga* 207
HANCOCK
Horace *aaffb f* 81
John 68 165
Susannah (Stodder) *aafbf f* 81
HANDSHAW
John 358
HANDY
Charles 531
Julia-Jenks *aabcf aea* 531
Margaret (Jenks) 531
HANEY
Annie A. 569
HANKINS
James 3
John 104
Mary (——) 366
HANKS
Benjamin 340
Dennis 334 338 340
John 340 465
Jonathan 357
Joseph 336 338 339 340
Lucy 338 340
Nancy *adaaa d* 204 334-42
Nancy (Shipley) 338 339
HANSCOM
Hannah 144
Lydia (Huntley) 433
Mary-Knight *aacdb ee* 433
Peter 433
HANSEN
Mahn 515
HARBISON
Mary 347 348
HARDAWAY
Louise (Nall) 200 201 202 204
HARDIN—Harding
Chester 282
Margaret 22
Martha (Martin) *adaga cag* 359
Rebecca ([Lincoln] Dyer) *adaaf f* 207
HARDWICK
Hannah-Lincoln (Kent) *aaffg h* 83
John *aaffg h* 83
HARDY
Evaline *adaaa abcg* 462
Harriet 558
HARKNESS
Sarah 385
HARLAN
Ann-Eliza (Peck) 567
James 567
Mary *adaaa dbd* 567-8
HARLOW
Catherine-Turner (Daniels) 318
Irene-Beal (Lincoln) *aafff gf* 318
James-Madison 318

HARLOW cont'd
James-Warren *aafff gf* 318
Sadie-Warren *aafff gfa* 318
HARRINGTON
Mary *abaec d* 87
Nellie-May *adaga gee* 363
Timothy 162
HARRIS
mr. 589
John 103
Jane G. (Hayden) 575
Laura-Frances *aacdb dd* 180
Mehitabel 70 71
Phila 393
Rebecca (——) 71
Thomas 71
William T. 575
Willie-Jane *adaah ebb* 575
HARRISON
Ann 208
Elizabeth ([Lincoln] Smith) *adaid hg* 378
Hannah 101
Hannah (Lincoln) *adaab* 98 101
Henry-Knabb *adaid hg* 378
Robert 101
William-Henry 278
HART
Flossie-May *adahb gbfa* 502
Mariah-Jackson *adaga ag* 487
Sarah *adaaf k* 353
HARTSOOK
James-Allen *adahb ghb* 370
Mary-Lavina (Smith) *adahb ghb* 370
HARTWELL
Chastine *aacbg c* 297-9
Nancy (——) 297
Samuel 297
HASEY
Amanda-Sophrona (Lincoln) *aacdb ib* 307
Bernice (Murphy) *aacdb iba* 307
Elijah-Williams 307
Hannah (Martin) 307
Harry-Leonard *aacdb iba* 307
Thomas-Brown *aacdb ib* 307
HASKELL
Josiah 128
Sarah *abbea cafd* 451
Sarah-Royce 445
Susan A. *adffd f* 134
HASKINS
Keziah 555
Nellie (Rutledge) *adaaa bbbga* 559
W. M. *adaaa bbbga* 559
HATCH
Adeline *adfba i* 132
Francis-Winsor *aabcg dh* 264
Mary G. (——) 264
Mary-Tidmarsh (Lincoln) *aabcg dh* 264
Winsor 264
HATFIELD
Bertha-Randolph *aacdb iea* 308
HATHAWAY
Abigail (Clarke) *akb* 9
Charles 547
Josiah *akb* 9
Polly 395
Rebecca *akc* 9
HAUGH-A-WONT
John *adahd a* 110
Nancy (Davis) *adahd a* 110
HAVEN
Welford 327
HAWKE
Elizabeth 10
Hannah (Mulligan) 605
Henry 605
John J. 605

HAWKE cont'd
Mary-Jane *abbea cacc* 605
Matthew 76
HAWKINS
Charles-Leonard 552
Emma-Baker (Davidson) 552
Grace-May *aacdc eca* 552
HAWLEY
Adeline-Elizabeth 520
Joseph 157
HAY
John 196 200 223
Maria *aabcj fe* 150
HAYDEN
Benjamin *adfaf* 127-8
Betty (Lincoln) 127
Catharine-Elliott (Pattangall) *aacdb db* 180
Charles *aacdb db* 180
Ellen B. *aacdd ea* 447
Ezekiel 127
Fanny *adfaf a* 128
Franklin-Willard 536
Ida-Adelia (McCarty) 536
Isabella-Weir (Smith) 447
James *adfaf b* 128
Jane G. 575
Joel 447
John 127
Mary-Florence *aabhg dba* 536
Ruth (Lincoln) *adfaf* 63 127-8
Tamsen 187
HAYES—Hays
Andrew 403
Andrew-Wayland *aabce cde* 403-4
Caroline (Gower) 403
Flora-Estella *abbea mh* 453
Gertrude-Lincoln *aabce cdea* 404
Hattie-Louise (Lincoln) *aabce cde* 403-4
Helena-Vesta *aabce cdeb* 404
Ivory 453
Lincoln *aabce cdec* 404
Margaret-Trimble 576
Olive (Plummer) 453
HAYMAKER
Hannah-Ann *adagb dj* 493
Leroy 493
Sallie (Sutton) 493
HAYMON
Sophia *aacdb i* 307-8
Susan *aacdb i* 306-8
HAYS see Hayes
HAYWARD—Haywood see Heyward
Edith-Viola (Cameron) *abbea cacaa* 555
Hannah 532
Oliver-Stodder *abbea cacaa* 555
HAZEL
Caleb 465
HAZEN
Eliza 311
HEAD
Jesse 339
HEALD
Deliverance (Blanchard) 300
John 300
Mary *aacda e* 300
Sybil *aacda e* 300-1
Thomas 300
Timothy 300
HEATH
Andrew J. *aabcd bac* 252
Anna-Maria (Curtis) *aabcd bac* 252
Emmeline (Balch) *adffd b* 133
William 68
HEBB
Ellen (Blackburn) *adaga cce* 359
Silas *adaga cce* 359

HEDDEN
Margaret *adagb h* 367
HEDRICK
Henry 561
HEISKELL
Frederick 349
Katherine (Steidinger) 349
Sophia-Williams *adaaf d* 349-51
HEISS
Barbara (Miller) 496
Mary-Loreno *adahb bbh* 496
Philip 496
HEMENWAY—Hemingway
Coleman 546
Jane G. *aabcf gd* 145
Kathareen (McCarger) 587
Mary A. (——) 546
Mary-Abbie *aacbc haa* 546
Rose-Jane *adahb gcd* 587-8
William 587
HEMING
Catharine 379
HEMMICK
Mary-Jane *adagb l* 367-8
HEMMIG
Anna-Louisa *adaii bb* 507-9
Mary (Yost) 507
Samuel-Warren 507
HENDERSON
Clemson 375
Margaret-Amelia *adaid a* 375
Margaret-Amelia (Moore) 375
Sarah E. *aacdb je* 181
HENDLY
James 66 note
Mary 66
HENDRICKSON
Caroline *adaga fg* 218
HENKEL
Alice-Rebecca (Pence) *adaae hbe* 345
Otto-Haining *adaae hbe* 345
HENLEY
Eunice 552
HENRY
Sarah 296
HENTON
Mary 474
Mary (Lincoln) *adaaf d* 206
HERNDON
William-Henry 328 333 338 340 342 467
HERRING
Bathsheba *adaaa* 193-204
Bethnel 200
Betsy 201
Charles-Griffin 202
John 200 201
Leonard 199 200 201 202
HERSEY
mr. 151
Abigail-Allen 251
Deborah *aa* 9 10
Ezekiel 33
Hannah 131
Joshua 73
Mary (——) 13
Mary-Catherine *aabad ge* 139 142
Mehitable-Lewis 302 304
Mercy 437
Mercy *aahd* 12
Polly 156
Rachel 79
Rebecca 10
Rebecca (Chubbuck) 9
Sarah *aaid* 12
Sarah-Leighton 437
Thomas 66 137
William 9

HERTZLER
Alice-May *adaid cca* 377
Anna-Mae (Millard) *adaid ccb* 377
Edward-Fendall *adaid ccb* 377
Elizabeth (Lincoln) *adaid cc* 377
John 377
John-Zook *adaid cc* 377
Martha (Reeser) 377
HEVENER
Elizabeth *adaae icb* 346
HEWENS
Hannah 519
HEWES
Susannah-Wendell 253
HEYWARD—Heywood see Hayward
Deborah 173
Lillian *abbec fdac* 458
HIBBARD—Hibbert
Clementina *aacdb ih* 440
Eliza (Smith) 433
John 433
Lidia (Hurd) 440
Lizzie-Smith *aacdb ee* 433-4
William 440
HICKMAN
Benjamin 375
Frances (Lincoln) *adahb dbg* 499
H. *adahb dbg* 499
Lucy (Cheyney) 375
Mary 375
HICKS
Amanda *adaaf ja* 212
Ezra *adaaf j* 209 210 211 212
John *adaaf jb* 212
Juliana (Lincoln) *adaaf j* 209 211 212
Lewis *adaaf jc* 212
HICKY
Charles A. 511
HIGGINS
Alice-Foster (Lincoln) *aacdb fcbb* 549
Alice-Susan (Crawford) 455
Earl-Rollins *aacdb fcbb* 549
Ethel (Johnson) *aacdb fcbb* 549
John-Ralph 549
Joseph-Henry 455
Nina-Elizabeth *abbec bg* 454-5
Olive (Barnard) 549
HIGHTONER
Annie-Pattie (Howard) *adaah efb* 355
Milton *adaah efb* 355
HILL—Hills
Alonzo 286
Charles *adaha dg* 224
Eliza-Rebecca *adaha dk* 225
Elizabeth *adaha dh* 224
James *adaha df* 224
John 26
John *adaha dc* 224
Jonathan *adaha d* 224
Julia (Stiff) *adaha df* 224
Lucy-Jane *adaha dl* 225
Lucy (Lincoln) *adaha d* 224
Malvina *adaha dj* 225
Margaret *adaha dd* 224
Maria (Shipman) *adaha dc* 224
Martha *adaha dm* 225
Mary-Priscilla *adaha di* 224
Sarah *adaha db* 224
Sena *adaha de* 224
Thomas 26
William 572
William-Jeffreys *adaha da* 224
Willie *adaae hfb* 572
HILLIARD
Esther 8
Mary 39
HILLMAN
Mary 522

HILLS see Hill
HILTON
  Elizabeth 58 114
  Esther *adba* 114
HISE
  Mary-Elizabeth 491
HITCHCOCK
  Caroline (Hanks) 339 340 341
  Elizabeth-Libbie (Johnson) *adagb fdb* 366
  Frederick-Russell *adagb fdb* 366
  May-Lib (Johnson) *adagb fdb* 366
HIXON
  Amelia *aabcf abd* 261
  Elizabeth *adaga cgc* 360
HOAR
  George-Frisbie 280
  John-Rogers 445
  Mary-Rogers *aacdd da* 445
  Sarah-Royce (Haskell) 445
HOARD
  Nancy *aacbc af* 418-9
  Nancy-Mary (Devillers) 418
  Silvius 418
HOBART
  Bertha (Loring) *aabha a* 69
  Caleb 21 138
  Caleb *aabad c* 138
  Caleb *aabad ce* 138
  Calvin *aabaf e* 66
  Catherine-Harris *aabad cg* 138
  Celia *aabag* 140
  Daniel *aabaf* 65
  Daniel *aabaf b* 66
  David 76 89 121
  Deborah (Sprague) 140
  Edmund 21 65 76 89 121 138 140
  Elijah-Fearing *aabad cf* 138
  Eliza W. (Ellis) *aabad ce* 138
  Frances-Elnathan (Pattangall) *aacdb dg* 180
  Hannah 82
  James 140
  James *aabaf f* 66
  Joanna *aabaf d* 66
  Joanna (Lincoln) *aabaf* 64 65-6
  Joseph *aabaf c* 66
  Louisa-Caroline (Muzzey) *aabad cb* 138
  Lydia 12
  Lydia *aacb* 76 89
  Lydia (Jacob) 76 89 121
  Lydia (Marsh) 65 138
  Lydia-Marsh *aabad ca* 138
  Mary *ad* 21
  Mary (Eliot) 21
  Mary-Fearing *aabad cc* 138
  Mary (Hendly) 66 and note
  Mary (Lincoln) *aabad c* 138
  Nehemiah 76 89 121
  Peter 8 13 65 76 79 89 121 138 183
  Rachel 68
  Reuben-Lincoln *aabaf a* 66 and note
  Samuel 65 138 140
  Samuel *aabha a* 69
  Sarah *abbe* 89-91 121 238 244
  Sarah-Ann *aabad cd* 138
  Sarah-Caroline *aacdb df* 180
  Seth-Lincoln *aabad cb* 138
  Susanna 67
  Thomas 21 65
  William-Thomas *aacdb dg* 180
HOBBS
  Abigail-Ripley *abaeg bc* 188
  Celia-Helen *adaae hi* 476
  Elizabeth (Lewis) *abaeb e* 87 188
  Elizabeth-Lewis *abaeg bf* 188
  Hannah *adcak b* 391-2
  Harriet-Joy (Lincoln) *abaeg b* 188

HOBBS cont'd
  Harriet-Lincoln *abaeg bb* 188
  Joshua 476
  Joshua-Barker-Flint *abaeg be* 188
  Josiah 188
  Lydia *abaeg bd* 188
  Lucretia-Lurena (Drake) 476
  Lydia (Child) 188
  Nathan 188
  Prentiss *abaeg b* 87 188
  Prentiss *abaeg ba* 188
HOBSON
  Leah 562
  Sarah-Frances 554
HOCKADAY
  mr. 484
  Betty (Whittington) *adaah eda* 354
  Birdie-Pixley (Bohart) *adaah edg* 355
  Dora *adaah edb* 354
  Edwin *adaah edf* 355
  Emma (Craig) *adaah eda* 354
  Fanny (Lincoln) *adaah ed* 354-5
  Isaac-Newton *adaah ed* 354-5
  Isaac-Newton *adaah edg* 355
  James-Winn *adaah edd* 355
  Jennie-Sullivan *adaah ede* 355
  John 354
  Louise R. (Canby) *adaah edc* 355
  Margaret (Doniphan) 354
  Mary (Rice) *adaah edd* 355
  Richard-Woodville *adaah eda* 354
  Urilla (Kunkle) *adaah edf* 355
  William-Doniphan *adaah edc* 355
HOCKLING
  Ebenezer *adbaa b* 114
  Elizabeth (Carter) *adbaa b* 114
HODDER
  Anna 185
HODGE—Hodges
  Elizabeth 58
  Frances 232
HOFFER
  Reuben 510
HOGSETT
  Rebecca *adagb jb* 221
HOLBROOK—Holbrooke
  Cornelius 69
  Eliza-Ann 256
  Eliza (Hyler) *aabce b* 255-6
  Elizabeth 146
  Elizabeth (Shaw) 69
  Elizabeth-Spring 538
  Emily-Rolfe *aacdb eba* 547-8
  Hannah 254
  Jane (Clapp) 62
  Lucy 394
  Lydia-Jane (Lindsey) 547-8
  Lydia ([Lincoln] Loring) *aabha* 69
  Mary 258
  Mary *adf* 62
  Molly *aaib* 12
  Samuel 62 69 131 256
  Sarah (Stockbridge) 69
  Silas 255-6
  Silas *aabha* 69
  Thomas 62
  Turner-Reed 547
  William 62 69
HOLL
  Nora *adaii bbab* 508
HOLLAND
  Mary 156
HOLLIS
  Ann *adahb ad* 226
  Elizabeth-Coats *adahb ae* 226
  Elizabeth-Coats (Hollis) *adahb ae* 226
  Elizabeth (Lincoln) *adahb a* 226
  George *adahb a* 225 226

HOLLIS cont'd
  Hannah *adahb ac* 226
  Sally-Ann (——) *adahb aa* 226
  Thomas *adahb ab* 226
  Washington *adahb aa* 226
  William *adahb ae* 226
HOLLOWELL
  Jesse 330 note
HOLLY
  Isabel *aabcd bad* 252
HOLMES
  Asa 456
  Julia-Ann *abbec fb* 456-7
  Lydia (Hobbs) *abaeg bd* 188
  Mary (Beals) 456
  S. Welles *abaeg bd* 188
HOLSTON
  Rachel (Dubois) 497
  Rachel-Potts *adahb bd* 497-8
  William 497
HOLT
  Winifred 544
HOLTZMAN
  Barbara (——) 475
  Eliza 475
  James 475
HOLUA
  Kala-Kepilino 533
HOMAN
  Caroline-Thomas *adaae ag* 472-3
  John 345
  Leannah (Thomas) 472
  Mary *adaae i* 345-7
  Mary (Robinson) 345
  Michael 472
HOMER
  Sarah *aagb* 11
HOOFSTITLER
  Henry 383
  Margaret (——) 383
  Phoebe-Speekman *adbcf b* 383-4
HOPE
  Abigail-Triphena 524
  Mary-Ann 383
  William 236
HOPKINS
  Asenath 192
  Hannah-Mayo 413
  Thomas 352
HORNBROOK
  Marie *adaaa bbbgb* 559
HORSWELL
  Francis 15 40
  Mary *abb* 15 40-2
  Mary (Cantlebury) 40
  Sarah 15 40
HORTON
  Caroline *adbca ce* 232
  John 149
HOSFORD
  Hannah-Maria 502
HOTTEN
  John-Camden 5
HOSKINSON
  Elizabeth (Crume) 203 note
HOUSEKEEPER
  Mary (Hickman) 375
  Rachel *adahf d* 375
  Philip 375
  Thomas 375
HOW—Howe
  Clara *aacbk bga* 270
  Eliza-Turner 420
  Elizabeth-Lewis (Hobbs) *abaeg bf* 188
  Sally 423
  Susan-Caroline *abaea af* 187
  William-Wirt *abaeg bf* 188

HOWARD
  Amelia *aacbe i* 296
  Anne (Pattie) 355
  Annie-Pattie *adaah efb* 355
  Ernest-Doniphan *adaah efc* 355
  Gordon 489
  Hannah 597
  Harriet *aabad dc* 139
  Henrietta (Campbell) 489
  Jane-Cordelia (Lincoln) *adaah ef* 355 481
  John-Day 296
  John-Leland *adaah ef* 355 481
  Julia-George *adaah efa* 355
  Lucy (Clark) 296
  Lucy D. (Gatewood) 354 note 355
  Martha *aacbe* 165-6 296
  Mary *adaga gdh* 489
  Thomas 355
HOWE see How
HOWELL
  Deborah 52 53 note
  Luke 68
HOWLAND
  Charles F. 444
HOYLE
  Jacob 102
HOYT—Hoyte
  Joseph-Dibble *adcak eb* 243
  Lucia-Caroline (Whitcomb) *adcak eb* 243
  Mary-Knight (Hanscom) *aacdb ee* 433
  Otis 433
HUBBARD
  Aaron D. 292
HUDSON
  Abigail (Marble) *agdi* 26 71
  Benjamin 26 note
  Charlotte *aacaa a* 71
  Elizabeth 26 note
  Elizabeth (——) *agde* 26 and note
  Ezra *agdf* 25 26
  Frost *agdg* 25 26
  Hezekiah *agdi* 25 26 71
  Hittie *agdh* 25 26
  John 26 note
  John *agdd* 25 26
  Joseph 26 note
  Joseph *agd* 25 26 71
  Joseph *agdb* 26
  Joseph *agde* 25 26 and note
  Martha *agda* 25 26
  Martha (Lincoln) *agd* 25 26 27 71
  Mary *aacaa a* 33
  Mary (Lincoln) *aacaa* 26 33 71
  Mary (Woodward) *agdi* 26 71
  Mehitable *agdh* 25 26
  Sarah (——) *agdg* 26
  Susan (Moore?) *adahb d* 369
  Thomas *agdc* 26 and note
  William 26 note
HUEY
  Albert-Baldwin 612
  Hazel-Rees *adaii bbba* 612
  Jennie-Virginia (Green) 612
HUGH—Hughes
  Edward 474
  Ellis 48
  Hannah *adafh* 53 and note
  Hester 562
  Margaret 376
  Mary (Henton) 474
  Mary-Elizabeth *adaae ah* 474-5
HULL
  Flossie-May (Hart) *adahb gbfa* 502
  Isaac 502
  John 23
  John M. *adahb gbf* 502
  Lydia 586
  Lydia-Augusta (Lincoln) *adahb gbf* 502

HULL cont'd
  Mary *adahb gbfb* 502
  Mary (Finley) 502
  Thomas *adahb gbfa* 502
HUMMEL
  Valentine 103
HUMPHREY—Humphreys
  Almira 402
  Elizabeth (Wheeler) 565
  George 125
  George *adcbf* 125
  George *adcbf a* 125
  Harriet *adcbf b* 125
  Harriett-Elizabeth *adaaa bbibc* 565
  Harriot *adcbf e* 125
  Harry *adcbf d* 125
  Hollis-Mordecai *adaaa bbiba* 565
  Howard-William *adaaa bbib* 565
  Jeremiah 565
  John 125
  Mahulda (Lincoln) *adaaa bbib* 565
  Mary (Bates) 125
  Mary (Orcutt) 125
  Peter 125
  Peter *adcbf* 125
  Peter *adcbf c* 125
  Ralph-Franklin *adaaa bbibb* 565
  Sally (Lincoln) *adcbf* 125
  Sally ([Lincoln] Humphrey) *adcbf* 125
  Sophia-Lucille *adaaa bbibd* 565
  Susan (——) 125
  Susanna 81
  Susannah-Davis 315
  Thankful 143
  Thomas 125
HUNDEVARD
  Anna 25
HUNT
  Anne (Ovis) 218
  Benjamin-Lincoln *adaga fb* 218
  Caroline (Hendrickson) *adaga fg* 218
  Daniel 547
  Daniel *adaga fc* 218
  Edwin-Marshall *adahf cha* 374
  Ella-Frances (Reynolds) *adahf cha* 374
  Hannah (Lincoln) *adaga f* 218
  Ilvira (Inks) *adaga fd* 218
  Isaac-Laning *adaga f* 218
  Isaac-Laning *adaga fd* 218
  Jacob 218
  Jacob *adaga fa* 218
  James-Lewis *aabcg ca* 147
  Louisa (Hall) 547
  Margaret (Sembower) *adaga fh* 218
  Martha-Ann *aacbe lfb* 547
  Mordecai-Lincoln *adaga fe* 218
  Rebecca E. *adahf cac* 373
  Sarah *adaga ff* 218
  Sarah (Thompson) *adaga fb* 218
  Susan-Lincoln (Thaxter) *aabcg ca* 147
  Thomas-Lincoln *adaga fg* 218
  William *adaga fh* 218
HUNTER
  Amelia-Robinson (Lincoln) *aacdb gd* 305
  David 305
  Lydia-Ann *aacdb gdb* 305
  Lydia-Ann (Belcher) 305
  Mary-Washington (Mason) *aacdb jh* 181
  Samuel-Belcher *aacdb gd* 305
  Sarah-Lincoln *aacdb gda* 305
  William *aacdb jh* 181
HUNTING
  Ella-Louise (Stewart) *abbea cabca* 553
  Frank-Loverell *abbea cabca* 553
HUNTLY
  Lydia 433
HUP—Hupp
  Elizabeth *adaaa bbd* 561

HUP—Hupp cont'd
  Emma-Catherine *adaae agi* 570
  George 330
  Hetty (Rimer) 570
  Samuel D. 570
HURBAUGH
  Catherine 563
  John 563
  Rachel-Ann *adaaa bbf* 563
HURD
  Lidia 440
HURT
  James *adaah efa* 355
  Julia-George (Howard) *adaah efa* 355
HUSTON
  Alice (Carroll) *adagb dba* 364
  Caleb-Stetson *aacdb cb* 180
  Martha ([——] Lincoln) *adagb de* 492
  Zelinda-Ray (Appleby) *aacdb cb* 180
HUTCHINS
  Alice-Lincoln (Rand) *aabcf daaa* 406
  George-Edward *aabcf daaa* 406
HUTCHINSON
  Clayanna (Lloyd) 589
  Edward-Stanley 589
  J. R. 44 196 328 341
  James *adbcf cd* 383 385
  Margaret 385
  Mary-Ann 385
  Rachel-Lloyd *adahf cea* 589
  Rebecca (Lincoln) *adbcf cd* 383 385
  Thomas 72
HUTTON
  Margaret 373
HUYETT
  Sarah 508
HYERS
  Ann 461
HYLAND
  Hannah (Studley) 450
  John 450
  Samuel 450
  Sarah *abbea ca* 450-2
  Thomas 450
  William 450
HYLER
  Eliza *aabce b* 255-6

ILES
  Elijah 466
ILGENFRITZ
  Eliza ([Moore] Lincoln) 369
  Jacob 369
INFANT
  Gilbert 136
INGHAM
  James-Clegg 535
  Lillian-Shaw (Lincoln) *aabck bfca* 535
  Mary-Burns (Partelow) 535
  William-Partelow *aabck bfca* 535
INGRAHAM
  Alice-Choate *aabce hac* 260
INKS
  Ilvira *adaga fd* 218
INSKEEP
  John 266
IRWIN
  Andrew-Jackson *adahb bbf* 495
  Anna-Elizabeth *adahb bbfb* 495
  Caroline-Leland 601
  Caroline (Lincoln) *adaah eia* 481-2
  Charles 495
  Frances-Allen *adaah eiab* 482
  Helen-Cecilia *adahb bbfd* 495
  James-Chiles *adaah eia* 481-2
  Joseph-Chambers 481
  Joseph-Chambers *adaah eiac* 482
  Julia-Lincoln *adaah eiaa* 481

IRWIN cont'd
Mary (Chiles) 481
Mary-Lincoln *adahb bbfc* 495
Nancy (Kirkpatrick) 495
Olivia-Elizabeth (Lincoln) *adahb bbf* 495
Ruth-Catheryn (McLeod) *adaah eiad* 482
Ruth-Lillian *adahb bbfa* 495
Susan *adaah eiad* 482
ISHAM
Charles *adaaa dbaa* 567-8
Julia (Burhans) 567
Lincoln *adaaa dbaaa* 568
Mary (Lincoln) *adaaa dbaa* 567-8
William-Bradley 567
IVES
Stephen-Bradshaw 446

JACKMAN
Benjamin *aacdb af* 179
Louisa-Maria *aacdb ad* 179
Mary-Lincoln (Gardner) *aacdb af* 179
JACKSON
Andrew 122 328 417 466 478
Charles 546
John 93
Lydia 10
Lyman B. *adaga gdaa* 580
Margaret (Hughes) 376
Maria *adaid c* 376-7
Mary 374
Mary-Elizabeth (Lincoln) *adaga gdaa* 580
Michael 81
S. R. 395
Sarah-Alice *aacbe ldf* 546-7
Sarah-Ann (Young) 546
Thomas 376
JACOB—Jacobs
David 34
Elizabeth (Coal) 360
Elizabeth (Hixon) *adaga cgc* 360
Emma *adaga cga* 360
Hannah *adaga cgb* 360
Hannah-Elizabeth (Cresswell) *adaid bca* 376
Henry 360
J. Howard *adaid bca* 376
John 68 240
Joseph 68
Lincoln *aacbh k* 78
Lydia 76 89 121
Lydia *aabh* 68-70
Mary 31
Mary *aac* 32 34
Mary (Lincoln) *adaga cg* 360
Nicholas 268
Olive (Fearing) *aacbh k* 78
Peter 68
Ruth (Wilson) 68
Samuel 8
Sarah (Cushing) 34
William *adaga cg* 360
William *adaga cgc* 360
JAMES
Abigail 260
Abner-Evans *adaid cb* 377
Bessie-Lincoln *adaid cbc* 377
Betsey *abaeg* 184-5 187-8
Bette (Beal) 184 187
Clarence-Alan *adaid cbb* 377
Ebenezer *aafff e* 184-5
Edward-Lincoln *adaid cba* 377
Eleazer 181
Elizabeth-Jane (Millard) *adaid cbb* 377
Francis 184 187
Galen 184 187
Galen *aafff ec* 185

JAMES cont'd
Hannah-James (Marshall) *aafff ha* 185
Jesse 377
Margaret (Allen) 377
Margaret (Lincoln) *adaid cb* 377
Mary (Nichols) *abcb* 14
Philip 184 187
Philip *abcb* 14
Polly *adcaj a* 123
Priscilla (Lincoln) *aafff e* 184-5
Priscilla-Lincoln *aafff eb* 92 185
Sarah-Wales *adffb g* 133
Susannah-Beal *aafff ea* 185
Thomas 17 184 187
JAMESON
Jamesena 533 534
JAQUETH—Jaquith
Ella *aacda hb* 175
Moses 268
JARVIS
Melinda 479
JASPER
Eliza (Holtzman) 475
Mary-Isabella *adaae hf* 475-6
William-Woodson 475
JAYNES
Ezekiel-Woods 412
Lula-DeEtta *aabhe ab* 412-3
Mary-Adeline (Sibley) 412
JEFFERSON
Thomas 159 160 161
JEFFERY
Joseph-Alexander *adahb ghd* 370
Lucy-Adelia (Smith) *adahb ghd* 370
JEFFREYS
Sarah *adaha* 224
JENKINS
Aurelia 144
Betsy (Dill) *adcag d* 122
Chloe *adcaj j* 123
Clarissa *adcaj i* 123
Cummings *adcag d* 122
David 377
Davis *adcaj c* 123 320
Dora-Emma *adaaa bbebb* 562
Edward 122 123
Elizabeth 221
Elizabeth-Tilestone *adffb f* 133
Elizabeth-Tilestone (Jenkins) *adffb f* 133
Gideon *adcaj* 122 123
Gideon *adcaj d* 123 133
Hannah-Chandler (Cole) *adcaj g* 123
Isaac *adcag e* 122
James 122 123
James *adcag* 122
James *adcag c* 122
John 377
John *adcag g* 122
Joshua 320
Josiah 144
Josiah *adcaj f* 123
Leah (Webb) *adcaj b* 123
Lucy *adcag h* 122
Lucy *adcag i* 122
Lucy ([Vinal] Collier) *adcaj b* 123
Luther *adcaj b* 123
Martha 506
Mary *adffb h* 133
Mary D. (McCalmant) 377
Mary (Lincoln) 27
Mary-Thomas (Young) *adcaj a* 123
Mary (Vinal) 122 123
Mercy *adcaj e* 123 133
Mercy (Lincoln) *adcaj* 122 123 133
Mercy-Little ([Otis] Curtis) *adcaj b* 123
Nancy *abbea m* 320-1
Nancy *adcaj c* 123 320
Nancy (Jenkins) *adcaj c* 123 320

JENKINS cont'd
Peleg *adcaj a* 123
Polly *adcag a* 122
Polly ([James] Cole) *adcaj a* 123
Prudence (Davis) 144
Rachel (Cole) *adcag d* 122
Rachel (Thaxter) *aacbd d* 77
Ruth *adcag b* 122
Ruth *adcag f* 122
Ruth (Lincoln) *adcag* 121
Sarah-Anderson *adaid g* 377
Shadrach *adcaj h* 123
Solon *adcaj g* 123
Thomas 27 122 123
JENKS
Margaret 531
JENNINGS
Penelope-Catharine 571
JENNISON
Elizabeth (Cushing) *aabce baa* 256
Emma 424
Nathaniel 161
William H. *aabce baa* 256
JENSEN—Jenson
Ane 556
Carl 602
Mary-Evangeline *aabce aeba* 602
Mary (Robishan) 602
JERMYN
Sarah 225
JEWETT
Eliza 263
Lydia 405
JOAB
Frances *adaga cch* 360
JOHANSON
Anna-Maria 605
Anna-Maria (Johnson) 605
Carl-August 605
Ellen-Harriet 605
JOHNSON
miss *adaae aed* 344
Alice (Thomas) 568
Andrew 204 351
Ann B. *adcac eh* 239
Benjamin 10
Charles 366
Charles N. *adagb fd* 366
Edward-Whiting 568
Elizabeth-Libbie *adagb fdb* 366
Enoch *adahb eb* 226 500
Esther *abbed g* 90 521
Ethel *aacdb fcbb* 549
Frank-Edward *adaaa dbdc* 568
Hannah-Elizabeth *adahb fa* 500-1
Hilma-Justine 556
Humphrey 10
Isaac 9 76
Jessie ([Lincoln] Beckwith) *adaaa abdc* 568
John 10 76 465
Lovina 565
Lydia (Lincoln) *adagb fd* 366
Martha 232
Mary 351
Mary-Libbie *adagb fda* 366
May-Lib *adagb fdb* 366
Olive (Briggs) 366
Rebecca (Hersey) 10
Sally 303
Sarah 10 75
Sarah-Ann (Steigers) *adahb eb* 226 500
Viola 432
JOHNSTON
Daniel 341
James 349
John 341
Matilda 341

JOHNSTON cont'd
Sarah 341
Sarah (Bush) *adaaa d* 341
JONES
Abraham 20 21
Adaline (Eastman) 549
Ann *adaig c* 112
Ann-Maria (Sturgis) *adagb gg* 221
Benjamin 21
Benjamin-Reynolds 549
Benjamin-Richards 302 304
Betsey (Ellmes) *aaffj. h* 84
Blanche (Armstrong) 604
Caleb 112 230 364
Charles H. *adbfa fd* 387-8
Clara (——) 613
David 112 230 364 376 494
David *adaig* 112 364
Eleanor *adage c* 109
Elizabeth *adaid* 112 230
Elizabeth *adaig f* 112
Elizabeth (Graham) 376
Ellen-Mehitable *aacdb fcb* 549
Frances *aaca* 64-5 71
Frances *aacbc acdd* 604
George 475
Hannah *adaid b* 376
Hannah *adaig b* 112 364-5
Hannah (Runnels) 434
Hannah (Samuels) 112 230
Henry 434
Ida P. *adbcf bedb* 613
Isaac 479
Jane (VanHorn) *adage e* 109
Jane ([Usrey] [Lincoln] Mercer) 479
John 376
John *adage* 104 107 108-9
John *adage e* 104 106 109
John-Ellsworth 604
Jonathan 376
Julia-Sophia *aacdb ef* 434
Lillie-Willits 591
Lucy A. (Lincoln) *adbfa fd* 387-8
Luella *adaaa ca* 203
Margaret 379
Martha *adaig d* 112
Mary 233
Mary *adage a* 108
Mary *aabcf bc* 144
Mary-Richards *aacdb e* 302-3
Matilda 561
Mehitable-Lewis (Hersey) 302 304
Nancy *adage d* 109
Phebe *adaig g* 112
Phebe (Lincoln) *adaig* 112 364
Rebecca *adaaa beg* 566
Robert *adagb gg* 221
Samuel 613
Samuel *aaffj h* 84
Samuel *adaig e* 112
Sarah 67
Sarah *ad* 20 21
Sarah *adaae hf* 475
Sarah-Dargue 257
Sarah (Graham) *adaig a* 112
Sarah-Leighton *aacdb g* 304-5
Sarah (Lincoln) *adage* 104 105 106 107 108-9
Sarah (Pendleton) 475
Sarah (Whitman) 20 21
Thomas 21
Thomas-Lincoln *adaig a* 112
William *adage b* 106 107 109
JORDAN
Anthony J. *adbcf a* 382
Charles D. 418
Eliza ([——] Lincoln) *adbcf a* 382
Helen 298

JORDAN cont'd
Helen-Lincoln (Stevens) *aacbg cga* 298 299
James-Clark *aacbg cga* 299
Marion 298

JOSSELYN
Abraham 166
Bethia (Bourne) 166
Eleazer 166
Eliza (Bronsden) 166
Eliza-Maria 166
Eliza-Maria (Lincoln) *aacbe m* 166
Frances-Revere *aacbe mb* 166
Frances-Revere (Lincoln) *aacbe k* 166
Henry 166
Josephine 166
Lucretia-Smith 166
Mary-Vinal *aacbe ma* 166
Mary-Vinal (Lincoln) *aacbe j* 166
Nathan *aacbe j* 166 295
Nathan-Lincoln *aacbe ka* 166
Nathan-Webster 166
Nathaniel 166
Rebecca 8

JOY
Abigail 36 71
Abnah 87
Amos 243
Andrew-Eliot 88
Anna 88
Ann (Eliot) 88
Benjamin *aagf* 11
Bethia (Sprague) *aagb* 11
Charles H. 430
Deborah *aagd* 11
Elisha 244
Elizabeth (Andrews) 11
Elizabeth-Eliot 88
Elizabeth G. 521
Emma-Jane ([Williams] Lincoln) 427
Harriet *abaed a* 88
Huldah *aagg* 11
Jared 243-4
John *aag* 11
John *aagb* 11
Joseph 11 87 243
Joseph-Franklin 88
Lefe *aagc* 11
Lillis 244
Lot 244
Lydia *aaga* 11
Lydia (Lincoln) *aag* 11
Mary *aage* 11
Mary (Eliot) 88
Mary-Pynchem 88
Melzar *abaed* 87-8
Olive 244
Olive (Lincoln) *abaed* 87-8
Olive ([Litchfield] Lincoln) 243-4
Patience (Bates) 243
Paulina-Snow *adcai bab* 390
Prince 87 243
Ruth 10
Sarah (Curtis) 87
Sarah (Homer) 11
Thomas 11 87 243 427
Warren 244
Susanna 79

JUDD
Julia-Louisa 428

JUNK
Elizabeth (Lincoln) *adaga h* 218
Henry *adaga he* 218
James *adaga h* 218
John 218
John *adaga ha* 218
Robert *adaga hf* 218
Samuel *adaga hb* 218

JUNK cont'd
Sarah *adaga hd* 218
Sarah (Preston) 218
Thomas 218
Thomas *adaga hc* 218

KAMAKAI
Haalou-Kaleikoa 533

KAUB
Augustus-Lincoln *adaii aa* 230
Daniel 230
John *adaii a* 230-1
Linda-Barbara (Stine) *adaii aa* 230
Martha (Lincoln) *adaii a* 230-1
Washington-Lincoln *adaii ab* 231

KAUFMAN—Kauffman
Catherine *adaga gdcb* 489
David 489
George-Conant *adbcf becd* 513
Isadore-Lincoln *adaga gdc* 489
Kenneth *adaga gdcc* 489
Louisa-Jones (McConnell) *adbcf becd* 513
Mabel-Marie *adaga gdca* 489
Mary-Jane (Lincoln) *adaga gdc* 489
Mary (Poundstone) 489

KAY
Elizabeth *adahb gc* 502
Rachel-Malinda *adahb gb* 501-2
Sarah (Fought) 501 502
William 501 502

KEEFE
Ellen 519

KEELING
Rosannah 332

KEFFER
Albert *adaga gfc* 490
Matilda-Craig (Lincoln) *adaga gfc* 490

KELLAR—Keller
Harriet *adagb dd* 364
Nancy 355

KELLEM
Rebecca (Lincoln) *adaha a* 224
William *adaha a* 224

KELLEY—Kelly
Catherine 606
Celia (St. John) 531
Eunice 511
Florence 545
Hannah 371
John 327 330
Mabel-Harriett *aabce cdba* 531
Wyatt 531

KELLOGG
Anna-Mary (Lincoln) *adcai fbc* 520
Elijah 260
Mary-Isabel *adcai fbca* 520
Orville-William *adcai fbc* 520
Sally 271

KELLY see Kelley

KENDALL
Almira 456

KENDIG
Hannah-Elvina *adahb bbi* 583
Henry 583
Mary-Dehaven (Squib) 583

KENNEDY
Agnes 439
Alameda (Dougherty) *adaaf dba* 574-5
Augusta-Maria (Lincoln) *abbea cada* 555-6
Ellen *adagb dh* 493
James-Andrew *abbea cada* 555-6
John 555
Martha J. *adaaa bed* 464

KENNERSEG
Edna *adaga gja* 363

KENNY
Hannah 150

KENT
Abel 82
Abel *aaffg* 82-3
Betsey *aaffg e* 83
Betsey (Fletcher) 82
Betsey (Kent) *aaffg e* 83
Charles *aaffg e* 83
Chloe ([Lincoln] Stephenson) *aaffg* 82-3
Ebenezer 40 82
Edward 149
Hannah 37 38
Hannah (Gannett) 40
Hannah (Hobart) 82
Hannah-Lincoln *aaffg h* 83
Henrietta *aaffg i* 83
Isaac *aaffg b* 83
John 40 82
Justin *aaffg c* 83
Mercy 40 63
Perez *aaffg d* 83
Sally-Fletcher 83
Sarah (Worrick) *aaffh d* 83
KENTON
John-Alexander 587
Martha (Purdy) 587
Mary-Etta *adahb gcd* 587
KEPILINO
Henrietta *aabcg dga* 533
KERNOGHAN see Cunningham
Abraham *adaga cea* 360
Benjamin *adaga ce* 360
George *adaga ced* 360
Hannah (Lincoln) *adaga ce* 360
Martha-Elizabeth *adaga ceb* 360
Mary-Catherine *adaga cef* 360
Rhoda *adaga ceh* 360
Robert *adaga ceg* 360
Sturgeon *adaga cee* 360
William *adaga cec* 360
KERR
miss *adaga gaa* 488
Esther 575
KERSHAW
James 531
Jennie-Elizabeth *aabcf aea* 531
Martha (Hall) 531
KEYLE
Estella *adaga ged* 363
KEYS
Eliza 583
KIBLER
Ann-Eliza (Koontz) *adaae aed* 344
Isaac *adaae aed* 344
KIDDER
mr. 271
KILBY
Abigail (Cushing) 85
Annie-Sophia *aacdb iac* 307
Bethia *aaffd c* 82
Catherine *abad* 85
Cushing 42 81 240 246
Cyrus-Hamlin *aacdb ia* 307
Elvira-Kingsley (Lincoln) *aacdb ia* 307
Fanny *adcai* 240-1
Harriet *aaffd g* 82
Hipzabah *aaffd d* 82
Huldah *adfae* 245-6
Huldah (Orcutt) 81 240 246
John 81 85 240 246 307
John D. *aacdb iaa* 307
Katherine *aaffd a* 82
Lincoln-Hamlin *aacdb iab* 307
Lydia (Wilder) 307
Maria *aaffd h* 82
Merriel *aaffd e* 82
Phebe (Byrom) *aaffd b* 82
Rebecca (Allyne) *abae* 86
Richard 81 85 240 246

KILBY cont'd
Sally *aaffd f* 82
Sarah 85
Thomas *aaffd* 81
Thomas *aaffd b* 81 82
William 85 86
Winifred (Lincoln) *aaffd* 81-2
KILGORE
Anna-Amelia (Lincoln) *aacbe lfe* 428
Emerson 428
Herbert *aacbe lfe* 428
Ida-Lincoln *aacbe lfea* 428
KILLIAN
Alfred-Lincoln *adaii bbad* 508
Caleb *adaii bbae* 508
Caleb-Ruth *adaii bba* 508
Elizabeth (Ruth) 508
Heister *adaii bbah* 508
Luke *adaii bbaf* 508
Mark *adaii bbag* 508
Oscar-Lincoln *adaii bbac* 508
Nora (Holl) *adaii bbab* 508
Ralph-Lincoln *adaii bbab* 508
Samuel-Lincoln *adaii bbaa* 508
Samuel-Quinter 508
Sarah-Clara (Lincoln) *adaii bba* 508
KIMBALL
Amos 318
Ellen-Augusta (Lincoln) *aafff gg* 318
George-William *aafff gg* 318
Herbert-Francis *adffe cea* 396
Herbert-Mortimer *adffe ce* 396
Jedediah 318
Jefferson-Liberty 396
Jesse 318
John 318
Lydia-Maria (Lincoln) *adffe ce* 396
Mary-Amanda (Gardner) 396
Mary-Ann (Baker) 318
Nettie-Grace (Litchfield) *aafff gga* 318
Peter-Cammett 318
Peter-Cammett *aafff gga* 318
Richard 318
KIMBER
Elizabeth (Jones) *adaig f* 112
Emmor *adaig g* 112
John *adaig f* 112
Phebe (Jones) *adaig g* 112
KINCH
Barbara *adbcf* 234
KING
Bessie-Amanda (McConnell) *adbcf beca* 513
Charles-Gedney 422
Gedney 421
George F. *adagb fca* 366
Jennie-Hannah (Kirk) *adahf cga* 374
Jerusha 346
Mary 21
Mary-Jemima (Lincoln) *adagb fc* 366
Robert *adagb fc* 366
William 389
William-Harry *adbcf beca* 513
William-Preston *adahf cga* 374
KINGMAN
Mary-Jane 398
Pliny E. 308
KINGSBURY
Elizabeth-Ann (Reed) 560
Elsie-Cordelia *adaaa bbcec* 560
Ethel (Glick) *adaaa bbcea* 560
Everett-Earl *adaaa bbcea* 560
Grace-May *adaaa bbceb* 560
Martha-Ann (Lincoln) *adaaa bbce* 560
Theodore-Harley *adaaa bbce* 560
Vern-Eldon *adaaa bbced* 560
Worster P. 560

KINGSLEY
Susan 306
KINNICUTT
Elizabeth-Waldo (Parker) *aacbc cb* 163
Francis-Harrison *aacbc cb* 163
KINSEY
Elizabeth 373
KIRBY
Harriet 524
Sarah-Ann *adaaf ga* 211
KIRK
Charles-Benton *adahf cgc* 374
Clara-Lincoln *adhf cgb* 374
Elizabeth (Rogers) *adahf cgc* 374
Francina-Knight (Lincoln) *adahf cg* 373-4
Hannah-Brown (Stubbs) 373
Isaac-Stubbs *adahf cg* 373-4
Jacob-Reynolds 373
Jennie-Hannah *adahf cga* 374
Mary 431
Mary (Stubbs) *adahf cgd* 374
Pinckney-Jacob *adahf cgd* 374
KIRKPATRICK
Arthur-Welles *aabce abab* 527
Gordon-Welles *aabce ababb* 527
John-William 527
Mary-Ellen (Wells) 527
Maude-Winthrop (Lincoln) *aabce abab*
527
Nancy 495
Priscilla *aabce ababa* 527
KISSINGER
Betsey-Viola *adaga gic* 582
Elizabeth (Fell) 582
Harry-Reaux-Martin *adahb bcba* 497
Margaret-Mae (Lincoln) *adahb bcba* 497
William 582
KITTENGER
Ellen-Elizabeth (Lincoln) *adahb dcda* 584
Frank-Lincoln *adahb dcdaa* 584
Frank M. *adahb dcda* 584
John-Alvin *adahb dcdab* 584
KLINE
Amanda-Alice *adaae aha* 571
Asa 571
Rebecca(McKever) 571
KNAPP
Annie (Lincoln) *adahb gbeb* 586
James-William *adahb gbeb* 586
KNIGHT
Elizabeth-Starr (Parvin) *adaid hab* 378
Hannah *adahc aba* 371
John-Lincoln *adahc abb* 371
Mary-Ann *aabcf aba* 261
Mary E. 372
Mary-Hathorne *aacbe d* 293-4
Rachel-Thompson (Lincoln) *adahc ab*
371
Richard-Warren *adaid hab* 378
Samuel H. *adahc ab* 371
KNOTT
James 324
Susan *abbhc d* 324
Susannah (Reynolds) 324
KNOWLES
Abigail (Hall) *abaec c* 87
Ann 232
Caleb *abaec c* 87
KNOWLTON
Clarence-Hinckley *aacdb gdb* 305
Hannah (Guptil) 431
Helen-Martha *aacdb bd* 431-2
Joel 431
Lydia-Ann (Hunter) *aacdb gdb* 305
KNOX
Henry 133 186
Sarah 443
42

KOCH
Anna 116 note
Peter 116 note
KOON
Katharine 118
KOONTZ
Abraham-William *adaae aeh* 344
Ann (Thomas) *adaae aec* 344
Ann-Eliza *adaae aed* 344
Betsy-Ann (Lincoln) *adaae ae* 343-4 568
Carrie (West) *adaae aef* 344
Dale-Lillie (Speck) *adaae aeh* 344
David-Edward *adaae aeb* 344
Diana-Catherine *adaae aea* 344
Elizabeth 343
Elizabeth (Koontz) 343
Lucy-Bell (Speck) *adaae aeh* 344
Mary-Elizabeth *adaae aee* 344 568-9
Mary (Strole) *adaae aeg* 344
Peter-Perry *adaae ae* 343-4 568
Philip 343
Philip-Peter-Perry *adaae aef* 344
Reuben-Franklin *adaae aec* 344
Wilson-Asbury *adaae aeg* 344
KUEHN
Anthony *adaaa bbceb* 560
Grace-May (Kingsbury) *adaaa bbceb* 560
KUNKLE
Urilla *adaah edf* 355
KUPFER
Margaret-Elizabeth 429
KYLE
Margaret 343
Thomas 204 332

LACEY
Mary-Elizabeth 442
LAFFERTY
Mary *adagb* 219-22
LAIR
Joseph 97
LAIRD
Elizabeth (Twining) 503
Margaret *adahb ge* 503
Thomas 503
LAKEMAN
William 143
LAMBERT
Anna 255
Bethia (Kilby) *aaffd c* 82
Charles *aaffd a* 82
James *aaffd c* 82
Katherine (Kilby) *aaffd a* 82
LAMON
Ward-Hill 337 338 342
LANCASTER
Sarah-Jane 581
Sewall 149
LANDERS
mr. 562
Margaret ([Lincoln] [Way] Leach) *adaaa bbed* 562
LANDRILL
mr. 562
LANE
Abigail 10
Abigail-Allen (Hersey) 251
Abby-Allen *aabcd aca* 251
Andrew 251
Anna-May *adbfa fga* 388
Anne-Otis *abbea ccb* 319
Belle E. (Lincoln) *adbfa fg* 388
Caroline-Hayden (Lincoln) *aabcd ac* 251-2
Caroline-Lincoln *aabcd acd* 252
Deliverance 321
Ebenezer 11
George 11

LANE cont'd
Hannah 11 83
Hannah (Hersey) 11
Herbert *adbfa fgb* 388
Jane M. *adbcf bdf* 384
John 388
Jonathan 251
Lydia 10
Mary-Agnes (——) *aabcd acc* 252
Mary N. *adbcf bda* 383
Oscar-Dana *aabcd acb* 251
Rufus 251
Rufus *aabcd ac* 251-2
Rufus-Allen *aabcd acc* 252
Sarah 42
Thomas 350
W. Arthur *adbfa fg* 388
William 11 251
LANG
Sarah 564
LANGDON
Elizabeth 88
Joanna 292
LANGER
Margaret 13 14
Richard 14
LANMAN
Gabriel *adaga ba* 217
Rhoda (Woodnancy) *adaga ba* 217
LANTZ
Annie *adagb dgf* 365
LARD
Annie-Shannon *adaah gda* 578
Moses E. 578
LARRABEE
Betsey-Roxanna 428
LARRICK
Ellen 570
LARSEN—Larson
Laura-Caroline *adbfa fh* 515-6
Mahn (Hansen) 515
Mary *adahb gbba* 501
Rasmus 515
LASLEY
Lucy-Jane (Hills) *adaha dl* 225
Manoah-Smith *adaha dl* 225
LATHROP
John 168
LAUTENSCHLAGER
Christina 606
LAWES
Francis 5 6
Liddea 5
Mary 5
LAWRENCE
Bernard-Whitman *aabce bhb* 257
Edith-Louisa (Snelling) *aabce bhb* 257
Emily-Augusta 520
Fayette-Washington 599
Katherine 595
Mabel-Bettina *adcai fba* 599
Rebecca 249
Mary (Sargent) 599
Samuel 430
LAWSHE
E. Irland *adahc aaaa* 588
Marie-Reed (Lincoln) *adahc aaaa* 588
LAWSON
Gustave 556
Hilma-Justine (Johnson) 556
Jennie-Louise *abbea mhc* 556-7
LAYTON
Robinson *adaga bf* 217
Sarah (Zearing) *adaga bf* 217
LEA—Lee
Charles-Carroll 430
Charles-Carroll *aacbg ckfc* 431
Charity-Emma *adaaf ac* 348 477-8

LEA—Lee cont'd
Clara-Lothrop *aacbg ckfa* 431
Clara-Lothrop (Lincoln) *aacbg ckf* 430-1
Fitzhugh 568
Helen *aacbg ckfb* 431
Helen (Parrish) 430
Isaac *adafd* 53
James Henry 44 196 200 223 324 note
328 329 330 333 note 335 341
James-Parrish *aacbg ckf* 430-1
Marion-Inez 614
Mary (Boone) *adafd* 53
Mary-Henderson (Peck) 477
Mildred *aacbg ckfd* 431
Philena *adahf be* 229
Preston-Jornegan 477
Robert Edmund 249
LEACH—Leech
Arthur B. 598
Fay *adaaa bbede* 562
Henry *adaaa bbed* 562
Huldah *adaga ga* 487-8
Jesse 487 488
Laura 438
Margaret ([Lincoln] Way) *adaaa bbed* 562
Susanna (——) 487
LEARMENT
Andrew A. *adagb fdc* 366
Andrew-Witherspoon *adagb fd* 366
John 366
Lydia ([Lincoln] Johnson) *adagb fd* 366
Sarah (Martin) 366
LEARNED
Martin-Dexter 44
LEAVITT
Abraham 11
Abraham *aae* 10 11
Almira (Humphrey) 402
Deborah 140 252
Deborah *aaeb* 10 11 138
Elijah 151
Elisha 42
Elizabeth *abbdb* 42
Hannah (Lane) 11
Israel 10 42
John 10 42
Joshua 402
Lydia (Jackson) 10
Martha (Lincoln) *abbd* 39 42
Nehemiah *abbd* 42
Rebecca *aaea* 11
Rebecca (Lincoln) *aae* 10 11
Sarah 174 402
Sarah *abbda* 42
Sarah (Lane) 42
LEBKICKER
Nellie *adaii bda* 379
LECLARE
Caroline 580
LEE see Lea
LEECH see Leach
LEEDS
Lida *adbcf becb* 513
LeFLORE
Elizabeth 482
LeGROW
Jennie 534
LEIBFRIED
Elizabeth-Skiles (Rutter) *adahb bceb* 497
Frederick *adahb bceb* 497
LEIGHTON
Elizabeth (Lincoln) *aacdb bc* 301 302
Ellen-Caroline 306
Ellen-Eliza *aacdb bcc* 302
Ellen-Elizabeth *aacdb bce* 302
Frederic *aacdb bab* 301
George *aacdb ba* 301 302

LEIGHTON cont'd
Hermon *aacdb hdb* 306
Jane (Cockran) 301
Lucy-Jane *aacdb* bcd 302
Mary-Martha (Lincoln) *aacdb ba* 301 302
Mary-Matilda *aacdb baa* 301
Samuel 301
Sarah-Augusta (Nutt) *aacdb hdb* 306
Sarah-Capen *aacdb bcb* 302

LEIMBACH
Catherine ([Biehl] Lincoln) *adaii be* 510
Charles *adaii be* 510

LELAND
Harriet 309 389

LEMARR
Elsie-Irene (Allen) *adaaa bbefb* 562
Isaac-Thomas *adaaa bbefb* 562

LENGEL
J. Harvey *adaii bjc* 379
Susan-Rebecca (Biehl) *adaii bjc* 379

LENNON
Gabriel *adaga ba* 217
Rhoda (Woodnancy) *adaga ba* 217

LEONARD
Addie *abbea caaj* 451

LERCH
Amos B. 502
Jessie-Belle (Lincoln) *adahb gbg* 502
John-Harvey-Carlton *adahb gbg* 502
Laura-Carlton (McFarland) 502

LESLIE
Annie-Louise (Brown) *aacdb hfa* 306
James-Edward *aacdb hfa* 306

LETHBRIDGE
Emeline (Lincoln) *aabce cf* 258
Franklin *aabce cfc* 258
Mary (Holbrook) 258
Richard 258
Susan-Fairbanks *aabce cfa* 258
Willard-Fairbanks *aabce cf* 258
Willard-Henry *aabce cfb* 258

LEVERETT
Betsey 247
James *adffe fa* 248
John 4
Lucy (Lincoln) *adffe f* 248
William *adffe f* 248

LEVIS
Elizabeth-Lincoln (Lukens) *adbca ib* 233
John *adbca ib* 233

LEWIS
Alice-Grace *aabce aeb* 528-9
Charlotte 309
David 382
Ebenezer 143
Edward-Lincoln 143
Elizabeth 322
Elizabeth *abaeb e* 87 188
Elizabeth-Curd 482
Elizabeth ([Vickery] Dixon) 79
Francis-Edward 528-9
George 36 79 143 405
George *aabcf b* 143-4
Harriet-McLellan *aabcf bb* 144
Henry 425
James 36 79 143
James-Hawke 86
Jane-Robinson (Thomas) *aabcj c* 267
Jerusha-Lincoln *aabcf be* 144
John *abaeb* 86-7 88 188
John *abaeb c* 87
Joseph 36 79
Letty-Miner *adahf ae* 228
Lothrop *aabcf bc* 144
Lucy 79
Lucy *aacab f* 72
Lydia (Pratt) 86
Mary 267

LEWIS cont'd
Mary (Davis) 143
Mary (Jones) *aabcf bc* 144
Mary (Marrett) *aabcf ba* 144
Mary-Parsons *abaeb a* 87
Mary (Thorla) 405
Mary-Waite *aabcf ae* 405
Mehitable *aabab f* 65
Royal-Lincoln *aabcf ba* 144
Ruth (Lincoln) *aabcf b* 143-4
Sarah *aaf* 33 36-38
Sarah *abaeb b* 87
Sarah-Kimball 518
Sarah-Maria (Penhallow) 528
Sarah (Marsh) 36
Sarah-Peabody *aabcf bf* 144
Stephen-Longfellow 269
Susan *aacbe hb* 425
Susan (Pickett) 425
Susanna 40 86
Susanna *abaeb d* 87
Susanna (Lincoln) *abaeb* 86-7 188
Tabitha 267
Tabitha-Longfellow *aabcf bd* 144

LILLIE
Sarah 310

LIME—Lyme
Isaac 220

LINCOLN
Abbie-Lucy *aabcg dgab* 533
Abbie (Morse) *aafff fc* 185
Abbie-Smith (Patrick) *aabcg dg* 408-9
Abby-Frothingham *aacbe be* 293
Abby-Hope *adffe dfa* 525
Abel *aabad a* 138
Abel *aabad b* 138
Abel-Thomas *adahf d* 229 374-5
Abel-Thomas *adahf ce* 373 505
Abiah (Eels) *adbf* 119-21 137
Abiah-Eels *adbfa d* 237 238
Abigail 153
Abigail *aah* 11 72
Abigail *aahg* 12
Abigail *adcah* 122-3
Abigail *adffa* 37 132
Abigail *aafff j* 185
Abigail *adaae j* 207-8
Abigail *adagb e* 220
Abigail *adagb m* 105 219 222
Abigail *adaae af* 344
Abigail *adaga gj* 361 362 363
Abigail *adagb hf* 367
Abigail (Andrews) *aaib* 12
Abigail (Curtis) *adfb* 131
Abigail-Frances *aabce aea* 401
Abigail H. *adaaf fe* 352
Abigail (Lincoln) *aah* 11 72
Abigail (Mellus) 63
Abigail (Mitchell) *adcak* 242-3
Abigail-Reed (Walker) *aacbe d* 293-4
Abigail-Tower *abbec bd* 322
Abraham *adb* 18 22 43 44 53-9 94 113 119
Abraham *adai* 49 50 53 59 110-2 509
Abraham *adba* 54 55 56 58 59 112-4 115
    116 117
Abraham *adff* 62 122 132-4
Abraham *aacbj* 75 78 169-73
Abraham *adaaa* 43 93 95 100 101 108
    193-204 206 222 324 and note 325 326
    327 335 469
Abraham *adbca* 116 117 118 231-3
Abraham *adffi* 62 134 250
Abraham *adaae i* 205 207 345-7
Abraham *adaaf c* 101 210
Abraham *adaah d* 213 214 215
Abraham *adaga c* 216 217 359-60
Abraham *adaic c* 229
Abraham *adaid g* 230 377

LINCOLN cont'd

Abraham *adbca f* 117 118 232 273 381-2
Abraham *adffe l* 249 397-8
Abraham *adaaa aa* 43 329 459-61
Abraham *adaaa db* 43 94 99 162 180 200 204 223 224 249 275 279 314 324 note 328 337 338 339 340 341 342 345 392 435 464-71 530
Abraham *adaae ah* 343 344 472 473-5
Abraham *aabce adi* 401
Abraham *adaaf acba* 478
Abraham *adaaa dbab* 568
Abraham *adaaf dbad* 575
Abraham-Dickinson *adahb gcd* 502 586-8
Abraham-Jairus *adffi c* 250
Abraham-Lucius *adaae ahca* 571
Abraham-Orne *aacbe l* 166 294 296-7
Abraham-Orne *aacbe le* 296 297
Abraham-Randolph *adaae hi* 345 476
Achsah *aafh* 36 37
Ada B. (——) *adahb bcd* 584
Ada-Etherage *adaaa bbeaa* 608
Ada-Lee *adaaf abc* 477
Ada-Maude (McLaughlin) *adffe cg* 524
Ada-May *adaaa befb* 566
Ada-Tyler *aacbe hab* 424
Adaline F. (Bancroft) *aabhe a* 275-6
Adaline-Sever *aacbc ahh* 421
Addie *adahb dbi* 499
Addie-Kimball *aabcg dca* 407
Addie L. *aacbe haaa* 546
Addie (Long) *abbhc dba* 458
Adelaide *aabhg af* 275 277
Adelaide-Cook (Franklin) *adaid bba* 592
Adelaide-Gertrude (Copithorn) *aacdd dae* 552
Adelbert *aacdb bdd* 431
Adelia-Lane *adaaf acd* 478
Adeline *aacbi m* 168 169 313
Adeline *aacbg cb* 298
Adeline (Lincoln) *aacbi m* 168 169 313
Adeline-Louise (Bodge) *abbhc dc* 459
Adrianna *aabce cbb* 402
Agatha (——) *adaah d* 214 215
Agnes-Catherine *adaaa bbcba* 606
Aida-Golden *aabce aebad* 602
Alameda ([Dougherty] Kennedy) *adaaf dba* 574-5
Albert *aabhg d* 156 277
Albert-Curtis *adaae aba* 344 471 568-9
Albert-Edward *aacdb fcb* 436 549
Albert-Robinson *aacdb fc* 304 434-6
Albert-Robinson *aacdb fcbg* 549
Albert-Sidney *adaaa befg* 566
Albertie-Mae *adaae abad* 568 569
Alexander *aacdc eac* 441 551
Alexander *aacdc eaca* 551
Alexander-Edwards *aacbi a* 168 299
Alexander-Scammell *aabce bc* 255-6 257
Alexander-Scott *adbcf baabc* 613
Alfred 313
Alfred *adcai fc* 391
Alfred *adbcf baa* 512 592-3
Alfred-Gilbert *adaii bb* 378 507-9
Alfred-Hawkes *abbea cacca* 605
Alfred-Stone *abbea cacc* 555 605
Alfred-Whitington *abbec bbb* 454
Alfred-Wiles *adbcf baa* 512 593 613
Alfred-Wiles *adbcf baaba* 613
Alice *aacdb bdc* 431
Alice *adaaa bbef* 562
Alice (Dehaven) *adaii* 230-1
Alice-Ella (Capeheart) *adahf dac* 591
Alice-Foster *aacdb fcbb* 549
Alice-Grace (Lewis) *aabce aeb* 528-9
Alice-Louise *abbhc dbf* 459
Alice-North (Towne) *aacdc ee* 310
Alice-Olive (Murr) *adaaa bbfd* 608-9

LINCOLN cont'd

Alice-Revere *aacdd dea* 313
Alice-Revere *aacbe ldfb* 547
Alice (Rout) *adaga gfe* 490
Alice-Zook (Evans) *adaid abc* 591-2
Allan-Mawson *adaid bbab* 592
Allen 278 313
Allen *abaea* see Allyne
Allen *abbec a* 190 191
Allen *abbec fb* 323 456-7
Allen-Augustus 278
Allyne *abaea* 85 86 185-7
Alma-Chipman *abbea cabga* 604
Alma G *abbea cabf* 553-4
Almira *abbea caa* 450-1
Alpha-Berenice *abbec fbda* 558
Alta (Schanck) *adahb gbd* 586
Altha-May *adaaa bbcl* 560-1
Alvah-Thaxter *aabcd bcb* 399
Amanda *adagb dk* 365
Amanda-Alice (Kline) *adaae aha* 571
Amanda (Collins) 515
Amanda-Emeline *adaaa bbck* 560
Amanda F. *adaah ga* 357
Amanda-Melvina (Pierce) *aacdd dd* 446
Amanda (Ogden) *adbcf be* 512-3
Amanda-Sophrona *aacdb ib* 307
Amanda-Stella *adaaa bbig* 565
Amasa-Lyman *aabcg dg* 264 408-9
Amelia 368
Amelia *adaii ba* 378
Amelia (Howard) *aacbe i* 296
Amelia-Robinson *aacdb gd* 305
Amer-Ogden *adbcf bcd* 513 593-
America-Sanders (Gatewood) *adaah g* 356-7
Amey-Gaskill ([Daniels] [Martin] Norwood) *adffe df* 524-5
Amos *aacbe* 74 75 77 164-6 296
Amos *adfae* 127 245-6
Amos *aacbe h* 166 294-5
Amos *abbea k* 190
Amos *aacbe ha* 295 423-4
Amos A. *aacbe haa* 424 545-6
Amy (Trout) *adagb dh* 493
Ananias 226 note
Andrew *aacbj d* 173
Andrew *aacdb ige* 439
Andrew-Crocker *aacdc fd* 311
Angeline *adaae hg* 345
Angeline (Burton) *adaaa bbb* 558-9
Angie *adaah ele* 483
Angie (Smith) *adaah el* 483
Anjanette (Bailey) *adffe dg* 525
Ann *adaih* 111 112
Ann *adaaf h* 101 see Nancy-Ann
Ann *adaic b* 229
Ann *adbca c* 118 232
Ann *adaga ac* 358
Ann *adaii bh* 379
Ann *adbca aa* 118 380
Ann *aacbc acdda* 604
Ann (Babb) 137
Ann (Boone) *adai* 111-2
Ann-Boone *adaid f* 230
Ann-Eliza *adbcf cc* 383 385
Ann-Eliza ([Taylor] Foy) *adagb fa* 366
Ann-Jane (Hall) *abbea mb* 452-3
Ann-Lucette *aabcf de* 263
Ann-Maria *aabcd ba* 140 141 252
Ann-Maria *aabck fb* 272
Ann-Taliaferro *adaah ea* 354
Ann (Wilkinson) *aacab f* 72
Anna *adaie* 111 112
Anna *adbcc* 114 116 117
Anna *abbea n* 190
Anna *adcai e* 241
Anna *adaah eib* 482

LINCOLN cont'd

Anna *adbcf cab* 514
Anna *adahb dcia* 500
Anna-Albright *adahc aaeb* 588
Anna-Amelia *aacbe lfe* 428
Anna-Amelia *adaii bbd* 508
Anna (Bates) *aabce a* 254-5
Anna-Bates *aabce ac* 255
Anna-Belle *adaae abaa* 569
Anna-Blake *aabcg dgbc* 534
Anna-Frances (Baker) *aacdd ec* 449
Anna (Hodder) 185
Anna-Jackson (Steward) *aacbg ckb* 547
Anna-Louisa *aabcf ah* 261-2
Anna-Louisa (Hemmig) *adaii bb* 507-9
Anna M. (White) *aacdb bd* 431
Anna-Mae (Billette) *aacdc eaa* 441
Anna-Maria (Pellman) *adahc aa* 504
Anna-Mary *adcai fbc* 520
Anna-Matilda *aacbe o* 166
Anna-Phoebe *adbcf bec* 513
Anna R. (Reed) *aabcd bcb* 399
Anna-Rebecca *adahc aag* 504
Anna (Reynolds) *adahf da* 506
Anna-Reynolds *adahf dabb* 590
Anna T *adahb bde* 498
Anna (Wyman) *aabck bdb* 411
Anne *adae* 47 49-52
Anne-Boone *adaid hf* 378
Anne-Devillers *aacbc afa* 419
Anne-Elizabeth *adaga ghab* 582
Anne (Rambo) *adbc* 113 114 116-8
Anne-Warren *aacbc ag* 283
Anne-Warren *aacbc adc* 417
Annette *adffe i* 248-9
Annie *aabhg ed* 278
Annie *adahb gbeb* 586
Annie (Cato) *adaaa bef* 566
Annie-Cottrell *adffe caa* 522
Annie-Eleanora *aabea mbac* 556
Annie-Elizabeth *abbea mi* 321
Annie-Ellen (Bye) *adaaa bbca* 605-6
Annie-Emily (Lindsey) *abbec fdc* 558
Annie-Leaver *aabcg dbf* 406
Annie-Marston *aacbc ahe* 420
Annie-May *aacdb gfe* 438
Annie-Merton (Stanwood) *aabcg dgb* 533-4
Annie-Robinson *aacdb hf* 305 306
Annie-Sarah *adbfa fb* 387
Annie-Shannon (Lard) *adaah gda* 578
Annie-Stubbs *adahf cba* 505
Anslem *adcai f* 241 391
Anslem *adcai ff* 391 520
Apphia-Jordan (Snow) *aabhg e* 277-8
Arabella-May (Whitcomb) *adfae adc* 600
Arnold *aacbc ahc* 420
Arthur *aacbe bc* 292
Arthur *aacdd eb* 314 447-8
Arthur-Earle *aabhg aaac* 536
Arthur-Frederick *aacdb eed* 434
Arthur-Huntington *aacbg ckc* 430
Arthur-Lyman *aabcg dgac* 533
Asa *aabcb* 67
Asa *aabcd a* 6 140 141 167 251-2
Asa-Carl *adbfa fhb* 516
Asa-Liggett *adaae ahaa* 571
Asa S. *adbfa f* 237 238 387-8
Asa S. *adbfa fe* 388
Ashby-Abraham *adaae hfh* 476 572-3
Augusta *aabce cc* 258
Augusta-Caroline (Nearing) *adbfa bd* 514-5
Augusta-Clark *aacbe lfa* 427
Augusta-Eugenie (Prentice) *adffe cd* 523
Augusta-Maria *abbea cada* 555-6
Augustus *adagb le* 368
Augustus-Clark *aacbe lf* 297 427-8

LINCOLN cont'd

Augustus-Clark *aacbe lfba* 547
Austin *adaha b* 223 224
Azariah *adahb g* 225 226 369-70
Azariah-Thomas *adahb ged* 503
Azariah-William *adahb gbc* 502 585-6
Barbara *adaaa ba* 332
Barbara *adaga ghac* 582
Barbara (Kinch) *adbcf* 234
Barnabas 278 313
Bash (Graham) *adaah ebd* 576
Bathsheba (Herring) *adaaa* 193-204 329
Beatrice *adahb bcda* 584
Becky (Pierce) *adfae a* 393-4
Belinda (McDonough) *aacda e* 300
Belle *adaga gdf* 489
Belle *adagb dea* 492
Belle E *adbfa fg* 388
Benjamin 30 34 68 72-3 85 142 146 151 176 242
Benjamin *adaga* 104 105 107 108 216-9
Benjamin *adaga cd* 360
Benjamin *adbca fc* 382 511-2
Benjamin *adaaa bbb* 463 558-9
Benjamin-Clark *aabcf dad* 406
Benjamin-Franklin *adaae ac* 343
Benjamin-Franklin *adaga gh* 361 362 363 491-2 581
Benjamin-Franklin *adagb de* 364 492
Benjamin-Franklin *adaga aab* 486
Benjamin-Franklin *adaga gfa* 490 581
Benjamin-Franklin *adaga gfab* 581
Benjamin-Jones *aacdb eee* 434
Benjamin-Thompson *aacdb ga* 304
Benton *adahf cj* 374
Bernice *adaaa bbfib* 609
Bertha *aacdb iga* 439
Bertha-Adelaide *aacdb bdf* 431
Bertha D (Eaton) *aabcg dea* 408
Bertha-Louise *abbea cabc* 553
Bertha-Louise *abbea cabdc* 604
Bertha-Lovell *adcac bajc* 597
Bertha-May *adaii bbf* 509
Bertram-Francis *abbea caccb* 605
Beryl *adahb gbea* 586
Bessie *aacdd eaa* 447
Bessie (Fisher) *aacdb igc* 551
Bessie-Maude *adaaa bbidh* 610
Bethia *aacba* 31 74 75 76 79 149 152
Bethia (Thaxter) *aacba b* 76 149-51
Bethia-Thaxter *aabcj f* 150
Bethia (Whiton) *adac* 34-5 70
Bethiah 10
Betsey *aabce d* 142
Betsey *aacbi b* 168
Betsey *aacbi j* 168 169
Betsey *abaeg a* 188
Betsey *adcac a* 238
Betsey-Ann *adaae ae* 343-4 568
Betsey (Edwards) *aacbi* 168
Betsey (James) *abaeg* 184-5 187-8
Betsey ([James] Lincoln) *aafff* 184-5
Betsey-Pierce *adfae ac* 394
Betsey (Thompson) *aabcf d* 262-3
Betsey-Viola (Kissinger) *adaga gic* 582
Betsey-Wade *adcai bf* 391
Betsy *abbec j* 190 191
Betsy *adfad e* 245
Betty 127
Betty *aaffe* 36 82
Beza *aabcg* 66 67 146
Beza *aabck h* 146 153 154 274
Beza-Holbrook *aabcg db* 264 406
Birdie V. *adaah ecaa* 480
Blanche-Adeline *aacdd dad* 445
Blanche-Winifred (Wadleigh) *aacbe ldd* 426
Boatner-Chapman *adaah ebbb* 575

LINCOLN cont'd
C. W. *adahc bba* 372
Caleb 66
Caleb *adfd* 62
Caleb *adfg* 61 62-3 124 131
Caleb *adffe* 62 134 246-9 395
Caleb *adaid a* 230 375
Caleb *adffe k* 249
Carl-Clifford *adaga gdae* 580
Carl-Frederick *aabce aebae* 602
Caroline *aabck bi* 271
Caroline *adaah eia* 481-2
Caroline-Alma (Brett) *aacdc gb* 443
Caroline-Amanda *adaae ic* 346-7
Caroline-Augusta *aacdb hd* 305 306
Caroline-Augusta-Elizabeth (Pratt) *aafff cc* 315
Caroline-Frances *abbea caca* 555
Caroline-Franklin (Bates) *abbea cac* 554
Caroline-Hayden *aabcd ac* 251-2
Caroline-Homan *adaae agg* 473
Caroline-Howard *aacbe q* 166
Caroline-Howard *aacbe lb* 294 297
Caroline-Jones *aacdb ea* 303
Caroline-Maria (Barton) *adfae ada* 600
Caroline-Matilda *aabce bh* 257
Caroline-Matilda (Wood) *aacdb ee* 433
Caroline-Parker *aabck fa* 272
Caroline-Taft *adffe cdab* 601
Caroline-Thomas (Homan) *adaae ag* 472-3
Carolyn-Louise (Whipple) *adffe dfb* 601
Carrie *adaaa bbga* 564
Carrie-Abbot *aacbe lff* 428
Carrie-Downs *aabcf acb* 404
Carrie H. (Pierce) *adahc aac* 504
Carrie-Thaxter *aabcj ha* 268
Casner *adaah fa* 215
Catarina *adbcb* 117 231
Catharine *adaah c* 213 215 471
Catharine *adaaa bf* 331
Catharine *adaaa bbfa* 563
Catharine (Barlow) *adaaa b* 330-3
Catherine *aabch e* 148
Catherine *aabcj g* 150-1
Catherine *adbca b* 232 383
Catherine *aacbg cg* 298 299
Catherine *adaga cf* 360
Catherine (Biehl) *adaii be* 510
Catherine (Bright) *adaae a* 343-4
Catherine-Elizabeth *adahc ac* 371
Catherine (Kilby) *abad* 85
Catherine-Kilby-Thaxter *aabcd dh* 253 254
Catherine M. *adaaf dc* 351
Catherine-Wild *aabck bc* 270
Cathleen *aacdd daea* 552
Celeste-Jane (Albright) *adahc aae* 588
Celia-Frances (Smith) *aacdc ea* 441-2
Celia-Helen (Hobbs) *adaae hi* 476
Celia (Hobart) *aabag* 140
Charity-Emma (Lea) *adaaf ac* 348 477-8
Charles *agi* 24 25 26 27
Charles *aabai* 66
Charles *aabck* 66 68 76 80 149 151-4
Charles *aabag b* 140
Charles *aabck b* 152 153 154 268-71
Charles *adbch f* 235 236
Charles *abbec fe* 323
Charles *adagb ld* 368
Charles *aacdb ebc* 432
Charles *aacdb iha* 440
Charles *adaaa bej* 464
Charles *adaaa bbfc* 563
Charles *adaaa befi* 566
Charles-Augustus *aacbi k* 169
Charles-Augustus *aabce ada* 168 169 400
Charles-Benton-Fremont *adaga gaa* 362 488

LINCOLN cont'd
Charles-Beza *aabck baa* 410
Charles-Broaddus *adaae hfi* 476 573
Charles-Cleveland *adbfa bgb* 515
Charles-Cushing *abbea mh* 321 453
Charles-Cushing *adcac baic* 597
Charles-Edmund *adffe dc* 397
Charles-Edward *adffe cg* 396 523-4
Charles-Edward *adaga gfd* 490
Charles-Egbert *adagb fbb* 494
Charles-Eliot *aabcg dea* 408
Charles-Elliot-Ware *aabcd dfc* 254
Charles-Ernest *aacdb ebgc* 548
Charles F. *abbea cabe* 553
Charles-Francis *abbea mhda* 557
Charles-Frederic *aacbc ahd* 420
Charles-Gatewood *adaah ekad* 576
Charles-Harold *aabce abce* 528
Charles-Henry *adaga gdb* 489
Charles-Henry *abbea mbaa* 556
Charles-Herman *adbcf beed* 594
Charles-Hobart *abbec fbd* 457 557-8
Charles-Howard *adaah el* 355 482-3
Charles-Howard *adaah eld* 483
Charles-Jairus *aabce aba* 400 526-7
Charles-James *abbea mbe* 453
Charles-Jennings *adaga agd* 487 579
Charles-Levi *aacbc acbb* 537
Charles-Minot *aabck bdc* 411
Charles-Nathaniel-Minot *aabck ba* 270 274 409-10
Charles-Otis *aacdb fa* 304
Charles-Otis *aacdb ebd* 432-3
Charles-Parker *aacdc gc* 313
Charles-Prentiss *adaaa abf* 462
Charles-Princeton *adaah eme* 485
Charles-Rapp *adfad bab* 521 599
Charles-Russell *adbfa fh* 388 515-6
Charles-Sanford *adcai ffe* 520
Charles-Shippen *adahf da* 375 506
Charles-Shippen *adahf dabd* 590
Charles-Sprague *aacbg cca* 429
Charles-Stuart-Fessenden *adcac dac* 518 597-8
Charles-Wesley *adaaa begb* 566
Charles-White *adffe la* 397
Charles-William *aacdc ecae* 552
Charles-Willis *aacdb igf* 439
Charlotte 168
Charlotte *aacbg a* 167 251-2 298
Charlotte *aacbj e* 172 173
Charlotte *aacdc ecb* 442
Charlotte *adahb dbk* 499
Charlotte-Ann-Lewis (French) *aacdc e* 309-10
Charlotte-Cushing *adaga* 141 251
Charlotte-Lewis *aacdc ed* 310
Charlotte (Lincoln) *aacbg a* 167 251-2 298
Charlotte-Mabel *adaaa bbei* 562
Charlotte-Otis *adcai bb* 390
Charlotte-Wells (Brevoort) *adfad bab* 599
Chastine *aacbg ca* 298
Chastine (Hartwell) *aacbg c* 297-9
Chester-Franklin *abbea cabe* 553
Chloe *aaffg* 36 82-3
Chloe *adcal* 122 123 244-5
Chloe *adcak e* 243
Chloe *adfad d* 245
Chloe (Lincoln) *adcal* 123 244-5
Chloe ([Whiton] Fearing) *aabad* 138
Christine-Lee *adaah emca* 577
Christopher *aacdf* 80
Christopher *abaeg* 86 89 184 187-8
Claiborne-Bird *adaah gf* 357
Claire *adaae hfacc* 611
Clara *adaid ha* 378

LINCOLN cont'd

Clara *adaga gde* 487
Clara-Amanda (Lothrop) *aacbg ck* 430-1
Clara-Eudora *aacdb icc* 439
Clara-Francis *adcai bgb* 519
Clara-Gilbert *adbcf bei* 513
Clara-Ida (Parker) *aacbc ahg* 544
Clara-Lothrop *aacbg ckf* 298 430-1
Clara-Louise (Wyman) *aabcg dbd* 533
Clara (Paul) *adaaf d* 349-51
Clara-Wentworth (Makepeace) *aabce abc* 527-8
Clarence-Amer *adbcf beda* 593
Clarence-Arthur *aabcg dbca* 532
Clarence-Blanchard *adaaa bbidb* 610
Clarence-Frederick *aabce aebc* 529 602-3
Clarence-Henry *adffe df* 397 524-5
Clarissa-Emily (Greenwood) *adffe cb* 522-3
Clarissa-Nodding *aacdb ii* 308
Clement-Robert *adahb dcga* 585
Clementina (Hibbard) *aacdb ih* 440
Clifford *adaga agdb* 579
Clifford-Franklin *adaid bbaa* 592
Clifford-Mitchell *adaaa bbcfb* 607
Cora-Alice (Tissue) *adaga gfa* 490 581
Cora (Breeden) *adaaa bbcg* 607
Cordelia-Etta (Makepeace) *aabce abc* 527-8
Cornelia *adahf ci* 374
Cotton *aabcf d* 144 262-3
Cullen-Melone *adaah ebb* 480 575
Cummings *adcab* 122
Cummings *adcam* 122 123
Cummings *adfad c* 245
Cushing *aabhe* 70 155-6 275
Cyrus S. *aacda ec* 301
Daisy-Maude *adaaa bbih* 565
Daisy-May *adagb fbe* 494
Dallas-Abraham *adaaa bbifa* 611
Damietta-Clapp *aabcg dd* 264
Damietta-Dennison (Clapp) *aabcg d* 263-4
Daniel 1 5 14 42 66 67 177 185 311 451
Daniel *ab* 3 4 7 12 13-5 17
Daniel *abad* 13 38 39 84-6 89
Daniel *abbea a* 189
Daniel-Bertie *adbfa bga* 515
Daniel-Boone *adagb ha* 367
Daniel-Bray *abbhc h* 193
Daniel-Lewis *adahb faea* 585
Daniel-Savage *adbfa b* 238 385-6
Daniel-Savage *adbfa bg* 386 515
Daniel W. *aafff fb* 185
Daniel-Waldo *aacbc b* 162-3
Daniel-Waldo *aacbc ad* 283 416-7
Daniel-Waldo *aacbc addd* 543
Daniel-Webster *adcac bac* 516 595-6
David 10 11 72 242 254 423
David *adaae a* 98 206 342-4
David *adaah g* 213 215 356-7
David *adaae hh* 345
David *adagb lb* 368
David-Francis *aacdc ga* 312-3
David-Franklin *adaae abf* 472
David-Hollis *adahb gbe* 502 586
David-Jones *adaid h* 230 377-8
David-Jones *adagb dd* 364
David-Pratt *aabce abc* 400 527-8
David-Roosevelt *aabce abci* 528
Davis *adaha c* 223 224
Davis Jenkins *abbea mc* 320
Deborah *aaa* 10 34
Deborah *aabb* 29 30 31 67 76 77
Deborah *adab* 50 109
Deborah *aabab* 64 65
Deborah *adagf* (?) 109
Deborah *aabad d* 138-9

LINCOLN cont'd

Deborah *adcai ba* 390
Deborah-Ann (Denton) *adaaa bbe* 561-2
Deborah (Denton) *adaaa bbe* 561-2
Deborah (Hersey) *aa* 9 10
Deborah-Leavitt *aabcd bb* 140 141 252
Deborah (Lincoln) *aaa* 10
Deborah-Otis (Wade) *adcai b* 390
Deborah (Revere) *aacbe* 165-6
Deborah-Revere *aacbe e* 166
Deborah-Reynolds (Foster) *aacdb fc* 436
Deborah (Souther) *aabcd b* 140 252
Deborah ([Thaxter] Thaxter) *aacba c* 76 80 152-3
Della-Frances *adaga gdag* 580
Della-Mae (Coil) *adahb fae* 585
Deloras-Adeline *adaaa bbifb* 611
Diadama (Briggs) *adagb f* 365-6
Diana-McKelva *adaae ahb* 474
Dickinson *adahb gc* 370 502
Dimple-Mae *adaaa bbidd* 610
Dolly (Epstein) *adahb bcd* 584
Donald *adahf daba* 590
Donald-Jason *aabcj hbaa* 534
Donald-Morton *aacdb fcdb* 549
Doniphan-Rice *adaah gdd* 485
Dora-Dell *adagb flf* 494
Dorcas *adaae e* 206-7
Dorcas *adaae ad* 343
Dorcas *adaae ha* 344
Dorcas-Lavina *adaae ib* 346
Dorcas (Robinson) *adaae* 205-8
Dorcas-Sarah *adaae ie* 347
Dorcas-Sarah-Emeline (Maupin) *adaae iac* 346 475
Dorothy *aacbc addf* 539 544
Dorothy *aacdb fcda* 550
Dorothy *adbcf baabg* 613
Dorothy-Davis *abbea mhca* 557
Dorothy-Evangeline *aabce aebaa* 602
Dorothy-Frances *aacdb efba* 549
Dorothy-Hardy (Richardson) *aacbc adde* 543-4
Dorothy-Louise *adcac baiba* 614
Dorothy-Maie *aacdb ebgb* 548
Dorothy-Pitkin *aacdc geb* 443 444
Drury-Harris *adaah ebba* 575
Edgar C. *adaga aae* 486
Edgar-Thomas *adaaa bbii* 566
Edith *aabhg ee* 278
Edith *adagb deb* 492
Edith (Anderson) *adaaa bbid* 610
Edith-Buckingham (Morse) *aacbe dad* 545
Edith-Estelle *abbea mha* 453
Edith-Hattie *abbhc dbb* 458
Edith-Lillian *aabce aebb* 528-9
Edith-Marian *adaid bbad* 592
Edith-May *aacdb ebad* 548
Edith-Myrtle *adaga gica* 582
Edith-Olivia *adahb fad* 501
Edmund-Sabine *aacdb ebg* 433 548
Edna-Alice *adagb fbc* 494
Edna-Earl (Moreland) *adaae agcd* 570
Edna-Phyllis *aabhg dbaa* 536
Edward 1 2 4 5 6 14
Edward *adaah eh* 355
Edward *adagb dl* 365
Edward *adaid ca* 377
Edward *adaah ecd* 481
Edward *adaga bbfi* 563 609
Edward-Baker *adaaa dbb* 471
Edward-Blake *aacbc acde* 538
Edward-Buck *adbfa bh* 386
Edward G. *adbfa bdg* 515
Edward-Gilpin *adaga gf* 361 362 489-91
Edward-Hall *abbea mba* 452 556

LINCOLN cont'd

Edward-Henry *adbcf baabb* 613
Edward-Henry *adbcf baabd* 613
Edward-Leland *abbea mbda* 556
Edward-Louis *aabck bdb* 411
Edward-Madison *adaga gfac* 581
Edward-Maynard *abbec fdc* 458 558
Edward-Return *adaae agce* 570
Edward-Reynold *abbhc dbe* 458
Edward-Rose *adaga gda* 489 580-1
Edward-Ross *aabcj cb* 267
Edward-Turner *abbce cdb* 403 530-1
Edward-Winslow *aacbc ah* 283 418 419-21
Edward-Winslow *aacbc ahga* 544
Edwin *aabhg da* 277
Edwin-Litchfield *adcai ffc* 520
Edwin-Saville *aabcg dba* 406 531-2
Edwina *adaah eea* 481
Edwina-Lewis (Seaverns) *abbea cabg* 604
Effie-Amelia-Florence *adaae agf* 473
Effie-Florence *abbec bia* 455
Effie-Julia (Garwood) *adahf dae* 591
Effie (Martin) *adaaf dbc* 575
Effie-Pearl *adaaa befc* 566
Elbridge-Bangs *aabck bab* 410 534-5
Eleanor (Ames) *aacdc eac* 551
Eleanor-Fessenden *adcac dacc* 598
Eleanor-Louise *aabcg dbdc* 533
Eleanor M. (Gove) *aacdb b* 301-2
Eleazer *adffj* 134
Electa-Nobles *adfad bc* 245 393
Elias-Hudson *adaga gfe* 490
Elijah 15
Elijah-Franklin *abbea cabi* 554 605
Elisha *aaf* 11 35-8 91 184
Elisha *aafd* 36 37
Elisha *aafe* 37
Elisha *aafff* 36 43 82 184-5 188
Elisha *aafff c* 184 314-6
Elisha L *aafff cc* 315
Eliza *aabcg a* 146
Eliza *aabck d* 153 154 274
Eliza *adffe e* 248
Eliza *aabcj ca.* 267
Eliza *adbcf bd* 232 383-4
Eliza (——) *adbcf a* 382-3
Eliza (——) *adbch f* 236
Eliza-Ann (Livingston) *abbec bi* 455
Eliza-Beal *aabcf h* 145-6
Eliza (Fogg) *aabcj c* 267
Eliza (Fraser) *adcai bga* 598
Eliza-Hall (Tower) *abbea md* 320
Eliza (Hyler) Holbrook *aabce b* 255-6
Eliza-Jackson (Copeland) *adfad ba* 521
Eliza-James *abbea caf* 451
Eliza-Langdon (Frothingham) *aacbe b* 292-3
Eliza M. *adbfa bc* 385 386
Eliza-Maria *aacbe m* 166
Eliza (Moore) *adahb f* 369
Eliza (Murry) *aacbe lfba* 547
Eliza-Paddleford *aacbc aha* 420
Eliza (Pratt) 185
Eliza (Robertson) *adbca d* 380-1
Eliza-Swift (Gardner) *aacdb efb* 549
Elizabeth 30 77
Elizabeth *ab* 13-5
Elizabeth *abc* 13-4 41
Elizabeth *ade* 18 22
Elizabeth *agf* 26
Elizabeth *aahc* 12
Elizabeth *abab* 38
Elizabeth *abbb* 14 39 41 88
Elizabeth *adfi* 63
Elizabeth *adahg* 110
Elizabeth *adfab* 63 127 189
Elizabeth *aacdb c* 179-80

LINCOLN cont'd

Elizabeth *abbea j* 189
Elizabeth *adaae k* 208
Elizabeth *adaah a* 215
Elizabeth *adaga h* 218
Elizabeth *adahb a* 226
Elizabeth *adbca h* 117 231 233
Elizabeth *aacdb bc* 301 302
Elizabeth *adaaa ad* 329
Elizabeth *adaaa bc* 332 561
Elizabeth *adaga ab* 358
Elizabeth *adaga cb* 359
Elizabeth *adaga ge* 361 362-3
Elizabeth *adahb da* 369
Elizabeth *adahb gd* 370
Elizabeth *adahf cd* 373
Elizabeth *adaid aa* 375
Elizabeth *adaid be* 376
Elizabeth *adaid cc* 377
Elizabeth *adaid hg* 378
Elizabeth *adaii bd* 378-9
Elizabeth *adbca da* 380-1
Elizabeth *adbca fb* 381-2
Elizabeth *adbcf ce* 383 385
Elizabeth *adbch bc* 118 236
Elizabeth *adaaa abb* 462
Elizabeth *adaaa bee* 464
Elizabeth *aabcf aeab* 531
Elizabeth *adaii bbbf* 592
Elizabeth *adbcf baabh* 613
Elizabeth (——) 127
Elizabeth (——) *aacbc ahj* 421
Elizabeth [Agner] Whartenby) *adahb dce* 499
Elizabeth (Alderson) *adaga gfd* 490
Elizabeth-Ann *adahb bcb* 496-7
Elizabeth (Beal) *aaic* 12
Elizabeth-Beal *aabce bgb* 402
Elizabeth (Casner) *adaah* 97 213-5 471
Elizabeth (Coffman) *adaah ca* 215 471-2
Elizabeth-Cushing *aabcd dd* 253-4
Elizabeth (Davis) *adah* 109-10
Elizabeth (Dickinson) *adahf* 225 228-9
Elizabeth (Doty) *adaga agd* 579
Elizabeth (DuRoss) *adahb b* 368
Elizabeth (Erb) *adahb bc* 496-7
Elizabeth-Esther *adbfa bdfa* 595
Elizabeth (Fillebrown) *aabce c* 257-8
Elizabeth-Fillebrown *aabce ca* 258
Elizabeth-Frothingham *aacbe bb* 292
Elizabeth-Gertrude *adaae abac* 569
Elizabeth (Haines) *adahf ce* 505
Elizabeth (Hawke) 10
Elizabeth-Hopkins *aabcf ad* 261
Elizabeth (Hupp) *adaaa bbd* 561
Elizabeth-Hutchinson *adahf ccac* 589
Elizabeth-Jacobs (Clarke) *aacdb fc* 436
Elizabeth (Jones) *adaid* 230
Elizabeth-Jones *adaid ga* 377
Elizabeth (Kay) *adahb gc* 502
Elizabeth-Lewis *aafff h* 185
Elizabeth (Lincoln) *ab* 13-5
Elizabeth (Lincoln) *adfab* 63 127 189-90
Elizabeth-Lincoln (Cushing) *aacdc gf* 444
Elizabeth (Lovett) *adahb dc* 499
Elizabeth M. (Edwards) *aabcf gg* 145
Elizabeth-Maria *aacdb fca* 436
Elizabeth-Marian (Gulick) *abbhc dca* 459
Elizabeth (Mudd) *adaaa aa* 459-61
Elizabeth (Neville) *abbec be* 454
Elizabeth (Noble) *adbcf ca* 514
Elizabeth (Norton) *aahf* 12
Elizabeth (Oaves) *adaga* 216-9 361
Elizabeth (Phipps) *adbcf aa* 382-3
Elizabeth (Revere) *aacbe* 165-6
Elizabeth (Richards) *adahf cb* 505
Elizabeth (Robbins) *adffe* 247 248-9

LINCOLN cont'd
Elizabeth (Ruth) *adaii bbb* 592
Elizabeth-Scammell *aabce ba* 255 256-7
Elizabeth (Severance) *adfad ba* 521
Elizabeth (Shrum) *adbca* 118 231-3
Elizabeth (Stoddard) *adcai b* 390-1
Elizabeth T. *adaah gb* 357
Elizabeth-Theresa *adaae agd* 473
Elizabeth (Thompson) *aacdb* 176-81
Elizabeth (Trumbull) *aacbc ac* 414-5
Elizabeth-Trumbull *aacbc acdb* 538
Elizabeth-Waterhouse *aabcd dfa* 254
Elizabeth (Whitcomb) *aaff* 36 80-4 91
Ella *adbfa ed* 386
Ella A. *aabce ade* 401
Ella B. *adaah ebc* 480
Ella-Frances (Ramsdell) *aabcg dbc* 532
Ella-Lee (Long) *adaae ahd* 474
Ella-Lightburn (Parker) *adaah gdb* 578
Ella (McClernan) *adagb dje* 583
Ellen *aabhg ab* 276
Ellen *aafff gd* 317
Ellen *adaaa aag* 460 461
Ellen-Augusta *aafff gg* 318
Ellen-Augusta *aabck bda* 411
Ellen B. (Hayden) *aacdd ea* 447
Ellen-Clark *adagb djed* 583
Ellen-Deane (Simonds) *aabce cd* 403
Ellen (Dyer) *aabcj cb* 267
Ellen-Elizabeth *adahb dcda* 584
Ellen-Elizabeth-Longfellow (Fessenden)
  adcac da 518
Ellen-Harriet (Carlson) *abbea cabi* 605
Ellen-Harriet (Johanson) *abbea cabi* 605
Ellen (Kennedy) *adagb dh* 493
Ellen-Maria *adcai fh* 391
Ellen-Maria *aacdb bda* 431
Ellen-Maria *abbea cai* 452
Ellen-Mehitable (Jones) *aacdb fcb* 549
Ellen B. (Sykes) *adaah ek* 482
Ellen (Spencer) *adahb dcd* 584
Ellen-Theresa (McKenna) *aabcg dbcb*
  532
Elliott-Curtis *aacdd deb* 313
Elmer-Ellsworth *aabce cdbd* 531
Elmer-Ray *adaga gdab* 580
Elmira-Taylor (Melone) *adaah eb* 480
Elsie *aacdc ead* 441-2
Elsie-Minnie (French) *aabcf acg* 404
Elvira-Kingsley *aacdb ia* 307
Elwyn-Russell *adahb gbcc* 586
Emelia-Carlson (Ahlberg) *aacdb eeb* 433
Emeline *aabce cf* 258
Emeline *aacbg cf* 298 299
Emeline E. (Bacon) *aafff cb* 315
Emeline (Hall) *aacbe da* 423
Emelyn-Irwin (Taft) *adffe cda* 601
Emily *adahb gga* 370
Emily-Bean *adcai fa* 391
Emily-Burling (Garrigues) *adaid hc* 507
Emily-Caroline *aacbe da* 423
Emily-Caroline *aacbe dabe* 545
Emily-Caroline (Lincoln) *aacbe da* 423
Emily-Rolfe (Holbrook) *aacdb eba* 547-8
Emily-Susan *adaaa abd* 462
Emily-Virginia (Mawson) *adaid bb* 507
Emma *adahb dbj* 499
Emma-Bicknell *adffe cc* 396
Emma-Catherine (Hupp) *adaae agi* 570
Emma-Cushman *aabch dd* 148 266
Emma-Eliza *adaga aag* 486-7
Emma-Frances *adahb bcc* 497
Emma-Gerard (Lyle) *adaah eka* 576
Emma-Hamlin (Torrey) *aabcg de* 407-8
Emma-Jane (Spicer) *adcai ff* 520
Emma-Jane (Williams) *aacbe lf* 427
Emma-Louisa *adahb fac* 500
Emma-Souther *aabcd bcc* 399-400

LINCOLN cont'd
Enfield (Stogdale) *adaah emc* 577
Enoch *aacb* 10 32 33 35 65 72-8 79 89
  176
Enoch *aacbb* 75 76
Enoch *aacbc e* 163 287-9
Ephraim 66 185
Erastus-Churchill 241
Ernest-Erdine *adaae agca* 569-70
Ernest-Francis *abbec fdcd* 558
Ernest-Wilbur *aacdd de* 313
Ernest-William *adahb gcdb* 588
Err-Ralston *adagb he* 367
Esther *aabce abcf* 528
Esther-Eliza (Bates) *adfae ad* 394 521-2
Esther (Hilton) *adba* 114
Esther-Nora *adaii bcd* 509
Ethel *aacbg chb* 298 430
Ethel *aacdb igba* 551
Ethel *adaaa bbeg* 562
Ethel-Agnes (Wentworth) *abbhc dbe* 458
Ethel-Forester *aabcg dbad* 532
Ethel-May *aacdc ecab* 552
Etta-Bearl *adaga gdaf* 580
Etta-Belle (Franks) *adaga gda* 580-1
Etta-Harriet *aabce abcg* 528
Etta-Lyman *aabcg dbe* 406
Ettie-Frances *adahb fab* 500
Ettie-Frances *adaaa befa* 566
Eugenia-Bryant (Outlaw) *adaaf ace* 573-
  4
Eugenia L. (Barbour) *aabcg dc* 407
Eunice *aaffa* 36 80
Eunice *abbhf* 92
Eunice-Adaline *adaae agcf* 570
Eunice-Eliza *adbca dca* 511
Eunice (Lincoln) *aaffa* 80 91-2
Eunice R. (Swett) *aacdb h* 305-6
Eunice-Viola *aabce cdbb* 531
Eva *adaaa bbbh* 559
Eva-Gwendoline *adaaa bbfea* 609
Eva-Malissa *adahb gca* 502
Eva-May (Mullen) *adaaa bbfi* 609
Eva (Mohring) *adahb dci* 500
Eva-Orilla *adahb geb* 503
Eva-Richards *aacdb eg* 303
Evalina-Barry *aabck fd* 273 274
Evalina-Barry (Lincoln) *aabck fd* 273
  274
Evalyn-Mae *adaaa bbcfd* 607
Eve-Marie *adaaa bbeab* 608
Evert-Wendell *aacbe dada* 545
Ezekiel *aaff* 36 37 80-4 91
Ezekiel *aabch* 66 67 146 147-8 259
Ezekiel *aabce c* 142 184 257-8
Ezekiel *aabch d* 148 264-6
Ezekiel *aacdb i* 177 180 306-8
Ezekiel *aafff a* 80 184
Ezekiel *aafff i* 185
Ezekiel *aafff gc* 317
Ezekiel *abbea cah* 450 452 552 553 554
Ezekiel-Wallis *abbec bl* 323 455-6
Ezra *aacbg* 74 75 77 167 251
Ezra *aacbg c* 167 297-9
Ezra *aacbg cc* 298 428-9
Ezra *aacbg cke* 298 430
Fannie *aacda g* 175
Fannie (Bell) *aacdb ebd* 432-3
Fannie-Biddle *abbhc dbd* 458
Fannie-Esther *adfae adab* 600
Fannie-Forester *aabcg dbb* 406
Fannie-Webster *adcac bacb* 596
Fanny *adaah ed* 354-5
Fanny (Chandler) *aacbc add* 541-4
Fanny-Clark *aabcf dab* 262 406
Fanny-Elizabeth *adaae abd* 472
Fanny-Ellen *abbec bga* 455
Fanny (Kilby) *adcai* 240-1

LINCOLN cont'd
Fanny-Kilby *adcai fe* 391
Fanny-Kilby *adcai bge* 519
Fanny-Mitchell *aacdc eb* 309
Fanny (Young) *adbcf beb* 593
Felix-Zollicoffer *adaaf aba* 477
Fern-Bell *adaaa bbcac a* 615
Flora-Dell (Mitchell) *adaaa bbcf* 607
Flora-Estella (Hayes) *abbea mh* 453
Flora-Page *aacdd daa* 445
Florence *aacbe daba* 545
Florence-Alberta (Bartlett) *aabce abca* 602
Florence-Bates *adcac bajb* 597
Florence-Cornelia *adffe dga* 525
Florence-Eva (Crane) *aacdb fcd* 550
Florence-Hayes *abbea mhb* 453
Florence-Lillian *adaae hfae* 572
Florence-Mary *adaaa bbfh* 563
Florence-May *aabce aecc* 529
Florilla (Buck) *adbfa b* 385-6
Floyd *adaah ela* 483
Frances *aacde* 79-80
Frances *aabaa b* 135 136-7
Frances *aacdb d* 180
Frances *aacdc a* 182
Frances *aabhg dbb* 413-4
Frances *adahb dbg* 499
Frances *aabcg dgca* 534
Frances-Ann (Brown) *adbca fc* 511-2
Frances (Day) *adaaa ab* 461-2
Frances-Ellen (Coney) *abbec bg* 454-5
Frances-Eloise *adagb fba* 494
Frances-Fiske (Merrick) *aacbc ad* 416-7
Frances-Gordon (Currier) *aabhg d* 277
Frances (Jones) *aaca* 64-5 71
Frances (Jones) *aacbc acdd* 71 604
Frances ([Jones] Lincoln) *aaba* 64-5
Frances-Josselyn *aacbe lc* 297
Frances-Katharine *adaah ge* 357
Frances-Louisa (Parr) *adagb fb* 494
Frances-Louisa (Smith) *abbec bla* 455-6
Frances-Maud (Monroe) *aacdb ebg* 548
Frances-Merrick *aacbc ada* 417
Frances (Nickerson) *adaga agf* 579
Frances-Revere *aacbe k* 166
Francina *aacdb igca* 551
Francina-Knight *adahf cg* 373-4
Francina (Reynolds) *adahf c* 372-4
Francis *abbe* 39 42 89-91 121 238
Francis *aacbe b* 166 291-3 294
Francis *adcac b* 238 388
Francis *aacbe ba* 292
Francis *adcac bab* 516
Francis-Henry *aacdd ec* 314 448
Francis-Henry *aabce bga* 402
Francis-Henry *aacdd eca* 449
Francis-Herbert *adffe cab* 522
Francis-Mayhew *abbea e* 189
Francis-Mayhew *abbea ca* 319 450-2
Francis-Mayhew *abbea cac* 450 451 552 554-5
Francis-Stone *adffe ca* 396 522
Frank *aabhg ec* 278
Frank-Abraham *adaaa bbfg* 563
Frank-Alvin *adahb dcd* 499 584
Frank-Antonio *aabce cdab* 530
Frank-Boynton *adffe cgb* 524
Frank-Buckingham *adaah gdbc* 578
Frank-Fitzhugh *adaae abab* 569
Frank-Louis *aacbe lda* 426
Frank-Louis *aacbe ldfa* 547
Frank-Thorla *aabcf aeb* 405
Franklin-Jones *aacdb gb* 304
Franklin-Philbrook *aacdb efb* 434 549
Fred E *aabck bfd* 412
Fred-Eugene *aabcd bcdd* 526
Fred-Jerome *abbea mhc* 453 556-7

LINCOLN cont'd
Fred-Royal *aabcf acg* 404
Frederic *aabce aeb* 401 528-9
Frederic-Ernest *adaaa bbcac* 606 614-5
Frederic-Fuller *adcai fbb* 520
Frederic-Revere *aacbe la* 296 297
Frederic-Revere *aacbe lfb* 427 547
Frederic-Walker *aacbe i* 166 168 294 295-6
Frederic-Walker *aacbe da* 294 421-3
Frederic-Walker *aacbe dab* 296 423 544-5
Frederic-Walker *aacbe dabb* 545
Frederick *aabce* 66 67 141-2 184
Frederick *aabce b* 142 255-7
Frederick *aacdb ebf* 433
Frederick-Albert *adaaf acf* 478 574
Frederick-Edwin *aabhg dba* 413 536
Frederick-Ernest *aabce aebba* 528
Frederick-Herbert *abbhc dba* 458
Frederick-Lewis *aafff gh* 316 318 449
Frederick-Oliver *aabce bb* 257
Galen *adfc* 62
Galen *adfaa* 127 243
Galen *adfaa a* 244
Gatewood-Saunders *adaah emc* 485 576-7
Geneva *adaaa bbcgb a* 615
George *abbhd* 91 92
George *adcbe* 125
George *adcbi* 125
George *aacbi e* 168
George *adaah e* 213 214 215 353-6
George *adbcf b* 118 234 382 383-4
George *aacbc af* 283 417-9
George *adagb lf* 368
George *adbcf bg* 384
George *adaha eca* 480
George-Albert *aacdb eea* 433 548-9
George-Augustus *aacbe lfd* 428
George-Bronson *aabcg de* 264 407-8
George-Bronson *aabcg dec* 408
George-Chandler *aacbc adde* 543-4
George-Cook *aabcf gg* 145
George-Cummings *adfae adc* 522 600
George-Eckert *adahb bbh* 496 584
George-Edmands *aabce cda* 403 529-30
George-Edward *aabce adb* 401
George-Frederick-Handel *aabce bg* 256 257 401-2
George-Gibbins *aabce bi* 257
George-Gifford *aabcf acf* 404
George-Henry *abbhc dc* 324 459
George-Henry *adffe cb* 247 396 522-3
George-Henry *aabcd bcd* 400 526
George-Henry *adbcf beb* 513 593
George-Henry *adcac bai* 517 596-7
George-Henry *adbcf bebb* 593
George-Herbert *aacdb ebb* 432
George-Jones *adaid bb* 376 507
George-Jones *adaid hd* 378
George-Jones *adaid bba* 507 592
George-Jones *adaid bbac* 592
George-Lewis *adahb bca* 496
George-Lowell *aacdb bdb* 431
George-Luther *abbhc dca* 459
George-Lyle *adaah ekab* 576
George-Lyman *aabcg dbd* 406 532-3
George-Martin *abbea mbd* 453 556
George-Morton *adaah eka* 482 576
George-Morton *adcai fba* 520 598-9
George-Morton *adcai fbaa* 599
George-Otis *aacdb eb* 303 432-3
George-Peter *aabce adg* 401
George-Pottle *aacdb ih* 307 308 440
George-Reynolds *adahf daea* 591
George-Russell *aabch de* 148 266
George-Ruth *adaii bbbe* 592
George-Thomas *adaah ek* 355 482
George-Thomas *adaae hfc* 475

LINCOLN cont'd
George-Thomas *adaaa bbda* 561
George-Trumbull *aacbc acc* 415
George-Vashtine *adahb bb* 368 495-6
George W. *aacbe haab* 546
George-Washington *adahf dd* 375
George-Washington *adaga gie* 492
George-Washington *adahb dcb* 499
George-Washington *adahf dae* 506 591
George-Washington *adaaa bbbe* 559
George-Washington-Henry *adbcf beef* 594
George-William *aabcf aea* 405 531
George-Winslow *abbea mbab* 556
Georgia *adaah eba* 480
Georgianna-Devillers *aacbc afa* 419
German *adahb h* 226
German-Dickenson *adahb bd* 368 497-8
Gertrude-Abby (Berry) *aacdb efc* 434
Gertrude (Reed) *adahc aaa* 588
Gladys-Adelia *aabce aecb* 529
Gladys-Maie *aabcd bcdc* 526
Gladys-Victoria *aacdb eeaa* 549
Glen-Washington *adaaa bbeae* 608
Gordon-Pfeiffer *adaaa bbgba* 610
Gorham *aabcd d* 140 141 252-4
Gorham-Edgar *aacdb igb* 439 551
Gorham-Prentice *aabcd dc* 253
Grace *aafa* 90 132
Grace *adaaa bbfda* 609
Grace-Ann *adbca dcb* 511
Grace-Caroline *aacdb efa* 434
Grace-Isabel *aabhg aaab* 536
Grace-May *adahb gcda* 587
Grace-May (Hawkins) *aacdc eca* 552
Grace ([Stockbridge] Thaxter) *aab* 28-31
Graham-Cullen *adaah ebda* 576
Grant *adahb dbh* 499
Grover-James *adaaa befe* 566
Gussie-Lou *adaaf dbac* 575
Guy-Alvin-Theodore *abbec bea* 454
Hannah (——) *adf* 61
Hannah *aafc* 37
Hannah *aafj* 36 37 38
Hannah *adac* 47 50 51
Hannah *adaab* 95 98 100 101
Hannah *adagd* 108 223
Hannah *adbfc* 120 121
Hannah *adffb* 133 320
Hannah *aabcd f* 140 141
Hannah *adaae g* 207
Hannah *adaaf b* 101
Hannah *adaah h* 213 215
Hannah *adaga f* 218
Hannah *adagb g* 219 220-1
Hannah *aabcd ad* 141 252
Hannah *adaga ce* 360
Hannah *abbea cae* 189 451
Hannah-Amelia *aacbe lg* 297
Hannah-Ann (Haymaker) *adagb dj* 493
Hannah (Clapp) *adcai f* 391
Hannah E. ([——] Norwood) *aacdb i* 307
Hannah-Elizabeth (Johnson) *adahb fa* 500-1
Hannah-Elvina (Kendig) *adahb bbi* 583
Hannah-Farrar-Jewett (Clark) *aabcf da* 405-6
Hannah (Hobbs) *adcak b* 391-2
Hannah-Jane *adfae af* 394
Hannah-Jane ([Taylor] Wiser) *adbcf beb* 593
Hannah (Jones) *adaid b* 376
Hannah (Jones) *adaig b* 112 364-5
Hannah M. *adbfa bb* 386
Hannah-Manson *adffi b* 250
Hannah-Margaret *adagb djee* 583
Hannah-Maria (Sears) *aabhg aa* 413
Hannah-Mary *adahc aad* 504
Hannah-Mehitabel (Brewer) *aabcf ac* 404

LINCOLN cont'd
Hannah-Pratt (Dunbar) *aabce ae* 401
Hannah-Prentiss (Perry) *adffe d* 396
Hannah (Ritter) *adaii bc* 509-10
Hannah (Salter) *ada* 44-53 100
Hannah-Samuels *adaid e* 230
Hannah-Sprague (Wales) *aacbe l* 294 296-7
Hannah (VanBuskirk) *adahc a* 371
Hannah-Young (Stoner) *adaii bf* 510-1
Hannaniah *adaha* 108 110 194 222
Harold-George *aabcd bcdb* 526
Harold-Thomas *adahb gbcb* 586 612
Harold-Wilbur *aabhg aaad* 536
Harriet *aabcj e* 150
Harriet *aacbj c* 172 173
Harriet *aacda h* 175
Harriet *aabck gb* 274
Harriet-Abbot *aacbe daa* 423
Harriet-Amelia *aacdb bdj* 432
Harriet-Ann (Elliott) *adaaa bbi* 564-6
Harriet-Ann (Zell) *adbca dc* 511
Harriet-Brayton (Nichols) *aacbc adde* 543
Harriet-Clementina *aabck bg* 270
Harriet-Cook (Fithian) *adbcf bee* 594
Harriet-DeLucy *adaah gg* 357
Harriet-Eveline *adaaa bbcj* 560
Harriet (Flenniken) *adaga agc* 487
Harriet-Holbrook (Nickerson) *abbec fdca* 558
Harriet-Joy *abaeg b* 188
Harriet (Keller) *adagb dd* 364
Harriet (McLellan) *aabcf a* 260-2
Harriet-McLellan *aabcf ab* 261
Harriet-Maria *aacbe lfc* 427-8
Harriet-Maria *adcac bafa* 596
Harriet-Maria ([White] Bean) *aacbe lf* 427-8
Harriet-Moody *aacbe db* 294 297
Harriet-Priscilla *aabce abb* 400
Harriet-Priscilla *abbec fdcc* 558
Harriet (Robie) *aabck g* 149 273 274
Harriet (Tufts) *abbec fd* 457-8
Harriot *aabhc e* 192
Harriot-Souther *aafff ga* 316-7
Harrison-Gilbert *adaii bc* 110 378 509-10
Harrison-Tilden *adaii bed* 510
Harry *adahb bdc* 498
Harry-Benjamin *adaga gdh* 489
Harry-Davis *adahb bdf* 498
Harry-Foster *aacdb fcd* 436 550
Harry-Francis *abbea mhd* 454 557
Harry-Francis *aabcg dbcb* 532
Harry-Gordon *aabcg dgad* 533
Harry-Grealy *aabcg dbab* 532
Harry-Irven *aacbe lfg* 428
Harry-Lewis *adbcf begd* 594
Harry-Newton *adcac baib* 597 613-4
Harry-Preston *adaaa bbeaf* 608
Harry-Reaves *adahb dcj* 500
Harry-Ward *aabcg dbc* 406 532
Harry-Willard *adcai bgf* 519
Hartwell *aacbg cd* 298
Hartwell *aacbg ce* 298
Harvey-Preston *adaae agc* 473 569-70
Harvey-Ruth *adaii bbbd* 592
Harvie-Gilpin *adahf cbb* 505
Hattie A. *adbfa bda* 514
Hattie-Green *aabcg dbac* 532
Hattie-Louise *aabce cde* 403-4
Hattie-Simons *adbfa bdc* 515
Hawkes 254
Hazel-Adeline *aabhe aba* 413
Hazel-Irene *adaga gdai* 581
Hazel-Rees (Huey) *adaii bbba* 612
Helen *aacbc ahi* 421
Helen *aacdb fcdb* 550
Helen *adaaa bbfdc* 609

LINCOLN cont'd
Helen-Abigail *aabce aecd* 529
Helen-Alma *aacdc gbb* 443
Helen ([Benedict] Burnett) *adaah gda* 578
Helen-Blake (Webber) *aacbc acd* 537-8
Helen-Brevoort *adfad baba* 599
Helen-Conoly *adaid bbb* 507
Helen-Elizabeth (Sprague) *aacbg cc* 429
Helen-Eugenia *adffe cdaa* 601
Helen-Francenia (Philbrick) *abbhc db* 458-9
Helen-Frances *aabch dc* 148 266
Helen-Frances *aacdc eab* 441
Helen-Francis *adffe cad* 522
Helen-Geraldine *adaaa bbeac* 608
Helen-Gertrude *abbea cabdb* 604
Helen-Hale (Story) *aacdb eec* 434
Helen-Irene *adaaa bbidg* 610
Helen-Maria *aabck bfb* 412
Helen-Maria *aacbg ccb* 429
Helen-Maria (Shedd) *aabck bf* 411-2
Helen-Martha (Knowlton) *aacdb bd* 431-2
Helen-Mary *adagb fbd* 494
Helen-Pauline *adaga gicc* 582
Helen-Revere *aacdd dab* 445
Heman 66 137
Henrietta *adcac h* 125 239-40
Henrietta ([Baugh] Scales) *adaaᶠ aa* 348
Henrietta-Brewer *aabcf aca* 404
Henrietta-Frances (Grandle) *adaae agc* 569-70
Henrietta (Kepilino) *aabcg dga* 533
Henrietta-Wallis *adcac baca* 595
Henry *aacdc* 79 181-3
Henry *aacda f* 175
Henry *aacdc e* 183 308-10 311
Henry *abbec e* 191
Henry *adaga j* 217 219
Henry *aabce cg* 258
Henry *aabhg ad* 276
Henry *aabhg db* 277 413-4
Henry *aacdc gg* 313
Henry *abbec bb* 84 321 453-4
Henry *adaga ga* 362 487-8
Henry *adbcf bb* 383
Henry *aacdb bde* 431
Henry *aacdc eaa* 441
Henry *aabce cdaa* 530
Henry *adbcf baabi* 613
Henry-Barry *aabck bf* 270 274 411-2
Henry-Brewer *aabcf acd* 404
Henry-Greenwood *adffe cba* 523
Henry-Harrison *abbea mf* 320
Henry-Huston *adagb djec* 583
Henry M. *aacda eb* 301
Henry-Moorhead *aabck bfa* 412
Henry-Mordecai *adaaa bbcab* 606
Henry-Patrick *aabcg dgb* 409 533-4
Henry-Philip *adahf dc* 375
Henry-Philip *adahf daa* 108 110 223 506 590
Henry-Philip *adaaa bbfb* 563 608
Henry-Richardson *aacdc eca* 442 552
Henry-Thomas *adfae adb* 522
Henry-Wadsworth *abbec bbaa* 557
Henry-Ware *aabcd df* 254
Henry-Ware *aabcd dfe* 254
Hepzibah *aaffi* 36 83-4 453
Hepzibah (Bouvé) *aabce b* 255-6
Herbert-Austin *abbea cabda* 604
Herbert-Henry *adbfa bda* 514
Herbert-Randolph *adbcf bedd* 594
Herbert-Richmond *aacdb ee* 303 433-4
Herman-Cushing *aabhe ab* 275 276 412-3
Herod-Franklin *adaae age* 473
Hester *adbab* 59 113 114
Hester *adagb dha* 364 493

LINCOLN cont'd
Hester *adaaa bbbf* 559
Hester-Ann (———) *adaae aa* 343
Hezekiah *abb* 13 14 15 39-43
Hezekiah *abbh* 39 42 80 88 91-2
Hezekiah *abbha* 92
Hezekiah *aacab f* 12 note 72
Hezekiah *adaaa aae* 460 461
Holbrook *aacdb ebab* 548
Homer-Fielden *adaaa bbfba* 608
Hope-Kirby *adffe cgd* 524
Horace-Greeley *adaga agf* 358 486 487 579
Horace-McKee *adbcf bej* 513
Horace-William *adbcf bedb* 594 613
Hosea *aaih* 12
Howard *adahb dci* 499-500
Howard *adaii bea* 510
Howard-Abbot *aacbe ldd* 426
Howard-Amasa *aabcg dgaa* 533
Howard-Andrew *aacdb igbb* 551
Howard-Bicknell *adffe cbd* 523
Howard-Nearing *adhfa bdf* 515 595
Howard-Thomas *adaaa bbead* 608
Howard-Walter *adfae adaa* 600
Hugh-Brown *adaaf aa* 348
Hugh-Brown *adaaf abe* 477
Hugh-Brown *adaaf acc* 478
Huldah *adfae ab* 394
Huldah (Kilby) *adfae* 127 245-6
Huldah (Leech) *adaga ga* 362 487-8
Ida *adbcf bebc* 593
Ida-Beatrice (Sharp) *adaaf ac* 478
Ida-Berenice (Tabbut) *abbec fbd* 558
Ida-Eliza *adaae hfd* 475
Ida-Ella *aacdb gfa* 437
Ida-Louise *aabce cdad* 530
Ida P. (Jones) *adbcf bedb* 613
Ida (Young) *adbcf baa* 592-3
Ina-Belle (Porter) *adbfa bdf* 595
Ira-Briggs *adagb fa* 365-6
Irene *adfae adca* 600
Irene-Beal *aafff gf* 318
Isaac 10 63 234 note 242
Isaac *abd* 14
Isaac *adc* 16 18 19 22 59-61 127 388
Isaac *adbb* 55 56 58 113 114-5 119
Isaac *adca* 59 60 61 89 121-3 132 244
Isaac *adaad* 43 93 95 100 101 204-5 348
Isaac *adcaa* 122
Isaac *adcbb* 125
Isaac *adaaf f* 101 209 210 211 351-2 353
Isaac *adbca d* 118 232 379 380-1
Isaac *adcac d* 239 388-9
Isaac *adcac ba* 388 516-7
Isaac *adcac daa* 518
Isaac-Buck *adbfa bd* 385 386 514-5
Isaac-Newton *adcac bag* 516
Isaac R. *adbcf ca* 383 384 514
Isaac-Warren *adcac bae* 516
Isaac-Wells *adaah gd* 356 357 485-6
Isaac-Wells *adaah gde* 485-6
Isaac-Wilber *adbca dcc* 511
Isabel *aabhg ae* 276
Isabel *adaae abe* 472
Isabel *adaae hfia* 573
Isabel R. 446
Isabella (McCain) *adaga gff* 490 491
Isaiah *aahi* 12
Isaiah *aaig* 12
Isaiah *abbea f* 189 190 240
Isaiah *abbea cab* 451 552-4
Isaiah-Austin *abbea cabd* 553 604
Israel 278 313
Israel *adbch g* 118 235 236
Jackson-Steward *aacbg ckbc* 547
Jacob *adf* 18 19 23 62-3 130 131
Jacob *adbc* 55 58 113 114 116-8 231

LINCOLN cont'd
Jacob *adfb* 62 128-32
Jacob *adaae* 43 94 95 96 97 98 100 101 205-8 213
Jacob *adbch* 116 117 118 234-7
Jacob *adfad* 61 63 123 127 128 244-5
Jacob *adaae h* 207 344-5
Jacob *adbcf a* 118 234 382-3 384
Jacob *adbch b* 118 235 236
Jaeob *adfad g* 244 245
Jacob *adaaa be* 332 333 464
Jacob *adbcf cb* 383 384
Jacob *adbcf bf* 384
Jacob *adaaa bbd* 463 561
Jacob-Arthur *aacdb ebac* 548
Jacob-Broaddus *adaae hf* 345 346 475-6
Jacob-Broaddus *adaae hfha* 573
Jacob-Lafferty *adagb da* 364
Jacob-Nicholas *adaae ag* 343 344 472-3
Jacob-Stannels *aacdb eba* 432 547-8
Jacob-Thomas *adaae agi* 473 570
Jael *aahh* 12
Jael (Curtis) *adfa* 63 127-8 189 190
Jael (Cushing) *aacda* 174-5
Jael (Garrett) *adc* 59-61
Jairus 254
Jairus *adffk* 134
Jairus *aabce h* 142 148 259-60
Jairus B *aabce h* 259
Jairus-Beals *aabce ab* 355 400
Jairus-Horace *aabce abca* 527 602
James 65 67 76 80 139 140 141 143 147 242
James *aaa* 10-11
James *aaaa* 10
James *adaid* 112 230
James *adcad* 121
James *adcaf* 122
James *adcak* 122 123 242-3
James *adaid ba* 376
James *adaid hb* 378
James *adbcf bc* 383
James *adaaa bbi* 463 564-6
James-Anderson *adaaa bbida* 610
James-Boone *adaid abc* 506 691-2
James-Bradford *adaaa ab* 43 329 461-2
James-Capeheart *adahf daca* 591
James-Carter *adcai bd* 390
James-Carter *adcai bgd* 519
James-Claiborne *adaah gda* 357 note 485 577-8
James-Claiborne *adaah gdaa* 578
James-Dallas *adcac bah* 517
James-Davis *abbea md* 320
James-Dernell *adaga gic* 492 582
James-Edward *aacdb bb* 301
James-Edwin *adaah em* 355 483-5
James-Edwin *adaah emd* 485 577
James F. *adaaa bbgb* 564 609-10
James-Francis *aabck bh* 152 270 274 412
James-Hamilton *adaaf ac* 205 348 477-8
James-Handshaw *adaqa aa* 358 486-7
James-Hubert *adahb faeb* 585
James-McCain *adaga gff* 490 491
James-Martin *abbea mhcb* 557
James-Minor 367 371
James-Moore *adahb fa* 226 369 500-1
James-Morris *adaaa bbgbd* 610
James-Otis *aacdc ge* 313 443-4
James-Preston *adaga gicb* 582
James-Riley *adaaa abe* 462
James-Russell *adcai bgaa* 598
James-Silliman *adaga agb* 487
James-Stephen *adaga aaaa* 579
James T. *adaga aaf* 486
James-Thomas *adaaa bbca* 559 605-6
James-Warren *adcak bb* 392
James-Washington *adaaa bed* 464

LINCOLN cont'd
James-Wesley *adahb faf* 501
Jane *aabah* 64 66 148 259
Jane *aabaa d* 135 137
Jane *aabch b* 148 259-60
Jane *aabcf aa* 260
Jane *adbca db* 381
Jane *adaga ghaa* 582
Jane-Cordelia *adaah ef* 355 481
Jane (Gilpin) *adaga g* 361-3 488
Jane (Lincoln) *aabah* 66 148 259
Jane (Lincoln) *aabch b* 148 259-60
Jane-Robinson ([Thomas] Lewis) *aabcj c* 267
Jane-Russell *aabce ha* 148 260
Jane-Thaxter (Burrell) *aabce ae* 401
Jane (Usrey) *adaaf db* 479
Janet-Sallie *adaae hfaca* 611
Janette-Ann *adaae hfaf* 572
Jared *aacab g* 12 note 72
Jeannette-Carlson *abbea cabic* 605
Jedediah *aac* 10 31-5 70
Jedediah *aaca* 35 64 70-2
Jedediah *aacbi* 74 75 78 167-9 293 313
Jedediah *aacab a* 12 note 72
Jedediah *aacbi c* 168
Jedediah *aacbi aa* 299
Jemima *adagb b* 219 220
Jennett *adffe h* 248 249
Jennett *adffe j* 249
Jennette-Emeline (Carpenter) *adahb ged* 503
Jennie-Catherine (Elofson) *abbea mba* 556
Jennie-Elizabeth (Kershaw) *aabcf aea* 531
Jennie-Louise (Lawson) *abbea mhc* 556-7
Jennie M. (Crockett) *aacbe lfd* 428
Jennie-Margaret (Adams) *adahb gbc* 586
Jennie-May (Morse) *aabcg dba* 532
Jennings-Sipe *adaae ahcb* 571
Jeremiah 157
Jeremiah *aaid* 12 80
Jermyn *adahb h* 226
Jerom *aacbg ch* 298 299 429-30
Jerome *abbea* 89 127 188-90
Jerome *abbea c* 189 318-9
Jerome-Bates *aacbg cha* 298 430
Jerusha *aabcf f* 144
Jerusha (Waterman) *aabcf* 142-6
Jesse *adaaf a* 101 209 210 347-8
Jesse *adagb d* 112 219 220 363-5
Jesse *adaaf aca* 478
Jesse *adaaa bbfia* 609
Jesse-Hampton *adaaf dbca* 575
Jesse-Leroy *adagb djc* 493
Jessie *adaaa dbac* 568
Jessie-Amanda *adbcf bck* 514
Jessie-Belle *adahb gbg* 502
Jessie-Florence *adbcf beee* 594
Jessie-Mary *adcai ffb* 520
Jessie (Schultz) *adaaa bbic* 610
Jetson-Jackson *adaae ahc* 474 571
Joanna 39
Joanna *aabaf* 64 65-6
Joanna E. (Bacon) *aafff cb* 315
Joanna-Frothingham *aacbe bf* 293
Joanna (Low) *aaa* 10
Job *aahd* 12
Joel *adffh* 134
Joel-Kay *adahb gbd* 502 586
Joel-Willcutt *adbec bj* 322-3
John *agg* 24 26
John *aabh* 29 30 31 68-70
John *adaa* 47 49 50 51 52 92-103 335
John *adbg* 54 55 59 94 113
John *aabcj* 66 68 76 141 143 148-51
John *adaaf* 43 94 95 96 98 99 100 101 208-12

LINCOLN cont'd

John *adagb* 94 104 105 106 108 219-22 367
John *adaij* 112 229
John *adbcd* 117 233
John *aabcj b* 150
John *aabck c* 154
John *aabhg a* 156 276-7
John *adaae b* 206
John *adaaf k* 101 209 210 211 212 352-3
John *adaah f* 213 214 215
John *adagb c* 105 219 220 366
John *adahc a* 227 371
John *adahf c* 229 372-4
John *adaid b* 230 375-6
John *adbca a* 118 232 379-80
John *adbch e* 118 235 236
John *adcai b* 241 389-91
John *aabhg aa* 276 413
John *adaae hc* 345
John *adagb hb* 367
John *adagb la* 368
John *adahb dc* 369 499
John *adahb ga* 370
John *adahc bb* 372
John *adaid ac* 375
John *adbcf ba* 383 512
John *adbfa eg* 387
John *adcai fb* 391 519-20
John *adahb dba* 498
John *adahc baa* 372
John *adahb dcgb* 585
John *adbcf baaa* 593
John-Anselm *adcai bgc* 519
John-Anslem *adcai ffa* 520
John-Barker *aabhg bh* 293
John-Bumstead *aacbe bh* 293
John-Clarence *adaaa bbeh* 562
John-Craigin *adaaf db* 210 349 351 478-9
John-Crocker *aacdc f* 183 310-1
John-Davie *adaae hfb* 475 572
John-Dehaven *adaii b* 112 231 378-9
John-Dunlap *adcac da* 389 517-8
John-Dunlap *adcac dacb* 598
John-Edward *adaae aha* 474 570-1
John-Egbert *adbfa a* 237
John-Egbert *adbfa ff* 388
John-Erb *adahb bcd* 497 584
John-Fillebrown *aabce cd* 258 403-4
John-Gilbert *adaii be* 379 510
John-Henry *aacdc fc* 311
John-Henry *adaae hfbb* 572
John-Hobart *abbec d* 190 191
John-Hobart *abbec bk* 323
John-Hobart *adcac baf* 516 596
John-Howard *aacdb ig* 307 308 439
John-James *adcai bg* 391 518-9
John-Joseph *adahf cea* 505 589
John-Joseph *adahf ceab* 589
John-Karsner *adaah eb* 354 479-80 481
John-Karsner *adaah ebd* 480 576
John-Mason *aacdb hc* 305 306
John-Melvin *aacdb gc* 305 436-7
John-Mordecai *adaaf ab* 348 476-7
John-Mordecai *adaaa bbcbb* 607
John-Morton *adaah ekac* 576
John-Nathan *aacdb icab* 550
John-Patterson *adagb dh* 364 365 493
John-Percy *adaae hfacd* 611
John-Robertson *adbca dc* 381 511
John-Robie *aabcj hb* 268 409
John-Russel *adaaa bbifc* 611
John-Spencer *aabcg dgc* 409 534
John-Strother *adaae aa* 343
John T. *aabce add* 401
John-Taylor *adahf db* 375
John-Thomas *adahb gec* 503
John-Thompson *aacdb gca* 437

LINCOLN cont'd

John-Thompson *aacdb gfd* 438
John-Waldo *aacbc d* 163 284-6 414
John-Waldo *aacbc ah* 283 419
John-Waldo *aacbc ahb* 420
John-Wesley *adahb fb* 369
John-Wesley *adahb dce* 499
John-Wesley *adahc aaa* 504 588
John-Winthrop *aabhg aaaa* 536
Jonathan *aabc* 29 30 31 66-8
Jonathan *aabcd* 66 67 140-1
Jonathan *aabcd e* 140 141
Jonathan-Jones *adaaa bef* 464 566
Joseph 278 313
Joseph *aaic* 12
Joseph *adahf* 110 225 227-9
Joseph *abbec b* 191 321-3
Joseph *adahb c* 226
Joseph *abbec be* 322 454
Joseph *adbca fa* 381
Joseph *adbfa ea* 386
Joseph *adaaa bbg* 463 563-4
Joseph *adaaa beg* 464 566-7
Joseph *adaaa bbec* 562
Joseph-David *adaaa bbcg* 560 607
Joseph-Gardner *abbec fbe* 457
Joseph H. *adaga gib* 492
Joseph-Henry *adahf cb* 373 504-5
Joseph-Hollis *adahb ge* 370 502-3
Joseph-Howard *adbcf bee* 513 594
Joseph-Howard *adbcf beeb* 594
Joseph-Waterman *adbfb* 120 121
Joseph-Waterman *adbfa c* 238
Josephine *aabhe aa* 276
Josephine *adaae he* 345
Josephine *adaaf dbb* 479
Josephine-Amy (Wands) *aabce aebc* 603
Josephine (Clapp) *aabck bh* 412
Josephine-Elizabeth *adaae abb* 471-2
Josephine-Marion (Barnard) *aacbc acbaa* 614
Josephine-Rebecca *adaae id* 347
Josephine-Rice *aabce cdac* 530
Josephine-Rose *aacbc addb* 542
Joshua 63
Joshua-Revere *aacbi i* 168 169
Joshua-Thompson *aabcf da* 405
Josiah *aai* 12 36
Josiah *aaib* 12
Josiah *adaaa b* 43 44 108 194 196 197 201 202 327 329-33 336 463
Jotham *aabhe a* 155 156 274-6
Julia *adaah eo* 355-6
Julia *adaah elf* 483
Julia-Ann (Caldwell) *adbfa e* 386-7
Julia-Ann (Holmes) *abbec fb* 456-7
Julia ([Brown] Colston) *adaah ebb* 575
Julia-Hall (Robbins) *aabcj hb* 409
Julia-Holmes *abbec fbc* 457
Julia-Jenks (Handy) *aabcf aea* 531
Julia-Maria (Ross) *adffe cg* 524
Julia O'Neal (Whitehead) *adaae hfh* 573
Julia-Sophia (Jones) *aacdb ef* 434
Juliana *adaaf j* 101 209 212
Julian (Boone) *adaic* 229
Julian (Mayberry) *adaic* 229
Juliann (Gatewood) *adaah e* 354-6
Kate-May (Bowles) *adaae hfi* 572
Kate-Von-Weber (Marston) *aacbc ah* 420-1
Katharine *adaaa bf* 331 333
Katharine *aacdc gea* 444
Katharine *adaaa bei* 464
Katharine-Bird *adaah emb* 484-5
Katharine (Dorflinger) *adbfa bg* 515
Katharine-May *adaaa beff* 566
Katharine-VonWeber *aacbc ahk* 421
Katherine-Marie *aabck bdd* 411

LINCOLN cont'd

Katherine-Mary *adaga ghc* 492
Katherine-Russell *aabch db* 148 265-6
Kathleen-Malinda (Zirkel) *adaae agca* 569-70
Kathryn *adaga agfd* 579
Kathryn-Gould (Wait) *adaah gde* 486
Katie-Bright *adaae ahf* 475
Kenneth *aacdb igbc* 551
Lafferty *adagb l* 105 219 222 367-8
LaForrest *aabce aec* 401 529
LaForrest-Webster *aabce aeca* 529
Langdon *aacbe bg* 293
Larkin F. *adaah gh* 357
Laura *adbcf cba* 384
Laura-Ashbury (Arnold) *adffe dd* 397
Laura-Caroline ([Larsen] Anderson) *adbfa fh* 515-6
Laura-Elcena (Tegarden) *adaaa bbea* 608
Laura-Flint *aabcf daa* 405-6
Laura-Maria (Simmons) *aabhg a* 276
Lavina *adahb dbc* 498
Lavina (Gibbs) *adaaa bbif* 611
Lawrence *adaaa bbic* 565 610
Lawrence-Franklin *abbea cabia* 605
Lawrence-Litchfield *aabck bfc* 412 535
Lazarus *adcai* 123 240-1
Leah *aacbh* 74 75 77-8 156
Leavitt *aacda d* 175
Leavitt *aacda e* 175 299-301
Lee (Moore) *adaaf dba* 574
Lelia *adaaa bbff* 563
Lemuel-Saunders *adaah ei* 355 481-2
Lena *adaaa bbfde* 609
Leon-Girard *abbec bla* 455-6
Leona-Adria (Parminter) *adaaf acf* 474
Leroy-Sherman *adagb dje* 493 582-3
Leroy-Sherman *adagb djeb* 583
Leslie-Alberta (Bigelow) *adffe dfc* 601
Leslie-Parker *aabce abch* 528
Lethea *adaaf fa* 352
Levi *aace* 35
Levi *aafg* 37
Levi *aahf* 12
Levi *aacbc* 75 76 157-64 169
Levi *aacbc a* 162 170 172 278-83 285 286 287 289 467
Levi *abbea d* 189 190
Levi *abbhc a* 192
Levi *adffe m* 249
Levi *aacbc ab* 74 283
Levi *aacbc acb* 415 536-7
Levi *aacbc acbaa* 603 614
Levi *aacbc acbaa a* 614
Levi-Bates *aacbe ldf* 426 546-7
Levi-Cook *adffe dg* 397 525
Levi-Louis *aacbe ld* 297 425-6
Levi-Thaxter *aabcj h* 151 153 267-8
Lewis *aafff b* 184
Lewis *aafff g* 185 316-8
Lewis-Craigin *adaaf dbc* 479 575
Lewis-Francis *abbea cacb* 554 555
Lewis-Jones *aacdb ec* 303
Lewis-Jones *aacdb ebe* 433
Lewis-Wadsworth *aacdb gcb* 437
Lillian *adaaa bbfdd* 609
Lillian *adbcf baabe* 613
Lillian-Cora (Shaw) *aabck bfc* 535
Lillian-Gertrude *aacdb icb* 438-9
Lillian-Haskell *aacdd dac* 445
Lillian-Hogsett *adaga gdg* 489
Lillian-Josephine *aabcg dbaa* 532
Lillian-May (Schuyler) *adbcf baab* 613
Lillian-Shaw *aabck bfca* 535
Lillian (Steiger) *adaae hfac* 611
Lillian (Taylor) *adbcf beg* 594
Lillie-Jane *adahb bdd* 498

LINCOLN cont'd

Linford-Rogers *adaid adb* 506
Lizzie (Deffenbaugh) *adaga gdb* 489
Lizzie (Miller) *adaaa bbcac* 615
Lizzie-Robbins *adffe lb* 398
Lizzie-Smith ([Hibbert] Norton) *aacdb ee* 433-4
Lloyd-Stanley *adahf ceaa* 589
Lodena *adahb dbd* 498
Lois *aaffj* 36 84
Lois (Pardee) *adbfa* 237-8
Lola (Pfeiffer) *adaaa bbgb* 609-10
Lora-Bird *adaah ema* 484
Lot *adcai d* 241
Lot-Rogers *adaid abd* 506
Lot-Whitmarsh *aabce f* 142 258-9
Louis *aacbe a* 165
Louis *aacbe d* 166 293-4
Louis-Dewolf *aacdb igd* 439
Louis-Manson *adffe cda* 523 600-1
Louis-Nichols *abbec bi* 322 455
Louis-Pellman *adahc aae* 504 588
Louis-Pellman *adahc aaec* 588
Louis-Revere *aacbe dad* 423 545
Louis-Russell, *aacbe hac* 424
Louisa *abbhc da* 324
Louisa *aubhg aab* 413
Louisa-Ann *adaaf de* 351
Louisa-Elizabeth *adagb djea* 583
Louisa-Grace *adaii bbbb* 592
Louisa-Jane *aabce ce* 258
Louise *adaah gdbb* 578
Louise (Stanwood) *aabcg dgc* 534
Lovell-Bicknell *adffe de* 397
Lovell-Bicknell *adcac baj* 517 597
Lowell *aacbg cj* 299
Lowell *aacbg ck* 167 298 299 430-1
Lowell *aacbg cka* 430
Lowell *aacbg ckb* 430 547
Lowell-Lothrop *aacbg ckbb* 547
Lucena *adcbm* 126
Lucia *adcak a* 242
Lucinda *aabhg b* 156
Lucinda *aabce fa* 259
Lucinda (Fearing) *aacbh d* 78 156
Lucinda-Fearing *aabhg ea* 278
Lucinda (Gates) *aabce f* 259
Lucretia (Bell) *aacdb ec* 303
Lucy *aabca* 66 67 68
Lucy *aabce g* 142 260
Lucy *aabcg g* 147
Lucy *aabcg i* 146 147
Lucy *adaha d* 224
Lucy *adffe f* 248
Lucy *aacdb if* 308
Lucy *adaah ecc* 481
Lucy A. *adbfa fd* 387-8
Lucy-Agnes *adcai ffd* 520
Lucy-Allen *abbec fba* 457
Lucy-Ann *aabcd bca* 399
Lucy-Ann (Briggs) *aabcd bc* 399-400
Lucy-Ann-Lombard *aabcg df* 264
Lucy-Ann (Moast) *adaga gf* 490-1
Lucy-Augusta *aacbe p* 166
Lucy-Coolidge *adffe cbb* 523
Lucy-Coolidge (Stone) *adffe c* 395-6
Lucy (Deno) *adgba fe* 366
Lucy-Ellen *aabhg aaaf* 536
Lucy-Ellen (Marsh) *adcac bai* 596-7
Lucy-Ellen (Simonds) *aabce aba* 526-7
Lucy-Emma *aacbe hbb* 425
Lucy-Frances *adfah ab* 395
Lucy-Gatewood *adaah ej* 355
Lucy-Isabella *adbfa fha* 516
Lucy-Jane (Souther) *aabhg aaa* 536
Lucy-Josephine-Elizabeth *abbec beb* 454
Lucy-Knox *adaae ahe* 474
Lucy (Lewis) *aacab f* 72

LINCOLN cont'd
Lucy-May *adaga gfaa* 581
Lucy (Post) *adbfa f* 387-8
Lucy (Richardson) *abbec fb* 456-7
Lula ([Adams] Brown) *adaae hfb* 572
Lula-DeEtta (Jaynes) *aabhe ab* 412-3
Lulu (Goodwin) *adaaf acb* 478
Luretta-Cushing *abbea cc* 319
Luther-Axtell *adaga age* 487
Luther-Jenkins *abbea me* 320
Lydia 142
Lydia *aag* 11
Lydia *aaia* 12
Lydia *aaie* 12
Lydia *adfj* 62 63 130
Lydia *aabha* 69
Lydia *adaac* 95 100 101
Lydia *adfag* 128
Lydia *aabcd c* 140-1
Lydia *aacdd c* 184
Lydia *adaae c* 206
Lydia *aacdd dc* 313
Lydia *adagb fd* 366
Lydia-Abbott *aabcd dfd* 254
Lydia-Augusta *adahb gbf* 502
Lydia (Bates) *aacdd* 183-4
Lydia (Cushing) *aaha* 12
Lydia-Ellen *aacdb be* 302
Lydia-Ellen (Breed) *adcac bag* 516
Lydia-Elmirah *adahf ch* 374
Lydia (Hobart) 12
Lydia ([Hobart] Ripley) *aacb* 74 76 89
Lydia (Jacob) *aabh* 68-70
Lydia-Jacob *aabhg c* 156
Lydia-James (Cushing) *aafff fb* 185
Lydia-Jane (Gilpatrick) *aacdb ec* 303
Lydia-Maria *adffe ce* 396
Lydia (Myers) *adahb b* 368
Lydia (Nichols) *aabcd* 140-1
Lydia-Nichols *aabcd db* 253
Lydia-Nichols (Bates) *aacbe ld* 426
Lydia-Priscilla *adahb bbd* 495
Lydia ([Whiton] Beal) *aaha* 12
Lyman-Putnam *aabcg dga* 409 533
Mabel *aacdc ecd* 442
Mabel *adaaa bbfdb* 609
Mabel ([Anson] Hammer) *adbca dcc* 511
Mabel-Bettina (Lawrence) *adcai fba* 599
Mabel-Gertrude (Pinkham) *abbea cabd* 604
Mabel-Harriet (Kelley) *aabce cdba* 531
Mabel-Louise (Champney) *abbea mbd* 556
Mabel (Sawyer) *aacdb igb* 551
Madeline *abbec fdb* 457-8
Mahulda *adaaa bbib* 565
Major-Wetherford *adaaa bbcb* 559 606-7
Malinda (Morris) *adahc ba* 372
Malinda (Morris) *adahc bb* 372
Mamie-Elizabeth *adaae hfib* 573
Mamie-Maria (Swarens) *adaaa bbfb* 608
Marcia-Dunlap *adcac daca* 598
Marcia-Maria (Bangs) *aabck ba* 409-10
Marcia-Scott (Dunlap) *adcac d* 389
Marcy (Vinal) *adfah* 246
Margaret 11 77 101
Margaret *aabi* 28 29 30 31
Margaret *adaah b* 215
Margaret *adahf a* 228
Margaret *adaic d* 229
Margaret *adaic e* 229
Margaret *adagb dc* 364
Margaret *adagb df* 364
Margaret *adahb gf* 370
Margaret *adaid cb* 377
Margaret *adaah elc* 483
Margaret *aacdb igcb* 551
Margaret *adaaa bbbg* 559

LINCOLN cont'd
Margaret *adaaa bbed* 562
Margaret *adaga* 582
Margaret (——) 10
Margaret-Alice (Rardin) *adaga aaa* 579
Margaret-Amelia (Henderson) *adaid a* 375
Margaret (Caldwell) *adcb* 124-126
Margaret-Eliza *adcai bgab* 598
Margaret-Elizabeth ([Greene] Merrill) *aabck bab* 535
Margaret-Ellen *adahb gcc* 502
Margaret-Ellen (Thurston) *adcac baf* 596
Margaret-Ellen (Yaw) *adaga gi* 492
Margaret-Evans *adaid abca* 592
Margaret (Frazer) *adaah gdaa* 578
Margaret (Hedden) *adagb h* 367
Margaret-Hoxson *adaid bbae* 592
Margaret-Hudson *adaid abb* 506
Margaret-Jameson *aabcg dgbb* 534
Margaret-Jane *adagb dja* 493
Margaret-Jane *adahb dch* 499
Margaret-Jane (Patrick) *adahb bbi* 583
Margaret L. (Beal) *aabce bg* 402
Margaret (Laird) *adahb ge* 503
Margaret (Langer) 13 14
Margaret (Lincoln) 11
Margaret-Louise *adahb gbcba* 612
Margaret-Louise (Sims) *adahb gbcb* 612
Margaret-May *adahb dcdb* 584
Margaret-Permilla *adaii bbe* 508-9
Margaret-Pixley (Bird) *adaah em* 484-5
Margaret-Priscilla *adahb bce* 497
Margaret ([Ringrose] McHugh) *adcac daa* 518
Margaret (Smith) *adbca d* 380-1
Margaret (Tibbons or Gibbons) *adaaa abe* 462
Margaret-Winslow *aacbc acda* 537-8
Margaret-Worthington *adahf cf* 373
Margarete H. *adaaf ka* 353
Margaretta *adahb be* 368
Marguerite *aabce abcaa* 602
Marguerite-Beatrice *adaaf acfa* 574
Maria *aabcj d* 150 153
Maria *adcak c* 242
Maria *adfad f* 245
Maria (Brandt) *adbcf ba* 512
Maria-Elizabeth *aacdb fd* 304
Maria H. *aabce bd* 257
Maria H. *aabce be* 257
Maria-Heald *aacda ea* 300
Maria (Jackson) *adaid c* 376-7
Maria L. (Copp) *aacdb f* 304
Maria-Revere *aacbe n* 166
Maria (Watson) *aacdb i* 307-8
Mariah-Jackson (Hart) *adaga ag* 487
Marian *aabcg dgcb* 534
Marian-Vinal *aacbc ahf* 420-1
Marie *adaga agfb* 579
Marie-Louisa (Gilkey) *adaah gd* 485-6
Marie-Reed *adahc aaaa* 588
Marie-Rosina (Seissler) *aacdb ica* 550
Marietta *adbcf baabf* 613
Marietta-Foster (Bennett) *abbea mhd* 557
Marinda-Ellen *adaaa bega* 567
Marion *adahf daab* 590
Marion-Josephine *aabce aebca* 603
Marion-Whitney *aabce abaa* 527
Mark-Halfpenny *adahc aac* 504
Marston *aacbc ahg* 421 544
Martha *ah* 4 8 9
Martha *abe* 14
Martha *aga* 24
Martha *agd* 25 26 27 71
Martha *abbd* 39 42
Martha *abbhc* 92

LINCOLN cont'd
Martha *adaib* 112
Martha *aacbc c* 163
Martha *adaii a* 230-1
Martha *adaaa af* 329
Martha *adaae hd* 345
Martha *adaii bg* 379
Martha *aabcf dac* 406
Martha *adaii bce* 510
Martha (——) *a* 6 7
Martha (——) *adagb de* 492
Martha-Adelia (Vinal) *aabce aec* 529
Martha-Ann *adaaa bbce* 560
Martha-Ann (——) *adbch g* 236
Martha-Ann-Chloe *adfad d* 245
Martha-Ann (Hunt) *aacbe lfb* 547
Martha-Ann-Robinson *aacdb ha* 306
Martha-Biddle (Fimple) *adbca a* 379-80
Martha-Blake (Minott) *aabck b* 269-70
Martha-Blake-Minot *aabck bhc* 412
Martha (Cole) *adaga c* 359-60
Martha-Elizabeth *aabcf dc* 263
Martha-Elizabeth *aabck bb* 270 274
Martha-Elizabeth *adahb fag* 501
Martha-Emma (Covington) *adbcf bed* 593-4
Martha (Gardner) *abbec fb* 456-7
Martha (Gibbs) *adaaa be* 464
Martha-(Golding) *aacdb ig* 439
Martha ([Howard] Robb) *aacbe* 165-6 296
Martha I. (Cook) *adaaa beg* 566
Martha J. (Kennedy) *adaaa bed* 464
Martha-Jane (Bures) *adaaa aba* 462
Martha-Jane (Newcomb) *adcac bai* 596-7
Martha-Josephine (Forester) *aabcg db* 406
Martha-Kathleen *abbea cabgb* 604
Martha (Lincoln) *abe* 14
Martha-Louise *adagb di* 365
Martha-Louise *adaaa bbicb* 610
Martha-Maria *abbea cabh* 554
Martha (Morrill) *aafff fc* 185
Martha (Parker) *adagb da* 364
Martha-Rogers *adaid aba* 506
Martha-Roy (Raymond) *adaah emd* 577
Martha-Stockbridge (Litchfield) *abbea cab* 552-4
Martha (Waldo) *aacbc* 162-4
Martin 176
Martin *abbea m* 133 190 319-21
Martin *adfad b* 245 392-3
Martin *abbea ma* 320
Martin-Jerome *abbea mb* 320 452-3
Martin-Volney *adfad ba* 393 521
Mary 10 34
Mary *af* 4 8
Mary *aad* 10
Mary *agc* 25 26
Mary *aacc* 35
Mary *abbc* 39 41-2 186
Mary *adad* 47 50-1 209
Mary *adfe* 62 131
Mary *aabae* 64 65
Mary *aacaa* 26 71
Mary *abbeb* 89 238-40
Mary *abbhb* 92
Mary *adahe* 110
Mary *adaia* 112
Mary *adbcg* 117 118
Mary *adcbl* 126
Mary *adfac* 127 190-1
Mary *adfba* 62 128 130 131-2
Mary *aabaa a* 135 136
Mary *aabad c* 138
Mary *aabce e* 142 251
Mary *aabck a* 153-4
Mary *aacbi g* 168 169
Mary *aacdb a* 178 179

LINCOLN cont'd
Mary *aacdd a* 183
Mary *abbea l* 190
Mary *abbec h* 191
Mary *adaaa c* 202-3
Mary *adaae d* 206
Mary *adaaf i* 101 212
Mary *adaga e* 217-8
Mary *adagb i* 219 221
Mary *adahf b* 229
Mary *adbca e* 117 118 231 232-3
Mary *adbch d* 118 235 236
Mary *adffe g* 248
Mary *aabcf af* 261
Mary *aabhg ac* 276
Mary *aacdc gd* 313
Mary *aacdd de* 313
Mary *adaga ad* 358
Mary *adaga cg* 360
Mary *adaii bj* 379
Mary *adbch ba* 118 236
Mary *aabce cbc* 402
Mary *aacdc gfb* 444
Mary *abbea cag* 451
Mary *adaaa bea* 464
Mary *adahb dbb* 498
Mary *aacbc addc* 543
Mary *adaaa bbbd* 559
Mary *adaaa dbaa* 567-8
Mary *adahf dabc* 590
Mary (——) 2 3 4 7
Mary (——) *ag* 23
Mary (——) *aabaa* 135-7
Mary ([——] Barker) *aac* 32 34
Mary ([——] Lucas) *adaah ek* 482
Mary-Abbie (Hemingway) *aacbe haa* 546
Mary-Adella (Ward) *aafff gh* 449
Mary-Alice (Daniell) *aabce cdb* 530-1
Mary-Alma *aacdb bdi* 432
Mary-Amanda *adbcf beea* 594
Mary-Amelia *aacbe ldb* 426
Mary-Ann *aabcj i* 151
Mary-Ann *aacdc d* 182-3
Mary-Ann *adagb db* 364
Mary-Ann *adcak ba* 392
Mary-Ann *adaaa bbeb* 561-2
Mary-Ann (Anderson) *abbea cac* 554-5
Mary-Ann (Bennett) *aacbe hb* 424-5
Mary-Ann-Binney *aabcd da* 253
Mary-Ann-Binney *aabcd dg* 254
Mary-Ann (Brown) *aabcj h* 267-8
Mary-Ann (Call) *aacbe ha* 424
Mary-Ann (Nelson) *adaah ee* 481
Mary-Ann (Sampson) *abbea cad* 555-6
Mary-Ann (Shattuck) *aabck ba* 409-10
Mary-Ann (Whiton) *adcac bac* 595-6
Mary-Anna *adcai fd* 391
Mary-Anna-Ludlow *aacbg ckba* 547
Mary-Augusta *aacdd db* 313
Mary-Avery (Souther) *aafff g* 316-8
Mary-Balkon *aabcf acc* 404
Mary (Barry) *aabck* 152-4
Mary (Bates) *aaba* 64-6 78 148
Mary-Birch *abbhc c* 192
Mary-Blanche *adahb gbda* 586
Mary (Booth) *adagb fbb* 494
Mary (Bowker) *aacbc adda* 542
Mary ([Brightman] Gifford) *adcai bgc* 519
Mary (Burr) *abea* 15
Mary-Catherine *adaae abc* 471 note 472
Mary-Catherine *adaii bbc* 508
Mary-Cecilia *adahg bbg* 496
Mary-Cornelia (Switzer) *adaae agce* 570
Mary-Cotton (Ware) 254
Mary (Cushing) *aabcd d* 253-4
Mary-Davies *adaid he* 378

43

LINCOLN cont'd
Mary E. ([——] Northorp) *adbfa ea* 386
Mary E. Celia (Crowell) *abbea cacb* 555
Mary E. (Coffey) *aacbc ahj* 421
Mary-Edmands *aabce cdc* 403
Mary-Eliot *aabch da* 148 265
Mary-Eliza *aabck ff* 273
Mary-Eliza *adahf ca* 372-3
Mary-Eliza (Trumbull) *aacdb ig* 439
Mary-Elizabeth *aafff gb* 317
Mary-Elizabeth *adaae ia* 346 475
Mary-Elizabeth *adahb fc* 369
Mary-Elizabeth *adcac db* 389
Mary-Elizabeth *aabcf ace* 404
Mary-Elizabeth *aacbe hba* 425
Mary-Elizabeth *aacdc ecc* 442
Mary-Elizabeth *adaga gia* 492
Mary-Elizabeth *adahb gba* 501
Mary-Elizabeth *adahb gea* 503
Mary-Elisabeth *adffe cac* 522
Mary-Elizabeth *adaga gdaa* 580
Mary-Elizabeth *adahb dcgc* 585
Mary-Elizabeth (Bourne) *abbec bba* 557
Mary-Elizabeth (Cottrell) *adffe ca* 522
Mary-Elizabeth (Hughes) *adaae ah* 474-5
Mary-Elizabeth (Koontz) *adaae aee* 344 568-9
Mary-Elizabeth (O'Keefe) *adaaa bbcb* 606-7
Mary-Elizabeth (Osman) *adaga gh* 491-2
Mary-Elizabeth (Rose) *adaga gd* 489
Mary-Elizabeth (Spencer) *adaaa bbc* 559-60
Mary-Elizabeth (Wallace) *adahb dcg* 585
Mary-Ellen *adaga aac* 486
Mary-Ellen *adaaa bbci* 560
Mary-Ellen *adbcf beba* 593
Mary-Elmina *abbea caba* 553
Mary-Emma *aabce cdd* 403
Mary-Emma *adahb bdb* 498
Mary-Ermina (Buchanan) *adaid abd* 506
Mary-Etta (Kenton) *adhab gcd* 587
Mary-Evangeline (Jenson) *aabce aeba* 602
Mary (Evans) *adaga a* 358-9
Mary (Farnum) *agi* 26 27
Mary (Fearing) *aabad* 138-9
Mary-Fleet (Eliot) *aabchd* 264-6
Mary-Florence *adaaa bbcaa* 606
Mary-Florence (Hayden) *aabhg dba* 536
Mary-Frances *aafff fa* 185
Mary-Frothingham *aacbe bd* 292
Mary-Garrigues *adaid hca* 507
Mary-Gertrude (Wiseman) *adaaa bbcgb* 615
Mary-Gilligan *aacdb fcc* 436
Mary (Harlan) *adaaa dba* 567-8
Mary-Hathorne (Knight) *aacbe d* 293
Mary ([Heald] Shattuck) *aacda e* 300
Mary (Holbrook) *adf* 62
Mary ([Hobart] Chapin) *ad* 18 19 21-3
Mary (Homan) *adaae i* 345-7
Mary (Horswell) *abb* 15 40-2
Mary (Howard) *adaga gdh* 489
Mary-Humphrey (Nichols) *abbec b* 321-3
Mary-Huntington (Fuller) *adcai fb* 519-20
Mary-Isabel *adaae hfab* 572
Mary-Isabella (Jasper) *adaae hf* 475-6
Mary-Ives (Davis) *adaid h* 378
Mary ([Jacob] Barker) *aac* 32 34
Mary-Jane *adagb hc* 367
Mary-Jane *adaaa aad* 459 460 461
Mary-Jane *adaga gdc* 489
Mary-Jane (Campbell) *aacdb bd* 431-2
Mary-Jane (Downs) *adcai bgf* 519
Mary-Jane (Galbraith) *adffe l* 397-8
Mary-Jane (Hawke) *abbea cacc* 605

LINCOLN cont'd
Mary-Jane (Hemmick) *adagb l* 367-8
Mary-Jane-Savage *adbfa ec* 386
Mary-Jemima *adagb fc* 366
Mary-Knight *aacbe dac* 423
Mary-Knight *aacbe dabc* 545
Mary-Knight ([Hanscom] Hoyte) *aacdb ee* 433
Mary L. *adbfa fc* 387
Mary (Lafferty) *adagb* 105 106 219-22
Mary-Leannah *adaae agb* 473
Mary-Lee (Curtis) 313
Mary (Lincoln) *abbeb* 238-40
Mary (Lincoln) *adfac* 127 190-1
Mary (Lincoln) *aacdd de* 313
Mary-Loreno (Heiss) *adahb bbh* 496
Mary-Louise *adaaa befj* 566
Mary-Louise *adaah gdac* 578
Mary-Lyon (Raymond) *abbea cacb* 555
Mary (McKenly) *aabcg dc* 407
Mary-Maria *adfad bb* 245 393
Mary-Martha *aacdb ba* 301 302
Mary (Miles) *adahb g* 370
Mary-Mitchell *adcak f* 243
Mary-Moore (Francis) *aacdc g* 312-3
Mary (Morris) *adahb bb* 495-6
Mary (Mudd) *adaaa a* 325-9 462
Mary-Nichols *abbec bc* 321-2
Mary (Otis) *aacd* 79-80
Mary-Otis *aacdb ed* 303
Mary-Otis *aacdb fcbc* 549
Mary P. *abbec fda* 457
Mary-Rebecca *adbcf bea* 512-3
Mary-Rebecca (Missimer) *adahb bd* 497-8
Mary (Revere) *aacbi* 168-9 313
Mary-Richards (Jones) *aacdb e* 302-3
Mary-Richardson *adcac dab* 518
Mary (Robeson) *ada* 47 49-53
Mary-Rogers (Hoar) *aacdd da* 445
Mary-Rowena *adaaa ae* 329
Mary Rowena *adaaa abc* 462
Mary-Ruth *adbca fca* 512
Mary (Scarlett) *aaca* 70-2
Mary ([Sampson] Packard) *adfah a* 394-5
Mary (Schoonover) *adaaa bbc* 559-61
Mary ([Seaman] Martin) *adaaf f* 352
Mary-Shattuck *aabck bac* 410
Mary-Shepard (Blanchard) *aabhg db* 413-4
Mary (Shute) *adbb* 115
Mary ([Smith] Gale) *aabhe* 155
Mary-Sophia *adaaf df* 349 350 351
Mary-Sophronia (Robertson) *aacbg cca* 429
Mary-Susan (Maynard) *aacbc acb* 537
Mary T. *adaah gc* 357
Mary (Taylor) *adbch* 235-7
Mary-Thaxter *aabcd bd* 140 141 252
Mary-Tidmarsh *aabcg dh* 264
Mary (Todd) *adaaa db* 470-1
Mary (Upham) *adffi* 250
Mary-Vinal *aacbe j* 166
Mary-Vinal *adfah aa* 395
Mary-Waite (Lewis) *aabcf ae* 405
Mary-Waldo *aacbc adb* 417
Mary (Ward) *adaad* 204-5
Mary-Warren *aabcg deb* 264 408
Mary (Webb) *adag* 103-9 216 223
Mary (Yarnall) *adadd* 51 100 101 209-12
Mary (Yates) *adahb bbh* 496
Matilda *adaga ae* 358
Matilda *adaaa beh* 464
Matilda (Aldridge) *adagb c* 219 220
Matilda-Craig *adaga gfc* 490
Matilda-Frances *adaga ag* 361 362 363
Matilda-May *adahb dcc* 499
Matthew 10 12 note 72

LINCOLN cont'd
Matthew *aah* 11
Matthew *aahe* 12 72
Mattie-Belle *adaae hff* 476
Mattie ([Halsey] Davis) *adaah ek* 482
Mattie-Joe *adaaf dbaa* 574
Maude-Anne *adaga ghb* 491
Maude-Bell *adaaa befh* 566
Maude-Minnie (Russell) *adaae abab* 569
Maude-Olivia *adahb faec* 585
Maude-Winthrop *aabce abab* 527
May-Anna-Adelaide (Schultz) *adffe df* 524-5
Mayme (Presley) *adaaf aca* 478
Mehitable *agb* 24 25
Mehitable *aacdd e* 314
Mehitable-Ellen (Wilder) *aacdb gc* 437
Mehitable (Frost) *ag* 23 24
Mehitable (Lincoln) *aacdd e* 314
Mehitable (Townsend) 14
Melissa (Daugherty) *adaaa bbg* 564
Melissa-Etta *adaaa bbch* 560
Mercy *aacbk* 75 78
Mercy *adcaj* 122 123 133
Mercy (Hersey) *aahd* 12
Mercy-Maria *adfah ac* 395
Mercy-Thomas (Merritt) *adcac baj* 597
Meriel *adcac c* 238-9
Merrick *aacbc adda* 541-2
Michael *adbcf c* 118 234 382 384-5
Mildred *aabce abcc* 527
Millicent-Roma *adaaf acfb* 574
Milton-Webber *aabce aebe* 529
Minerva *adaaa bbia* 565
Minerva-Wright *adffe cbc* 523
Minnie-Sadie (Catlett) *adaaa bbii* 566
Mira S. *aacda ed* 301
Mishal *adahc* 110 223 226-7
Molly (Holbrook) *aaib* 12
Mordecai *ac* 6 7
Mordecai *ad* 4 6 7 12 15 16-23 24 43 44 46 58 335 388 516
Mordecai *ada* 18 22 43-53 91 100 119 335
Mordecai *adag* 46 47 49 53 103-9 110 111 216 223
Mordecai *adbf* 44 55 58 59 115 118-21
Mordecai *adcb* 59 60 61 62 123-6 240
Mordecai *adaic* 111 112 229
Mordecai *adcbk* 125-6
Mordecai *adffg* 62 134 249-50
Mordecai *adaaa a* 43 195 196 197 198 201 202 324-9 330 336
Mordecai *adaaf d* 101 209 210 211 212 348-51 353
Mordecai *adaga g* 216 218 360-3 488
Mordecai *adagb a* 219 220
Mordecai *adaid d* 230
Mordecai *adaaa ac* 44 329
Mordecai *adaah gj* 357
Mordecai *adaga gd* 361 362 488-9
Mordecai *adaaa bbc* 463 559-61
Mordecai *adaga aad* 486
Mordecai-Abel *adaaa bbcgb* 607 615
Morton-Francis *aacdc gfa* 444
Moses 177 234 note 314
Moses *abe* 14-5
Moses *abea* 13 15
Moses *adbcf* 117 118 233-4 and note
Moses *aafff f* 185
Moses *adbch a* 234 235 236
Moses *aafff fc* 185
Moses *adbcf be* 384 512-3
Moses-Maris 234 note
Myra *abbec fa* 323
Nancy *adagc* 104 106 108
Nancy *aacbj a* 172 173
Nancy *adaaa e* 200 201 203-4
Nancy *adaga b* 216 217

LINCOLN cont'd
Nancy *adagb k* 105 219 221-2
Nancy *adaaa bd* 333
Nancy *adaae hia* 476
Nancy-Agnes *adaga gc* 361 362
Nancy-Ann *adaaf h* 101 209 212 353
Nancy (Barber) *aabce cb* 402
Nancy (Bicknell) *adffe* 247-8 395
Nancy-Bicknell *adffe b* 247-8
Nancy (Bigelow) *aacbj* 172-3
Nancy (Brown) *adaaf a* 347-8
Nancy (Driver) *adaae hc* 345
Nancy-Elizabeth (Burke) *aacbe hac* 424
Nancy-Franklin (Brown) *abbec bl* 455-6
Nancy (Gray) *aacab f* 72 note
Nancy (Hanks) *adaaa d* 334 335 336-42
Nancy (Hoard) *aacbc af* 418-9
Nancy-Jane *aabce adf* 401
Nancy-Jane (Porter) *aabce ad* 400-1
Nancy (Jenkins) *abbea m* 320-1
Nancy ([Lionberger] Rhodes) *adaae h* 344-5
Nancy (Norcross) *abbec f* 323
Nancy (Parker) *aabck f* 153 272-3 274
Nancy (Pratt) *abbea c* 318-9
Nancy (Simons) *abbec f* 323
Nanne *adcbd* 125
Nanette-Brown *adaaf abd* 477
Nannie-Margaret *adaae hfad* 572
Nathan-Harrison *adaaa bbif* 565 610-1
Nathan-Pattangall *aacdb ic* 307 438-9
Nathaniel *aaii* 12
Nellie *aacdb bdh* 432
Nellie (Brown) *adaga gh* 491
Nellie-Jane *adaga gfb* 490
Nellie-Josephine (Perkins) *adcac baib* 613-4
Nellie-Kilby *aacdb fcbh* 549
Nellie-May *aacdb gfb* 438
Nellie (Merrifield) *adaga aa* 486-7
Nellie-Olmsted (Pitkin) *aacdc ge* 443-4
Nellie-Pryor *adaah ekaa* 576
Nellie-Thomas *adcac baja* 597
Newcomb-Bourne *abbea cb* 319
Newton *adahb bbb* 495
Nicholas *adaaa aaf* 460 461
Nichols *aabcd b* 140 141 252 455
Nichols *aabcd bc* 140 141 252 399-400
Nina-Elizabeth (Higgins) *abbec bg* 454-5
Noah 423
Noah *aahb* 12
Nora-Abigail *adaae agh* 473
Nora-Anne *adahc aafa* 589
Nora-Arbel (Cain) *adaga aaaa* 579
Nora-Bell (Taylor) *adahc aaf* 589
Norman-Covington *adbcf bede* 594
Obadiah *aba* 13 14 38-39
Obadiah *abbg* 39 42 126 127
Obadiah *adfa* 60 61 62 126-8 131 189 190 394
Obadiah *abbhc* 92 191-3
Obadiah *adfah* 128 246
Odessa-Oleon *adaae agcb* 570
Olberson *adaaa befd* 566
Olive 142
Olive *aaij* 12
Olive *aaffc* 81
Olive *abaed* 86 87-8
Olive *adahb dbf* 498
Olive *adaaa bbgbc* 610
Olive-Augusta *adffe lc* 249 398
Olive (Cook) *adffe d* 396-7
Olive-Elkins *aacdb fce* 436
Olive-Irvette (Pike) *aabcf dad* 406
Olive (Litchfield) *adfaa* 243-4
Olive-May *adaga gdad* 580
Oliver *aabck g* 149 153 154 273-4

LINCOLN cont'd
Oliver *aabce ae* 255 401
Oliver *adahb dbe* 498
Oliver-Fessenden *aabck ga* 273-4
Oliver-Francis *aabce aeba* 528 602
Oliver-Gibbins *aabce bi* 255 257
Olivia-Elizabeth *adahb bbf* 495
Opal-Marie *adaae agib* 570
Ophelia (Whittington) *abbec bb* 84 453-4
Orianna-Augusta *abbea cabb* 553
Orpha-Theresa *adaaf fc* 352
Oscar *aabcf dd* 263
Oscar *adaii bk* 379
Oscar-Hemmig *adaii bbb* 508 592
Oscar-Moses *adbcf beec* 594
Oscar-Samuel *adagb fe* 366
Otis *aacdb* 79 175-181
Otis *aacdb e* 177 180 302-3 304 and note
Otis *aacdb ef* 303 434
Otis *aacdb efc* 434
Otis-Wade *adcai bc* 390
Pamela *aabhf* 70
Parmelia *adaaa aab* 460 461
Paschal-Hoopes *adbcf beh* 513
Patterson *adagb h* 105 219 221 366-7
Paul-Revere *aacbe g* 166
Paul-Revere *aacbe dadb* 545
Paulina-Emily *adaaf da* 349 350-1
Paulina (Stannels) *aacdb eb* 432-3
Pauline *aacdb ebaa* 548
Pauline *adahb bcda* 584
Pauline *adaaa bbgbb* 610
Pauline (Burns) *adahb gbca* 611-2
Pauline-Revere *aacdd daec* 552
Peggy *aabhb* 69
Peggy *adcba* 60 124-5
Peggy (Nichols) *adcac b* 388
Pelham-Winslow *aacbc ahj* 421
Pemberton-Hutchinson *adahf cead* 589
Penelope-Sever *aacbc ae* 283
Penelope-Winslow (Sever) *aacbc a* 282-3
Penelope-Winslow *aacbc acdc* 538
Percilla *abba* 13 39 40-1
Percilla (Farrow) *abb* 39-41
Percy-Woodson *adaae hfac* 572 611
Persis (Tower) *abaea* 42 186-7
Peter *aabce a* 142 254-5
Peter-Gatewood *adaah ee* 354 note 355 481
Peter-Whitmarsh *aabce aa* 255
Peter-Whitmarsh *aabce ad* 255 400-1
Phebe *adaig* 112 364
Phebe *adagb dg* 364-5
Phebe-Maria (Blake) *aacbg cc* 429
Phebe-Waterman *adbfa g* 237 238
Phoebe *adaaf g* 101 209 211
Phoebe *adaga i* 218-9
Phoebe *adaga cc* 359-60
Phoebe *adbcf bi* 384
Phoebe A. *adaga gk* 361 363
Phoebe-Ann (Brewer) *adaaa aae* 461
Phoebe-Gorham (Childs) 278
Phoebe-Speekman (Hoofstitler) *adbcf b* 383-4
Philena-Hope *aacbe dabd* 545
Philena (Prentice) *aacbe dab* 545
Philinda-Gates (Bates) *aacbg ch* 429-30
Philip-Jones *aacdb fcba* 549
Phineas *aacab e* 12 note 72
Polly *aacbe f* 166
Polly *adcac f* 239
Polly *adfad a* 244 245
Polly-Otis *aacda b* 174
Preston *adaae ab* 215 343 471-2
Priscilla *abbed* 37 89 90
Priscilla *aafff e* 184-5
Priscilla *abbea g* 189
Priscilla *abbec i* 191

LINCOLN cont'd
Priscilla *adahb e* 226
Priscilla *adcac e* 239
Priscilla *adaaa aaa* 460
Priscilla-Bates *adfae add* 522
Priscilla (Dickinson) *adahb* 225-6 228
Priscilla-Eastman *aacdb fcbe* 549
Priscilla-Nichols (Tower) *abbec bj* 323
Priscilla-Shaw (Pratt) *aabce ab* 400
Rachel *aacbd* 31 74 75 76-7
Rachel *adaif* 111 112
Rachel *aacbg h* 167
Rachel *aacdb j* 180-1
Rachel *abbea b* 189
Rachel *abbea i* 189
Rachel *adaaf e* 99 100 101 353
Rachel *adaic a* 229
Rachel *adaaa bba* 463
Rachel *adahc bab* 372
Rachel *adaaa bbbb* 559
Rachel (——) *adfb* 130 131
Rachel-Ann (Hurbaugh) *adaaa bbf* 563
Rachel-Ann (Noble) *aacbe ld* 426
Rachel-Burr (Sprague) *aabhg a* 276-7
Rachel (Cushing) *aacbg* 167 251
Rachel-Cushing *aabcd ab* 142 251
Rachel-Elizabeth *adaaa bbcc* 559-60
Rachel (Fearing) *aacb* 10 75-8
Rachel (Housekeeper) *adahf d* 375
Rachel-Housekeeper *adahf ck* 374
Rachel-Irene *adaaf fb* 352
Rachel-Lloyd (Hutchinson) *adahf cea* 589
Rachel-Malinda (Kay) *adahb gb* 501-2
Rachel-Potts (Holston) *adahb bd* 497-8
Rachel (Rogers) *adaid ab* 506
Rachel (Thompson) *adahc* 227
Rachel-Thompson *adahc ab* 371
Ralph-Albert *adaaa bbica* 610
Ralph-Augustus *adaae agia* 570
Ralph-Edward *adffe dfc* 525 601
Ralph-Freeman *aabhg aaae* 536
Ralph-Hamilton *adffe cgc* 524
Ralph-Herbert *aacdb eec* 434
Ralph-Nickerson *adaga agfa* 579
Ralph-Prosser *adaaa bbid* 565 610
Raymond-Emerson *aabcd bcda* 526
Raymond-Henry *aacdc ecaa* 552
Raymond-Taylor *adbcf bedc* 594
Rebecca *ak* 2 8 14
Rebecca *aae* 10
Rebecca *adbe* 55 58 114
Rebecca *aacab* 12 33 72
Rebecca *abaee* 88
Rebecca *abaef* 86 88-9
Rebecca *adaai* 94 95 100 101-3 208
Rebecca *adbaa* 59 113 114
Rebecca *adbce* 114 116 117-8 232
Rebecca *aabad f* 139
Rebecca *aacbc g* 163-4
Rebecca *adaae f* 207
Rebecca *adaha a* 224
Rebecca *adbca g* 118 232 233
Rebecca *aacbe hc* 295
Rebecca *adaae hb* 344-5
Rebecca *adbcf cd* 383 385
Rebecca (——) *adb* 58 94
Rebecca (R——) *adbcf c* 384-5
Rebecca ([Allyne] Kilby) *abae* 86-9
Rebecca (Edmonson) *adaaa beg* 566-7
Rebecca ([Flowers] Morris) *adaa* 93-103
Rebecca-Frances *adahf cc* 373
Rebecca-Hill (Butler) *aacbe d* 293
Rebecca (Jones) *adaaa beg* 566
Rebecca (Lincoln) *aacab* 12 72
Rebecca (Sherburn) *adcak bab* 392
Rebecca-Trevett (Bartol) *aacbe h* 295
Rebeckah *adfae ae* 394
Rees-Evans *adaid bd* 376

LINCOLN cont'd
Remington-King *adbfa bde* 515
Reuben *aabac* 65
Reuben *aabhc* 69
Revere *aacdd dd* 313 445-6
Rhoda *adaga gb* 361 362
Richard *aacdc ece* 442
Richard-Edward *adffe dfca* 601
Richard-Ellsworth *adagb djab* 493
Richard-Gilbert *adaii bf* 379 510-1
Richard-Hawkins *aacdc ecac* 552
Richard-Henry *abbec bba* 453 454 557
Richard-Mitchell *aacdc ec* 309 442
Richard-Newcomb *adcac baibb* 614
Richard-Stokes *adagb dj* 365 493
Richard-VanBuskirk *adahc aa* 223 371 503-4
Richard-VanBuskirk *adahc aaea* 588
Richmond-Jackson *adffe cf* 396
Robert *aacbi d* 168
Robert *adaaa aac* 460 461
Robert *aacdb igcc* 551
Robert *adahb bcdc* 584
Robert-Abraham *adaaf ace* 478 573-4
Robert-Allen *adahb dcg* 499 584-5
Robert-Beals *abbhc d* 192 323-4
Robert-Beals *abbhc db* 324 458-9
Robert-Beals *abbhc dbg* 459
Robert-Bicknell *adffe dfba* 601
Robert-Brewster *adahf daaa* 590
Robert-Burl *adaaa bbide* 610
Robert-Edmund *auvdb ebga* 548
Robert-Edson *adaae ahab* 570
Robert-Eugene *adaaa bbicc* 610
Robert-Golding *aacdb igc* 439 551
Robert-Herman *adbcf begb* 594
Robert M. *adaga gidc* 582
Robert-Ruth *adaii bbba* 592 612
Robert-Taliaferro *adaah ec* 354 480-1
Robert-Todd *adaaa dba* 471 567-8
Robert-Todd *adaga agda* 487 579
Robert-Webster *aabcg dbdb* 533
Roberta-Alice *adaaf dbcb* 575
Roberta-Beatrice *adaaf acea* 574
Robie-Thaxter *aabcj hba* 409 534
Robinson *aacdb h* 77 180 302 305-6
Roger-Bates *aacbe ldfc* 547
Roland-Crocker *aacdc ee* 310
Rosa-Bell *adaaa bbfe* 609
Rosa-Bell (Priest) *adaaa bbfe* 609
Rosa-Johrton *adaae hfaa* 572
Rosalie-Morgan *adaid bbc* 507
Rosanna *adaaa bek* 464
Roscoe-Murl *adaaa bbidf* 610
Rose *adahc bd* 372
Rose-Jane (Hemenway) *adahb gcd* 587
Roswell-Stoner *adaii bfa* 511
Roxanna ([Wood] Moody) *aabhe* 155-6
Roy-Bancroft *aabhe abb* 413
Roy-Lester *aabhg aaag* 536
Royal *aabcf* 66 67 143-6
Royal *aabcf a* 143 260-2
Royal *aabcf hd* 145
Royal *aabce abcd* 528
Royal-Waterman *aabcf ac* 261 404
Ruby-Hunt (Dean) *adaga gha* 581-2
Rufus *aabcg d* 264
Rufus-VanBuskirk *adahc aaf* 504 589
Rufus-Warren *aabcg d* 146 147 148 263-4 407
Rufus-Warren *aabcg dc* 264 406-7
Russell *aabch a* 148
Russell *aabch c* 148
Russell *adaah elb* 483
Russell *adaga gdah* 581
Russell-Phipps *adbcf begc* 594
Ruth *aabe* 31
Ruth *aabf* 31

LINCOLN cont'd
Ruth *aabg* 29 31
Ruth *aabcc* 67
Ruth *aabhd* 69
Ruth *adcag* 122 123
Ruth *adfaf* 127-8
Ruth *adffd* 133-4
Ruth *aabcf b* 143-4
Ruth *aabec fc* 323
Ruth *adbcf bedba* 613
Ruth-Ann *aabhg ec* 278
Ruth-Ann *adahb bba* 495
Ruth-Ann (Lincoln) *aabhg ec* 278
Ruth (Bates) *aacab g* 72
Ruth-Bates (Barker) *adcai bg* 518-9
Ruth (Beal) *adca* 121-3 132
Ruth ([Collier] [Willcutt] Tower) *adffg* 249-50
Ruth (Cushing) *aab* 30-1
Ruth-Elizabeth *adahb bbia* 583
Ruth-Eugenia (Martin) *adaah ebba* **575**
Ruth-Jessie *adaii bbbaa* 612
Ruth-Lillian *adaac hfacb* 611
Ruth (Manson) *abbea m; adffb d* **133** 320-1
Ruth-Marion *abbea mg* 320
Ruth-Pearl *aacdc ecad* 552
Ruth (Prater) *adbca f* 381-2
Ruth-Stannels *aacdb ebae* 548
Sadie-Countas *adbcf bef* 513
Sallie-Ann (Shewey) *adaae hfa* 571-2
Sallie-Haymaker *adagb djd* 493
Sallie-Josephine *adaae hfe* 476
Sallie-Knight *adaah gdc* 485
Sallie-Rebecca *adaae hfhb* 573
Sallie-Stuart (Sipe) *adaae ahc* 571
Sally *aaffh* 36 83
Sally *adcbf* 125
Sally *aabad g* 139
Sally *aabcg e* 147
Sally *aabcg h* 146 147
Sally *aacbe c* 166
Sally *aacda c* 174-5
Sally *adcac g* 239
Sally *adcak d* 242
Sally-Andora *adaii bca* 509
Sally (Howe) 423
Sally-Thaxter *aabcj a* 149
Sally (Thompson) *adaah ec* 480-1
Samuel 136 137 148
Samuel *a* 1 2 3 4 5-8 11 43 **44 91** 335
Samuel *aa* 3 4 7 9-12 16 91
Samuel *aab* 9 10 28-31
Samuel *aaba* 29 30 64-6 71 78 **148**
Samuel *aafi* 36 37
Samuel *aabag* 64 66 139-40 **143**
Samuel *adfff* 134
Samuel *aabad h* 139
Samuel *aabag a* 140
Samuel *aabcj c* 150 153 266-7
Samuel *aabhg e* 156 277-8
Samuel *aabci f* 168
Samuel *adahb f* 225 226 369
Samuel *adaid c* 230 376-7
Samuel *adbch c* 235 236
Samuel *adffe d* 247 395 396-7
Samuel *adahb db* 369 498-9
Samuel *adahb gg* 370
Samuel *adaid ab* 375 506
Samuel *adbch bb* 118 236
Samuel *abbea cad* 451 555-6
Samuel *adaah ece* 481
Samuel-Bicknell *adffe dfb* 525 601
Samuel-Darling *adffe dd* 397
Samuel-Enoch *adahb fae* 501 585
Samuel-Humphrey *adahb fd* 369
Samuel-James *aabce hb* 148 260
Samuel-Jones *adagb dm* 365

LINCOLN cont'd

Samuel-Kilby *adcai a* 241
Samuel-Kilby *adcai c* 241
Samuel-Nichols *aafff cb* 315
Samuel-Nichols *abbec bf* 322
Samuel-Pellman *adahc aab* 504
Samuel-Russell-Trevett *aacbe hb* 295 424-5
Samuel-Thomas *adahb dca* 499
Samuel-Walden *adaae ahd* 474
Samuel-Wilson *adahb bbi* 496 583
Sarah 15
Sarah *ai* 8
Sarah *aj* 4 8
Sarah *add* 18 22
Sarah *agj* 26 27
Sarah *aafb* 37
Sarah *aafl* 35 36 38
Sarah *abbf* 39 42
Sarah *adaf* 47 49 52-3
Sarah *adbd* 55 58 115
Sarah *aacbf* 75 77
Sarah *abaec* 86 87
Sarah *abbee* 89 90
Sarah *adaag* 95 98 100 101
Sarah *adage* 104 105 106 107-8
Sarah *adahd* 110 223
Sarah *adcae* 60 122 132-4
Sarah *adcbc* 125
Sarah *aacbj b* 172 173
Sarah *abaea a* 86 186-7
Sarah *abbec c* 191
Sarah *abbhc b* 192
Sarah *adaga d* 217
Sarah *adagb j* 219 221
Sarah *adahb i* 226
Sarah *adahc c* 227
Sarah *adffe a* 247
Sarah *abbec ba* 321
Sarah *adaaa da* 336 342
Sarah *adaga af* 358-9
Sarah *adahb ba* 368
Sarah *adahc bc* 372
Sarah *adaii bi* 379
Sarah *adaaa bbba* 559
Sarah-Adaline *adahb gbb* 501
Sarah-Adaline *adcai ffg* 520
Sarah-Alice (Jackson) *aacbe ldf* 546-7
Sarah (Allen) *adaah ei* 481-2
Sarah-Amelia *adaaf dd* 351
Sarah-Anderson (Jenkins) *adaid g* 377
Sarah-Ann *adaga gdd* 489
Sarah-Ann (Tripple) *adaid ca* 377
Sarah-Anna (Stubbs) *adahf cb* 504-5
Sarah (Bates) *adcac ba* 516-7
Sarah-Binney *aabcd df* 253 254
Sarah-Binney (Lincoln) *aabcd df* 254
Sarah (Brewster) *adahf daa* 590
Sarah ([Bush] Johnson) *adaaa d* 341
Sarah-Butler ([Shiverick] Nye) *aacdc f* 310
Sarah-Campbell *aacdb gfc* 438
Sarah-Clara *adaii bba* 508
Sarah (Cummings) *adc* 59
Sarah (Davis) *aacdc f* 310-1
Sarah-Elizabeth *adffe da* 396
Sarah-Elizabeth *adahb faa* 226 note 500
Sarah (Gilbert) *adaii b* 378-9
Sarah ([Guinn] Wright) *adaaf ab* 477
Sarah (Hart) *adaaf k* 353
Sarah (Hersey) *aaid* 12
Sarah (Hobart) *abbe* 89-91 121 244
Sarah ([Hobart] Lincoln) *abbe* 89 121-3 238 244
Sarah (Hyland) *abbea ca* 450-2
Sarah-James (Beal) *aabce h* 260
Sarah-Jane *aabcf db* 262-3

LINCOLN cont'd

Sarah-Jane *aabce adc* 401
Sarah-Jane *adahb bbe* 495
Sarah-Jane *adaaa bbcd* 560
Sarah-Jane (David) *adahb db* 498-9
Sarah-Jane (Luey) *aabck bd* 410-1
Sarah-Janette (White) *adffe l* 397
Sarah (Jeffreys) *adaha* 224
Sarah (Jones) *ad* 20 21
Sarah ([Jones] Shipman) *adaae hf* 475
Sarah-Legrow (Pollock) *aabcj hba* 534
Sarah-Leighton (Jones) *aacdb g* 304-5
Sarah (Lewis) *aaf* 36-8
Sarah-Lewis *aafff f* 185
Sarah-Lewis *aafff ge* 316 317
Sarah-Lewis *aafff gha* 318 449
Sarah-Lewis (Lincoln) *aafff f* 185
Sarah (Lincoln) *adcae* 122 132-4
Sarah-Maria (Campbell) *aacdb gf* 437-8
Sarah-Marjorie *adaaa bbcfc* 607
Sarah-Minot *aabck be* 270
Sarah (Nichols) 14
Sarah (Nichols) *aafff c* 314-6
Sarah-Nichols *aafff cd* 316
Sarah-Nitsel *adbca i* 118 232 233
Sarah-Nitzel *adbca ab* 118 380
Sarah-Priscilla *adahb gh* 370
Sarah-Rhodes (Arnold) *aacbc ah* 420
Sarah-Rosetta (Eberline) *aacbc ahb* 420
Sarah-Vinal *adcac bad* 516
Sarah (Ward) *aabcg* 146-7
Sarah-Ward *aabcg da* 264
Sarah-Warren *aacbc aa* 283
Sarah (Watts) *aacbi a* 299
Sarah (Weathers) *adaaa bb* 463
Selwyn-Randall *aacdd dae* 445 552
Serafina *aacdd eba* 448
Serafina (Loring) *aacdd eb* 448
Serena-Lambert *aacbi l* 169
Serena-Morgan (Brown) *aacdb ic* 438-9
Seth *aabd* 31
Seth *aabad* 64 65 137-9
Seth *aabad e* 139
Sherman *adbfa ba* 385-6
Sherman *adbfa be* 386
Shirley-Ada *aabce aebab* 602
Shubal *aacab d* 12 note 72
Sidney-Lindsey *abbec fdcb* 558
Silas *abbea h* 189
Silas-Woodson *adaah gdab* 578
Silence (Bates) *aacab g* 72
Silence (Tower) 451
Solomon 63
Solomon *aacdd* 72 79 176 183-4
Solomon *aacdb b* 177 179 301-2
Solomon *aacdd e* 43 44 168 183 184 313-4
Solomon *adahc ba* 372
Solomon *aacdd ea* 314 446-7
Solomon-Henry *aacdb bd* 302 431-2
Sophia *aabcf c* 144
Sophia *adaga ch* 360
Sophia (Gibbs) *aacdb i* 306-8
Sophia-Gibbs *aacdb ie* 308
Sophia (Haymon) *aacdb i* 307-8
Sophia-Merrill *aabcf ag* 261
Sophia-Opal *adaaa bbie* 565
Sophia-Williams (Heiskell) *adaaf d* 349-51
Stella *adaaa bbcga* 607
Stella-May (Cheney) *aacdb eea* 548-9
Stephen 10 11 12 13 34 72 77 242 254 423 426
Stephen *aaha* 12
Stephen *adaah ecb* 480
Stephen-Mason *aacdb icac* 550
Sukey *aabcg b* 146
Susan 426
Susan *aabaa c* 135 136 137

LINCOLN cont'd

Susan *adbcf caa* 514
Susan-Anne *adaae hface* 611
Susan-Beals *aabck fe* 273
Susan-Caroline *aabck bi* 271
Susan-Congdon (Allen) *aacdc gf* 444
Susan-Crocker *aacdc fb* 310-1
Susan-Elizabeth *adfad baa* 521
Susan (Groomes) *adaga agb* 487
Susan (Haymon) *aacdb i* 306-8
Susan (Knott) *abbhc d* 324
Susan ([Lewis] Mansfield) *aacbe ha* 425
Susan-Louise (Edgar) *aabce cda* 529-30
Susan-Maria *aacdb he* 305 306
Susan ([Moore] Hudson) *adahb d* 369
Susan-Patterson ([Coolidge] Low) *aabck b* 269-71
Susan-Permilla *adaii bec* 510
Susan-Russell *abbhc dbc* 458
Susan-White (Freeman) *adfad b* 392-3
Susanna *aai* 12
Susanna *aabc* 66-8
Susanna *aafk* 38
Susanna *aaif* 12
Susanna *aaii* 12
Susanna *abac* 38 39
Susanna *abbi* 13 39 42-3 88 184
Susanna *aabci* 66 67 68 142
Susanna *aaffb* 36 81 390
Susanna *abaeb* 86-7 188
Susanna *adcbg* 125
Susanna *adcbh* 125 239
Susanna *aabcf g* 145
Susanna *aabcg c* 146 147
Susanna *aacab b* 72
Susanna *aacab c* 12 note 72
Susanna *aafff d* 184
Susanna (——) 2
Susanna (Beal) *abbid* 43 184-5
Susanna (Beal) *aacab a* 72
Susanna-Crocker *aacdc c* 182
Susanna (Gill) 314
Susanna (Gill) *aba* 13 38-9
Susanna (Gill) *aahe* 12 38-9 72
Susanna (Lincoln) *aai* 12
Susanna (Lincoln) *aabc* 66-8
Susanna (Lincoln) *aaii* 12
Susanna ([Worrick] Marble) *adf* 61 62
Susannah *abbhc f* 191 193
Susannah (Crocker) *aacdc* 182
Susannah-Nichols *aafff ca* 315
Susannah-Stoddard *adcai be* 390-1
Susie-Ella (Thompson) *aabcd bcd* 526
Sybil (Heald) *aacda e* 300-1
Sylvanus-Gibbs *aacdb id* 308
Sylvia-Delphine (Vanatta) *adahb gbe* 586
Tabitha (Whitmarsh) *aabce* 142
Tamar *adcbj* 125
Tamar (Nichols) *abbhc* 191-3
Tamar-Nichols *abbhc g* 193
Tennessee *adaaf abb* 477
Thamazine *adaid bc* 376
Thankful *aabcf e* 144
Theresa-Eveline *adaaa bbcgc* 607
Thomas 1 2 3 4 6 7 10 11 12 13 14 63 68 77 128 142 145 157 278 313 367
Thomas *ae* 7
Thomas *ag* 4 8 23-7
Thomas *age* 26
Thomas *agh* 26
Thomas *abaa* 38
Thomas *abae* 13 39 85-9
Thomas *adah* 46 47 49 50 53 108 109-10 223
Thomas *adfh* 62 63 130
Thomas *adaah* 43 95 97 98 100 101 212-5 471

LINCOLN cont'd

Thomas *adahb* 110 223 225-6 228
Thomas *adaii* 111 112 229 230-1
Thomas *adffc* 133
Thomas *abbec f* 191 323
Thomas *adaaa d* 43 197 200 201 202 203 204 328 330 333-42
Thomas *adaga a* 107 109 216 217 357-9
Thomas *adahb d* 226 368-9
Thomas *adahc b* 227 371-2
Thomas *adffe c* 248 395-6
Thomas *abbec bh* 322
Thomas *abbec fd* 323 457-8
Thomas *adaaa bb* 44 331 332 463
Thomas *adaaa dc* 342
Thomas *adahb bc* 368 496-7
Thomas *adahb gb* 370 501-2
Thomas *adaaa beb* 464
Thomas *adaaa dbd* 471
Thomas *adaaa bbbc* 559
Thomas *adaga agfc* 579
Thomas-Abraham *adaga aaa* 486 579
Thomas-Boone *adaga ag* 359 487
Thomas-Bouvé *aabce bf* 257
Thomas-Franklin *abbec fdca* 558
Thomas-Gatewood *adaah gi* 357
Thomas J *adaga gfae* 581
Thomas-Jefferson *adaga gi* 361 363 492
Thomas-Jefferson *adaaa aba* 462
Thomas-Lionel *adaga agc* 487
Thomas-Manson *adffe cd* 396 253
Thomas-Osborn *adahb bbc* 495
Thomas-Pryor *adaah ekae* 576
Thomas-Ransom *aabce cdbc* 531
Thompson *aacdb g* 177 180 304-5
Thompson *aabcf da* 262 405-6
Thorla *aabcf aeaa* 531
Tillie-May (Zimmerman) *adaga gid* 582
Uriah *adcac* 21 22 60 89 121 122 238-40 516
Uriah *adcac baa* 516
Villroy-Augusta (Goulding) *aacbc ccba* 603
Viola-Maria *abbea cabib* 605
Viola-Zitella *aabce aebd* 529
Virgil-Ashmead *adaga aga* 487
Virgil-Edgar *adaaa bbidc* 610
Virginia *adaii bfb* 511
Virginia *adahf dabe* 590
Virginia-Catherine *adaae aga* 472
Virginia-Mabel (Murray) *aacdc ec* 442
Virginia-May (Gibb) *adahf dab* 590
Virginia-Morton (Pryor) *adaah ek* 482
Virginia-Thorn *adagb djef* 583
Wakefield-Gale *aacdb ge* 305
Waldo *aacbc f* 163
Waldo *aacbc h* 164
Waldo *aacbc i* 164
Waldo *aacbc add* 162 163 282 417 418 538-44
Walter *aacdb bdg* 432
Walter *adaah ecf* 481
Walter *adaii beb* 510
Walter-Bowdlear *aacbe lde* 426
Walter-Daniell *aabce cdba* 531
Walter F. *aabck bha* 412
Walter-Foster *adfae ada* 522 599-600
Walter-Kendall *adaga gha* 491 581-2
Walter-Moore *aacdc ge* 313 444
Walter-Rodman *adahf dac* 506 590-1
Ward-Clapp *aabcg ded* 408
Warden *adaaa bbf* 463 563
Warren *aabcg f* 117
Warren *aabck f* 153 154 271-3 274
Warren *adcak b* 242 391-2
Warren *adcai fg* 391
Warren *adfae adcb* 600
Warren-Parker *aabck fc* 272-3

LINCOLN cont'd
Warren-Silvester *aacdb eeb* 433
Warren-Stanwood *aabcg dgba* 534
Warren T. *aabcc adh* 401
Washington *adaaa bbe* 463 561-2
Welcome 15 314
Wiley-Ethelbert *adaaa bbcfa* 607
Willard-Emmanuel *adaaa bbfe* 563 609
Willard-Moore *adcai fff* 520
William 368
William *aacd* 33 35 78-80
William *aacda* 79 173-5
William *adbfa* 120 237-8
William *aabaa e* 135 136 137
William *aabcf i* 146
William *aabck e* 154
William *aabhg f* 156
William *aacbc j* 163 164 287 289-91 414 415
William *aacda a* 174
William *aacdb f* 177 180 303-4 and note
William *aacdc g* 182 308 311-3
William *aacdd b* 183
William *adagb f* 219 220 365-6
William *adahb b* 226 368
William *adbch h* 118 235 236
William *adfae a* 63 246 393-4
William *aabce cb* 258 462
William *aacda ee* 301
William *aacdc fa* 310
William *adagb hd* 367
William *adagb lc* 368
William *adbcf aa* 236 382-3 514
William *adbcf bh* 384
William *adbfa ee* 387
William *adfae a* 394
William *adfae ad* 394 521-2
William *aabce cba* 402
William *aacbc aca* 415
William *aacdc gfc* 444
William *adaaa bbh* 463
William *adaaa bec* 464
William *adahb gcb* 502
William *adaaa bbfd* 563 608-9
William *adaaf dbab* 574
William-Adams *adahb gbca* 586 611-2
William-Andrew *adagb fbg* 494
William-Brant *adaae hfba* 572
William-Burns *adahb gbcaa* 612
William-Crowell *adffe cga* 524
William-Curtis *aacdb igg* 439
William-David *adaah gdb* 485 578
William-David *adaah gdba* 578
William-Dickinson *adahb dcf* 499
William-Edmond *adbcf bega* 594
William-Edward *adaga gdac* 580
William-Edwards *aacdc gb* 312 313 442-3
William-Effiah *adaae hfa* 475 571-2
William-Ellis *abbea mbc* 452
William-Grim *adaga agg* 487
William H. *adbfa eb* 386
William-Harrison *adagb fb* 366 494
William-Harry *adaah ecab* 480
William-Henry *aacbi h* 169
William-Henry *aacdc b* 182
William-Henry *aacdb fb* 304
William-Henry *aacdb gf* 305 437-8
William-Henry *aacdc ea* 308 309 440-2
William-Henry *aabck bhb* 412
William-Henry *aacdb gcc* 437
William-Henry *adaaf dba* 479 574-5
William-Henry *adagb fbh* 494
William-Irving *abbea cabg* 554 604
William-Ives *adaid hc* 378 507
William M. *adbfa e* 238 386-7
William-Ogden *adbcf beg* 513 594
William-Oliver *aabck bd* 270 274 410-1
William-Otis *aacdd d* 168 169 183 184 313

LINCOLN cont'd
William-Otis *aacdd da* 313 444-5
William-Otis *aacdc gba* 443
William-Otis *aacdd daeb* 552
William-Penn *adahf cl* 374
William-Penn *adahf de* 375
William-Perry *adffe db* 397
William-Preston *adaaf acb* 478
William-Reynolds *adahf dah* 506 590
William-Robie *aabcj hbab* 534
William-Rogers *adaga gid* 492 582
William-Sever *aacbc ac* 283 414-5 419
William-Sever *aacbc acba* 537 603
William-Sherman *adaaa bbcf* 560 607
William-Taylor *adahb bda* 498
William-Thomas *adaaa bbea* 561 607-8
William-Vinal *adafh a* 246 394-5
William-Wallace *adaaa dbc* 471
William-Waterman *aabcf ae* 261 404-5
William-Weaver *adbcf bebd* 593
William-Wesley *adaae agcd* 570
William-Wharton *adaah eg* 355
William-Zimmerman *adaga gidb* 582
Willie-Beatrice *adaaf acbb* 478
Willie (Hill) *adaae hfb* 572
Willie-Jane (Harris) *adaah ebb* 575
Williette-Woodside (Eastham) *adcac dac* 598
Winfield-Scott *adaga gfad* 581
Winifred *aaffd* 36 81-2
Winslow-Hall *abbea mbb* 452
Winslow-Sever *aacbc acd* 415 537-8
Winslow-Sever *aacbc acdd* 538 603-4
Winthrop *aabhg aaa* 413 530-6
Winthrop-Clinton *aacdb ica* 438 550
Winthrop-Dallas *abbec bec* 454
Winthrop-Seissler *aacdb icaa* 550
Wyman-Forester *aabcg dbda* 533
Wyman-Russell *adcai bga* 519 598
Zadock *aabaa* 64 65 135-7
Zenas *abbec* 89 127 190-1
Zenas *abbed g* 191
Zenas-Dallas *abbec bg* 322 454-5
Zeroda *adaaa bbee* 562
LINDEN
John 353
LINDER
Usher F. 328
LINDSEY
Annie-Emily *abbec fdc* 558
Harriet (Hardy) 558
Lydia-Jane 547-8
Mary 566
Thomas 558
LINFIELD
Jonathan *abbhc bf* 192
Josephine 581
Mary-Lincoln (Shaw) *abbhc bf* 192
LIONBERGER
David 344
Mary (——) 344
Nancy *adaae h* 344-5
LITCHFIELD
Abigail-Joy 529
Abigail (Studley) 126
Abner *adfba f* 132
Abner-Hersey *adfba* 131-2
Adeline (Hatch) *adfba i* 132
Alfred 241
Ann *adcbm i* 126
Anne (Cushing) 270
Ann (Gary) *adcai ea* 241
Anna (Lincoln) *adcai e* 241
Anna (Stoddard) *adfba a* 131
Asa *adcai ef* 241
Benjamin-Sewell *abbea caff* 451
Bethiah 319
Betsey *adcbm h* 126

LITCHFIELD cont'd
Betsey (Stetson) *adcbm b* 126
Billings *adcbm f* 126
Celia *adfba b* 63 131
Daniel 452
Deborah 554
Edwin-Lawrence *adcai ec* 241
Eliza *adfba h* 132
Eliza (Litchfield) *adfba h* 132
Elizabeth-Maria (Cowdin) *adcai el* 241
Elizabeth-Strickland (Smith) *adcai ed* 241
Ellen-Maria (Lincoln) *abbea cai* 452
Elwin-Lewis *adcai ed* 241
Eunice *adcbm c* 126
Eunice (Litchfield) *adcbm c* 126
Eunice (Witherell) *adfba d* 132
Fanny-Kilby *adcai eb* 241
Fanny ([Kilby] Lincoln) 240-1
Francis *adcbm* 126
Francis *adcbm c* 126
Freeman 452
George *adcbm a* 126
Hannah *aafaa* 37
Hannah (Hersey) 131
Hannah-Hersey *adfba d* 132
Hannah-Hersey (Litchfield) *adfba d* 132
Harriet *adcbm g* 126
Hersey *adfba d* 132
Howard-Ellms *abbea caah* 450
Howland *adcai ea* 241
Hubbard *adfba h* 63 132
Ida-May (Williams) *abbea caah* 450
Isaac 131
Isabella (Merrett) *adfba i* 132
Israel 240-1
Jacob *adfba a* 131
Joshua *aaffj j* 84
Josiah 17 126 131 240 243
Laban-Hersey *adcai el* 241
Lawrence 126 131 240 241 243 452
Lawrence *aabck be* 270 274
Lendall *aaffd h* 82
Lewis *adcbm b* 126
Liba-Lincoln *adcai ee* 241
Lily W. ([Peterson] Eldred) *abbea caic* 452
Lincoln *adfba i* 63 132
Lizzie-Maria *abbea caia* 452
Louisa-Jane (Williams) *abbea caab* 450
Lucena(Lincoln) *adcbm* 126
Lucy (Damon) 452
Lucy-Lincoln *adcbm d* 126
Lucy (Randall) *adcbm a* 126
Lucy (Studley) *adcbm b* 126
Luther *adcai e* 241
Lydia 90 91
Lydia (Cole) 90
Maria (Kilby) *aaffd h* 82
Martha (Brown) *adfba h* 132
Martha ([Brown] Litchfield) *adfba h* 132
Martha-Stockbridge *abbea cab* 553-4
Mary *adcbm e* 126
Mary-Elizabeth *aabck bea* 270
Mary-Elizabeth *abbea caib* 452
Mary-Eva (Ainslie) *abbea caff* 451
Mary (Lincoln) *adfba* 131-2
Mary-Ray (Tinkcom) *adcai ec* 241
Mary (Simmons) *adcbm f* 126
Maryetta (Bonsteel) *adcai ef* 241
Meshech 553
Nettie-Grace *aafff gga* 318
Nicholas 126 131 240 452
Nichols 270
Olive *adfaa* 243-4
Perez *adfba g* 132
Polly *adfba g* 132
Polly (Damon) *adcbm a* 126
Polly (Ellmes) *aaffj j* 84

LITCHFIELD cont'd
Polly (Litchfield) *adfba g* 132
Priscilla *aaflc* 38
Priscilla (Vinal) 243
Rachel *adfba c* 63 132
Rachel-Anna *adcai eh* 241
Rachel (Clapp) 241
Rehtse-Louisa *adcai ei* 241
Roxanna (Shattuck) *adfba e* 132
Ruth-Beal *adcai ek* 241
Ruth ([Snow] Pratt) *adcbm c* 126
Samuel 243
Samuel *adfba e* 63 131
Sarah-Ann *adcai ej* 241
Sarah (Case) 240
Sarah-Kilby *adfba f* 132
Sarah-Kilby (Litchfield) *adfba f* 132
Sarah-Minot (Lincoln) *aabck be* 270 274
Sarah (Weisz) *adcai ee* 241
Serissa 241
Silas 452
Silas-Damon *abbea cai* 452
Silas-Damon *abbea caic* 452
Sophia (Patten) *adcbm c* 126
Susan (Wall) *adcbm b* 126
Susanna (Morey) 240
Temperance (Stoddard) 553
Thankful (Simmons) *adcbm f* 126
Thomas 90
William *abbea caab* 450
LITHCOE
Elizabeth 255
LITTLE
Amelia (Hixon) *aabcf abd* 261
Cornelia *aabad ga* 139
Cornelia-Woodhull *aabcf abe* 261
David 20
Edward 287 note
Elizabeth (Malbon) *aabad gc* 139
Emily-Shaw *aabcf abf* 261
Harriet 261
Harriet-Lincoln *aabcf abg* 261
Harriet-McLellan (Lincoln) *aabcf ab* 261
Helen (Graham) *aabcf abi* 261
Henry-Augustus *aabcf aba* 261
Henry-Otis *aabad ge* 139
Isaac 139
Isaac *aabad g* 139
Jane-Lincoln *aabcf abh* 261
Joseph-Vaill *aabcf abc* 261
Martha-Merrill *aabcf abb* 261
Mary-Ann (Knight) *aabcf aba* 261
Mary-Catherine (Hersey) *aabad ge* 139 142
Rebecca (Dodge) 261
Sally (Lincoln) *aabad g* 139
Samuel *aabad gc* 139
Sarah *aabad gd* 139
Stephen 261
Thomas-Jones *aabcf abd* 261
Welthea (Winsor) 139
William-Dodge *aabcf ab* 261
William-Frederick *aabcf abi* 261
LITTLEFIELD
John 311
Nellie B. *aacdb eae* 303
LIVINGSTON
Abigail (———) 455
Eliza-Ann *abbec bi* 455
John 455
LLOYD
Clayanna 589
Thomas 93
LOCKE
Abigail (Nichols) *adcah f* 123
Augustus *aacdc gbb* 443
Augustus W. 443
Charles *adcah f* 123

LOCKE cont'd
Elizabeth (Berry) 25
Helen-Alma(Lincoln) *aacdc gbb* 443
James-Frederick 145
James W. 145
John 25
Louise F. (——) 145
Martha (Perkins) 443
LOCKWOOD
Ambrose-Sanford *adffe bd* 248
Emeline-Corbett (Dickinson) *adffe bd* 248
LOFLAND
Ada-Winslow *adaae adj* 343
Anna-McKelvin *adaae adj* 343
Cornelia-Smith *adaae adh* 343
Dorcas (Lincoln) *adaae ad* 343
Dorman 343
Dorman-David *adaae adf* 343
Frances-Elizabeth *adaae ade* 343
Franklin-Lincoln *adaae adi* 343
Henrietta *adaae add* 343
Ida (Smith) *adaae adf* 343
James-Preston *adaae ada* 343
Margaret-Catherine *adaae adb* 343
Margaret (Kyle) 343
Mary-Jane *adaae adc* 343
Sallie (Rumple) *adaae adi* 343
Smith *adaae ad* 343
LOFTUS
Ralph 208
LOGAN
Stephen T. 467
LOMBARD
Elizabeth 88
LONG
Abigail 249
Addie *aabhc dba* 458
Charles M. *adaae ici* 347
Edna-Earle (Brock) *adaae ici* 347
Ella-Lee *adaae ahd* 474
George 375
John *adaid a* 375
Josiah-Campbell 458
Margaret *adaae jc* 207
Margaret-Amelia ([Henderson] Lincoln) *adaid a* 375
Rebecca (Young) 458
LONGFELLOW
Arethusa *aacdb df* 180
Ellen-Elizabeth *adcac da* 518
Tabitha 150
LONIGAN
Anna-Mabel *adaaa bbgab* 564
Carrie (Lincoln) *adaaa bbga* 564
Edward-Francis *adaaa bbga* 564
Guy-Lincoln *adaaa bbgaa* 564
Jessie-Maud *adaaa bbgac* 564
John-William 564
Sarah (Lang) 564
LOOMIS
Eliza P. (Sheldon) 393
Horace 393
Lewis-Harris *adfad bb* 393
Mary-Maria (Lincoln) *adfad bb* 393
Phila (Harris) 393
LORD
Samuel 129
Sarah 277
LORIN—Loring
Benjamin 69 448
Bertha *aabha a* 69
Bethia (Smith) 69
Charles *aabha b* 69
George 448
Harriet 69 note
Harriet *aabha e* 69
James 311

LORIN—Loring cont'd
John 69 448
John *abbec fad* 323
Joseph 448
Joseph-George 448
Josias 4
Jotham 77
Lucy-Richardson (Souther) *abbec fad* 323
Lydia (Lincoln) *aabha* 69
Peter 75
Reuben *aabha c* 69
Serafina *aacdd eb* 448
Serafina (Martinez) 448
Thomas 69 448
Thomas *aabha* 69
Thomas *aabha d* 69
LOTHROP
Abigail 8
Amand-Sophia (Forbes) 430
Ann B. (Johnson?) *adcac eh* 239
Anselm 239
Anselm *adcac e* 239
Clara 239
Clara-Amanda *aacbg ck* 430-1
Cummings-Lincoln *adcac eh* 239
Elizabeth-Lincoln *adcac ec* 239
Elizabeth (Whittington) *aaffi b* 84
Eunice (Burr) 239
Eunice-Burr *adcac eb* 239
George-Beal *adcac ee* 239
George-Beal *adcac ef* 239
James-Burr 239
John 239
John-Jacob *aaffi b* 84
Joseph 239
Loring 430
Marcia-Dunlap *adcac eg* 239
Peter 83 92 185 189 191 240 314 321
Priscilla (Lincoln) *adcac e* 239
Priscilla-Lincoln *adcac ed* 239
Priscilla-Nichols 453
Ruth 390
Ruth (Nichols) 239
Ruth-Nichols *adcac ei* 239
Sarah 92
Thomas 239
Thornton K. 447
Uriah-Lincoln *adcac ea* 239
LOURY
William M. 350
LOVELY
Amanda (Burrow) *adaaa abca* 462
John 462
Mary (French) 462
Mary-Rowena (Lincoln) *adaaa abc* 462
William *adaaa abc* 462
William *adaaa abca* 462
LOVETT
Elizabeth *adahb dc* 499
Joshua 272
LOW
Albert F. *aabce faa* 259
Charlotte F. 259
Dolly (Crosby) 259
Elizabeth (Stone) 269
Francis 259
Francis *aabce fa* 259
Isaiah 269
Jacob *aabaa a* 136
Joanna *aaa* 10
John 10 269
Lucinda (Lincoln) *aabce fa* 259
Margaret ([Robinson] Phillips) 259
Mary (Lincoln) *aabaa a* 135 136
Ruth (Joy) 10
Susan-Patterson (Coolidge) *aabck b* 269-71
William 259

LOWELL
Daniel *aabcf fc* 144
Emma-Chapman ([Woodbury] Rounds) *aabcf fc* 144
John 176
Lydia (——) 431
Thomas 431
LOWENBACH
Sarah-Aramenta-Nannie (Brock) *adaae icf* 347
William-Moritz *adaae icf* 347
LOWNES
Benanuel 56
LOWRIE
Catherine (Zearing) 217
LUCAS
Benedick 203
Mary (——) *adaah ek* 482
LUDWIG
Lucia 611
LUEY
Elizabeth (——) 410
James 410
Sarah-Jane *aabck bd* 410-1
LUKENS
Elizabeth-Lincoln *adbca ib* 233
Levi 233
Levi *adbca ia* 233
Mary-Elizabeth (Shaffner) *adbca ia* 233
Mary (Jones) 233
Nathan-Jones *adbca i* 233
Sarah-Nitsel (Lincoln) *adbca i* 233
LULL
Emmelyn-Ticknor (Guild) *aabck bic* 271
George-Summers *aabck bic* 271
LYLE
Emma-Gerard *adaah eka* 576
John-Newton 576
Margaret-Trimble (Hays) 576
LYMAN
Caleb 41
LYME see Lime
LYNDE
Samuel 25

McALLISTER
Elinor 587
McCAIN
Isabella *adaga gff* 490 491
McCALMANT
Mary D. 377
McCARGER
Kathareen 587
McCARTHY—McCarty
Ellen 421
Elizabeth (MacVeagh) *adahf ac* 228
Henry *adahf ac* 228
Ida-Adelia 536
James *adahf ab* 228
Rebecca (MacVeagh) *adahf ab* 228
McCAULEY
Benjamin-Lincoln *adagb dic* 365
Harry-Lincoln *adagb dib* 365
John C. *adagb di* 365
Martha-Louise ([Lincoln] Bailes) *adagb di* 364 365
McCLAIN—McClean
Eliza 358
Mary-Jane 514
Samuel 107
McCLENNEN
Albert *aacbe hbb* 425
Arthur-Raymond *aacbe hbbb* 425
Emma-Gertrude *aacbe hbba* 425
Lucy-Emma (Lincoln) *aacbe hbb* 425
Mary-Ann (Pigeon) 425
Robert 425

McCLERNAN
Ella *adagb dje* 583
Louisa-Ann (Snyder) 583
William-Leroy 583
McCLOUD
Mary-Ann 458
McCONNELL
Anna-Phoebe (Lincoln) *adbcf bec* 513
Bessie-Amanda *adbcf beca* 513
Charles-Maxwell *adbcf bece* 513
Harry-Bonsall *adbcf becb* 513
John 513
Lida (Leeds) *adbcf becb* 513
Louisa-Jones *adbcf becd* 513
Mary (——) 513
Rose-Lelia (Small) *adbcf bece* 513
Susan-Bailey *adbcf becc* 513
William *adbcf bec* 513
McCORKLE
F. A. 351
McCRAY—McCrea
Eliza *adaga ia* 219
Jane 494
McCULLOUGH
Anna 572
Anna-Newman (Mason) *aacdb jg* 181
Ella-Catherine 591
George W. *aacdb jg* 181
McDANIEL
B. 350
McDONALD
Ettie *adaaa beia* 464
McDONOUGH
Belinda *aacda e* 300
McDOUGALL
Alexander 224
McFANN
Mary-Holmes 602
McFARLAND
Bessie-Lincoln (James) *adaid cbc* 377
Isaac-Trego *adaid cbc* 377
Laura-Carlton 502
Lodena (Lincoln) *adahb dbd* 498
McGAW
Jacob 78
Margaret 78
McGILL
Charles C. *adaaa aaaa* 460
Clement C. 460
James *adaha dd* 224
Margaret (Hills) *adaha dd* 224
Mary E. 460
Priscilla-Florida ([Smith] Anderson) *adaaa aaaa* 460
Robert 351
Robert J. 460
McGREGOR
Jessie 421
McGRUFFIN
Hannah-Martha 571
McHUGH
Margaret (Ringrose) *adcac daa* 518
McINTIRE
Buford *adaha db* 224
Sarah (Hills) *adaha db* 224
MACKAY—McKay
James 93
Lydia (——) 93
Margaret *adffa d* 132
Mary (——) 93
Moses 93
Robert 93
Zechariah 93
McKEEVER
Rebecca 571
McKENLY
Mary *aabcg dc* 407
Patrick 407

McKENLY cont'd
  Rosanna (——) 407
McKENNA
  Ellen-Theresa *aabcg dbcb* 532
  John-Joseph 532
  Mary-Elizabeth (Mullen) 532
McKENZIE
  Mabel-Louise *abbea cabbd* 553
McKEON
  Almira-Hall (Guild) *aabck bie* 271
  John *aabck bie* 271
McKINNEY
  Harry *adaii bde* 379
  Rachel-Lincoln (Hafer) *adaii bde* 379
McKINSEY
  George *adahf ccg* 373
  Rachel-Emma (Haines) *adahf ccg* 373
McLAREN
  Ian 435
McLAUGHLIN
  Ada-Maude *adffe ce* 524
  Archibald-Arnold 524
  Harriet (Kirby) 524
McLAUTHLIN
  John-Thomas *adfah ab* 395
  Lewis 395
  Lucy-Frances (Lincoln) *adfah ab* 395
  Polly (Hathaway) 395
McLELLAN
  Bryce 260
  Eunice 150
  Harriet *aabcf a* 260-2
  Jane (——) 260
  William 260
McLEOD—MacLeod
  Daniel *abbdb* 42
  Elizabeth (Leavitt) *abbdb* 42
  Ruth-Catheryn *adaah eiac* 482
McLURE
  Nancy 370
McMASTER
  Charlotte *aacdc ecbb* 442
  Charlotte (Lincoln) *aacdc ecb* 442
  Edith *aacdc ecba* 442
  Harry-Austin *aacdc ecb* 442
  Henry-Austin 442
  Mary-Celia (Rhymes) 442
  Virginia *aacdc ecbc* 442
McMICHAEL
  Clara *adaah eod* 356
  Fanny *adaah eob* 356
  Hannah (Morgan) 355
  John-Morgan *adaah eo* 355-6
  John-Morgan *adaah eof* 356
  Julia *adaah eoc* 356
  Julia (Lincoln) *adaah eo* 355-6
  Lenore *adaah eoa* 356
  Thomas 355
  Thomas *adaah eoe* 356
McNEAL—McNeil
  miss *adahb d* 369
  Elizabeth (Bailey) 83
  Jane 305
McNEY
  Harry-Benjamin *adaga abc* 358
  Sara-Frances (Carson) *adaga abc* 358
McQUEANIE
  Jennie 598
McTONER
  Martin *adaaf he* 212
  Rachel (Williams) *adaaf he* 212
MacVEAGH—MacVeigh
  Delila (——) *adahf aa* 228
  Elizabeth *adahf ac* 228
  Ellen *adahf af* 228
  Emily (Eames) *adahf ag* 228
  Franklin *adahf ag* 228 and note
  Isaac-Wayne *adahf ae* 228 note

MacVEAGH cont'd
  Letty-Miner (Lewis) *adahf ae* 228
  Major-John *adahf a* 228
  Margaret (Lincoln) *adahf a* 228
  Mary-Ann *adahf ad* 228
  Nathan *adahf aa* 228
  Rebecca *adahf ab* 228
  Sarah 229
  Virginia-Rolette (Cameron) *adahf ae* 228
  Wayne *adahf ae* 228 and note
MADDISON—Madison
  Gabriel 222
  James 159 160
MAITLAND
  Ann (Hollis) *adahb ad* 226
  Joseph *adahb ad* 226
MAKEPEACE
  Clara-Wentworth *aabce abc* 527-8
  Cordelia-Etta *aabce abc* 527-8
  Horace-Mann 527
  Mary-Julia (Parker) 527
MALBON
  Elizabeth *aabad gc* 139
MALIN
  Elizabeth (Paschall) *adbca cb* 232 233
  Levi *adbca cb* 232
MANN
  Charlotte 250
  Joshua *aabgc* 31
  Molly (Cushing) *aabgc* 31
  Peggy 38
MANNING
  Abigail-Ripley (Hobbs) *abaeg bc* 188
  Albert 256
  Eliza-Ann (Holbrook) 256
  William W. *abaeg bc* 188
MANSFIELD
  Isaac *aacbe hb* 425
  John 425
  Lydia-Hersey (Breed) 425
  Susan (Lewis) *aacbe hb* 425
MANSON
  Ann-Stephen (Ellms) *adffb e* 133
  Elizabeth-Tilestone ([Jenkins] Jenkins)
    adffb f 133
  George *adffb g* 133
  Hannah (Lincoln) *adffb* 63 133 320
  Joel-Lincoln *adffb h* 133
  John 133
  John *adffb a* 133
  John *adffb e* 133
  Mary (Jenkins) *adffb h* 133
  Mary (Turner) *adffb b* 133
  Mercy (Jenkins) *adcaj e* 123 133
  Miriam (Curtis) 133
  Nehemiah *adffb* 123 133 320
  Nehemiah *adffb f* 133
  Ruth *adffb c* 133
  Ruth *adffb d* 133 320-1
  Sarah-Wales (James) *adffb g* 133
  Thomas-Lincoln *adffb b* 133
MANUEL
  Caroline-Adelaide *abbea caag* 450
MARBLE
  Abigail *agdi; aacaa* 26 71
  Abigail (Joy) 71
  David 71 82
  Elizabeth 138
  Gershom 71 82
  Nathaniel 62
  Joseph-Russel 421
  Susanna 82
  Susanna (Tower) 82
  Susanna (Worrick) *adf* 62
MARCH
  Emily *aabcj aa* 149
MARCY
  Emeline-Josephine (Perham) 537-8

MARCY cont'd
Helen *acbca acdaa* 538
Henry-Sullivan 537-8
Lincoln *acbca acdab* 538
Margaret-Winslow (Lincoln) *aacbc acda* 537-8
William *aacbc acda* 537-8
MARDEN
Harry-Nixon *adffe lba* 398
Horace-Kingman *adffe lb* 398
Lizzie-Robbins (Lincoln) *adffe lb* 398
Mary-Jane (Kingman) 398
Shadrach-Sever 398
MARENDAZ
Edith *adbfa fbb* 387
MARKLEY
Sarah 513
MARRETT
Mary *aabcf ba* 144
MARSH
Abigail-Tower (Lincoln) *abbec bd* 322
Ada-Frances *abbec bde* 322
Caleb 10
Eliza-Ann 397
Elizabeth *aabbh* 31 147
Frederic-Alonzo *abbec bdb* 322
George W. 322
Henry-Lincoln *abbec bdc* 322
Isaac 322
John 596
Louisa-Frances *abbec bda* 322
Lucy (——) 322
Lucy-Dunbar (Studley) 596
Lucy-Ellen *adcac bai* 596-7
Lydia 65 138
Mary (——) 322
Mary A. (Woodbury) *abbec bdb* 322
Mary-Frances (Lincoln) *aafff fa* 185
Sarah 10 36
Stephen-Puffer *aafff fa* 185
Warren *abbec bd* 322
MARSHALL
Ann-Maria *aafff hc* 185
Arthur-Lincoln *abbea cabbb* 553
Elizabeth-Lewis (Lincoln) *aafff h* 185
Esther (Wilson) 185
Hannah-James *aafff ha* 185
John 355
Joseph 185
Orianna-Augusta (Souther) *abbea cabbb* 553
Samuel *aafff h* 185
MARSTON
Kate-Von-Weber *aacbc ah* 420-1
Mary (Von Weber) 420
Ward 420
MARTIN
Amey-Gaskill (Daniels) *adffe df* 524-5
Anna (Morton) 144
Bryan 144
Betty (Chaplin) 174
Calvin *adaga cah* 359
Effie *adaaf dbc* 575
Elizabeth *adaga caf* 359
Esther (Kerr) 575
Eugene 525
Fannie (Thrash) 575
Hannah 144 307
Irene (Whittington) *aaffi e* 84
J. E. 575
James *adaga cad* 359
Jasper *adaga caa* 359
John 174
John *adaga cac* 359
John-Harry *adahb bcea* 497
Lincoln *adaga cae* 359
Luther *adaga cah* 359
Martha *adaga cag* 359

MARTIN cont'd
Mary 489
Mary (Seaman) *adaaf f* 352
Minnie-Lytle (Rutter) *adahb bcea* 497
Richard *aaffi e* 84
Ruth-Eugenia *adaah ebba* 575
Samuel *adaga ca* 359
Sarah 366
Sarah (Lincoln) *adaga ca* 359
Susanna 174
Tilley-Alexander 575
MARTINDALE
Alice M. *adahf caa* 373
MARTINEZ
Serafina 448
MASON
mr. 486
Andrew-Jackson *adcai ej* 241
Anna-Frances (Cox) *aacdb jf* 181
Anna-Newman *aacdb jg* 181
Ebenezer-Erskine *aacdb ja* 180 181
Elizabeth-Thompson (Pattangall) *aacdb de* 180 181
Ezra-Lincoln *aacdb jb* 181
John *aacdb j* 181
John-Lincoln *aacdb jc* 181
Joseph *aacbc cc* 163
Joseph-Parker 539
Mary-Washington *aacdb jh* 181
Otis-Tufton *aacdb je* 181
Rachel (Lincoln) *aacdb j* 177 180-1
Robert-Tufton 181
Sarah-Ann (Litchfield) *adcai ej* 241
Sarah E. (Henderson) *aacdb je* 181
Sarah-Elizabeth *aacdb jd* 181
Sarah (Gilman) 181
Sarah-Rebecca (Parker) *aacbc cc* 163
William-Henry *aacdb jf* 181
MASTEN
Elisha *abbhb b* 92
Lucenia (Birch) *abbhb b* 92
MATTERS
Mary-Louisa *adahb faca* 500
MATTESON
Elinor (McAllister) 587
Grace-May (Lincoln) *adahb gcda* 587
Harry-Ashley *adahb gcda* 587
John-Lincoln *adahb gcdaa* 587
John-Richard 587
MATTHEWS
Alice ([Lincoln] [O'Brien] Briery) *aacdb bdc* 431
Don *aacdb bdc* 431
MATTOON
Charles 155
MAUGRIDGE
Mary 52
MAUPIN
Abraham-Lincoln *adaae iaa* 346
David-Spencer 346
Dorcas-Sarah-Emeline *adaae iac* 346 475
Emma (Campbell) *adaae iaa* 346
Jerusha (King) 346
Mary-Elizabeth (Lincoln) *adaae ia* 346 475
Richard-Snow *adaae ia* 346 475
MAWSON
Emily-Virginia *adaid bb* 507
MAXEY
Anna-Helen 446
MAXIM
Caroline-Franklin ([Lincoln] Cameron) *abbea caca* 555
Charles-Herbert *abbea caca* 555
Dwight-Thornton *abbea cacab* 555
Harriet (Swift) 555
Pelham W. 555

MAY
Cornelia F. *abbec faa* 323
William 335
MAYBERRY
Julian *adaic* 229
Margaret *adafe* 53
MAYER
David 445
MAYNARD
Annie R. *adaae icj* 347
Asa 537
Lyman-Allen 537
Mary-Susan *aacbc acb* 537
Susan-Hyde (Walker) 537
MAYO
Amy-Eliot *adfad baab* 521
Edward-Richards 521
Eliot-Belknap *adfad baa* 521
Lincoln *adfad baaa* 521
Nancy-Pierce (Reed) 521
Sarah (Ellmes) *aaffj i* 84
Susan-Elizabeth (Lincoln) *adfad baa* 521
William *aaffj i* 84
MAYS
Elizabeth 573
MEACHAM
Ida 408
MEAD
Joseph 154
Sarah 595
MEAHAN
Ellen 584
MEALY
Charlotte-Otis (Snow) *adcai bef* 391
George W. *adcai bef* 391
MELLUS
Abigail 63
MELONE
Cullen 480
Elmira-Taylor *adaah eb* 480
Louisiana (Schroder) 480
MELTON see Milton
MERCER
Effie 479
Flora 479
Jane ([Usrey] Lincoln) 479
Nicholas 479
MERRETT
Isabella *adfba i* 132
MERRIAM
Elbridge 457
Eliot (——) 457
Harriet E. *abbec fdaa* 457
Mary P. (Lincoln) *abbec fda* 457
Nathan-Albert *abbec fda* 457
MERRICK
Frances-Fiske *aacbc ad* 416-7
Francis-Taliaferro 416
James 416
Mary-Buckminster (Fiske) 416
Noah 416
Phiny 416
Thomas 416
MERRICKS
Elisha-Hobson 572
James-Wesley *adaae hfad* 572
James-Wesley *adaae hfada* 572
Mary-Elizabeth (Mullins) 572
Nannie-Margaret (Lincoln) *adaae hfad* 572
Robert-Lincoln *adaae hfadb* 572
MERRIFIELD
Nellie *adaga aa* 486-7
MERRILL
Frances M. (Allen) 535
Frank-Allen *aabck bab* 535
John-Foster 535

MERRILL cont'd
Margaret-Elizabeth (Greene) *aabck bab* 535
MERRITT
Elizabeth (Cole) *adea* 23
Hannah (Howard) 597
Harry *adcac baja* 597
Henrietta (Bates) 597
Isabella 132
James *adea* 22 23
James-Cummings 597
Joseph-Ensign 597
Mercy-Thomas *adcac baj* 597
Nellie-Thomas (Lincoln) *adcac baja* 597
MESSICK
Margaret (Long) *adaae jc* 207
MESSIER
Josephine 603
MILES
Augusta-Holyoke (Moore) 260
Helen-Augusta *aabce ha* 260
Henry-Adolphus 260
John 370
Margaret (Dickinson) 370
Mary *adahb g* 370
MILLARD
Anna-Mae *adaid ccb* 377
Barbara *adacd* 50
Elizabeth-Jane *adaid cbb* 377
Hannah (Lincoln) *adac* 50
James *adacc* 50
Joseph *adac* 50
Joseph *adacb* 50
Mary (——) 50
Mordecai *adaca* 50
Thomas 46
MILLER
Alfred-Kelley *adaaf hf* 212
Annie L. *aafff gbb* 317
Barbara 496
Belle (Lincoln) *adagb dea* 492
Betsey (Rimel) *adaai i* 102 103
Cyrus 496
Elijah 119
Elizabeth 474
Elizabeth-Anna (Eaby) 496
Elizabeth-Ann (Lincoln) *adahb bcb* 496-7
Elsie-Reidenbach (Eberly) *adahb bcbb* 497
Emily *adaaf gb* 211
Eusebe *adaaf gc* 211
George W. 615
Harrison *adaaf ga* 211
Hattie E. (Rosebrooks) 615
John *adagb dea* 492
Jonathan-Roland *adahb bcb* 496-7
Joseph-Clyde *adahb bcbb* 497
Lizzie *adaaa bbcac* 615
Margaret 473
Margaret-Mae *adahb bcba* 497
Nancy-Ann (Williams) *adaaf hf* 212
Phoebe (Lincoln) *adaaf g* 209 211
Samuel *adaaf g* 209 211
Sarah 218
Sarah-Ann (Kirby) *adaaf ga* 211
Susan 471 475
MILLS
Almira 515
MILTENBERGER
Eunice-Eliza (Lincoln) *adbca dca* 511
Christopher 511
Frank *adbca dca* 511
Jane (Decker) 511
Mildred *adbca dcaa* 511
Milo *adbca dcab* 511
MILTON—Melton
Charles 335 337

MINCER
Hannah-Lincoln (Williams) *adaaf hd* 212
Robert *adaaf hd* 212
MINER
George A. 317
Sabra-Lucinda *adagb ga* 221
MINICK
Catherine ([Lincoln] Swords) *adaga cf* 360
David *adaga cf* 360
John *adaga cfd* 360
MINOTT
Martha-Blake *aabck b* 269-70
Nathaniel 269
Rachel (Wilde) 269
MISSIMER
Henry-Gregg 497
Mary-Rebecca *adahb bd* 497-8
Rachel-Logan (Brown) 497
MITCHELL
Abigail *adcak* 242-3
Alice-Josephine *aacdb bdff* 431
Amelie-Hill *aacdc ad* 182
Ann (Shiverick) *aacdc aa* 182
Bertha-Adelaide (Lincoln) *aacdb bdf* 431
Charlotte-Frances (Morton) *aacdc ac* 182
Doris-Blanche *aacdb bdfe* 431
Experience 242
Flora-Dell *adaaa bbcf* 607
Frances (Lincoln) *aacdc a* 182
Frances-Lincoln *aacdc ah* 182
Harry-Allen *aacdb bdfb* 431
Jacob 242
James 233
John-Augustine *aacdb bdf* 431
John-Lester *aacdb bdfd* 431
John-Lincoln *aacdc ae* 182
Lincoln *aacdc ag* 182
Mary-Ann *aacdc af* 182
Mary (Kirk) 431
Mary (Wade) 242
Merah (Coffin) 182
Nellie-May *aacdb bdfc* 431
Paul 182
Rachel 70
Richard *aacdc a* 182
Richard *aacdc ac* 182
Sarah-Ann (Graves) 607
Seth 242
Susan-Lincoln *aacdc ab* 182
Thomas 242 431
Wallace-Ezekiel-Clark 607
Walter-Augustine *aacdb bdfa* 431
William *aacdb bdfg* 431
William-Henry *aacdc aa* 182
MOAST
Lucy-Ann *adaga gf* 490-1
Mary (Sweitser) 490
Zebley 490
MOCK
Polly 102
MOHRING
Eva *adahb dci* 500
MOLLENEAUX
Mary 302
MONROE—Munroe
Abigail 263
Edmund 312
Frances-Maud *aacdb ebg* 548
John-Wilson 548
Margaret-Rosetta (Rudolf) 548
Rebecca 139
MONTGOMERY
William 195
MOODY
Abijah 155
Joshua 24
Roxanna (Wood) *aabhe* 155

MOONE
John *adahb bcda* 584
Pauline (Lincoln) *adhab bcda* 584
MOORE—Moores
Andrew 506
Anna 506
Anna (McCullough) 572
Annie-Elizabeth (Carson) *adaga abd* 358
Augusta-Holyoke 260
Bernice-Luin *adaae agdb* 473
Edward C. *adbfa fc* 387
Eliza 118
Eliza *adahb f* 369
Ellen-Deane ([Simonds] Lincoln) *aabce cd* 403
Emma (Pirtle) 574
Eunice (Southworth) 387
Frederick W. 403
George 574
Harriet H. (——) 403
Jairus 387
James 369
James-Osborne 572
James-Osborne *adaae hfabb* 572
John-DeRosset *adaae hfab* 572
John-Lincoln *adaae hfaba* 572
John-William *adaga abd* 358
Joseph 506
Lee *adaaf dba* 574
Manda 579
Margaret-Amelia 375
Mary 312
Mary-Cathlin 522
Mary-Isabel (Lincoln) *adaae hfab* 572
Mary-Jane (Earle) 369
Mary L. (Lincoln) *adbfa fc* 387
Maurice-McCullough *adaae hfabc* 572
Mercy (Cutler) 506
Phebe-Dinah 374
Robert B. *aabce cd* 403
Ruth 493
Susan *adahb d* 369
MORELAND
Albert-Sample 570
Edna-Earl *adaae agcd* 570
Susan-Thompson (Foster) 570
MOREMAN
Mary-Priscilla (Hills) *adaha di* 224
Richard *adaha di* 224
MOREY
Susanna 240
Thomas 139
MORGAN
Alice *aabce abccb* 527
Charles-Lincoln *aabck aa* 151 153
Clarence-Augustus *adbfa bba* 386
David 363
David *aabck aa* 153
Edgar *adbfa bbb* 386
Hannah 535
Hannah (Jacobs) *adaga cgb* 360
Hannah M. (Lincoln) *adbfa bb* 386
Harold-Fairbanks *aabce abcca* 527
Hiram *adbfa bb* 386
Irving-Weston *aabce abcc* 527
John 112
John *adaga cgb* 360
Mai *adaaf dbaab* 574
Marianne (Pierce) *aabck aa* 153
Michael 527
Mildred (Lincoln) *aabce abcc* 527
Sarah-Jane (——) 527
MORRILL
Martha *aafff fc* 185
MORRIS
mr. 471
James 99 100

MORRIS cont'd
Jonathan 99 100
Malinda *adahc ba* 372
Malinda *adahc bb* 372
Mary *adahb bb* 495
Mary-Burnside *aabch dcb* 266
Mary (Smith) 495
Rebecca (Flowers) *adaa* 99 100
Rose (Lincoln) *adahc bd* 372
Samuel *adahc bc* 372
Samuel *adahc bd* 372
Sarah (Lincoln) *adahc bc* 372
Stacy 495
Walter 471
William 128
MORRISON
Isaac 199
MORROW
Josiah 99
MORSE
Abbie *aafff fc* 185
David 532
Edith-Buckingham *aacbe dad* 545
Jennie-May *aabcg dba* 532
Johanna-Paige (Emmons) 545
John-Crafts 545
Ruth 151
Sarah-Shaw (Morton) 532
MORTON
Anna 144
Charlotte-Frances *aacdc ac* 182
John 56
Lydia-Atearn 444
Mary-Anna 519
Sarah-Shaw 532
MOSES
George W. *adaae hfia* 573
Isabel (Lincoln) *adaae hfia* 573
MOSHER
Chauncy-Henry *adffe ba* 247
Jenny 145
Nancy-Bicknell (Dickinson) *adffe ba* 247
MOSLEY
Robert 222
MOTLEY
Blanche-Duncan *adaah embb* 485
Dorothy-Margaret *adaah emba* 485
Katharine-Bird (Lincoln) *adaah emb* 484-5
M. E. 485
Mary-Ellen (Duncan) 485
Robert-Lee *adaah emb* 485
Thomas 430
MOTT
Ebenezer 20
MOULTON
Mary-Frances 405
MOWRY
Emma *adaii bcaa* 509
MOXLEY
Elizabeth 489
MOYER
Sarah 508
MUDD
Benjamin 459
Benjamin *adaaa ad* 329
Elizabeth *adaaa aa* 459-61
Elizabeth (Lincoln) *adaaa ad* 329
Mary *adaaa a* 328-9 462
MUDGE
E. R. 430
MUHLENBERG
Alice-May (Hertzler) *adaid cca* 377
George-Henry *adaid cca* 377
MULLEN
Amelia-Ann (Priest) 609
Eva-May *adaaa bbfi* 609
Louis-Henry 609

MULLEN cont'd
Mary-Elizabeth 532
Rosa-Bell *adaaa bbfe* 609
MULLIGAN
Hannah 605
MULLINS
Mary-Elizabeth 572
MUNROE see Monroe
MURDOCK
Andrew 179
MURPHY
Bernice *aacdb iba* 307
Charles 575
Gussie-Lou (Lincoln) *adaaf dbac* 575
Lena (Young) 575
William *adaaf dbac* 575
MURR
Alice-Olive *adaaa bbfd* 608-9
Lucinda (Burgess) 608
Thomas 608
MURRAY—Murry
Eliza *aacbe lfba* 547
Mary-Elizabeth (Lacey) 442
Virginia-Mabel *aacdc ec* 442
William-Lewis 442
MUZZY
Benjamin 139
John 139
John *aabad f* 139
Joseph 139
Julia A. *aabad fa* 139
Louisa-Caroline *aabad cb* 138
Rebecca (Lincoln) *aabad f* 139 148
Rebecca (Munroe) 139
Robert 139
MYERS
Charles-Ralph *adagb fbad* 494
Ethel-Elizabeth ([Bradley] Russell) *adahb dcha* 499
Florence-Edna *adagb fbab* 494
Frances-Eloise (Lincoln) *adagb fba* 494
George-Henry *adagb fba* 494
Helen-Mary *adagb fbaa* 494
Joseph-Conrad 494
Lydia *adahb b* 368
Mary (Ayres) 494
Mary-Frances *adagb fbac* 494
Rexford-LeRoy *adahb dcha* 499
MYLIN
Carrie-Lincoln (Rutter) *adahb bcef* 497
Walter-Franklin *adahb bcef* 497

NALL
Elizabeth (Brumfield) *adaaa eb* 204
J. L. 200 201 202
Louise 200 201 202 204
William P. *adaaa eb* 204
NASH
James 555
Mary-Ann 406
Mary E. Celia ([Crowell] Lincoln) *abbea cacb* 555
Sarah 35
Sophia 401
Thomas 191 240
NASSAN
William 118
NAYLIS
George 222
NEAL—Neale
A. 192
Charles *adaaf dac* 350
Emily-Oneal ([Dinges] Simrill) *adaaf dac* 350
Joseph 82
Mary-Birch (Lincoln) *abbhc c* 192
Michael-Anthony 192

NEARING
Augusta-Caroline *adbfa bd* 514-5
Emily (Eno) 514
Heman L. 514
NEIGHBORS
Martha (Lincoln) *adaaa af* 329
Washington *adaaa af* 329
NENSON
Elizabeth (Davis) *adahd d* 110
Mary Ann *adaah ee* 481
NEVILLE
Elizabeth *abbec be* 454
Elizabeth (Northey) 454
William-Henry 454
NEWCOMB
Ann-Maria-(Arnold) 452
AnnieMay (Lincoln) *aacdb gfe* 438
Ellen-Frances *abbea caid* 452
Ellen-Maria (|Lincoln] Damon) *abbea cai* 452
Hattie-Colberth *abbea caie* 452
Joseph W. 163
Laura-Annie *aacdb gfea* 438
Laura (Leach) 438
Martha-Jane *adcac bai* 596-7
Oscar-Elmer *aacdb gfe* 438
Robert 438
Ruth (Cook) 452
Silas 452
Susanna (Cushing) 596
Warren *abbea cai* 452
William-James 596
NEWELL
Carrie-Dexter (Colburn) 413
Daniel 63 note
Frances (Lincoln) *aabhg dbb* 413-4
Gurdon-Tucker *aabhg dbb* 413-4
Josiah-Benjamin 413
Rebecca-Battles 63 and note
Susanna (Battles) 63 note
NEWTON
Abner 163
Caroline-Matilda 408
Daniel-Lincoln *aacbc ga* 164
Henry *aaflg* 38
Hester *aacbc gc* 164
Hester (Grennell) 163
Isaac 163
John 163 164
Levi-Lincoln *aacbc gb* 164
Olive (Whitcomb) *aaflg* 38
Rebecca (Lincoln) *aacbc g* 163-4
Rejoice *aacbc g* 163-4 290 414
Roger 163
Samuel 163
NICELY
George *adaaa ae* 329
Mary-Rowena (Lincoln) *adaaa ae* 329
NICHOLAS
Bernice-Luin (Moore) *adaae agdb* 473
Bessie-Lincoln *adaae agba* 473
Carrie-Taylor *adaae agbb* 473
Charles-Henry *adaae agd* 473
Edna-Virginia *adaae agbf* 473
Elizabeth (Coiner) 473
Elizabeth-Lincoln *adaae agda* 473
Elizabeth-Theresa (Lincoln) *adaae agd* 473
Georgia-Winifred *adaae agdc* 473
Grover-Cleveland *adaae agbe* 473
Jacob-Bright 473
Jacob-Bright *adaae agbc* 473
Jefferson-Jacob *adaae agb* 473
John-Homan *adaae agbd* 473
Mary-Leannah (Lincoln) *adaae agb* 473
Roselie (Baxter) *adaae agbe* 473
William-Franklin *adaae agdb* 473

NICHOLS
col. 78
Aaron 314 315
Abigail 323
Abigail *aafae* 37
Abigail *adcah f* 123
Abigail (Beal) *abca* 14
Abigail (Lincoln) *adcah* 122-3
Amos *adahb ed* 226
Anna 321
Anna (Nichols) 321
Bethia *addb* 22 88 186
Caroline8Frances *aafff cac* 315
Catherine (Cushing) *abce* 14 140
Catherine (Russell) 315
Charles-Lemuel 543
Daniel 191 388
Daniel *abca* 13 14
Daniel *abbaf* 41 191
Daniel-Burril *adcah c* 123
Edward *adahb i* 226
Edward *adahb ee* 226
Elizabeth 41
Elizabeth *abcd* 14
Elizabeth *abbba* 41
Elizabeth *abbbg* 41
Elizabeth *adcah b* 123
Elizabeth (Beal) *abcf* 14 122
Elizabeth (Gowan) *adcah c* 123
Elizabeth (Lincoln) *abc* 13 14 41
Elizabeth (Lincoln) *abbc* 14 39 41 88
Elizabeth (Steigers) *adahb ee* 226
Emily (Fitts) *aafff cab* 315
Hannah 133
Harriet-Brayton *aacbc addd* 543
Ichabod 288
Isaac *adcah e* 123
Isaac-Lincoln;*adcah g* 123
Isabella L. (Bates) *abbed h* 90
Israel 388
Israel *ak* 8 9 14 41 122 140 191 315 321
James-Franklin *aafff cai* 315
James-Hall *adcai bee* 320 391
Jazaniah 315
Lazarus *adcah h* 123
Lot *abbb* 41
Lydia *aabcd* 140-1
Lydia (Steigers) *adahb ed* 226
Martha *abcg* 14
Martha *abbbd* 41
Martin *aaffi i* 84
Martin *aafff cab* 315
Mary 66
Mary *abcb* 14
Mary *abbbc* 41
Mary (——) 8
Mary-Humphrey *abbec b* 321-3
Mary-Janette (Brayton) 543
Mary ([Pratt] Orcutt) 14
Mary (Sumner) 8 14
Mary (Whittington) *aaffi i* 84
Molly (Tower) 388
Nathaniel 188 388
Nathaniel *abc* 14 41 122 140 191 321
Nathaniel *abce* 14 140
Nathaniel *aafaf* 37
Noah 81 88 122 321
Noah *abcf* 14
Noah *adcah* 122-3
Peggy *adcac b* 388
Peter 388
Priscilla *abbbh* 41 88
Rebecca (Josselyn) 8
Rebecca (|Lincoln] Clark) *ak* 8 14
Ruth 239
Ruth *abch* 14
Ruth-Nichols (Snow) *adcai bee* 320 391
Sabiah (Bate) *aafaf* 35 37

44

NICHOLS cont'd
Samuel-Allen *aafff ca* 315
Samuel-Herbert *aafff cah* 315
Sarah 14
Sarah *abbbe* 41
Sarah *aafff c* 314-6
Sarah-Hobart (Bates) *abbed f* 90
Sarah (Lincoln) *adahb i* 226
Sarah-Lincoln *aafff cad* 315
Stephen 315
Susan-Lincoln *aafff cak* 315
Susannah *adcah a* 123
Susannah-Davis (Humphrey) 315
Susannah-Nichols (Lincoln) *aafff ca* 315
Tamar *abbhc* 191-3
Tamar (Beal) *abbaf* 41 191
Thankful (Tower) *abbbb* 41
Thomas 8 14 41 122 140 191 315 321 388
Thomas *abcc* 14 41 88
Thomas *abbbf* 41
William *abbed f; abbed h* 90
William *adcah d* 123
Willie *aafff caj* 315
Zibiah (Bates) *aafaf* 37
NICKERSON
Alvans-Thomas 558
Elijah *abaeb d* 87
Frances *adaga agf* 579
Harriet-Holbrook *abbec fdca* 558
John-Holland *aabhg b* 156
Laurietta (——) 558
Lucinda (Lincoln) *aabhg b* 156
Mary (Holland) 156
Sparrow 156
Susanna (Lewis) *abaeb d* 87
NICOLAY
John-George 196 200 223
NITSELL—Nitzell
Jacob 232 235
NIXON
Caroline 501
NOAH
Sarah-Rosetta 420
NOBLE
Eliza-Jane (Barnes) *adaga chc* 360
Elizabeth *adbcf ca* 514
Ewing *adaga chc* 360
John 426
Mary (French) 426
Rachel-Ann *aacbe ld* 426
NOECKER
Mary *adaid hac* 378
NORCROSS
James-Alonzo 421
Nancy *abbec f* 323
Orlando-Whitney 421
NORMON
Nellie 574
NORRIS
Charles 287 note
NORTH
Charles-Weed *adffe cbc* 522 523
Gideon-Leeds 523
Howard-Lincoln *adffe cbcb* 523
Mildred-Brown *adffe cbca* 523
Minerva-Wright (Lincoln) *adffe cbc* 522 523
Sarah-Ann (Weed) 523
NORTHEY
Elizabeth 454
NORTHORP
Mary E. *adbfa ea* 386
NORTON
Augusta 527
Elizabeth *aahf* 12
Helen-Virginia *adbca abc* 380
Lizzie-Smith (Hibbert) *aacdb ee* 433-4
Martha 120

NORTON cont'd
Mercy 61
Seth B. 433
NORWOOD
Amey-Gaskill ([Daniels] Martin) *adffe df* 524-5
Hannah E. (——) *aacdb i* 307
NOWELL
Rachel ([——] Lincoln) 130 131
Silas 130 131
NUTE
Asa *aaffe g* 82
Lucinda (Pratt) *aaffe g* 82
NUTT
Caroline-Augusta *aacdb hdd* 306
Caroline-Augusta (Lincoln) *aacdb hd* 306
Eliza-Ann 306
Ellen-Caroline (Leighton) 306
James 306
James-Robinson *aacdb hdc* 306
Jethro-Brown *aacdb hd* 306
Ruth-Brown *aacdb hda* 306
Sarah-Augusta *aacdb hdb* 306
Sarah (Brown) 306
NUTTING
Edwin-Augustus *abbhc bb* 192
Sarah-Asenath (Shaw) *abbhc bb* 192
NYE
mr. 33
Sarah-Butler (Shiverick) *aacdc f* 310
OAKES—Oaks
Abigail (——) 276
Albert 276
Hannah (Whitcomb) *aafha* 37
Harry *aabhe aaa* 275 276
Jefferson G. *aabhe aa* 276
John 276
Josephine (Lincoln) *aabhe aa* 276
Samuel *aafha* 37
Theodosia *aaffb d* 81
OAVES—Oves
Elizabeth 361
Elizabeth *adaga* 216 217-9
OBERLIN
Jesse-Lincoln *adagb dfa* 364
Margaret (Lincoln) *adagb df* 364
Simon *adagb df* 364
O'BRIEN
Alice (Lincoln) *aacdb bdb* 431
John *aacdb bdc* 431
O'BRION
Abigail (Wilson) 262
Charles-Carroll *aabcf dbc* 263
Clara-Wilson *aabcf dbc* 263
Daniel-Wilson *aabcf db* 262-3
Ellen *aabcf dba* 263
Hattie-Eliza (Bailey) *aabcf dbc* 263
John 262
Sarah-Jane (Lincoln) *aabcf db* 262-3
OFFUTT
Denton 465
OGDEN
Aaron 380
Amanda *adbcf be* 512-3
Amer 512
Amory 233
Anning-Asbury *adbca ab* 380
David 380
George-Lybrand *adbca abb* 380
Helen-Virginia (Norton) *adbca abc* 380
Hugh-Walker 551
James-Asbury *adbca abc* 380
Jennie (Wright) *adbca aba* 380
John-Lincoln *adbca aba* 380
Joseph 380
Lucretia (Gorman) 380
Rebecca (Weed) 512

OGDEN cont'd
Sarah-Nitzel (Lincoln) *adbca ab* 233 380
Selina (Sharp) *adbca abb* 380
Stephen 380
OGLE
miss *adaga cea* 360
OGLENEE
Rebecca (——) 492
Joseph 492
O'KEEFE
Catherine (Kelly) 606
Daniel 606
Mary-Elizabeth *adaaa bbcb* 606-7
OLDSHUE
Daniel *adagb bj* 220
Eliza *adagb bd* 220
Jacob *adagb bi* 220
James *adagb bg* 220
Jane *adagb ba* 220
Jemima (Lincoln) *adagb b* 219 220
John *adagb b* 219 220
John *adagb bf* 220
Lincoln *adagb be* 220
Martha-Ann (West) *adagb be* 220
Martha J. *adagb bh* 220
Mary *adagb bb* 220
Nancy *adagb bc* 220
OLIVER
Arnett-Stanton *adaaf dbaab* 574
Betty (Crutchfield) 574
Campbell *adaaf dbaa* 575
Luther 574
Mai (Morgan) *adaaf dbaab* 574
Mattie-Joe (Lincoln) *adaaf dbaa* 574
Willie-Lee *adaaf dbaaa* 574
Willie-May *adaaf dbbb* 479
ONAN
John *adaah b* 213 215
Margaret (Lincoln) *adaah b* 213 215
O'NEAL
Elizabeth 381
OOTS
Virginia 578
ORCUTT
Ebenezer 81
Edward *agdh* 26
Ephraim *aaffc* 81
Hittie (Hudson) *agdh* 25 26
Huldah 81 240 246
John 81
Mary 125
Mehitable (Hudson) *agdh* 25 26
Mercy (Pratt) 14
Meribah 595
Olive *aaffe a* 36 81
Olive (Lincoln) *aaffc* 81
Ruth (Worrick) 81
Samuel 14 81
Susanna 191
Susanna (Bates) 81
William 81
ORNE
Sarah 165 168
OSMAN
Mary-Elizabeth *adaga gh* 491-2
Mary-Elizabeth (Hise) 491
William 491
OSTRANDER
Eunice (Birch) *abbhb h* 92
James *abbhb h* 92
OSWALD
Caroline (Strayer) *adaae eb* 207
OTIS
Charlotte 390
Desire 252
Ephraim 79
Job 79
John 79

OTIS cont'd
Mary *aacd* 79-80
Mercy-Little *adcaj b* 123
Rachel (Hersey) 79
OTT
Amanda-Marthaette *adaaa bbaa* 463
Dora (Campbell) *adaaa bbai* 463
Florence-May *adaaa bbaj* 463
George-McLean *adaaa bbai* 463
Harriet-Anne *adaaa bbag* 463
Harriet-Anna (Seacat) *adaaa bbac* 463
Henry-Thomas *adaaa bbac* 463
Hester-Rosanna *adaaa bbah* 463
John-Patterson *adaaa bbad* 463
Joseph-Davis *adaaa bba* 463
Joseph-Marion *adaaa bbaf* 463
Mary-Abigail *adaaa bbae* 463
Mary-Flora 564
Rachel (Lincoln) *adaaa bba* 463
Samuel M. 463
Sarah-Elizabeth *adaaa bbab* 463
OUTLAW
Eugenia-Bryant *adaaf ace* 573-4
Eugenia D. (Whitfield) 573
OVERTON
Elizabeth-Ann (Clapp) *abbea ccd* 319
Francis *abbea ccd* 319
OVES see Oaves
OVIS
Anne 218
OWEN
Juliet 480

PACKARD
Emma-Frances 317
Mary (Sampson) *adfah a* 394-5
Samuel *adfai a* 394
PADDLEFORD
Elizabeth 420
PAGE
James W. 411
Samuel 309
Mary-Chadbourne 287
PAINE
Nancy-Armstrong 525
PALFREY
Elizabeth ([Bailey] McNeil) 83
PALMER
Josephine 604
Sarah 499
Temperance 310
PANCOAST
Abigail (Boone) *adafa* 52 53 and note
Adin *adafa* 52 53 and note
Anna-Thompson *adbca bb* 232
John 53 note
Mary (——) 53 note
PARDEE
Daniel 237
Lois *adbfa* 237-8
Phebe (Woodruff) 237
PARKE
Martha *adagb da* 364
PARKER
Aaron 272
Abraham 272
Alexander-Tennett 578
Ann-Eliza 470
Anna-Maria *abbec bc* 322
Clara-Ida *aacbc ahg* 544
Daisy-Maude (Lincoln) *adaaa bbih* 565
Ebenezer 272
Edward-Sidney *aabce cdbb* 531
Elizabeth (Lewis) 322
Elizabeth-Waldo *aacbc cb* 163
Ella-Lightburn *adaah gdb* 578
Eunice-Viola (Lincoln) *aabce cdbb* 531
Florence-Bates *aabce cdbbc* 531

PARKER cont'd
Fred-Allen *adaaa bbih* 565
James 13 163
Jane 508
John-Davis 531
Josephine *aabce cdbbb* 531
Julia-Ann (Eskew) 565
Leonard 163
Leonard-Moody *aacbc c* 163
Luther 322
Margery *aabce cdbbd* 531
Martha *adagb da* 364
Martha (Lincoln) *aacbc c* 163
Martha-Lincoln *aacbc ca* 163
Mary-Annie (Bates) 531
Mary-Julia 527
Mary-Maria (Phelps) 544
Moses 272
Nancy *aabck f* 272-3 274
Phineas 163
Richard 197
Robert-Lincoln *aabce cdbba* 531
Sally (Bowers) 272
Sarah (Dickenson) 163
Sarah-Rebecca *aacbc cc* 163
Shadrach 565
Virginia (Oots) 578
William-Henry 544
PARKHURST
Edward 317
PARKMAN
Sarah 175
PARKS
Susanna *adafc* 53
PARMINTER
Leona-Adria *adaaf acf* 574
Nellie (Norman) 574
Percy-Elwyn 574
PARR
Frances-Louisa *adagb fb* 494
Mary-Araminta (Trumbull) 494
Stephen-Vanranselar 494
PARRISH
Helen 430
PARROTT
John H. 339
PARRY
Carter *adbaa aa* 114
Hester (Carter) *adbaa a* 114
Roland *adbaa a* 114
PARSONS
Susan 553
PARTELOW
Mary-Burns 535
PARTRIDGE
John 135
PARVIN
Benjamin 378
Benjamin *adaid hae* 378
Clara (Lincoln) *adaid ha* 378
Edward-Lincoln *adaid haa* 378
Elizabeth (Starr) 378
Elizabeth-Starr *adaid hab* 378
Elizabeth-Weida (Raser) *adaid haa* 378
George-Brooke *adaid hac* 378
Jeremiah-Starr *adaid ha* 378
Lucia *adaid haf* 378
Mary-Ives *adaid had* 378
Mary (Noecker) *adaid hac* 378
PASCHALL
Abraham *adbca ce* 232
Abraham-Johnson *adbca c* 232
Ann 235
Ann *adbca cg* 232
Ann (Garrett) 232
Ann (Lincoln) *adbca c* 118 232 233
Anna-Frances *adbcf bdg* 384
Anna-Thompson (Pancoast) *adbca bb* 232

PASCHALL cont'd
Benjamin 232
Benjamin *adbca ca* 232
Beulah-Worth *adbcf bdc* 383
Caroline (Horton) *adbca ce* 232
Catherine (Lincoln) *adbca b* 232 383
Catherine-Lincoln *adbcf bdd* 383
Eliza-Irene *adbcf bdh* 384
Eliza (Lincoln) *adbcf bd* 232 383-4
Elizabeth *adbca cb* 232
Elizabeth (Smedley) *adbca ca* 232 233
Ellen (Weise) *adbcf bde* 384
Fanny (Boone) *adaaf dag* 350
Frances (Hodge) 232
George-Henry *adbcf bda* 383
Harriet (Rogers) *adbca cc* 232
Henry *adbca b* 232 382 383
Henry-Lincoln *adbca bb* 232
Isaac *adbca ch* 232 233
Jane M. (Lane) *adbcf bdf* 384
Jesse *adbca cc* 232
John 232
Joseph *adbca ba* 232 383-4
Joseph *adbcf bdb* 383
Joseph-Albin *adbcf bde* 384
Martha *adbca cf* 232 233
Martha (Johnson) 232
Mary *adbca cd* 232 233
Mary-Amelia (Acker) *adbca ch* 232
Mary N. (Lane) *adbcf bda* 383
Moses-Lincoln *adbcf bdf* 384
Nellie (Sherman) *adbcf bde* 384
Stephen 235
Thomas 232
Thomas J. 235
PASSMORE
Alice M. (Martindale) *adahf caa* 373
Charles-Sumner *adahf cae* 373
Deborah (Brown) 372
Ellen F. (Faxon) *adahf cab* 373
Ellis-Pusey *adahf ca* 372-3
Ellis-Pusey *adahf cag* 373
Emily-Pusey (Shelmire) *adahf cag* 373
Emma-Frances *adahf cad* 373
John-Wardell 372
John-Wardell *adahf caa* 373
Leroy-Chase *adahf cac* 373
Lincoln-Knight *adahf cab* 373
Lillian P. (Haines) *adahf caf* 373
Mary-Eliza (Lincoln) *adahf ca* 372-3
Rebecca E. (Hunt) *adahf cac* 373
Susan M. (Came) *adahf cae* 373
Walter-Channing *adahf caf* 373
PASTORIUS
Samuel *adbd* 58 115
Sarah (Lincoln) *adbd* 58 115
PATRICK
Abbie-Smith *aabcg dg* 408-9
Eliza (Keys) 583
John 583
Johnson 408
Margaret-Jane *adahb bbi* 583
Mary (Foster) 408
PATTANGALE—Pattangall
Arethusa (Longfellow) *aacdb df* 180
Bethia C. ([Baker] Wheldon) *aacdb da* 180
Catharine-Elliott *aacdb db* 180
Catherine (Wright) 180
Daniel 180
Elizabeth-Thompson *aacdb de* 180 181
Ezra-Lincoln *aacdb df* 180
Frances-Elnathan *aacdb dg* 180
Frances (Lincoln) *aacdb d* 177 180
Frances-Mehitable (Foster) *aacdb dc* 180
Laura-Frances (Harris) *aacdb dd* 180
Moses 180
Nathan *aacdb d* 180

PATTANGALE—Pattangall cont'd
Nathan-Page *aacdb dd* 180
Nathaniel 180
Otis-Lincoln *aacdb da* 180
Rebecca (Crowell) *aacdb da* 180
Richard 180
Sarah-Caroline (Hobart) *aacdb df* 180
Susan-Maria (Appleby) *aacdb da* 180
William-Robinson *aacdb dc* 180
PATTEE
Laura (Saltonstall) 538
Penelope-Pelham *aacbc acdca* 538
Penelope-Winslow (Lincoln) *aacbc acdc* 538
Richard-Saltonstall *aacbc acdc* 538
William-Greenleaf-Appleton 538
PATTEN
Sophia *adcbm c* 126
PATTERSON
Eleanor (Jones) *adage c* 109
Isaac *adage c* 109
Louisa 269
PATTIE
Anne 355
PAUL
Catherine (See) 349 350
Clara *adaaf d* 348-51
William 349
PAXON
Letitia *adahf cdb* 373
PAYSON
Althea (Train) 441
Edith-Cushing *aacdc eadb* 442
Elsie (Lincoln) *aacdc eab* 441-2
Gilbert-Russell 441
Samuel-Cushing *aacdc ead* 441-2
William-Lincoln *aacdc eada* 442
PEABODY
Henry-Wayland 545
PEAKES
John-Quincy-Adams *aafff ea* 185
Susannah-Beal (James) *aafff ea* 185
PEARCE—Pearse see Pierce
Isaac 104 216
Sarah 216
PEARL
Susan-Margaret 363
PEARSON
Charlotte-Price (Ward) *aacdc fbe* 311
Franklin *aacdc fbe* 311
Isaac 56
PEAVEY
miss 304
PECK
Ann-Eliza 567
Mary-Henderson 477
PELHAM
Herbert 282
Penelope 282
Penelope (West) 282
PELLMAN
Anna-Maria *adahc aa* 504
Mary (Wolfe) 504
Samuel 504
PENCE
Alice-Rebecca *adaae hbe* 345
Beal-Steambergen *adaae hb* 344-5
Charles-Lee *adaae hbd* 345
Edith (Rynard) 344
Ida-Angeline *adaae hbc* 345
Jacob 344
John-Lincoln *acaae hbb* 345
Mary-Lavenia *adaae hba* 345
Rebecca (Lincoln) *adaae hb* 344-5
PENDLEBERG
Hannah (Zearing) *adaga be* 217
Henry *adaga be* 217

PENDLETON
Fleming *adaah gdc* 485
Sallie-Knight (Lincoln) *adaah gdc* 485
Sarah 475
PENHALLOW
Sarah-Maria 528
PENN
William 49
PENNINGTON
Sarah 498
PENNY
Charles-Henry *aafff cda* 316
Charles L. *aafff cda* 316
John 316
Sarah-Ellis *aafff ccb* 316
Sarah-Nichols (Lincoln) *aafff cd* 316
Temperance (Cushing) 316
Uriah *aafff cd* 316
PENNYBACKER
Amanda (Strayer) *adaae ea* 206 207
Derrick-Dehaven *adaae ea* 207
Isaac-Samuels 346
John-Dyer *adaae ia* 346
John-Dyer *adaae iaf* 346
Kate-Abigail *adaae iae* 346
Mary-Elizabeth ([Lincoln] Maupin) *adaae ia* 346
Mary-Lee *adaae iad* 346
Sarah-Ann (Dyer) 346
PERCIVAL
John 279
PERHAM
Emeline-Josephine 537-8
PERKINS
mrs. 33
Martha 443
Nellie-Josephine *adcac baib* 613-4
Nellie (Tarr) 613
Perry 613
Thomas-Nelson 538
PERRIN
Elizabeth 590
PERRY
Elizabeth 84
Fred H. 545
Hannah-Prentiss *adffe d* 396-7
Horatio-Nelson 421
Jessie (McGregor) 421
Malvina (Wilson) 421
Margaret-Elizabeth 576
Marian-Vinal ([Lincoln] Bogert) *cbc ahf* 421
Marsden-Jasael *aacbc ahf* 421
Marsden-Jasael *aacbc ahfc* 421
Oliver-Hazard 212
William 396
PERSHING
John-Joseph 614
PETERS
Enfield 577
PETERSON
Lily W. *abbea caic* 452
PETTIS
Naomi-Downs *adcai baa* 390
PFEIFFER
Julia (Priest) 610
Lola *adaaa bbgb* 609-10
Lewis-Cass 610
PHELAN
Mary-Ann (MacVeagh) *adahf ad* 228
William *adahf ad* 228
PHELPS
Adaline (——) 395
Annie-May *aabcd bccb* 400
Arthur-Chester *aabcd bcca* 400
Eliza *aabcd cc* 141
Eliza (Thompson) 399
Emily-Augusta (Lawrence) 520

PHELPS cont'd
  Emma-Souther (Lincoln) *aabcd bcc* 399-400
  Horace W. *adfah aa* 395
  Joshua 395
  Jerome-Porter *aahcd bcc* 399-400
  Joel F. 399
  Luman-Edwin 520
  Mary-Maria 544
  Mary-Vinal (Lincoln) *adfah aa* 395
PHILBRICK
  Helen-Francenia *abbhc db* 458
  Ira-Rowell 458
  Louisa (Daniels) 458
  William D. 312
PHILLIPS
  John 41
  Margaret (Robinson) 259
  Rachel (Bates) *afd* 8
  Thomas *afd* 8
PHIPPS
  Albert-Loammi *aacbe hba* 425
  Charles-Walker *aacbe hbaa* 425
  Eliza *aabcd cc* 141
  Elizabeth *adbcf aa* 382-3
  George-Albert *aacbe hbab* 425
  Joseph 383
  Laurana (Pincin) 425
  Loammi-Walker 425
  Mary-Ann (Hope) 383
  Mary-Elizabeth (Lincoln) *aacbe hba* 42
PICKETT
  Mary 164
  Susan 425
PIERCE—Peirce see Pearce
  Abigail 189
  Amanda-Melvina *aacdd dd* 446
  Anna-Helen (Maxey) 446
  Anna (Tuttle) 153
  Becky *adfae a* 393-4
  Caroline 432
  Carrie H. *adahc aac* 504
  Cromwell 504
  Eliza-Lincoln *aabck ab* 154
  Elizabeth (Lincoln) *adaid aa* 375
  Ella-Ruth (Gaul) *adaid aab* 375
  Haywood 393
  Henrietta-Lamson *aabck ad* 154
  Horace-Martin 446
  James-Lincoln *adaid aab* 375
  John *adaid aaa* 375
  Josiah *aabck a* 153-4
  Josiah *aabck ac* 154
  Judith (Bailey) 393
  Lydia 505
  Margaret-Amelia *adaid aac* 375
  Marianne *aabck aa* 153
  Mary (Lincoln) *aabck a* 152 153
  Mehitabel (Harris) 70 71
  Nicholas 153
  Patty 456
  Richard *adaid aa* 375
  Samuel 71
  Sarah H. (Taylor) 504
  Sarah-Robie *aabck ae* 154
PIERSOL
  Archibald *adaig d* 162
  Martha (Jones) *adaig d* 112
PIERSON
  Elizabeth 505
PIGEON
  Mary-Ann 425
PIKE
  Amanda (Stone) 406
  Elizabeth *abaef b* 88
  Elizabeth (Lombard) 88
  George 88
  George *abaef* 88-9

PIKE cont'd
  Henry-Bennett 406
  Leonard 88
  Olive-Irvette *aabcf dad* 406
  Rebecca-Allen *abaef a* 89
  Rebecca (Lincoln) *abaef* 88-9
PINCIN see Pynchon
  Laurana 425
PINKHAM
  James-Henry 604
  Josephine (Palmer) 604
  Mabel-Gertrude *abbea cabd* 604
PIRTLE
  Emma 574
PITCAIRN
  John 152
PITKIN
  Nellie-Olmsted *aacdc ge* 443-4
  Robert 443
  Sarah (Knox) 443
PITTLE
  Henry 330
PITTMAN
  Mary (Steigers) *adahb ej* 226
PITTS
  Edmund 4
PIXLEY
  Catherine 484
PLACE
  Fanny-Kilby (Litchfield) *adcai eb* 241
  Horace *adcai eb* 241
PLANK
  Effie-Thornton (Rutter) *adahb bceh* 497
  Park-Leaman *adahb bceh* 497
PLATT
  Charles H. *adahf ck* 374
  Elizabeth-Reybold *adahf ckc* 374
  Florence-Francina *adahf ckb* 374
  Helen *adahf cke* 374
  John 374
  John-Lincoln *adahf ckd* 374
  Mary-Cornelia *adahf cka* 374
  Mary (Jackson) 374
  Rachel-Housekeeper (Lincoln) *adahf ck* 374
PLUM
  Reuben 119
PLUMER—Plummer
  Daniel 516
  Ira-Newton *adcac bag* 516
  Lydia-Ellen ([Breed] Lincoln) *adcac bag* 516
  Olive 453
  Persis (Stevens) 516
POLAND
  William C. 397
POLLOCK
  Frederic 534
  Jennie (Le Grow) 534
  Sarah-Legrow *aabcj hba* 534
POOR
  Hannah 294 297
POPE
  Benjamin 197
  Jemima 91
  Olive 490
  Saloam 183
POPHAM
  Sally 203 note
POPPLETON
  Ezra 600
  Grace-May *adfae adcba* 600
  Grace (Riggs) 600
  Irene (Lincoln) *adfae adca* 600
  Ralph-Riggs *adfae adca* 600
PORTER
  Alexander S. 448
  Andrew 217

PORTER cont'd
Frederick-Nelson 595
Ina-Belle *adbfa*, *bdf* 595
John 35
John *aacc* 35
Joseph 35
Katherine (Lawrence) 595
Luzina 568
Mary 35
Mary (Lincoln) *aacc* 35
Mercy 35
Mercy (Randall) 35
Nancy-Jane *aabce ad* 400-1
Nancy (Spence) 400
Nehemiah 120
Richard 35
Samuel 614
Sarah (Nash) 35
Suryyer 35
Temperance (Shaw) 35
Thomas 400

POST
John-Reed *aacbc adbb* 417
Lucy *adbfa f* 387-8
Mabel (Davis) *aacbc adbb* 417

POTTS
Thomas A. 382

POTTER
Bessie (Lincoln) *aacdd eaa* 447
Edward-Edmund 447
Murray-Anthony *aacdd eaa* 447
Susan (Anthony) 447

POUNDSTONE
Mary 489

POWELL
Abigail (Lincoln) *adaga gj* 363
Atwood *adbcf aa* 383
Charles-Francis *adaga gje* 363
David 363
David-William *adaga gj* 363
Edna (Kennerseg) *adaga gja* 363
Elizabeth ([Phipps] Lincoln) *adbcf aa* 383
Emily-Wells (Scheller) *adaga gjd* 363
Henry-George *adaga gjc* 363
Nellie-Lincoln (Towle) *aabcf deb* 263
Olive-Frances (Woodburn) *adaga gje* 363
Philip-Thales *adaga gja* 363
Rhoda-Estella *adaga gjf* 363
Stephen-Lincoln *adaga gjb* 363
Susan-Margaret (Pearl) 363
William *aabcf deb* 263
William *adaga gjd* 363

POWERS
Margaret 451

POWNALL
Thomas 68

PRATER
Elizabeth (O'Neal) 381
Ruth *adbca f* 381-2
Zachariah 381

PRATT
Aaron 14 17 27 82 238 315 318 390
Abigail 142
Abner 247
Anna *aafhc* 37
Anna *aaffe d* 82
Anne (Eustis) *aaffe a* 82
Asa 185
Bernard *agja* 27
Betsy *aaffe b* 82
Betsey (Willcutt) 315
Betty (Lincoln) *aaffe* 82
Bridget (Collier) 82 238
Caleb *adffe aa* 247
Caroline-Augusta-Elizabeth *aafff cc* 315
Caroline (Gaylord) *aaffe f* 82
Clara (Lothrop) 239
Constantine *agjc* 27

PRATT cont'd
David 400
Deborah (Lincoln) *adcai ba* 390
Dorcas (Ashley) *agje* 27
Ebenezer 142 247
Eliza 185
Eliza (Stone) 185
Elizabeth (———) *aaffe f* 82
Eunice-Burr (Lothrop) *adcac eb* 239
Ezekiel 239
Ezekiel *adcac c* 238-9
Ezekiel *adcac cd* 239
Francis-Lincoln *adcac cc* 239
Francis-Lincoln *adcac ce* 239
Gerard see Jared
Gershom 390
Hannah (———) *agjh* 27
Harriet (Loring) *aabha e* 69
Henrietta-Lincoln *adcac cf* 239
Henry *adcac cb* 239
Ira-Norton 38
Jairus 256
James 315 405
Jane 239
Jane (Chandler) *aabhf e* 70
Jared *agjb* 27
Jared *agjf* 27
Jared *adffe a* 247
Job 315
John *aaflf* 38 189 314 321
John *adcai ba* 390
John L. *adcai bab* 390
Jonathan *aabha e* 69
Joseph 318
Lucinda *aaffe g* 82
Lucy *adffe bb* 247
Lydia 86
Mary *addd* 22
Mary (———) *agja* 27
Mary (Byron) *aaffe f* 82
Mary-Jane 555
Mary L. 408
Mary-Lincoln *adcac ca* 239
Mercy 14
Meriel (Lincoln) *adcac c* 238-9
Molly 247
Nabby 247
Nabby (Pratt) 247
Nancy *abbea c* 318-9
Naomi-Downs (Pettis) *adcai baa* 390
Nichols 239
Olive *agjg* 27
Olive *aaffe e* 82
Otis-Lincoln *adcai baa* 390
Paul *aaffe a* 82
Paulina-Snow (Joy) *adcai bab* 390
Phineas 27 82 238 315 318 390
Phineas *agj* 27
Phineas *agjh* 27
Polly *aaffe c* 82
Polly (Shaw) 400
Priscilla-Shaw *aabce ab* 400 ·
Relief (Bourne) 318
Rhoda *agjd* 27
Ruth (Lothrop) 390
Ruth (Snow) *adcbm c* 126
Samuel 400
Samuel *aaffe* 82
Samuel *aaffe f* 82
Sarah 14
Sarah *agje* 27
Sarah (Lincoln) *agj* 27
Sarah (Lincoln) *adffe a* 247
Sarah (Pratt) 14
Sarah (Stoddard) *adcac ce* 239
Sarah ([Wright] Cummings) 27
Susan-Lincoln (Whiton) 142
Thomas 315

PRATT cont'd
Timothy *aabhf e* 70
Zoa (Whitcomb) *aaflf* 38
PREBLE
William P. 287
PRENTICE—Prentiss
Augusta-Eugenie *adffe cd* 523
Daniel 462
Daniel-Anthony 523
Florence (Kelly) 545
Mary-Sampson (Bogman) 523
Philena *aacbe dab* 545
William-Packer 545
PRESCOTT
Mabel *adahb ghc* 370
PRESLEY
Mayme *adaaf aca* 478
PRESTON
Sarah 218
PRICE
Celia ([Hobart] Lincoln) *aabag* 140
George *aabag* 140
Philip 116 117
Rebecca 509
Sarah 346
Sterling 483
PRIEST
Alice-Ann 512
Amelia-Ann 609
Julia 610
Mary-Olivia *aabcj ac* 149
PRIME
Joseph 131
PRINTZ
Angeline (Lincoln) *adaae hg* 345
Ida-Angeline (Pence) *adaae hbc* 345
Ida-Annie *adaae hgb* 345
Isaac 345
Isaiah *adaae hbc* 345
John-David *adaae hga* 345
Lavinia-Arribella *adaae hga* 345
Lavinia-Arribella (Printz) *adaae hga* 345
Lorenzo-Sibert *adaae hg* 345
Mamie-Rhodes *adaae hffb* 476
Martha-Hill (Grayson) 345
PRIOR
Jonathan 461
PRITCHARD
Abigail (Tower) 37
Hannah (Lincoln) *aafj* 36 37 38
John 37
Oliver 37
Peggy (Mann) 38
Theodore *aafj* 37 38
PROBST
Ann ([Lincoln] Glasgow) *adaih* 112
Catharine *adaih b* 112
Eliza (Fisher) *adaih c* 112
Elizabeth *adaih a* 112
George 112
George-Michael *adaih* 112
William *adaih c* 112
PROUTY
Philinda-Gates 429
PRYOR
Elizabeth-Curd (Lewis) 482
George-Morton 482
Virginia-Morton *adaah ek* 482
PUGH
Clara-Lincoln (Kirk) *adahf cgb* 374
Harold-Brown *adahf cgb* 374
PULLMAN
George-Mortimer 567
PULTZ
Ashby-Lincoln *adaae hfda* 475
David 475
Erasmus *adaae hfd* 475
Graham-Moore *adaae hfdb* 475

PULTZ cont'd
Ida-Eliza (Lincoln) *adaae hfd* 475
Jacob-DeWitt *adaae hfdd* 475
Mamie-Bell *adaae hfdc* 475
Susan (Miller) 475
PURCELL
Mary 511
PURDY
Martha 587
PURMETT
Joseph 23
PUTNAM
Andrew 128
Ann-Maria (Cushing) *aabce bab* 256
John-Howard *aabce bab* 256
PYATT
Edith (Lincoln) *adagb deb* 492
Willis *adagb deb* 492
PYNCHEM—Pynchon see Pincin
Abner 36
Hannah (Cowing) 36
Mary 88

QUAIN
Daniel 49
QUINCY
Josiah 85

RADFORD
Agnes-Margaret *aacbe lbb* 297
RALSTON
Ann *adagb kh* 222
Err *adagb kc* 221
James *adagb k* 219 221-2
Jane *adagb kf* 221
John-Lincoln *adagb ka* 221
Martha *adagb* 222
Mary *adagb kd* 221
Nancy (Lincoln) *adagb k* 219 221-2
Robert *adagb kb* 221
Silas *adagb ke* 221
RAMBO
Anne *adbc* 114 116-8
Anna (Koch) 116 note
Catharine (Boon) 116 and note
Gaumer 116 and note
Mounce 116 and note
Peter 116 and note
RAMSDELL
Ella-Frances *aabcg dbc* 532
Hannah (Haywood) 532
Henry 532
Lydia *aafhe* 37 243
RAND
Alice-Lincoln *aabcf daaa* 406
Elizabeth 429
Elizabeth F. 189
George-Frank 405
John-Frank *aabcf daa* 405-6
Laura-Flint(Lincoln) *aabcf daa* 405-6
Mary-Frances (Moulton) 405
RANDALL
Hollis *aabcf ga* 145
John 401
Lucy *adcbm a* 126
Mary-Ann (———) 401
Mercy 35
Sophia L. (Edwards) *aabcf ga* 145
RANDOLPH
Beverly 195
RANKIN
Mary-Ann 561
RANNO
Pernicia-Ann 429
RANSFORD
Susan *aabcd baa* 252
RARDIN
Manda (Moore) 579

RARDIN cont'd
Margaret-Alice *adaga aaa* 579
Steven-Decatur 579
RASER
Elizabeth-Weida *adaid haa* 378
RATTRAY
Alice *aacda he* 175
RAUSCHNER
John Christian 162
RAVENEL
Caroline-Elise *aabch dda* 266
RAY
Lizzie-Herbert *aabce acb* 255
RAYMOND
Enos D. 555
Martha-Roy *adaah emd* 577
Martha-Roy (Wilson) 577
Mary-Jane (Pratt) 555
Mary-Lyon *abbea cacb* 555
Richard-Lee 577
READ see Reed
Lydia-Jane (Watson) *adaga gbf* 362
William *adaga gbd* 362
REAGAN
Catherine ([Lincoln] [Swords] Minick)
adaga cf 360
Patrick *adaga cf* 360
REDDICK
George 103
REDDING
Jerome 295
Rebecca (Brown) 295
REDMAN
George 336
REDWINE •
Catherine 479
REECE
Lurisia 582
REED—Reid see Read
Agnes-Catherine (Lincoln) *adaaa bbcba*
606
Anna R. *aabcd bcb* 399
Caroline (Bergstrasser) 588
Elizabeth-Ann 560
Frances (Bucknall) *aabcf dcb* 263
Gertrude *adahc aaa* 588
John *aabcf dcb* 263
Mary 293
Mary-Ann (Townsend) 399
Mary (Wheatly) 606
Nancy-Pierce 521
Rhoda 399
Robert 588
Tobias-Davis 399
William 606
William-Harvey *adaaa bbcba* 606
William-Joseph *adaaa bbcba a* 606
REEL
Sarah 565
REESER
Martha 377
REIFSNYDER
Ann (Lincoln) *adaii bh* 379
Joel 379
John-Frederick *adaii bh* 379
Margaret (Jones) 379
RELYEA
Benjamin *abbhb g* 92
Emily (Birch) *abbhb g* 92
RENSHAW
Aaron *adaga ccd* 359
Martha (Blackburn) *adaga ccd* 359
REVERE
Deborah *aacbe* 165-6
Elizabeth *aacbe* 165-6
Joseph W. 168 294 295
Mary *aacbi* 168-9 313
Paul 164 165 166 168 169 note

REVERE cont'd
Sarah (Orne) 165 168
REYNOLDS
Anna *adahf da* 506
Anna (Moore) 506
Cornelia *adahf chf* 374
Edwin H. *adahf ch* 374
Elizabeth *adahf chd* 374
Elizabeth (Lincoln) *adahf cd* 373
Ella-Frances *adahf cha* 374
Francina *adahf c* 372-4
Georgiana *adahf che* 374
Haines 374
Henry 372 506
Isaac 373
Isaac-Wayne *adahf cdb* 373
Jacob 506
Janette *adahf chg* 374
Jonathan *adahf cd* 373
Letitia (Paxon) *adahf cdb* 373
Lydia-Elmira (Lincoln) *adahf ch* 374
Margaret *adahf chb* 374
Mary E. (Knight) 372
Mary-Emma *adahf cda* 373
Mira (Haines) 373
Phebe-Dinah (Moore) 374
Sarah-Rosene *adahf chc* 374
Susannah 324
RHODES—Rodes
Ann 344
Charles-Lincoln *adaae hffb* 476
Charles-Preston *adaae hff* 476
Fannie-Clarissa *adaae el* 207
Greenberry 476
Hamilton 344
Helen-Margaret *adaae hffc* 476
Joseph 344
Mamie-Rhodes (Printz) *adaae hffb* 476
Mary-Anna *adaae hffa* 476
Mary-Hansbarger(Anderson) 476
Mattie-Belle (Lincoln) *adaae hff* 476
Nancy (Lionberger) *adaae h* 344-5
Robert-Preston *adaae hffd* 476
RHYMES
Mary-Celia 442
RICE
Ada-Gertrude 486
Arthur 419
David *adaah a* 214 215
Edmund 419
Edward 419
Elizabeth *adaae icc* 346
Elizabeth-Chandler (Blake) 419
Elizabeth (Lincoln) *adaah a* 213 215
Francis-Blake 419
Francis-Blake *aacbc afa* 419
George-Graham 441
George-Tilly 419
Georgianna-de-Villers (Lincoln) *aacbc*
afa 419
Gertrude-Austin 419
Jacob 419
Mary *adaah edd* 355
Obadiah 419
Sally-Blake (Austin) 419
Thomas 419
Tilly 419
RICH
Abigail ([Hall] Knowles) *abaec c* 87
Betsey 253
James *abaec e* 87
Mary-Elizabeth *abbea caac* 450
Sarah (Hall) *abaec e* 87
Zaccheus *abaec c* 87
RICHARDS
Ada-Frances (Marsh) *abbec bde* 322
Clarissa-Emeline 398
Clarissa-Emeline (Richards) 398

RICHARDS cont'd
David L. *abbec bde* 322
Ebenezer-William 398
Elizabeth *adahf cb* 505
Florence-Eveline (Sulis) *adffe lca* 398
Frank-Winslow *adffe lc* 398
Fred-Lincoln *adffe lca* 398
John 23
Olive-Augusta (Lincoln) *adffe lc* 398
Rebecca (Stubbs) 505
Stephen 505
RICHARDSON
Albert E. 408
Alice-Lyndon (Bowen) 543
Almira (Kendall) 456
Arthur *aacdc ebc* 309
Charles-Marshall *abbec fbaa* 457
Cyrus 457
Cyrus-Bowen *abbec fba* 457
Cyrus-Wilmarth *adcak ec* 243
Dorothy-Hardy *aacbc adde* 543-4
Ellen (———) 457
Fanny-Leland *aacdc ebd* 309
Fanny-Mitchell (Lincoln) *aacdc eb* 309
Frank-Lincoln *abbec fbad* 457
Grace *aacdc ebb* 309
Harriet (Leland) 309 389
Henry-Lincoln *aacdc eb* 309
John 153
John-Green *adcac db* 389
Lucy *abbec fb* 456-7
Lucy-Allen *abbec fbac* 457
Lucy-Allen (Lincoln) *abbec fba* 457
Marcia-Dunlap *adcac dba* 389
Mary-Abigail (Whitcomb) *adcak ec* 243
Mary-Elizabeth (Lincoln) *adcac db* 389
Rufus-Byam 543
Stephen 456
William 309 389
William-King *aacdc eba* 309
RICHMOND
Ann 234 note
RIDDLE
Adeline L. *aacbi gd* 169
Ann (Aiken) 78 169
Charles-Lincoln *aacbi gc* 168 169
Charles-Wisner 169 note
David *aacbi g* 169
Frances-Eliza (Field) *aacbi gc* 169
Gawm 78 169
Gilman *aacbi gb* 169
Isaac *aacbk* 78 169
Margaret (McGaw) 78
Mary (Bell) 78
Mary E. *aacbi ga* 169
Mary (Lincoln) *aacbi g* 168 169
Mercy ([Lincoln] Vinal) *aacbk* 78
RIFFE
Christopher 326
RIGGS
Grace 600
RIMEL—Rymel
Abraham *adaai e* 103
Alpha (Fannon) *adaai e* 103
Betsey *adaai i* 102 103
Christena (Willhoite) *adaai d* 103
Dorcas *adaai g* 102 103
Elias *adaai f* 103
George *adaai j* 102 103
Isaac *adaai a* 102 103
Jacob *adaai d* 102 103
Jenny (Dunkin) *adaai f* 103
John *adaai* 94 101-3
John *adaai b* 102 103
Kezia (Williamson) *adaai a* 103
Polly *adaai c* 102 103
Rebecca (Lincoln) *adaai* 94 101-3
Sally *adaai h* 102 103

RIMEL cont'd
Sarah (Williamson) *adaai b* 103
RIMER
Hetty 570
RINEY
Zachariah 465
RINGROSE
Margaret *adcac daa* 518
RIPLEY
George 23 322
Lydia (Hobart) *aacb* 76
Lydia-Jacobs 449
Nehemiah 76
Sarah (———) 23
RITENOUR
Elizabeth-Augusta (Shaw) *adagb jg* 219
221
John-Sturgis 105 108
Leah-Jane (Sturgis) *adagb gd* 221
William-Mandeville *adagb gd* 221
RITTER
Esther (Tobias) 509
Hannah *adaii bc* 509-10
Joseph 509
ROBB
Ann (Tolait) 165
James 165
Martha 165
Martha (Howard) *aacbe* 165-6 296
Thomas 165
ROBBINS
Betsey (Leverett) 247
Elizabeth *adffe* 247-9
Grace (Hamlin) 409
Julia-Hall *aabcj hb* 409
Nelson-Collingwood 409
William 247
ROBERTS
Anne *aabce ccdb* 403
Bennet 305
Joshua 129
Ruth (———) 129
ROBERTSON
Annie B. *abbec fdb* 458
Eliza *adbca d* 380-1
George B. 458
John 380
John-Johnson 429
Mary (———) 458
Mary-Sophronia *aacbg cca* 429
Pernicia-Ann (Ranno) 429
Susannah 322
ROBESON
Andrew 49
Israel 48
Jonathan 47
Mary *ada* 47 49-53
ROBIDSON
Lucinda 611
ROBIE
Charles *aacbj aa* 149
Edward 149 274
Eliza ([Stevens] Cross) 149
Emily (March) *aabcj aa* 149
Frances-Maria (Barrett) *aabcj ab* 149
Francis B. 149
Frederick *aabcj ac* 149
George *aabcj ab* 149
Harriet *aabck g* 149 273 274
Henry 149
Lydia (Brown) 149 274
Martha-Ellen (Cressey) *aabcj ac* 149
Mary-Olivia (Priest) *aabcj ac* 149
Sally-Thaxter (Lincoln) *aabcj a* 149
Sarah (Smith) 149
Thomas S. 149
Toppan *aabcj a* 149 274

ROBINSON
Andrew 259
David 205
Dorcas *adaae* 205-8
Dorcas (——) 205
Ebenezer *adbb* 115
Eliza-Folsom 441
H. E. 108
John *adaga gbb* 362
Margaret 259
Mary 345
Mary-Frances (Watson) *adaga gbb* 362
Mary ([Shute] Lincoln) *adbb* 115
Sarah (——) 259
Susannah 182
ROBISHAN
Mary 602
ROBY
W. J. 198
ROCHAMBEAU
count de 418
ROCKWELL
James *abbhb a* 92
Loretta (Birch) *abbhb a* 92
RODES see Rhodes
ROE
Mary-Josephine 51 93
RODGES—Rogers
Abner 269
Elizabeth *adahf cgc* 374
Harriet *adbca cc* 232
Jacob 23
James 197
Lot 506
Martha (Jenkins) 506
Mary ([Robeson] Lincoln) *ada* 49 50 52 109 110
Rachel *adaid ab* 506
Roger *ada* 49 50 52
ROLLIN
Ichabod 130
ROMIG
Rachel 379
ROOP
Alice-Lincoln *adahb bdda* 498
Francis-Asbury 498
Hubert-Armitage *adahb bdd* 498
Keziah-Jane (Stewart) 498
Lillie-Jane (Lincoln) *adahb bdd* 498
ROPES
John-Codman 538
ROSE
Edward 489
Josephine 541
Mary-Elizabeth *adaga gd* 489
Mary (Martin) 489
ROSEBROOKS
Hattie E. 615
ROSS
Barbara 267
Elsie (Briggs) 524
Ichabod-Henry 524
Julia-Maria *adffe cg* 524
ROUNDS
Emma-Chapman (Woodbury) *aabcf fc* 144
George *aabcf fc* 144
ROUSH
Michall *adahc c* 227
Sarah (Lincoln) *adahc c* 227
ROUT—Routt
Alice *adaga gfe* 490
Henry L. 483
ROUTH
Edward *adaaa bbae* 463
Mary-Abigail (Ott) *adaaa bbae* 463
ROWE
Pauline-Isabelle *aabck fda* 273

ROWELL
George P. 273
ROY
Frank *adaaf dbaaa* 474
Willie-Lee (Oliver) *adaaf dbaaa* 474
RUDOLPH
Margaret-Rosetta 548
RUEBUSH
Frank *adaae abea* 472
Isabel (Lincoln) *adaaf abe* 472
John *adaaf abe* 472
RUGGLES
Harriet (Litchfield) *adcbm g* 126
Samuel-Oakman *adcbm g* 126
RUMPLE
Sallie *adaae adi* 343
RUNDIO
Albert J. *adagb dhab* 493
Rosalie-Amy (Collins) *adagb dhab* 493
RUNELL
Andromicha-Wright (Cummins) 569
RUNNELS
Hannah 434
RUPPERT
Adam-Lincoln *adaii bbda* 508
Anna-Amelia (Lincoln) *adaii bbd* 508
Clara *adaii bbdc* 508
Cyrus *adaii bbd* 508
Earl-Lincoln *adaii bbdb* 508
Florence *adaii bbdg* 508
Frank-Lincoln *adaii bbdf* 508
George-Lincoln *adaii bbde* 508
Helen-Lincoln *adaii bbdd* 508
Jonathan 508
Sarah (Huyett) 508
RUSH
Abraham *adbed* 58
Benjamin 58
Catharine 58
Elizabeth *adbea* 58
Elizabeth (Hilton) 58 114
Elizabeth (Hodges) 58
Esther 58
James 58
John 58
Joseph *adbe* 58 114
Martha (Wallace) *adbec* 58
Mary *adbeb* 58
Rebecca (Lincoln) *adbe* 58 114
Sarah 58
Susanna 58
William 58
William *adbec* 58
RUSO
Ellen-Frances (Newcomb) *abbea caie* 452
Joseph *abbea caie* 452
RUSSELL
Catherine 315
Ethel-Elizabeth (Bradley) *adahb dcha* 499
James *adaga d* 217
Judith-Cooper 254
Martha (Ellmes) *aaffj g* 84
Maude-Minnie *adaae abab* 569
Rebecca 86
Sarah (Lincoln) *adaga d* 217
Steven *adahb dcha* 499
Thomas 176
William *aaffj g* 84
William-Wakefield 569
RUST
Henry 131
Nathaniel 255
Susannah (Scannell) 255
RUTH
Clarence *adaii bib* 379
Elizabeth 508
Elizabeth *adaii bbb* 592

RUTH cont'd
    Elizabeth *adaii bia* 379
    Elizabeth (Spayd) 379
    Gertrude(Brown) *adaii bib* 379
    John 592
    Lewis P. *adaii bi* 379
    Mary-Seifert (Wicklein) 592
    Samuel 379
    Sarah (Lincoln) *adaii bi* 379
RUTLAND
    Irene *adaaf dbbc* 479
RUTLEDGE
    A. G. 559
    Elizabeth *adahf bg* 229
    Margaret (Lincoln) *adaaa bbbg* 559
    Marie (Hornbrook) *adaaa bbbgb* 559
    Mary E. (———) 559
    Mary-Isabel *adaaa bbbge* 559
    Nellie *adaaa bbbga* 559
    Ralph-Lincoln *adaaa bbbgb* 559
    Ray-Jesse *adaaa bbbgd* 559
    Ruth-Hester *adaaa bbbgc* 559
    William-Jesse *adaaa bbbg* 559
RUTTER
    Carrie-Lincoln *adahb bcef* 497
    Effie-Thornton *adahb bceh* 497
    Eli 497
    Eli *adahb bced* 497
    Elizabeth (Skiles) 497
    Elizabeth-Skiles *adahb bceb* 497
    Harriet-Cleveland *adahb bceg* 497
    Jacob-Blance *adhb bcec* 497
    Jacob R. *adahb bce* 497
    Lydia-Magdalene (Bair) *adahb bcee* 497
    Maggie-Carey *adahb bcei* 497
    Margaret-Priscilla (Lincoln) *adahb bce* 497
    Minnie-Lytle *adahb bcea* 497
    William-Evans *adahb bcee* 497
RYERSON
    William 180
RYNARD
    Edith 344

SABINE
    Edward-Andrews *aacdb eg* 303
    Eliphalet-Young 303
    Eva-Richards (Lincoln) *aacdb eg* 303
    Paulina-Fletcher (Coney) 303
SAFFORD
    Augustus 128
    George *adfag a* 128
    Polly (Stevenson) *adfag a* 128
SAGE
    Eliza-Ann ([Arnold] Lincoln) 397
    Oliver F. 397
ST CLAIR
    Charles *aabcf ahc* 262
    Louisa-Harding ([Sawyer] Barrett) *aabcf ahc* 262
ST JOHN
    Celia 531
SALISBURY
    Nancy ([Hoard] Lincoln) *aacbc af* 418
    Rebecca 162
    Stephen 418
SALTAR—Salter
    Hannah *ada* 44-53
    Hannah (Bowne) 49
    John 45
    Richard 45 49
SALTONSTALL
    Laura 538
SALYEARS
    Edward-Leslie *adaaa bbcha* 560
    Maggie-Fern (Christian) *adaaa bbcha* 560

SAMPSON
    Elisha 555
    Joshua 394
    Lucy (Holbrook) 394
    Mary *adfah a* 394-5
    Mary-Ann *abbea cad* 555-6
    Relief 273
    Sylvia (Gurney) 555
    William-Thomas 577
SAMUELS
    Hannah 112 230
SANDERS
    Alvin-Vernette *adaaa bbcib* 560
    Lincoln-Ellsworth *adaaa bbcia* 560
    Malinda (Smith) 560
    Marion-Ellsworth *adaaa bbci* 560
    Mary-Ellen (Lincoln) *adaaa bbci* 560
    Thomas-Jefferson 560
SARGENT
    mr. 269
    Mary 599
SAVAGE
    Abiah 120
    Abiah ([Eels] Lincoln) *adbf* 120
    Daniel *adbf* 120
    Martha (Norton) 120
    Sarah 120
    Sarah (Savage) 120
    William 120 237
SAWYER
    mr. 409
    Alice (Crowley) 551
    Anna-Louisa (Lincoln) *adbcf ah* 261-2
    Charlotte-Elizabeth (Smith) *aabec bad* 321
    David-Tilden-Stinson *aabcf ahb* 262
    Emma-Maria *aabcf ahd* 261 262
    Frances-Lincoln *aabcf acba* 404
    Frank-Lincoln *aabcf ahe* 262
    George-Aholiab 404
    Harriet (Little) 261
    Howard-George *aabcf ace* 404
    John 551
    Julia-Putnam *aabcf aha* 262
    Laura-Whitehouse (Decker) 404
    Louisa-Harding *aabcf ahb* 261 262
    Mabel *aacdb igb* 551
    Mary-Elizabeth (Lincoln) *aabcf ace* 404
    Nancy *aacbd c* 77
    Nathan 261
    Otis-Vinal *abbec bad* 321
    Reuben *aabcf ah* 261-2
    Reuben-Frank *aabcf ahf* 262
SCALES
    Henrietta (Baugh) *adaaf aa* 348
    Joseph *adaaf aa* 348
SCAMMELL
    Alexander 255-6
    Elizabeth 255
    Elizabeth (Lithcoe) 255
    Mary (———) 255
    Susannah 255
SCARLETT
    Humphrey 70 71
    Mary *aaca* 70-2
    Mary (Wentworth) 71
    Mehitable ([Harris] Pierce) 70
SCHANCK
    Alta *adahb gbd* 586
    James 586
    Rebecca-Jane (Stevens) 586
SCHAUMBERG
    George-William *aacda hd* 175
    Sarah-Elizabeth (Wheeler) *aacda hd* 175
SCHEIFLEY
    Eliza (Bowman) *adaaa abcb* 462
    George *adaaa abcb* 462

SCHELLER
Emily-Wells *adaga gjd* 363
SCHERFF
Beryl (Lincoln) *adahb gbea* 586
Harold-Christopher *adahb gbea* 586
SCHLESINGER
Leopold 445
SCHOFIELD
Mary 613
SCHOOLCRAFT
Caroline-Cornelia (Canfield) 283
John-Lawrence 283
SCHOONOVER
Alice 609
Mary *adaaa bbc* 459-61
SCHRADER
Louisiana 480
SCHRAM
Cleas 231
SCHREIER
Charles-Christopher *adbfa fbl* 387
Pearl-Amelia (Botelle) *adbfa fbl* 387
SCHUCK
Harry S. *adaii bjb* 379
Sarah-Lincoln (Biehl) *adaii bjb* 379
SCHULTZ
Abigail-Triphena (Hope) 524
Christopher 524
Jessie *adaaa bbic* 610
John 610
Lissa (Blister) 610
May-Anna-Adelaide *adffe df* 524-5
SCHUTT
Pauline 599
SCHUYLER
Henry 613
Lillian-May *adbcf baab* 613
Mary (Schofield) 613
SCOTT
Amelia-Margaret 578
Daisy *adahb bccb* 497
Elizabeth (Kinsey) 373
Emma-Frances (Lincoln) *adahb bcc* 497
Florence-May *adahf cfc* 373
George-Miltenberger *adahf cfa* 373
Grover *adahb bccg* 497
Howard *adahb bccd* 497
Ira *adahb bcca* 497
James *adahb bcc* 497
James *adahb bccf* 497
James-Henry *adahf cf* 373
Lewis *adahb bcce* 497
Margaret-Lincoln *adahf cfb* 373
Margaret-Worthington (Lincoln) *adahf cf* 373
Ralph *adahb bccc* 497
Samuel 373
Sarah-Anna *adahf cfd* 373
Winfield 467
SEACAT
Harriet-Anna *adaaa bbac* 463
SEAGRAVE
Arnold 601
SEAHORN
Julia *adaaf dae* 350
SEALY
Sarah 283
SEAMAN
Mary *adaaf f* 352
SEARS
Hannah-Maria *aabhg aa* 413
Hannah-Mayo (Hopkins) 413
John 413
Joshua 311
Orin 413
Paul 413
Reuben 413
Richard 413

SEARS cont'd
Willard 413
William-Richard 551
SEATON
Jacob *adaai h* 102 103
Joseph-Crawford *adaga aba* 358
Mary-Bianco (Carson) *adaga aba* 358
Sally (Rimel) *adaai h* 102 103
SEAVER see Sever
Hepsey-Ann 423
Norman 173
SEAVERNS
Charles 604
Edwina-Lewis *abbea cabg* 604
Martha-Jane (Webb) 604
SEACOMB
Eben-Dennis *aafff gbe* 317
Mary-Gertrude (Beal) *aafff gbe* 317
SEE
Catherine 349
SEISSLER
Ella (Blackman) 550
John 550
Marie-Rosina *aacdb ica* 550
SEMBOWER
Margaret *adaga fh* 218
SEVER see Seaver
Caleb 282
James-Warren 417
Mary (Chandler) 282
Nicholas 282
Penelope-Winslow *aacbc a* 282-3
Robert 282
William 282
SEVERANCE
Elizabeth *adfad ba* 521
Elizabeth G. (Joy) 521
Samuel 521
SERVICE
Hugh *adaig* 112
Phebe ([Lincoln] Jones) *adaig* 112
SEWALL
David *aacbe l* 296
Elizabeth C. (———) 296
Hannah-Sprague ([Wales] Lincoln) *aacbe l* 296-7
Henry 296
Joseph 25
Sarah (Henry) 296
SEWARD
Louisa-Cornelia 283
Samuel-Swezy 283
William Henry 468
SEXTON
George-Lytton *adaaa bbcca* 560
Rose-Ada (Gott) *adaaa bbcca* 560
SHACKFORD
Elizabeth (Lincoln) *aacdb c* 179-80
Esther (Woodwell) 179
John 179
Joshua 179
Mary-Maria (Tinkham) *aacdb ca* 180
Samuel 179
Samuel *aacdb c* 179-80
Samuel *aacdb ca* 44 180
William 179
SHAFFNER
Mary-Elizabeth *adbca ia* 233
SHALLCROSS
Ella *adahb dcc* 499
SHALLENBERGER
Caroline-Winters (Bogardus) *adagb dgh* 365
John-Parkhill *adagb dgh* 365
SHANNAMAN
Mary (Barto) *adaic ec* 229
SHARON
Samuel 110 note

SHARON cont'd
Samuel *adahd i* 110 and note
Sarah (Davis) *adahd i* 110
Susan (Davis) *adahd f* 110
William *adahd f* 110 and note
William W. 110 note
SHARP
Barrington-Symrad *adaaf aba* 477
Barrington-Symrad *adaaf abae* 477
Elizabeth-Emily *adaaf abaa* 477
Felix-Zollicoffer (Lincoln) *adaaf aba* 477
Helen *adaaf abac* 477
Ida-Beatrice *adaaf ac* 478
McAllen *adaaf abab* 477
Mary-Earle (Hackett) 477 478
Robert *adaaf abad* 477
Selina *adbca abb* 380
William-Monroe 477 478
SHATTUCK
Francis 300
Henry 409
Mary 155
Mary-Ann *aabck ba* 409-10
Mary (Heald) *aacda e* 300
Olive-Pratt (Turner) 409
Roxanna *adbfa e* 132
SHAVER
Abigail (Lincoln) *adaae af* 344
John *adaae af* 344
Lincoln *adaae afb* 344
Smith *adaae afa* 344
SHAW
Abigail 318
Arthur-Augustus *abbhc bg* 192
Asenath (Hopkins) 192
Benjamin *abbhc b* 192
Benjamin-Franklin *abbhc bc* 192
David-Downey *adagb j* 219 221
David-Downey *adagb ji* 221
Dorcas (Smith) 318
Elizabeth 69
Elizabeth-Augusta *adagb jg* 219 220 221
Fanny A. *aacdb eab* 303
George-Nichols *abbhc ba* 192
Harriet-Lincoln *abbhc bd* 192
Hester *adagb je* 219 221
Jane (Downey) 221
John-Jackson 535
John-Lincoln *adagb jh* 219 220 221
Lillian-Cora *aabck bfc* 535
Lydia (Eldredge) 535
Martha-Annie (Webber) *aabhc bc* 192
Mary-Jane *adagb ja* 219 221
Mary-Jane (Gamble) *adagb jf* 221
Mary-Lincoln *abbhc bf* 192
Mary-Maria (Chase) *abbhc bg* 192
Polly 400
Rebecca (Hogsett) *adagb jb* 221
Robert 221
Robert-Beals *abbhc be* 192
Robert-Patterson *adagb jf* 219 220 221
Roland *adagb jb* 219 221
Sarah-Ann *adagb jd* 219 221
Sarah-Asenath *abbhc bb* 192
Sarah (Lincoln) *abbhc b* 192
Sarah (Lincoln) *adagb j* 219 221
Temperance 35
William 181 192 318
William *adagb jc* 219 221
SHEDD
Helen-Maria *aabck bf* 411-2
Mary (Foster) 411
Zachariah 411
SHELDON
Eliza P. 393
SHELMIER
Emily-Pusey *adahf cag* 373

SHEPARD
Edward 119
SHEPLER
Joseph T. 490
SHEPLE
Annette (Lincoln) *adffe i* 248-9
Curtis 249
Rebecca (Lawrence) 249
Samuel-Curtis *adffe i* 249
SHERBURNE
Harriet *aabcg ia* 147
Joseph 392
Rebecca *adcak bb* 392
Zerviah (Sweetland) 392
SHERIDAN
Philip-Henry 345
SHERMAN
Nellie *adbcf bde* 384
SHERRIFF
Eva-Moody *abbec bcc* 322
SHERWIN
Nancy *adffa g* 133
SHEWEY
Hannah-Martha (McGuffin) 571-2
John L. 571-2
Sallie-Ann *adaae hfa* 571-2
SHIELDS
James 467
SHIPLEY
Lucy 339
Mary 200 201
Nancy 338 339
SHIPMAN
John *adaaf hf* 475
Maria *adaha dc* 224
Sarah (Jones) *adaae hf* 475
SHIVELY
Eliza (Bowman) *adaaa abcb* 462
SHIVERICK
Ann *aacdc aa* 182
Olive (Butler) 310
Sarah-Butler *aacdc f* 310
William 310
SHRUM
Elizabeth *adbca* 231-3
SHULL
Henry-Giger *adagc ha* 108
M. L. *adagc haa* 108
Samuel *adagc h* 108
Sarah (Giger) *adagc h* 108
SHUTE
Daniel 167
Mary 115
Mary *adbb* 115
Rebecca 115
Thomas 115
SIBERT
Arbelia 570
SIBLEY
Mary-Adeline 412
SIEGFRIED
Adele-Lincoln (Hafer) *adaii bdb* 379
John *adaii bdb* 379
SIMMONS—Simonds—Simons—Symmons
Alden 392
Alvan 526
Betsey (Litchfield) *adcbm h* 126
Christiana *aabci a* 68
Ellen-Deane *aabce cd* 403
Freeman *adcbm h* 126
John 403
Laura-Maria *aabhg a* 276
Leonard 276
Louisa-Lavina 370
Lucy-Ellen *aabce aba* 526-7
Lucy-Whitney (Day) 526
Mary 501
Mary *adcbm f* 126

SIMMONS cont'd
Mary-Ann ([Lincoln] Doyle) *adcak ba* 392
Mary (Deane) 403
Nancy *abbec f* 323
Sally B. (——) 276
Sarah *aabgd* 31
Thankful *adcbm f* 126
SIMPSON
Louis *adaaa bbee* 562
Zeroda (Lincoln) *adaaa bbee* 562
SIMRILL
Emily-Oneal (Dinges) *adaaf dac* 350
Marion *adaaf dac* 350
SIMS
Lizzie (——) 612
Margaret-Louise *adahb gbcb* 612
Matthew 612
SINCLAIR
Elizabeth-Fillebrown (Lincoln) *aabce ca* 258
William *aabce ca* 258
SINGLETON
Patience 256
SIPE
Emanuel 571
Penelope-Catharine (Jennings) 571
Sallie-Stuart *adaae ahc* 571
SKINNER
Alonzo A. *aabcf ad* 261
Elizabeth-Hopkins (Lincoln) *aabcf ad* 261
Cornelia 525
Otis A. 424
SLACK
William 198
SLATER
John-Tom 335 336 337
SMALL
Albion K. P. *aabcf fb* 144
Elizabeth 221
Rose-Lelia *adbcf bece* 513
Thankful-Lincoln (Woodbury) *aabcf fb* 144
SMEDLEY
Elizabeth *adbca ca* 232
SMITH
Abner 155
Agnes-Irene *adahb ghe* 370
Albert-Francis *adahb gha* 370
Aldo *adaga aaca* 486
Alexander-Watson *adfae af* 394
Alice-Jane (Dinsdale) *adahb gha* 370
Angie *adaah el* 483
Anne 6
Bethia 89
Caroline-Louise (Wahle) *abbec baf* 321
Celia-Frances *aacdc ea* 441-2
Charles-Harris 455-6
Charles-Marcus 528
Charles-Mighill *abbec bae* 321
Charles P *abbec bab* 321
Charlotte-Elizabeth *abbec baa* 321
Charlotte-Elizabeth *abbec bad* 321
Clara 430
Clara-Elizabeth *adahb ghf* 370
Deliverance (Lane) 321
Dorcas 318
Douglas *adaid hg* 378
Edward 495
Eliza 433
Elizabeth 403
Eliza-Folsom (Robinson) 441
Elizabeth (Lincoln) *adaid hg* 378
Elizabeth-Strickland *adcai ed* 241
Elmer-Ellsworth *aafff geb* 317
Ernest-Welcome *aabce aebb* 528
Fannie-Biddle (Lincoln) *abbhc dbd* 458

SMITH cont'd
Florence-Jeannette *abbhc dbda* 458
Frances-Louisa *abbec bla* 455-6
Frank-Bulkeley 542
George 483
Grace-Ann (Lincoln) *adbca dcb* 511
Hannah-Jane (Lincoln) *adfae af* 394
Harry-Austin *abbhc dbd* 458
Henry-Lincoln *abbec baf* 321
Ida *adaae adf* 343
Ida E. (Soule) 528
Isabella-Weir 447
James-Wiggin 441
Jennie-Warren (Beal) *aafff geb* 317
John *adaaa aaa* 460
John-Edwin 416
John-Henry *adbca dcb* 511
Joseph 321
Julia-Ann (——) 483
Louisa-Frances (Adams) 455-6
Louisa-Lavina (Simons) 370
Lucy-Adelia *adahb ghd* 370
Mabel-Edith *abbhc dbca* 458
Mabel (Prescott) *adahb ghc* 370
Malinda 560
Margaret *adbca d* 380-1
Maria-Jane (Hall) 458
Martha-Ann 439
Mary 495
Mary *aabhe* 155
Mary *adaga gba* 362
Mary (Bromley) *abbec bae* 321
Mary-Lavina *adahb ghb* 370
Mighill *abbec ba* 321
Nathan 458
Nathan *abbhc dbcb* 458
Nathan-Ellsworth *abbhc dbc* 458
Nathaniel 511
Priscilla-Florida *adaaa aaaa* 460
Priscilla (Lincoln) *adaaa aaa* 460 461
Putnam-David *adahb ghc* 370
Ralph T. 370
Robert 394
Samuel 107
Sarah 149
Sarah-Ann *abbec bac* 321
Sarah (Lincoln) *abbec ba* 321
Sarah-Priscilla (Lincoln) *adahb gh* 370
Sarah-Stubbs (Haines) *adahf ccf* 373
Susan (Ellis) 511
Susan-Hardy (Chadbourne) 458
Susan-Russell (Lincoln) *abbhc dbc* 458
Taylor-Fillmore 458
Walter-Loraine *adahb gh* 370
William *adahf ccf* 373
William *adaid hga* 378
SNELL
Lucy-Maria *adffd c* 134
SNELLING
Caroline-Matilda (Lincoln) *aabce bh* 256 257
Carrie-Maria *aabce bhc* 257
Edith-Louisa *aabce bhb* 257
Enoch-Howes 257
Enoch-Howes *aabce bh* 256 257
James-Fowler *aabce bha* 257
Sarah-Dargue (Jones) 257
SNOW
Amelia-Ripley *abbea caed* 451
Ann-Frances *adcai bec* 391
Anthony 390
Apphia-Jordan *aabhg e* 277-8
Benjamin-Lincoln *adcai beg* 391
Betsy (Pratt) *aaffe b* 82
Charlotte-Otis *adcai bef* 391
David 390
Deliverance (Dyer) 390
Henry 390

SNOW cont'd
Henry *adcai be* 390-1
James H. *adcai beb* 390
John 390
Mary-Jane 558
Nicholas 390
Ruth *adcbm c* 126
Ruth-Nichols *adcai bee* 320 391
Samuel *aaffe b* 82
Sarah (Lord) 277
Susan-Elizabeth *adcai bed* 391
Susannah-Stoddard (Lincoln) *adcai be* 390-1
William 277
SNYDER
Ashville *adaga bg* 217
Louisa-Ann 583
Mary (Zearing) *adaga bg* 217
SONER
Julia-Ann 464
SOPPENFIELD
Margaret-Jane *adaaa bdc* 333
SOULE
Ida E. 528
Nancy-Deering (Chandler) *aabhf a* 70
Timothy-Davis *aabhf a* 70
SOUTHARD
Clara-Ellen (O'Brion) *aabcf dbb* 263
William F. *aabcf dbb* 263
SOUTHER
Abigail-Kent (Tower) 553
Allen-Lincoln *abbec fac* 323
Ann (Bent) *aabcd ce* 141
Bertha-Orilla *abbea cabbe* 553
Caleb *abbec fa* 323
Catherine-Cushing *aabcd ci* 141
Charles-Nichols *aabcd cg* 141
Cornelia F. (May) *abbec faa* 323
Cynthia (Spear) *aabcd ca* 141
Daniel 536
David *abbea cabbd* 553
Deborah *aabcd b* 252
Deborah (Leavitt) 140 252
Edward-Brush *aabcd cj* 141
Eliza (Phelps) *aabcd cc* 141
Emery *aabcd ch* 141
Frederick *aabcd ce* 141
George *aabcd cd* 141
Hannah-Lincoln *aabcd ch* 141
Hannah-Lincoln (Souther) *aabcd ch* 141
Henry *aabcd cc* 141
John 140 252 553
John *aabcd c* 140-1
John-Albert-Lincoln *abbea cabba* 553
John B. *abbec faa* 323
John-Lincoln *aabcd ca* 141
Joseph 140 252 316 323 536 553
Louise (Stoddard) *abbea cabbc* 553
Lucy-Jane *aabhg aaa* 536
Lucy-Richardson *abbec fad* 323
Lydia (Lincoln) *aabcd c* 140-1
Lydia-Lincoln *aabcd cf* 141
Mabel-Louisa (McKenzie) *abbea cabba* 553
Mary-Avery *aafff g* 316-8
Mary E. (Chubbuck) *aabcd cj* 141
Myra-Elizabeth *abbec fad* 323
Myra (Lincoln) *abbec fa* 323
Nathan 316 323 553
Nathaniel 316 323 536 553
Orianna-Augusta *abbea cabbc* 553
Orianna-Augusta (Lincoln) *abbea cabb* 553
Sally (Wilson) 316 323
Samuel-Cushing 536
Sarah H. (Adams) *aabcd cj* 141
Sarah-Jane (Tower) 536
Sarah-Wilson-Hobart *abbec fab* 323

SOUTHER cont'd
William-Lincoln *aabcd cb* 141
William-Otis *abbea cabb* 553
William-Otis *abbea cabbc* 553 604
SOUTHWORTH
Eunice 387
SPARRELL
Catherine-Wild (Lincoln) *aabck bc* 270
Elbridge-Kirkwood *aabck bc* 270
John 270
Sylvia-Sampson (Turner) 270
SPAYD
Elizabeth 379
SPEAR
Cynthia *aabcd ca* 141
SPECK
Dale-Lillie *adaae aeh* 344
Lucy-Bell *adaae aeh* 344
SPENCE
Nancy 400
SPENCER
Elizabeth 332
Ellen *adahb dcd* 584
Ellen-Maria (Whitcomb) *adffd h* 134
Ellen (Meahan) 584
James 559
John H. *adffd e* 134
Mary-Elizabeth *adaaa bbc* 559-60
Nancy C. 563
Sabrina 391
Sarah (Whitcomb) *adffd e* 134
Thomas 584
SPICER
Adaline-Elizabeth (Hawley) 520
Alexander 520
Emma-Jane *adcai ff* 520
SPONSELLOR
Stella 570
SPOTTS
Henry-Kupp *adaid aac* 375
Margaret-Amelia (Pierce) *adaid aac* 375
SPRAGUE
Adrianna (Lincoln) *aabca cbb* 402
Ann-Maria *aabce eg* 142
Annie W. (Vinal) *aabce cbba* 402
Anthony 69 156 276 402
Bethia *aagb* 11
Betsey *aacbf d* 77
Caroline 296
Charles 429
Clarinda (Curtis) *aabhb b* 69
Daniel 402
Deborah 140
Ebed *aabhb b* 69
Ebed *aabhg c* 156
Ebed *aabhg ca* 156
Elizabeth (Rand) 429
Elizabeth (Whiton) 69
Fred-Lincoln *aabce cbba* 402
Fremont-Jesse *aacdb ead* 303
Helen-Elizabeth *aacbg cc* 429
Isaac 156 276
Jeremiah 69
John 158
Josiah 156 276 402
Josiah *aabce cbb* 402
Lincoln *aabhb c* 69
Lucy (Whiton) *aabce ee* 142
Luther *aabce ee* 142
Lydia *aabhb d* 69
Lydia-Jacob (Lincoln) *aabhg c* 156
Mary (Burr) 276
Mary-Eva (Fisher) *aacdb ead* 303
Mary-Lincoln (Whiton) *aabce ed* 142
Mary W. (Fuller) *aabhb a* 69
Matilda 299
Miles *aabhb* 69
Miles *aabhb a* 69

SPRAGUE cont'd
Moses 156
Myra-Ellen 402
Peggy (Lincoln) *aabhb* 69
Polly-Hersey 156
Rachel-Burr *aabhg a* 276-7
Samuel *aabhb e* 69
Sarah (Leavitt) 402
Sidney *aabce ed* 142
Tamar (Stoddard) 402
William 69 156 276 402
SPRING
Mary (Zearing) *adaga bg* 217
SPRINGER
Christopher 221
Dennis 221
Elizabeth (Jenkins) 221
Elizabeth (Small) 221
Hester (Shaw) *adagn je* 219 221
Jacob 221
Jacob *adagb i* 219 221
James-Hidden *adagb je* 219-221
M̲a̲y (Lincoln) *adagb i* 219 221
SQUIB
Mary-Dehaven 583
STACKPOLE
Eliza 70
STAHLE
Benjamin *adaih b* 112
Catharine (Probst) *adaih b* 112
STALEY
Caleb 513
Charles-Markley *adbcf bei* 513
Clara-Gilbert (Lincoln] Blythe) *adbcf ' ei* 513
Sarah (Markley) 513
STANNELS
Caroline (Pierce) 432
Jacob 432
Paulina *aacdb eb* 432-3
STANWOOD
Annie-Merton *aabcg dgb* 533-4
Jamesena (Jameson) 533 534
Louise *aabcg dgc* 534
William-Henry 533 534
STAPLES
Ai 150
Alexander-McLellan *aabcf f* 150
Bethia-Thaxter (Lincoln) *aabcf f* 150 153
Charles-Alpheus *aabcf fe* 150
Eunice (McLellan) 150
Harriet-Stephenson *aabcj fd* 150
Jeremiah 150
John-Alexander *aabcj fc* 150
John-L8ncoln 150
Lincoln-Thaxter *aabcj ff* 150
Lydia-Ann-Thaxter *aabcj fa* 150
Maria (Hay) *aabcj fe* 150
Statira-Curtis *aabcf fb* 150
Susan *abbea ja* 190
STARK
Elmira-Juliet (Weller) *adaah ebab* 480
John 165
John-Walker *adaah ebab* 480
STARR
Eizabeth 378
STAUFFER
Peter-Jacob *adaga ie* 219
Sarah (Yeagley) *adaga ie* 210
STEAD
J. Walter 581
William H. 491 581
STEARN
Betty (Fridley) *adaae abbb* 471
Bishop-Weaver *adaae abbd* 472
Charles-Albert *adaae abbb* 471
John-William 471
John-William *adaae abb* 471-2

STEARN cont'd
Josephine-Elizabeth (Lincoln) *adaae abb* 471-2
Lucy (Doval) *adaae abbd* 472
Maud (Vanpelt) *adaae abbe* 472
Stuart-Samuel *adaae abbe* 472
Susan (Miller) 471
Susan-Pansy *adaae abba* 471
Virginia-Davis *adaae abbc* 471
STEARNS
Urania-Anderson *aacda gc* 175
STEIDINGER
Katherine 349
STEIGER—Steigers—Stiger
Edward 611
Elizabeth *adahb ee* 226
Jacob *adahb ec* 226
James *adahb e* 226
James *adahb eg* 226
James *adahb eh* 226
John *adahb ea* 226
Joseph *adahb ea* 226
Lillian *adaae hfac* 611
Lucia (Ludwig) 611
Lydia *adahb ed* 226
Mary *adahb ej* 226
Priscilla *adahb ef* 226
Priscilla (Lincoln) *adahb e* 226
Sarah-Ann 500
Sarah-Ann *adahb eb* 226
William *adahb ei* 226
STEPHENS—Stevens
Agnes-Lillian (Watson) *aabcg dbea* 406
Benjamin 299
Benjamin-Franklin *aacbg cg* 299
Catherine (Lincoln) *aacbg cg* 299
E. P. 566
Ebenezer 122
Eleanor-MacVeigh *adahf bc* 229
Eliza 149
Elizabeth *adahf bb* 229
Elizabeth (Rutledge) *adahf bg* 229
Etta-Lyman (Lincoln) *aabcg dbe* 406
Everett *aabcg dbe* 406
George 406
George-Everett *aabcg dbea* 406
George H. 89
Helen-Lincoln *aacbg cga* 298 299
Henrietta *aacbg cgd* 299
Henry-Clifford *aacbg cgc* 299
Henry-Woodman *adahf bd* 229
Jeremiah *adahf b* 229
John L. *adahf bg* 229
John-Percival *aacbg cgb* 299
Joseph-Lincoln *adahf be* 229
Lucy-Amelia (Abbot) *aacbe lbc* 297
Mary (Lincoln) *adahf b* 229
Matilda (Sprague) 299
Melvina 569
Moses 129 130
Nathan 11
Persis 516
Philena (Lee) *adahf be* 229
Rebecca (——) 11
Rebecca *adahf bf* 229
Rebecca-Jane 586
Ruth 432
Samuel-Dale *aacbe lbc* 297
Sarah *adahf ba* 229
Sarah (MacVeigh) 229
Stephen 229
William 149
STEPHENSON—Stevenson
Alice 124
Anna-Maria *aabcj ec* 150
Betsy *adfag b* 128
Chloe (Lincoln) *aaffg* 82-3
Francis *aaffg* 82-3

45

STEPHENSON cont'd
Francis *aaffg a* 82 83
Galen-Lincoln *adfag d* 128
Harriet (Lincoln) *aabcj e* 150 153
Harriet-Lincoln (Little) *aabcf abg* 261
James-Watt *aabcf abg* 261
Jerome *abbae* 41 82
John 82 128 150
John *abcg* 14
John-Lincoln *aabcj eb* 150
John-Martin *adfag f* 128
Lucy (Beal) 124
Lucy-Rugg *adfag g* 128
Luther 124
Lydia *adfag c* 128
Lydia (Lincoln) *adfag* 63 128
Martha (Nichols) *abcg* 14
Martin *adfag* 128
Mary (Beal) *abbae* 41 82
Polly *adfag a* 128
Sarah (Baldwin) *adfag d* 128
Solon *abbac* 41 128
Susanna (Beal) *abbac* 41 128
Susanna (Marble) 82
Tabitha (Longfellow) 150
Tabitha Longfellow *aabcj ea* 150
Thomas-Curtis *adfag e* 128
William *aabcj e* 150
STERNE
Thomas-Edward 538
STETSER
Mary-Rebecca 585
STETSON
Betsey (——) *adcbm b* 126
STEVENS see Stephens
STEVENSON see Stephenson
STEWARD
Anna-Jackson *aacbg ckb* 547
Charles *adaga cb* 359
Elizabeth (Lincoln) *adaga cb* 359
Jackson 547
Mary-Anna (Bogart) 547
STEWART—Stuart
Allen *adaga cca* 359
Bertha-Louise (Lincoln) *abbea cabc* 553
Edwin-Gleason *abbea cabc* 553
Elizabeth 594
Elizabeth-Calief (Damon) 553
Ella-Louise *abbea cabca* 553
Georgianna-Almena *abbea cabcb* 553
James 118 495
John *adahb bba* 495
John T. 467
Kate 560
Keziah-Jane 498 and note
Phoebe (Blackburn) *adaga cca* 359
Ralph-Aldace 543
Ruth-Ann (Lincoln) *adahb bba* 495
William 553
William-Temple-Stanley 553
STICKLEMAN
Eliza-Wise 352
STIFF
Julia *adaha df* 224
STIGER see Steiger
STINE
Linda-Barbara *adaii aa* 230
STOCKBRIDGE
Grace *aab* 30
Joseph 30
Lydia (Barrell) 22
Margaret (Turner) 30
Persis *add* 22
Samuel 22
Sarah 69
STODDARD—Stodder
Anna *adbfa a* 131
Anna (Pratt) *aaffe d* 82

STODDARD cont'd
Bertha *adbfa fbg* 387
Betsey *aaffb b* 81
Elizabeth *aaffb b* 390-1
Hannah *aaffb a* 81
Hannah (Todd) *aabcc a* 67
Harriet 437
Isaiah *abbaa* 41
James 81 390
James *aaffb* 81 390
James *aaffh e* 81 83
Jane (Worrick) *aaffh e* 81 83
Jeremiah 81 390
John 63 81 390
Lincoln *aaffb c* 81
Louise *abbea cabbc* 553
Lydia (Lincoln) *adfj* 62 63
Mercy (Kent) 40 63
Nathaniel *aabcc a* 67
Percilla (Beal) *abbaa* 41
Ruth (Beal) *abbic* 43 88
Sally *adfja* 63
Sally (Stodder) *adfja* 63
Samuel 63 81 390
Sarah *adcac ce* 239
Simeon *adfj* 63
Stephen 40 63
Susannah 453
Susannah *aaffb f* 81
Susanna (Humphrey) 81
Susanna (Lincoln) *aaffb* 81 390
Tamar 402
Temperance 553
Theodosia (Oakes) *aaffb d* 81
Thomas *adfja* 63
William-Humphrey *aaffb d* 81
Zenas *abbic* 43 88
Zenas *aaffe d* 82
STODDER see Stoddard
STOGDALE
Enfield *adaah emc* 577
Enfield (Peters) 577
Robert-Miller 577
STOKER
Mame *adahb gbbc* 501
STONE
Amanda 406
Asa 395
Ebenezer 395
Eliza 185
Elizabeth 269
John 395
Lucy-Coolidge *adffe c* 395-6
Mary (Coolidge) 395
Simon 395
William W. 430
STONER
Catherine (Young) 510
George 510
Hannah-Young *adaii bf* 510-1
STORY
Helen-Hale *aacdb eec* 434
Herbert-Austin 434
Martha-Amelia (Hale) 434
STOUT
Mary-Lincoln (Biehl) *adaii bje* 379
William-Joseph *adaii bje* 379
STOUTIMORE
America E. *adaah gac* 357
Amanda F. (Lincoln) *adaah ga* 357
Casper 357
Catharine (Trout) 357
Charles-Claiborn *adaah gag* 357
David-Lincoln *adaah gad* 357
Francis D. *adaah gab* 357
George B. *adaah gaa* 357
Isaac-Newton *adaah gae* 357
Jonathan-DeWit *adaah gai* 357

STOUTIMORE cont'd
Josiah *adaah ga* 357
Josie *adaah gaj* 357
Virginia-Ann *adaah gaf* 357
William-Henry-Harrison *adaah gah* 357
STOVER
Daniel 351
Elizabeth *adaae hea* 345
Josephine (Lincoln) *adaae he* 345
Mary (Johnson) 351
Nannie *adaae heb* 345
Samuel *adaae he* 345
William 204
STOWER
Seth 68
STRAYER
Alfred-Gossler *adaae ek* 207
Amanda *adaae ea* 207
Calvin *adaae ed* 207
Caroline *adaae eb* 207
Catharine-Mary *adaae ei* 207
Dorcas (Lincoln) *adaae e* 206-7
Elizabeth *adaae eg* 207
Emily-Susan *adaae ef* 207
Fannie-Clarissa (Rodes) *adaae el* 207
Henrietta *adaae ej* 207
Hiram-Lincoln *adaae ec* 207
Jacob 206
Jacob-Williamson-Lincoln *adaae ee* 207
John *adaae e* 206-7
John-Romulus *adaae eh* 207
Joseph-Beveridge *adaae el* 207
STREETER
Sebastian 257 258 259 277 402
STRICKLAND
William 119
STRICKLER
Albertie-Mae (Lincoln) *adaae abad* 568 569
Benjamin-Franklin 569
Elizabeth 207
Ethel-Irene *adaae abadd* 569
Eula-Lucille *adaae abadc* 569
Luther-John *adaae abad* 569
Mary-Gertrude *adaae abadb* 569
Melvina (Stephens) 569
Raymond-Rush *adaae abada* 569
STROLE
Mary *adaae aeg* 344
STUART see Stewart
STUBBS
Annie-(Cutler) 504
Annie-Stubbs (Lincoln) *adahf cba* 505
Benjamin-Passmore *adahf chc* 374
Cornelia (Winterson) *adahf cbab* 505
Elizabeth (Pierson) 505
Hannah-Brown 373
Harvie-Lincoln *adahf cbaa* 505
Isaac-Hopper *adahf cba* 505
John 504
Mary *adahf cgd* 374
Rebecca 505
Rupert-Isaac *adahf cbab* 505
Sarah-Anna *adahf cb* 504-5
Sarah-Rosene (Reynolds) *adahf chc* 374
Vincent-Gilpin 505
STUDLEY
Abigail 126
Amiel *adfba b* 63 131
Celia (Litchfield) *adfba b* 63 131
Charles-Amiel 63
Hannah 450
Lucy *adcbm b* 126
Lucy-Dunbar 596
Zoa *aaffj f* 84
STURGEON
Ettie-Frances (Lincoln) *adaaa befa* 566

STURGIS
Alfred-Gallatin *adagb ga* 221
Ann-Maria *adagb gg* 221
Hannah (Lincoln) *adagb g* 219 220-1
James-Sansom *adagb gh* 221
John-Phineas *adagb g* 219 220-1
Leah-Jane *adagb gd* 221
Mary-Ann *adagb gc* 221
Phineas M. *adagb gb* 221
Sabra-Lucinda (Miner) *adagb ga* 221
William-Barnes *adagb ge* 221
STUTERVILLE
Bell *adaga geb* 363
STUTLER
Cecil-Ernest *adaga gfbc* 490
Hayward-Lawrence *adaga gfba* 490
Hiram-Lakin *adaga gfb* 490
Lilla-Pearl *adaga gfbe* 490
Nellie-Estelle *adaga gfbd* 490
Nellie-Jane ([Lincoln] Farr) *adaga gfb* 490
Olive (Pope) 490
William-Edward *adaga gfbb* 490
William-Winfield 490
STYER
Katharine-Rebecca (Paschall) *adbca bbd* 234
SULIS
Florence-Eveline *adffe lca* 398
SULLENGER
John *adaaa bf* 333
Katharine (Lincoln) *adaaa bf* 333
SULLIVAN
Ellen (Lincoln) *adaaa aag* 461
James 160 162 227
John 136
John *adaaa aag* 461
SUMMERFIELD
Anna 494
SUMMERS
Clara E. 607
Mary-Elizabeth 559
SUMNER
Charles 46
Mary 8 14
SURRATT
John H. 530
Mary E. 530
SUTHERLAND
Almira (Crosman) 596
Jesse *adcac baf* 596
John-Prout 596
Margaret-Ellen([Thurston] Lincoln) *adcac baf* 596
SUTTON
Andrew *adcba d* 125
Alice ([Stevenson] Cole) 124
Anna *adcba e* 125
Anna *adaga gbd* 362
Betty *adcba c* 125
Eben 447
Elizabeth 62
George 124
John 124
John *adcba* 124-5
John *adcba b* 124
Josephine-Augusta 550
Lidia 362
Peggy *adcba f* 125
Peggy (Lincoln) *adcba* 124-5
Sallie 493
Tamar-Lincoln *adcba a* 124
SWAIN
Edgar-Arnold *aacdb fce* 436
Edgar-Arnold *aacdb fcea* 436
Ellen-Elizabeth (Arnold) 436
James-Roscoe 436
Olive-Elkins (Lincoln) *aacdb fce* 436

SWANER
Isabel-Ugenia 586
SWANSON
Brigitta 116 note
Catharine (——) 116 note
Swan 116 note
SWARENS
Caroline (Brawley) 608
John-Wesley 608
Mamie-Maria *adaaa bbfb* 608
SWATZEL
Polly (Rimel) *adaai c* 103
Samuel *adaai c* 103
SWAZEY
mr. 465
SWEARINGEN—Swearington
William 106 217
SWEET
Dessy-May (Walk) *adaaa beif* 464
Edgar-Lee *adaaa beif* 464
SWEETLAND
Zerviah 392
SWEETSER
Ann-Maria 151
Catherine (Lincoln) *aabcj g* 150-1 153
Joseph *aabcj g* 150-1
Rebecca (Wood) 150
Seth 150
SWEITSER
Mary 490
SWETT
Aurelia (Jenkins) 144
Benjamin 144
Daniel 305
Eunice R. *aacdb h* 305-6
Hannah *aabcf ca* 144
Hannah (Hanscom) 144
Hannah (Martin) 144
James *aabcf c* 144
Jane (McNeil) 305
John 144
Josiah 144
Josiah *aabcf cb* 144
Moses 144
Parsons *aabcf cc* 144
Sophia (Lincoln) *aabcf c* 144
Stephen 144
SWIFT
Hannah-Boyden 549
Harriet 555
SWINK
Arvilla (Goodwin) *adaaf fce* 352
Clarence-John *adaaf fce* 352
David-Reed *adaaf fcc* 352
Elizabeth-Louella *adaaf fcd* 352
Enos-Jones 352
Eliza-Wise (Stickleman) 352
John-Lawrence *adaaf fc* 352
Lucy-Bell *adaaf fca* 352
Orpha-Theresa (Lincoln) *adaaf fc* 352
Wirter-Lincoln *adaaf fcb* 352
SWITZER
Frank-Ward 570
Mary-Cornelia *adaae agce* 570
Stella (Sponsellor) 570
SWORDS
Catherine (Lincoln) *adaga cf* 360
George *adaga cfb* 360
Lincoln *adaga cfa* 360
Martha *adaga cfc* 360
William *adaga cf* 360
SYBERT
Peter 198 199
SYKES
Ellen S. *adaah ek* 482
William J. 482
SYMMONS see Simmons

TABBUT
Ida-Berenice *abbec fbd* 558
Jotham-Merett 558
Mary-Jane (Snow) 558
TAFT
Caroline-Leland (Irwin) 601
Emelyn-Irwin *adffe cda* 601
Nellie *adahf cca* 373
Orsemus A. 601
William-Howard 228 note
TAGE
miss *adbch b* 236
Benjamin 118 236
TALBOT
Priscilla *aacbe lfaa* 427
Thomas 446
TALIAFERRO
Lucy-Ann 354 note
TALL
Adeline 459
TALLMAN
Ann *adaei* 52
Ann (Lincoln) *adae* 51-2
Anna *adaek* 52
Benjamin 51
Benjamin *adaeb* 51 52
Dinah (Boone) *adaeb* 52
Hannah *adaej* 52
Mary *adaec* 52
Mary *adaef* 52
Patience *adaea* 52
Patience (Durfee) 51
Peter 51
Sarah *adaed* 52
Thomas *adaee* 52
Thomas *adaeg* 52
William *adae* 49 50,51 52
William *adaeh* 52
TAPHAM
Mary 389
TAPPAN
Charles-Alfred *adffe bg* 248
Lucy-Ashley (Dickinson) *adffe bg* 248
TARBELL
Ida M. 194 197 328 339 341
TARR
Nellie 613
TATEM
Joseph *adbeb* 58
Mary (Rush) *adbeb* 58
TAYLOR
Abner 372
Albert-Samuel *adbca fbd* 381
Ann-Eliza *adagb fa* 366
Carrie-Emma (Warwick) *adbca fbd* 381
Charles-Edmund 589
Clara E. (Summers) 607
Clara-Virginia (Gilbert) *adbcf bia* 384
Cora-Augusta *abbhc ed* 193
Dorothy E. *adaaa bbcga a* 607
Douglas 607
Edmond H. 594
Edward-Thompson *adbcf bia* 384
Elizabeth (Stewart) 594
Hannah-Jane *adbcf beb* 593
Hester (——) 235 236
Horace 366
James 465
John-Wesley *adaae aga* 472
Joseph 225
Joseph M. *adaaa bbcga* 607
Lillian *adbcf beg* 594
Lucetta (Erskine) 366
Margaret D. 424
Margaret (Dawson) 593
Margaret (Dickinson) 225
Mary *adbch* 235-7
Mary-Elizabeth (Lincoln) *adahb gea* 503

TAYLOR cont'd
Nancy (Eppard) 472
Nora-Bell *adahc aaf* 589
Nora-Bell (Berry) 589
Robert 56 113
Sarah H. 504
Stella (Lincoln) *adaaa bbcga* 607
Stephen-Harvey *adahb gea* 503
Virginia-Catherine (Lincoln) *adaae aga* 472
Washington 593
Zachary 418 419 472
TEA
Ann *adaff* 53
TEGARDEN
Emily-Jane (Evans) 608
Laura-Elcena *adaaa bbea* 608
Preston 608
TEMPLE
Hannah (Hollis) *adahb ac* 226
John *adahb ac* 226
TEMPLIN
Terah 327
TEVIS
Maria-Rebecca 310
THAXTER
major 33
Alice (Chubbuck) 31
Anna *aacbd f* 77
Benjamin 79
Bethia *aacba b* 76 149-51 153
Bethia (Lincoln) *aacba* 31 74 75 76 79 149 152
Daniel *aabbj* 31
David 30 76 147 149 152
David *aabb* 30 31 67 76 147 149 152
David *aabba* 31
David *aabcg cb* 147
Deborah *aabbf* 31
Deborah *aabbg* 31
Deborah *aacba c* 76 80 152-3
Deborah (Lincoln) *aabb* 29 30 31 67 76 77 79
Deborah (Thaxter) *aacba c* 76 79-80 152-3
Duncan-McBean *aabab b* 65 147
Duncan-McBean *aabcg i* 147
Duncan-McBean *aabcg ia* 147
Elizabeth 30
Elizabeth (Marsh) *aabbh* 31 147
Frances (Lincoln) *aacde* 79-80
Francis 79
Francis *aacde* 76 79-80 152
Francis *aacde a* 80
George *aabcg c* 147
George-Warren *aabcg cc* 147
Grace (Stockbridge) *aab* 30
Hannah (Gridley) 30
Harriet (Sherburne) *aabcg ia* 147
Jacob *aabbd* 31 74 76-7
Jacob *aacbd a* 77
James 80
John 30 79 147
Jonathan *aabbb* 31 74 76 79 149 152
Jonathan *aacba e* 76 153
Joseph 64 74
Laban *aabbi* 31
Levi 153
Levi *aacba f* 76 153
Lucy (Blake) *aabbj* 31
Lucy (Lincoln) *aabcg i* 147
Lucy (White) *aacba f* 76
Lydia (Bond) *aacba f* 76
Margaret (Bennet) *aacdb b* 77
Martha *aabbc* 31 67
Mary-Ann (Bennet) *aacbd e* 77
Mary (Gill)*aabab b* 65 147
Mary (Groves) *aacbd a* 77
Nancy (Sawyer) *aacbd c* 77

THAXTER cont'd
Perez *aacbd e* 77
Rachel *aacbd d* 77
Rachel (Lincoln) *aacbd* 31 74 76-7
Samuel 30 34 68 76 79 147 149 152
Sarah *aacba d* 76
Seth *aabbe* 31
Seth *aabbh* 31 147
Seth *aacbd b* 77
Sophia B. *aabcg cd* 147
Susan-Lincoln *aabcg ca* 147
Susanna (Joy) 79
Susanna (Lincoln) *aabcg c* 147
Thomas 30 76 79 147 149 152
Warren *aacbd c* 77
THAYER
Abby-Hope (Lincoln) *adffe dfa* 525
Clarence-Richmond *adffe dfaa* 525
Donald-Francis *adffe dfac* 525
Francis-Lincoln *adffe dfab* 525
Francis-Nicholas 525
Frank N. 440
Horace-Richmond *adffe dfa* 525
Nancy-Armstrong (Paine) 525
Richard-Nelson *adffe dfad* 525
Susan-Elizabeth 521
THOMAS
Alice 568
Ann *adaae aec* 344
Barbara (Ross) 267
Jane-Robinson *aabcj c* 267
Leannah 472
Margaret 225 228
Mary-Elizabeth 427
Sarah (Jermyn) 225
Stephen 267
Thomas 225
William 225
THOMASON
America-Agnes *adaah gcb* 357
Mary T. (Lincoln) *adaah gc* 357
William F. *adaah gca* 357
THOMPSON—Thomson
Archibald 177 178
Andrew 178
Betsey *aabcf d* 262-3
Betsey (Chadbourn) 262
Challoner-Guilford *aacdb bdha* 432
Elinor (Foley) 432
Eliza 178 399
Elizabeth *aacdb* 176-81
Elizabeth *aabce bag* 257
Emerson-Greenleaf 526
Isabella 178
James 178
John 178
John *adahb bbfa* 495
Joseph-Miller 262
Joshua 56 178
Mary 499
Nancy 178
Mary-Elizabeth (Emmons) 526
Nellie (Lincoln) *aacdb bdh* 432
Otis 178
Rachel *adahc* 227
Robert *aacdb bdh* 432
Robinson 178
Ruth-Lillian (Irwin) *adahb bbfa* 495
Sally *adaah ec* 480-1
Samuel 178
Sarah *adaga fb* 218
Susan 178
Susie-Ella *aabcd bcd* 526
William 222 432
Wilson 178
THORLA
Mary 405

THORN
mr. 269
THORNTON
Susan-Maria 427
THRASH
Fannie 575
THURSTON
Arthur-Lincoln *aabcj hab* 268
Brown 268
Carrie-Thaxter (Lincoln) *aabcj ha* 268
Charles-Brown *aabcj ha* 268
Edwin-Brown *aabcj haa* 268
Harriet (Chapman) 268
Eliza-Sparrow (Downing) 596
Jean-Mellen *aacbe daac* 423
John-Albert 596
Margaret-Ellen *adcac baf* 596
TIBBALS
John *agjg* 27
Olive (Pratt) *agjg* 27
TIBBONS (or Gibbons)
Margaret *adaaa abe* 462
TICKNOR
Owen-Only *adcai ek* 241
Ruth-Beal (Litchfield) *adcai ek* 241
TILDEN
Asenath (Bailey) 249
Charles-Henry *adffe jb* 249
Christopher 249
Jennett (Lincoln) *adffe j* 249
John 249
Joseph 249
Josephine 554
Julia-Frances 443
Miriam (Cooper) *adffe jb* 249
Nathaniel 249
Thomas 249
Thomas *adffe j* 249
Thomas-Lincoln *adffe ja* 249
William P. 408
TIMMONS
Anna (Lincoln) *adaah eib* 482
L. L. *adaah eib* 482
TINKCOM
Mary-Ray *adcai ec* 241
TINKHAM
Mary-Maria *aacdb ca* 180
TIRRELL
Alma G (Lincoln) *abbea cabf* 553-4
Herbert-Warren *abbea cabf* 553-4
Jennie-Baker *abbea cabfa* 554
Josephine (Tilden) 554
Martha-Josephine *abbea cabfb* 554
Warren 554
TISINGER
Anna-Eliza-Virginia *adaae haa* 344
Dorcas (Lincoln) *adaaa ha* 344
George *adaae ha* 344
TISSUE
Cora-Alice *adaga gfa* 490 581
James-Madison 581
Sarah-Jane(Lancaster) 581
TOBIAS
Esther 509
TODD
Andrew 67
Andrew *aabcc b* 67
Ann-Eliza (Parker) 470
Deborah (Thaxter) *aabbg* 31
Hannah *aabcc a* 66 67
James *aabbg* 31
Levi 470
Mary *adaaa db* 467 470-1
Robert-Smith 470
Ruth (Lincoln) *aabcc* 67
Samuel *aabcc* 67
Samuel *aabcc c* 66 67
Sarah (Bassett) 67

TODD cont'd
Susanna (Hobart) 67
TOGUE
Anna *abaea ac* 187
TOLAIT
Ann 165
TOLMAN
Thomas 294
TOMLINSON
Ann *adadc* 51 and note
John 51 note
TOMMINS
Esther ([Hilton] Lincoln) *adba* 114
Hester ([Hilton] Lincoln) *adba* 114
Patrick *adba* 114
TOOMEY
Julia M. 601
TOPPAN
Anne 272
TORREY
Emma-Hamlin *aabcg de* 407-8
Leavitt 408
Mary L. (Pratt) 408
TOTTON
Amanda-Marthaette (Lincoln) *adaaa bbaa* 463
John-Robert *adaaa bbaa* 463
Sallie *adaaa bde* 333
TOWER—Towers
Abigail 37 323
Abigail-Kent 553
Abraham 239
Abraham *addc* 22
Abraham-Hobart 22 87
Alvan 250
Asa-Cushing 249-50
Bethia (Nichols) *addb* 22 88 186
Carrie ([Lincoln] Lonigan) *adaaa bbga* 564
Charles-Noel *adaaa bbgad* 564
Charlotte (Mann) 250
Daniel *add* 19 22 88 186 320 323
Daniel *addb* 22 88 186 320 323
Eliza-Hall *abbea md* 320
Esther (Bates) *adffa j* 133
George-Andrew *adaaa bbga* 564
George-Andrew *adaaa bbgai* 564
Harriet-Hope *adaaa bbgah* 564
Ibrook 22 88 186 320 323
Jane (Bates) 320
Jesse 250
Job *addd* 22
John 6 22 88 117 186 320 323
John-Franklin *adaaa bbgae* 564
Levi 323
Levi *abaef* 41 43 88 239 320 323
Lloyd-Merlin *adaaa bbgaj* 564
Marcia-Dunlap (Lothrop) *adcac eg* 239
Margaret (——) 235
Margaret (Hardin) 22
Mary (Pratt) *addd* 22
Mildred-Arlene *adaaa bbgaf* 564
Molly 388
Mordecai *adde* 22
Nichols 320
Paul-Henry *adaaa bbgag* 564
Persis *abaea* 42 186-7
Persis ([Stockbridge] Curtis) *add* 22
Priscila 316
Priscilla (Nichols) *abbbh* 41 88
Priscilla-Nichols *abbec bj* 323
Rachel *adffa b* 132
Rebecca (Cushing) 250
Rebecca ([Lincoln] Pike) *abaef* 88
Robert 235
Ruth ([Beal] Stodder) 43 88
Ruth ([Collier] Willcutt) *adffg* 249-50
Sally (Bates) *adffa c* 132

TOWER cont'd
Sarah *adda* 22 80
Sarah *aafai* 37 516
Sarah-Jane 536
Sarah (Lincoln) *add* 18 22
Stoddard *adffa c; addfa j* 132 133
Susanna 82
Thankful *addf* 22
Thankful *addg* 22
Thankful *abbbb* 41
Thomas-Nichols 320
TOWLE
Amos 263
Ann-Lucette (Lincoln) *aabcf de* 263
Betsey (Andrews) 263
Daniel-Henry *aabcf aha* 262
Edward *aabcf dea* 263
Ezra *aabcf de* 263
Julia-Putnam (Sawyer) *aabcf aha* 262
Nellie-Lincoln *aabcf deb* 263
TOWNE
Alice-North *aacdc ee* 310
John-Henry 310
Maria-Rebecca (Levis) 310
TOWNSEND
Etta 393
Mary-Ann 399
Mary-Cecilia-Turner 557
Mehitable 14
TOWNSHEND
Emma-Birch 92
TOWNSLEY
Amanda-Stella (Lincoln) *adaaa bbig* 565
Charles-Bernard *adaaa bbigc* 565
Clarence *adaaa bbig* 565
Elmer-Roland *adaaa bbiga* 565
Margaret (Flock) 565
Margaret-Lillian *adaaa bbigd* 565
Orval-Clarence *adaaa bbigb* 565
Reuben 565
TRACY
Asaph *aabge* 31
Lydia (Cushing) *aabge* 31
TRADER
Eliza 360
TRAIN
Althea 441
TREAT
Samuel 167
TREVETT
Sally 295
TRIPPLE
Hannah (Cox) 377
John 377
Sarah-Ann *adaid ca* 377
TRITES
miss *adbcf ccb* 385
Ann-Eliza (Lincoln) *adbcf cc* 383 385
Daniel *adbcf cc* 383 385
Jacob-Lincoln *adbcf cca* 385
TROUT
Amy *adagb dh* 493
Catharine 357
TRUMBULL
Elizabeh *aacbc ac* 414-5
George-Augustus 414
John 414 439
Joseph 414
Louisa (Clapp) 414
Lyman 467 468
Mary-Araminta 494
Mary-Eliza *aacdb ig* 439
Nancy (Carlow) 439
TRUMP
Anna 588
TUCKERMAN
Grace (Richardson) *aacdc ebb* 309
Leverett-Salstonstall *aacdc ebb* 309

TUFTS
Abigail (——) 457
Harriet *abbec fd* 457-8
John 457
Otis 410
TUPPER
Meriba *aka* 9
TURNBULL
Robert 454
TURNER
Edward *adaaf dac* 350
Ella *adbca fbb* 381
Ellen 532
Emily-Oneal ([Dinges] [Simrill] Neal) *adaaf dac* 350
Lydia 410
Margaret 30
Mary *adffb b* 133
Mehitable (——) 22
Olive-Pratt 409
Rachel 61
Seth 22
Sylvia-Sampson 270
TURPIN
Guy-Edward *adaaa bbchc* 560
Ruth-Marie (Christian) *adaaa bbchc* 560
TUTTLE
Anna 153
Mary-Jane *abbea cca* 319
TWICHELL
Ginery 416
TWINING
Elizabeth 503
TYNG
Edward 4

UHVY
Emma (Jacobs) *adaga cga* 360
George *adaga cga* 360
UNDERWOOD
Emma 529
Emma *aabcd bae* 252
UPHAM
Ebenezer 250
John 250
Mary *adffi* 250
Phineas 250
Sarah (Warren) 250
Thaddeus 250
USREY
Jane *adaaf db* 479
Melinda (Jarvis) 479
William 479
UTTERTREP
Guinnie *adaai ejb* 355

VANATTA
James 586
Lydia (Hull) 586
Sylvia-Delphine *adahb gbe* 586
VANBUSKIRK
Hannah *adahc a* 371
Hannah (Kelly) 371
Richard 371
VANCE
Addison-Shannon *adagb gc* 221
Mary-Ann (Sturgis) *adagb gc* 221
VANDEGRAF
Isabel 530-1
VANDERGRIFT
Gertrude *adbcf bid* 384
VANDEVER
Mary 496
VANHORN
Abraham 53
Jane *adage e* 109
VANIER
Marie *aacdb hea* 306

VANPELT
Maud *adaae abbe* 472
Tanis 206
VANTASSEL
Elizer-Brown *adcai eh* 241
Rachel-Anna (Litchfield) *adcai eh* 241
VEDDER
Edmund-Burke *adcak ea* 243
Sarah-Maria (Whitcomb) *adcak ea* 243
VICKERY
Elizabeth 79
VINAL
Abigail-Joy (Litchfield) 529
Anna (——) 91 246
Annie W. *aabce cbba* 402
Chloe (Jenkins) *adcaj j* 123
Elizabeth 22
Elizabeth (Baker) 91
Elizabeth (Booth) 91
Israel 78 90 91 246
Israel *abbee* 90 91
Jacob 78 90 91 246
Jemina (Pope) 91
John 78 90 246
Jonathan 91
Lucy *adcaj b* 123
Lydia 90 91
Lydia (Litchfield) 90 91
Marcy *adfah* 246
Martha 91
Martha-Adelia *aabce aec* 529
Mary 122 123
Mary *aacbk* 75
Mary (Cudworth) 91
Mercy (Cushing) 78 90 91 246
Mercy (Lincoln) *aacbk* 75 78
Nathaniel-James 529
Priscilla 243
Rebecca (Bailey) 90 91
Rebeckah 91
Sally *abbee a* 90 91
Sarah (Briggs) 63 note
Sarah (Lincoln) *abbee* 90
Simeon 63 and note
Sophia 90 91
Stephen 91
Thomas *adcaj j* 123
William *aacbk* 65 75 78 246 394
VINTON
Frederic-Porter 541
VITTOR
Cora-Maud *adaga gea* 363
VON FEILGERS
Catherine-Gertrude 217
VON WEBER
Mary 420
VOSE
Julia 404
Mary 150 438

WADDILL
Rebecca-Rodes 573
WADE
Abigail (Bates) *aafah* 35 37
Anna 60 61
Charlotte (Otis) 390
Deborah-Otis *adcai b* 390
Elizabeth 61
Elizabeth *adfea* 62
Issachar 390
Jacob 60
John *aafah* 37
Joseph 20 60 61 300
Mary 242
Mary (Garrett) 61
Mercy (Norton) 61
Rachel (Turner) 61
Ruth 60 127

WADE cont'd
Ruth (Garrett) 60 61
Snell 390
Zebulon 61
WADLEIGH
Blanche-Winifred *aacbe ldd* 426
Elizabeth (Carlisle) 426
Royal-Hopkins 426
WADSWORTH
Marcus M. 444
WAGNER
George-Washington *adahb bbe* 495
Grace-Olivia *adahb bbea* 495
Sarah-Jane (Lincoln) *adahb bbe* 495
WAHLE
Caroline-Louise *abbec baf* 321
WAIT—Waite
Ada-Gertrude (Rice) 486
Arthur-Henry 486
Harriet *aabcj i* 151
Kathryn-Gould *adaah gde* 486
WAKEY
Susan 491
WALDO
Cornelius 162
Daniel 162 284
Martha *aacbc* 162-4
Rebecca (Salisbury) 162
WALES
Atherton 296
Caroline (Sprague) 296
Hannah-Sprague *aacbe l* 294 296-7
WALK
Andy-Grover *adaaa beib* 464
Charley-Eddy *adaaa beia* 464
Chloe-Marie *adaaa beig* 464
Claude-Elmer *adaaa beid* 464
Dessy-May *adaaa beif* 464
Ettie (McDonald) *adaaa beia* 464
Isaac-Wilford *adaaa bei* 464
Ivy-May *adaaa beic* 644
John-Jacob 464
Julia-Ann (Soner) 464
Katharine (Lincoln) *adaaa bei* 464
Lola-Florence *adaaa beie* 464
Oscar-Alonzo *adaaa beih* 464
WALKER
Abigail-Reed *aacbe d* 293-4
Catherine-Amelia 449
Jennie *abbea caai* 451
Mary (Reed) 293
Quork 161
Samuel 293
Susan-Hyde 537
WALL
Ashbell-Tingley *adffe cbb* 523
Ashbell-Tingley *adffe cbbc* 523
Beriah 523
Constance-Cole *adffe cbbb* 523
Helen-Lincoln *adffe cbba* 523
Lucretia (Cole) 523
Lucy-Coolidge (Lincoln) *adffe cbb* 523
Susan (——) *adcbm b* 126
WALLACE—Wallis
Anna-Eliza-Virginia (Tisinger) *adaae haa* 344
Arthur-Andrew *adaae hia* 476
Bodine *aabch ddc* 266
Charlotte *adcbh b* 125
Clement-Whittall 485
Ellen (Bates) *abbed b* 90 125
Ezekiel 189
Ezekiel *adcbh* 125 239
Ezekiel *adcbh c* 125 239-40
Henrietta (Lincoln) *adcac h* 125 239-40
John-William *adaae haa* 344
Louisa (Duane) *aabch ddc* 266
Maria (Bates) *abbed e* 90 125

WALLACE cont'd
Martha *adbec* 58
Mary-Elizabeth *adahb dcg* 585
Mary-Rebecca (Stetser) 585
Melvina *adaaf dae* 350
Mordecai-Lincoln *adcbh a* 90 125
Nancy (Lincoln) *adaae hia* 476
Susanna (Lincoln) *adcbh* 125 239
WALLEY
Ruth 26
WALLIS see Wallace
WALTON
Edgar-Bryant *adfad bcc* 393
Electa-Nobles (Lincoln) *adfad bc* 245 393
Elizabeth (Bryant) 393
Frances (——) 330
Frederick *adfad bcd* 393
George-Augustus *adfad bc* 245 393
George-Lincoln *adfad bcb* 393
Harriet-Pierce *adfad bca* 393
James 393
Mary-Alice *adfad bce* 393
Mathew 330
WANDS
Josephine-Amy *aabce aebc* 603
Josephine (Messier) 603
Rufus-Putnam 603
WARD
Adam-Price 310
Andrew-Lincoln *aacdc fbb* 311
Catherine-Amelia (Walker) 449
Charlotta-Price *aacdc fbe* 311
Eliza (Hazen) 311
Eliza-Thompson (Gardner) 179
Elizabeth (Holbrook) 146
Ezekiel-Gould *aacdc fb* 310-11
Ezekiel-Gould *aacdc fbc* 311
Frederick *aacdc fbf* 311
Henry 146
James-Edward 449
Mary *adag* 107
Mary *adaad* 204-5
Mary-Adella *aafff gh* 449
Samuel 146
Sarah *aabcg* 146-7
Sarah (Lillie) 310
Sarah-Lincoln *aacdc fba* 311
Susan-Crocker (Lincoln) *aacdc fb* 310-1
William 311
WARE
Mary-Cotton 254
WARFIELD
Elisha 214 356
WARNICK
Agnes (Kennedy) 439
Bertha (Lincoln) *aacdb iga* 439
Clowds 439
Ernest-Howard *aacdc igaa* 439
William *aacdb iga* 439
WARREN
Betsey-Roxanna (Larrabee) 428
Carl-Reed *aacbe lffa* 428
Carrie-Abbot (Lincoln) *aacbe lff* 428
Edward-Allen 560
Edward-Allen *adaaa bbcj* 560
Ernest-Eugene *aacbe lff* 428
Harriet-Eveline (Lincoln) *adaaa bbcj* 560
Joseph H. 428
Julia-Louisa (Judd) 428
Kate (Stewart) 560
Louis A. 193 note
Michael 93
Sarah 250
WARWICK
Albert-Elliot *adbca fb* 381-2
Carrie-Emma *adbca fbd* 381
Clayton-Raymond *adbca fbc* 381
Elizabeth (Lincoln) *adbca fb* 381

WARWICK cont'd
Ella (Turner) *adbca fbb* 381
Evelyn-Ophelia *adbca fba* 381
Joseph-Wilkins *adbca fbb* 381
Kate (Bloom) *adbca fbc* 381
Lizzie-Ada *adbca fbe* 382
Ruth-Anna *adbca fbf* 382
WASHBURN
Emory 283 295
Lefe (Joy) *aagc* 11
Nehemiah *aagc* 11
WASHINGTON
George 111 186
WATERMAN
Abiah 119
Elizabeth 10
Jerusha *aabcf* 142
Josiah 143
Lydia (Lincoln) *aaie* 12
Robert 143
Thankful (Humphrey) 143
Thomas 143
Thomas *aaie* 12
WATERS
Abigail 10 131
Sarah-Harding *aabce ec* 142
WATSON
Agnes-Lillian *aabcg dbea* 406
Anna (Sutton) *adaga gbd* 362
Benjamin 362
Benjamin-Milton *adaga gbc* 362
Charles-Ewing *adaga gbh* 362
Deborah (——) 307
Eva (Burnworth) *adaga gbh* 362
James *adaga ae* 358
James-Darby *adaga gbe* 362
Jehu-Brownfield *adaga gb* 361 362
Jonathan 307
Lidia (Sutton) 362
Lydia-Jane *adaga gbf* 362
Maria *aacdb i* 307-8
Mary-Frances *adaga gbb* 362
Mary (Smith) *adaga gba* 362
Matilda (Lincoln) *adaga ae* 358
Minnebanca *adaga gbg* 362
Rhoda (Lincoln) *adaga gb* 361 362
Robert-Hagan *adaga gbd* 362
William-Henry *adaga gba* 362
WATTS
Sarah *aacbi a* 299
WAUGH
Margaret 78
WAY
Alva-Washington *adaaa bbeda* 562
Irva-Franklin *adaaa bbedc* 562
Margaret (Lincoln) *adaaa bbed* 562
Pearl-Lucinda *adaaa bbedd* 562
William *adaaa bbed* 562
William-Ilva *adaaa bbedb* 562
WEATHERS
Benjamin 463
Mary (Ballington) 463
Sarah *adaaa bb* 463
WEAVER
Caroline-Homan (Lincoln) *adaae agg* 473
John 473
John-William *adaae agg* 473
Rhea-Lovetta *adaae agga* 473
Robert-Lincoln *adaae aggb* 473
Sally (Bowers) 473
WEBB
John 107
Joseph 68
Leah *adcaj b* 123
Martha-Jane 604
Mary *adag* 107-9 223
Mary (Boone) 107
Silas 244

WEBBER
Amelia (Wentzel) 509
Edwin-Augustus 537
Edwin-Harrison *adaii bca* 509
Emma (Mowry) *adaii bcaa* 509
Esther-Irene *adaii bcac* 509
Fidel 509
Harrison-Fidel *adaii bcaa* 509
Helen-Blake *aacbc acd* 537-8
Lydia McClellan (Blake) 537
Martha-Annie *abbhc bc* 192
Robert-Emery *adaii bcab* 509
Sally-Andora (Lincoln) *adaii bca* 509
WEBSTER
Ann-Rebecca 533
Edward 456
Daniel 280 456
Harriet-Stephenson (Staples) *aabcj fd* 150
Joseph-Henry *aabcj fd* 150
WEDGEWOOD
Ann-Maria 438
WEED
Rebecca 512
Sarah-Ann 523
WEISE
Ellen *adbcf bde* 384
WEISZ
Sarah *adcai ee* 241
WELLER
Benjamin 480
Benjamin-Owen *adaah eba* 480 481
Elmira-Juliet *adaah ebad* 480
Georgia (Lincoln) *adaah eba* 480
John-Theron *adaah ebaa* 480
Juliet (Owen) 480
WELLS
Henry 408
Mary-Ellen 527
Sarah 247
WELSH
Henry *aaffe c* 82
Polly (Pratt) *aaffe c* 82
WENTWORTH
Clarence-Llewellyn 458
Edith (Ashley) 458
Ethel-Agnes *abbhc dbe* 458
John 131
Mary 71
WENTZEL
Amelia 509
WEST
Carrie *adaae aef* 344
Martha-Ann *adagb be* 220
Penelope 282
Thomas 282
William 350
WESTCOTT
George 115
WETHERBEE
Clarissa R. (Edwards) *aabcf gf* 145
Levi *aabcf gf* 145
WETHERELL see Witherell
Hester (Newton) *aacbc gc* 164
John-Walcott *aacbc gc* 164
HARTENBY
WElizabeth (Agner) *adahb dce* 499
HARTON
WEliza (Moore) 118
Fanny 354
Joseph 115
HEATLY
WMary 606
HEELER
WAbiel-Heywood *aacda h* 175
Adelaide (Bliss) *aacda ha* 175
Alice (Rattray) *aacda he* 175
Charles-Parkman *aacda hb* 175

WHEELER cont'd
David 175
Edward 175
Elizabeth 565
Ella (Jaqueth) *aacda hb* 175
Ephraim 175
Ephraim *aacda hf* 175
George 175
George-Francis *aacda he* 175
Harriet (Lincoln) *aacda h* 175
Harriet-Lincoln *aacda hc* 175
Henry-Lincoln *aacda ha* 175
John 175
Mary-Coleman *aacda hg* 175
Sarah-Elizabeth *aacda hd* 175
Sarah (Parkman) 175
WHEELWRIGHT
Gershom *aaffj c* 84
Hannah (Ellmes) *aaffj c* 84
WHELDON
Bethia C. (Baker) *aacdb da* 180
WHIPPLE
Carolyn-Louise *adffe dfb* 601
Charles-Henry 601
Julia M. (Toomey) 601
Ormus-Mandel *adffa f* 133
Sherman Leland 551
Sybil (Bates) *adffa f* 133
WHISLER
Ann (——) 208
Henry 208
WHITCOMB
Abram *adffd g* 134
Achsah (Lincoln) *aafh* 36 37
Albert-Simeon *aacda cf* 175
Anna (Pratt) *aafhc* 37
Arabella-May *adfae adc* 600
Chloe (Lincoln) *adcak e* 243
Dolly (Barber) *aaflh* 38
Elijah *aafhd* 37
Elizabeth *aaff* 80 91
Elizabeth *aafla* 38
Elizabeth (Francis) *aafli* 38
Ellen-Maria *adffd h* 134
Elvira (Farrar) *aacda cf* 175
Emmeline ([Balch] Heath) *adffd b* 133
Ezekiel 37
Ezekiel *aafhf* 37
Hannah *aafha* 37
Hannah *adffd a* 133 and note
Hannah (Baker) 174
Hannah-Baker *aacda cg* 174 175
Hannah (Kent) 37 38
Hannah (Nichols) 133
Harlan-Page *aacda ci* 175
Harriet-Lincoln (Wheeler) *aacda hc* 175
Henry-Knox *adffd c* 134
Henry-Lincoln *aacda ch* 175
Israel 37 38 80 133 243
Israel *aafh* 37 243
Jacob *aafhc* 37
Jael-Cushing *aacda cc* 175
Jairus-Lincoln *adffd d* 134
Job 174
John 37 38 80 133 174 243
John *adda* 22
Jonathan 174
Joseph 133
Joseph *adffd f* 134
Levi 174
Levi *aafli* 38
Lincoln *adffd b* 133 and note
Lot *aafl* 38
Lot *aaflh* 38
Lucia-Caroline *adcak eb* 243
Lucy 37
Lucy-Maria (Snell) *adffd c* 134

WHITCOMB cont'd
Lydia (Ramsdell) *aafhe* 37 243
Martha K. (Willis) *aacda cf* 175
Mary-Abigail *adcak ec* 243
Mary (Fisher) *adffd g* 134
Olive *aaflg* 38
Perez *aaflc* 38
Phebe (Davis) *adffd d* 134
Priscilla (Litchfield) *aaflc* 38
Rachel *aafld* 38
Rachel (Gray) *aafhb* 37
Robert 37 38 80 133 243
Ruth (Lincoln) *adffd* 62 133
Sally *aafle* 38
Sally (Lincoln) *aacda c* 174-5
Sally-Lincoln *aacda cb* 175
Samuel *aafhe* 37 243
Sarah *adffd e* 134
Sarah-Leavitt *aacda ce* 175
Sarah (Lincoln) *aafl* 35 36 38
Sarah-Maria *adcak aa* 243
Sarah (Tower) *adda* 22 80
Shubael *adffd* 133
Simeon *aacda c* 174-5
Susan A. ([Haskell] Bowen) *adffd f* 134
Sylvester (Whitehead) 600
Thomas-Jefferson *adcak e* 243
Tyle *aaflb* 38
William 600
William-Cushing *aacda cd* 175
William-Lincoln *aacda ca* 174
Zadoc *aafhb* 37
Zoa *aaflf* 38
WHITE
Abigail 87
Anna M. *aacdb bd* 431
Carrie-Jarvis *aafff gbc* 317
Charlotte (Wallace) *adcbh b* 125
Elizabeth (Wade) 60 61
Earl P. 397
Frances 428
Harriet-Maria *aacbe lf* 427-8
John 301
Josiah *adcbh b* 125
Juline (Everett) 397
Lucy *aacba f* 76
Margaret 392
Mary 168
Mary-Adeline *adbca"daf* 381
Nathaniel 61
Olive *adaga bd* 217
Sarah-Janette *adffe l* 397
Susan-Maria (Thornton) 427
William-Charles 163
William-Henry 427
WHITEHEAD
Cubus 573
Julia-O'Neal *adaae hfh* 573
Rebecca-Rodes (Waddill) 573
Sylvesta 600
WHITESCARVER
Catharine-Ann (Dunn) 500
Charles-Strawther 500
Clara-May *adahb faab* 500
Etta-Elizabeth *adahb faaa* 500
James-Christopher *adahb faa* 500
Sarah-Elizabeth (Lincoln) *adahb faa*
226 note 500
WHITFIELD
Eugenia D. 573
WHITING
Hannah 432
Jotham 142
Mary 31
Susanna 142
Susanna (Wilder) 142
WHITMAN
John 21

WHITMAN cont'd
Ruby-Grace *aacbe lfca* 428
Sarah 20 21
Thomas 224
WHITMARSH
Abigail (Pratt) 142
Ezra 142
John 142
Peter 142
Tabitha *aabce* 142
WHITNEY
Abigail (Frothingham) 170
Benjamin 173
Daniel 173
Eleanor (Breasha) *aacda gd* 175
Fannie (Lincoln) *aacda g* 175
Francis *aacbj c* 172 73
Harriet (Lincoln) *aacbj c* 172 173
Harriet-Maria *aacda ge* 175
Henrietta-Frances *aacda gb* 175
John 91 173
John-Putnam *aacda gc* 175
Josiah 175
Mary (Barrett) 175
Myron *aacda ga* 175
Myron-William *aacda gd* 175
Nathaniel-Ruggles 173
Simon 173
Sophia (Vinal) 91
Urania-Anderson (Stearns) *aacda gc* 175
William *aacda g* 175
WHITON
Ann-Maria (Sprague) *aabce eg* 142
Bela-Herndon *aabee eb* 142
Bethia *aac* 34 35
Charlotte-Lincoln *aabcd a'bb* 251
Chloe *aabad* 138
Daniel 595
David 142 251
Dexter-Brigham *aabcd aba* 251
Elijah 142 251
Elijah *aabce e* 68 142 251
Elijah-Lincoln *aabce ea* 142 251
Elizabeth 69
Elizabeth (Marble) 138
Enoch 10 34
Erastus *aabce ef* 142
Frederick *aabce ec* 142
Hannah-Richmond *aabce eb* 142
Hannah-Richmond (Whiton) *aabce eb*
142
Isaac 138
Jacob 138
James 34 138 142 251 595
John-Chadwick *aabce eg* 142
Lucy *aabce ɔe* 142
Lydia *aaha* 12
Lydia (Lincoln) 142
Margaret 10
Mary-Ann *adcac bac* 595-6
Mary-Catherine ([Hersey] Little *aabce e*
142
Mary (Lincoln) 10 34
Mary (Lincoln) *aabce e* 142 251
Mary Lincoln *aabce ed* 142
Mary-Lincoln *aabcd abc* 251
Matthew 138 142 251
Maribah (Orcutt) 595
Nabby-Fearing *aacbh h* 78
Nahum 595
Priscilla (Burr) *aabce ef* 142
Rachel-Cushing (Lincoln) *aabcd ab* 142
251
Samuel 595
Sarah-Harding (Waters) *aabce ec* 142
Susan (Beal) *aabci b* 68 142
Susan-Lincoln 142
Sylvanus 595

WHITTINGTON
Alfred *aaffi g* 84
Ann (Franklin) *aaffi c* 84
Betty *adaah eda* 354
Cordelia (Wilder) *aaffi h* 84
Elizabeth *aaffi b* 84
Elizabeth ([Bailey] [McNeil] Palfrey) 83
George *adffi c* 84
Granville *aaffi h* 84
Hepzibah (Lincoln) *aaffi* 453
Hiram-Abith *aaffi f* 84
Irene *aaffi e* 84
Mary *aaffi i* 84
Mary-Ann (Bird) *aaffi d* 84
Mary (Burnham) *aaffi f* 84
Ophelia *aaffi j* 84 453-4
Ruth (Delano) *aaffi g* 84
Sarah *aaffi a* 84
William 83
William *aaffi* 83-4 453
William *aaffi d* 84

WHITTLE
Clara (How) *aabck bga* 270
George-Grant *aabck bgb* 270
George-Washington *aabck bg* 270
Hannah (Goldsmith) 270
Harriet-Clementina (Lincoln) *aabck bg* 270
Minot-Lincoln *aabck bga* 270
Parker 270

WICKES
Charles-Chidsey *adffe ba* 247
Nancy-Bicknell ([Dickinson] Mosher) *adffe ba* 247

WICKLEIN—Wickline
Edward-Sylvester 572
Janette-Ann (Lincoln) *adaae hfaf* 572
John-Preston *adaae hfaf* 572
Josephine (Cook) 572
Mary-Seifert 592

WIGHT
Alice-Burrington 265

WILBUR
Ann-Maria (Lincoln) *aabck fb* 272
Anne (Toppan) 272
Edward-Lincoln *aabck fba* 272
Edward-Payson *aabck fb* 272
Elinor-Lincoln *aabck fbb* 272
Harvey-Backus 272

WILD—Wilde
Benjamin-Elmer *adaga gfaab* 581
Catharine 154
Elmer-George *adaga gfaa* 581
Harriet (Joy) *abaed a* 88
Ida-May *adaga gfaaa* 581
Jonathan *abaed a* 88
Josephine (Linfield) 581
Lucy-May (Lincoln) *adaga gfaa* 581
Rachel 269
William 581

WILDER
Bela 437
Cordelia *aaffi h* 84
Eliza 436
Hannah-Cushing 304
Lydia 307
Matilda *aacbh b* 78 260
Mehitable-Ellen *aacdb gc* 437
Mercy (Hersey) 437
Susanna 142
Theophilus 90 190 240

WILDS
David *adaaf dfd* 351
Mary-Gertrude (Brown) *adaaf dfd* 351

WILKINS
Catherine 494

WILKINSON
Ann *aacab f* 72

WILLARD
Joseph 157
Simon 13

WILLCUTT
Betsey 315
Chloe (Beal) *abbai* 41 249
Daniel 249
James *aaffi j* 84 453-4
Joel *adcba a* 86 124
John *abbai* 41 249
Lewis *abbec fab* 323
Ophelia ([Whittington] Lincoln) *aaffi j* 84 453-4
Parmela 249
Priscilla-Nichols (Lothrop) 453
Rachel-Phillips *aaffh b* 83
Ruth (Collier) *adffg* 249
Sarah-Wilson-Hobart (Souther) *abbec fab* 323
Susan-Lothrop *abaea ag* 187
Susannah (Stoddard) 453
Tamar-Lincoln (Sutton) *adcba a* 124
Thomas 453

WILLEY
Stephen *aabcf bd* 144
Tabitha-Longfellow (Lewis) *aabcf bd* 144

WILLHOITE
Christena *adaai d* 103

WILLIAMS
Addie (Leonard) *abbea caaj* 451
Alexander *abaea ai* 187
Almira (Lincoln) *abbea caa* 450-1
Angie (Lincoln) *adaah ele* 483
Augusta (Burbank) *abbea caad* 450 597
Benjamin F. 329
Caroline-Adelaide (Manuel) *abbea caag* 450
Charles-Herbert *abbea caai* 451
David 212
Edward 427
Elizabeth (Collier) *abaea ai* 187
Elmer-Stanley *adcac bajb* 597
Emily-Elizabeth *adagb dgg* 365
Emma-Jane *aacbe lf* 427
Ezekiel-Thomas *abbea caag* 450
Florence-Bates (Lincoln) *adcac bajb* 597
George *abbea caaa* 450
Hannah (Evans) 212
Hannah-Lincoln *adaaf hd* 212
Harriet A. *aacbh g* 78
Ida-May *abbea caah* 450
James-Franklin *abbea caac* 450
Jennie (Walker) *abbea caai* 451
Jesse *adaaf ha* 212
John 461
Louisa-Jane *abbea caab* 450
Mary *adaaf hb* 212
Mary A. (——) 427
Mary-Elizabeth (Rich) *abbea caac* 450
Miranda *adaaf hc* 212
Nancy-Ann *adaaf hf* 212
Nancy-Ann (Lincoln) *adaaf h* 209 211 212 353
Nancy-Caroline *abbea caaf* 450
Rachel *adaaf he* 212
S. M. 96 97
Samuel-Lincoln *abbea caad* 450 597
Sarah-Frances *abbea caae* 450
Sarah-Jane *adaaf hg* 212
Thomas 53
Thomas *abbea caa* 450-1
Wallace-Clarence *abbea caaj* 451
William 212
William *adaaf h* 211 212 353

WILLIAMSON
Dorcas (Rimel) *adaai g* 102 103
John *adaai g* 102 103
Kezia *adaai a* 103

WILLIAMSON cont'd
Sarah *adaai* b 103
Thomas 102
WILLIS
Charles 236
Clara-Frances (Lincoln) *adcai* bgb 519
Edward 519
Hannah (Hewens) 519
Martha K. *aacda* cf 175
Stillman-Hewens *adcai* bgb 519
WILLS
E. H. 163
WILMARTH
Elizabeth-Jane 556
WILSON
Abigail 262
David *adcac* ca 239
Esther 185
George *afa* 8
Hipzabah (Kilby) *aaffd* d 82
John *aaffd* d 52
Malvina 421
Martha-Roy 577
Mary 486
Mary (Bates) *afa* 8
Mary-Lincoln (Pratt) *adcac* ca 239
Ruth 68
Sally 316 323
Susanna 38
W. 364
Woodrow 540
WILT
Harriet 431
WINCHESTER
Charles A. *aabcf* ahd 262
Emma-Maria (Sawyer) *aabcf* ahd 262
Sarah L. 248
WINDLE
Anna *adaae* icb 346
WINGFIELD
A. Waverly *adaae* hfib 573
Mamie-Elizabeth (Lincoln) *adaae* hfib 573
WINSLOW
Edward 66 282
John 64
Josiah 282
Penelope (Pelham) 282
WINSOR
Welthea 139
WINTERSON
Cornelia *adahf* cbab 505
WINTHROP
John 76
WISE
Abraham *adbcf* bdg 384
Anna-Frances (Paschall) *adbcf* bdg 384
WISEMAN
Adaline (Burgess) 615
George 615
Mary-Gertrude *adaaa* bbcgb 615
WISER
George-Hammond *adbcf* beb 593
Hannah-Jane (Taylor) *adbcf* beb 593
WITHERELL see Wetherell
Eunice *adfba* d 132
WOLFE
Mary 504
WOOD
Abigail (Shaw) 318
Barzillai 155
Belcher-Sylvester 433
Caroline-Matilda *aacdb* ee 433
Cyrus-William *abbea* cagc 451
Delilah (Cole) 472
Emily-Catherine *abbec* bcb 322
Emma-Melville *abbea* cagb 451

WOOD cont'd
Fanny-Elizabeth (Lincoln) *adaae* abd 472
Fred-Edward *adaae* abda 472
Gabriel 472
Hannah (Whiting) 433
John-Dickerson *adaae* abd 472
Julia (Lincoln) *adaah* elf 483
Martha-Cottle *abbea* cagd 451
Martha-Franklin (Curtis) *abbea* cagc 451
Mary (Lincoln) *abbea* cag 451
Mary-Matilda (Leighton) *aacdb* baa 301
Mary (Shattuck) 155
Mary-Snow *abbea* caga 451
Nancy ([Pratt] Lincoln) 318
Osburn 451
Osborn *aaffj* j 84
Polly ([Ellmes] Litchfield) *aaffj* j 84
Rebecca 150
Roxanna *aabhe* 155-6
Silence-Tower (Lincoln) 451
William-John *aacdb* baa 301
William-Osborn *abbea* cag 451
Willis *adaah* elf 483
Ziba 318 451
WOODBURN
Olive-Frances *adaga* gje 363
WOODBURY
Aaron *aabcf* bf 144
Ann-Augusta (Burleigh) *aabcf* fe 145
Ann-Maria (Wedgewood) 438
Calvin-Edwards *aabcf* ff 145
Emma-Chapman *aabcf* fc 144
Frank-Herbert *aacdb* gfb 438
Jerusha (Lincoln) *aabcf* f 144-5
Joseph 438
Mary A. *abbec* bdb 322
Miranda-Church *aabcf* fd 144
Nellie-May (Lincoln) *aacdb* gfb 438
Ormond-William *aabcf* fe 145
Sarah (Barker) *aabcf* ff 145
Sarah-Peabody (Lewis) *aabcf* bf 144
Susan-Byles *aabcf* fa 144
Susanna (Byles) 144
Thankful-Lincoln *aabcf* fb 144
William 144
William *aabcf* f 144-5
WOODNANCY
Daniel *adaga* b 217
Nancy (Lincoln) *adaga* b 217
Rhoda *adaga* ba 217
WOODRUFF
Phebe 237
WOODSON
W. H. 483
WOODWARD
Augusta-Clark (Lincoln) *aacbe* lfa 427
Daniel *aagd* 11
Deborah (Joy) *aagd* 11
Harry-Lincoln *aacbe* lfaa 427
Horace 427
Mary *agdi* 26 71
Mary-Elizabeth (Thomas) 427
Priscilla (Talbot) *aacbe* lfaa 427
William-Given *aacbe* lfa 427
WOODWELL
Esther 179
WOOL
John-Ellis 418
WOOLERTON
Elizabeth *aaffh* c 83
WORK
Alice-Mills *adbfa* bdcd 515
Almira (Mills) 515
Harold-Knowlton *adbfa* bdcb 515
Hattie-Simons (Lincoln) *adbfa* bdc 515
Lincoln-Thomas *adbfa* bdca 515
Norman-Porter *adbfa* bdc 515

WORK cont'd
  Ruth-Lincoln *adbfa bdcc* 515
  Thomas-Knowlton 515
WORRELL
  Emily *adbcg e* 118
WORRICK
  Chasling *aff* 8 62 81 83
  Elizabeth (Woolerton) *aaffh c* 83
  Hannah *aaffh a* 83 518
  Hannah (Lane) 83
  Hester (Bates) *aff* 8 62
  Hezekiah 83
  Jane *aaffh e* 81 83
  Jonathan 81
  Laban *aaffh* 83
  Levi-Lincoln *aaffh c* 83
  Lorette *aaffh f* 83
  Mary (Fetteridge) 81
  Paul-Baker *aaffh b* 83
  Rachel-Phillips (Willcutt) *aaffh b* 83
  Ruth 81
  Sally (Lincoln) *aaffh* 83
  Sarah *aaffh d* 83
  Susanna *adf* 62
WORRILOW
  Alice 50
WRIGHT
  Catherine 180
  Jennie *adbca aba* 380
  Mary (Williams) *adaaf hb* 212
  Peter *adaaf hb* 212
  Rosa-Anna 522
  Sarah 27 59
  Sarah (Guinn) *adaaf ab* 477
WYATT
  Sarah-Duxbury 455
WYMAN
  Ann-Rebecca (Webster) 533
  Anna *aabck bdb* 411
  Anna (Doyle) 411
  Clara-Louise *aabcg dbd* 533
  Daniel 533
  Edward 411
  Harvey *aacda cc* 175
  Jael-Cushing (Whitcomb) *aacda cc* 175
WYRICK
  Jacob T. *adaaf i* 212
  Mary (Lincoln) *adaaf i* 212

YANCEY
  Bessie-Lincoln (Nicholas) *adaae agba* 473
  Stuart M. *adaae agba* 473
YARNALL
  Alice (Worrilow) 50
  Ann (Tomlinson) *adadc* 51
  Francis 50
  Francis *adad* 50-1 100 209
  Francis *adadb* 51
  Jesse *adadc* 51
  Leah (——) *adada* 51
  Mary *adadd* 51 100 101 209-12
  Mary (Lincoln) *adad* 50-1 100 209
  Mordecai *adada* 51 100
  Peter 50
YATES
  Mary *adahb bbh* 496
  Mary (Vandever) 496
  Washington 496

YAW
  Margaret-Ellen *adaga gi* 492
YEAGLEY
  Andrew 218
  Andrew *adaga ic* 219
  Benjamin-Lincoln *adaga ig* 219
  Eliza (McCray) *adaga ia* 219
  Elizabeth *adaga id* 219
  George *adaga ia* 219
  Henry *adaga i* 218-9
  Henry *adaga ib* 218 219
  Jane (Flanigan) *adaga ig* 219
  Mary L. (Criley) *adaga ic* 219
  Phoebe (Lincoln) *adaga i* 218-9
  Rhoda-Louisa *adaga if* 219
  Sarah *adaga ie* 219
  Sarah (Miller) 218
  Sarah (Dibert) *adaga ib* 219
YORK
  Rufus R. 267
YOST
  Mary 507
YOUNG
  Alexander 185
  Catherine 510
  Fanny *adbcf beb* 593
  Ida *adbcf baa* 592-3
  George 592
  Lena 575
  Mary (——) 592
  Mary-Thomas *adcaj a* 123
  Rebecca 458
  Robert *abbbe* 41
  Sarah-Ann 546
  Sarah (Nichols) *abbbe* 41

ZEARING
  Benjamin *adaga c* 217
  Catherine 217
  Catherine-Gertrude (von Feilgers) 217
  Elizabeth *adaga bb* 217
  George *adaga bd* 217
  Hannah *adaga be* 217
  John-Henry *adaga b* 217
  Ludwig 217
  Mary *adaga bg* 217
  Nancy ([Lincoln] Woodnancy) *adaga b* 217
  Olive (White) *adaga bd* 217
  Sarah *adaga bf* 217
  William *adaga bh* 217
ZEISTER
  Michael 109
ZELL
  Eunice (Kelley) 511
  George 511
  Harriet-Ann *adbca dc* 511
ZIMMERMAN
  Lurisia (Reece) 582
  Tillie-May *adaga gid* 582
  William 582
ZIRKLE
  Edgar-Leigh 570
  Ellen (Larrick) 570
  Kathleen-Malinda *adaae agca* 569-70
ZWINGLER
  Catherine 462